The

RIVERSIDE
READER

The RIVERSIDE READER

SIXTH EDITION

Joseph F. Trimmer
Ball State University

Maxine Hairston
University of Texas at Austin

Houghton Mifflin Company   Boston   New York

Senior Sponsoring Editor: Dean Johnson
Project Editor: Kellie Cardone
Senior Production/Design Coordinator: Sarah Ambrose
Senior Manufacturing Coordinator: Marie Barnes
Senior Marketing Manager: Nancy Lyman

Cover designer: Harold Burch Design, NYC
Photographer: Ted Nierenberg from *The Beckoning Path,* Aperture

Printed in the U.S.A.

Library of Congress Catalog Card Number: 98-71519

ISBN: Student text 0-395-90354-8

123456789-DH-02 01 00 99 98

CONTENTS

2 week (handwritten)

COMPARISON AND CONTRAST   153

THEMATIC TABLE OF CONTENTS

The Other

Women

Science and Technology

Business and Ethics

PREFACE

The sixth edition of *The Riverside Reader*, like its predecessors, presents essays by acknowledged masters of prose style, including George Orwell, Flannery O'Connor, and Maya Angelou, along with many new voices such as Judith Ortiz Cofer, Natalie Angier, John Berendt, and Bill Barich. More than half of the selections are new to this edition. As always, introductions, readings, study questions, and writing assignments are simple, clear, and cogent.

FEATURES OF THE SIXTH EDITION

At the center of *The Riverside Reader* is our desire to assist students in their reading and writing by helping them to understand the interaction between the two processes:

- The **connection between the reading and writing process** is highlighted in the general introduction. The familiar terminology of *purpose, audience,* and *strategy* provides a framework for the introduction and for subsequent study questions and writing assignments.

- **Guidelines for Writing an Essay** is paired with **Guidelines for Reading an Essay** to enhance and advance the students' understanding of the reading/writing connection.

- **A new annotated essay** appears in the general introduction—"The Chain Gang Show" by Brent Staples. The annotations illustrate how a reader responds to his reading by writing.

- In each section introduction, an **annotated paragraph by a professional writer,** such as an excerpt from Maxine Hong Kingston's "A Song for a Barbarian Reed Pipe," concisely demonstrates reading and writing at work.

- In each section introduction, a **paragraph by a student writer,** such as Lauren Briner's "Deloris," is followed by questions about writing strategy.

- A **Points to Remember list** concludes each section introduction and provides a convenient summary of the essential tasks and techniques of each strategy.

- This edition contains **thirty-six new selections,** among them Doris Kearns Goodwin's "Keeping the Scorebook," Pico Iyer's "Of Weirdos and Eccentrics," and Terry McMillan's "The Movie That Changed My Life." The complete collection, which includes popular essays from previous editions, provides a variety of readings to engage the interest of all students.

- A **Thematic Table of Contents** is provided for teachers who wish to organize their course by themes or issues.

- **Selections in the Persuasion and Argument section are paired** to present different perspectives on the issues of race, technology, poverty, and education. This feature reflects our continuing emphasis on analytical and interpretive reading and writing.

- A **short story** concludes each section to provide an interesting perspective on a particular writing strategy and to give students opportunities to broaden their reading skills. New to this edition are Frank O'Connor's "Guests of the Nation," Kurt Vonnegut, Jr.'s "Harrison Bergeron," and Louise Erdrich's "Lyman's Luck."

- **Study questions and writing assignments** throughout the book have been extensively revised.

- A thematically organized final section, **Resources for Writing,** focuses on the subject of gambling and includes seven essays (each exemplifying one rhetorical mode), one short story, and a student essay. The writing assignments following each reading encourage students to use what they already know to *respond, analyze,* and *argue* about the essays.

- A **student essay,** Jason Rex's "Not a Bad Night," draws on the pieces in Resources for Writing to demonstrate how students can explore a subject and strategies to attract their audience and advance their purpose.

THE RIVERSIDE TRADITION

The first seven sections in this reader are arranged in a sequence that is familiar to most writing teachers. Beginning with narration and description, moving through the five expository patterns, and ending with persuasion and argument, these sections group readings according to traditional writing strategies.

Each section begins with a simple, direct introduction previewing that writing strategy and helping the student become an active reader of that type of writing. Each section introduction ends with a professional and a student paragraph illustrating the strategy in action and with a convenient Points to Remember summary of the strategy's essential tasks and techniques. The headnote for each selection contains basic biographical information about the writer. This introductory material focuses on four questions about the writing situation: *Who* is writing? What is the writer's *purpose? Whom* is the writer addressing? *How* does the writer accomplish his or her purpose?

The readings within each section have been chosen to illustrate what the section introductions say they illustrate: there are no strange hybrids or confusing models. Within each section, the selections are arranged in ascending order of length and complexity. The readings at the beginning are generally shorter and simpler than those near the end. The ultimate purpose of *The Riverside Reader* is to produce writing. For that reason, the writing assignments in this book are presented as the culminating activity of each section. Six assignments at the end of each section ask students to write essays that cover a range of writing tasks from personal response to analysis and argument.

Instructor's Guide

The new Instructor's Resource Manual by Rai Peterson of Ball State University is available to any instructor using *The Riverside Reader*. The Manual includes extensive rhetorical analysis of each essay and story, reading quizzes and vocabulary lists, and additional student essays and writing assignments. The Manual also includes advice on teaching the reading and writing strategies.

ACKNOWLEDGMENTS

We are grateful to the following writing instructors who have provided extensive commentary on *The Riverside Reader* for this revision:

Paul Andrews, St. Johns River Community College, FL
Lona Bassett, Jones County Junior College, MS
Carol A. Galbus, Winona State University, MN
Will Hochman, University of Southern Colorado, CO
Mary Ellen Jordan, Hamline University, MN
John Sherman, Moorhead State University, MN
Robert P. Sowada, Mesa State College, CO
E. Roger Stephenson, Canisius College, NY
Brad Van Alstyne, Academy of Art, CA

We are also thankful to our students for allowing us to reprint their work in this edition: Lauren Briner, Sara Temple,

Nathan Harms, Gareth Tucker, Jason Utesch, Emily Linderman, Jim Saloman, and Jason Rex. A special thanks goes to Karen Taylor for her help in manuscript preparation. And, of course, our debt to all our students is ongoing.

J. F. T.

M. H.

INTRODUCTION

As a college student, you are necessarily a reader and a writer. Not that either role is new to you—certainly you were a reader and a writer before you started college, and you read and write outside of college. In college, however, you're in a different kind of reading and writing environment: the stakes are higher and you often have to work under pressure. You have to read a broad variety of material, some of it difficult and unfamiliar, and write more demanding kinds of assignments, many of them about or in response to your reading. Your success in college depends, in part, on how well you can read and write and how well you can connect these two processes. Why is the connection important? Because the processes interact closely: as you become a more skillful and

1

knowledgeable reader, you will also become a better writer. In turn, as you become a more competent writer, you will become a more skilled reader.

BECOMING A READER WHO WRITES

The first time you read one of the essays or short stories in this book, move along steadily and enjoy it just because it's entertaining or because you are learning something. Unless you get lost or have to go back to pick up meaning, don't stop to analyze what you're reading. Instead, try to absorb the main ideas and come out with a dominant impression of the theme and of the essay's impact on you. Don't stop to annotate or underline.

When you've finished your first reading, take a look at the questions or comment that follows each selection. They are designed to start you thinking about your reactions to the reading and to get you ready for the second reading that is almost always necessary for mastering serious nonfiction writing.

The Second Reading

When you read the piece for the second time, you need to read more actively. Do more than notice your reactions. Think about why you have those reactions and how the author provoked them. Start moving back and forth between the roles of reader and writer, interacting with the piece of writing—looking for key points or weak spots and making associations and asking questions. Get ready to start making notes in the margins.

Begin an imaginary conversation with the author. Ask, "*Why* are you writing this? *For whom* are you writing? *What strategies* are you using?" If you keep these questions in mind during your second reading, you'll begin to get a picture of the writer behind the page, someone who has something to say and is working at getting it across to his or her readers.

React to what you're reading. Don't accept the author's

claims passively. Instead, ask questions, argue, comment, and test what the writer is saying against your own knowledge and experience. Say, "Yes, I agree," or ask, "What's your evidence?" or, "Why do you say that?" Such comments and questions help you to decide what an essay or story means *for you.*

The phrase *for you* is important because a piece of writing never means exactly the same thing for every reader. Nor should it. You are a special reader who brings unique experiences and attitudes with you, and you create your own meaning when you combine what you know and feel with what the writer tells you.

For example, as you read you may be comparing the author's account of something that happened to her—perhaps an encounter with stereotyping or sex discrimination—with a similar experience of yours and thinking about how differently you reacted. Or in reading another essay, you may disagree with the author's analysis of an American political problem and decide you'd like to refute him in your next paper. As you respond, write your reactions down. If you don't, you may forget them.

Notes and Questions in the Margins

On your second reading, interact with what you read by underlining and writing in the margins as you read—just highlighting usually isn't enough. Jot notes and questions in the margins (or on a separate piece of paper if you have to), and summarize key points. Also note any ideas the essay may trigger for your own writing.

This kind of reading is such an essential part of understanding serious material that most experienced readers underline and write in margins almost routinely when they are reading to absorb content. If they don't own the book they have to master, they buy it or photocopy parts of it so they can read with a pencil in hand. At the end of this introduction, we include a short annotated essay that shows how one reader used this method to interact with a piece of writing.

We believe that trying this method and using the guideline questions on pages 9–11 will help you to become a good reader who enjoys serious reading and knows how to use it for your own writing.

BECOMING A WRITER WHO READS

When you *write* college essays, you need to move back and forth between the roles of reader and writer. As you move through the writing process, you need to be aware that you are interacting with different readers.

The Self as Reader

Your first reader is yourself. You write, read what you've written, and in response to that reading write more. You're creating as you go. When you get to the revision stage, you rewrite because you realize, as a reader, that your essay didn't come out quite as you wanted it to. When you're satisfied with content but go back to tinker and polish, you're doing so in response to your own reading. And when you get to the final editing stage, you edit and proofread because you are acting as the most critical of all readers: an editor.

Other Readers

As you write, you need to think about the other people who will read what you write. To help you do so, look at the suggestions in Parts IV and VI of Guidelines for Writing an Essay (see pages 20–21). Ask yourself, "For whom am I writing, and what do my readers expect? How can I get my ideas across to them?" When you have finished your first draft, it's particularly important for you to stand back from it, put yourself in the place of your readers, and ask yourself what questions they might have for you.

READING TO BECOME MORE AWARE OF THE WRITING PROCESS

As you read and react to a piece of writing, you can sharpen your own writing skills by thinking about the writing process in the essay you're reading. Try to see what's going on beneath the surface of the words; try to get into the writer's mind and watch her or him at work. By asking certain questions, you can do a kind of simulation exercise that can help you understand the writer's thinking process.

Ask About Purpose

We know that most writers have goals when they write, certain things they want to accomplish. So ask yourself,

- Why is the author writing? What motivated him or her?
- Does the author tell me the purpose directly? How can I determine it?

Ask About Audience

We know that most writers—especially professionals—write for a definite audience and tailor their writing to meet that audience's needs and expectations. So ask yourself,

- For whom is the writer writing? Why did he or she choose that audience?
- What does the writer know about that audience? How does that knowledge affect his or her writing?

Ask About Strategies

You can learn from other writers by noticing how they work and what kinds of appeals they use. So ask yourself,

- How does the writer go about putting the essay together? How is it organized?
- What kind of strategies does the writer use? Is he or she

telling stories, giving evidence, using examples, employing metaphor and images? How well do those strategies work and why?

Reading a well-crafted essay critically is like watching a well-made movie on two levels: on one level you can enjoy the drama itself, and on another level you appreciate the talent and skill of the artists at work.

Do we guarantee that close analysis of a professional writer's work will make you a better writer? No, of course we don't. But we do believe that learning to read responsively, critically, and analytically will give you insights into the craft of writing and make it a less intimidating and more manageable process.

READING TO LEARN ABOUT WRITING STRATEGIES

In *The Riverside Reader* you will find essays and short stories that comment on events and concerns that affect all our lives—social programs such as welfare, the experiences of different ethnic groups, women's roles, and politics, to name just a few. The essays connect to other strands in your college education and are as pertinent in sociology, history, or environmental courses as they are in your college writing course. The short stories expand your understanding of the essay by showing how nonfiction connects with the worlds of fiction. All these readings touch on matters that affect your personal life or your job. The last section of the book, Resources for Writing, is devoted to issues about gambling.

Common Writing Strategies

The essays in *The Riverside Reader* are arranged according to common patterns of organization that have been serving writers well for centuries: *narration and description, process analysis, comparison and contrast, division and classification, definition, cause and effect,* and *persuasion and argument.*

These patterns can serve as *strategies* for the development of ideas in writing. Study how professional writers use these traditional strategies in their writing. If you know from your reading how these strategies are used, you will be able to choose one that fits your writing situation. For example, if you notice how Maya Angelou uses narrative to dramatize racial stereotyping, you may see how you can relate an incident from your life to illustrate a point. If you are convinced by Cathy Young's claim that radical feminists are harming the cause of women's liberation by portraying women as victims, you may want to use the same kind of cause-and-effect argument in a paper for sociology or ethnic studies.

Not that you have to limit yourself to a single strategy for the entire paper—certainly professional writers don't. Often, however, they do structure a piece of writing around one central pattern, and for *The Riverside Reader* we have chosen essays with one dominant strategy so that you can see particularly strong examples of each strategy in action.

Strategies for Your Writing

You can also use the traditional strategies to generate resources and then transform them into writing. Suppose you are trying to get started writing an essay on the early impressionist painters for a humanities course. One way to start thinking would be to *define* the impressionist school of painting. Another would be to explore what *caused* the rise of impressionism in the nineteenth century—what were the artists in the movement reacting to? Another potentially rich approach would be to *compare* these painters to other painters of the time. You could also *describe* an important early impressionist painting or relate a *narrative* about one of the early painters. Each of the strategies provides a kind of special lens for viewing your topic, a different way of looking at it so that you can see its possibilities.

When you become aware of how these lenses work—how each one helps you see and shape your subject—you can select one strategy or combine two or three to draft and revise your essay. That is the procedure you can follow in Resources for Writing. Each selection in that section uses one of the common writing strategies to explore a different aspect of gambling. As you read these selections, recalling what you know about that topic, you can expand and shift your perspective on the subject, uncovering all sorts of resources to develop in your writing.

USING *THE RIVERSIDE READER*

The Riverside Reader will help you become an active, critical reader and an effective writer. At the start of every section, you will find an introduction that previews the strategy, gives you clues about what to look for as you read, and concludes with the key "Points to Remember." Examples from both a professional and a student paragraph show how the strategy works. Before each essay and short story, you will find a headnote that tells you about the author's background and credentials and about how and where the selection originated. After each essay and short story, you will find study questions or commentary to help you connect your reading to the author's writing process. At the end of each section, you will find writing assignments that give you opportunities to respond to your reading using your own experiences and knowledge.

On the next few pages, you will find a set of questions titled Guidelines for Reading an Essay. The guidelines will help you to preview an essay, to read and respond to it critically, and to see it from a writer's point of view. After these guidelines, you will find a sample analysis of Brent Staples's essay "The Chain Gang Show"; it shows how one reader read, responded to, and annotated the essay. Also included are three writing topics that grew out of the reader's responses to Staples's piece. This Introduction to *The Riverside Reader* then closes with Guidelines for Writing an Essay, a brief review of the writing process that should help you to get started with your own writing.

Guidelines for Reading an Essay

Most of us don't sit down to read essays or anything else with a set of guidelines in our hand. Sometimes we read so casually that if someone were to ask about the article later, we'd have a hard time giving an accurate summary. That's fine—no one wants to be taking tests on his or her leisure reading.

However, when we read to grasp ideas and to appreciate the style and language of an essay, reading becomes serious work, something that we need to do intelligently and systematically. We have no magic formula for that kind of reading, but we think the following guidelines can be helpful.

I. READ THE ESSAY THROUGH COMPLETELY

a. Notice the title, and consider what it may mean. Note the author's name and whether it's familiar to you. Read any introduction and any summary sentence such as the one on the second page of each essay in this volume.

b. Read slowly, looking up important words if necessary, but don't stop to reread unless you think you've missed some major point.

c. When you finish, think about the dominant impression the essay made on you. Was it powerful? Persuasive? Comic? Moving? Baffling?

d. If there are questions at the end of the essay, read them through to determine their focus. Prepare to read the selection again, this time with a pencil in hand.

II. ANALYZE YOUR RESPONSE

a. Think about any personal experience that the essay brings to mind. How does that experience affect your response?

b. Jot down any questions the essay raised for you. Put a check in the margin where you want to say "Yes!" Put a cross where you want to say "No way!"

c. Consider what you'd say if you wanted to talk back to the author.

d. Reflect on the emotional or intellectual impact the essay had on you.

III. ANALYZE THE AUTHOR'S PURPOSE

a. Decide what the author is trying to accomplish with the essay. That goal can range from trying to amuse to inspiring outrage and action.

b. Ask yourself what in the writer's experience or background motivated him or her to write the essay. How does it seem to grow out of that experience?

c. Mark sentences or sections in the essay that show the writer's purpose.

d. When you finish, consider how well the writer achieved his or her purpose with you. What are some of the reasons he or she succeeded or failed with you?

IV. ANALYZE THE WRITER'S AUDIENCE

a. Identify the audience you think the writer is appealing to. If the essay was first published in a magazine, try to analyze the type of magazine and what characteristics its audience would have.

b. Identify the beliefs or values the author assumes the readers share with him or her. To what extent do you think that assumption is justified?

c. Authors also assume their readers have a certain amount of background knowledge. What knowledge does this author take for granted? How do you know?

d. Consider how well you fit the profile the author probably constructed of his or her readers. How does that fit, or lack of it, affect your response to the essay?

V. ANALYZE AND EVALUATE THE WRITER'S STRATEGIES

a. The most effective writers catch their readers at the very beginning of an essay. Read a few paragraphs, and decide how well they work and why.

b. Look for the dominant patterns—definition, narration, cause and effect, and so on—in the essay. How do they serve the writer's purpose?

c. Look for metaphor, vivid description, personal experience, the use of authority and statistics, or other strategies. What do they accomplish?

d. What strategies of the writer worked best with you? Why do you think so?

VI. IDENTIFY ISSUES RAISED BY THE ESSAY

a. What larger social issues do you think the essay raises? How does it contribute to the ongoing conversation about those issues?

b. What, if anything, has happened in the field the author is writing about since the time the essay was written? How is the essay still relevant, or is it?

c. What impact do you think the essay may have had on its original readers?

Sample Analysis of an Essay

BRENT STAPLES

Brent Staples was born in Chester, Pennsylvania, in 1951 and was educated at Widener College and the University of Chicago. He worked for several years as a reporter for the *Chicago Sun-Times* before moving on to an editorial position at the *New York Times*. He currently serves as assistant editor of the Metropolitan section of the *Times* and frequently publishes commentary and opinion pieces on the editorial page. Staples regularly contributes articles to the *New York Times Magazine* and to other magazines such as *Harper's*. He has also written a memoir about his youth and his relationship with his troubled brother: it is titled *Parallel Lives: Growing Up in Black and White* (1994).

"The Chain Gang Show" highlights Staples's gifts as an observer and a reporter. His grim opening sentence, "Any animal with teeth enough will chew off its leg to escape a trap," rivets the readers' attention and sets the desperate, sorrowful tone for the whole essay. He goes on to create a shocking image of chained prisoners who, like trapped animals, mutilated themselves in an effort to escape. The image is from the past, but the next paragraph moves the reader to modern-day chain gangs in Alabama. Staples comments that the reinstatement of these gangs signals "a resurgence of the American appetite for spectacles of punishment and humiliation."

In the third paragraph he reveals the spectacle for what it is: a staged show where reporters can sip lemonade in the shade while watching prisoners—in politically correct proportions of black and white—break rocks under the blazing sun. Staples uses his sharp descriptive powers here to create a vivid and concrete image. The next three paragraphs reveal his additional skill as an investigative reporter as he digs beneath the show to get the truth about these so-called vicious criminals. He finds that they're neither vicious nor dangerous; they're medium-security prisoners who have been put on display for political purposes. Moreover, he points out, chaining the prisoners together is grossly inefficient, and the publicized rock breaking is useless activity. It's a farce staged for the benefit of the public at the prisoners' expense. Staples theorizes, however, that such exploitation of captive men could backfire on the authorities, making prisoners more desperate, more like the vicious animals they're being treated as.

In addition to exposing the cynical political maneuvers that underlie the sad spectacle he describes, Staples's essay makes a chilling comment on a public that calls for such cruel and unusual punishment and delights in watching it. For many readers, the behavior of the crowd sounds all too similar to accounts of the crowds who, not so many years ago, loved to watch hangings and other executions or who gathered to watch people being stoned or tortured to death. So a larger issue emerges here. Staples suggests that our zeal for punishment and retribution may be eroding the American moral character. Who's on trial here?

Comments in the left margin summarize Staples's main points and note his strategies. In the right margin, the reader notes her responses to the essay and jots down ideas and questions the essay raises. This process of annotating and responding generates ideas for discussion and for possible written responses to Staples. Some possible paper topics are given after the essay.

The Chain Gang Show

Shocking image of horrors of early chain gangs

ANY ANIMAL WITH teeth enough will chew off its leg to escape a trap. Human beings behaved similarly when chain gang imprisonment—a successor to slavery—swept through the labor-starved South during Reconstruction. Beaten and driven like maltreated beasts, shackled to one another around the clock, prisoners turned to self-mutilation to make themselves useless for work. They slashed their bodies, broke their own legs, crippled themselves by cutting their tendons.

A public outcry beginning in the 30's gradually shamed even the most backward states into abolishing the gangs. Their return this spring to Alabama—followed by Florida and Arizona, with several other states mulling them over—signals an end to the fiction of rehabilitation and a resurgence of the American appetite for spectacles of punishment and humiliation. Calls for corporal punishment in schools and for the caning of petty criminals tell a similar story.

Return of gangs shows resurgence of Am. love of spectacles of punishment

Have to wonder about people who like to watch others suffer

In Alabama, highway gangs were reinstated to great fanfare. The debut of its rock-breaking gangs at the Limestone Correctional Facility near Huntsville in August was staged like a Sunday picnic. A tent was erected where reporters could sip cold lemonade in shaded comfort while the prisoners struggled under 10-pound sledgehammers in the blazing sun. Mindful of the chain gangs' racist past—and the sight of white, shotgun-wielding guards in mirrored sunglasses lording over shackled black men—Gov. Fob James Jr. decreed that the gangs, which consist of five-man groups, would "reflect the demographics of the prison." The gangs are thus racially correct—

Brutal show of contrasts

Vivid image

Ironic political correctness

three blacks and two whites apiece, where possible.

The prisoners were eager to be photographed, hoping that a shocked citizenry would rally to the rescue. The prison authorities were just as eager for publicity, given what one of Limestone's assistant wardens, Ralph Hooks, called "the perception that prison life was too easy." The prisoners spend one to three months on the gangs. To further combat the perception of easy living, the men are stripped of everything that makes prison life bearable: television, radio, smoking and the right to make purchases (except for necessities like soap and deodorant) at the prison store. Worst of all, they are denied personal visits, even from family members. Public opinion is thus far on the side of the wardens.

The chain gangs will furnish a handy campaign commercial if Governor James runs for re-election. But like most political symbols, this one is not what it seems. The men in shackles and white suits are medium-security prisoners—not quite the ax murderers, assassins and sundry death-row candidates that onlookers might wish to imagine. The gangs are made up of nonviolent criminals only—check forgers, deadbeat dads, safe crackers, parole violaters.

The "work" the gangs do is valueless. The rock breaking is pure photo opportunity. The highway crews allegedly clear weeds and debris, but this is impossible to do on any useful scale with five men chained eight feet apart, each stumbling when the next does. The real reason for stretching legions of chained, white-suited men for a mile or so along the highway is to let motorists gorge on a visible symbol of punishment and humiliation. Hanging, too, was once a public entertainment. No one should be

Margin notes (left): Vindictive penalties · It's a phony political gimmick · Work is useless · It's all for show

Margin notes (right): How can anyone think prison life is easy? · Like medieval executions

surprised if some ambitious politician suggests making it so again.

Many Alabamans delight in the chain gangs' **Gross behavior** reappearance. Drivers roll down their windows to taunt the prisoners, barking like dogs. Others look on the predominantly black gangs and feel nostalgia for the South they knew as children. "I love seeing 'em in chains," one elderly white woman said. "They ought to make them pick cotton."

Warden claims chain gangs make prisoners behave The warden thinks the experience of being trussed up in chains and paraded before a scornful public will make inmates better citizens. Inmates see it differently. Louis Bennett, a 25-year-old serving time for burglary, said being chained "makes you start hating." Chris Davis, a 26-year-old doing time for drug dealing, put it more strongly: **Opposite probably true** "It would make a person kill somebody to get away, if the police were chasing him, to not come back to this."

Prison officials in other parts of the country should heed these sentiments. Hard-core prisoners are bound to be less pliable, particularly in the Northern industrial states, where the history **Backlash possible** of prison activism is strong, the grip of authority tenuous. In such places, chain gangs might be more than morally repugnant. They could also be self-defeating.

Possible Writing Topics

1. In recent years, some commentators have proposed that the way to solve problems such as teenage pregnancies and juvenile delinquency would be to reinstate some of the sanctions of Victorian times, principally that of using ostracism and shame to influence youngsters into moral behavior. Many Victorians were also committed to the "spare the rod and spoil the child" theory

of behavior modification. Write an opinion column for your local or campus paper giving your reaction to these kinds of recommendations. Draw on your own experience or that of people you know well to support your stance. Make your essay reasoned as well as emotional. What do you think works best with children and why?

2. Write a historical account, supported by some research, of punishment practices of some earlier eras. What were public executions like? What was the public response? What seems to have been the purpose behind these punishments? Is there evidence that such punishments acted as deterrents? Some eras that you might look at are the reign of James I in England, persecution of heretics by the Inquisition, executions during the French Revolution, or punishments in our own colonial era. If you like, close with your own response to these practices. What effect do you think they may have had on spectators?

3. Find and read—or reread—Shirley Jackson's story "The Lottery," a story about a community that each year observed the ritual of stoning to death a young person chosen by lottery. Write your response to the story and the statement you think Jackson is making in it. What connections do you see between the story and Staples's account of "The Chain Gang Show?"

Guidelines for Writing an Essay

Because writing is a complex, often messy process that varies greatly from one writer to another and from one task to another, we're not going to offer you a formula that says "Here's how you write." It's never that simple. Nevertheless, it's possible to rough out guidelines that can be useful for getting started on a writing assignment. Here is what we suggest.

I. ANALYZE YOUR WRITING SITUATION

Every time you write, you write in a specific set of circumstances that has four elements to it: topic, purpose, audience, strategy. If one of these elements changes, so do the others. The successful writer always keeps that in mind. So start your writing process each time by analyzing the overall writing situation:

a. What do you want to say?
b. Why do you want to say it?
c. To whom do you want to say it?
d. How can you say it effectively?

Write out your analysis, and use it as a chart to keep you on course as you develop your paper. For instance, perhaps you are taking a children's literature course or have been reading to your own children and have noticed how few women heroes there are in traditional children's literature. Using that experience as a writing prompt, you could set up this writing situation:

> *I want to persuade librarians to look for more children's books that have women heroes because girls today need role models for bravery and leadership. I'll use my own experience in the argument.*

Now you have your writing situation in a nutshell. It will help get you started.

II. SELECT AND NARROW YOUR TOPIC

a. Select a topic you are genuinely interested in and about which you already have some information. The children's books topic meets both criteria.
b. Brainstorm, free-write, and talk to people to generate information on your topic. Narrow your topic to one main idea; for example, traditional children's books lack the strong women role models that today's youngsters need.
c. For a topic that requires factual information, research your topic to find out what material is available. For the topic given above, you could talk to librarians, elementary teachers, and the owners of children's bookstores.
d. Write a tentative thesis sentence to anchor your writing. For example, "Today's children, especially girls, need books showing women as heroines and leaders; traditional children's books have few powerful role models for girls."

III. DECIDE ON YOUR PURPOSE IN WRITING

a. Decide what you want to achieve by writing. Is your purpose to inform, entertain, persuade, bring about change? You will probably have more than one.
b. When you know what you want to do, decide what readers you need to reach. In an essay about children's books, the audience could be librarians and educators.
c. Consider how you want your readers to respond, what action you hope for. For the topic given above, you want librarians and educators to find books with strong role models for girls.

IV. ANALYZE YOUR AUDIENCE

a. Identify your target audience, and decide what is important to those readers. What kinds of appeals would they respond to? For example, librarians and educators want books that will appeal to young readers, and they want their readers to learn and benefit from the books they read.
b. Consider how much your audience already knows about the topic. What new information do they need? What examples would persuade them?
c. Anticipate what questions your argument will raise in readers' minds and plan to respond to those questions.
d. Identify a place where an essay like yours might be published. For the model topic, you could consider journals for librarians, *Scholastic* magazine, or an editorial on the school page of the local newspaper. Look over those publications.

V. DECIDE ON YOUR STRATEGIES

a. Make a plan of organization and rough out a working outline; jot down ideas for supporting evidence.
b. Decide what kind of arguments you can use. For instance, you could use *narration* to give your own experience, *definition* to show what kind of books girls need, and *comparison and contrast* to compare the number of men and women heroes in children's books.
c. Review the discussions of the strategies you're going to use to find what techniques you can use to develop the ones you've chosen.
d. Consider what kind of opening will catch and hold your readers' interest.
e. Find evidence to support your argument. For instance, examples of favorite children's books that focus on males could include *The Jungle Book, King Arthur and His Knights, Huckleberry Finn,* and the tales about Greek heroes.
f. Refine your thesis sentence to help you focus your topic.

For example, "Because strong role models are so important for a child's development, librarians and educators need to make special efforts to locate books with women heroes and leaders in order to compensate for the lack of such figures in most traditional children's literature."

VI. WRITE A DRAFT, REVISE, AND EDIT

a. Write your first draft, let it sit for several hours or overnight, and then reread it. Ask yourself: Does it have a clear, specific focus? Is your purpose clear? Do you keep your audience in mind? Have you supported your claims with evidence? Is it clearly organized? Do you need more examples?

b. Mark changes, deletions, and additions on your first draft and reorganize where you need to do so. Write a second draft.

c. Revise the second draft, pruning excess words and sentences, improving word choice, smoothing out transitions, and polishing the opening and closing paragraphs.

d. Edit for spelling, grammar, and typographical errors. Proofread once again, and print out or type a final clean copy.

NARRATION
AND
DESCRIPTION

꧁

The writer who *narrates* tells a story to make a point. The writer who *describes* evokes the senses to create a picture. Although you can use either strategy by itself, you will probably discover that they work best in combination if you want to write a detailed account of some memorable experience— your first trip alone, a last-minute political victory, a picnic in some special place. When you want to explain what happened, you will need to tell the story in some kind of chronological order, putting the most important events—I took the wrong turn, she made the right speech, we picked the perfect spot—in the most prominent position. When you want to give the texture of the experience, you will need to select words and images that help your readers see, hear, and feel what happened—the road snaked to a dead end, the crowd thundered into applause, the sunshine softened our scowls. When you show and tell in this way, you can help your readers see the meaning of the experience you want to convey.

PURPOSE

You can use narration and description for three purposes. Most simply, you can use them to introduce or illustrate a complicated subject. You might begin an analysis of the energy crisis, for example, by telling a personal anecdote that dramatizes wastefulness. Or you might conclude an argument for gun control by giving a graphic description of a shooting incident. In each case, you are using a few sentences or a detailed description to support some other strategy such as causal analysis or argument.

Writers use narration and description most often not as isolated examples but as their primary method when they are analyzing an issue or theme. For example, you might spend a whole essay telling how you came to a new awareness of patriotism because of your experience in a foreign country. Even though your personal experience would be the center of the essay, your narrative purpose (what happened) and your descriptive purpose (what it felt like) might be linked to other purposes. You might want to *explain* what caused your new awareness (why it happened) or to *argue* that everyone needs such awareness (why everyone should reach the same conclusion you did).

The writers who use narration and description most often are those who write autobiography, history, and fiction. If you choose to write in any of these forms, your purpose will be not so much to introduce an example or tell about an experience as to throw light on your subject. You may explain why events happened as they did or argue that such events should never happen again, but you may choose to suggest your ideas subtly through telling a story or giving a description rather than stating them as direct assertions. Your primary purpose is to report the actions and describe the feelings of people entangled in the complex web of circumstance.

AUDIENCE

As you think about writing an essay using narration and description, consider how much you will need to tell your readers and how much you will need to show them. If you are writing from personal experience, few readers will know the story before you tell it. They may know similar stories or have had similar experiences, but they do not know your story. Because you can tell your story in so many different ways—adding or deleting material to fit the occasion—you need to decide how much information your readers will need Do they need to know every detail of your story, only brief summaries of certain parts, or some mixture of detail and summary?

In order to decide what details you should provide, you need to think about how much your readers know and what they are going to expect. If your subject is unusual (a trip to see an erupting volcano), your readers will need a lot of information, much of it technical, to understand the novel experience you are going to describe. They will expect an efficient, matter-of-fact description of volcanoes but also want you to give them some sense of how it feels to see one erupting. If your subject is familiar to most people (your experience with lawn sprinklers), your readers will need few technical details to understand your subject. But they will expect you to give them new images and insights that create a fresh vision of your subject—for example, portraying lawn sprinklers as the languid pulse of summer.

STRATEGIES

The writers in this section demonstrate that you need to use certain strategies to write a successful narrative and descriptive essay. For openers, you must recognize that an experience and an essay about that experience are not the same thing.

When you have any experience, no matter how long it lasts, your memory of that experience is going to be disorganized and poorly defined, but the essay you write about that experience must have a purpose and be sharply focused. When you want to transform your experience into an essay, start by locating the central **conflict.** It may be (1) between the writer and himself, or herself, as when George Orwell finds himself in a quandary about whether to shoot the elephant; (2) between the writer and others, as when Maya Angelou responds to Mrs. Cullinan and her friends; or (3) between the writer and the environment, as when Judith Ortiz Cofer tries to explain the world of El Building.

Once you have identified the conflict, arrange the action so that your readers know how the conflict started, how it developed, and how it was resolved. This coherent sequence of events is called a **plot.** Sometimes you may want to create a plot that sticks to a simple chronological pattern. In "Keeping the Scorebook," Doris Kearns Goodwin simply begins at the beginning and describes events as they occur. At other times you may want to start your essay in the middle or even near the end of the events you are describing. In "The Village Watchman," Terry Tempest Williams begins at the end, after her Uncle Alan's death, and works back to the beginning as she searches for "proper instruction." Each author chooses a pattern according to her purpose: Goodwin wants to describe the evolution of an exciting game; Williams wants to describe the impact of a social stigma.

When you figure out what the beginning, middle, and end of your plot should be, you can establish how each event in those sections should be paced. **Pace** is the speed at which the writer recounts events. Sometimes you can narrate events quickly by omitting details, compressing time, and summarizing experience. For example, Cofer summarizes several episodes in her family's fractured history. At other times you may want to pace events more slowly and carefully because they are vital to your purpose. You will need to include every detail, expand on time, and present the situation as a fully realized scene rather than in summary form. Williams creates such a scene when she describes her Uncle Alan's baptism.

You can make your scenes and summaries effective by your careful **selection of details.** Just adding more details doesn't satisfy this requirement. You must select those special details that satisfy the needs of your readers and further your purpose in the essay. For example, sometimes you will need to give *objective* or *technical* details to help your readers understand your subject. Cofer provides this kind of detail when she describes the food her mother buys. At other times you will want to give *subjective* or *impressionistic* details to appeal to your readers' senses. Orwell provides much of this sort of detail as he tries to re-create his physical and psychological response to shooting the elephant. Finally, you may want to present your details so they form a *figurative image* or create a *dominant impression.* Williams uses both of these strategies: the first when she describes the "Wolf Pole," for example, and the second when she describes the pattern of her uncle's seizures.

In order to identify the conflict, organize the plot, vary the pace, and select details for your essay, you need to determine your **point of view:** the person and position of the narrator (*point*) and the attitude toward the experience being presented (*view*). You choose your *person* by deciding whether you want to tell your story as "I" saw it (as Maya Angelou does in her story about confrontation with Mrs. Cullinan), or as "he" saw it (as Williams does in her account of her uncle's last days).

You choose your *position* by deciding how close you want to be to the action in time and space. You may be involved in the action or view it from the position of an observer, or you may tell about the events as they are happening or many years after they have taken place. For example, George Orwell, the young police officer, is the chief actor in his narrative, but George Orwell, the author, still wonders, years after the event, why he shot the elephant. You create your attitude—how you view the events you intend to present and interpret—by the person and position you choose for writing your essay. The attitudes of the narrators in the following essays might be characterized as angry (Angelou), nostalgic (Goodwin), reverent (Williams), perplexed (Cofer), and ambivalent (Orwell).

USING NARRATION AND DESCRIPTION IN PARAGRAPHS

Here are two narration and description paragraphs. The first is written by a professional writer and is followed by an analysis. The second is written by a student writer and is followed by questions.

MAXINE HONG KINGSTON
from "A Song for a Barbarian Reed Pipe"

Not all of the children who were silent at American school found a voice at Chinese school. One new teacher said each of us had to get up and recite in front of the class, who was to listen. My sister and I had memorized the lesson perfectly. We said it to each other at home, one chanting, one listening. The teacher called on my sister to recite first. It was the first time a teacher had called on the second-born to go first. My sister was scared. She glanced at me and looked away; I looked down at my desk. I hoped that she could do it because if she could, then I would have to. She opened her mouth and a voice came out that wasn't a whisper, but it wasn't a proper voice either. I hoped that she would not cry, fear breaking up her voice like twigs underfoot. She sounded as if she were trying to sing though weeping and strangling. She did not pause or stop to end the embarrassment. She kept going until she said the last word, and then she sat down. When it was my turn, the same voice came

Sets up conflict

Conflict slows pace; heightens suspense

Appeals to sense

out, a <u>crippled animal running on broken legs.</u>

Confirms point of view

You could hear splinters in my voice, bones rubbing jagged against one another. I was loud, though. I was glad I didn't whisper.

Creates new image

Comment This paragraph, taken from the final section of *The Woman Warrior*, recounts an embarrassing scene involving two Chinese sisters. Kingston describes how she and her sister prepare for the expected recitation. The conflict occurs when the teacher calls on the second-born sister first—a breach of Chinese etiquette. By describing how she looks down at her desk, Kingston slows the pace and heightens the anxiety of the situation. She then selects details and images to evoke the sound of her sister's and then her own voice as they complete the lesson.

LAUREN BRINER
Deloris

"All right, how do you say 'dollars' in Spanish?" Mrs. Tyrrel was setting the rules for Spanish II, but we wanted the old rules. Last year Mr. Kreuger, who taught Spanish I, loved to throw parties. I guess he thought fiestas would make us want to learn Spanish. What we really wanted was more fiestas. But now, according to Mrs. Tyrrel, the party was over. She peered at us over the top of her glasses looking for a snitch. We avoided her eyes by thumbing the sides of our new books. "Lauren? How about you?" I looked for help. No luck! My party friends were faking it, staring at the unintelligible sentences in *Spanish II*. I was on my own. I looked up at Mrs. Tyrrel. "Lauren?" I was desperate, caught in her gaze. I panicked. In a really hokey accent, I suggested a possible answer, "Dellores?" "Deloris? Who's Deloris? Is she a friend of yours?" Mrs. Tyrrel was laughing. The whole class began laughing,

"Deloris! Deloris! Deloris!" The blood rushed to
my face and tears welled in my eyes. So much for
old rules and old friends.

1. How does Briner's description of the two teachers establish the
conflict in this episode?
2. How do the responses of the teacher and the class to Lauren's
answer reveal the writer's point of view?

NARRATION AND DESCRIPTION

Points to Remember

1. Focus your narrative on the "story" in your story—
that is, focus on the conflict that defines the plot.
2. Vary the pace of your narrative so that you can summarize some events quickly and render others as fully
realized scenes.
3. Supply evocative details to help your readers experience the dramatic development of your narrative.
4. Establish a consistent point of view so that your readers know how you have positioned yourself in your
story.
5. Represent the events in your narrative so that your
story makes its point.

MAYA ANGELOU

Maya Angelou (given name, Marguerita Johnson) was born in St. Louis, Missouri, in 1928 and spent her early years in California and Arkansas. A woman of varied accomplishments, she is a novelist, poet, playwright, stage and screen performer, composer, and singer. She is perhaps best known for her autobiographical novels: *I Know Why the Caged Bird Sings* (1970), *Gather Together in My Name* (1974), *Singin' and Swingin' and Gettin' Merry Like Christmas* (1976), *Heart of a Woman* (1981), *All God's Children Need Traveling Shoes* (1986), *Wouldn't Take Nothing for My Journey Now* (1993), and *A Brave and Startling Truth* (1995). Angelou's poetry is equally well respected and is published in her *Complete Collected Poems* (1994). In the following selection from *I Know Why the Caged Bird Sings*, Angelou recounts how she maintained her identity in a world of prejudice.

My Name Is Margaret

Recently a white woman from Texas, who would quickly describe herself as a liberal, asked me about my hometown. When I told her that in Stamps my grandmother had owned the only Negro general merchandise store since the turn of the century, she exclaimed, "Why, you were a debutante." Ridiculous and even ludicrous. But Negro girls in small Southern towns, whether poverty-stricken or just munching along on a few of life's necessities, were given as extensive and irrelevant preparations for adulthood as rich white girls shown in magazines. Admittedly the training was not the same. While white girls learned to waltz and sit gracefully with a tea cup balanced on their

1

knees, we were lagging behind, learning the mid-Victorian values with very little money to indulge them. (Come and see Edna Lomax spending the money she made picking cotton on five balls of ecru tatting thread. Her fingers are bound to snag the work and she'll have to repeat the stitches time and time again. But she knows that when she buys the thread.)

We were required to embroider and I had trunkfuls of colorful dishtowels, pillowcases, runners and handkerchiefs to my credit. I mastered the art of crocheting and tatting, and there was a lifetime's supply of dainty doilies that would never be used in sacheted dresser drawers. It went without saying that all girls could iron and wash, but the finer touches around the home, like setting a table with real silver, baking roasts and cooking vegetables without meat, had to be learned elsewhere. Usually at the source of those habits. During my tenth year, a white woman's kitchen became my finishing school.

Mrs. Viola Cullinan was a plump woman who lived in a three-bedroom house somewhere behind the post office. She was singularly unattractive until she smiled, and then the lines around her eyes and mouth which made her look perpetually dirty disappeared, and her face looked like the mask of an impish elf. She usually rested her smile until late afternoon

---

During my tenth year, a white woman's kitchen became my finishing school.

---

when her women friends dropped in and Miss Glory, the cook, served them cold drinks on the closed-in porch.

The exactness of her house was inhuman. This glass went here and only here. That cup had its place and it was an act of impudent rebellion to place it anywhere else. At twelve o'clock the table was set. At 12:15 Mrs. Cullinan sat down

to dinner (whether her husband had arrived or not). At 12:16
Miss Glory brought out the food.

It took me a week to learn the difference between a salad 5
plate, a bread plate and a dessert plate.

Mrs. Cullinan kept up the tradition of her wealthy parents. 6
She was from Virginia. Miss Glory, who was a descendant of
slaves that had worked for the Cullinans, told me her history.
She had married beneath her (according to Miss Glory). Her
husband's family hadn't had their money very long and what
they had "didn't 'mount to much."

As ugly as she was, I thought privately, she was lucky to 7
get a husband above or beneath her station. But Miss Glory
wouldn't let me say a thing against her mistress. She was very
patient with me, however, over the housework. She explained
the dishware, silverware and servants' bells. The large round
bowl in which soup was served wasn't a soup bowl, it was a
tureen. There were goblets, sherbet glasses, ice-cream glasses,
wine glasses, green glass coffee cups with matching saucers,
and water glasses. I had a glass to drink from, and it sat with
Miss Glory's on a separate shelf from the others. Soup
spoons, gravy boat, butter knives, salad forks and carving
platter were additions to my vocabulary and in fact almost
represented a new language. I was fascinated with the novelty,
with the fluttering Mrs. Cullinan and her Alice-in-Wonder-
land house.

Her husband remains, in my memory, undefined. I 8
lumped him with all the other white men that I had ever seen
and tried not to see.

On our way home one evening, Miss Glory told me that 9
Mrs. Cullinan couldn't have children. She said that she was
too delicate-boned. It was hard to imagine bones at all under
those layers of fat. Miss Glory went on to say that the doctor
had taken out all her lady organs. I reasoned that a pig's
organs included the lungs, heart and liver, so if Mrs. Cullinan
was walking around without those essentials, it explained why
she drank alcohol out of unmarked bottles. She was keeping
herself embalmed.

When I spoke to Bailey about it, he agreed that I was right, 10

but he also informed me that Mr. Cullinan had two daughters
by a colored lady and that I knew them very well. He added
that the girls were the spitting image of their father. I was
unable to remember what he looked like, although I had just
left him a few hours before, but I thought of the Coleman
girls. They were very light-skinned and certainly didn't look
very much like their mother (no one ever mentioned Mr.
Coleman).

My pity for Mrs. Cullinan preceded me the next morning   11
like the Cheshire cat's smile. Those girls, who could have
been her daughters, were beautiful. They didn't have to
straighten their hair. Even when they were caught in the rain,
their braids still hung down straight like tamed snakes. Their
mouths were pouty little cupid's bows. Mrs. Cullinan didn't
know what she missed. Or maybe she did. Poor Mrs. Cullinan.

For weeks after, I arrived early, left late and tried very hard   1
to make up for her barrenness. If she had had her own
children, she wouldn't have had to ask me to run a thousand
errands from her back door to the back door of her friends.
Poor old Mrs. Cullinan.

Then one evening Miss Glory told me to serve the ladies   13
on the porch. After I set the tray down and turned toward
the kitchen, one of the women asked, "What's your name,
girl?" It was the speckled-faced one. Mrs. Cullinan said, "She
doesn't talk much. Her name's Margaret."

"Is she dumb?"   14

"No. As I understand it, she can talk when she wants to   15
but she's usually quiet as a little mouse. Aren't you, Margaret?"

I smiled at her. Poor thing. No organs and couldn't even   16
pronounce my name correctly.

"She's a sweet little thing, though."   17

"Well, that may be, but the name's too long. I'd never   18
bother myself. I'd call her Mary if I was you."

I fumed into the kitchen. That horrible woman would   19
never have the chance to call me Mary because if I was
starving I'd never work for her. I decided I wouldn't pee on

her if her heart was on fire. Giggles drifted in off the porch
and into Miss Glory's pots. I wondered what they could be
laughing about.

Whitefolks were so strange. Could they be talking about   20
me? Everybody knew that they stuck together better than the
Negroes did. It was possible that Mrs. Cullinan had friends
in St. Louis who heard about a girl from Stamps being in
court and wrote to tell her. Maybe she knew about Mr.
Freeman.

My lunch was in my mouth a second time and I went   21
outside and relieved myself on the bed of four-o'clocks. Miss
Glory thought I might be coming down with something and
told me to go on home, that Momma would give me some
herb tea, and she'd explain to her mistress.

I realized how foolish I was being before I reached the   22
pond. Of course Mrs. Cullinan didn't know. Otherwise she
wouldn't have given me two nice dresses that Momma cut
down, and she certainly wouldn't have called me a "sweet
little thing." My stomach felt fine, and I didn't mention
anything to Momma.

That evening I decided to write a poem on being white,   23
fat, old and without children. It was going to be a tragic
ballad. I would have to watch her carefully to capture the
essence of her loneliness and pain.

The very next day, she called me by the wrong name. Miss   24
Glory and I were washing up the lunch dishes when Mrs.
Cullinan came to the doorway. "Mary?"

Miss Glory asked, "Who?"   25

Mrs. Cullinan, sagging a little, knew and I knew. "I want   26
Mary to go down to Mrs. Randall's and take her some soup.
She's not been feeling well for a few days."

Miss Glory's face was a wonder to see. "You mean Mar-   27
garet, ma'am. Her name's Margaret."

"That's too long. She's Mary from now on. Heat that soup   28
from last night and put it in the china tureen and, Mary, I
want you to carry it carefully."

Every person I knew had a hellish horror of being "called   29
out of his name." It was a dangerous practice to call a Negro

anything that could be loosely construed as insulting because of the centuries of their having been called niggers, jigs, dinges, blackbirds, crows, boots and spooks.

Miss Glory had a fleeting second of feeling sorry for me. 30 Then as she handed me the hot tureen she said, "Don't mind, don't pay that no mind. Sticks and stones may break your bones, but words . . . You know, I been working for her for twenty years."

She held the back door open for me. "Twenty years. I 31 wasn't much older than you. My name used to be Hallelujah. That's what Ma named me, but my mistress give me 'Glory,' and it stuck. I likes it better too."

I was in the little path that ran behind the houses when 32 Miss Glory shouted, "It's shorter too."

For a few seconds it was a tossup over whether I would 33 laugh (imagine being named Hallelujah) or cry (imagine letting some white woman rename you for her convenience). My anger saved me from either outburst. I had to quit the job, but the problem was going to be how to do it. Momma wouldn't allow me to quit for just any reason.

"She's a peach. That woman is a real peach." Mrs. Ran- 34 dall's maid was talking as she took the soup from me, and I wondered what her name used to be and what she answered to now.

For a week I looked into Mrs. Cullinan's face as she called 35 me Mary. She ignored my coming late and leaving early. Miss Glory was a little annoyed because I had begun to leave egg yolk on the dishes and wasn't putting much heart in polishing the silver. I hoped that she would complain to our boss, but she didn't.

Then Bailey solved my dilemma. He had me describe the 36 contents of the cupboard and the particular plates she liked best. Her favorite piece was a casserole shaped like a fish and the green glass coffee cups. I kept his instructions in mind, so on the next day when Miss Glory was hanging out clothes and I had again been told to serve the old biddies on the porch, I dropped the empty serving tray. When I heard Mrs. Cullinan scream, "Mary!" I picked up the casserole and two

of the green glass cups in readiness. As she rounded the
kitchen door I let them fall on the tiled floor.

I could never absolutely describe to Bailey what happened   37
next, because each time I got to the part where she fell on
the floor and screwed up her ugly face to cry, we burst out
laughing. She actually wobbled around on the floor and
picked up shards of the cups and cried, "Oh, Momma. Oh,
dear Gawd. It's Momma's china from Virginia. Oh, Momma,
I sorry."

Miss Glory came running in from the yard and the women   38
from the porch crowded around. Miss Glory was almost as
broken up as her mistress. "You mean to say she broke our
Virginia dishes? What we gone do?"

Miss Cullinan cried louder, "That clumsy nigger. Clumsy   39
little black nigger."

Old speckled-face leaned down and asked, "Who did it,   40
Viola? Was it Mary? Who did it?"

Everything was happening so fast I can't remember   41
whether her action preceded her words, but I know that Mrs.
Cullinan said, "Her name's Margaret, goddamn it, her
name's Margaret." And she threw a wedge of the broken
plate at me. It could have been the hysteria which put her
aim off, but the flying crockery caught Miss Glory right over
the ear and she started screaming.

I left the front door wide open so all the neighbors could   42
hear.

Mrs. Cullinan was right about one thing. My name wasn't   43
Mary.

For Study and Discussion

QUESTIONS FOR RESPONSE

1. In what ways do you identify with your name? How do you feel
   when someone mispronounces, changes, or forgets it?
2. What questions do you have about some of the unresolved issues

in the narration? For example, what do you think will happen when Margaret loses her job?

QUESTIONS ABOUT PURPOSE

1. In what sense does Mrs. Cullinan's kitchen serve as Angelou's "finishing school"? What is she supposed to learn there? What does she learn?
2. How does Angelou's description of Mrs. Cullinan's house as *exact* and *inhuman* support her purpose in recounting the events that take place there?

QUESTIONS ABOUT AUDIENCE

1. How does Angelou's comment about the liberal woman from Texas identify the immediate audience for her essay?
2. What assumptions does Angelou make about her other readers when she comments on the laughter of the white women on the porch?

QUESTIONS ABOUT STRATEGIES

1. How does Angelou use the three discussions of her name to organize her narrative? How does she pace the third discussion to provide an effective resolution for her essay?
2. How does Angelou's intention to write a poem about Mrs. Cullinan establish her initial attitude toward her employer? What changes her attitude toward Mrs. Cullinan's "loneliness and pain"?

QUESTIONS FOR DISCUSSION

1. How did you feel about Glory's and Bailey's reactions to the destruction of the fish-shaped casserole? Explain their strengths and weaknesses as a teacher or adviser.
2. Angelou admits that poor black girls in small southern towns and rich white girls in magazines do not receive the same training. What evidence in the essay suggests that both girls were given "extensive and irrelevant preparations for adulthood"?

DORIS KEARNS GOODWIN

Doris Kearns Goodwin was born in 1943 in Rockville Centre, New York, and educated at Colby College and Harvard University. She worked in Washington, D.C. at various government agencies, eventually becoming special consultant to President Lyndon Johnson. That appointment enabled her to write *Lyndon Johnson and the American Dream* (1976). She has worked since at Harvard University where she has written *The Fitzgeralds and the Kennedys: An American Saga* (1987) and *No Ordinary Time—Franklin and Eleanor Roosevelt: The Home Front in World War II* (1994), which won the Pulitzer Prize. In "Keeping the Scorebook," reprinted from her memoir *Wait till Next Year* (1997), Goodwin explains how she recorded the deeds of her favorite baseball team, the Brooklyn Dodgers.

Keeping the Scorebook

W HEN I WAS six, my father gave me a bright-red score- 1 book that opened my heart to the game of baseball. After dinner on long summer nights, he would sit beside me in our small enclosed porch to hear my account of that day's Brooklyn Dodger game. Night after night he taught me the odd collection of symbols, numbers, and letters that enable a baseball lover to record every action of the game. Our score sheets had blank boxes in which we could draw our own slanted lines in the form of a diamond as we followed players around the bases. Wherever the baserunner's progress stopped, the line stopped. He instructed me to fill in the unused boxes at the end of each inning with an elaborate checkerboard design which made it absolutely clear who had been the last to bat and who would lead off the next inning. By the time I had mastered the art of scorekeeping, a lasting bond had been forged among my father, baseball, and me.

All through the summer of 1949, my first summer as a fan,   2
I spent my afternoons sitting cross-legged before the squat Philco radio which stood as a permanent fixture on our porch in Rockville Centre, on the South Shore of Long Island, New York. With my scorebook spread before me, I attended Dodger games through the courtly voice of Dodger announcer Red Barber. As he announced the lineup, I carefully printed each player's name in a column on the left side of my

---

The nightly recountings to
my father of the Dodgers' progress
provided my first lessons
in the narrative art.

---

sheet. Then, using the standard system my father had taught me, which assigned a number to each position in the field, starting with a "1" for the pitcher and ending with a "9" for the right fielder, I recorded every play. I found it difficult at times to sit still. As the Dodgers came to bat, I would walk around the room, talking to the players as if they were standing in front of me. At critical junctures, I tried to make a bargain, whispering and cajoling while Pee Wee Reese or Duke Snider stepped into the batter's box: "Please, please, get a hit. If you get a hit now, I'll make my bed every day for a week." Sometimes, when the score was close and the opposing team at bat with men on base, I was too agitated to listen. Asking my mother to keep notes, I left the house for a walk around the block, hoping that when I returned the enemy threat would be over, and once again we'd be up at bat. Mostly, however, I stayed at my post, diligently recording each inning so that, when my father returned from his job as bank examiner for the State of New York, I could re-create for him the game he had missed.

When my father came home from the city, he would change from his three-piece suit into long pants and a short-sleeved sport shirt, and come downstairs for the ritual Manhattan cocktail with my mother. Then my parents would summon me for dinner from my play on the street outside our house. All through dinner I had to restrain myself from telling him about the day's game, waiting for the special time to come when we would sit together on the couch, my scorebook on my lap.

"Well, did anything interesting happen today?" he would begin. And even before the daily question was completed I had eagerly launched into my narrative of every play, and almost every pitch, of that afternoon's contest. It never crossed my mind to wonder if, at the close of a day's work, he might find my lengthy account the least bit tedious. For there was mastery as well as pleasure in our nightly ritual. Through my knowledge, I commanded my father's undivided attention, the sign of his love. It would instill in me an early awareness of the power of narrative, which would introduce a lifetime of storytelling, fueled by the naive confidence that others would find me as entertaining as my father did.

Michael Francis Aloysius Kearns, my father, was a short man who appeared much larger on account of his erect bearing, broad chest, and thick neck. He had a ruddy Irish complexion, and his green eyes flashed with humor and vitality. When he smiled his entire face was transformed, radiating enthusiasm and friendliness. He called me "Bubbles," a pet name he had chosen, he told me, because I seemed to enjoy so many things. Anxious to confirm his description, I refused to let my enthusiasm wane, even when I grew tired or grumpy. Thus excitement about things became a habit, a part of my personality, and the expectation that I should enjoy new experiences often engendered the enjoyment itself.

These nightly recountings of the Dodgers' progress provided my first lessons in the narrative art. From the scorebook, with its tight squares of neatly arranged symbols, I could unfold the tale of an entire game and tell a story that seemed to last almost as long as the game itself. At first, I was unable to resist the temptation to skip ahead to an important play in later innings. At times, I grew so excited about a Dodger victory that I blurted out the final score before I had hardly begun. But as I became more experienced in my storytelling, I learned to build a dramatic story with a beginning, middle, and end. Slowly, I learned that if I could recount the game, one batter at a time, inning by inning, without divulging the outcome, I could keep the suspense and my father's interest alive until the very last pitch. Sometimes I pretended that I was the great Red Barber himself, allowing my voice to swell when reporting a home run, quieting to a whisper when the action grew tense, injecting tidbits about the players into my reports. At critical moments, I would jump from the couch to illustrate a ball that turned foul at the last moment or a dropped fly that was scored as an error.

 "How many hits did Roy Campanella get?" my dad would ask. Tracing my finger across the horizontal line that represented Campanella's at bats that day, I would count. "One, two, three. Three hits, a single, a double, and another single." "How many strikeouts for Don Newcombe?" It was easy. I would count the Ks. "One, two . . . eight. He had eight strikeouts." Then he'd ask me more subtle questions about different plays—whether a strikeout was called or swinging, whether the double play was around the horn, whether the single that won the game was hit to left or right. If I had scored carefully, using the elaborate system he had taught me, I would know the answers. My father pointed to the second inning, where Jackie Robinson had hit a single and then stolen second. There was excitement in his voice. "See, it's all here. While Robinson was dancing off second he rattled the pitcher so badly that the next two guys walked to load the bases. That's the impact Robinson makes, game after game. Isn't he something?" His smile at such moments inspired me to take my responsibility seriously.

 7

Sometimes, a particular play would trigger in my father a   8
memory of a similar situation in a game when he was young,
and he would tell me stories about the Dodgers when he was
a boy growing up in Brooklyn. His vivid tales featured strange
heroes such as Casey Stengel, Zack Wheat, and Jimmy
Johnston. Though it was hard at first to imagine that the
Casey Stengel I knew, the manager of the Yankees, with his
colorful language and hilarious antics, was the same man as
the Dodger outfielder who hit an inside-the-park home run
at the first game ever played at Ebbets Field, my father so
skillfully stitched together the past and the present that I felt
as if I were living in different time zones. If I closed my eyes,
I imagined I was at Ebbets Field in the 1920s for that celebrated game when Dodger right fielder Babe Herman hit a
double with the bases loaded, and through a series of mishaps
on the base paths, three Dodgers ended up at third base at
the same time. And I was sitting by my father's side, five
years before I was born, when the lights were turned on for
the first time at Ebbets Field, the crowd gasping and then
cheering as the summer night was transformed into startling
day.

When I had finished describing the game, it was time to   9
go to bed, unless I could convince my father to tally each
player's batting average, reconfiguring his statistics to reflect
the developments of that day's game. If Reese went 3 for 5
and had started the day at .303, my father showed me, by
adding and multiplying all the numbers in his head, that his
average would rise to .305. If Snider went 0 for 4 and started
the day at .301 then his average would dip four points below
the .300 mark. If Carl Erskine had let in three runs in seven
innings, then my father would multiply three times nine,
divide that by the number of innings pitched, and magically
tell me whether Erskine's earned-run average had improved
or worsened. It was this facility with numbers that had made
it possible for my father to pass the civil-service test and
become a bank examiner despite leaving school after the
eighth grade. And this job had carried him from a Brooklyn

tenement to a house with a lawn on Southard Avenue in
Rockville Centre.

All through that summer, my father kept from me the   10
knowledge that running box scores appeared in the daily
newspapers. He never mentioned that these abbreviated histories had been a staple feature of the sports pages since the
nineteenth century and were generally the first thing he and
his fellow commuters turned to when they opened the *Daily
News* and the *Herald Tribune* in the morning. I believed that,
if I did not recount the games he had missed, my father would
never have been able to follow our Dodgers the proper way,
day by day, play by play, inning by inning. In other words,
without me, his love of baseball would be forever unfulfilled.

I had the luck to fall in love with baseball at the start of   11
an era of pure delight for New York fans. In each of the nine
seasons from 1949 to 1957—spanning much of my childhood—we would watch one of the three New York teams—
the Dodgers, the Giants, or the Yankees—compete in the
World Series. In this golden era, the Yankees won five con-
secutive World Series, the Giants won two pennants and one
championship, and my beloved Dodgers won one championship and five pennants, while losing two additional pennants
in the last inning of the last game of the season.

In those days before players were free agents, the starting   12
lineups remained basically intact for years. Fans gave their
loyalty to a team, knowing the players they loved would hold
the same positions and, year after year, exhibit the same
endearing quirks and irritating habits. And what a storied
lineup my Dodgers had in the postwar seasons: Roy Campanella started behind the plate, Gil Hodges at first, Jackie
Robinson at second, Pee Wee Reese at short, Billy Cox at
third, Gene Hermanski in left, Duke Snider in center, and
Carl Furillo in right. Half of that lineup—Reese, Robinson,
Campanella, and Snider—would eventually be elected to the
Hall of Fame; Gil Hodges and Carl Furillo would likely have
been enshrined in Cooperstown had they played in any other
decade or for any other club. Never would there be a better
time to be a Dodger fan.

For Study and Discussion

QUESTIONS FOR RESPONSE

1. What kind of special skill has one of your parents taught you—cooking, fishing, car repair—that has created a "lasting bond" between you?
2. How has the business of contemporary sports changed your loyalties to *your* team?

QUESTIONS ABOUT PURPOSE

1. What does Goodwin learn about the power of narrative by telling her father the story of the day's game?
2. Why is Goodwin so devoted to keeping the scorebook for her father?

QUESTIONS ABOUT AUDIENCE

1. How does Goodwin anticipate the needs and questions of her primary audience (her father)?
2. How does she make this story about old baseball games "come alive" for her contemporary readers?

QUESTIONS ABOUT STRATEGY

1. How does Goodwin learn "to build a dramatic story with a beginning, middle, and end"?
2. How does Goodwin's father use effective narrative strategies to tell his daughter about the games he saw when he was a boy?

QUESTIONS FOR DISCUSSION

1. Why does Goodwin's father fail to mention the box scores published in the daily newspaper?
2. How does Goodwin's attitude toward baseball demonstrate her realization that expecting to enjoy new experiences "often engendered the enjoyment itself."

Terry Tempest Williams was born in 1955 in the Salt Valley of Utah and educated at the University of Utah. She has taught on a Navajo reservation and in the women's studies program at the University of Utah. She currently serves as the curator of education and naturalist-in-residence at the Utah Museum of Natural History in Salt Lake City. Williams has written children's books with nature themes, including *The Secret Language of Snow* (1984); a collection of short stories set in Utah, *Coyote's Canyon* (1989); and three works of nonfiction that blend natural history and personal experience: *Pieces of White Shell: A Journey to Navajo-Land* (1984), *Refuge: An Unnatural History of Family and Place* (1991), and *An Unspoken Hunger: Stories from the Field* (1994). In "The Village Watchman," reprinted from *An Unspoken Hunger,* Williams describes the remarkable lessons she learned from her Uncle Alan.

The Village Watchman

S TORIES CARVED IN cedar rise from the deep woods of 1
Sitka. These totem poles are foreign to me, this vertical lineage of clans; Eagle, Raven, Wolf, and Salmon. The Tlingit craftsmen create a genealogy of the earth, a reminder of mentors, that we come into this world in need of proper instruction. I sit on the soft floor of this Alaskan forest and feel the presence of Other.

The totem before me is called "Wolf Pole" by locals. The 2
Village Watchman sits on top of Wolf's head with his knees drawn to his chest, his hands holding them tight against his body. He wears a red-and-black-striped hat. His eyes are

direct, deep-set, painted blue. The expression on his face reminds me of a man I loved, a man who was born into this world feet first.

"Breech—" my mother told me of her brother's birth. 3
"Alan was born feet first. As a result, his brain was denied oxygen. He is special."

As a child, this information impressed me. I remember 4 thinking fish live underwater. Maybe Alan had gills, maybe he didn't need a face-first gulp of air like the rest of us. His sweet breath of initiation came in time, slowly moving up through the soles of his tiny webbed feet. The amniotic sea

---

Alan was wild, like a mustang in the desert and, like most wild horses, he was eventually rounded up.

---

he had floated in for nine months delivered him with a fluid memory. He knew something. Other.

Wolf, who resides in the center of this totem, holds the tail 5 of Salmon with his feet. The tongue of Wolf hangs down, blood-red, as do his front paws, black. Salmon, a sockeye, is poised downriver—a swish of a tail and he could be gone, but the clasp of Wolf is strong.

There is a story of a boy who was kidnapped from his 6 village by the Salmon People. He was taken from his family to learn the ways of water. When he returned many years later to his home, he was recognized by his own as a Holy Man privy to the mysteries of the unseen world. Twenty years after my uncle's death, I wonder if Alan could have been that boy.

But our culture tells a different story, more alien than those 7 of Tlingit or Haida. My culture calls people of sole-births retarded, handicapped, mentally disabled or challenged. We see them for who they are not, rather than for who they are.

My grandmother, Lettie Romney Dixon, wrote in her 8

journal, "It wasn't until Alan was sixteen months old that a busy doctor cruelly broke the news to us. Others may have suspected our son's limitations but to those of us who loved him so unquestionably, lightning struck without warning. I hugged my sorrow to myself. I felt abandoned and lost. I wouldn't accept the verdict. Then we started the trips to a multitude of doctors. Most of them were kind and explained that our child was like a car without brakes, like an electric wire without insulation. They gave us no hope for a normal life."

Normal. Latin: *normalis; norma,* a rule; conforming with   9
or constituting an accepted standard, model, or pattern, especially corresponding to the median or average of a large group in type, appearance, achievement, function, or development.

Alan was not normal. He was unique; one and only; single;   10
sole; unusual; extraordinary; rare. His emotions were not measured, his curiosity not bridled. In a sense, he was wild like a mustang in the desert and, like most wild horses, he was eventually rounded up.

He was unpredictable. He created his own rules and they   11
changed from moment to moment. Alan was twelve years old, hyperactive, mischievous, easily frustrated, and unable to learn in traditional ways. The situation was intensified by his seizures. Suddenly, without warning, he would stiffen like a rake, fall forward and crash to the ground, hitting his head. My grandparents could not keep him home any longer. They needed professional guidance and help. In 1957 they reluctantly placed their youngest child in an institution for handicapped children called the American Fork Training School. My grandmother's heart broke for the second time.

Once again, from her journal: "Many a night my pillow is   12
wet from tears of sorrow and senseless dreamings of 'if things had only been different,' or wondering if he is tucked in snug and warm, if he is well and happy, if the wind still bothers him. . . ."

The wind may have continued to bother Alan, certainly   13
the conditions he was living under were less than ideal, but as a family there was much about his private life we never

knew. What we did know was that Alan had an enormous capacity for adaptation. We had no choice but to follow him. I followed him for years.   14

Alan was ten years my senior. In my mind, growing up, he   15 was mythic. Everything I was taught not to do, Alan did. We were taught to be polite, to not express displeasure or anger in public. Alan was sheer, physical expression. Whatever was on his mind was vocalized and usually punctuated with colorful speech. We would go bowling as a family on Sundays. Each of us would take our turn, hold the black ball to our chest, take a few steps, swing our arm back, forward, glide, and release—the ball would roll down the alley, hit a few pins, we would wait for the ball to return, and then take our second run. Little emotion was shown. When it was Alan's turn, it was an event. Nothing subtle. His style was Herculean. Big man. Big ball. Big roll. Big bang. Whether it was a strike or a gutter, he clapped his hands, spun around in the floor, slapped his thighs and cried, "God-damn! Did you see that one? Send me another ball, sweet Jesus!" And the ball was always returned.

I could always count on my uncle for a straight answer.   16 He was my mentor in understanding that one of the remarkable aspects of being human was to hold opposing views in our mind at once.

"How are you doing?" I would ask.   17

"Ask me how I am feeling?" he answered.   18

"Okay, how are you feeling?"   19

"Today? Right now?"   20

"Yes."   21

"I am very happy and very sad."   22

"How can you be both at the same time?" I asked in all   23 seriousness, a girl of nine or ten.

"Because both require each other's company. They live in   24 the same house. Didn't you know?"

We would laugh and then go on to another topic. Talking   25 to my uncle was always like entering a maze of riddles. Ask a question. Answer with a question and see where it leads you.

My younger brother Steve and I spent a lot of time with   26 Alan. He offered us shelter from the conventionality of a

Mormon family. At our home during Christmas, he would direct us in his own nativity plays. "More—" he would say to us, making wide gestures with his hands. "Give me more of yourself." He was not like anyone we knew. In a culture where we were taught socially to be seen not heard, Alan was our mirror. We could be different too. His unquestioning belief in us as children, as human beings, was in startling contrast to the way we saw the public react to him. It hurt us. What we could never tell was if it hurt him.

Each week, Steve and I would accompany our grandparents south to visit Alan. It was an hour's drive to the training school from Salt Lake City, mostly through farmlands.   27

We would enter the grounds, pull into the parking lot of the institution where a playground filled with huge papier-mâché storybook figures stood (a twenty-foot pied piper, a pumpkin carriage with Cinderella inside, the old woman who lived in a shoe), and nine out of ten times, Alan would be standing outside his dormitory waiting for us. We would get out of the car and he would run toward us, throwing his powerful arms around us. His hugs cracked my back and at times I had to fight for my breath. My grandfather would calm him down by simply saying, "We're here, son. You can relax now."   28

Alan was a formidable man, now in his early twenties, stocky and strong. His head was large with a protruding forehead that bore many scars, a line-by-line history of seizures. He always had on someone else's clothes—a tweed jacket too small, brown pants too big, a striped golf shirt that didn't match. He showed us appearances didn't matter, personality did. If you didn't know him, he could look frightening. It was an unspoken rule in our family that the character of others was gauged in how they treated him. The only thing consistent about his attire was that he always wore a silver football helmet from Olympus High School where my grandfather was coach. It was a loving, practical solution to protect Alan when he fell. Quite simply, the helmet cradled his head and absorbed the shock of the seizures.   29

"Part of the team," my grandfather Sanky would say as he   30 slapped him affectionately on the back. "You're a Titan, son, and I love you—you're a real player on our team."

The windows to the dormitory were dark, reflecting Mount Timpanogos to the east. It was hard to see inside, but I knew what the interior held. It looked like an abandoned gymnasium without bleachers, filled with hospital beds. The stained white walls and yellow-waxed floors offered no warmth to its residents. The stench was nauseating, sweat and urine trapped in the oppression of stale air. I recall the dirty sheets, the lack of privacy, and the almond-eyed children who never rose from their beds. And then I would turn around and face Alan's cheerfulness, the open and loving manner in which he would introduce me to his friends, the pride he exhibited as he showed me around his home. I kept thinking, Doesn't he see how bad this is, how poorly they are being treated? His words would return to me, "I am very happy and I am very sad." 31

For my brother and me, Alan was our guide, our elder. He was fearless. But neither one of us will ever be able to escape the image of Alan kissing his parents good-bye after an afternoon with family and slowly walking back to his dormitory. Before we drove away, he would turn toward us, take off his silver helmet, and wave. The look on his face haunts me still. Alan walked point for all of us. 32

Alan liked to talk about God. Perhaps it was in these private conversations that our real friendship was forged. 33

"I know Him," he would say when all the adults were gone. 34

"You do?" I asked. 35

"I talk to Him every day." 36

"How so?" 37

"I talk to Him in my prayers. I listen and then I hear His voice." 38

"What does He tell you?" 39

"He tells me to be patient. He tells me to be kind. He tells me that He loves me." 40

In Mormon culture, children are baptized a member of the Church of Jesus Christ of Latter-Day Saints when they 41

turn eight years old. Alan had never been baptized because
my grandparents believed it should be his choice, not something simply taken for granted. When he turned twenty-two,
he expressed a sincere desire to join the Church. A date was
set immediately.

The entire Dixon clan convened in the Lehi Chapel, a few   42
miles north of the group home where Alan was now living.
We were there to support and witness his conversion. As we
walked toward the meetinghouse where this sacred rite was
to be performed, Alan had a violent seizure. My grandfather
and Uncle Don, Alan's elder brother, dropped down with
him, holding his head and body as every muscle thrashed on
the pavement like a school of netted fish brought on deck. I
didn't want to look, but to walk away would have been worse.
We stayed with him, all of us.

"Talk to God," I heard myself saying under my breath. "I   43
love you, Alan."

"Can you hear me, darling?" It was my grandmother's   44
voice, her hand holding her son's hand.

By now, many of us were gathered on our knees around   45
him, our trembling hands on his rigid body.

> *And we, who have always thought*
> *Of happiness as rising, would feel*
> *The emotion that almost overwhelms us*
> *Whenever a happy thing falls.*
> *—Rainer Maria Rilke*

Alan opened his eyes. "I want to be baptized," he said.   46
The men helped him to his feet. The gash on his left temple
was deep. Blood dripped down the side of his face. He would
forgo stitches once again. My mother had her arm around
my grandmother's waist. Shaken, we all followed him inside.

Alan's father and brother ministered to him, stopped the   47
bleeding and bandaged the pressure wound, then helped him
change into the designated white garments for baptism. He
entered the room with great dignity and sat on the front pew

with a dozen or more eight-year-old children seated on either side. Row after row of family sat behind him.

"Alan Romney Dixon." His name was called by the presiding bishop. Alan rose from the pew and met his brother Don, also dressed in white, who took his hand and led him down the blue-tiled stairs into the baptismal font filled with water. They faced the congregation. Don raised his right arm to the square in the gesture of a holy oath as Alan placed his hands on his brother's left forearm. The sacred prayer was offered in the name of the Father, the Son, and the Holy Ghost, after which my uncle put his right hand behind Alan's shoulder and gently lowered him into the water for a complete baptism by immersion. 48

Alan emerged from the holy waters like an angel. 49

> *The breaking away of childhood*
> *Left you intact. In a moment,*
> *You stood there, as if completed*
> *In a miracle, all at once.*
> —*Rainer Maria Rilke*

Six years later, I found myself sitting in a chair across from my uncle at the University Hospital, where he was being treated for a severe ear infection. I was eighteen. He was twenty-eight. 50

"Alan," I asked. "What is it really like to be inside your body?" 51

He crossed his legs and placed both hands on the arms of the chair. His brown eyes were piercing. 52

"I can't tell you what it's like except to say I feel pain for not being seen as the person I am." 53

A few days later, Alan died alone; unique; one and only; single; in American Fork, Utah. 54

The Village Watchman sits on top of his totem with Wolf and Salmon—it is beginning to rain in the forest. I find it curious that this spot in southeast Alaska has brought me back into 55 relation with my uncle, this man of sole-birth who came into the world feet first. He reminds me of what it means to live and love with a broken heart; how nothing is sacred, how everything is sacred. He was a weather vane—a storm and a clearing at once.

Shortly after his death, Alan appeared to me in a dream. 56
We were standing in my grandmother's kitchen. He was leaning against the white stove with his arms folded.

"Look at me, now, Terry," he said smiling. "I'm normal— 57
perfectly normal." And then he laughed. We both laughed.

He handed me his silver football helmet that was resting 58
on the counter, kissed me, and opened the back door.

"Do you recognize who I am?" 59

On this day in Sitka, I remember. 60

For Study and Discussion

QUESTIONS FOR RESPONSE

1. In what ways does our culture (television, movies) portray "special" people?
2. In what ways does Williams's essay correct or enrich your understanding of "special" people?

QUESTIONS ABOUT PURPOSE

1. How does Williams's title suggest the purpose of her description of her Uncle Alan's life?
2. How does Williams's description of the Wolf Pole present the purpose of her narrative?

QUESTIONS ABOUT AUDIENCE

1. How does Williams's use of the pronoun *our* in the following phrase identify her audience: "our culture tells a different story, more alien"?
2. How does the following sentence separate Williams's family from her audience: "His unquestioning belief in us . . . was in startling contrast to the way we saw the public react to him"?

QUESTIONS ABOUT STRATEGIES

1. How does Williams use the quotations from Rilke's poetry to interpret Alan's baptism?
2. How does she use the visits at the school, and particularly her last visit at the hospital, to slow the pace of her narrative?

QUESTIONS FOR DISCUSSION

1. What do the words *normal* and *special* mean in our culture?
2. How is it possible to hold opposing views in the mind at once? How does Alan do it?

Judith Ortiz Cofer was born in Hormigueros, Puerto Rico, in 1952. She emigrated to the United States in 1956 and was educated at Augusta College, Florida Atlantic University, and Oxford University. She has taught in the public schools of Palm Beach County, Florida, as well as at several universities such as Miami University and the University of Georgia. Her poetry is collected in *Reading for the Mainland* (1987) and *Terms of Survival* (1987), and her first novel, *The Line of the Sun* (1989), was nominated for the Pulitzer Prize. Her recent books include *The Latin Deli: Prose and Poetry* (1993) and *An Island Like You: Stories of the Barrio* (1995). In "Silent Dancing," the title essay from her collection of personal essays (1990), Cofer describes how a silent home movie helps her understand her family heritage.

Silent Dancing

We have a home movie of this party. Several times my mother   1
and I have watched it together, and I have asked questions about
the silent revelers coming in and out of focus. It is grainy and
of short duration, but it's a great visual aid to my memory of
life at that time. And it is in color—the only complete scene in
color I can recall from those years.

W E LIVED IN Puerto Rico until my brother was born   2
in 1954. Soon after, because of economic pressures
on our growing family, my father joined the United States
Navy. He was assigned to duty on a ship in Brooklyn Yard—a
place of cement and steel that was to be his home base in the
States until his retirement more than twenty years later. He

left the Island first, alone, going to New York City and
tracking down his uncle who lived with his family across the
Hudson River in Paterson, New Jersey. There my father
found a tiny apartment in a huge tenement that had once
housed Jewish families but was just being taken over and
transformed by Puerto Ricans, overflowing from New York
City. In 1955 he sent for us. My mother was only twenty
years old, I was not quite three, and my brother was a toddler
when we arrived at *El Building,* as the place had been chris-
tened by its newest residents.

My memories of life in Paterson during those first few years 3
are all in shades of gray. Maybe I was too young to absorb
vivid colors and details, or to discriminate between the slate
blue of the winter sky and the darker hues of the snow-bear-
ing clouds, but that single color washes over the whole period. The building we lived in was gray, as were the streets,

---

*It became my father's obsession to get out of
the barrio, and thus we were never
permitted to form bonds with the place or
with the people who lived there.*

---

filled with slush the first few months of my life there. The
coat my father had bought for me was similar in color and
too big; it sat heavily on my thin frame.

I do remember the way the heater pipes banged and rat- 4
tled, startling all of us out of sleep until we got so used to
the sound that we automatically shut it out or raised our
voices above the racket. The hiss from the valve punctuated
my sleep (which has always been fitful) like a nonhuman
presence in the room—a dragon sleeping at the entrance of
my childhood. But the pipes were also a connection to all the
other lives being lived around us. Having come from a house

designed for a single family back in Puerto Rico—my
mother's extended-family home—it was curious to know that
strangers lived under our floor and above our heads, and that
the heater pipe went through everyone's apartments. (My
first spanking in Paterson came as a result of playing tunes on
the pipes in my room to see if there would be an answer.)
My mother was as new to this concept of beehive life as I
was, but she had been given strict orders by my father to keep
the doors locked, the noise down, ourselves to ourselves.

It seems that Father had learned some painful lessons   5
about prejudice while searching for an apartment in Paterson.
Not until years later did I hear how much resistance he had
encountered with landlords who were panicking at the influx
of Latinos into a neighborhood that had been Jewish for a
couple of generations. It made no difference that it was the
American phenomenon of ethnic turnover which was changing the urban core of Paterson, and that the human flood
could not be held back with an accusing finger.

"You Cuban?" one man had asked my father, pointing at   6
his name tag on the Navy uniform—even though my father
had the fair skin and light-brown hair of his northern Spanish
background, and the name Ortiz is as common in Puerto
Rico as Johnson is in the United States.

"No," my father had answered, looking past the finger into   7
his adversary's angry eyes. "I'm Puerto Rican."

"Same shit." And the door closed.   8

My father could have passed as European, but we couldn't.   9
My brother and I both have our mother's black hair and olive
skin, and so we lived in El Building and visited our great-uncle and his fair children on the next block. It was their private
joke that they were the German branch of the family. Not
many years later that area too would be mainly Puerto Rican.
It was as if the heart of the city map were being gradually
colored brown—*café con leche*[1] brown. Our color.

---

[1] *café con leche:* Coffee with cream. In Puerto Rico it is sometimes prepared
with boiled milk.—COFER'S NOTE.

The movie opens with a sweep of the living room. It is "typical" 10
immigrant Puerto Rican decor for the time: The sofa and chairs
are square and hard-looking, upholstered in bright colors (blue
and yellow in this instance), and covered with the transparent
plastic that furniture salesmen then were so adept at convincing
women to buy. The linoleum on the floor is light blue; if it had
been subjected to spike heels (as it was in most places), there were
dime-sized indentations all over it that cannot be seen in this
movie. The room is full of people dressed up: dark suits for the
men, red dresses for the women. When I have asked my mother
why most of the women are in red that night, she has shrugged,
"I don't remember. Just a coincidence." She doesn't have my
obsession for assigning symbolism to everything.

The three women in red sitting on the couch are my mother, 11
my eighteen-year-old cousin, and her brother's girlfriend. The
novia is just up from the Island, which is apparent in her body
language. She sits up formally, her dress pulled over her knees.
She is a pretty girl, but her posture makes her look insecure, lost
in her full-skirted dress, which she has carefully tucked around
her to make room for my gorgeous cousin, her future sister-in-
law. My cousin has grown up in Paterson and is in her last year
of high school. She doesn't have a trace of what Puerto Ricans
call la mancha *(literally, the stain: the mark of the new immi-*
grant—something about the posture, the voice, or the humble
demeanor that makes it obvious to everyone the person has just
arrived on the mainland). My cousin is wearing a tight, se-
quined, cocktail dress. Her brown hair has been lightened with
peroxide around the bangs, and she is holding a cigarette ex-
pertly between her fingers, bringing it up to her mouth in a
sensuous arc of her arm as she talks animatedly. My mother, who
has come up to sit between the two women, both only a few years
younger than herself, is somewhere between the poles they repre-
sent in our culture.

It became my father's obsession to get out of the barrio, 12
and thus we were never permitted to form bonds with the
place or with the people who lived there. Yet El Building was

a comfort to my mother, who never got over yearning for *la isla*. She felt surrounded by her language: The walls were thin, and voices speaking and arguing in Spanish could be heard all day. *Salsas* blasted out of radios, turned on early in the morning and left on for company. Women seemed to cook rice and beans perpetually—the strong aroma of boiling red kidney beans permeated the hallways.

Though Father preferred that we do our grocery shopping 13 at the supermarket when he came home on weekend leaves, my mother insisted that she could cook only with products whose labels she could read. Consequently, during the week I accompanied her and my little brother to *La Bodega*—a hole-in-the-wall grocery store across the street from El Building. There we squeezed down three narrow aisles jammed with various products. Goya's and Libby's—those were the trademarks that were trusted by *her mamá*, so my mother bought many cans of Goya beans, soups, and condiments, as well as little cans of Libby's fruit juices for us. And she also bought Colgate toothpaste and Palmolive soap. (The final *e* is pronounced in both these products in Spanish, so for many years I believed that they were manufactured on the Island. I remember my surprise at first hearing a commercial on television in which Colgate rhymed with "ate.") We always lingered at La Bodega, for it was there that Mother breathed best, taking in the familiar aromas of the foods she knew from Mamá's kitchen. It was also there that she got to speak to the other women of El Building without violating outright Father's dictates against fraternizing with our neighbors.

Yet Father did his best to make our "assimilation" painless. 14 I can still see him carrying a real Christmas tree up several flights of stairs to our apartment, leaving a trail of aromatic pine. He carried it formally, as if it were a flag in a parade. We were the only ones in El Building that I knew of who got presents on both Christmas day AND *dia de Reyes,* the day when the Three Kings brought gifts to Christ and to Hispanic children.

Our supreme luxury in El Building was having our own 15 television set. It must have been a result of Father's guilt feelings over the isolation he had imposed on us, but we were among the first in the barrio to have one. My brother quickly became an avid watcher of Captain Kangaroo and Jungle Jim, while I loved all the series showing families. By the time I started first grade, I could have drawn a map of Middle America as exemplified by the lives of characters in "Father Knows Best," "The Donna Reed Show," "Leave It to Beaver," "My Three sons," and (my favorite) "Bachelor Father," where John Forsythe treated his adopted teenage daughter like a princess because he was rich and had a Chinese houseboy to do everything for him. In truth, compared to our neighbors in El Building, *we* were rich. My father's Navy check provided us with financial security and a standard of life that the factory workers envied. The only thing his money could not buy us was a place to live away from the barrio—his greatest wish, Mother's greatest fear.

In the home movie the men are shown next, sitting around a 16 *card table set up in one corner of the living room, playing dominoes. The clack of the ivory pieces was a familiar sound. I heard it in many houses on the Island and in many apartments in Paterson. In "Leave It to Beaver," the Cleavers played bridge in every other episode; in my childhood, the men started every social occasion with a hotly debated round of dominoes. The women would sit around and watch, but they never participated in the games.*

Here and there you can see a small child. Children were 17 *always brought to parties and, whenever they got sleepy, were put to bed in the host's bedroom. Babysitting was a concept unrecognized by the Puerto Rican women I knew: A responsible mother did not leave her children with any stranger. And in a culture where children are not considered intrusive, there was no need to leave the children at home. We went where our mother went.*

Of my preschool years I have only impressions: the sharp 18 bite of the wind in December as we walked with our parents toward the brightly lit stores downtown; how I felt like a stuffed doll in my heavy coat, boots, and mittens; how good it was to walk into the five-and-dime and sit at the counter drinking hot chocolate. On Saturdays our whole family would walk downtown to shop at the big department stores on Broadway. Mother bought all our clothes at Penney's and Sears, and she liked to buy her dresses at the women's specialty shops like Lerner's and Diana's. At some point we'd go into Woolworth's and sit at the soda fountain to eat.

We never ran into other Latinos at these stores or when eating out, and it became clear to me only years later that the women from El Building shopped mainly in other places—stores owned by other Puerto Ricans or by Jewish merchants who had philosophically accepted our presence in the city and decided to make us their good customers, if not real neighbors and friends. These establishments were located not downtown but in the blocks around our street, and they were referred to generically as *La Tienda, El Bazar, La Bodega, La Botánica*. Everyone knew what was meant. These were the stores where your face did not turn a clerk to stone, where your money was as green as anyone else's.

One New Year's Eve we were dressed up like child models in the Sears catalogue: my brother in a miniature man's suit and bow tie, and I in black patent-leather shoes and a frilly dress with several layers of crinoline underneath. My mother wore a bright red dress that night, I remember, and spike heels; her long black hair hung to her waist. Father, who usually wore his Navy uniform during his short visits home, had put on a dark civilian suit for the occasion: We had been invited to his uncle's house for a big celebration. Everyone was excited because my mother's brother Hernan—a bachelor who could indulge himself with luxuries—had bought a home movie camera, which he would be trying out that night.

Even the home movie cannot fill in the sensory details such a gathering left imprinted in a child's brain. The thick sweetness of women's perfumes mixing with the ever-present smells of food cooking in the kitchen: meat and plantain *pasteles*, as well as the ubiquitous rice dish made special with pigeon peas—*gandules*—and seasoned with precious *sofrito*[2] sent up from the Island by somebody's mother or smuggled in by a recent traveler. *Sofrito* was one of the items that women hoarded, since it was hardly ever in stock at La Bodega. It was the flavor of Puerto Rico.

The men drank Palo Viejo rum, and some of the younger   22 ones got weepy. The first time I saw a grown man cry was at a New Year's Eve party: He had been reminded of his mother by the smells in the kitchen. But what I remember most were the boiled *pasteles*—plantain or yucca rectangles stuffed with corned beef or other meats, olives, and many other savory ingredients, all wrapped in banana leaves. Everybody had to fish one out with a fork. There was always a "trick" pastel— one without stuffing—and whoever got that one was the "New Year's Fool."

There was also the music. Long-playing albums were   23 treated like precious china in these homes. Mexican record- ings were popular, but the songs that brought tears to my mother's eyes were sung by the melancholy Daniel Santos, whose life as a drug addict was the stuff of legend. Felipe Rodríguez was a particular favorite of the couples, since he sang about faithless women and brokenhearted men. There is a snatch of one lyric that has stuck in my mind like a needle on a worn groove: *De piedra ha de ser mi cama, de piedra la cabezera . . . la mujer que a mi me quiera . . . ha de quererme de veras. Ay, Ay, Ay, corazón, porque no amas.*[3] . . . I must have heard it a thousand times since the idea of a bed made of stone, and its connection to love, first troubled me with its disturbing images.

---

[2] *sofrito:* A cooked condiment. A sauce composed of a mixture of fatback, ham, tomatoes, and many island spices and herbs. It is added to many typical Puerto Rican dishes for a distinctive flavor.—COFER'S NOTE.

[3] *De piedra ha de ser . . . amas:* Lyrics from a popular romantic ballad (called a *bolero* in Puerto Rico). Freely translated: "My bed will be made of stone, of stone also my headrest (or pillow), the woman who (dares to) loves me, will have to love me for real. Ay, Ay, Ay, my heart, why can't you (let me) love. . . ."—COFER'S NOTE.

The five-minute home movie ends with people dancing in   24
a circle—the creative filmmaker must have set it up, so that
all of them could file past him. It is both comical and sad to
watch silent dancing. Since there is no justification for the
absurd movements that music provides for some of us, people
appear frantic, their faces embarrassingly intense. It's as if you
were watching sex. Yet for years I've had dreams in the form
of this home movie. In a recurring scene, familiar faces push
themselves forward into my mind's eyes, plastering their features into distorted close-ups. And I'm asking them: "Who
is *she*? Who is the old woman I don't recognize? Is she an
aunt? Somebody's wife? Tell me who she is."

"See the beauty mark on her cheek as big as a hill on the lunar   25
landscape of her face—well, that runs in the family. The women
on your father's side of the family wrinkle early; it's the price they
pay for that fair skin. The young girl with the green stain on her
wedding dress is *La Novia*—just up from the Island. See, she
lowers her eyes when she approaches the camera, as she's supposed to. Decent girls never look at you directly in the face.
Humilde, humble, a girl should express humility in all her actions. She will make a good wife for your cousin. He should
consider himself lucky to have met her only weeks after she
arrived here. If he marries her quickly, she will make him a good
Puerto Rican-style wife; but if he waits too long, she will be
corrupted by the city—just like your cousin there."

"She means me. I do what I want. This is not some primitive   26
island I live on. Do they expect me to wear a black mantilla on
my head and go to mass every day? Not me. I'm an American
woman, and I will do as I please. I can type faster than anyone
in my senior class at Central High, and I'm going to be a
secretary to a lawyer when I graduate. I can pass for an American
girl anywhere—I've tried it. At least for Italian, anyway—I never
speak Spanish in public. I hate these parties, but I wanted the
dress. I look better than any of these *humildes* here. *My* life is
going to be different. I have an American boyfriend. He is older

and has a car. My parents don't know it, but I sneak out of the house late at night sometimes to be with him. If I marry him, even my name will be American. I hate rice and beans—that's what makes these women fat."

"Your *prima*[4] is pregnant by that man she's been sneaking   27
around with. Would I lie to you? I'm your *Tía Política*,[5] your great-uncle's common-law wife—the one he abandoned on the Island to go marry your cousin's mother. *I* was not invited to this party, of course, but I came anyway. I came to tell you that story about your cousin that you've always wanted to hear. Do you remember the comment your mother made to a neighbor that has always haunted you? The only thing you heard was your cousin's name, and then you saw your mother pick up your doll from the couch and say: 'It was as big as this doll when they flushed it down the toilet.' This image has bothered you for years, hasn't it? You had nightmares about babies being flushed down the toilet, and you wondered why anyone would do such a horrible thing. You didn't dare ask your mother about it. She would only tell you that you had not heard her right, and yell at you for listening to adult conversations. But later, when you were old enough to know about abortions, you suspected.

"I am here to tell you that you were right. Your cousin was   28
growing an *Americanito* in her belly when this movie was made. Soon after she put something long and pointy in her pretty self, thinking maybe she could get rid of the problem before breakfast and still make it to her first class at the high school. Well, *Niña*, her screams could be heard downtown. Your aunt, her mamá, who had been a midwife on the Island, managed to pull the little thing out. Yes, they probably flushed it down the toilet. What else could they do with it—give it a Christian burial in a little white casket with blue bows and ribbons? Nobody wanted that baby—least of all the father, a teacher at her school with a house in West Paterson that he was filling with real children, and a wife who was a natural blonde.

"Girl, the scandal sent your uncle back to the bottle. And guess   29

[4]*prima:* Female cousin.—COFER'S NOTE.
[5]*Tía Política:* Aunt by marriage.—COFER'S NOTE.

where your cousin ended up? Irony of ironies. She was sent to a village in Puerto Rico to live with a relative on her mother's side: a place so far away from civilization that you have to ride a mule to reach it. A real change in scenery. She found a man there—women like that cannot live without male company—but believe me, the men in Puerto Rico know how to put a saddle on a woman like her. *La Gringa,* they call her. Ha, ha, ha. *La Gringa* is what she always wanted to be. . . ."

The old woman's mouth becomes a cavernous black hole I **30** fall into. And as I fall, I can feel the reverberations of her laughter. I hear the echoes of her last mocking words: *La Gringa, La Gringa!* And the conga line keeps moving silently past me. There is no music in my dream for the dancers.

When Odysseus visits Hades to see the spirit of his mother, **31** he makes an offering of sacrificial blood, but since all the souls crave an audience with the living, he has to listen to many of them before he can ask questions. I, too, have to hear the dead and the forgotten speak in my dream. Those who are still part of my life remain silent, going around and around in their dance. The others keep pressing their faces forward to say things about the past.

My father's uncle is last in line. He is dying of alcoholism, **32** shrunken and shriveled like a monkey, his face a mass of wrinkles and broken arteries. As he comes closer I realize that in his features I can see my whole family. If you were to stretch that rubbery flesh, you could find my father's face, and deep within *that* face—my own. I don't want to look into those eyes ringed in purple. In a few years he will retreat into silence, and take a long, long time to die. *Move back, Tio,* I tell him. *I don't want to hear what you have to say. Give the dancers room to move. Soon it will be midnight. Who is the New Year's Fool this time?*

For Study and Discussion

QUESTIONS FOR RESPONSE

1. What sorts of "visual aids"—photographs, home movies, artifacts—do you use to remember events in the life of your family?
2. What painful lessons about prejudice have you learned when you lived in or visited a different culture?

QUESTIONS ABOUT PURPOSE

1. Why do Cofer and her mother watch the home movie about the party? Why is it significant that Cofer sees this film in color?
2. What do the film and the commentary on it reveal about the problems of assimilation?

QUESTIONS ABOUT AUDIENCE

1. How do Cofer's footnotes identify her primary audience?
2. What assumption does Cofer make about her audience when she does *not* translate certain Spanish terms and phrases?

QUESTIONS ABOUT STRATEGY

1. How does Cofer use Uncle Hernan's new camera to fuse the memories in her narrative with the scenes in the movies?
2. How does she use the commentary of her mother, cousin, and aunt to answer her questions about the film?

QUESTIONS FOR DISCUSSION

1. What does Cofer's narrative reveal about the cost of assimilation? Explain how her cousin's nickname is the "irony of ironies."
2. What does Cofer's story reveal about the attitudes toward race *(la mancha)* and gender *(humildes)* in Puerto Rican culture?

George Orwell, the pen name of Eric Blair (1903–1950), was born in Motihari, Bengal, where his father was employed with the Bengal civil service. He was brought to England at an early age for schooling (Eton), but rather than completing his education at the university, he served with the Indian imperial police in Burma (1922–1927). He wrote about these experiences in his first novel, *Burmese Days.* Later he returned to Europe and worked at various jobs (described in *Down and Out in Paris and London,* 1933) before fighting on the Republican side in the Spanish civil war (see *Homage to Catalonia,* 1938). Orwell's attitudes toward war and government are reflected in his most famous books: *Animal Farm* (1945), *1984* (1949), and *Shooting an Elephant and Other Essays* (1950). In the title essay from the last volume, Orwell reports a "tiny incident" that gave him deeper insight into his own fears and "the real motives for which despotic governments act."

Shooting an Elephant

I N MOULMEIN, IN lower Burma, I was hated by large num- 1
bers of people—the only time in my life that I have been important enough for this to happen to me. I was sub-divisional police officer of the town, and in an aimless, petty kind of way anti-European feeling was very bitter. No one had the guts to raise a riot, but if a European woman went through the bazaars alone somebody would probably spit betel juice over her dress. As a police officer I was an obvious target and was baited whenever it seemed safe to do so. When a nimble Burman tripped me up on the football field and the

referee (another Burman) looked the other way, the crowd yelled with hideous laughter. This happened more than once. In the end the sneering yellow faces of young men that met me everywhere, the insults hooted after me when I was at a safe distance, got badly on my nerves. The young Buddhist priests were the worst of all. There were several thousands of them in the town and none of them seemed to have anything to do except stand on street corners and jeer at Europeans.

All this was perplexing and upsetting. For at that time I had already made up my mind that imperialism was an evil thing and the sooner I chucked up my job and got out of it 2

As soon as I saw the elephant I knew with perfect certainty that I ought not to shoot him.

---

the better. Theoretically—and secretly, of course—I was all for the Burmese and all against their oppressors, the British. As for the job I was doing, I hated it more bitterly than I can perhaps make clear. In a job like that you see the dirty work of Empire at close quarters. The wretched prisoners huddling in the stinking cages of the lock-ups, the gray, cowed faces of the long-term convicts, the scarred buttocks of the men who had been flogged with bamboos—all these oppressed me with an intolerable sense of guilt. But I could get nothing into perspective. I was young and ill educated and I had had to think out my problems in the utter silence that is imposed on every Englishman in the East. I did not even know that the British Empire is dying, still less did I know that it is a great deal better than the younger empires that are going to supplant it. All I knew was that I was stuck between my hatred of the empire I served and my rage against the evil-spirited little beasts who tried to make my job impossible. With one part of my mind I thought of the British Raj as an unbreakable tyranny, as something clamped down, in *saecula saeculorum,* upon the will of prostrate peoples; with another part I thought that the greatest joy in the world would be to drive a bayonet into a Buddhist priest's guts. Feelings like these are the normal by-products of imperialism; ask any Anglo-Indian official, if you can catch him off duty.

One day something happened which in a roundabout way   3
was enlightening. It was a tiny incident in itself; but it gave me a better glimpse than I had had before of the real nature of imperialism—the real motives for which despotic governments act. Early one morning the sub-inspector at a police station the other end of town rang me up on the 'phone and said that an elephant was ravaging the bazaar. Would I please come and do something about it? I did not know what I could do, but I wanted to see what was happening and I got on to a pony and started out. I took my rifle, an old .44 Winchester and much too small to kill an elephant, but I thought the noise might be useful *in terrorem.* Various Burmans stopped me on the way and told me about the elephant's doings. It was not, of course, a wild elephant, but a tame one which had gone "must." It had been chained up, as tame elephants always are when their attack of "must" is due, but on the previous night it had broken its chain and escaped. Its mahout, the only person who could manage it when it was in that state, had set out in pursuit, but had taken the wrong direction and was now twelve hours' journey away, and in the morning the elephant had suddenly reappeared in the town. The Burmese population had no weapons and were quite helpless against it. It had already destroyed somebody's bamboo hut, killed a cow and raided some fruit-stalls and devoured the stock; also it had met the municipal rubbish van and, when the driver jumped out and took to his heels, had turned the van over and inflicted violences upon it.

The Burmese sub-inspector and some Indian constables   4
were waiting for me in the quarter where the elephant had been seen. It was a very poor quarter, a labyrinth of squalid bamboo huts, thatched with palm-leaf, winding all over a steep hillside. I remember that it was a cloudy, stuffy morning

at the beginning of the rains. We began questioning the people as to where the elephant had gone and, as usual, failed to get any definite information. That is invariably the case in the East; a story always sounds clear enough at a distance, but the nearer you get to the scene of events the vaguer it becomes. Some of the people said that the elephant had gone in one direction, some said that he had gone in another, some professed not even to have heard of any elephant. I had almost made up my mind that the whole story was a pack of lies, when we heard yells a little distance away. There was a loud, scandalized cry of "Go away, child! Go away this instant!" and an old woman with a switch in her hand came round the corner of a hut, violently shooing away a crowd of naked children. Some more women followed, clicking their tongues and exclaiming; evidently there was something that the children ought not to have seen. I rounded the hut and saw a man's dead body sprawling in the mud. He was an Indian, a black Dravidian coolie, almost naked, and he could not have been dead many minutes. The people said that the elephant had come suddenly upon him round the corner of the hut, caught him with its trunk, put its foot on his back and ground him into the earth. This was the rainy season and the ground was soft, and his face had scored a trench a foot deep and a couple of yards long. He was lying on his belly with arms crucified and head sharply twisted to one side. His face was coated with mud, the eyes wide open, the teeth bared and grinning with an expression of unendurable agony. (Never tell me, by the way, that the dead look peaceful. Most of the corpses I have seen looked devilish.) The friction of the great beast's foot had stripped the skin from his back as neatly as one skins a rabbit. As soon as I saw the dead man I sent an orderly to a friend's house nearby to borrow an elephant rifle. I had already sent back the pony, not wanting it to go mad with fright and throw me if it smelt the elephant.

The orderly came back in a few minutes with a rifle and 5
five cartridges, and meanwhile some Burmans had arrived and told us that the elephant was in the paddy fields below, only a few hundred yards away. As I started forward practically the

whole population of the quarter flocked out of the houses and followed me. They had seen the rifle and were all shouting excitedly that I was going to shoot the elephant. They had not shown much interest in the elephant when he was merely ravaging their homes, but it was different now that he was going to be shot. It was a bit of fun to them, and it would be to an English crowd; besides they wanted the meat. It made me vaguely uneasy. I had no intention of shooting the elephant—I had merely sent for the rifle to defend myself if necessary—and it is always unnerving to have a crowd following you. I marched down the hill, looking and feeling a fool, with the rifle over my shoulder and an ever-growing army of people jostling at my heels. At the bottom, when you got away from the huts, there was a metalled road and beyond that a miry waste of paddy fields a thousand yards across, not yet ploughed but soggy from the first rains and dotted with coarse grass. The elephant was standing eight yards from the road, his left side toward us. He took not the slightest notice of the crowd's approach. He was tearing up bunches of grass, beating them against his knees to clean them, and stuffing them into his mouth.

I had halted on the road. As soon as I saw the elephant I knew with perfect certainty that I ought not to shoot him. It is a serious matter to shoot a working elephant—it is comparable to destroying a huge and costly piece of machinery—and obviously one ought not to do it if it can possibly be avoided. And at that distance, peacefully eating, the elephant looked no more dangerous than a cow. I thought then and I think now that his attack of "must" was already passing off; in which case he would merely wander harmlessly about until the mahout came back and caught him. Moreover, I did not in the least want to shoot him. I decided that I would watch him for a little while to make sure that he did not turn savage again, and then go home.

But at that moment I glanced round at the crowd that had followed me. It was an immense crowd, two thousand at the least and growing every minute. It blocked the road for a long distance on either side. I looked at the sea of yellow faces above the garish clothes—faces all happy and excited over this bit of fun, all certain that the elephant was going to be shot. They were watching me as they would watch a conjurer about to perform a trick. They did not like me, but with the magical rifle in my hands I was momentarily worth watching. And suddenly I realized that I should have to shoot the elephant after all. The people expected it of me and I had got to do it; I could feel their two thousand wills pressing me forward, irresistibly. And it was at this moment, as I stood there with the rifle in my hands, that I first grasped the hollowness, the futility of the white man's dominion in the East. Here was I, the white man with his gun, standing in front of the unarmed native crowd—seemingly the leading actor of the piece; but in reality I was only an absurd puppet pushed to and fro by the will of those yellow faces behind. I perceived in this moment that when the white man turns tyrant it is his own freedom that he destroys. He becomes a sort of hollow, posing dummy, the conventionalized figure of a sahib. For it is the condition of his rule that he shall spend his life in trying to impress the "natives," and so in every crisis he has got to do what the "natives" expect of him. He wears a mask, and his face grows to fit it. I had got to shoot the elephant. I had committed myself to doing it when I sent for the rifle. A sahib has got to act like a sahib; he has got to appear resolute, to know his own mind and do definite things. To come all that way, rifle in hand, with two thousand people marching at my heels, and then to trail feebly away, having done nothing— no, that was impossible. The crowd would laugh at me. And my whole life, every white man's life in the East, was one long struggle not to be laughed at.

But I did not want to shoot the elephant. I watched him 8 beating his bunch of grass against his knees with that preoccupied grandmotherly air that elephants have. It seemed to me that it would be murder to shoot him. At that age I was not squeamish about killing animals, but I had never shot an elephant and never wanted to. (Somehow it always seems worse to kill a *large* animal.) Besides, there was the beast's owner to be considered. Alive, the elephant was worth at least a hundred pounds; dead, he would only be worth the value of his tusks, five pounds, possibly. But I had got to act quickly.

I turned to some experienced-looking Burmans who had been there when we arrived, and asked them how the elephant had been behaving. They all said the same thing: he took no notice of you if you left him alone, but he might charge if you went too close to him.

It was perfectly clear to me what I ought to do. I ought 9 to walk up to within, say, twenty-five yards of the elephant and test his behavior. If he charged, I could shoot; if he took no notice of me, it would be safe to leave him until the mahout came back. But also I knew that I was going to do no such thing. I was a poor shot with a rifle and the ground was soft mud into which one would sink at every step. If the elephant charged and I missed him, I should have about as much chance as a toad under a steam-roller. But even then I was not thinking particularly of my own skin, only of the watchful yellow faces behind. For at that moment, with the crowd watching me, I was not afraid in the ordinary sense, as I would have been if I had been alone. A white man mustn't be frightened in front of "natives"; and so, in general, he isn't frightened. The sole thought in my mind was that if anything went wrong those two thousand Burmans would see me pursued, caught, trampled on, and reduced to a grinning corpse like that Indian up the hill. And if that happened it was quite probable that some of them would laugh. That would never do. There was only one alternative. I shoved the cartridges into the magazine and lay down on the road to get a better aim.

The crowd grew very still, and a deep, low, happy sigh, as 10 of people who see the theater curtain go up at last, breathed from innumerable throats. They were going to have their bit of fun after all. The rifle was a beautiful German thing with cross-hair sights. I did not then know that in shooting an elephant one would shoot to cut an imaginary bar running from ear-hole to ear-hole. I ought, therefore, as the elephant was sideways on, to have aimed straight at his ear-hole; actually I aimed several inches in front of this, thinking the brain would be further forward.

When I pulled the trigger I did not hear the bang or feel 11 the kick—one never does when a shot goes home—but I heard the devilish roar of glee that went up from the crowd. In that instant, in too short a time, one would have thought, even for the bullet to get there, a mysterious, terrible change had come over the elephant. He neither stirred, nor fell, but every line of his body had altered. He looked suddenly stricken, shrunken, immensely old, as though the frightful impact of the bullet had paralyzed him without knocking him down. At last, after what seemed a long time—it might have been five seconds, I dare say—he sagged flabbily to his knees. His mouth slobbered. An enormous senility seemed to have settled upon him. One could have imagined him thousands of years old. I fired again into the same spot. At the second shot he did not collapse but climbed with desperate slowness to his feet and stood weakly upright, with legs sagging and head drooping. I fired a third time. That was the shot that did for him. You could see the agony of it jolt his whole body and knock the last remnant of strength from his legs. But in falling he seemed for a moment to rise, for as his hind legs collapsed beneath him he seemed to tower upward like a huge rock toppling, his trunk reaching skyward like a tree. He trumpeted, for the first and only time. And then down he came, his belly toward me, with a crash that seemed to shake the ground even where I lay.

I got up. The Burmans were already racing past me across the mud. It was obvious that the elephant would never rise again, but he was not dead. He was breathing very rhythmically with long rattling gasps, his great mound of a side painfully rising and falling. His mouth was wide open—I could see far down into caverns of pale pink throat. I waited a long time for him to die, but his breathing did not weaken. Finally I fired my two remaining shots into the spot where I thought his heart must be. The thick blood welled out of him like red velvet, but still he did not die. His body did not even jerk when the shots hit him, the tortured breathing continued without a pause. He was dying, very slowly and in great agony, but in some world remote from me where not even a bullet could damage him further. I felt that I had got to put an end to that dreadful noise. It seemed dreadful to see the great beast lying there, powerless to move and yet powerless to die, and not even to be able to finish him. I sent back for my small rifle and poured shot after shot into his heart and down his throat. They seemed to make no impression. The tortured gasps continued as steadily as the ticking of a clock.

In the end I could not stand it any longer and went away. 13 I heard later that it took him half an hour to die. Burmans were bringing dahs and baskets even before I left, and I was told they had stripped his body almost to the bones by the afternoon.

Afterward, of course, there were endless discussions about 14 the shooting of the elephant. The owner was furious, but he was only an Indian and could do nothing. Besides, legally I had done the right thing, for a mad elephant has to be killed, like a mad dog, if its owner fails to control it. Among the Europeans opinion was divided. The older men said I was right, the younger men said it was a damn shame to shoot an elephant for killing a coolie, because an elephant was worth more than any damn Coringhee coolie. And afterward I was very glad that the coolie had been killed; it put me legally in the right and it gave me a sufficient pretext for shooting the elephant. I often wondered whether any of the others grasped that I had done it solely to avoid looking a fool.

For Study and Discussion

QUESTIONS FOR RESPONSE

1. How do you feel when you are laughed at? What do you do in order to avoid looking like a fool?
2. How did you react to Orwell's long introduction (paragraphs 1 and 2) to the incident? Were you attentive, bored, or confused? Now that you have finished the essay, reread these two paragraphs. How does your second reading compare with your first?

QUESTIONS ABOUT PURPOSE

1. What thesis about "the real nature of imperialism" does Orwell prove by narrating this "tiny incident"?
2. List the reasons Orwell considers when he tries to decide what to do. According to his conclusion, what was his main purpose in shooting the elephant?

QUESTIONS ABOUT AUDIENCE

1. How does Orwell wish to present himself to his readers in paragraphs 6 through 9? Do you follow the logic of his argument?
2. Which of the three positions stated in the final paragraph does Orwell expect his readers to agree with? Why is he "glad that the coolie had been killed"?

QUESTIONS ABOUT STRATEGIES

1. Although Orwell begins narrating the incident in paragraph 3, we do not see the elephant until the end of paragraph 5. What details do we see? How do they intensify the dramatic conflict?
2. How does Orwell pace the shooting of the elephant in paragraphs 11 and 12? How does the elephant's slow death affect Orwell's point of view toward what he has done?

QUESTIONS FOR DISCUSSION

1. Orwell was young, frightened, and tormented by strangers in a strange land. What parallels do you see between Orwell's plight and the plight of young American soldiers who served in Vietnam?
2. Much of Orwell's essay assumes a knowledge of the words *imperialism* and *despotism*. What do these words mean? How do they apply to the essay? What current events can you identify in which these words might also apply?

Alice Adams was born in 1926 in Fredericksburg, Virginia, and educated at Radcliffe College. After twelve years of marriage, she began working at various office jobs, including secretary, clerk, and bookkeeper, while she mastered the skills of a writer. Adams published her first book of fiction, *Careless Love* (1966), at the age of forty. Since that time she has published five widely acclaimed novels, *Families and Survivors* (1975), *Listening to Billie* (1978)—the title refers to the legendary blues singer Billie Holiday—*Rich Rewards* (1980), *Superior Women* (1984), and *Caroline's Daughter* (1991), as well as three collections of short stories, *Beautiful Girl* (1979), *To See You Again* (1982), and *Return Trips* (1985). She has also contributed numerous short stories to magazines such as *The New Yorker, The Atlantic,* and *Paris Review.* The narrator of "Truth or Consequences," reprinted from *To See You Again,* tries to understand the "consequences" that resulted from her truthful answer in a childhood game.

Truth or Consequences

THIS MORNING, WHEN I read in a gossip column that a man named Carstairs Jones had married a famous former movie star, I was startled, thunderstruck, for I knew that he must certainly be the person whom I knew as a child, one extraordinary spring, as "Car Jones." He was a dangerous and disreputable boy, one of what were then called the "truck children," with whom I had a most curious, brief and frightening connection. Still, I noted that in a way I was pleased at such good fortune; I was "happy for him," so to

1

speak, perhaps as a result of sheer distance, so many years. And before I could imagine Car as he might be now, Carstairs Jones, in Hollywood clothes, I suddenly saw, with the most terrific accuracy and bright sharpness of detail, the schoolyard of all those years ago, hard and bare, neglected. And I relived the fatal day, on the middle level of that schoolyard, when we were playing truth or consequences, and I said that I would rather kiss Car Jones than be eaten alive by ants.

Our school building then was three stories high, a formidable brick square. In front a lawn had been attempted, some years back; graveled walks led up to the broad, forbidding entranceway, and behind the school were the playing fields, the playground. This area was on three levels: on the upper level, nearest the school, were the huge polished steel frames for the creaking swings, the big green splintery wooden seesaws, the rickety slides—all for the youngest children. On the middle level older girls played hopscotch, various games, or jumped rope—or just talked and giggled. And out on the lowest level, the field, the boys practiced football, or baseball, in the spring.

To one side of the school was a parking space, usually filled with the bulging yellow trucks that brought children from out in the country in to town: truck children, country children. Sometimes they would go back to the trucks at lunchtime to eat their sandwiches, whatever; almost always there were several overgrown children, spilling out from the trucks. Or Car Jones, expelled from some class, for some new acts of rebelliousness. That area was always littered with trash, wrappings from sandwiches, orange peel, Coke bottles.

Beyond the parking space was an empty lot, overgrown with weeds, in the midst of which stood an abandoned trellis, perhaps once the support of wisteria; now wild honeysuckle almost covered it over.

The town was called Hilton, the seat of a distinguished university, in the middle South. My widowed mother, Charlotte Ames, had moved there the previous fall (with me, Emily, her only child). I am still not sure why she chose

Hilton; she never much liked it there, nor did she really like the brother-in-law, a professor, into whose proximity the move had placed us.

An interesting thing about Hilton, at that time, was that there were three, and only three, distinct social classes. (Negroes could possibly make four, but they were so separate, even from the poorest whites, as not to seem part of the social system at all; they were in effect invisible.) At the scale's top were professors and their families. Next were the townspeople, storekeepers, bankers, doctors and dentists, none of whom had the prestige nor the money they were later to acquire. Country people were the bottom group, families living out on the farms that surrounded the town, people who sent their children in to school on the yellow trucks. 6

The professors' children of course had a terrific advantage, academically, coming from houses full of books, from parental respect for learning; many of those kids read precociously and had large vocabularies. It was not so hard on most of the town children; many of their families shared qualities with the faculty people; they too had a lot of books around. But the truck children had a hard and very unfair time of it. Not only were many of their parents near-illiterates, but often the children were kept at home to help with chores, and sometimes, particularly during the coldest, wettest months of winter, weather prevented the trucks' passage over the slithery red clay roads of that countryside, that era. A child could miss out on a whole new skill, like long division, and fail tests, and be kept back. Consequently many of the truck children were overage, oversized for the grades they were in. 7

In the seventh grade, when I was eleven, a year ahead of myself, having been tested for and skipped the sixth (attesting to the superiority of Northern schools, my mother thought, and probably she was right), dangerous Car Jones, in the same class, was fourteen, and taller than anyone. 8

There was some overlapping, or crossing, among those three social groups; there were hybrids, as it were. In fact, I was such a crossbreed myself: literally my mother and I were 9 town people—my dead father had been a banker, but since his brother was a professor we too were considered faculty people. Also my mother had a lot of money, making us further élite. To me, being known as rich was just embarrassing, more freakish than advantageous, and I made my mother stop ordering my clothes from Best's; I wanted dresses from the local stores, like everyone else's.

Car Jones too was a hybrid child, although his case was less visible than mine: his country family were distant cousins of the prominent and prosperous dean of the medical school, Dean Willoughby Jones. (They seem to have gone in for fancy names, in all the branches of that family.) I don't think his cousins spoke to him.

In any case, being richer and younger than the others in my class made me socially very insecure, and I always approached the playground with a sort of excited dread: would I be asked to join in a game, and if it were dodge ball (the game I most hated) would I be the first person hit with the ball, and thus eliminated? Or, if the girls were just standing around and talking, would I get all the jokes, and know which boys they were talking about?

Then, one pale-blue balmy April day, some of the older girls asked me if I wanted to play truth or consequences with them. I wasn't sure how the game went, but anything was better than dodge ball, and, as always, I was pleased at being asked.

"It's easy," said Jean, a popular leader, with curly red hair; her father was a dean of the law school. "You just answer the questions we ask you, or you take the consequences."

I wasn't at all sure what consequences were, but I didn't like to ask.

They began with simple questions. How old are you? What's your middle name?

This led to more complicated (and crueler) ones.

"How much money does your mother have?"

"I don't know." I didn't, of course, and I doubt that she did either, that poor vague lady, too young to be a widow, too old for motherhood. "I think maybe a thousand dollars," I hazarded.

At this they all frowned, that group of older, wiser girls, 19 whether in disbelief or disappointment, I couldn't tell. They moved a little away from me and whispered together.

It was close to the end of recess. Down on the playing field 20 below us one of the boys threw the baseball and someone batted it out in a long arc, out to the farthest grassy edges of the field, and several other boys ran to retrieve it. On the level above us, a rutted terrace up, the little children stood in line for turns on the slide, or pumped with furious small legs on the giant swings.

The girls came back to me. "Okay, Emily," said Jean. "Just 21 tell the truth. Would you rather be covered with honey and eaten alive by ants, in the hot Sahara Desert—or kiss Car Jones?"

Then, as now, I had a somewhat literal mind: I thought of 22 honey, and ants, and hot sand, and quite simply I said I'd rather kiss Car Jones.

Well. Pandemonium: Did you hear what she said? Emily 23 would kiss Car Jones! *Car Jones.* The truth—Emily would like to kiss Car Jones! Oh, Emily if your mother only knew! Emily and Car! Emily is going to kiss Car Jones! Emily said she would! Oh, Emily!

The boys, just then coming up from the baseball field, cast 24 bored and pitying looks at the sources of so much noise; they had always known girls were silly. But Harry McGinnis, a glowing, golden boy, looked over at us and laughed aloud. I had been watching Harry timidly for months; that day I thought his laugh was friendly.

Recess being over, we all went back into the schoolroom, 25 and continued with the civics lesson. I caught a few ambiguous smiles in my direction, which left me both embarrassed and confused.

That afternoon, as I walked home from school, two of the 26 girls who passed me on their bikes called back to me, "Car Jones!" and in an automatic but for me new way I squealed out, "Oh no!" They laughed, and repeated, from their distance, "Car Jones!"

The next day I continued to be teased. Somehow the boys   27
had got wind of what I had said, and they joined in with
remarks about Yankee girls being fast, how you couldn't tell
about quiet girls, that sort of wit. Some of the teasing
sounded mean; I felt that Jean, for example, was really out
to discomfit me, but most of it was high-spirited friendliness.
I was suddenly discovered, as though hitherto I had been
invisible. And I continued to respond with that exaggerated,
phony squeal of embarrassment that seemed to go over so
well. Harry McGinnis addressed me as Emily Jones, and the
others took that up. (I wonder if Harry had ever seen me
before.)

Curiously, in all this new excitement, the person I thought   28
of least was the source of it all: Car Jones. Or, rather, when
I saw the actual Car, hulking over the water fountain or
lounging near the steps of a truck, I did not consciously
connect him with what felt like social success, new popularity.
(I didn't know about consequences.)

Therefore, when the first note from Car appeared on my   29
desk, it felt like blackmail, although the message was innocent, was even kind. "You mustn't mind that they tease you.
You are the prettiest one of the girls. C. Jones." I easily
recognized his handwriting, those recklessly forward-slanting
strokes, from the day when he had had to write on the
blackboard, "I will not disturb the other children during
Music." Twenty-five times. The note was real, all right.

Helplessly I turned around to stare at the back of the   30
room, where the tallest boys sprawled in their too small desks.
Truck children, all of them, bored and uncomfortable. There
was Car, the tallest of all, the most bored, the least contained.
Our eyes met, and even at that distance I saw that his were
not black, as I had thought, but a dark slate blue; stormy
eyes, even when, as he rarely did, Car smiled. I turned away
quickly, and I managed to forget him for a while.

Having never witnessed a Southern spring before, I was   31
astounded by its bursting opulence, that soft fullness of petal
and bloom, everywhere the profusion of flowering shrubs
and trees, the riotous flower beds. Walking home from
school, I was enchanted with the yards of the stately houses
(homes of professors) that I passed, the lush lawns, the rows
of brilliant iris, the flowering quince and dogwood trees,
crepe myrtle, wisteria vines. I would squint my eyes to see
the tiniest pale-green leaves against the sky.

My mother didn't like the spring. It gave her hay fever,   32
and she spent most of her time languidly indoors, behind
heavily lined, drawn draperies. "I'm simply too old for such
exuberance," she said.

"Happy" is perhaps not the word to describe my own state   33
of mind, but I was tremendously excited, continuously. The
season seemed to me so extraordinary in itself, the colors, the
enchanting smells, and it coincided with my own altered
awareness of myself: I could command attention, I was pretty
(Car Jones was the first person ever to say that I was, after
my mother's long-ago murmurings to a late-arriving baby).

Now everyone knew my name, and called it out as I walked   34
onto the playground. Last fall, as an envious, unknown new
girl, I had heard other names, other greetings and teasing-
insulting nicknames, "Hey, Red," Harry McGinnis used to
shout, in the direction of popular Jean.

The new note from Car Jones said, "I'll bet you hate it   35
down here. This is a cruddy town, but don't let it bother
you. Your hair is beautiful. I hope you never cut it. C. Jones."

This scared me a little: the night before I had been arguing   36
with my mother on just that point, my hair, which was long
and straight. Why couldn't I cut it and curl it, like the other
girls? How had Car Jones known what I wanted to do? I
forced myself not to look at him; I pretended that there was
no Car Jones; it was just a name that certain people had made
up.

I felt—I was sure—that Car Jones was an "abnormal"   37
person. (I'm afraid "different" would have been the word I

used, back then.) He represented forces that were dark and strange, whereas I myself had just come out into the light. I had joined the world of the normal. (My "normality" later included three marriages to increasingly "rich and prominent" men; my current husband is a surgeon. Three children, and as many abortions. I hate the symmetry, but there you are. I haven't counted lovers. It comes to a normal life, for a woman of my age.) For years, at the time of our coming to Hilton, I had felt a little strange, isolated by my father's death, my older-than-most-parents mother, by money. By being younger than other children, and new in town. I could clearly afford nothing to do with Car, and at the same time my literal mind acknowledged a certain obligation.

Therefore, when a note came from Car telling me to meet   38 him on a Saturday morning in the vacant lot next to the school, it didn't occur to me that I didn't have to go. I made excuses to my mother, and to some of the girls who were getting together for Cokes at someone's house. I'd be a little late, I told the girls. I had to do an errand for my mother.

It was one of the palest, softest, loveliest days of that   39 spring. In the vacant lot weeds bloomed like the rarest of flowers; as I walked toward the abandoned trellis I felt myself to be a sort of princess, on her way to grant an audience to a courtier.

Car, lounging just inside the trellis, immediately brought   40 me up short. "You're several minutes late," he said, and I noticed that his teeth were stained (from tobacco?) and his hands were dirty: couldn't he have washed his hands, to come and meet me? He asked, "Just who do you think you are, the Queen of Sheba?"

I am not sure what I had imagined would happen between   41 us, but this was wrong; I was not prepared for surliness, this scolding. Weakly I said that I was sorry I was late.

Car did not acknowledge my apology; he just stared at me,   42 stormily, with what looked like infinite scorn.

Why had he insisted that I come to meet him? And now   43 that I was here, was I less than pretty, seen close up?

A difficult minute passed, and then I moved a little away.   44
I managed to say that I had to go; I had to meet some girls,
I said.

At that Car reached and grasped my arm. "No, first we   45
have to do it."

Do it? I was scared.   46

"You know what you said, as good as I do. You said kiss   47
Car Jones, now didn't you?"

I began to cry.   48

Car reached for my hair and pulled me toward him; he   49
bent down to my face and for an instant our mouths were
mashed together. (Christ, my first kiss!) Then, so suddenly
that I almost fell backward, Car let go of me. With a last look
of pure rage he was out of the trellis and striding across the
field, toward town, away from the school.

For a few minutes I stayed there in the trellis; I was no   50
longer crying (that had been for Car's benefit, I now think)
but melodramatically I wondered if Car might come back and
do something else to me—beat me up, maybe. Then a
stronger fear took over: someone might find out, might have
seen us, even. At that I got out of the trellis fast, out of the
vacant lot. (I was learning conformity fast, practicing up for
the rest of my life.)

I think, really, that my most serious problem was my utter   51
puzzlement: what did it mean, that kiss? Car was mad, no
doubt about that, but did he really hate me? In that case, why
a kiss? (Much later in life I once was raped, by someone to
whom I was married, but I still think that counts; in any case,
I didn't know what he meant either.)

Not sure what else to do, and still in the grip of a monu-   52
mental confusion, I went over to the school building, which
was open on Saturdays for something called Story Hours, for
little children. I went into the front entrance and up to the
library where, to the surprise of the librarian, who may have
thought me retarded, I listened for several hours of tales of
the Dutch Twins, and Peter and Polly in Scotland. Actually
it was very soothing, that long pasteurized drone, hard even
to think about Car while listening to pap like that.

When I got home I found my mother for some reason in   53
a livelier, more talkative mood than usual. She told me that
a boy had called while I was out, three times. Even before
my heart had time to drop—to think that it might be Car,
she babbled on, "Terribly polite. Really, these *bien élevé*
Southern boys." (No, not Car.) "Harry something. He said
he'd call again. But, darling, where were you, all this time?"

I was beginning to murmur about the library, homework,   54
when the phone rang. I answered, and it was Harry McGinnis, asking me to go to the movies with him the following
Saturday afternoon. I said of course, I'd love to, and I giggled
in a silly new way. But my giggle was one of relief; I was saved,
I was normal, after all. I belonged in the world of light, of
lightheartedness. Car Jones had not really touched me.

I spent the next day, Sunday, in alternating states of agita-   55
tion and anticipation.

On Monday, on my way to school, I felt afraid of seeing   56
Car, at the same time that I was both excited and shy at the
prospect of Harry McGinnis—a combination of emotions
that was almost too much for me, that dazzling, golden first
of May, and that I have not dealt with too successfully in later
life.

Harry paid even less attention to me than he had before;   57
it was a while before I realized that he was conspicuously not
looking in my direction, not teasing me, and that that in itself
was a form of attention, as well as being soothing to my
shyness.

I realized too, after a furtive scanning of the back row, that   58
Car Jones was *not at school* that day. Relief flooded through
my blood like oxygen, like spring air.

Absences among the truck children were so unremarkable,   59
and due to so many possible causes, that any explanation at
all for his was plausible. Of course it occurred to me, among
other imaginings, that he had stayed home out of shame for
what he did to me. Maybe he had run away to sea, had joined
the Navy or the Marines? Coldheartedly, I hoped so. In any
case, there was no way for me to ask.

Later that week the truth about Car Jones did come out—   60 at first as a drifting rumor, then confirmed, and much more remarkable than joining the Navy: Car Jones had gone to the principal's office, a week or so back, and had demanded to be tested for entrance (immediate) into high school, a request so unprecedented (usually only pushy academic parents would ask for such a change) and so dumbfounding that it was acceded to. Car took the test and was put into the sophomore high-school class, on the other side of town, where he by age and size—and intellect, as things turned out; he tested high—most rightfully belonged.

I went to a lot of Saturday movies with Harry McGinnis, 61 where we clammily held hands, and for the rest of that spring, and into summer, I was teased about Harry. No one seemed to remember having teased me about Car Jones.

Considering the size of Hilton at that time, it seems sur- 62 prising that I almost never saw Car again, but I did not, except for a couple of tiny glimpses, during the summer that I was still going to the movies with Harry. On both those occasions, seen from across the street, or on the other side of a dim movie house, Car was with an older girl, a high-school girl, with curled hair, and lipstick, all that. I was sure that his hands and teeth were clean.

By the time I had entered high school, along with all those 63 others who were by now my familiar friends, Car was a freshman in the local university, and his family had moved into town. Then his name again was bruited about among us, but this time was an underground rumor: Car Jones was reputed to have "gone all the way"—to have "done it" with a pretty and most popular senior in our high school. (It must be remembered that this was more unusual among the young then than now.) The general (whispered) theory was that Car's status as a college boy had won the girl; traditionally, in Hilton, the senior high-school girls began to date the freshmen in the university, as many and as often as possible. But this was not necessarily true; maybe the girl was simply

drawn to Car, his height and his shoulders, his stormy eyes.
Or maybe they didn't do it after all.

The next thing I heard about Car, who was by then an
authentic town person, a graduate student in the university,
was that he had written a play which was to be produced by
the campus dramatic society. (Maybe that is how he finally
met his movie star, as a playwright? The column didn't say.)
I think I read this item in the local paper, probably in a
clipping forwarded to me by my mother; her letters were
always thick with clippings, thin with messages of a personal
nature.

My next news of Car came from my uncle, the French
professor, a violent, enthusiastic partisan in university affairs,
especially in their more traditional aspects. In scandalized
tones, one family Thanksgiving, he recounted to me and my
mother, that a certain young man, a graduate student in
English, named Carstairs Jones, had been offered a special
sort of membership in D.K.E., his own beloved fraternity,
and "Jones had *turned it down.*" My mother and I laughed
later and privately over this; we were united in thinking my
uncle a fool, and I am sure that I added, Well, good for him.
But I did not, at that time, reconsider the whole story of
Car Jones, that most unregenerate and wicked of the truck
children.

But now, with this fresh news of Carstairs Jones, and his
wife the movie star, it occurs to me that we two, who at a
certain time and place were truly misfits, although quite differently—we both have made it: what could be more American dream-y, more normal, than marriage to a lovely movie
star? Or, in my case, marriage to the successful surgeon?

And now maybe I can reconstruct a little of that time;
specifically, can try to see how it really was for Car, back then.
Maybe I can even understand that kiss.

Let us suppose that he lived in a somewhat better than
usual farmhouse; later events make this plausible—his family's
move to town, his years at the university. Also, I wish him
well. I will give him a dignified white house with a broad

front porch, set back among pines and oaks, in the red clay countryside. The stability and size of his house, then, would have set Car apart from his neighbors, the other farm families, other truck children. Perhaps his parents too were somewhat "different," but my imagination fails at them; I can easily imagine and clearly see the house, but not its population. Brothers? sisters? Probably, but I don't know.

Car would go to school, coming out of his house at the honk of the stained and bulging, ugly yellow bus, which was crowded with his supposed peers, toward whom he felt both contempt and an irritation close to rage. Arrived at school, as one of the truck children, he would be greeted with a total lack of interest; he might as well have been invisible, or been black, *unless* he misbehaved in an outright, conspicuous way. And so he did: Car yawned noisily during history class, he hummed during study hall and after recess he dawdled around the playground and came in late. And for these and other assaults on the school's decorum he was punished in one way or another, and then, when all else failed to curb his ways, he would be *held back,* forced to repeat an already insufferably boring year of school. 69

One fall there was a minor novelty in school: a new girl (me), a Yankee, who didn't look much like the other girls, with long straight hair, instead of curled, and Yankee clothes, wool skirts and sweaters, instead of flowery cotton dresses worn all year round. A funny accent, a Yankee name: Emily Ames. I imagine that Car registered those facts about me, and possibly the additional information that I was almost as invisible as he, but without much interest. 70

Until the day of truth or consequences. I don't think Car was around on the playground while the game was going on; one of the girls would have seen him, and squealed out, "Oooh, there's Car, there *he is!*" I rather believe that some skinny little kid, an unnoticed truck child, overheard it all, and then ran over to where Car was lounging in one of the school buses, maybe peeling an orange and throwing the peel, in spirals, out the window. "Say, Car, that little Yankee girl, she says she'd like to kiss you." 71

"Aw, go on." 72

He is still not very interested; the little Yankee girl is as   73
dumb as the others are.

And then he hears me being teased, everywhere, and   74
teased with his name. "Emily would kiss Car Jones—Emily
Jones!" Did he feel the slightest pleasure at such notoriety?
I think he must have; a man who would marry a movie star
must have at least a small taste for publicity. Well, at that point
he began to write me those notes: "You are the prettiest one
of the girls" (which I was not). I think he was casting us both
in ill-fitting roles, me as the prettiest, defenseless girl, and
himself as my defender.

He must have soon seen that it wasn't working out that   75
way. I didn't need a defender, I didn't need him. I was having
a wonderful time, at his expense, if you think about it, and I
am pretty sure Car did think about it.

Interestingly, at the same time he had his perception of my   76
triviality, Car must have got his remarkable inspiration in
regard to his own life: there was a way out of those miserably
boring classes, the insufferable children who surrounded him.
He would demand a test, he would leave this place for the
high school.

Our trellis meeting must have occurred after Car had taken   77
the test, and had known that he did well. When he kissed me
he was doing his last "bad" thing in that school, was kissing
it off, so to speak. He was also insuring that I, at least, would
remember him; he counted on its being my first kiss. And he
may have thought that I was even sillier than I was, and that
I would tell, so that what had happened would get around
the school, waves of scandal in his wake.

For some reason, I would also imagine that Car is one of   78
those persons who never look back; once kissed, I was readily
dismissed from his mind, and probably for good. He could
concentrate on high school, new status, new friends. Just as,
now married to his movie star, he does not ever think of
having been a truck child, one of the deprived, the disappointed. In his mind there are no ugly groaning trucks, no
hopeless littered playground, no squat menacing school
building.

But of course I could be quite wrong about Car Jones. He   79

could be another sort of person altogether; he could be as
haunted as I am by everything that ever happened in his life.

COMMENT ON "TRUTH OR CONSEQUENCES"

"Truth or Consequences" is an excellent illustration of how
narration and description are used in short fiction. The cata-
lyst for the story is the narrator's reading in a gossip column
about Car Jones's marriage to a famous former movie star.
His name sparks a memory, and the narrator (Emily) tries to
reconstruct the events that occurred during her school years.
The story is paced at two speeds: the opening is slow as Emily
describes the various social divisions on the playground; the
action speeds up once Emily says she would rather kiss Car
Jones than be eaten by ants. The plot reaches its climax when
Car Jones calls Emily's bluff and asks her to meet him by the
trellis near the school. The story concludes as Emily (older
and wiser?) continues to wonder about the "truth" and "consequences" of this brief encounter.

Narration and Description as a Writing Strategy

1. Recount the details of an accident or disaster in which you were a witness or a victim. You may wish to retell the events as a reporter would for a front-page story in the local newspaper, or you may recount the events from a more personal point of view, as Maya Angelou does in her description of the "disaster" in Mrs. Cullinan's kitchen. If you were a witness, consider the points of view of the other people involved so that you can give your readers an objective perspective on the event. If you were a victim, slow the pace of the major conflict, which probably occurred quickly, so you can show your readers its emotional impact.

2. Report an experience in which you had to commit an extremely difficult or distasteful deed. You may wish to begin, as George Orwell does, by telling your readers about the conditions you encountered before you confronted the problem of whether to commit the questionable act. Be sure to list all the options you considered before you acted, and conclude by reflecting on your attitude toward your choice. And, of course, make sure to plot your essay so that the *act* is given the central and most dramatic position.

3. In "Keeping the Scorebook," Doris Kearns Goodwin recounts her experience telling the stories of the daily baseball game. Study the lessons she learned about "storytelling." Then make a list of the difficulties your friends and relatives have telling an effective story. Finally, write a narrative illustrating "how to tell a good story" or "how to ruin a good story."

4. Chronicle a significant event in your life that occurred during a major crisis in the life of the nation—the civil rights movement, the Persian Gulf War, some environmental disaster. Or like Judith Ortiz Cofer, consider how the experience of your family was affected by living in another culture.

5. Describe how people who are different are treated within your community. Like Terry Tempest Williams, you may want to compare the way different communities explain experiences (or people) that are different. For example, you may want to focus on a public ceremony—wedding, baptism, funeral—to illustrate how people deal with the problem of difference.

6. Demonstrate the effects of perception on values (how "seeing is believing"). All the writers in this section deal with this subject. Angelou demonstrates how white people's inability to "see" black people distorts their belief about them. Goodwin describes how a scorekeeper's code or a good story can make you believe you are seeing the real thing. Williams reveals how words such as *normal* and *handicapped* encourage people to form opinions about people who are different. Cofer explains how stories about the people in her home movie help her understand her culture. Orwell shows how seeing the crowd's mocking faces convinces him to shoot the elephant. And Emily Ames, the narrator in Alice Adams's short story, tells how her concern for social acceptance made her misread the actions of someone who was different.

PROCESS
ANALYSIS

◌

A **process** is an operation that moves through a series of steps to bring about a desired result. You can call almost any procedure a process, whether it is getting out of bed in the morning or completing a transaction on the stock exchange. A useful way to identify a particular kind of process is by its principal function. A process can be *natural* (the birth of a baby), *mechanical* (starting a car engine), *physical* (dancing), or *mental* (reading).

Analysis is an operation that divides something into its parts in order to understand the whole more clearly. For example, poetry readers analyze the lines of a poem to find meaning. Doctors analyze a patient's symptoms to prescribe treatment. Politicians analyze the opinions of individual voters and groups of voters to plan campaigns.

If you want to write a process-analysis essay, you need to go through three steps: (1) divide the process you are going to explain into its individual steps; (2) show the movement of the process, step by step, from beginning to end; and (3) explain how each step works, how it ties into other steps in the sequence, and how it brings about the desired result.

PURPOSE

Usually you will write a process analysis to accomplish two purposes: *to give directions* and *to provide information.* Sometimes you might find it difficult to separate the two purposes. After all, when you give directions about how to do something (hit a baseball), you also have to provide information on how the whole process works (rules of the game—strike zone, walks, hits, base running, outs, scoring). But usually you can separate the two because you're trying to accomplish different goals. When you give directions, you want to help your readers do something (change a tire). When you give information, you want to satisfy your readers' curiosity about some process they'd like to know about but are unlikely to perform (pilot a space shuttle).

You might also write a process analysis to demonstrate that (1) a task that looks difficult is really easy or (2) a task that looks easy is really quite complex. For instance, you might want to show that selecting a specific tool can simplify a complex process (using a microwave oven to cook a six-course dinner). You might also want to show why it's important to have a prearranged plan to make a process seem simple (explaining the preparations for an informal television interview).

AUDIENCE

When you write a process-analysis essay, you must think carefully about who your audience will be. First, you need to decide whether you're writing *to* an audience (giving directions) or writing *for* an audience (providing information). If you are writing *to* an audience, you can address directly readers who are already interested in your subject: "If you want to plant a successful garden, you must follow these seven steps." If you are writing *for* an audience, you can write from a more detached point of view, but you have to find a way to catch the interest of more casual readers: "Although many Americans say they are concerned about nuclear power, few understand how a nuclear power plant works."

Second, you have to determine how wide the knowledge gap is between you and your readers. Writing about a process suggests you are something of an expert in that area. If you can be sure your readers are also experts, you can make certain assumptions as you write your analysis. For instance, if you're outlining courtroom procedure to a group of fellow law students, you can assume you don't have to define the special meaning of the word *brief.*

On the other hand, if you feel sure your intended audience knows almost nothing about a process (or has only general knowledge), you can take nothing for granted. If you are explaining how to operate a VCR to readers who have never used one, you will have to define special terms and explain all procedures. If you assume your readers are experts when they are not, you will confuse or annoy them. If you assume they need to be told everything when they don't, you will bore or antagonize them. And, finally, remember that to analyze a process effectively, you must either research it carefully or have firsthand knowledge of its operation. It's risky to try to explain something you don't really understand.

STRATEGIES

The best way to write a process analysis is to organize your essay according to five parts:

Overview
Special terms

Sequence of steps
Examples
Results

The first two parts help your readers understand the process, the next two show the process in action, and the last one evaluates the worth of the completed process.

Begin your analysis with an *overview* of the whole process. To make such an overview, you take these four steps:

1. Define the objective of the process
2. Identify (and number) the steps in the sequence
3. Group some small steps into larger units
4. Call attention to the most important steps or units

For example, Edward Hoagland begins his analysis of the jury system by pointing out that the jurists' objective was to be fair, "to be better than themselves." Nikki Giovanni makes her recommendations for black students in sequence and then goes on to illustrate some of the common problems that occur with each recommendation.

Each process has its own *special terms* to describe tools, tasks, and methods, and you will have to define those terms for your readers. You can define them at the beginning so your readers will understand the terms when you use them, but often you do better to define them as you use them. Your readers may have trouble remembering specialized language out of context, so it's often practical to define your terms throughout the course of the essay, pausing to explain their special meaning or use the first time you introduce them. Ann Zwinger follows this strategy by describing the various drawing tools she keeps in her purse.

When you write a process-analysis essay, you must present the *sequence of steps* clearly and carefully. As you do so, give the reason for each step and, where appropriate, provide these reminders:

1. *Do not omit any steps.* A sequence is a sequence because all steps depend on one another. Nikki Giovanni explains the

importance of going to class to establish "a consistent presence in the classroom."

2. *Do not reverse steps.* A sequence is a sequence because each step must be performed according to a necessary and logical pattern. Lars Eighner reminds readers that if they start eating something before they have inspected it, they are likely to discover moldy bread or sour milk after they have put it into their mouth.

3. *Suspend certain steps.* Occasionally, a whole series of steps must be suspended and another process completed before the sequence can resume. Natalie Angier analyzes how male dolphins must first reach consensus before they start their courtship rituals.

4. *Do not overlook steps within steps.* Each sequence is likely to have a series of smaller steps buried within each step. Edward Hoagland reminds his readers that selecting a jury may involve another procedure—agreeing to plea bargain.

5. *Avoid certain steps.* It is often tempting to insert steps that are not recommended but that appear "logical." Ann Zwinger warns her readers that beginning a drawing with an outline can trap you in a corner.

You may want to use several kinds of examples to explain the steps in a sequence:

1. *Pictures.* You can use graphs, charts, and diagrams to illustrate the operation of the process. Although none of the writers in this section uses pictures, Ann Zwinger's purpose is to demonstrate what you can learn by drawing them.

2. *Anecdotes.* Since you're claiming some level of expertise by writing a process analysis, you can clarify your explanation by using examples from your own experience. Eighner uses this method when he describes his experience selecting discarded pizzas and waiting for the "junk" that will be pitched at the end of a semester.

3. *Variants.* You can mention alternative steps to show that the process may not be as rigid or simplistic as it often

appears. Angier suggests that male dolphins can change alliances and courtship procedures every day.

4. *Comparisons.* You can use comparisons to help your readers see that a complex process is similar to a process they already know. Hoagland uses this strategy when he compares jury duty to other universal experiences "like getting married or having a child, like voting."

Although you focus on the movement of the process when you write a process-analysis essay, finally you should also try to evaluate the *results* of that process. You can move to this last part by asking two questions: How do you know it's done? How do you know it's good? Sometimes the answer is simple: the car starts; the trunk opens. At other times, the answer is not so clear: the student may need further instruction; the jury may have difficulty reaching a decision.

USING PROCESS ANALYSIS IN PARAGRAPHS

Here are two process-analysis paragraphs. The first is written by a professional writer and is followed by an analysis. The second is written by a student writer and is followed by questions.

SCOTT RUSSELL SANDERS
from "Digging Limestone"

Dealing with the stone itself involves a whole new set of machines. Great mobile engines called channelers, powered by electricity, chug on rails from one side of the bed to the other, chiseling ten-foot-deep slots. Hammering and puffing along, they look and sound and smell like small locomotives. By shifting rails, the quarriers eventually slice the bed into a grid of blocks. The first of these to be removed is called the keyblock, and

Topic sentenc predicts conte

Names specia tools

Identifies first step

it always provokes a higher than usual proportion of curses. There is no way to get to the base of this first block to cut it loose, so it must be wedged, hacked, splintered and worried at, until something like a clean hole has been excavated. Men can then climb down and, by drilling holes and driving wedges, split the neighboring block free at its base, undoing in an hour a three-hundred-million-year-old cement job.

Describes subsequent steps

Makes comparison (earth's crust to cement job)

Comment This paragraph, excerpted from "Digging Limestone," analyzes the complicated process of removing large slabs of limestone from the earth. The opening sentences name the special machines required to begin the work. Sanders makes sure his readers understand the importance of removing the keyblock. Only after this slice of stone is removed can the workers proceed with the rest of the process, "undoing in an hour a three-hundred-million-year-old cement job."

SARA TEMPLE
Making Stained Glass

Before you begin making stained glass, you will need to purchase the right tools—most of which you can find at your local hardware store. First, select a glass cutter. It looks like a steel fork with a wheel at one end. The wheel is the blade that allows you to cut out the shape of each piece of glass. Second, you will need another tool to "break" the glass along the line you have scored with your cutter. I've always called this object "the tool." Tell the hardware clerk what you want and she'll show you what you need. Third, pick out a glass grinder to polish each piece of glass to the right size. Finally, buy a soldering iron to fuse the various pieces of glass into your design. These last two tools can be "pricey," so you may want to find a partner to share the cost. In the process, you may discover that your stained glass will become more creative when you design it with a friend.

1. How does Temple list and describe the special tools needed in the process?
2. What advice does Temple provide about how to purchase and use the "pricey" tools?

PROCESS ANALYSIS

Points to Remember

1. Arrange the steps in your process in an orderly sequence.
2. Identify and explain the purpose of each of the steps in the process.
3. Describe the special tools, terms, and tasks needed to complete the process.
4. Provide warnings, where appropriate, about the consequences of omitting, reversing, or overlooking certain steps.
5. Supply illustrations and personal anecdotes to help clarify aspects of the process.

Ann Zwinger was born in Muncie, Indiana, in 1925, and was educated at Wellesley College and Indiana University. She has taught art at Smith College and the University of Arizona, and served as naturalist-in-residence at Carleton College. She is best known for books she has written and illustrated about the environment, such as *Beyond the Aspen Grove* (1970), *Run, River Run: A Naturalist's Journey Down One of the Great Rivers of the West* (1975), and *The Mysterious Lands: The Four Deserts of the United States* (1989). Her artwork has been exhibited throughout the country and in her home town, Colorado Springs, and she has published (with her daughter) a book of writings and photographs, *Women in the Wilderness* (1995). In "Drawing on Experience," reprinted from a collection of essays on nature and culture from *Orion* magazine, *Finding Home* (1992), Zwinger explains the "simple act of pencil rotating softly on paper."

Drawing on Experience

I T REALLY DOESN'T matter whether you can draw or not— just the time taken to examine in detail, to turn a flower or a shell over in your fingers, opens doors and windows. The time spent observing pays, and you can better observe with a hand lens than without one. A hand lens is a joy and a delight, an entrée to another world just below your normal vision. Alice in Wonderland never had it so good—no mysterious potions are needed, just a ten- or fifteen-power hand lens hung around your neck. There's a kind of magic in seeing stellate hairs on a mustard stem, in seeing the retrorsely

1

barbed margin of a nettle spine—there all the time but never visible without enhancement.

But to take the next step—to draw these in the margin of your notebook, on the back of an envelope, in a sketch pad, or even in the sand—establishes a connection between hand and eye that reinforces the connection between eye and memory. Drawing fastens the plant in memory. 2

I speak of plants because they are what I enjoy drawing. I find small plants easier to translate to paper than a minute ant's antennae or a full-blown, horizon-to-horizon landscape. Landscapes are beautiful for what you leave out; the most magnificent landscapes I know are those Rembrandt did 3

I think of drawing not as an end in itself but as a learning process, of doing research with a hand lens and pencil instead of a book and note cards.

---

with a wash from a couple of brush strokes enlivened with a crisp pen. But that took years of practice and a large dose of genius, which are not the point here—I speak of the enjoyment of learning from precise observation.

With a plant, I start with a small detail and build up because it's easier to extend outward into the infinite space of the page than to be caught in the finite space of an outline. If you begin with the big outline and fill in, and if you have any of the proportion problems I do, you often draw yourself into a corner. I begin with the stigma and stamens, or perhaps a petal, or perhaps the part that's closest, and work outward, relating each part to what's been put down before rather than blocking in a general outer shape and working down to detail. 4

When I begin in the center, as it were, and move outward, I build up a reality in which each detail relates to the one 5 before. I wonder if this is also a way of apprehending a world, of composing it from many observations, a detail here, a detail there, creating an infinitely expandable universe. I always thought I worked this way because I was myopic, but maybe it's deeper than that and has to do with judgments, perceived realities, and whether there are five or six stamens.

Small things, large enough to see easily, but small enough 6 to hold in the hand or put on the table in front of you, small enough to translate more or less one-to-one, seem to me the easiest subjects for the neophyte illustrator. Why deal with complex proportions if you don't have to? Forget the tea rose and the peony. Forgo the darlings of the garden that have been bred into complex, complicated flowers with multiple petals and fancy shapes. Try instead an interesting leaf, noting how the veining webs, or the edges curl or notch. Or try a simple flower—a phlox or lily-of-the-valley or an open, five-petaled wild rose.

Pale-colored plants are easier to draw: dark or brilliant 7 colors often obscure the shape and character of the flower. Seedheads, summer's skeletons, are often felicitous subjects. So are cow parsnip's umbrella ribs or pennycress's orbicular pods, shepherd's purse or lily pods, which likewise give a sense of seasons past and springs to come.

Plants are nice because they stay still. I draw insects but 8 only deceased ones, collected, pinned, and dried. Trying to portray a moving bug is a ridiculous task ending only in frustration.

Quick sketches of larger moving animals are difficult but 9 greatly rewarding. If you are a birdwatcher and have the patience, drawing is a good way to learn how birds move, orient and tilt their bodies, and to pick up a lot on animal behavior because the observation is focused. (I happen to find birds hard to draw but suspect it's because I don't practice.) An afternoon sketching at the zoo with pencil and pad will astound anyone who's never tried it before. Pick out the movement, never mind the details, and by the end of the afternoon the improvement, both in drawing and observation, is measurable.

Shells, beach debris, offer endless possibilities. Think of 10 what you are doing as doodling, not immortalizing a shell for posterity. Play with different points of view and different scales. Find out how a snail builds its shell by the Fibonacci numbers, how the inside of an oyster shell reveals in color and pattern where the oyster was attached and how it lived.

Or go to your local natural history museum and draw stuffed animals, although a weasel in the bush is worth two in the display. I remember wanting to draw a pocket gopher, and the sole specimen easily available was in a natural history museum. Only the front part was visible, the rest of the specimen having presumably been blown to bits on capture. It was not a successful drawing, and I never used it.   11

Drawing is like practicing the piano: you have to do it on a fairly regular basis to keep your hand in.   12

I have no patience with the "Oh,-if-I-could-only-draw!" school. Drawing is a state of mind—how much you want to do it, how much time you're willing to practice. It is, after all, simply a neural connection between eye and mind and hand, and the more that connection is reinforced, the more satisfying the result is going to be. I knew an art teacher who required students in his class to draw their own hand, once a week. His theory was that the subject was always on the premises, had infinite possibilities of outline and pose and was not very easy to draw. The difference between the first hand drawn and the last was remarkable, a real confidence builder.   13

I'm also impatient with those who say "It doesn't *look* like what I wanted it to look like!" So what? Don't demand of yourself what you're not able to do at the time. Enjoy the feel of pencil on paper without imposing goals you can't meet.   14

I don't know why this setting of impossible goals happens more with drawing than with other creative endeavors. People who accept that they can't sit down and write a symphony in a week expect to produce a skilled drawing the first time out. Potters spend hours learning how to center on the wheel; violinists practice scales all their lives. Drawing is in the same category: it takes time to develop the basic skills. And patience. When you hit a wrong note on the piano it   15 fades off into the air before you play the correct one. If you make a wrong line, you can erase it. Or start over.

There are some wonderful books on drawing—Frederick   16
Franck's *The Zen of Drawing* and, best of all, *Drawing on the Right Side of the Brain* by Betty Edwards. The exercises she suggests, along with her practical how-tos, open a whole new way of looking and seeing.

A drawing class can also be useful, but it's not necessary.   17
What *is* necessary is to toss out some preconceived notions, and to accept and appreciate your fallibility and then forget it. Masterpieces of self-expression are not devoutly to be wished. Drawing is an experience of the facts and figures of a visual world that you can learn about in no other way.

Fancy tools aren't necessary either. Although I used to   18
carry a full complement of pencils, I now carry a single automatic one with a .5 mm lead that I buy at the supermarket. I prefer a spiral sketch pad because the papers remain anchored better, and I like one with little "tooth," as smooth as will comfortably take pencil. And if there's space in your pack or purse, carry a can of workable spray fixative. It's dismaying in the extreme to see a labored-over drawing reduced to a smear, and know that it can't be restored.

Colored pencils are a delight to use, but there's a great   19
deal to be said for learning with black pencil on white paper. The analogy of black-and-white and color photography comes to mind: color is lively, but color obfuscates. I don't learn as much about a plant when I draw with color. The structure and the detail are clearer in black and white.

When I am drawing I am usually very content in the   20
pleasures of focusing outward. I think of drawing not as an end in itself but as a learning process, of doing research with a hand lens and pencil instead of a book and note cards. I think of it as seeing what I did not see before, of discovering, of walking around in the stamens and the pistil, of pacing off the petals, of touching the plant and knowing who it is.

In touch, you are given knowledge in an immediate and   21
practical way. You find out quickly that a cholla spine stings, that a blue spruce stabs, that a juniper prickles, that a mullein

leaf is soft. There is also a communication established, an intimacy between mind and plant.

I remember a morning an April ago. I had been out in the desert for three days and had an ice chest full of plants. No matter how hard I worked in the evening, I couldn't catch up with all there was to draw, so I took that morning just to draw. And I'm not sure but what it isn't a good time for drawing—your mind is yet uncluttered, energy is high, the capacity for concentration undiluted. The light tends to be bright and cool and better for drawing than the artificial light needed at night.

Two days prior a kindly hostess had said, "Let me get you a glass to put the lily in so you don't have to hold it in your hand." I had replied without thinking, "No thank you—I need to see what's on the other side." I thought of that that morning as I drew the lily, which had been carefully cossetted in the ice chest since.

When I had acquired the lily, it had five buds. That morning only one remained closed, two were open, and two were spent. It was a delicate, difficult flower, spreading its sepals and petals into a six-pointed star, stretching out gold-powdered sepals that would attract no pollinator, extending a white, three-partite stigma beyond where it could catch its own pollen, a stigma that now, in the end, would catch none. But even as I had plucked the stalk (there was no time to draw it on site) I knew the bulb would endure, to produce another stalk of flowers next year, nourished by the ruffled leaves that spread across the dry, hard ground.

I propped the lily up in the folds of the bedspread, arranged it so that the two open flowers gave different aspects of the same reality, arranged it so it said not only *Hemerocallis* but *undulata* and Sonoran Desert at ten o'clock on an April morning. A light breeze came in the window at my right shoulder and the perfect light, bright but soft, illuminated the ruffled edges of the petals, revealing a trace of where they had overlapped in the bud.

The quintessential lily, based on a trinity of shapes: I drew three lines, enough to put a turned-back sepal on paper, layered pencil lines to limn the greenish stripe down the middle, checked the proportions, width against length, ruffle against sweep of edge. And picked it up. Unconsciously. Turned it over, looked it round, set it back, realized that knowing what was on the other side mattered a great deal. How do you know where you're going if you don't know where you've been?

The appearance of the lily on the page is the future, but I've already seen it in my mind's eye, turned it in my hand, seen all lilies in this lily, known dryness in my roots, spreading in my leaves, sunshine polishing my stalk. Because of this lily, which I never saw until a few days ago, I know all about waiting for enough warmth, all about cool dawns and wilting noons. Because of this lily I know about desert heat and winter sleep and what the desert demands. 27

This lily is fixed in my mind's memory, on the page and blowing in a desert spring. No matter what the season, this lily blooms as part of experience, part of understanding, a deep part of knowledge beyond words. Words, visual images, straight memory—none bring that lily to flower in the mind like the notation of its curve and the line of its flare, a memory of the eye and the hand inscribed in the simple act of pencil rotating softly on paper. 28

For Study and Discussion

QUESTIONS FOR RESPONSE

1. When was the last time you tried to draw a picture? Why does the prospect of drawing produce anxiety?
2. How do you respond to the "mistakes" you see in your drawing?

QUESTIONS ABOUT PURPOSE

1. According to Zwinger, what is the purpose of drawing?
2. Why does she encourage her readers to enjoy "the feel of pencil on paper without imposing goals you can't meet"?

QUESTIONS ABOUT AUDIENCE

1. How does Zwinger address her readers who belong to the "Oh,-if-I-could-only-draw!" school?
2. How does she respond to those readers who say "It doesn't *look* like what I wanted it to look like"?

QUESTIONS ABOUT STRATEGY

1. Why does Zwinger recommend drawing small things? Why does she begin at the center?
2. What sort of tools and techniques does Zwinger recommend? Why is black and white more effective than color?

QUESTIONS FOR DISCUSSION

1. How does Zwinger use the example of the lily to illustrate how "drawing is an experience of the facts and figures of a visual world that you can learn about in no other way"?
2. In what way is "drawing a state of mind"? How does it depend on practice?

LARS EIGHNER

Lars Eighner was born in 1948 in Corpus Christi, Texas, and attended the University of Texas at Austin. He held a series of jobs, including work as an attendant at the state mental hospital in Austin, before he became homeless. For five years he drifted between Austin and Hollywood, living on the streets and in abandoned buildings. Then he began to contribute essays to the *Threepenny Review*; these writings are collected in his memoir, *Travels with Lizabeth* (1993). In one of these essays, "My Daily Dives in the Dumpster," Eighner analyzes the "predictable series of stages that a person goes through in learning to scavenge."

My Daily Dives in the Dumpster

I BEGAN DUMPSTER diving about a year before I became 1
homeless.

I prefer the term "scavenging" and use the word "scroung- 2
ing" when I mean to be obscure. I have heard people, evidently meaning to be polite, use the word "foraging," but I prefer to reserve that word for gathering nuts and berries and such which I do also, according to the season and opportunity.

I like the frankness of the word "scavenging." I live from 3
the refuse of others. I am a scavenger. I think it a sound and honorable niche, although if I could I would naturally prefer to live the comfortable consumer life, perhaps—and only perhaps—as a slightly less wasteful consumer owing to what I have learned as a scavenger.

Except for jeans, all my clothes come from Dumpsters. 4
Boom boxes, candles, bedding, toilet paper, medicine, books,

a typewriter, a virgin male love doll, change sometimes amounting to many dollars: All came from Dumpsters. And, yes, I eat from Dumpsters too.

There are a predictable series of stages that a person goes 5 through in learning to scavenge. At first the new scavenger is filled with disgust and self-loathing. He is ashamed of being seen and may lurk around trying to duck behind things, or

---

Scavenging, more than most other pursuits, tends to yield returns in some proportion to the effort and the intelligence brought to bear.

---

he may try to dive at night. (In fact, this is unnecessary, since most people instinctively look away from scavengers.)

Every grain of rice seems to be a maggot. Everything 6 seems to stink. The scavenger can wipe the egg yolk off the found can, but he cannot erase the stigma of eating garbage from his mind.

This stage passes with experience. The scavenger finds a 7 pair of running shoes that fit and look and smell brand-new. He finds a pocket calculator in perfect working order. He finds pristine ice cream, still frozen, more than he can eat or keep. He begins to understand: People do throw away perfectly good stuff, a lot of perfectly good stuff.

At this stage he may become lost and never recover. All 8 the Dumpster divers I have known come to the point of trying to acquire everything they touch. Why not take it, they reason, it is all free. This is, of course, hopeless, and most divers come to realize that they must restrict themselves to items of relatively immediate utility.

The finding of objects is becoming something of an urban 9 art. Even respectable, employed people will sometimes find something tempting sticking out of a Dumpster or standing beside one. Quite a number of people, not all of them of the bohemian type, are willing to brag that they found this or that piece in the trash.

But eating from Dumpsters is the thing that separates the dilettanti from the professionals. Eating safely involves three principles: using the senses and common sense to evaluate the condition of the found materials; knowing the Dumpsters of a given area and checking them regularly; and seeking always to answer the question, Why was this discarded?   10

Perhaps everyone who has a kitchen and a regular supply of groceries has, at one time or another, eaten half a sandwich before discovering mold on the bread, or has gotten a mouthful of milk before realizing the milk had turned. Nothing of the sort is likely to happen to a Dumpster diver because he is constantly reminded that most food is discarded for a reason.   11

Yet perfectly good food can be found in Dumpsters. Canned goods, for example, turn up fairly often in the Dumpsters I frequent. All except the most phobic people would be willing to eat from a can even if it came from a Dumpster. I have few qualms about dry foods such as crackers, cookies, cereal, chips, and pasta if they are free of visible contaminants and still dry and crisp. Raw fruits and vegetables with intact skins seem perfectly safe to me, excluding, of course, the obviously rotten. Many are discarded for minor imperfections that can be pared away. Chocolate is often discarded only because it has become discolored as the cocoa butter de-emulsified.   12

I began scavenging by pulling pizzas out of the Dumpster behind a pizza delivery shop. In general, prepared food requires caution, but in this case I knew what time the shop closed and went to the Dumpster as soon as the last of the help left.   13

Because the workers at these places are usually inexperienced, pizzas are often made with the wrong topping, baked   14

incorrectly, or refused on delivery for being cold. The products to be discarded are boxed up because inventory is kept
by counting boxes: A boxed pizza can be written off; an
unboxed pizza does not exist. So I had a steady supply of
fresh, sometimes warm pizza.

The area I frequent is inhabited by many affluent college   15
students. I am not here by chance; the Dumpsters are very
rich. Students throw out many good things, including food,
particularly at the end of the semester and before and after
breaks. I find it advantageous to keep an eye on the academic
calendar.

A typical discard is a half jar of peanut butter—though   16
non-organic peanut butter does not require refrigeration and
is unlikely to spoil in any reasonable time. Occasionally I find
a cheese with a spot of mold, which, of course, I just pare
off, and because it is obvious why the cheese was discarded,
I treat it with less suspicion than an apparently perfect cheese
found in similar circumstances. One of my favorite finds is
yogurt—often discarded, still sealed, when the expiration
date has passed—because it will keep for several days, even in
warm weather.

I avoid ethnic foods I am unfamiliar with. If I do not know   17
what it is supposed to look or smell like when it is good, I
cannot be certain I will be able to tell if it is bad.

No matter how careful I am I still get dysentery at least   18
once a month, oftener in warm weather. I do not want to
paint too romantic a picture. Dumpster diving has serious
drawbacks as a way of life.

Though I have a proprietary feeling about my Dumpsters,   19
I don't mind my direct competitors, other scavengers, as
much as I hate the soda-can scroungers.

I have tried scrounging aluminum cans with an able-   20
bodied companion, and afoot we could make no more than
a few dollars a day. I can extract the necessities of life from
the Dumpsters directly with far less effort than would be
required to accumulate the equivalent value in aluminum.
Can scroungers, then, are people who *must* have small
amounts of cash—mostly drug addicts and winos.

I do not begrudge them the cans, but can scroungers tend   21
to tear up the Dumpsters, littering the area and mixing the
contents. There are precious few courtesies among scavengers, but it is a common practice to set aside surplus items:
pairs of shoes, clothing, canned goods, and such. A true
scavenger hates to see good stuff go to waste, and what he
cannot use he leaves in good condition in plain sight. Can
scroungers lay waste to everything in their path and will stir
one of a pair of good shoes to the bottom of a Dumpster to
be lost or ruined in the muck. They become so specialized
that they can see only cans and earn my contempt by passing
up change, canned goods, and readily hockable items.

Can scroungers will even go through individual garbage   22
cans, something I have never seen a scavenger do. Going
through individual garbage cans without spreading litter is
almost impossible, and litter is likely to reduce the public's
tolerance of scavenging. But my strongest reservation about
going through individual garbage cans is that this seems to
me a very personal kind of invasion, one to which I would
object if I were a homeowner.

Though Dumpsters seem somehow less personal than gar-   23
bage cans, they still contain bank statements, bills, correspon-
dence, pill bottles, and other sensitive information. I avoid
trying to draw conclusions about the people who dump in
the Dumpsters I frequent. I think it would be unethical to
do so, although I know many people will find the idea of
scavenger ethics too funny for words.

Occasionally a find tells a story. I once found a small paper   24
bag containing some unused condoms, several partial tubes
of flavored sexual lubricant, a partially used compact of birth
control pills, and the torn pieces of a picture of a young man.
Clearly, the woman was through with him and planning to
give up sex altogether.

Dumpster things are often sad—abandoned teddy bears,   25
shredded wedding albums, despaired-of sales kits. I find dia-
ries and journals. College students also discard their papers;
I am horrified to discover the kind of paper that now merits
an A in an undergraduate course.

Dumpster diving is outdoor work, often surprisingly pleas-   26
ant. It is not entirely predictable; things of interest turn up
every day, and some days there are finds of great value. I am
always very pleased when I can turn up exactly the thing I
most wanted to find. Yet in spite of the element of chance,
scavenging, more than most other pursuits, tends to yield
returns in some proportion to the effort and intelligence
brought to bear.

I think of scavenging as a modern form of self-reliance.   27
After ten years of government service, where everything is
geared to the lowest common denominator, I find work that
rewards initiative and effort refreshing. Certainly I would be
happy to have a sinecure again, but I am not heartbroken to
be without one.

I find from the experience of scavenging two rather deep   28
lessons. The first is to take what I can use and let the rest go.
I have come to think that there is no value in the abstract. A
thing I cannot use or make useful, perhaps by trading, has
no value, however fine or rare it may be. (I mean useful in
the broad sense—some art, for example, I would think valuable.)

The second lesson is the transience of material being. I do   29
not suppose that ideas are immortal, but certainly they are
longer-lived than material objects.

The things I find in Dumpsters, the love letters and rag   30
dolls of so many lives, remind me of this lesson. Many times
in my travels I have lost everything but the clothes on my
back. Now I hardly pick up a thing without envisioning
the time I will cast it away. This, I think, is a healthy state of
mind. Almost everything I have now has already been cast
out at least once, proving that what I own is valueless to
someone.

I find that my desire to grab for the gaudy bauble has been   31
largely sated. I think this is an attitude I share with the very
wealthy—we both know there is plenty more where whatever
we have came from. Between us are the rat-race millions who
have confounded their selves with the objects they grasp and

who nightly scavenge the cable channels looking for they know not what.

I am sorry for them. 32

For Study and Discussion

QUESTIONS FOR RESPONSE

1. What assumptions do you make about someone sorting through a Dumpster?
2. What things that you throw away in the weekly garbage might others find valuable?

QUESTIONS ABOUT PURPOSE

1. Why does Eighner prefer the term *scavenging* to *scrounging* or *foraging* to characterize the process he analyzes?
2. In what ways does Eighner's analysis demonstrate that Dumpster diving is "a sound and honorable niche"?

QUESTIONS ABOUT AUDIENCE

1. How does Eighner anticipate his audience's reaction to his subject by presenting the "predictable series of stages that a person goes through in learning to scavenge"?
2. How do Eighner's "scavenger ethics" enhance his standing with his readers?

QUESTIONS ABOUT STRATEGIES

1. How does Eighner use the example of pizza to illustrate the three principles of eating from a Dumpster?
2. How does Eighner's analysis of the process of "soda-can scrounging" help distinguish that process from "scavenging"?

QUESTIONS FOR DISCUSSION

1. How do the two lessons Eighner has learned demonstrate that his "work" rewards initiative and effort?
2. What attitudes toward consumption and waste does Eighner claim he shares with the very wealthy? Why does he feel sorry for "the rat-race millions"?

NIKKI GIOVANNI

Nikki Giovanni was born in 1943 in Knoxville, Tennessee, and was educated at Fisk University, the University of Pennsylvania, and Columbia University. She has taught creative writing at Rutgers University and Virginia Tech and worked for the Ohio Humanities Council and the Appalachian Community Fund. Her poems have appeared in the collections *My House* (1972), *The Women and the Men* (1975), and *Those Who Ride the Night Winds* (1983). Her nonfiction work appears in books such as *Gemini: An Extended Autobiographical Statement on My First Twenty-five Years Being a Black Poet* (1971), *Sacred Cows . . . and Other Edibles* (1988), and *Racism 101* (1994). In "Campus Racism 101," Giovanni tells black students how to succeed at predominantly white colleges.

Campus Racism 101

T HERE IS A bumper sticker that reads: TOO BAD IGNO- RANCE ISN'T PAINFUL. I like that. But ignorance is. We just seldom attribute the pain to it or even recognize it when we see it. Like the postcard on my corkboard. It shows a young man in a very hip jacket smoking a cigarette. In the background is a high school with the American flag waving. The caption says: "Too cool for school. Yet too stupid for the real world." Out of the mouth of the young man is a bubble enclosing the words "Maybe I'll start a band." There could be a postcard showing a jock in a uniform saying, "I don't need school. I'm going to the NFL or NBA." Or one showing a young man or woman studying and a group of young people saying, "So you want to be white." Or something equally demeaning. We need to quit it.

I am a professor of English at Virginia Tech. I've been here 2 for four years, though for only two years with academic rank. I am tenured, which means I have a teaching position for life, a rarity on a predominantly white campus. Whether from malice or ignorance, people who think I should be at a predominantly Black institution will ask, "Why are you at Tech?" Because it's here. And so are Black students. But even if Black students weren't here, it's painfully obvious that this nation and this world cannot allow white students to go

---

Your job is not to educate white people; it is to obtain an education.

---

through higher education without interacting with Blacks in authoritative positions. It is equally clear that predominantly Black colleges cannot accommodate the numbers of Black students who want and need an education.

Is it difficult to attend a predominantly white college? 3 Compared with what? Being passed over for promotion because you lack credentials? Being turned down for jobs because you are not college-educated? Joining the armed forces or going to jail because you cannot find an alternative to the streets? Let's have a little perspective here. Where can you go and what can you do that frees you from interacting with the white American mentality? You're going to interact; the only question is, will you be in some control of yourself and your actions, or will you be controlled by others? I'm going to recommend self-control.

What's the difference between prison and college? They 4 both prescribe your behavior for a given period of time. They both allow you to read books and develop your writing. They both give you time alone to think and time with your peers to talk about issues. But four years of prison doesn't give you a passport to greater opportunities. Most likely that time only gives you greater knowledge of how to get back in. Four years of college gives you an opportunity not only to lift yourself but to serve your people effectively. What's the difference when you are called nigger in college from when you are called nigger in prison? In college you can, though I admit with effort, follow procedures to have those students who called you nigger kicked out or suspended. You can bring issues to public attention without risking your life. But mostly, college is and always has been the future. We, neither less nor more than other people, need knowledge. There are discomforts attached to attending predominantly white colleges, though no more so than living in a racist world. Here are some rules to follow that may help:

Go to class. No matter how you feel. No matter how you   5
think the professor feels about you. It's important to have a consistent presence in the classroom. If nothing else, the professor will know you care enough and are serious enough to be there.

Meet your professors. Extend your hand (give a firm hand-   6
shake) and tell them your name. Ask them what you need to do to make an A. You may never make an A, but you have put them on notice that you are serious about getting good grades.

Do assignments on time. Typed or computer-generated.   7
You have the syllabus. Follow it, and turn those papers in. If for some reason you can't complete an assignment on time, let your professor know before it is due and work out a new due date—then meet it.

Go back to see your professor. Tell him or her your name   8
again. If an assignment received less than an A, ask why, and find out what you need to do to improve the next assignment.

Yes, your professor is busy. So are you. So are your parents   9
who are working to pay or help with your tuition. Ask early what you need to do if you feel you are starting to get into academic trouble. Do not wait until you are failing.

Understand that there will be professors who do not like you;   10 there may even be professors who are racist or sexist or both. You must discriminate among your professors to see who will give you the help you need. You may not simply say, "They are all against me." They aren't. They mostly don't care. Since you are the one who wants to be educated, find the people who want to help.

Don't defeat yourself. Cultivate your friends. Know your 11 enemies. You cannot undo hundreds of years of prejudicial thinking. Think for yourself and speak up. Raise your hand in class. Say what you believe no matter how awkward you may think it sounds. You will improve in your articulation and confidence.

Participate in some campus activity. Join the newspaper 12 staff. Run for office. Join a dorm council. Do something that involves you on campus. You are going to be there for four years, so let your presence be known, if not felt.

You will inevitably run into some white classmates who are 13 troubling because they often say stupid things, ask stupid questions—and expect an answer. Here are some comebacks to some of the most common inquiries and comments:

Q: What's it like to grow up in a ghetto? 14
A: I don't know. 15

Q (from the teacher): Can you give us the Black perspective 16 on Toni Morrison, Huck Finn, slavery, Martin Luther King, Jr., and others?
A: I can give you *my* perspective. (Do not take the burden 17 of 22 million people on your shoulders. Remind everyone that you are an individual, and don't speak for the race or any other individual within it.)

Q: Why do all the Black people sit together in the dining 18 hall?
A: Why do all the white students sit together? 19

Q: Why should there be an African-American studies course? 20
A: Because white Americans have not adequately studied the 21

contributions of Africans and African-Americans. Both Black and white students need to know our total common history.

Q: Why are there so many scholarships for "minority" students?

A: Because they wouldn't give my great-grandparents their forty acres and the mule.

Q: How can whites understand Black history, culture, literature, and so forth?

A: The same way we understand white history, culture, literature, and so forth. That is why we're in school: to learn.

Q: Should whites take African-American studies courses?

A: Of course. We take white-studies courses, though the universities don't call them that.

Comment: When I see groups of Black people on campus, it's really intimidating.

Comeback: I understand what you mean. I'm frightened when I see white students congregating.

Comment: It's not fair. It's easier for you guys to get into college than for other people.

Comeback: If it's so easy, why aren't there more of us?

Comment: It's not our fault that America is the way it is.

Comeback: It's not our fault, either, but both of us have a responsibility to make changes.

It's really very simple. Educational progress is a national concern; education is a private one. Your job is not to educate white people; it is to obtain an education. If you take the racial world on your shoulders, you will not get the job done. Deal with yourself as an individual worthy of respect, and make everyone else deal with you the same way. College is a little like playing grown-up. Practice what you want to be. You have been telling your parents you are grown. Now is your chance to act like it.

For Study and Discussion

QUESTIONS FOR RESPONSE

1. How have you responded to situations in which you were convinced that your teacher did not like you?
2. How have you felt when a teacher or fellow student placed you in a group (characterized by stereotypes) and then asked you to speak *for* that group?

QUESTIONS ABOUT PURPOSE

1. How does Giovanni explain her reasons for teaching at a predominantly white school?
2. In what ways does the issue of control, particularly self-control, explain the purpose of her advice?

QUESTIONS ABOUT AUDIENCE

1. How do the examples in the first paragraph and the advice in the last paragraph identify Giovanni's primary audience?
2. How does Giovanni's status as professor at a predominantly white college establish her authority to address her audience on "Racism 101"?

QUESTIONS ABOUT STRATEGIES

1. How does Giovanni arrange her advice? Why is her first suggestion—"Go to class"—her *first* suggestion? Why is her last suggestion—"Participate in some campus activity"—her *last* suggestion?
2. How does she use sample questions and answers to illustrate the experience of learning on a white campus?

QUESTIONS FOR DISCUSSION

1. What does Giovanni's attitude toward *individual* as opposed to *group* perspective suggest about the nature of "racism"?
2. How might white students learn as much as black students from following her advice?

Natalie Angier was born in New York City in 1958, and educated at the University of Michigan and Barnard College. She worked as a staff writer for *Discover* and *Time* and as an editor for *Savvy* before becoming the science correspondent for the *New York Times* where she won the Pulitzer Prize for best reporting. Her books include *Natural Obsessions* (1988) and *The Beauty of the Beastly* (1995). In "Dolphin Courtship: Brutal, Cunning, and Complex," reprinted from *The Beauty of the Beastly,* Angier analyzes the complex process by which dolphins mate.

Dolphin Courtship: Brutal, Cunning, and Complex

A S MUCH AS puppies or pandas or even children, dolphins are universally beloved. They seem to cavort and frolic at the least provocation, their mouths are fixed in what looks like a state of perpetual merriment, and their behavior and enormous brains suggest an intelligence approaching that of humans—even, some might argue, surpassing it.

Dolphins are turning out to be exceedingly clever, but not in the loving, utopian-socialist manner that sentimental Flipperophiles may have hoped. Researchers who spent thousands of hours observing the behavior of bottle-nose dolphins off the coast of Australia have discovered that the males form social alliances that are far more sophisticated and devious than any seen in animals other than human beings. In these sleek submarine partnerships, one team of dolphins will recruit the help of another band of males to gang up against a third group, a sort of multitiered battle plan that requires considerable mental calculus.

The purpose of these complex alliances is not exactly spor-   3
tive. Males collude with their peers in order to steal fertile females from competing bands. And after they succeed in spiriting a female away, the males remain in their tight-knit group and perform a series of feats, at once spectacular and threatening, to guarantee that the female stays in line. Two or three males will surround her, leaping and bellyflopping, swiveling and somersaulting, all in perfect synchrony. Should the female be so unimpressed by the choreography as to attempt to flee, the males will chase after her, bite her, slap her with their fins, or slam into her with their bodies. The

---

*Dolphins become conspicuously charmless
when they want to mate or avoid mating.*

---

scientists call this effort to control females "herding," but they acknowledge that the word does not convey the aggressiveness of the act. As the herding proceeds, the sounds of fin swatting and body bashing rumble the waters, and sometimes the female emerges with deep tooth rakes on her sides.

Although biologists have long been impressed with the   4
intelligence and social complexity of bottle-nose dolphins—the type of porpoise often enlisted for marine mammal shows because they are so responsive to trainers—they were nonetheless surprised by the Machiavellian flavor of the males' stratagems. Many primates, including chimpanzees and baboons, are known to form gangs to attack rival camps, but never before had one group of animals been seen to solicit a second to go after a third. Equally impressive, the multipart alliances among dolphins seemed flexible, shifting from day

to day depending on the dolphins' needs, whether one group owed a favor to another, and the dolphins' perceptions of what they could get away with. The creatures seemed to be highly opportunistic, which meant that each animal was always computing who was friend and who was foe.

In an effort to thwart male encroachment, female dolphins likewise formed sophisticated alliances, the sisterhood sometimes chasing after an alliance of males that had stolen one of their friends from the fold. What is more, females seemed to exert choice over the males that sought to herd them, sometimes swimming alongside them in apparent contentment, at other times working furiously to escape, and often succeeding. Considered together, the demands of fluid and expedient social allegiances and counterallegiances could have been a force driving the evolution of intelligence among dolphins. 5

Lest it seem that a dolphin is little more than a thug with fins and a blowhole, biologists emphasize that it is in general a remarkably good-natured and friendly animal, orders of magnitude more peaceful than a leopard or even a chimpanzee. Most of the thirty species of dolphins and small whales are extremely social, forming into schools of several to hundreds of mammals, which periodically break off into smaller clans and come back together again in what is called a fission-fusion society. Among other things, their sociality appears to help them evade sharks and forage more effectively for fish. 6

Species like the bottle-nose and the spinner dolphins make most of their decisions by consensus, spending hours dawdling in a protected bay, nuzzling one another, and generating an eerie nautical symphony of squeaks, whistles, barks, twangs, and clicks. The noises rise ever louder until they reach a pitch that apparently indicates the vote is unanimous and it is time to take action—say, to go out and fish. "When they're coordinating their decisions, it's like an orchestra tuning up, and it gets more impassioned and more rhythmic," said Dr. Kenneth Norris, a leader in dolphin research. "Democracy 7 takes time, and they spend hours every day making decisions."

As extraordinary as the music is, dolphins do not possess 8
what can rightly be called a complex language, where one
animal can say unequivocally to another "Let's go fishing."
But the vocalizations are not completely random. Each bottle-nose dolphin has, for example, its own call sign—a signature whistle unique to that creature. A whistle is generated
internally and sounds more like a radio signal than a human
whistle. The mother teaches her calf what its whistle will be
by repeating the sound over and over. The calf retains that
whistle, squealing it out at times as though declaring its
presence. On occasion, one dolphin will imitate the whistle
of a companion, in essence calling the friend's name.

But dolphin researchers warn against glorifying dolphins 9
beyond the realms of mammaldom. "Everybody who's done
research in the field is tired of dolphin lovers who believe
these creatures are floating Hobbits," said one dolphin trainer
and scientist. "A dolphin is a healthy social mammal, and it
behaves like one, sometimes doing things that we don't find
very charming."

Dolphins become conspicuously charmless when they 10
want to mate or to avoid being mated. Female bottle-nose
dolphins bear a single calf only once every four or five years,
so a fertile female is a prized commodity. Because there is
almost no size difference between the sexes, a single female
cannot be forced to mate by a lone male. That may be part
of the reason that males team into gangs.

One ten-year study covered a network of about three 11
hundred male dolphins off western Australia. The researchers
discovered that early in adolescence, a male bottle-nose will
form an unshakable alliance with one or two other males.
They stick together for years, perhaps a lifetime, swimming,
fishing, and playing together, and flaunt their fast friendship
by always traveling abreast and surfacing in exact synchrony.

Sometimes that pair or triplet is able to woo a fertile female 12 on its own, although what happens once the males have herded in a female, and whether she goes for one or all of them, is not known: dolphin copulations occur deep under water and are almost impossible to witness. Nor do researchers understand how the males determine that a female is fertile, or at least nearly so, and is thus worth herding. Males do sometimes sniff around a female's genitals, as though trying to smell her receptivity; but because bottlenose dolphins give birth so rarely, males may attempt to keep a female around even when she is not ovulating, in the hope that she will require their services when the prized moment of estrus arrives.

At other times potential mates are scarce, and male alliances grow testy. That is when pairs or triplets seek to steal females from other groups. They scout out another alliance of lonely bachelors and, through a few deft strokes of their pectoral fins or gentle pecks with their mouths, persuade that pair or triplet to join in the venture.   13

The pact sealed, the two dolphin gangs then descend on a third group that is herding along a female. They chase and assault the defending team, and, because there are more of them, they usually win and take away the female. Significantly, the victorious joint alliance then splits up, with only one pair or triplet getting the female; the other team apparently helped them strictly as a favor.   14

That buddy-buddy spirit, however, may be fleeting. Two groups of dolphins that cooperated one week may be adversaries the next, and a pair of males will switch sides to help a second group pilfer the same female they had helped the defending males capture in the first place.   15

The instability and complications of the mating games may explain why males are so aggressive and demanding toward the females they do manage to capture. Male pairs or triplets guard the female ferociously, jerking their heads at her, charging her, biting her, and leaping and swimming about her in perfect unison, as though turning their bodies into fences. They may swim up under her, their penises extruded and   16 erect but without attempting penetration. Sometimes a male will make a distinctive popping noise at the female, a vocalization that sounds like a fist rapping on hollow wood. The noise probably indicates "Get over here!" for if the female ignores the pop, the male will threaten or attack her.

At some point, the female mates with one or more of the   17
males, and once she gives birth, the alliance loses interest in her. Female dolphins raise their calves as single mothers for four to five years.

The pressure to cooperate and to compete with their fel-   18
lows may have accelerated the evolution of the dolphin brain. The dolphin has one of the highest ratios of brain size to body mass in the animal kingdom, and such a ratio is often a measure of intelligence. A similar hypothesis has been proposed for the flowering of intelligence in humans, another big-brained species. Like dolphins, humans evolved in highly social conditions, where kin, friends, and foes are all mingled together, and the resources an individual can afford to share today may become dangerously scarce tomorrow, igniting conflict. In such a setting, few relationships are black or white; it is the capacity to distinguish subtle shades of gray that demands intelligence.

But keep in mind that the dolphin's big brain does not,   19
on its own, rank it as a big thinker. After all, the creature endowed with what may be the largest brain-to-body ratio in nature is none other than the sheep.

For Study and Discussion

QUESTIONS FOR RESPONSE

1. How have you responded to movies about "Flipper," or marine mammal shows featuring dolphins?
2. In what ways has figuring out the friends and foes in your shifting peer groups made you more savvy about social relationships?

QUESTIONS ABOUT PURPOSE

1. Why does Angier begin her essay by characterizing dolphins as "universally beloved"?
2. Why does she end her essay by speculating about the evolution of the dolphin's brain?

QUESTIONS ABOUT AUDIENCE

1. What assumptions does Angier make about her audience when she uses the term "Flipperophiles"?
2. How does she use the testimony of dolphin trainers and researchers to convince her readers that dolphins are not always "charming"?

QUESTIONS ABOUT STRATEGY

1. According to Angier, what are the primary steps in dolphin courtship?
2. How does she account for the steps researchers cannot explain (determining fertility) or have not seen (copulation)?

QUESTIONS FOR DISCUSSION

1. How does Angier's comparison of dolphins to other animals explain the uniqueness of their courtship rituals?
2. In what ways does the male-female behavior of dolphins remind you of the male-female behavior of human beings?

Edward Hoagland was born in New York City in 1932 and was educated at Harvard University. Although he has written several novels and books on travel, Hoagland considers himself a personal essayist, a writer who is concerned with expressing "what I think" and "what I am." He has published essays in *Commentary*, *Newsweek*, the *Village Voice*, and the *New York Times* on an intriguing range of subjects such as tugboats, turtles, circuses, city life in Cairo, and his own stutter. His essays have been collected in books such as *The Courage of Turtles* (1971), *The Edward Hoagland Reader* (1979), *Notes from the Century Before: A Journal from British Columbia* (1982), and *Balancing Acts* (1992). He has also published a collection of stories, *City Tales/Wyoming Stories* (1986), with Gretel Ehrlich. In "In the Toils of the Law," reprinted from *Walking the Dead Diamond River* (1973), Hoagland uses his own experience to explain the process of being selected for and serving on a jury.

In the Toils of the Law

LATELY PEOPLE SEEM to want to pigeonhole themselves ("I'm 'into' this," "I'm 'into' that"), and the anciently universal experiences like getting married or having a child, like voting or jury duty, acquire a kind of poignancy. We hardly believe that our vote will count, we wonder whether the world will wind up uninhabitable for the child, but still we do vote with a rueful fervor and look at new babies with undimmed tenderness, because who knows what will become of these old humane responsibilities? . . .

Jury duty. Here one sits listening to evidence: thumbs up   2

1

for a witness or thumbs down. It's unexpectedly moving; everybody tries so hard to be fair. For their two weeks of service people really try to be better than themselves. In Manhattan eighteen hundred are called each week from the voters' rolls, a third of whom show up and qualify. Later this third is divided into three groups of two hundred, one for the State Supreme Court of New York County, one for the Criminal Court, and one for the Civil Court. At Civil Court, 111 Centre Street, right across from the Tombs, there are jury rooms on the third and eleventh floors, and every Monday a new pool goes to one or the other. The building is relatively modern, the chairs upholstered as in an airport lounge, and the two hundred people sit facing forward like

---

Jury duty is unexpectedly moving; everybody tries so hard to be fair.

---

a school of fish until the roll is called. It's like waiting six or seven hours a day for an unscheduled flight to leave. They read and watch the clock, go to the drinking fountain, strike up a conversation, dictate business letters into the pay telephones. When I served, one man in a booth was shouting, "I'll knock your teeth down your throat! I don't want to hear, I don't want to know!"

. . . There are lots of retired men and institutional employees from banks, the Post Office or the Transit Authority whose bosses won't miss them, as well as people at loose ends who welcome the change. But some look extremely busy, rushing back to the office when given a chance or sitting at the tables at the front of the room, trying to keep up with their work. They'll write payroll checks, glancing to see if you notice how important they are, or pore over statistical charts or contact sheets with a magnifying glass, if they are in public relations or advertising. Once in a while a clerk emerges to rotate a lottery box and draw the names of jurors, who go into one of the challenge rooms—six jurors, six alternates—to be interviewed by the plaintiff's and defendant's lawyers. Unless the damages asked are large, in civil cases the jury has six members, only five of whom must agree on a decision, and since no one is going to be sentenced to jail, the evidence for a decision need merely seem preponderant, not "beyond a reasonable doubt."

The legal fiction is maintained that the man or woman you   4 see as defendant is actually going to have to pay, but the defense attorneys are generally insurance lawyers from a regular battery which each big company keeps at the courthouse to handle these matters, or from the legal corps of the City of New York, Con Edison, Hertz Rent A Car, or whoever. If so, they act interchangeably and you may see a different face in court than you saw in the challenge room, and still another during the judge's charge. During my stint most cases I heard about went back four or five years, and the knottiest problem for either side was producing witnesses who were still willing to testify. In negligence cases, so many of which involve automobiles, there are several reasons why the insurers haven't settled earlier. They've waited for the plaintiff to lose hope or greed, and to see what cards each contestant will finally hold in his hands when the five years have passed. More significantly, it's a financial matter. The straight-arrow companies that do right by a sufferer and promptly pay him off lose the use as capital of that three thousand dollars or so meanwhile—multiplied perhaps eighty thousand times, for all the similar cases they have.

Selecting a jury is the last little battle of nerves between   5 the two sides. By now the opposing attorneys know who will testify and have obtained pretrial depositions; this completes the hand each of them holds. Generally they think they know what will happen, so to save time and costs they settle the case either before the hearing starts or out of the jury's earshot during the hearing with the judge's help. Seeing a good sober jury waiting to hear them attempt to justify a bad case greases the wheels.

In the challenge room, though, the momentum of con-   6
frontation goes on. With a crowded court calendar, the judge
in these civil cases is not present, as a rule. It's a small room,
and there's an opportunity for the lawyers to be folksy or
emotional in ways not permitted them later on. For example,
in asking the jurors repeatedly if they will "be able to convert
pain and suffering into dollars and cents" the plaintiff's attorney is preparing the ground for his more closely supervised
presentation in court. By asking them if they own any stock
in an insurance company he can get across the intelligence,
which is otherwise *verboten,* that not the humble "defendant"
but some corporation is going to have to pay the tab. His
opponent will object if he tells too many jokes and wins too
many friends, but both seek not so much a sympathetic jury
as a jury that is free of nuts and grudge-holders, a jury
dependably ready to give everybody "his day in court"—a
phrase one hears over and over. The questioning we were
subjected to was so polite as to be almost apologetic, however, because of the danger of unwittingly offending any of
the jurors who remained. Having to size up a series of strangers, on the basis of some monosyllabic answers and each
fellow's face, profession and address, was hard work for these
lawyers. Everybody was on his best behavior, the jurors too,
because the procedure so much resembled a job interview,
and no one wanted to be considered less than fair-minded,
unfit to participate in the case; there was a vague sense of
shame about being excused.

The six alternates sat listening. The lawyers could look at   7
them and draw any conclusions they wished, but they could
neither question them until a sitting juror had been challenged, nor know in advance which one of the alternates
would be substituted first. Each person was asked about his
work, about any honest bias or special knowledge he might
have concerning cases of the same kind, or any lawsuits he
himself might have been involved in at one time. Some questions were probably partly designed to educate us in the
disciplines of objectivity, lest we think it was all too easy, and
one or two lawyers actually made an effort to educate us in

the majesty of the law, since, as they said, the judges sometimes are "dingbats" and don't. We were told there should
be no opprobrium attached to being excused, that we must
not simply assume a perfect impartiality in ourselves but
should help them to examine us. Jailhouse advocates, or
Spartan types who might secretly believe that the injured
party should swallow his misfortune and grin and bear a
stroke of bad luck, were to be avoided, of course, along with
the mingy, the flippant, the grieved and the wronged, as well
as men who might want to redistribute the wealth of the
world by finding for the plaintiff, or who might not limit their
deliberations to the facts of the case, accepting the judge's
interpretation of the law as law. We were told that our common sense and experience of life was what was wanted to sift
out the likelihood of the testimony we heard.

Most dismissals were caused just by a lawyer's hunch—or   8
figuring the percentages as baseball managers do. After the
first day's waiting in the airport lounge, there wasn't anybody
who didn't want to get on a case; even listening as an alternate in the challenge room was a relief. I dressed in a suit and
tie and shined my shoes. I'd been afraid that when I said I
was a novelist no lawyer would have me, on the theory that
novelists favor the underdog. On the contrary, I was accepted
every time; apparently a novelist was considered ideal, having
no allegiances at all, no expertise, no professional link to the
workaday world. I stutter and had supposed that this too
might disqualify me [but] these lawyers did not think it so.
What they seemed to want was simply a balanced group,
because when a jury gets down to arguing there's no telling
where its leadership will arise. The rich man from Sutton
Place whom the plaintiff's lawyer almost dismissed, fearing
he'd favor the powers that be, may turn out to be a fighting
liberal whose idea of what constitutes proper damages is
much higher than what the machinist who sits next to him
has in mind. In one case I heard about, a woman was clonked
by a Christmas tree in a department store and the juror whose
salary was lowest suggested an award of fifty dollars, and the
man who earned the most, fifty thousand dollars (they

rounded it off to fifteen hundred dollars). These were the kind of cases Sancho Panza did so well on when he was governor of Isle Barataria, and as I was questioned about my prejudices, and solemnly looking into each lawyer's eyes, shook my head—murmuring, No, I had no prejudices—all the time my true unreliable quirkiness filled my head. All I could do was resolve to try to be fair.

By the third day, we'd struck up shipboard friendships. There was a babbling camaraderie in the jury pool, and for lunch we plunged into that old, eclipsed, ethnic New York near City Hall—Chinese roast ducks hanging in the butcher's windows on Mulberry Street next door to an Italian store selling religious candles. We ate at Cucina Luna and Giambone's. Eating at Ping Ching's, we saw whole pigs, blanched white, delivered at the door. We watched an Oriental funeral with Madame Nhu the director waving the limousines on. The deceased's picture, heaped with flowers, was in the lead car, and all his beautiful daughters wept with faces disordered and long black hair streaming down. One of the Italian bands which plays on feast days was mourning over a single refrain—two trumpets, a clarinet, a mellophone and a drum.

As an alternate I sat in on the arguments for a rent-a-car crash case, with four lawyers, each of whom liked to hear himself talk, representing the different parties. The theme was that we were New Yorkers and therefore streetwise and no fools. The senior fellow seemed to think that all his years of trying these penny-ante negligence affairs had made him very good indeed, whereas my impression was that the reason he was still trying them was because he was rather bad. The same afternoon I got on a jury to hear the case of a cleaning woman, sixty-four, who had slipped on the floor of a Harlem ballroom in 1967 and broken her ankle. She claimed the floor was overwaxed. She'd obviously been passed from hand to hand within the firm that had taken her case and had wound up with an attractive young man who was here cutting his teeth. What I liked about her was her abusive manner, which expected no justice and made no distinction at all between her own lawyer and that of the ballroom owner, though she was confused by the fact that the judge was black. He was from the Supreme Court, assigned to help cut through this backlog, had a clerk with an Afro, and was exceedingly brisk and effective.

The porter who had waxed the floor testified—a man of good will, long since at another job. The ballroom owner had operated the hall for more than thirty years, and his face was fastidious, Jewish, sensitive, sad, like that of a concertgoer who is not unduly pleased with his life. He testified, and it was not *his* fault. Nevertheless the lady had hurt her ankle and been out of pocket and out of work. It was a wedding reception, and she'd just stepped forward, saying, "Here comes the bride!"   11

The proceedings were interrupted while motions were heard in another case, and we sat alone in a jury room, trading reading material, obeying the injunction not to discuss the case, until after several hours we were called back and thanked by the judge. "They also serve who stand and wait." He said that our presence next door as a deliberative body, passive though we were, had pressured a settlement. It was for seven hundred and fifty dollars, a low figure to me (the court attendant told me that there had been a legal flaw in the plaintiff's case), but some of the other jurors thought she'd deserved no money; they were trying to be fair to the ballroom man. Almost always that's what the disputes boiled down to: one juror trying to be fair to one person, another to another.   12

On Friday of my first week I got on a jury to hear the plight of a woman who had been standing at the front of a bus and had been thrown forward and injured when she stooped to pick up some change that had spilled from her purse. The bus company's lawyer was a ruddy, jovial sort. "Anybody here have a bone to pick with our New York City buses?" We laughed and said, no, we were capable of sending her away without any award if she couldn't prove negligence. Nevertheless, he settled with her attorney immediately after we left the challenge room. (These attorneys did not necessarily run to type. There was a Transit Authority man who   13 shouted like William Kunstler; five times the judge had an officer make him sit down, and once threatened to have the chap bound to his chair.)

I was an alternate for another car crash. With cases in progress all over the building, the jury pool had thinned out, so that no sooner were we dropped back into it than our names were called again. Even one noteworthy white-haired fellow who was wearing a red velvet jump suit, a dragon-colored coat and a dangling gold talisman had some experiences to talk about. I was tabbed for a panel that was to hear from a soft-looking, tired, blond widow of fifty-seven who, while walking home at night five years before from the shop where she worked, had tripped into an excavation only six inches deep but ten feet long and three feet wide. She claimed that the twists and bumps of this had kept her in pain and out of work for five months. She seemed natural and truthful on the witness stand, yet her testimony was so brief and flat that one needed to bear in mind how much time had passed. As we'd first filed into the courtroom she had watched us with the ironic gravity that a person inevitably would feel who has waited five years for a hearing and now sees the cast of characters who will decide her case. This was a woeful low point of her life, but the memory of how badly she'd felt was stale.

The four attorneys on the case were straightforward youngsters getting their training here. The woman's was properly aggressive; Con Edison's asked humorously if we had ever quarreled with Con Edison over a bill; the city's, who was an idealist with shoulder-length hair, asked with another laugh if we disliked New York; and the realty company's, whether we fought with our landlords. Of course, fair-minded folk that we were, we told them no. They pointed out that just as the code of the law provides that a lone woman, fifty-seven, earning a hundred dollars a week, must receive the same consideration in court as a great city, so must the city be granted an equal measure of justice as that lone woman was.

Our panel included a bank guard, a lady loan officer, a

young black Sing Sing guard, a pale, slim middle-aged executive from Coca-Cola, a hale fellow who sold package tours from an airline and looked like the Great Gildersleeve, and me. If her attorney had successfully eliminated Spartans from the jury, we'd surely award her something; the question was how much. I wondered about the five months. No bones broken—let's say, being rather generous, maybe two months of rest. But couldn't the remainder be one of those dead-still intermissions that each of us must stop and take once or twice in a life, not from any single blow but from the accumulating knocks and scabby disappointments that pile up, the harshness of winning a living, and the rest of it—for which the government in its blundering wisdom already makes some provision through unemployment insurance?

But there were no arguments. The judge had allowed the   17
woman to testify about her injuries on the condition that her physician appear. When, the next day, he didn't, a mistrial was declared.

For Study and Discussion

QUESTIONS FOR RESPONSE

1. What preconceptions do you have about the American jury system? What is the source of these preconceptions—television, books, movies?
2. What aspects of Hoagland's description of jury duty would encourage or discourage you from serving on a jury?

QUESTIONS ABOUT PURPOSE

1. Does Hoagland's analysis suggest that jury duty is a simple or a complex process? What do the first few sentences in paragraph 2 suggest about the process? What does the rest of the essay demonstrate?
2. In what ways does Hoagland's analysis support or contradict his theories about contemporary attitudes toward "anciently universal experiences"?

QUESTIONS ABOUT AUDIENCE

1. How does Hoagland's use of the pronoun "we" in the first paragraph identify his audience?
2. How does Hoagland's description of his fellow jurors show his readers the difficulties a jury faces when it tries to arrive at a fair decision?

QUESTIONS ABOUT STRATEGIES

1. How does Hoagland use the lawyers' questions to illustrate the selection process? What kind of people are these questions designed to eliminate?
2. How does Hoagland use the five cases he heard as examples to illustrate different problems with the jury process? For example, what problem does the jury face in the last case?

QUESTIONS FOR DISCUSSION

1. Hoagland argues that jurors "really try to be better than themselves." What does this assertion suggest about how we judge people in our everyday lives?
2. Hoagland is assigned to Civil Court, where most of the cases are at least five years old. Having read Hoagland's testimony about these cases, how would you evaluate the effectiveness of the American legal system?

Elizabeth Winthrop was born in 1948 in Washington, D.C., and educated at Sarah Lawrence College. She worked for Harper and Row editing "Harper Junior Books" before she began her own career as author of books for children. She has written more than thirty such books, including *Bunk Beds* (1972), *Potbellied Possums* (1977), *In My Mother's House* (1988), and *The Battle for the Castle* (1993). Winthrop has twice won the PEN Syndicated Fiction Contest, once in 1985 with her story "Bad News" and again in 1990 with "The Golden Darters." In the latter story, reprinted from *American Short Fiction*, a young girl betrays her father by using their creation for the wrong purpose.

The Golden Darters

I WAS TWELVE years old when my father started tying flies. 1
It was an odd habit for a man who had just undergone a serious operation on his upper back, but, as he remarked to my mother one night, at least it gave him a world over which he had some control.

The family grew used to seeing him hunched down close 2
to his tying vise, hackle pliers in one hand, thread bobbin in the other. We began to bandy about strange phrases—foxy quills, bodkins, peacock hurl. Father's corner of the living room was off limits to the maid with the voracious and destructive vacuum cleaner. Who knew what precious bit of calf's tail or rabbit fur would be sucked away never to be seen again?

Because of my father's illness, we had gone up to our 3
summer cottage on the lake in New Hampshire a month

early. None of my gang of friends ever came till the end of July, so in the beginning of that summer I hung around home watching my father as he fussed with the flies. I was the only child he allowed to stand near him while he worked. "Your brothers bounce," he muttered one day as he clamped the vise onto the curve of a model-perfect hook. "You can stay and watch if you don't bounce."

So I took great care not to bounce or lean or even breathe   4
too noisily on him while he performed his delicate maneu-
vers, holding back hackle with one hand as he pulled off the final flourish of a whip finish with the other. I had never been so close to my father for so long before, and while he studied his tiny creations, I studied him. I stared at the large pores of his skin, the sleek black hair brushed straight back from the soft dip of his temples, the jaw muscles tightening and slackening. Something in my father seemed always to be ticking. He did not take well to sickness and enforced confinement.

When he leaned over his work, his shirt collar slipped down   5
to reveal the recent scar, a jagged trail of disrupted tissue. The tender pink skin gradually paled and then toughened during those weeks when he took his prescribed afternoon nap, lying on his stomach on our little patch of front lawn. Our house was one of the closest to the lake and it seemed to embarrass my mother to have him stretch himself out on the grass for all the swimmers and boaters to see.

"At least sleep on the porch," she would say. "That's why   6
we set the hammock up there."

"Why shouldn't a man sleep on his own front lawn if he   7
so chooses?" he would reply. "I have to mow the bloody thing. I might as well put it to some use."

And my mother would shrug and give up.   8

At the table when he was absorbed, he lost all sense of   9
anything but the magnified insect under the light. Often when he pushed his chair back and announced the comple-
tion of his latest project to the family, there would be a bit of down or a tuft of dubbing stuck to the edge of his lip. I

did not tell him about it but stared, fascinated, wondering
how long it would take to blow away. Sometimes it never did,
and I imagine he discovered the fluff in the bathroom mirror
when he went upstairs to bed. Or maybe my mother plucked
it off with one of those proprietary gestures of hers that
irritated my brothers so much.

In the beginning, Father wasn't very good at the fly-tying.   10
He was a large, thick-boned man with sweeping gestures, a
robust laugh, and a sudden terrifying temper. If he had not
loved fishing so much, I doubt he would have persevered
with the fussy business of the flies. After all, the job required
tools normally associated with woman's work. Thread and
bobbins, soft slippery feathers, a magnifying glass, and an
instruction manual that read like a cookbook. It said things
like, "Cut off a bunch of yellowtail. Hold the tip end with
the left hand and stroke out the short hairs."

But Father must have had a goal in mind. You tie flies   11
because one day, in the not-too-distant future, you will attach
them to a tippet, wade into a stream, and lure a rainbow trout
out of his quiet pool.

There was something endearing, almost childish, about his   12
stubborn nightly ritual at the corner table. His head bent
under the standing lamp, his fingers trembling slightly, he
would whisper encouragement to himself, talk his way
through some particularly delicate operation. Once or twice
I caught my mother gazing silently across my brothers' heads
at him. When our eyes met, she would turn away and busy
herself in the kitchen.

Finally, one night, after weeks of allowing me to watch, he   13
told me to take his seat. "Why, Father?"

"Because it's time for you to try one."   14

"That's all right. I like to watch."   15

"Nonsense, Emily. You'll do just fine."   16

He had stood up. The chair was waiting. Across the room,   17
my mother put down her knitting. Even the boys, embroiled
in a noisy game of double solitaire, stopped their wrangling
for a moment. They were all waiting to see what I would do.
It was my fear of failing him that made me hesitate. I knew

that my father put his trust in results, not in the learning process.

"Sit down, Emily." 18

I obeyed, my heart pounding. I was a cautious, secretive 19 child, and I could not bear to have people watch me doing things. My piano lesson was the hardest hour in the week. The teacher would sit with a resigned look on her face while my fingers groped across the keys, muddling through a sonata that I had played perfectly just an hour before. The difference was that then nobody had been watching.

"—so we'll start you off with a big hook." He had been 20 talking for some time. How much had I missed already?

"Ready?" he asked. 21

I nodded. 22

"All right then, clamp this hook into the vise. You'll be 23 making the golden darter, a streamer. A big flashy fly, the kind that imitates a small fish as it moves underwater."

Across the room, my brothers had returned to their game, 24 but their voices were subdued. I imagined they wanted to hear what was happening to me. My mother had left the room.

"Tilt the magnifying glass so you have a good view of the 25 hook. Right. Now tie on with the bobbin thread."

It took me three tries to line the thread up properly on the 26 hook, each silken line nesting next to its neighbor. "We're going to do it right, Emily, no matter how long it takes."

"It's hard," I said quietly. 27

Slowly I grew used to the tiny tools, to the oddly enlarged 28 view of my fingers through the magnifying glass. They looked as if they didn't belong to me anymore. The feeling in their tips was too small for their large, clumsy movements. Despite my father's repeated warnings, I nicked the floss once against the barbed hook. Luckily it did not give way.

"It's Emily's bedtime," my mother called from the 29 kitchen.

"Hush, she's tying in the throat. Don't bother us now." 30

I could feel his breath on my neck. The mallard barbules 31 were stubborn, curling into the hook in the wrong direction.

Behind me, I sensed my father's fingers twisting in imitation of my own.

"You've almost got it," he whispered, his lips barely moving. "That's right. Keep the thread slack until you're all the way around." 32

I must have tightened it too quickly. I lost control of the feathers in my left hand, the clumsier one. First the gold mylar came unwound and then the yellow floss. 33

"Damn it all, now look what you've done," he roared, and for a second I wondered whether he was talking to me. He sounded as if he were talking to a grown-up. He sounded the way he had just the night before when an antique teacup had slipped through my mother's soapy fingers and shattered against the hard surface of the sink. I sat back slowly, resting my aching spine against the chair for the first time since we'd begun. 34

"Leave it for now, Gerald," my mother said tentatively from the kitchen. Out of the corner of my eye, I could see her sponging the kitchen counter with small, defiant sweeps of her hand. "She can try again tomorrow." 35

"What happened?" called a brother. They both started across the room toward us but stopped at a look from my father. 36

"We'll start again," he said, his voice once more under control. "Best way to learn. Get back on the horse." 37

With a flick of his hand, he loosened the vise, removed my hook, and threw it into the wastepaper basket. 38

"From the beginning?" I whispered. 39

"Of course," he replied. "There's no way to rescue a mess like that." 40

My mess had taken almost an hour to create. 41

"Gerald," my mother said again. "Don't you think—" 42

"How can we possibly work with all these interruptions?" he thundered. I flinched as if he had hit me. "Go on upstairs, all of you. Emily and I will be up when we're done. Go on, for God's sake. Stop staring at us." 43

At a signal from my mother, the boys backed slowly away and crept up to their room. She followed them. I felt all 44 alone, as trapped under my father's piercing gaze as the hook in the grip of its vise.

We started again. This time my fingers were trembling so much that I ruined three badger hackle feathers, stripping off the useless webbing at the tip. My father did not lose his temper again. His voice dropped to an even, controlled monotone that scared me more than his shouting. After an hour of painstaking labor, we reached the same point with the stubborn mallard feathers curling into the hook. Once, twice, I repinched them under the throat, but each time they slipped away from me. Without a word, my father stood up and leaned over me. With his cheek pressed against my hair, he reached both hands around and took my fingers in his. I longed to surrender the tools to him and slide away off the chair, but we were so close to the end. He captured the curling stem with the thread and trapped it in place with three quick wraps.

"Take your hands away carefully," he said. "I'll do the whip finish. We don't want to risk losing it now."

I did as I was told, sat motionless with his arms around me, my head tilted slightly to the side so he could have the clear view through the magnifying glass. He cemented the head, wiped the excess glue from the eye with a waste feather, and hung my golden darter on the tackle box handle to dry. When at last he pulled away, I breathlessly slid my body back against the chair. I was still conscious of the havoc my clumsy hands or an unexpected sneeze could wreak on the table, which was cluttered with feathers and bits of fur.

"Now, that's the fly you tied, Emily. Isn't it beautiful?"

I nodded. "Yes, Father."

"Tomorrow, we'll do another one. An olive grouse. Smaller hook but much less complicated body. Look. I'll show you in the book."

As I waited to be released from the chair, I didn't think he meant it. He was just trying to apologize for having lost his temper, I told myself, just trying to pretend that our time together had been wonderful. But the next morning when I came down, late for breakfast, he was waiting for me with the materials for the olive grouse already assembled. He was ready to start in again, to take charge of my clumsy fingers with his voice and talk them through the steps.

That first time was the worst, but I never felt comfortable at the fly-tying table with Father's breath tickling the hair on my neck. I completed the olive grouse, another golden darter to match the first, two muddler minnows, and some others. I don't remember all the names anymore.   52

Once I hid upstairs, pretending to be immersed in my summer reading books, but he came looking for me.   53

"Emily," he called. "Come on down. Today we'll start the lead-winged coachman. I've got everything set up for you."   54

I lay very still and did not answer.   55

"Gerald," I heard my mother say. "Leave the child alone. You're driving her crazy with those flies."   56

"Nonsense," he said, and started up the dark, wooden stairs, one heavy step at a time.   57

I put my book down and rolled slowly off the bed so that by the time he reached the door of my room, I was on my feet, ready to be led back downstairs to the table.   58

Although we never spoke about it, my mother became oddly insistent that I join her on trips to the library or the general store.   59

"Are you going out again, Emily?" my father would call after me. "I was hoping we'd get some work done on this minnow."   60

"I'll be back soon, Father," I'd say. "I promise."   61

"Be sure you do," he said.   62

And for a while I did.   63

Then at the end of July, my old crowd of friends from across the lake began to gather and I slipped away to join them early in the morning before my father got up.   64

The girls were a gang. When we were all younger, we'd held bicycle relay races on the ring road and played down at the lakeside together under the watchful eyes of our mothers. Every July, we threw ourselves joyfully back into each other's lives. That summer we talked about boys and smoked illicit   65 cigarettes in Randy Kidd's basement and held leg-shaving parties in her bedroom behind a safely locked door. Randy was the ringleader. She was the one who suggested we pierce our ears.

"My parents would die," I said. "They told me I'm not allowed to pierce my ears until I'm seventeen." 66

"Your hair's so long, they won't even notice," Randy said. "My sister will do it for us. She pierces all her friends' ears at college." 67

In the end, only one girl pulled out. The rest of us sat in a row with the obligatory ice cubes held to our ears, waiting for the painful stab of the sterilized needle. 68

Randy was right. At first my parents didn't notice. Even when my ears became infected, I didn't tell them. All alone in my room, I went through the painful procedure of twisting the gold studs and swabbing the recent wounds with alcohol. Then on the night of the club dance, when I had changed my clothes three times and played with my hair in front of the mirror for hours, I came across the small plastic box with dividers in my top bureau drawer. My father had given it to me so that I could keep my flies in separate compartments, untangled from one another. I poked my finger in and slid one of the golden darters up along its plastic wall. When I held it up, the mylar thread sparkled in the light like a jewel. I took out the other darter, hammered down the barbs of the two hooks, and slipped them into the raw holes in my earlobes. 69

Someone's mother drove us all to the dance, and Randy and I pushed through the side door into the ladies' room. I put my hair up in a ponytail so the feathered flies could twist and dangle above my shoulders. I liked the way they made me look—free and different and dangerous, even. And they made Randy notice. 70

"I've never seen earrings like that," Randy said. "Where did you get them?" 71

"I made them with my father. They're flies. You know, for fishing." 72

"They're great. Can you make me some?" 73

I hesitated. "I have some others at home I can give you," 74
I said at last. "They're in a box in my bureau."

"Can you give them to me tomorrow?" she asked. 75

"Sure," I said with a smile. Randy had never noticed 76
anything I'd worn before. I went out to the dance floor,
swinging my ponytail in time to the music.

My mother noticed the earrings as soon as I got home. 77

"What has gotten into you, Emily? You know you were 78
forbidden to pierce your ears until you were in college. This
is appalling."

I didn't answer. My father was sitting in his chair behind 79
the fly-tying table. His back was better by that time, but he
still spent most of his waking hours in that chair. It was as if
he didn't like to be too far away from his flies, as if something
might blow away if he weren't keeping watch.

I saw him look up when my mother started in with me. 80
His hands drifted ever so slowly down to the surface of the
table as I came across the room toward him. I leaned over so
that he could see my earrings better in the light.

"Everybody loved them, Father. Randy says she wants a 81
pair, too. I'm going to give her the muddler minnows."

"I can't believe you did this, Emily," my mother said in a 82
loud, nervous voice. "It makes you look so cheap."

"They don't make me look cheap, do they, Father?" I 83
swung my head so he could see how they bounced, and my
hip accidentally brushed the table. A bit of rabbit fur floated
up from its pile and hung in the air for a moment before it
settled down on top of the foxy quills.

"For God's sake, Gerald, speak to her," my mother said 84
from her corner.

He stared at me for a long moment as if he didn't know 85
who I was anymore, as if I were a trusted associate who had
committed some treacherous and unspeakable act. "That is
not the purpose for which the flies were intended," he said.

"Oh, I know that," I said quickly. "But they look good 86
this way, don't they?"

He stood up and considered me in silence for a long time   87
across the top of the table lamp.

"No, they don't," he finally said. "They're hanging upside   88
down."

Then he turned off the light and I couldn't see his face   89
anymore.

COMMENT ON "THE GOLDEN DARTERS"

"The Golden Darters" questions the purpose of learning a
particular process. Emily's father decides to tie fishing flies to
help him recuperate from back surgery. Although he is clumsy
at first, he masters the tools, the procedure, and the artistry
of tying. He has a goal in mind—to "attach [the flies] to a
tippet, wade into a stream, and lure a rainbow trout out of
his quiet pool." Emily's father decides to teach her what he
has learned, even though his presence makes her nervous and
her mistakes complicate the work process. Emily eventually
escapes his obsession and joins her girlfriends to learn other
procedures—smoking, leg-shaving, ear-piercing. The last
procedure enables Emily to experiment—to wear two yellow
darters as earrings to the club dance. Although she dazzles
her friends, she disappoints her father, who sees her experiment as a betrayal.

Process Analysis as a Writing Strategy

1. Write an essay for readers of a popular magazine in which you give directions on how to complete a mechanical or artistic project. Like Ann Zwinger, anticipate the resistance of those readers who are certain before they start that they can't do it and won't learn anything by trying your project.

2. Provide information for the members of your writing class on the steps you followed to complete an educational project such as writing a research paper. Like Nikki Giovanni, you may want to explain these steps to a particular group of students.

3. Lars Eighner's "My Daily Dives in the Dumpster" raises significant questions about how our culture views the processes of consuming, disposing, and conserving. Construct a portrait of a conscientious consumer, and then analyze the processes he or she would use to maintain an ethically responsible relationship to the environment.

4. Analyze the various steps in a political process (casting a vote) or economic process (purchasing stock). Assume that your audience watches a lot of television. Explain how the process you are analyzing (selecting a jury) differs from the process they see represented on the tube.

5. Analyze a process that tests the ability to reach consensus and capture others. Like Natalie Angier, you may want to describe the behavioral process of certain animals. Or you may want to analyze the process illustrated in children's play, athletic contests, or human mating games.

6. Analyze a process that confuses or intimidates people, particularly when other people are watching. Elizabeth Winthrop's short story "The Golden Darters" is obviously a good source for this assignment. Your job is to describe the intricate steps of the physical tasks and to speculate on why the presence of the observer (a teacher, a relative, a friend) makes the task so difficult.

COMPARISON AND CONTRAST

Technically speaking, when you **compare** two or more things, you're looking for similarities; and when you **contrast** them, you're looking for differences. In practice, of course, the operations are opposite sides of the same coin, and one implies the other. When you look for what's similar, you will also notice what is different. You can compare things at all levels, from the trivial (plaid shoelaces and plain ones) to the really serious (the differences between a career in medicine and one in advertising). Often when you compare things at a serious level, you do so to make a choice. That's why it's helpful to know how to organize your thinking so that you can analyze similarities and differences in a systematic, useful way that brings out significant differences. It's particularly helpful to have such a system when you are going to write a comparison-and-contrast essay.

PURPOSE

You can take two approaches to writing comparison-and-contrast essays; each has a different purpose. You can make a *strict* comparison, exploring the relationship between things in the same class, or you can do a *fanciful* comparison, looking at the relationship among things from different classes.

When you write a *strict* comparison, you compare only things that are truly alike—actors with actors, musicians with musicians, but *not* actors with musicians. You're trying to find similar information about both your subjects. For instance, what are the characteristics of actors, whether they are movie or stage actors? How are jazz musicians and classical musicians alike, even if their music is quite different? In a strict comparison, you probably also want to show how two things in the same class are different in important ways. Often when you focus your comparison on differences, you do so in order to make a judgment and, finally, a choice. That's one of the main reasons people make comparisons, whether they're shopping or writing.

When you write a *fanciful* comparison, you try to set up an imaginative, illuminating comparison between two things that don't seem at all alike, and you do it for a definite reason: to help explain and clarify a complex idea. For instance, the human heart is often compared to a pump—a fanciful and useful comparison that enables one to envision the heart at work. You can use similar fanciful comparisons to help your readers see new dimensions to events. For instance, you can compare the astronauts landing on the moon to Columbus discovering the New World, or you can compare the increased drug use among young people to an epidemic spreading through part of our culture.

You may find it difficult to construct an entire essay around a fanciful comparison—such attempts tax the most creative energy and can quickly break down. Probably you can use this method of comparison most effectively as a device for enlivening your writing and highlighting dramatic similarities. When you're drawing fanciful comparisons, you're not very likely to be comparing to make judgments or recommend choices. Instead, your purpose in writing a fanciful comparison is to catch your readers' attention and show new connections between unlike things.

AUDIENCE

As you plan a comparison-and-contrast essay, think ahead about what your readers already know and what they're going to expect. First, ask yourself what they know about the items or ideas you're going to compare. Do they know a good deal about both—for instance, two popular television programs? Do they know very little about either item—for instance, Buddhism and Shintoism? Or do they know quite a bit about one but little about the other—for instance, football and rugby?

If you're confident that your readers know a lot about both items (the television programs), you can spend a little time pointing out similarities and concentrate on your reasons for making the comparison. When readers know little about either (Eastern religions), you'll have to define each, using concepts they are familiar with before you can point out important contrasts. If readers know only one item in a pair (football and rugby), then use the known to explain the unknown. Emphasize what is familiar to them about football, and explain how rugby is like it but also how it is different.

As you think about what your readers need, remember they want your essay to be fairly balanced, not 90 percent about Buddhism and 10 percent about Shintoism, or two paragraphs about football and nine or ten about rugby. When your focus seems so unevenly divided, you appear to be using one element in the comparison only as a springboard to talk about the other. Such an imbalance can disappoint your readers, who expect to learn about both.

STRATEGIES

You can use two basic strategies for organizing a comparison-and-contrast essay. The first is the *divided* or *subject-by-subject* pattern. The second is the *alternating* or *point-by-point* pattern.

When you use the *divided* pattern, you present all your information on one topic before you bring in information on the other topic. Mark Twain uses this method in "Two Views of the River." First he gives an apprentice's poetic view, emphasizing the beauty of the river; then he gives the pilot's practical view, emphasizing the technical problems the river poses.

When you use the *alternating* pattern, you work your way through the comparison point by point, giving information first on one aspect of the topic, then on the other. If Mark Twain had used an alternating pattern, he would have given the apprentice's poetic view of a particular feature of the river, then the pilot's pragmatic view of that same feature. He would have followed that pattern throughout, commenting on each feature—the wind, the surface of the river, the sunset, the color of the water—by alternating between the apprentice's and the pilot's points of view.

Although both methods are useful, you'll find that each has benefits and drawbacks. The divided pattern lets you present each part of your essay as a satisfying whole. It works especially well in short essays, such as Twain's, where you're presenting only two facets of a topic and your reader can easily keep track of the points you want to make. Its drawback is that sometimes you slip into writing what seems like two separate essays. When you're writing a long comparison essay about a complex topic, you may have trouble organizing your material clearly enough to keep your readers on track.

The alternating pattern works well when you want to show the two subjects you're comparing side by side, emphasizing

the points you're comparing. You'll find it particularly good
for longer essays, such as Pico Iyer's "Of Weirdos and Eccentrics," when you want to show many complex points of
comparison and need to help your readers see how those
points match up. The drawback of the alternating pattern is
that you may reduce your analysis to an exercise. If you use
it for making only a few points of comparison in a short essay
on a simple topic, your essay sounds choppy and disconnected, like a simple list.

Often you can make the best of both worlds by *combining
strategies*. For example, you can start out using a divided
pattern to give an overall, unified view of the topics you're
going to compare. Then you can shift to an alternating pattern to show how many points of comparison you've found
between your subjects. Deborah Tannen uses a version of this
strategy in "Rapport-Talk and Report-Talk." She begins by
establishing the difference between private conversations and
public speaking; then she uses an alternating pattern within
each category to demonstrate the contrasts between the
speaking styles of men and women.

When you want to write a good comparison-and-contrast
analysis, keep three guidelines in mind: (1) *balance parts,* (2)
include reminders, and (3) *supply reasons.* Look, for example,
at how Naomi Shihab Nye arranges her comparison of her
brother's house in Dallas and her house in San Antonio. She
provides the same kind of information on each house, uses
transitional phrases to show her readers when she is changing
topics, and comments on the reasons she finds the comparison significant.

Bill McKibben uses similar strategies when he contrasts his
firsthand experience with nature and his secondhand experience with nature by means of television, catalogs the various
ways television distorts the way we think about nature, and
reasons that our reliance on such images makes it difficult for
us to understand and accept nature on its own terms.

USING COMPARISON AND CONTRAST IN PARAGRAPHS

Here are two comparison-and-contrast paragraphs. The first is written by a professional writer and is followed by an analysis. The second is written by a student writer and is followed by questions.

DAVID McCULLOUGH
FDR and Truman

Uses alternating pattern

Both [FDR and Truman] were men of exceptional determination, with great reserves of personal courage and cheerfulness. They were alike too in their enjoyment of people. (The human race, Truman once told a reporter, was an "excellent outfit.") Each had an active sense of humor and was inclined to be dubious of those who did not. But Roosevelt, who loved stories, loved also to laugh at his own, while Truman was more of a listener and laughed best when somebody else told "a good one." Roosevelt enjoyed flattery, Truman was made uneasy by it. Roosevelt loved the subtleties of human relations. He was a master of the circuitous solution to problems, of the pleasing if ambiguous answer to difficult questions. He was sensitive to nuances in a way Harry Truman never was and never would be. Truman, with his rural Missouri background, and partly, too, because of the limits of his education, was inclined to see things in far simpler terms, as right or wrong, wise or foolish. He dealt little in abstractions. His answers to questions, even complicated questions, were nearly always direct and assured, plainly said, and followed often by a conclusive "And that's all there is to it," an old Missouri expression, when in truth there may have been a great deal more "to it."

Establishes points of comparison

Sets up points of contrast

Expands on significant difference between two men (circuitous versus direct)

Comment This paragraph illustrates how the alternating pattern can be used to point out many levels of comparison between two subjects. McCullough acknowledges that President Roosevelt and President Truman shared many common virtues—determination, courage, and cheerfulness. But he also contrasts (point by point) how the two men's personal styles—love of complex subtleties (FDR) versus preference for direct simplicity (Truman)—contributed to their uniqueness.

NATHAN M. HARMS
Howard and Rush

Howard [Stern] and Rush [Limbaugh] seem like the ying and yang of talk radio. Howard is thin and shaggy and loves to bash entrenched, stodgy Republicans. Rush is fat and dapper and loves to bash traditional liberal Democrats. Howard, the defender of individual freedom, wants to sleep with every woman in America. Rush, the defender of family values, wants every American woman to stay home and take care of the kids. Although they may think the world works in different ways, Howard and Rush work in the world in the same way. They focus their shows on controversy, belittle those who disagree with them, package their "philosophies" in best-selling books, and thrive on their ability to create publicity and fame for themselves.

1. What specific points of difference does Harms see between Howard Stern and Rush Limbaugh?
2. What major personality trait does Harms suspect they share?

COMPARISON AND CONTRAST

Points to Remember

1. Decide whether you want the pattern of your comparison to focus on complete units (*divided*) or specific features (*alternating*).
2. Consider the possibility of combining the two patterns.
3. Determine which subject should be placed in the first position and why.
4. Arrange the points of your comparison in a logical, balanced, and dramatic sequence.
5. Make sure you introduce and clarify the reasons for making your comparison.

Mark Twain (the pen name of Samuel Clemens, 1835–1910) was born in Florida, Missouri, and grew up in the river town of Hannibal, Missouri, where he watched the comings and goings of the steamboats he would eventually pilot. Twain spent his young adult life working as a printer, a pilot on the Mississippi, and a frontier journalist. After the Civil War, he began a career as a humorist and storyteller, writing such classics as *The Adventures of Tom Sawyer* (1876), *Life on the Mississippi* (1883), *The Adventures of Huckleberry Finn* (1885), and *A Connecticut Yankee in King Arthur's Court* (1889). His place in American writing was best characterized by editor William Dean Howells, who called Twain the "Lincoln of our literature." In "Two Views of the River," taken from *Life on the Mississippi,* Twain compares the way he saw the river as an innocent apprentice to the way he saw it as an experienced pilot.

Two Views of the River

N OW WHEN I had mastered the language of this water, and had come to know every trifling feature that bordered the great river as familiarly as I knew the letters of the alphabet, I had made a valuable acquisition. But I had lost something, too. I had lost something which could never be restored to me while I lived. All the grace, the beauty, the poetry, had gone out of the majestic river! I still keep in mind a certain wonderful sunset which I witnessed when steamboating was new to me. A broad expanse of the river was turned to blood; in the middle distance the red hue brightened into gold, through which a solitary log came floating

1

black and conspicuous; in one place a long, slanting mark lay
sparkling upon the water; in another the surface was broken
by boiling, tumbling rings that were as many-tinted as an
opal; where the ruddy flush was faintest, was a smooth spot
that was covered with graceful circles and radiating lines, ever
so delicately traced; the shore on our left was densely
wooded, and the somber shadow that fell from this forest was
broken in one place by a long, ruffled trail that shone like
silver; and high above the forest wall a clean-stemmed dead
tree waved a single leafy bough that glowed like a flame in
the unobstructed splendor that was flowing from the sun.

When I mastered the language of the river,
I made a valuable acquisition, but I lost
something too.

There were graceful curves, reflected images, woody heights,
soft distances; and over the whole scene, far and near, the
dissolving lights drifted steadily, enriching it every passing
moment with new marvels of coloring.

I stood like one bewitched. I drank it in, in a speechless   2
rapture. The world was new to me, and I had never seen
anything like this at home. But as I have said, a day came
when I began to cease from noting the glories and the charms
which the moon and the sun and the twilight wrought upon
the river's face; another day came when I ceased altogether
to note them. Then, if that sunset scene had been repeated,
I should have looked upon it without rapture, and should
have commented upon it, inwardly, after this fashion: "This
sun means that we are going to have wind to-morrow; that
floating log means that the river is rising, small thanks to it;
that slanting mark on the water refers to a bluff reef which is
going to kill somebody's steamboat one of these nights, if it
keeps on stretching out like that; those tumbling 'boils' show

a dissolving bar and a changing channel there; the lines and circles in the slick water over yonder are a warning that that troublesome place is shoaling up dangerously; that silver streak in the shadow of the forest is the 'break' from a new snag, and he has located himself in the very best place he could have found to fish for steamboats; that tall dead tree, with a single living branch, is not going to last long, and then how is a body ever going to get through this blind place at night without the friendly old landmark?"

No, the romance and beauty were all gone from the river. 3 All the value any feature of it had for me now was the amount of usefulness it could furnish toward compassing the safe piloting of a steamboat. Since those days, I have pitied doctors from my heart. What does the lovely flush in a beauty's cheek mean to a doctor but a "break" that ripples above some deadly disease? Are not all her visible charms sown thick with what are to him the signs and symbols of hidden decay? Does he ever see her beauty at all, or doesn't he simply view her professionally, and comment upon her unwholesome condition all to himself? And doesn't he sometimes wonder whether he has gained most or lost most by learning his trade?

For Study and Discussion

QUESTIONS FOR RESPONSE

1. Mark Twain is one of America's most famous historical personalities. Which of his books or stories have you read? What ideas and images from this selection do you associate with his other works?
2. Do you agree with Twain when he argues that an appreciation of beauty depends on ignorance of danger? Explain your answer.

QUESTIONS ABOUT PURPOSE

1. What does Twain think he has gained and lost by learning the river?

2. What does Twain accomplish by *dividing* the two views of the river rather than *alternating* them beneath several headings?

QUESTIONS ABOUT AUDIENCE

1. Which attitude—poetic or pragmatic—does Twain anticipate his readers have toward the river? Explain your answer.
2. How does he expect his readers to answer the questions he raises in paragraph 3?

QUESTIONS ABOUT STRATEGIES

1. What sequence does Twain use to arrange the points of his comparison?
2. Where does Twain use transitional phrases and sentences to match up the parts of his comparison?

QUESTIONS FOR DISCUSSION

1. Besides the pilot and the doctor, can you identify other professionals who lose as much as they gain by learning their trade?
2. How would people whose job is to create beauty—writers, painters, musicians, architects, gardeners—respond to Twain's assertion that knowledge of their craft destroys their ability to appreciate beauty?

Pico Iyer was born in Oxford, England, in 1957 and was educated at Oxford University and Harvard University. He has worked for *Time* magazine since 1982, but he is best known for his books about his travels through various Asian countries such as *Video Night in Kathmandu: And Other Reports from the Not-So-Far East* (1988), *The Lady and the Monk: Four Seasons in Kyoto* (1991), and *Falling Off the Map* (1993). In "Of Weirdos and Eccentrics," reprinted from *Tropical Classical: Essays from Several Directions* (1997), Iyer explains how the "weirdo" and the "eccentric" reveal the invisible line at which "oddness becomes menace."

Of Weirdos and Eccentrics

CHARLES WATERTON WAS just another typical eccentric. In his eighties, the eminent country squire was to be seen clambering around the upper branches of an oak tree with what was aptly described as the agility of an "adolescent gorilla." The beloved twenty-seventh lord of Walton Hall also devoted his distinguished old age to scratching the back part of his head with his right big toe and ministering to a young, but ailing, lady chimpanzee, whom he visited daily and left each day with a kiss on the cheek. Not that such displays of animal high spirits were confined to the gentleman's old age: when young, Waterton made four separate trips to South America, where he sought the wourali poison (a cure, he was convinced, for hydrophobia), and once spent months on end with one foot dangling from his hammock in the quixotic hope of having his toe sucked by a vampire bat.

James Warren Jones, by contrast, was something of a

weirdo. As a boy in the casket-making town of Lynn, Indiana, he used to conduct elaborate funeral services for dead pets. Later, as a struggling preacher, he went from door to door, in bow tie and tweed jacket, selling imported monkeys. After briefly fleeing to South America (a shelter, he believed, from an imminent nuclear holocaust), the man who regarded himself as a reincarnation of Lenin settled in northern California and opened a pet shelter, three convalescent homes, and some kitchens for the poor. Then, one humid day in the jungles of Guyana, the former human rights commissioner of

---

The eccentric raises a smile; the weirdo leaves a chill.

Indianapolis ordered his followers to drink a Kool-Aid–like punch soured with cyanide. By the time the world arrived at Jonestown, 911 people were dead.

The difference between the eccentric and the weirdo is, in 3 its way, the difference between a man with a teddy bear in his hand and a man with a gun. We are also, of course, besieged by other kinds of deviants—crackpots, oddballs, fanatics, quacks, and cranks. But the weirdo and the eccentric define between them that invisible line at which strangeness acquires an edge and oddness becomes menace.

The difference between the two starts with the words 4 themselves: "eccentric," after all, carries a distinguished Latin pedigree that refers, quite reasonably, to anything that departs from the center; "weird," by comparison, has its mongrel origins in the Old English *wyrd,* meaning fate or destiny; and the larger, darker forces conjured by the term—Macbeth's Weird Sisters and the like—are given an extra twist with the slangy bastard suffix *-o.*

Beneath the linguistic roots, however, we feel the differ- 5
ence on our pulses. The eccentric we generally regard as
something of a donny, dotty, harmless type, like the British
peer who threw over his Cambridge fellowship in order to
live in a bath, and became so ardent a champion of water that
he would press silver coins on anyone who drank his favorite
beverage; the weirdo is an altogether more shadowy figure—
Charles Manson acting out his messianic visions. The eccentric is a creature of fancy, the weirdo one of fantasy. The
eccentric is a distinctive presence; the weirdo something of
an absence, who casts no reflection in society's mirror. The
eccentric raises a smile; the weirdo leaves a chill.

All too often, though, the two terms are not so easily 6
distinguished. Many a criminal trial, after all, revolves around
precisely that gray area where the two begin to blur. Was
Bernhard Goetz just a volatile Everyman, ourselves pushed
to the limit, and then beyond? Or was he in fact an aberra-
tion? What do we make of Jerry Lee Lewis, the maniacal rock
'n' roller who boasts of how he earned his nickname, "the
Killer"? Or, conversely, of Gary Gilmore, the convicted killer
with a scrupulous, if erratic, sense of moral justice?

Often, moreover, eccentrics may simply be weirdos in pos- 7
session of a VIP pass, people rich enough or powerful enough
to live by their own laws. Who knows what Howard Hughes
might have done had he not enjoyed the resources to create
his own private world in which uncleanliness was next to
godliness? Elvis Presley could afford to pump bullets into
silhouettes of humans and never count the cost; lesser mor-
tals, however, after shooting their dummies, must find another kind of victim. Eccentricity can thus become almost a
sign of aristocracy, the calling card of those who do not have
to defer to convention, but live above it, amoral as Greek
gods. It is no coincidence, perhaps, that Charles Waterton
was a nobleman descended from Sir Thomas More, Saint
Matilda Queen of Germany, Saint Margaret Queen of Scotland, and Saint Vladimir of Russia. Or that the man who lived
in a tub, a beard stretching down to his knees, was a peer of

the realm, Lord Rokeby. These days, it is our modern ruling class—the Superstars—whose idiosyncrasies we devour in the tabloids.

To some extent, too, we tend to think of eccentricity as the prerogative, even the hallmark, of genius. And genius is its own vindication. Who cared that Glenn Gould sang along with the piano while playing Bach, so long as he played so beautifully? Or if Sir Ralph Richardson, the very patron saint of oddness, bursts into *The Tempest* in the middle of *Volpone,* so long as he can carry it off convincingly? Even the Herculean debauches of Babe Ruth did not undermine so much as confirm his status as a legend. 8

Indeed, the unorthodox inflections of the exceptional can lead to all kinds of dangerous assumptions. If geniuses are out of the ordinary and psychopaths are out of the ordinary, then geniuses are psychopaths and vice versa, or so at least runs the reasoning of many dramatists who set their plays in loony bins. If the successful are often strange, then being strange is a way of becoming successful, or so believe all those would-be artists who work on eccentric poses. And if celebrity is its own defense, then many a demagogue or criminal assures himself that he will ultimately be redeemed by the celebrity he covets. 9

All these distortions, however, ignore the most fundamental distinction of all: the eccentric is strange because he cares too little about society, the weirdo because he cares too much. The eccentric generally wants nothing more than his own attic-like space in which he can live by his own peculiar lights. The weirdo, however, resents his outcast status and constantly seeks to get back into society, or at least get back at it. His is the rage not of the bachelor but of the divorcé. 10

Thus the eccentric hardly cares if he is seen to be strange; that in a sense is what makes him strange. The weirdo, by contrast, wants desperately to be taken as normal and struggles to keep his strangeness to himself. "He was always such a nice man," the neighbors ritually tell reporters after a sniper's rampage. "He always seemed so normal." 11

And because the two mark such different tangents to the 12

norm, their incidence can, in its way, be an index of a society's health. In her very English and very eccentric book, *English Eccentrics,* Edith Sitwell asserts that "Eccentricity exists particularly in the English, and partly, I think, because of that peculiar and satisfactory knowledge of infallibility that is the hallmark and birthright of the British nation." She might have added that the height of British eccentricity coincided with the height of British power, if only, perhaps, because Britain in its imperial heyday presented so strong a center from which to depart. Nowadays, however, with the empire gone and the center vanishing, Britain is more often associated with the maladjusted weirdo—the orange-haired misfit or the soccer hooligan.

At the other extreme, the relentless and ritualized normalcy of a society like Japan's—there are only four psychiatrists in all of Tokyo—can, to Western eyes, itself seem almost abnormal. Too few eccentrics can be as dangerous as too many weirdos. For in the end, eccentricity is a mark of confidence, accommodated best by a confident society; whereas weirdness inspires fear because it is a symptom of fear, and uncertainty and rage. A society needs the eccentric as much as it needs a decorated frame for the portrait it fashions of itself; it needs the weirdo as much as it needs a hole punched through the middle of the canvas. 13

For Study and Discussion

QUESTIONS FOR RESPONSE

1. How do you use the word "weirdo" to label people you know? To what extent do you consider them dangerous or merely different?
2. Among the people you admire—musicians, athletes, movie or television stars—which ones exhibit weirdo or eccentric behavior?

QUESTIONS ABOUT PURPOSE

1. How does Iyer's illustration of "a man with a teddy bear in his hand and a man with a gun" demonstrate the distinction he is trying to demonstrate?
2. What is the "fundamental distinction" Iyer is trying to demonstrate by his comparison?

QUESTIONS ABOUT AUDIENCE

1. Which of Iyer's illustrations—eccentrics, weirdos—are likely to be more familiar to his readers? Explain your answer.
2. How do Iyer's definitions of the two words distinguish the two concepts for his readers?

QUESTIONS ABOUT STRATEGIES

1. How does Iyer make use of the alternating pattern to illustrate why the eccentric "raises a smile" while the weirdo "leaves a chill"?
2. What kind of examples does he use to illustrate why "all too often . . . the two terms are not so easily distinguished"?

QUESTIONS FOR DISCUSSION

1. How does Iyer use the comparison between geniuses and psychopaths to clarify his comparison?
2. How does he use the examples of Great Britain and Japan to illustrate the larger cultural implications of his comparison?

NAOMI SHIHAB NYE

Naomi Shihab Nye was born in St. Louis, Missouri, in 1952 and educated at Trinity University. Her poems focus on the connections between diverse people. Her first collection, *Different Ways to Pray* (1980), explores the shared experiences of cultures as varied as California, Mexico, and South America. Her other collections include *Hugging the Jukebox* (1982) and *Words Under the Words* (1995). She has also edited a book of poems for children, *This Same Sky: A Collection of Poems from Around the World* (1992), and written a book of essays, *Never in a Hurry: Essays of People and Places* (1996). In "My Brother's House," Nye compares her brother's house and her house to explain how she and her brother, although raised in the same house, have become "different people."

My Brother's House

IN THE GUEST bedroom at my brother's brand-new house 1
in the north Dallas suburbs are four sets of electrical
sockets with no cords coming out of them. The possibilities
feel overwhelming. My brother could plug in appliances I
haven't even heard of yet.

Our 90-year-old house in inner-city San Antonio sports 2
intricate ugly tangles of extension cords and multiple power
outlets. I am always stuffing them back under the skirt on the
bed. I have heard it is not good for one's electromagnetic
field to have electrical cords criss-crossing under your sleeping place, but have not yet learned how to activate my reading
lamp and alarm clock without them.

My brother's house smells of fresh paint and packaging— 3
those foam bubbles and peanuts that come in big boxes. It

171

smells like carpet no one has ever stepped on. I cannot imagine the bravado of white carpet. My brother prefers if you
remove your shoes at his front door. So do I, but no one ever
does it in our house.

We have dusty wooden floors and raggedy little rugs from   4
Turkey and Libya. We have throw rugs hand-knotted in Ap-
palachia in 1968. We have a worn Oriental carpet that once
belonged to my friend's reclusive father, a famous science
fiction writer. He lived on an island all by himself. Our house

---

If people grow up together, eating the same
whole grain cereals, under the same
mapped ceiling, how do they grow
up so different?

---

smells of incense and grandmother's attics in Illinois in the
1950s and vaguely sweetened shelf paper pressed into
drawers.

My brother and his family are the first people to live in   5
their house, which is part of a generically named and very
expensive subdivision—something like Fair Oaks (but there
aren't any oaks, so it couldn't be) or Placid Plains or Rampant
Meadows. They made some decisions about finishing details,
deciding which wallpaper would go in the bathrooms and the
shape of the pool and the color of its tiles. They chose a lion's
head to be spitting water into the pool from beneath the
flower bed. Even the curb beside their front sidewalk is sleek.

Our house with its high ceilings and columned wrap-   6
around front porch was built in 1905 a block from the San
Antonio River by a French family that started a "Steamship
and Travel Company" downtown. Their agency still exists,
mailing out travel tickets in blue envelopes imprinted with
elegant, floating steamships. I visit their offices, scribbling

checks under the watchful portrait of the man who built our house. His eyes say, "Can't you ever stay *home?*"

Later the house belonged to his son and daughter-in-law, 7 named Ruby, who left her screened windows open in summer, as everybody in the world used to do. She outlived both her husbands. Her rusting wedding gifts—a hand-cranked ice cream freezer, a giant oval platter—remained in their original, crumbling wrapping papers stacked out in the chicken shed, even after she moved. She did not want them back. The old-fashioned gift cards with fluted edges said, "Salutations! We wish you years of happiness!"

Ruby listened to a rectangular radio on her kitchen table. 8 It was the size of a box of saltine crackers. She served me Coca-Colas in squatty old-fashioned bottles when I first visited her here. I asked where she bought bottles like that, but she never answered. Maybe she had been saving them up under the sink for decades. To this day, sometimes we call this her house.

She raised one son in this house, as we are doing. More 9 than once I have caught a brief echo of her boy's feet running across the floors right behind our boy. Maybe he's leading him, or they're traveling side-by-side. I like the fact that in ninety years our house has known only three owners and two little boys.

My brother's house is made of pink recycled bricks. Recy- 10 cled bricks are more expensive than new red bricks. Someone told me that. They make the house look organically weather-beaten, but only slightly. The other houses on the street, very similar in design to my brother's, with high-pitched roofs and enormous windows and exalted dormers, are made of redder bricks. Most of the families have planted beds of petunias and hibiscus as borders.

These are words that could apply to my brother's neigh- 11 borhood: manicured, impeccable, formal, aloof. There are others: cookie-cutter, master plan. Words that could apply to ours: offbeat, down-at-the-heels.

Our house used to be made of old wooden boards, but a 12 few years ago we had our carpenter take the old boards off, stuff the thickest insulation he could find inside the walls (try facing west through a blazing Texas summer), and apply new boards. Then he painted them white so the house looked just like it used to look, but felt substantially cooler. Our neighbors thought we were crazy, wasting our money. Why didn't we put the old boards back on?

My husband said they were too thickly mottled with old   13
paint. It was hard to make the house look fresh when the paint was so lumpy. Plus, some of them were rotting. Our neighbors raised their eyebrows. Our neighbors, we think, lead mysterious lives themselves.

Gigantic pecan trees cast their shadows down on all of us.   14
We suffer collective web worm invasions. If you walk barefoot in the grass, fat nuts poke your feet. During autumn, various citizens—skinny black men in baseball caps, Latina *abuelas* in long, full skirts—appear in the city park across the street from our house with plastic bags and long poles, for poking the towering trees. Nuts shower down and they collect their bounty. I imagine them strolling home to their kitchens to make pecan pies more easily than I imagine them standing in line at the pecan cracking plant down the block (We Buy— $.50 a pound).

My brother has six fancy bathrooms in his house. One   15
offers two toilets in separate closets and two gigantic gleaming sinks. I think I would dream about Dutch cleanser if I lived there. His bathrooms have fan vents and special mirror lights for putting on makeup. I opened a sleek drawer under his sink and found 1,000 miniature bottles of hotel shampoo.

We have one old-fashioned bathroom downstairs tiled   16
with blue flying birds from Mexico. We hauled those tiles home in our car after visiting the hand-painted tile factory in Dolores Hidalgo. I was drinking Coca-Cola from a squatty Mexican bottle when we spotted them. Of course, we hadn't measured the bathroom back home, so we had to guess how many to buy which is why a plain navy blue border lines the bottom and top. We filled in. Our bathroom wall still features an ancient, ornately scrolled gas heater that we are afraid to turn on, but like to look at.

We have another bathroom upstairs with a claw foot bath-   17
tub. I found the tub on the front porch of an elderly lady's
house on Maverick Street. I knocked on her door. "This is
very brazen, but the fact that your bathtub is filled with—
leaves—makes me wonder if it is essential to your life anymore
or if you might consider selling it." She took twenty dollars
on the spot.

Four men almost died hoisting that bathtub up to our   18
second floor, which used to be the attic. We have a metal
spiral staircase heading up there, but the tub was too wide
for it. So the men had to build a scaffolding in the backyard
and haul the tub up with ropes. I wasn't home, but my
husband says there was a moment they lost control of it, like
a slippery bar of soap. We would never have voted for that
tub if we knew the risk they were taking.

My brother's kitchen has a ceiling that vaults like a cathe-   19
dral over two ovens, two sinks, and two gleaming dishwash-
ers. A commune could live there, a whole Girl Scout troop,
or an entire division of Simon & Schuster. My brother has a
trash compactor and a bread machine that cooks bread even
while you are sleeping and a giant refrigerator and a couple
of garbage disposals and a dozen cabinets filled with chips
and kiddie cereals and Dallas Cowboy beer mugs. His stove
is electric and has a memory, I think. Or maybe it's his ovens
that have memories. They have memories but not much to
remember, since they are so new.

Our stove (a red Magic Chef—people are always com-   20
menting on its unusual color) was purchased by our parents
when I was two. My brother wasn't born yet.

I was in love with it. I thought it had a face. Teeth. I   21
thought my dreams were stacked inside the double-boiler and
the steamer pans. There's a silver door on the left where the
pots live and an oven on the right that long ago gave up being
true to its own temperature. Every baked good is a gamble
in our house. The enchiladas come out like *flautas* sometimes, thoroughly crisped, and the birthday cakes—well, we
gave those up. Now we buy angel cakes and cut up fresh
Texas strawberries.

As a child, I begged my mother to save this stove for me   22
so I could have it when I grew up. This was a real burden for
her since she had to store it in somebody's barn while we
lived overseas, then have it hauled all the way down to Texas.
It waited for me to grow up. I have also managed to preserve
an archival, turquoise refrigerator from the rocky days of the
late '60s when my parents plummeted back into the United
States and had to start keeping house again from scratch. It
has bungee cords in the door for holding the mustard and
ketchup in place, instead of real shelf fronts anymore.

Sometimes I feel like a hobo. Just camping out.   23

Our refrigerator's freezer compartment is, intelligently, at   24
the bottom instead of the top. *Why don't you buy a new
refrigerator?* our parents ask me. The front panels of the
vegetable drawers are cracked, the rubber door seals dubious.
But I feel attached to it. What could go better with a red
stove than a turquoise refrigerator? Anyway, isn't there something to be said for waiting till things truly *give up the ghost*?

The main thing I admire in my brother's house is his   25
closets. Anyone who has lived in a 90-year-old closetless
house will appreciate this. My brother and his wife could
entertain guests in their closets. Children could have sleep-
overs in there, surrounded by racks of color-coded shirts,
fringed rodeo sections, neat shelves of shoes. My brother's
daughter and son have their own giant, well-lit, walk-in closets too. I think my brother's dogs have their own closets.
Even the Christmas tree ornaments have their designated
hideaway.

At our house, we have a few antique wooden wardrobes,   26
items of furniture which should never, ever be romanticized.
They don't hold much and they don't hold it very well,
either. Also, they take up a lot of room. My husband has never
yet figured out how to close the door to his, so it is always
standing slightly open. Mine came off a British train. The
drawers are efficiently labeled: underwear, shirts. It has a little
trough for "collar stays" too. Very useful in the 1990s. The
drawers are still lined with the British newspapers they held
when we discovered it.

When we turned part of our attic into an upstairs room, 27
we built in a single closet, but failed to air-condition it which
means, in the summer, its contents are held at approximately
200 degrees. Also, it is four feet tall. One must ask, *Is it worth
banging my head and sweltering to find that old velvet vest?*

When we added a workroom for me, we added another 28
(too skinny) closet that has turned out to be just perfect for
a few T-shirts and strips of (unlabeled) 35 millimeter negatives. Nothing else. Our son has no place to put his clothes
but on a toy shelf with his Monopoly game and his Star Trek
phasers. Is it any wonder the boy has not yet mastered organization? Is it any wonder his pajama pants pile up like
Mount Hood in the center of the floor? We will buy him a
wide set of drawers to inaugurate the new school year. We
will say those magic American words: *this goes here, that goes
there.*

When I spend the night in my brother's well-organized 29
house, I wake up thinking, *but there are no one else's legends
lodged in these walls.*

He likes it that way. His wife likes it that way. They are the 30
main characters.

I stand in their narrow front yard staring up into the sky, 31
which always feels like the real "terrain" of suburban neighborhoods.

The first years they lived here, no birds came. I thought— 32
well, there are no trees. Maybe the sky is too well-divided for
birds.

These days, when we sit by their pool, I catch a few blurry 33
flashes above our heads, which feels heartening. Over the
investment experts and interior decorators and corporate
executives, the birds are once again lifting their wings. Just
as they do in our own neighborhood over barbers and hospital maintenance workers and security guards and retired
alcoholic mechanics and mariachis in silver-studded black
suits.

I think the roots of old houses go deep down into the 34
ground before we were born and the roots of new houses go
out into the atmosphere, into the disembodied visions of

developers and the crisp edges of dollar bills rolled up at the bank.

The houses in his neighborhood are palm trees with very   35
short roots.

I realize the same kinds of things must go on in both our   36
houses: people eat, clean up, converse, pop videos into the
television, take showers, make love, and occasionally plow
through old family photographs with a forlorn sense of lost-
ness. *Who were those people? Did I really look that good, when
I thought I was looking bad?*

People say things they don't mean to say. *Not now! Later!*   37
People lie around on beds or couches planning their next
moves out into the world. My brother's children have dogs,
cats, and newts. Our son has a cat, nine hens, and newts.
Where did all these newts come from?

I would like to go nowhere. I would like to stay home,   38
learning slow secrets, harvesting the earthworms that live in
a ventilated composting tub on the back deck, pruning the
lanky Don Juan roses at the correct moment.

I would spread new hay on the bottom of our chickens'   39
coop as the hens butt me like young goats for the juicy prizes
they think I carry. I would take all day about it, collecting
the dried corn cobs and watermelon rinds, recycling them
into the worm tub. One thing could go on becoming another.

For years I've had a title in my mind: *Still Waiting for a*   40
Dull Moment.

I would continue my ongoing (extremely gradual) excava-   41
tion into the deep recesses of the storage sections of our
jumbled attic to find the handwritten air letter sheet that
Graham Greene, the British novelist, mailed to me in 1971.
He professed recurrent doubt about his work. He hoped I
would never locate a copy of his first book—a collection of
poems. I know his letter is pressed up against the large stack
of square, white envelopes from Stella Kerouac, last wife of
Jack, which I rubber banded together long ago.

But this is what happens: every time I get up into the attic,   42

I find a box or bag of baby clothes, little pants, small T-shirts rippling with sailboats, and have to smooth out each one dreamily and refold it or put it in a stack to give away.

This takes eons. 43

The air whistles through the spinning air vent in the top of the attic while I am musing. 44

The buses steam past along Main Avenue and the boy who will never be so little again goes on clacking away on his computer downstairs. I could be a squirrel trapped in a wall. 45

My brother and I grew up in the same houses together, in St. Louis, Jerusalem, and San Antonio, three cities as dissimilar as pretzels, *hummos,* and salsa. So how did we become such different people? 46

Our parents had Egyptian wall hangings, camel saddles, Moroccan hassocks. Such cultural exclamation points may still be found in both my brother's and my residences. 47

Our St. Louis house, a square, unassuming box with few distinguishing features on the outside, has now been swallowed up by the redbud trees my grandfather planted when we were babies. It is startling to consider how trees grow, while objects constructed by people stay the same or disintegrate. 48

This house once had a forest green, screened-in back porch which was all we needed to feel wealthy. How much air we owned! We could sleep out there on cots in the summer. We could follow the moon rising up over the vacant lot behind our house. 49

Recent owners have removed the porch. I knock and ask what's cooking. I don't know what comes over me, but it's the first thing out of my mouth. "Potatoes," the woman says. 50

"We lived here once." 51

She does not say "Come in" and I do not suggest they rebuild the old green porch back where it used to be. She is black and I am—sort of—white, and for one moment we stare past each other's eyes. 52

My brother has never been back to that house. 53

Why do I burst into tears beside the blue mailbox across 54 the street from our house where I mailed my first letters? I knew there was A Larger World out there. The scent of pine nuts and garlic sizzled in olive oil clung to my clothes. In Jerusalem we lived in a stone second floor flat eight miles north of the holy places. In those days, I thought a lot about what makes one place holy and another place not. Homes were holy. My brother was happier in that house than I was. Gypsies camped in the stony meadow beside it. I wanted to go live with them.

We could hear the guns in Israel from our own bedrooms.   55 The soldiers were practicing. Newspaper headlines back in the United States always pretended Israelis were just "keeping the peace"—after they'd stolen the land. Songs burst forth in my head. "Liar, liar, pants on fire." When our refugee father talked about being "back home," he referred to all of Palestine, not just our new address. Finally, in 1967, the situation exploded and we flew as far away from it as we could—to Texas.

In San Antonio, our parents bought the first house they   56 looked at. It had a tree in the backyard that seemed to whisper "yes" if you leaned against it long enough.

We were teenagers there, hot-blooded and melodramatic,   57 and my brother got so mad at me once he kicked a hole right through my bedroom door with his pointed cowboy boot. The hole outlived us in that house. No one, of course, could remember what had made us so mad.

If people grow up together, eating the same whole-grain   58 cereals, under the same mapped ceilings, how do they end up so different? College students discuss this as "Human Nature vs. Nurture." I have no conclusions.

When my husband and I married, I visited the local de-   59 partment store to "pick out our plates." I looked and looked through the fine chinas, the bone-thin frills, and elaborate floral glazes, and selected the thickest variety (gray with a single navy stripe and vertical sides, like a baby would eat from) called "Less Is Enough." Why is less enough for some and not for others?

Am I holding myself above my brother? Do I judge him 60
by his house? He has told me what his monthly mortgage
payment is—or maybe our father has told me—it is so large
whole parts of our house could fit inside it. He could be
eighty and still paying. Something like that.

He told me once, with a note of sadness in his voice, "It's 61
like a carnival ride—if you're on, you can't just jump off."

We have no monthly mortgage payment. Our modest 62
house was paid for long ago. The mortgage company
stamped the receipt in red—PAID IN FULL. We used it as
a centerpiece with flowers for a while.

What surprises me is this: my brother sometimes says he 63
imagines a slow going, rural-tinted existence. He mentions
stepping down, leafing out, taking the chance. Anyone who
has worked more than a decade for a major corporation must
carry these little bubbles inside. He delights his family with
a weekend at a rugged bed-and-breakfast ranch in the Texas
hill country. His son collects fresh eggs and his daughter
washes a horse. He imagines having less and being happy.

I sit on the steps of our front porch in the evenings. Our 64
son scrawls a picture on the sidewalk—blue chalk man with
a runny nose vast as a volcano's eruption. For him this feels
like spectacular, nasty fun.

Across the street, women and men walk arm-in-arm 65
around the quiet park, under the yellow lamplight, as they
do in Mexico. What are they thinking of? I imagine they carry
the days when their own sons and daughters were small
tucked deep inside them. When other children shout at dusk,
swinging wooden bats or skidding onto the gravel jogging
path on their bikes, something in them still shouts, *Come
back, come back! It's time for bed! It's time to go home!*

My brother and I used to answer to a call like that. His 66
skin smelled like pennies, the faint coppery twist of pockets
and salt inside a fist. He kept his little cars all lined up in
shoeboxes and would flip the doors of the milk truck and the
fire truck open now and then before going to bed, just to
make sure everything still worked.

For Study and Discussion

QUESTIONS FOR RESPONSE

1. Among your friends and relatives whose house do you admire? What individual rooms or features impress you? Explain your choices.
2. What feature or room in your house makes it feel like home?

QUESTIONS ABOUT PURPOSE

1. What are the major differences between Nye's brother's house and her own house?
2. How does Nye's description of the two houses demonstrate that she and her brother have become different people?

QUESTIONS ABOUT AUDIENCE

1. What statements suggest that Nye assumes her readers might *prefer* her brother's house?
2. What statements suggest that Nye feels the need to defend her house to her readers?

QUESTIONS ABOUT STRATEGIES

1. How does Nye use "little stories" (i.e., red stove, turquoise refrigerator) to make her house more "legendary"?
2. How does Nye's description of her parent's three houses help explain why she and her brother prefer different houses?

QUESTIONS FOR DISCUSSION

1. Nye says she realizes that "the same kinds of things must go on in both our houses." What information does she provide to contradict that statement?
2. How does Nye's comparison provide an illustration of "Human Nature vs. Nurture"?

DEBORAH TANNEN

Deborah Tannen was born in 1945 in Brooklyn, New York, and was educated at the State University of New York at Binghamton, Wayne State University, and the University of California at Berkeley. She has taught English at the Hellenic American Union in Athens, Greece; Herbert H. Lehman College of the City University of New York; and Georgetown University. She has contributed articles on language to numerous scholarly books, including *Language and Social Identity* (1982) and *Languages and Linguistics in Context* (1986), and she has written several books on language and gender, including *Gender and Discourse* (1994) and *Talking from 9 to 5* (1994). Tannen's *That's Not What I Meant! How Conversational Style Makes or Breaks Your Relations with Others* (1986) attracted national attention because of its engaging study of the breakdown of communication between the sexes. In "Rapport-Talk and Report-Talk," excerpted from *You Just Don't Understand* (1989), Tannen compares the public and private conversational styles of men and women.

Rapport-Talk and Report-Talk

W HO TALKS MORE, then, women or men? The seemingly contradictory evidence is reconciled by the difference between what I call *public* and *private speaking*. More men feel comfortable doing "public speaking," while more women feel comfortable doing "private" speaking. Another way of capturing these differences is by using the terms *report-talk* and *rapport-talk*.

For most women, the language of conversation is primarily

1

2

a language of rapport: a way of establishing connections and negotiating relationships. Emphasis is placed on displaying similarities and matching experiences. From childhood, girls criticize peers who try to stand out or appear better than others. People feel their closest connections at home, or in settings where they *feel* at home—with one or a few people they feel close to and comfortable with—in other words, during private speaking. But even the most public situations can be approached like private speaking.

For most men, talk is primarily a means to preserve independence and negotiate and maintain status in a hierarchical   3

To men, talk is for information. To women, talk is for interaction.

---

social order. This is done by exhibiting knowledge and skill, and by holding center stage through verbal performance such as story-telling, joking, or imparting information. From childhood, men learn to use talking as a way to get and keep attention. So they are more comfortable speaking in larger groups made up of people they know less well—in the broadest sense, "public speaking." But even the most private situations can be approached like public speaking, more like giving a report than establishing rapport.

PRIVATE SPEAKING: THE WORDY WOMAN AND THE MUTE MAN

What is the source of the stereotype that women talk a lot?   4
Dale Spender suggests that most people feel instinctively (if not consciously) that women, like children, should be seen and not heard, so any amount of talk from them seems like too much. Studies have shown that if women and men talk equally in a group, people think the women talked more. So

there is truth to Spender's view. But another explanation is that men think women talk a lot because they hear women talking in situations where men would not: on the telephone; or in social situations with friends, when they are not discussing topics that men find inherently interesting; or, like the couple at the women's group, at home alone—in other words, in private speaking.

Home is the setting for an American icon that features the silent man and the talkative woman. And this icon, which grows out of the different goals and habits I have been describing, explains why the complaint most often voiced by women about the men with whom they are intimate is "He doesn't talk to me"—and the second most frequent is "He doesn't listen to me."

A woman who wrote to Ann Landers is typical:

> *My husband never speaks to me when he comes home from work. When I ask, "How did everything go today?" he says, "Rough . . ." or "It's a jungle out there." (We live in Jersey and he works in New York City.)*
>
> *It's a different story when we have guests or go visiting. Paul is the gabbiest guy in the crowd—a real spellbinder. He comes up with the most interesting stories. People hang on every word. I think to myself, "Why doesn't he ever tell me these things?"*
>
> *This has been going on for 38 years. Paul started to go quiet on me after 10 years of marriage. I could never figure out why. Can you solve the mystery?*
>
> —THE INVISIBLE WOMAN

Ann Landers suggests that the husband may not want to talk because he is tired when he comes home from work. Yet women who work come home tired too, and they are nonetheless eager to tell their partners or friends everything that happened to them during the day and what these fleeting, daily dramas made them think and feel.

Sources as lofty as studies conducted by psychologists, as   7
down to earth as letters written to advice columnists, and as
sophisticated as movies and plays come up with the same
insight: Men's silence at home is a disappointment to women.
Again and again, women complain, "He seems to have everything to say to everyone else, and nothing to say to me."

The film *Divorce American Style* opens with a conversation   8
in which Debbie Reynolds is claiming that she and Dick Van
Dyke don't communicate, and he is protesting that he tells
her everything that's on his mind. The doorbell interrupts
their quarrel, and husband and wife compose themselves
before opening the door to greet their guests with cheerful
smiles.

Behind closed doors, many couples are having conversa-   9
tions like this. Like the character played by Debbie Reynolds,
women feel men don't communicate. Like the husband
played by Dick Van Dyke, men feel wrongly accused. How
can she be convinced that he doesn't tell her anything, while
he is equally convinced he tells her everything that's on his
mind? How can women and men have such different ideas
about the same conversations?

When something goes wrong, people look around for a   10
source to blame: either the person they are trying to communicate with ("You're demanding, stubborn, self-centered") or the group that the other person belongs to ("All
women are demanding"; "All men are self-centered"). Some
generous-minded people blame the relationship ("We just
can't communicate"). But underneath, or overlaid on these
types of blame cast outward, most people believe that something is wrong with them.

If individual people or particular relationships were to   11
blame, there wouldn't be so many different people having
the same problems. The real problem is conversational style.
Women and men have different ways of talking. Even with
the best intentions, trying to settle the problem through talk
can only make things worse if it is ways of talking that are
causing trouble in the first place.

BEST FRIENDS

Once again, the seeds of women's and men's styles are sown   12
in the ways they learn to use language while growing up. In
our culture, most people, but especially women, look to their
closest relationships as havens in a hostile world. The center
of a little girl's social life is her best friend. Girls' friendships
are made and maintained by telling secrets. For grown
women too, the essence of friendship is talk, telling each
other what they're thinking and feeling, and what happened
that day: who was at the bus stop, who called, what they said,
how that made them feel. When asked who their best friends
are, most women name other women they talk to regularly.
When asked the same question, most men will say it's their
wives. After that, many men name other men with whom they
do things such as play tennis or baseball (but never just sit
and talk) or a chum from high school whom they haven't
spoken to in a year.

When Debbie Reynolds complained that Dick Van Dyke   13
didn't tell her anything, and he protested that he did, both
were right. She felt he didn't tell her anything because he
didn't tell her the fleeting thoughts and feelings he experienced throughout the day—the kind of talk she would have
with her best friend. He didn't tell her these things because
to him they didn't seem like anything to tell. He told her
anything that seemed important—anything he would tell his
friends.

Men and women often have very different ideas of what's   14
important—and at what point "important" topics should be
raised. A woman told me, with lingering incredulity, of a
conversation with her boyfriend. Knowing he had seen his
friend Oliver, she asked, "What's new with Oliver?" He replied, "Nothing." But later in the conversation it came out
that Oliver and his girlfriend had decided to get married.
"That's nothing?" the woman gasped in frustration and disbelief.

For men, "Nothing" may be a ritual response at the start   15
of a conversation. A college woman missed her brother but

rarely called him because she found it difficult to get talk going. A typical conversation began with her asking, "What's up with you?" and his replying, "Nothing." Hearing his "Nothing" as meaning "There is nothing personal I want to talk about," she supplied talk by filling him in on her news and eventually hung up in frustration. But when she thought back, she remembered that later in the conversation he had mumbled, "Christie and I got into another fight." This came so late and so low that she didn't pick up on it. And he was probably equally frustrated that she didn't.

Many men honestly do not know what women want, and   16
women honestly do not know why men find what they want so hard to comprehend and deliver.

"TALK TO ME!"

Women's dissatisfaction with men's silence at home is cap-   17
tured in the stock cartoon setting of a breakfast table at which a husband and wife are sitting: He's reading a newspaper; she's glaring at the back of the newspaper. In a Dagwood strip, Blondie complains, "Every morning all he sees is the newspaper! I'll bet you don't even know I'm here!" Dagwood reassures her, "Of course I know you're here. You're my wonderful wife and I love you very much." With this, he unseeingly pats the paw of the family dog, which the wife has put in her place before leaving the room. The cartoon strip shows that Blondie is justified in feeling like the woman who wrote to Ann Landers: invisible.

Another cartoon shows a husband opening a newspaper   18
and asking his wife, "Is there anything you would like to say to me before I begin reading the newspaper?" The reader knows that there isn't—but that as soon as he begins reading the paper, she will think of something. The cartoon high- lights the difference in what women and men think talk is for: To him, talk is for information. So when his wife inter- rupts his reading, it must be to inform him of something that he needs to know. This being the case, she might as well tell him what she thinks he needs to know before he starts read-

ing. But to her, talk is for interaction. Telling things is a way to show involvement, and listening is a way to show interest and caring. It is not an odd coincidence that she always thinks of things to tell him when he is reading. She feels the need for verbal interaction most keenly when he is (unaccountably, from her point of view) buried in the newspaper instead of talking to her.

Yet another cartoon shows a wedding cake that has, on top, in place of the plastic statues of bride and groom in tuxedo and gown, a breakfast scene in which an unshaven husband reads a newspaper across the table from his disgruntled wife. The cartoon reflects the enormous gulf between the romantic expectations of marriage represented by the plastic couple in traditional wedding costume, and the often disappointing reality represented by the two sides of the newspaper at the breakfast table—the front, which he is reading, and the back, at which she is glaring.   19

These cartoons, and many others on the same theme, are funny because people recognize their own experience in them. What's not funny is that many women are deeply hurt when men don't talk to them at home, and many men are deeply frustrated by feeling they have disappointed their partners, without understanding how they failed or how else they could have behaved.   20

Some men are further frustrated because, as one put it, "When in the world am I supposed to read the morning paper?" If many women are incredulous that many men do not exchange personal information with their friends, this man is incredulous that many women do not bother to read the morning paper. To him, reading the paper is an essential part of his morning ritual, and his whole day is awry if he doesn't get to read it. In his words, reading the newspaper in the morning is as important to him as putting on makeup in the morning is to many women he knows. Yet many women, he observed, either don't subscribe to a paper or don't read it until they get home in the evening. "I find this very puzzling," he said. "I can't tell you how often I have picked up a woman's morning newspaper from her front door   21 in the evening and handed it to her when she opened the door for me."

To this man (and I am sure many others), a woman who 22 objects to his reading the morning paper is trying to keep him from doing something essential and harmless. It's a violation of his independence—his freedom of action. But when a woman who expects her partner to talk to her is disappointed that he doesn't, she perceives his behavior as a failure of intimacy: He's keeping things from her; he's lost interest in her; he's pulling away. A woman I will call Rebecca, who is generally quite happily married, told me that this is the one source of serious dissatisfaction with her husband, Stuart. Her term for his taciturnity is *stinginess of spirit*. She tells him what she is thinking, and he listens silently. She asks him what he is thinking, and he takes a long time to answer, "I don't know." In frustration she challenges, "Is there nothing on your mind?"

For Rebecca, who is accustomed to expressing her fleeting 23 thoughts and opinions as they come to her, *saying* nothing means *thinking* nothing. But Stuart does not assume that his passing thoughts are worthy of utterance. He is not in the habit of uttering his fleeting ruminations, so just as Rebecca "naturally" speaks her thoughts, he "naturally" dismisses his as soon as they occur to him. Speaking them would give them more weight and significance than he feels they merit. All her life she has had practice in verbalizing her thoughts and feelings in private conversations with people she is close to; all his life he has had practice in dismissing his and keeping them to himself. . . .

PUBLIC SPEAKING: THE TALKATIVE MAN AND THE SILENT WOMAN

So far I have been discussing the private scenes in which many 24 men are silent and many women are talkative. But there are other scenes in which the roles are reversed. Returning to Rebecca and Stuart, we saw that when they are home alone, Rebecca's thoughts find their way into words effortlessly, whereas Stuart finds he can't come up with anything to say. The reverse happens when they are in other situations. For example, at a meeting of the neighborhood council or the parents' association at their children's school, it is Stuart who stands up and speaks. In that situation, it is Rebecca who is silent, her tongue tied by an acute awareness of all the negative reactions people could have to what she might say, all the mistakes she might make in trying to express her ideas. If she musters her courage and prepares to say something, she needs time to formulate it and then waits to be recognized by the chair. She cannot just jump up and start talking the way Stuart and some other men can.

Eleanor Smeal, president of the Fund for the Feminist Majority, was a guest on a call-in radio talk show, discussing abortion. No subject could be of more direct concern to women, yet during the hour-long show, all the callers except two were men. Diane Rehm, host of a radio talk show, expresses puzzlement that although the audience for her show is evenly split between women and men, 90 percent of the callers to the show are men. I am convinced that the reason is not that women are uninterested in the subjects discussed on the show. I would wager that women listeners are bringing up the subjects they heard on *The Diane Rehm Show* to their friends and family over lunch, tea, and dinner. But fewer of them call in because to do so would be putting themselves on display, claiming public attention for what they have to say, catapulting themselves onto center stage.

I myself have been the guest on innumerable radio and television talk shows. Perhaps I am unusual in being completely at ease in this mode of display. But perhaps I am not unusual at all, because, although I am comfortable in the role of invited expert, I have never called in to a talk show I was listening to, although I have often had ideas to contribute. When I am the guest, my position of authority is granted before I begin to speak. Were I to call in, I would be claiming that right on my own. I would have to establish my credibility by explaining who I am, which might seem self-aggrandizing, or not explain who I am and risk having my comments ignored or not valued. For similar reasons, though I am comfortable lecturing to groups numbering in the thousands, I rarely ask questions following another lecturer's talk, unless I know both the subject and the group very well.

My own experience and that of talk show hosts seems to   27
hold a clue to the difference in women's and men's attitudes toward talk: Many men are more comfortable than most women in using talk to claim attention. And this difference lies at the heart of the distinction between report-talk and rapport-talk.

REPORT-TALK IN PRIVATE

Report-talk, or what I am calling public speaking, does not   28
arise only in the literally public situation of formal speeches delivered to a listening audience. The more people there are in a conversation, the less well you know them, and the more status differences among them, the more a conversation is *like* public speaking or report-talk. The fewer the people, the more intimately you know them, and the more equal their status, the more it is like private speaking or rapport-talk. Furthermore, women feel a situation is more "public"—in the sense that they have to be on good behavior—if there are men present, except perhaps for family members. Yet even in families, the mother and children may feel their home to be "backstage" when Father is not home, "on-stage" when he is: Many children are instructed to be on good behavior when Daddy is home. This may be because he is not home often, or because Mother—or Father—doesn't want the children to disturb him when he is.

The difference between public and private speaking also   29
explains the stereotype that women don't tell jokes. Although some women are great raconteurs who can keep a group spellbound by recounting jokes and funny stories, there are fewer such personalities among women than among men. Many women who do tell jokes to large groups of people come from ethnic backgrounds in which verbal performance is highly valued. For example, many of the great women

stand-up comics, such as Fanny Brice and Joan Rivers, came from Jewish backgrounds.

Although it's not true that women don't tell jokes, it is true that many women are less likely than men to tell jokes in large groups, especially groups including men. So it's not surprising that men get the impression that women never tell jokes at all. Folklorist Carol Mitchell studied joke telling on a college campus. She found that men told most of their jokes to other men, but they also told many jokes to mixed groups and to women. Women, however, told most of their jokes to other women, fewer to men, and very few to groups that included men as well as women. Men preferred and were more likely to tell jokes when they had an audience: at least two, often four or more. Women preferred a small audience of one or two, rarely more than three. Unlike men, they were reluctant to tell jokes in front of people they didn't know well. Many women flatly refused to tell jokes they knew if there were four or more in the group, promising to tell them later in private. Men never refused the invitation to tell jokes. 30

All of Mitchell's results fit in with the picture I have been drawing of public and private speaking. In a situation in which there are more people in the audience, more men, or more strangers, joke telling, like any other form of verbal performance, requires speakers to claim center stage and prove their abilities. These are the situations in which many women are reluctant to talk. In a situation that is more private, because the audience is small, familiar, and perceived to be members of a community (for example, other women), they are more likely to talk. 31

The idea that telling jokes is a kind of self-display does not imply that it is selfish or self-centered. The situation of joke telling illustrates that status and connection entail each other. Entertaining others is a way of establishing connections with them, and telling jokes can be a kind of gift giving, where the joke is a gift that brings pleasure to receivers. The key issue is asymmetry: One person is the teller and the others are the audience. If these roles are later exchanged— for example, if the joke telling becomes a round in which one person after 32 another takes the role of teller—then there is symmetry on the broad scale, if not in the individual act. However, if women habitually take the role of appreciative audience and never take the role of joke teller, the asymmetry of the individual joke telling is diffused through the larger interaction as well. This is a hazard for women. A hazard for men is that continually telling jokes can be distancing. This is the effect felt by a man who complained that when he talks to his father on the phone, all his father does is tell him jokes. An extreme instance of a similar phenomenon is the class clown, who, according to teachers, is nearly always a boy.

RAPPORT-TALK IN PUBLIC

Just as conversations that take place at home among friends can be like public speaking, even a public address can be like private speaking: for example, by giving a lecture full of personal examples and stories. 33

At the executive committee of a fledgling professional organization, the outgoing president, Fran, suggested that the organization adopt the policy of having presidents deliver a presidential address. To explain and support her proposal, she told a personal anecdote: Her cousin was the president of a more established professional organization at the time that Fran held the same position in this one. Fran's mother had been talking to her cousin's mother on the telephone. Her cousin's mother told Fran's mother that her daughter was preparing her presidential address, and she asked when Fran's presidential address was scheduled to be. Fran was embarrassed to admit to her mother that she was not giving one. This made her wonder whether the organization's professional identity might not be enhanced if it emulated the more established organizations. 34

Several men on the committee were embarrassed by Fran's reference to her personal situation and were not convinced by her argument. It seemed to them not only irrelevant but unseemly to talk about her mother's telephone conversations at an executive committee meeting. Fran had approached the 35 meeting—a relatively public context—as an extension of the private kind. Many women's tendency to use personal experience and examples, rather than abstract argumentation, can be understood from the perspective of their orientation to language as it is used in private speaking.

A study by Celia Roberts and Tom Jupp of a faculty meeting at a secondary school in England found that the women's arguments did not carry weight with their male colleagues because they tended to use their own experience as evidence, or argue about the effect of policy on individual students. The men at the meeting argued from a completely different perspective, making categorical statements about right and wrong.   36

The same discussion is found in discussions at home. A man told me that he felt critical of what he perceived as his wife's lack of logic. For example, he recalled a conversation in which he had mentioned an article he had read in *The New York Times* claiming that today's college students are not as idealistic as students were in the 1960s. He was inclined to accept this claim. His wife questioned it, supporting her argument with the observation that her niece and her niece's friends were very idealistic indeed. He was incredulous and scornful of her faulty reasoning; it was obvious to him that a single personal example is neither evidence nor argumentation—it's just anecdote. It did not occur to him that he was dealing with a different logical system, rather than a lack of logic.   37

The logic this woman was employing was making sense of the world as a more private endeavor—observing and integrating her personal experience and drawing connections to the experiences of others. The logic the husband took for granted was a more public endeavor—more like gathering information, conducting a survey, or devising arguments by rules of formal logic as one might in doing research.   38

Another man complained about what he and his friends call women's "shifting sands" approach to discussion. These men feel that whereas they try to pursue an argument logically, step by step, until it is settled, women continually   39 change course in mid-stream. He pointed to the short excerpt from *Divorce American Style* quoted above as a case in point. It seemed to him that when Debbie Reynolds said, "I can't argue now. I have to take the French bread out of the oven," she was evading the argument because she had made an accusation—"All you do is criticize"—that she could not support.

This man also offered an example from his own experience.   40
His girlfriend had told him of a problem she had because her boss wanted her to do one thing and she wanted to do another. Taking the boss's view for the sake of argumentation, he pointed out a negative consequence that would result if she did what she wanted. She countered that the same negative consequence would result if she did what the boss wanted. He complained that she was shifting over to the other field of battle—what would happen if she followed her boss's will—before they had made headway with the first— what would happen if she followed her own.

For Study and Discussion

QUESTIONS FOR RESPONSE

1. How would you characterize your own conversational style?
2. How does context affect the way you talk? What situations make you shift styles?

QUESTIONS ABOUT PURPOSE

1. What does Tannen want to demonstrate about the relationship between communication failure and conversational style?
2. How do size (the number of people) and status (those people claiming authority) contribute to Tannen's comparison of rapport-talk and report-talk?

QUESTIONS ABOUT AUDIENCE

1. What assumptions does Tannen make about the probable gender of most of her readers?

2. How does Tannen assume her audience can benefit from her analysis?

QUESTIONS ABOUT STRATEGIES

1. How does Tannen use advice columns, movies, and cartoons to illustrate the problems of domestic communication?
2. How does Tannen use her own experience as a lecturer to compare the way men and women talk in public?

QUESTIONS FOR DISCUSSION

1. Do the men and women you know construct arguments according to Tannen's format? How many men use personal experience as evidence? How many women make categorical assertions?
2. To what extent do conversational styles depend on innate skill (personality type) or learned behavior (acquired habits)? To what extent is it possible (or desirable) to change styles?

BILL McKIBBEN

Bill McKibben was born in 1960 in Palo Alto, California, and educated at Harvard University. He began his career as a staff writer for *The New Yorker*, focusing on environmental issues. In *The End of Nature* (1989) he assesses the ecological disasters that will occur if the industrialized world does not change its habits. In *The Age of Missing Information* (1992) he speculates on how television has changed our lives. In "Nature and Televised Nature," excerpted from the latter book, McKibben argues that television's representation of certain forms of nature destroys our understanding of the larger context of environmental systems.

Nature and Televised Nature

U NABLE THOUGH I was to forecast the weather, I retained sufficient mother wit to recognize that it had turned into a gorgeous day, and so I set out to climb Blackberry Mountain, Crow's smaller neighbor.

From the pond I followed a brook down to the valley between the peaks—it is a mossy cool trickle in the summer, and instead of clambering over deadfall along the banks you can hop easily from rock to rock down the creek. I stopped occasionally at the small clear pools to admire the water striders, their legs dimpling the tense surface, their small bodies casting impressive shadows on the creek bottom as they went about their inscrutable business.

When I reached the valley between the mountains, I could look up at the open cliffs at the top of Blackberry. Since there's no trail to the summit, I just hit out along a compass bearing through the woods. The bottom slopes have been logged in the last couple of decades—the sun pours into the clearings, which of course are luxuriant with thorny berry cane. I fought my way through, and after twenty minutes or so, as the slope steepened, rock patches began to appear—the trees were fewer and bigger, and in the shade of one hemlock I lay down to rest. After about ten minutes, at least a dozen small birds began to resume the activity I had interrupted with my noisy arrival. They were mostly small thrushes, and they flew in and out of the branches in what looked like a

---

When you get most of your information about nature through television, the "real" nature around you begins to seem dull.

---

high-speed game of tag, over and over, lighting now on a swaying bough, then launching themselves off into the air once more.

After my rest I climbed the remaining distance to Black-berry's long summit ridge, and walked out along the top of the steep cliffs that faced back to Crow. The wind was blowing below—I could hear it rush like white water and see where it was riffling the maple tops in the mountain valley—but up on top it was still, and the sun baked the fragrant pine needles. I was sitting, drinking from my canteen, when I saw a vulture appear way below in the draw between the mountains. He circled slowly and methodically up, holding his wings in a stiff, lacquered bow, never flapping, always soaring. Eventually, after perhaps a half hour, he was directly above me on the cliffs, perhaps a hundred feet in the air, still circling. He was joined there by four, then five, finally six others, circling so close I could count feathers. When they passed directly overhead it was nearly unbearable—almost erotic—this feeling of being watched. At moments I felt small and vulnerable, like prey; if they disappeared from view for a minute I wanted to know where they were. But by the time I finally rose to go back to my tent on Crow, I felt almost protected, watched over. It had been thrilling—my heart was beating hard.

Still and all, by the standards of television nature, the water 5 striders and the thrushes and even the vultures were hardly worth mentioning. I had not been gored, chased, or even roared at. I had failed to tranquilize anything with a dart; no creature had inflated stupendous air sacs in a curious and ancient mating ritual, or eaten its young, or done any of the other prodigious tricks that happen around the clock on nature television. You could spend nearly the whole day watching nothing but nature documentaries, and if you did you would emerge exhausted. Nature on TV is the job of a man named Graham or Ian or Nigel who makes every announcement ("Using his incisors like a comb, the marmot attends to his thick underfleece") sound like Churchill in wartime. The point of the show can be that, say, elephants are all but exterminated in a certain African refuge, but you can be sure that our host will find one. Not one—dozens. "I think there's a jolly good chance of sketching this lot," the host is saying as he piles out of his Land-Rover. "There's the matriarch—she's the one to watch. I'd be crazy to get too close to her. If I can reach that anthill I can get some good sketches. She's accompanied by uncles and aunties of all ages—the young males get kicked out because they get stroppy." On the voiceover, the narrator may be confessing the boring truth: "Lions are lazy—the males are the worst. They'll sleep twenty hours a day if they get the chance." But on the screen the lions are training their young by chasing jackals and other exotic game—Oooh, so much for that zebra. The man in the jeep, obligatory spare tire on the hood, tracks the lion pack toward a watering hole, never losing sight of them. He spies some ostriches: "Ostriches mean water, and water means life—and the lion feels an ancient urge. Perhaps she's come upon a place to start a pride." Oooh—lion sex! Cubs come tumbling out after a two- or three-minute gestation, full of play, and the timeless predatory cycle repeats—

Oooh, poor wildebeest. Switch the channel and someone is releasing a seal from a California aquarium. He starts to travel north, but suddenly a killer whale is on his tail. A brief respite in a kelp bed ("It's the life of Riley, lying on your back and eating crab so fresh it tries to walk away") and then our seal resumes his trip up the coast to the Pribilofs, where the breeding beach is a great heaving mass of flippers. At the precise moment our hero washes ashore, the men appear with the baseball bats for the annual fur harvest; fortunately he retreats to the safety of the ocean before they can get him, still alive for the documentaries that will surely follow.

It would be churlish to complain about these gorgeous films. It would be even more churlish to quote from a recent interview in *Entertainment Weekly* with Wolfgang Bayer. An acclaimed nature photographer who's made dozens of TV films, he tells of hoisting tame, declawed jaguars into trees for action scenes, and spray-painting pet-shop ferrets till they're ringers for the nearly extinct black-footed variety, and starving piranhas so they'll attack with more ferocity. He once did a show on an Amazonian tarantula that occasionally eats birds. How often does it eat birds, asked the reporter? "As often as you throw them to him," he says. It would be churlish because TV nature films have without any question done an immense amount of good—species exist today that would be fossil records if Philo Farnsworth hadn't invented the picture tube. Your can of tuna has a little "dolphin-safe" symbol on it because in 1963 Chuck Connors starred in a film called *Flipper,* which gave birth to a TV show of the same name. The movie version was shown on May 3—in the month of May alone it was on the Disney Channel five times and on Cinemax twice, so presumably each new generation sees the boy battle his stern, old-fashioned father, who actually believes dolphins are a threat to his fishery. "If they come, we'll kill them. We have no choice," the father says. The rise of environmental consciousness over the intervening three decades can be felt in just how shocking this attitude now seems. Some fishermen still kill dolphins, but they try to hide their work because nearly everyone agrees it is a sick waste;

6

in 1963, obviously, *not* killing dolphins was regarded as revolutionary, and *Flipper* is a key reason for the change.

In 1963, too, the sperm-whale kill reached its peak, claiming about thirty thousand of the great beasts. We think of whaling as being at its height in the last century, when Nantucket men and Gloucester men and Mystic men and the men of a dozen other ports that are now pricy tourist attractions sailed the globe in search of lamp oil. But the slaughter continued, except of those species that were already reduced below commercial levels, until about the time that a slight Frenchman took to the TV screens. On any given time that day you can see Jacques Cousteau, the John Muir of the deep, two or three times—here he is in the sea grass beds of Australia, a safe pasture for sea cows now threatened by sand-mining; here he is working to "cweate a weef, shimmawing with life." His son Michel is apparently taking over the family trade, and has perfected the sad Gallic intonations of his dad. He is swimming next to a giant grouper—"I hardly ever see a fish so large anymore, which were my constant companions when I began diving. I cannot resist reaching out to this veteran of living, as if to touch the past, the time when big fish were nothing more than that." Cousteau's success can be measured in the sea, where remnant populations of some species survive because of great human efforts, and even more in the popular mind—a four-year-old boy just spent the weekend with us, and his conversation rarely strayed from the topic of killer whales, a species that until quite recently stirred loathing and not love.

Still, measured in the largest terms, such appeals aren't working. That is, virtually everyone in the industrialized world has a television and has presumably, if only by accident, seen many hours of gorgeous nature films—seen a more diverse and wondrous natural world than man could ever have seen before. And yet we're still not willing to do anything very drastic to save that world. We'll buy dolphin-safe tuna if it doesn't cost much extra, but we won't cut back on driving and consuming electricity and doing the other things that lead to global warming, even though the world now loses as much as 5 percent of its coral reefs annually due to higher water temperatures likely caused by the greenhouse effect. Species continue to disappear, and at an accelerating rate; presidents continue to propose, say, drilling for oil in the Arctic National Wildlife Refuge, square in the middle of an enormous caribou herd. Why can't Graham and Ian and Nigel stop this?

They can't, I think, because for all their dart guns and millions of feet of film they actually get across remarkably little information—much less than you'd acquire almost unconsciously from a good long hike. Half the time they specialize in misinformation, undercutting their message with their pictures. The Englishman is telling you that this great flightless bird is on the edge of extinction, but for half an hour he is showing you endless pictures of this great flightless bird, so how bad could it be? The actual numbers of surviving big mammals are astoundingly small—grizzly bears in the lower forty-eight states can be counted in the hundreds. In fact, you've probably seen a large fraction of them at one time or another, wandering slowly through the telephoto field of a Yellowstone camera. But they appear so often they seem numerous. No one shows film of the weeks in camp waiting for the damned gorillas to appear—a documentary of trees that used to be inhabited by the ancient manlike primates but no longer are is a documentary people wouldn't watch, though that void is the true revelation about an awful lot of the world.

Something even more insidious happens when you get most of your nature through television, though—the "real" nature around you, even when it's intact, begins to seem dull. Mr. Bayer, the man with the spray-painted ferrets, said, "If we showed viewers only natural, unadulterated filmmaking, wildlife filmmakers would be out of business in a year, it'd be so boring." So, instead, nature films are like the highlight clips they show on the evening sportscast, all rim-bending slam dunks and bleachers-clearing home runs and knee-crumpling knockout punches. If you'd been raised on a steady diet of such footage and then you went to a game,

9

10

you'd feel cheated—what is all this business with singles and pop flies? Why do the hockey players skate around for so long between fights? The highlights films erode appreciation for the various beauties of the game, some of which are small and patient.

The problem is even more severe with the natural world,   11 where the ratio of observable high drama is much lower. A movie like *Benji the Hunted,* which was on the Disney Channel, presents the forest as a place where, in the space of a day, you encounter and must vanquish mountain lions, wolves, grizzlies, badgers, and so on right down Noah's list—it is a car-chase flick with animals. (And as impossible in its outcome as most car chases—Benji, a domesticated dog, has somehow retained the instinct necessary to outwit every predatory mammal of the North American continent, while acquiring a remarkably un-Darwinian compassion for the young of other species.) How disappointing, then, to go for a walk in a healthy Eastern woods and see so few bared claws. In many years hiking in the East I've happened across bears twice. Once, in Maine, I rounded a corner in a trail and there, three feet away, as lost in thought as I had been, sat a black bear. One look at me and she dived for the bushes—total contact time perhaps four seconds. A few years later, walking near my house with my wife, I heard a noise in a treetop and all of a sudden another black bear, roughly the size and shape of a large sofa, dropped to the ground a few yards away. She glowered in our direction and then lit out the opposite way. Time of engagement: maybe seven seconds. Those were grand encounters, and they've spiced every other day I've spent in the woods—on the way up Blackberry Mountain, for instance, I sang as I waded through the berry bushes, aware that this is where any bear with a stomach would be. But if I counted as dramatic only those days when I actually saw a big fierce mammal, I would think the forest a boring place indeed.

Big animals are fairly scarce in the best of conditions, and   12 understandably shy—an Adirondack hunter last fall shot a bear that biologists, studying his teeth, determined was forty-three years old. That is, he'd been hiding out up here since before Truman beat Dewey. When you do see large animals it's usually at a pretty good distance, not right up close as on TV—you can rarely sneak up on, say, a heron the way you can with a zoom lens. (On the other hand, you need a big, natural field of vision to get a sense of the graceful spookiness with which they glide.) But even if you did see a rare animal, and somehow managed to creep up real close, chances are it wouldn't be doing anything all that amazing. Chances are it would be lying in the sun, or perhaps grooming itself, or maybe, like the duck on the pond, swimming back and forth. A lot of animals are remarkably good at sitting still (especially when they suspect they're under surveillance), and this is something TV never captures. The nature documentaries are as absurdly action-packed as the soap operas, where a life's worth of divorce, adultery, and sudden death are crammed into a week's worth of watching—trying to understand "nature" from watching *Wild Kingdom* is as tough as trying to understand "life" from watching *Dynasty*.

This is particularly true because, even at its best, TV covers only a small slice of the natural world. There are perhaps ten million (some say thirty million) species on earth; of those that we know about and have catalogued, only a few meet the requirements for extensive television coverage—cuteness (or grotesqueness so complete it borders on the cute), great amiability or ferocity, accessibility (it lives on grassland plains or beaches, not in the deep ocean, badly lit caves, or rain-forest canopies), correct size to show up well on camera, and so on. Species with these characteristics seem to exist in roughly the same ratio as human television actors to the general population, and they are as consistently overexposed. But even the most unengaging, hard-to-get-at, drab little animal has a great advantage over any plant except a Venus's-flytrap, and that is mobility. In its immense fear that we might grow bored, TV has not yet acquired the courage necessary to show an unmoving picture for very long, and so the only hope of star-struck vegetation is time-lapse photography, which works okay for orchids but doesn't do much for, say, evergreens. Someone sent me a "working treatment" recently for a television program celebrating trees that is being made by a leading wildlife filmmaker. The "tease opening" features "intercutting of striking tree images with interview characters expressing

Wonder

Concern

Reverence .

followed by opening credits over breathtaking images of trees and forests" against an "*engaging mix of forest sounds, rain, and music.*" The film covers rain forest, swamps, and the autumn blaze of color; it looks at furniture and at musical instruments made from wood; it covers bonsai and the Yellowstone fires, all in forty-seven and a half minutes, leaving twelve and a half for commercials. Beautiful, no doubt, but perhaps the wrong way to nurture appreciation for trees, whose most glorious characteristic is that they stay in the same place forever. Any time spent in a real forest gives you this information: a tree is of a piece with the soil from which it grows and the sky it rises into, part and parcel of the insect that eats at its middle and the bird that eats the insect, inseparable from the forest of other trees and yet perfect in its humped and gnarly isolation. And yet this is so hard to show—much easier to flash a sequoia on the screen and say this counts because it's big.

The upshot of a nature education by television is a deep   14
fondness for certain species and a deep lack of understanding of systems, or of the policies that destroy those systems. For instance, one of the ads that may come on during this celebration of trees, as it did several times on May 3, is paid for by the Forest Products Council. "Today we have more trees than we did back in 1920," it says, "thanks in part to something our forest products companies do three million times a day—plant a tree." The visuals accompanying this reassuring voice are stunning—from the air we see a bend in a wilderness river with a rich and exuberant old forest spilling

forth to the bank. There's a lot less of this kind of forest than there was in 1920, thanks in part (in whole, really) to something else the forest products companies do every day, which is cut down virgin stands of climax forest, the biologically diverse, marvelously complex ancient forest that covered much of this country when Europeans arrived. The forest products companies *do* plant trees. They plant them in nice straight rows, every sapling the same age and the same height and the same species, and then they drop herbicides from helicopters to keep down undesirable varieties; they create, in other words, sterile plantations for growing timber and pulp. And the forest products companies often perform this public service on public lands, under the guidance of government employees. The great national forests, which cover so much of the western part of the nation, are mostly managed as timber farms; the trees, in many cases old-growth forests, are sold to lumber companies and then cut down. One of these public servants is Smokey Bear, whose commercials run all day and night. We all grew up believing Smokey hated forest fires because they fried Bambi's kin, but the truth is Smokey doesn't want you to burn the forest down because his employer, the Forest Service, wants to cut it down instead. You don't see this when you drive through a national forest, because the government employs an enormous corps of landscape architects whose whole job is to make sure the clearcuts are invisible. And you don't see it on TV because it's political, and a tree is a tree, and it's time to look at the fur seals again.

In 1990, according to the *New York Times,* the not-to-be-lived-without accessory was the "personal meadow, a mini-expanse of green grass growing ever-so-sweetly out of a gently rusticated plywood box." "They couldn't walk by without coming in to touch it," said one florist. "It's such a fresh look. People have very strong reactions to it." An interior designer who changes the sod in his foyer every two weeks when it begins to yellow says, "I see it as Eastern in its concept." 15

Like urban living, TV cuts us off from context—stops us   16
from understanding plants and animals as parts of systems,
from grounding them in ideas larger than "fresh" or fierce or
cute. And so we don't know what to make of them. We are
still pulled toward this natural world, with a tug so strong it
must be primal, but TV helps turn it into a zoo; hence most
of our responses are artificial. Animals amble across the screen
all day and night—I saw the same squad of marching fla-
mingos twice during the day on different networks. ("They're
stupid," said the handler on one of the programs. "It took
me six months to get them to walk in formation.") CNN, in
just a few hours, reported on a new virus that was spreading
among macaws, parrots, and cockatoos; an orphanage that
had been established for African elephants whose mothers
had been killed by poachers; a group of manatees in the
waterways of Florida who were being gouged by outboard
propellers; a white tiger being born in a zoo; some home
videos of dolphins dying in the tuna nets that a man had
risked his life to take; a debate about whether people should
be permitted to swim in tanks with dolphins; some "doomsday dolphins" that might be trained for ordnance work; and
a Navy plan to kill thirty-five thousand feral goats on San
Clemente island. The day's main animal feature was a constantly repeated story on the abuses of puppy breeders, a
story that also appeared on virtually every network's broadcast. The Humane Society had issued a report that morning—most pet store dogs, it turns out, come from breeders
in six Midwestern states, who in many cases raise them in
such horrid conditions that they sicken and die after purchase. Two big dogs and their owner came on the *Today* show
to chat with Bryant Gumbel about the problem; other networks aired film of puppies crowded together in wire cages.
"Her ear canal has been inflamed so long there's no longer
any hole in there," said one vet. "Her skin is dry, cracking,
bleeding in spots. Boy—I can imagine how uncomfortable
she is."

We all can. That's the marvelous thing about pets—our   17
visceral and natural affection for them offers an easy door for

human minds to enter into a larger than normal world, a world where our preoccupations count for less. A dog or a cat or a rabbit is a constant reminder that there is more than us out there—our love for them is a healthy recognition of that more. But when that love lacks a larger context, the relationship turns mawkish. Everyone knows about pet cemeteries, but CNN carried the story of a cemetery where people could be buried *with* their pets. The Fox affiliate offered news of a New York company that will freeze-dry your dead pet so you can keep him in your living room. A twenty-pound dog will run you $1,200—"We charge by the pound, but on birds we've got a flat price"—and take four months to prepare. "After we got him back, we'd just put him in his normal position, and people would walk up to him, pet him, joke with him, and then notice he was dead," said one satisfied owner. "Archie was our whole life. Everything we did was for Archie. . . . Even though he wasn't going to be living, we could still stroke him, still tell him how much we loved him."

The healthier relationships always had some content to them—one of the local channels, for instance, carried a fine report about the members of the Fairfax County police K-9 squad, German shepherds who live at the homes of their handlers. "You get very used to grabbing the dog and loving him up," said one cop. But it's a relationship based more on respect—on an appreciation of a dog's nature, his gifts—than on sentiment. "When he gets in the cruiser his personality changes. You can actually see the transition. He has a little dance he does—a twirl like 'Let's get rolling.'" One of the German shepherds, Jake, was stabbed seven times but kept on going—he collared the criminal despite his fatal wounds. "They become such a part of you—it's like losing an arm or a leg or a baby," said his distraught handler. But there was no suggestion that Jake should be freeze-dried—he was too real for that. [18]

In somewhat the same way, the men on a few of the angling programs showed some real connection with their catch—they were both competitors and, in a strange sense, colleagues. "This fish is exhausted beyond any of our beliefs, [19] it's fought so hard," said one hip-booted host of *Fish'n Canada*. "It's your duty as an angler to wait till she's fully revived before releasing her." Don Meissner, the host of *Rod 'n' Reel Streamside*, caught a big old brookie: "I tell you, my heart's just a poundin'. Holy cow, oh, oh, holy cow, look at that fish. . . . Since I got older, my feelings on fishing have changed tremendously. It's just to be out there. Not to kill something. Oh my—I'm shaking like a leaf." Now, you could argue that there's something perverse about catching a fish and letting him go, and you could argue that if people really *admired* a fish they wouldn't stick a barb through its lip and pull on it for a quarter of an hour. And if you argued any of those things you might be right. Still, there is an echo of something here, of the traditional respectful relationship between hunters and their quarry.

Even in the most civilized, that tug remains. A Cousteau 20
special on the Turner Broadcasting System showed crowds of Australians climbing off buses to wade along a beach where dolphins lolled in the surf. Some of the people were painfully stupid—sticking their fingers down the dolphin's blowhole. But most seemed genuinely filled with

> Wonder
>
> Concern
>
> Reverence

"In ze welcome of ze dolphins lies ze test of human wisdom," said Cousteau, right as usual. Do we appreciate dolphins for the tricks they can perform, for being like limited humans?— the trainer at a Hawaii dolphin show said that she knew her charge was "smart" because "he wants something for nothing." Do we appreciate them as an economic and recreational "resource," like the striped bass described by a hatchery director on *Virginia Wildlife*? (Captured fish are weighed to determine how much hormone, collected from the pituitaries of pregnant women, to inject them with—"Fish in captivity tend to hold back on their eggs, but this overrides that.") Or do we begin to understand again what once was common knowledge—that they're marvelous for their own reasons, that they matter independently of us?

That piece of information can come only when you accept nature and its component parts on their own terms—small and placid and dull and parts of systems, as well as big and flashy and fierce and soulful. Alone on a mountain you do start slowly to learn this lesson—it's inevitable if you lie on your back for hours and watch the hawks just circle, or lie on your stomach and watch the ducks just swim. They are not there for you—they are there because the world belongs to them too. Learn this lesson too well and you are in trouble, for in our current world it will mostly bring pain, mostly breed hysteria. Even on television this pain occasionally surfaces. HBO was showing Diane Fossey's story, *Gorillas in the Mist*—it is the story of a kook, driven mad by her understanding of what was happening around her. On paper her actions look insane—she kidnaps poachers, imprisons them. But watching the gorillas, tugged by that old tug, you know why she did what she did. The gorillas so clearly *belong.* An even better film, and more remarkable considering it was made way back in 1958, is John Huston's *The Roots of Heaven,* an elephant story starring Errol Flynn that aired on the American Movie Channel. "Anyone who's seen the great herds on the march across the last free spaces knows it is something the world can't afford to lose," says the Flynn character, and of course he is right. 21

But the world *is* losing them—CNN is filled with the pictures of dying elephants and of a dozen other creatures. This is perhaps the ultimate loss of information—too sophisticated to burn books, we burn the planet. Each day information leaks away—some branch of life that evolved for millions of years is gone, and the next day two more, and six the day after that. The world grows stupider, less substantial. And those of us who would fight have little ground on which to stand, for the tug at our hearts from the sad picture on the screen is no substitute for the deep and lifelong understandings we've let slip away. 22

For Study and Discussion

QUESTIONS FOR RESPONSE

1. What kind of "nature stories" do you watch on television?
2. What aspect of the show—the scenery, the animals, the plot, the narrator—engages your attention?

QUESTIONS ABOUT PURPOSE

1. Why does McKibben admit that "It would be churlish to complain about these gorgeous films?"
2. What thesis does he attempt to prove about the difference between "real nature" and televised nature?

QUESTIONS ABOUT AUDIENCE

1. What assumptions does McKibben make about his readers' "environmental consciousness"?
2. What assumptions does he make about their television viewing habits?

QUESTIONS ABOUT STRATEGIES

1. How does McKibben use the first four paragraphs to demonstrate the *complexity* of his experience with nature and its *inappropriateness* for a television show?
2. How do McKibben's comparisons of nature films with sports-highlight films, car-crash flicks, and soap operas clarify the purpose of his essay?

QUESTIONS FOR DISCUSSION

1. In what ways does "televised nature" provide us with "fondness for certain species" and a "lack of understanding of systems"?
2. Why does "televised nature" prevent us from understanding "what was once common knowledge" about "real nature"?

FRANK O'CONNOR

Frank O'Connor (1903–1966), the pen name for Michael John O'Donovan, was born in Cork, Ireland. Although he briefly attended the Christian Brothers School in Cork, his family's poverty forced him to forgo more education. While still in his teens, O'Connor joined the Irish Republican Army (IRA) and fought in the civil war from 1922 to 1923. Arrested and imprisoned, O'Connor served as the prison librarian until he was released in 1923. His stories, which attempt to record the distinctive vernacular of the Irish people and which appear in more than twenty volumes, are most accessible in *Collected Stories* (1981). O'Connor also wrote novels, such as *Dutch Interior* (1940); travel literature, *Irish Miles* (1947); literary criticism, *The Lonely Voice* (1963); and two volumes of an autobiography, *An Only Child* (1961) and *My Father's Son* (1969). "Guests of the Nation," reprinted from *Collected Stories*, recounts the experiences of several Irishmen who must choose between loyalty to their guests and duty to their nation.

Guests of the Nation

A T DUSK THE big Englishman Belcher would shift his long legs out of the ashes and ask, "Well, chums, what about it?" and Noble or me would say, "As you please, chum" (for we had picked up some of their curious expressions), and the little Englishman 'Awkins would light the lamp and produce the cards. Sometimes Jeremiah Donovan would come up of an evening and supervise the play, and grow excited over 'Awkins's cards (which he always played badly), and shout at him as if he was one of our own, "Ach, you divil you, why didn't you play the tray?" But, ordinarily, Jeremiah was a sober and contented poor devil like the big Englishman Belcher, and was looked up to at all only because he was a fair hand at documents, though slow enough at these, I vow. He wore a small cloth hat and big gaiters over his long pants. He reddened when you talked to him, tilting from toe to heel and back and looking down all the while at his big farmer's feet. His uncommon broad accent was a great source of jest to me, I being from the town as you may recognize.

I couldn't at the time see the point of me and Noble being   2
with Belcher and 'Awkins at all, for it was and is my fixed belief you could have planted that pair in any untended spot from this to Claregalway and they'd have stayed put and flourished like a native weed. I never seen in my short experience two men that took to the country as they did.

They were handed on to us by the Second Battalion to   3
keep when the search for them became too hot, and Noble and myself, being young, took charge with a natural feeling of responsibility. But little 'Awkins made us look right fools when he displayed he knew the countryside as well as we did and something more, "You're the bloke they calls Bonaparte?" he said to me. "Well, Bonaparte, Mary Brigid Ho'Connell was arskin abaout you and said 'ow you'd a pair of socks belonging to 'er young brother." For it seemed, as they explained it, that the Second used to have little evenings of their own, and some of the girls of the neighborhood would turn in, and seeing they were such decent fellows, our lads couldn't well ignore the two Englishmen, but invited them in and were hail-fellow-well-met with them. 'Awkins told me he learned to dance "The Walls of Limerick" and "The Siege of Ennis" and "The Waves of Tory" in a night or two, though naturally he could not return the compliment, because our lads at that time did not dance foreign dances on principle.

So whatever privileges and favors Belcher and 'Awkins had   4
with the Second they duly took with us, and after the first

evening we gave up all pretense of keeping a close eye on their behavior. Not that they could have got far, for they had a notable accent and wore khaki tunics and overcoats with civilian pants and boots. But it's my belief they never had an idea of escaping and were quite contented with their lot.

Now, it was a treat to see how Belcher got off with the old 5 woman of the house we were staying in. She was a great warrant to scold, and crotchety even with us, but before ever she had a chance of giving our guests, as I may call them, a lick of her tongue, Belcher had made her his friend for life. She was breaking sticks at the time, and Belcher, who hadn't been in the house for more than ten minutes, jumped up out of his seat and went across to her.

"Allow me, madam," he says, smiling his queer little smile; 6 "please allow me," and takes the hatchet from her hand. She was struck too parlatic to speak, and ever after Belcher would be at her heels carrying a bucket, or basket, or load of turf, as the case might be. As Noble wittily remarked, he got into looking before she leapt, and hot water or any little thing she wanted Belcher would have it ready for her. For such a huge man (and though I am five foot ten myself I had to look up to him) he had an uncommon shortness—or should I say lack—of speech. It took us some time to get used to him walking in and out like a ghost, without a syllable out of him. Especially because 'Awkins talked enough for a platoon, it was strange to hear big Belcher with his toes in the ashes come out with a solitary "Excuse me, chum," or "That's right, chum." His one and only abiding passion was cards, and I will say for him he was a good card-player. He could have fleeced me and Noble many a time; only if we lost to him, 'Awkins lost to us, and 'Awkins played with the money Belcher gave him.

'Awkins lost to us because he talked too much, and I think 7 now we lost to Belcher for the same reason. 'Awkins and Noble would spit at one another about religion into the early hours of the morning; the little Englishman as you could see worrying the soul out of young Noble (whose brother was a priest) with a string of questions that would puzzle a cardinal. And to make it worse, even in treating of these holy subjects, 'Awkins had a deplorable tongue; I never in all my career struck across a man who could mix such a variety of cursing and bad language into the simplest topic. Oh, a terrible man was little 'Awkins, and a fright to argue! He never did a stroke of work, and when he had no one else to talk to he fixed his claws into the old woman.

I am glad to say that in her he met his match, for one day   8
when he tried to get her to complain profanely of the drought she gave him a great comedown by blaming the drought upon Jupiter Pluvius (a deity neither 'Awkins nor I had ever even heard of, though Noble said among the pagans he was held to have something to do with rain). And another day the same 'Awkins was swearing at the capitalists for starting the German war, when the old dame laid down her iron, puckered up her little crab's mouth and said, "Mr. 'Awkins, you can say what you please about the war, thinking to deceive me because I'm an ignorant old woman, but I know well what started the war. It was that Italian count that stole the heathen divinity out of the temple in Japan, for believe me, Mr. 'Awkins, nothing but sorrow and want follows them that disturbs the hidden powers!" Oh, a queer old dame, as you remark!

So one evening we had our tea together, and 'Awkins lit the   9
lamp and we all sat in to cards. Jeremiah Donovan came in too, and sat down and watched us for a while. Though he was a shy man and didn't speak much, it was easy to see he had no great love for the two Englishmen, and I was surprised it hadn't struck me so clearly before. Well, like that in the story, a terrible dispute blew up late in the evening between 'Awkins and Noble, about capitalists and priests and love for your own country.

"The capitalists," says 'Awkins, with an angry gulp, "the   10
capitalists pays the priests to tell you all abaout the next world, so's you won't notice what they do in this!"

"Nonsense, man," says Noble, losing his temper, "before   11 ever a capitalist was thought of people believed in the next world."

'Awkins stood up as if he was preaching a sermon. "Oh, they did, did they?" he says with a sneer. "They believed all the things you believe, that's what you mean? And you believe that God created Hadam and Hadam created Shem and Shem created Jehoshophat? You believe all the silly hold fairy-tale about Heve and Heden and the happle? Well, listen to me, chum. If you're entitled to 'old to a silly belief like that, I'm entitled to 'old to my own silly belief—which is, that the fust thing your God created was a bleedin' capitalist with mirality and Rolls Royce complete. Am I right, chum?" he says then to Belcher. 12

"You're right, chum," says Belcher, with his queer smile, and gets up from the table to stretch his long legs into the fire and stroke his mustache. So, seeing that Jeremiah Donovan was going, and there was no knowing when the conversation about religion would be over, I took my hat and went out with him. We strolled down towards the village together, and then he suddenly stopped, and blushing and mumbling, and shifting, as his way was, from toe to heel, he said I ought to be behind keeping guard on the prisoners. And I, having it put to me so suddenly, asked him what the hell he wanted a guard on the prisoners at all for, and said that so far as Noble and me were concerned we had talked it over and would rather be out with a column. "What use is that pair to us?" I asked him. 13

He looked at me for a spell and said, "I thought you knew we were keeping them as hostages." "Hostages—?" says I, not quite understanding. "The enemy," he says in his heavy way, "have prisoners belong' to us, and now they talk of shooting them. If they shoot our prisoners we'll shoot theirs, and serve them right." "Shoot them?" said I, the possibility just beginning to dawn on me. "Shoot them exactly," said he. "Now," said I, "wasn't it very unforeseen of you not to tell me and Noble that?" "How so?" he asks. "Seeing that we were acting as guards upon them, of course." "And hadn't you reason enough to guess that much?" "We had not, Jere- 14 miah Donovan, we had not. How were we to know when the men were on our hands so long?" "And what difference does it make? The enemy have our prisoners as long or longer, haven't they?" "It makes a great difference," said I. "How so?" said he sharply; but I couldn't tell him the difference it made, for I was struck too silly to speak. "And when may we expect to be released from this anyway?" said I. "You may expect it tonight," says he. "Or tomorrow or the next day at latest. So if it's hanging round here that worries you, you'll be free soon enough."

I cannot explain it even now, how sad I felt, but I went   15
back to the cottage, a miserable man. When I arrived the discussion was still on, 'Awkins holding forth to all and sundry that there was no next world at all and Noble answering in his best canonical style that there was. But I saw 'Awkins was after having the best of it. "Do you know what, chum?" he was saying, with his saucy smile. "I think you're jest as big a bleedin' hunbeliever as I am. You say you believe in the next world and you know jest as much abaout the next world as I do, which is sweet damn-all. What's 'Eaven? You dunno. Where's 'Eaven? You dunno. Who's in 'Eaven? You dunno. You know sweet damn-all! I arsk you again, do they wear wings?"

"Very well then," says Noble, "they do; is that enough for   16
you? They do wear wings." "Where do they get them then? Who makes them? 'Ave they a fact'ry for wings? 'Ave they a sort of store where you 'ands in your chit and tikes your bleedin' wings? Answer me that."

"Oh, you're an impossible man to argue with," says Noble.   17
"Now listen to me—" And off the pair of them went again.

It was long after midnight when we locked up the Eng-   18
lishmen and went to bed ourselves. As I blew out the candle I told Noble what Jeremiah Donovan had told me. Noble took it very quietly. After we had been in bed about an hour he asked me did I think we ought to tell the Englishmen. I having thought of the same thing myself (among many others) said no, because it was more than likely the English wouldn't shoot our men, and anyhow it wasn't to be sup-

posed the Brigade who were always up and down with the Second Battalion and knew the Englishmen well would be likely to want them bumped off. "I think so," says Noble. "It would be sort of cruelty to put the win up them now." "It was very unforeseen of Jeremiah Donovan anyhow," says I, and by Noble's silence I realized he took my meaning.

So I lay there half the night, and thought and thought, and picturing myself and young Noble trying to prevent the Brigade from shooting 'Awkins and Belcher sent a cold sweat out through me. Because there were men on the Brigade you daren't let nor hinder without a gun in your hand, and at any rate, in those days disunion between brothers seemed to me an awful crime. I knew better after.

It was next morning we found it so hard to face Belcher and 'Awkins with a smile. We went about the house all day scarcely saying a word. Belcher didn't mind us much; he was stretched into the ashes as usual with his usual look of waiting in quietness for something unforeseen to happen, but little 'Awkins gave us a bad time with his audacious gibing and questioning. He was disgusted at Noble's not answering him back. "Why can't you tike your beating like a man, chum?" he says. "You with your Hadam and Heve! I'm a Communist—or an Anarchist. An Anarchist, that's what I am." And for hours after he went round the house, mumbling when the fit took him "Hadam and Heve! Hadam and Heve!"

I don't know clearly how we got over that day, but get over it we did, and a great relief it was when the tea things were cleared away and Belcher said in his peaceable manner, "Well, chums, what about it?" So we all sat round the table and 'Awkins produced the cards, and at that moment I heard Jeremiah Donovan's footsteps up the path, and a dark presentiment crossed my mind. I rose quietly from the table and laid my hand on him before he reached the door. "What do you want?" I asked him. "I want those two soldier friends of yours," he says reddening. "Is that the way it is, Jeremiah Donovan?" I ask. "That's the way. There were four of our

lads went west this morning, one of them a boy of sixteen."
"That's bad, Jeremiah," says I.

At that moment Noble came out, and we walked down   22
the path together talking in whispers. Feeney, the local intelligence officer, was standing by the gate. "What are you going
to do about it?" I asked Jeremiah Donovan. "I want you and
Noble to bring them out: you can tell them they're being
shifted again; that'll be the quietest way." "Leave me out of
that," says Noble suddenly. Jeremiah Donovan looked at him
hard for a minute or two. "All right so," he said peaceably.
"You and Feeney collect a few tools from the shed and dig a
hole by the far end of the bog. Bonaparte and I'll be after
you in about twenty minutes. But whatever else you do, don't
let anyone see you with the tools. No one must know but
the four of ourselves."

We saw Feeney and Noble go round to the houseen where   23
the tools were kept, and sidled in. Everything if I can so
express myself was tottering before my eyes, and I left Jeremiah Donovan to do the explaining as best he could, while
I took a seat and said nothing. He told them they were to
go back to the Second. 'Awkins let a mouthful of curses out
of him at that, and it was plain that Belcher, though he said
nothing, was duly perturbed. The old woman was for having
them stay in spite of us, and she did not shut her mouth until
Jeremiah Donovan lost his temper and said some nasty things
to her. Within the house by this time it was pitch dark, but
no one thought of lighting the lamp, and in the darkness the
two Englishmen fetched their khaki top-coats and said good-
bye to the woman of the house. "Just as a man mikes a 'ome
of a bleedin' place," mumbles 'Awkins, shaking her by the
hand, "some bastard at Headquarters thinks you're too cushy
and shunts you off." Belcher shakes her hand very hearty. "A
thousand thanks, madam," he says, "a thousand thanks for
everything . . ." as though he'd made it all up.

We go round to the back of the house and down towards   24
the fatal bog. Then Jeremiah Donovan comes out with what
is in his mind. "There were four of our lads shot by your
fellows this morning so now you're to be bumped off." "Cut

that stuff out," says 'Awkins, flaring up. "It's bad enough to be mucked about such as we are without you plying at soldiers." "It's true," says Jeremiah Donovan, "I'm sorry, 'Awkins, but 'tis true," and comes out with the usual rigmarole about doing our duty and obeying our superiors. "Cut it out," says 'Awkins irritably. "Cut it out!"

Then, when Donovan sees he is not being believed he 25 turns to me, "Ask Bonaparte here," he says. "I don't need to arsk Bonaparte. Me and Bonaparte are chums." "Isn't it true, Bonaparte?" says Jeremiah Donovan solemnly to me. "It is," I say sadly, "it is." 'Awkins stops. "Now, for Christ's sike. . . ." "I mean it, chum," I say. "You daon't saound as if you mean it. You knaow well you don't mean it." "Well, if he don't I do," says Jeremiah Donovan. "Why the 'ell sh'd you want to shoot me, Jeremiah Donovan?" "Why the hell should your people take out four prisoners and shoot them in cold blood upon a barrack square?" I perceive Jeremiah Donovan is trying to encourage himself with hot words.

Anyway, he took little 'Awkins by the arm and dragged 26 him on, but it was impossible to make him understand that we were in earnest. From which you will perceive how difficult it was for me, as I kept feeling my Smith and Wesson and thinking what I would do if they happened to put up a fight or ran for it, and wishing in my heart they would. I knew if only they ran I would never fire on them. "Was Noble in this?" 'Awkins wanted to know, and we said yes. He laughed. But why should Noble want to shoot him? Why should we want to shoot him? What had he done to us? Weren't we chums (the word lingers painfully in my memory)? Weren't we? Didn't we understand him and didn't he understand us? Did either of us imagine for an instant that he'd shoot us for all the so-and-so brigadiers in the so-and-so British Army? By this time I began to perceive in the dusk the desolate edges of the bog that was to be their last earthly bed, and, so great a sadness overtook my mind, I could not answer him. We walked along the edge of it in the darkness, and every now and then 'Awkins would call a halt and begin again, just as if he was wound up, about us being chums, and I was in despair that nothing but the cold and open grave made ready for his presence would convince him that we meant it all. But all the same, if you can understand, I didn't want him to be bumped off.

At last we saw the unsteady glint of a lantern in the distance   27
and made towards it. Noble was carrying it, and Feeney stood somewhere in the darkness behind, and somehow the picture of the two of them so silent in the boglands was like the pain of death in my heart. Belcher, on recognizing Noble, said "'Allo, chum" in his usual peaceable way, but 'Awkins flew at the poor boy immediately, and the dispute began all over again, only that Noble hadn't a word to say for himself, and stood there with the swaying lantern between his gaitered legs.

It was Jeremiah Donovan who did the answering. 'Awkins   28
asked for the twentieth time (for it seemed to haunt his mind) if anybody thought he'd shoot Noble. "You would," says Jeremiah Donovan shortly. "I wouldn't, damn you!" "You would if you knew you'd be shot for not doing it." "I wouldn't, not if I was to be shot twenty times over; he's my chum. And Belcher wouldn't—isn't that right, Belcher?" "That's right, chum," says Belcher peaceably. "Damned if I would. Anyway, who says Noble'd be shot if I wasn't bumped off? What d'you think I'd do if I was in Noble's place and we were out in the middle of a blasted bog?" "What would you do?" "I'd go with him wherever he was going. I'd share my last bob with him and stick by 'im through thick and thin."

"We've had enough of this," says Jeremiah Donovan,   29
cocking his revolver. "Is there any message you want to send before I fire?" "No, there isn't, but . . ." "Do you want to say your prayers?" 'Awkins came out with a cold-blooded remark that shocked even me and turned to Noble again. "Listen to me, Noble," he said. "You and me are chums. You won't come over to my side, so I'll come over to your side. Is that fair? Just you give me a rifle and I'll go with you wherever you want."

Nobody answered him.   30

"Do you understand?" he said. "I'm through with it all.   31
I'm a deserter or anything else you like, but from this on I'm
one of you. Does that prove to you that I mean what I say?"
Noble raised his head, but as Donovan began to speak he
lowered it again without answering. "For the last time have
you any messages to send?" says Donovan in a cold and
excited voice.

"Ah, shut up, you, Donovan; you don't understand me,   32
but these fellows do. They're my chums; they stand by me
and I stand by them. We're not the capitalist tools you seem
to think us."

I alone of the crowd saw Donovan raise his Webley to the   33
back of 'Awkins's neck, and as he did so I shut my eyes and
tried to say a prayer. 'Awkins had begun to say something
else when Donovan let fly, and, as I opened my eyes at the
bang, I saw him stagger at the knees and lie out flat at Noble's
feet, slowly, and as quiet as a child, with the lantern light
falling sadly upon his lean legs and bright farmer's boots. We
all stood very still for a while watching him settle out in the
last agony.

Then Belcher quietly takes out a handkerchief, and begins   34
to tie it about his own eyes (for in our excitement we had
forgotten to offer the same to 'Awkins), and, seeing it is not
big enough, turns and asks for a loan of mine. I give it to
him and as he knots the two together he points with his foot
at 'Awkins. "'E's not quite dead," he says, "better give 'im
another." Sure enough 'Awkins's left knee as we see it under
the lantern is rising again. I bend down and put my gun to
his ear; then, recollecting myself and the company of Belcher,
I stand up again with a few hasty words. Belcher understands
what is in my mind. "Give 'im 'is first," he says. "I don't
mind. Poor bastard, we dunno what's 'appening to 'im now."
As by this time I am beyond all feeling I kneel down and
skilfully give 'Awkins the last shot so as to put him forever
out of pain.

Belcher who is fumbling a bit awkwardly with the hand-   35
kerchiefs comes out with a laugh when he hears the shot. It

is the first time I have heard him laugh, and it sends a shiver down my spine, coming as it does so inappropriately upon the tragic death of his old friend. "Poor blighter," he says quietly, "and last night he was so curious abaout it all. It's very queer, chums, I always think. Naow, 'e knows as much abaout it as they'll ever let 'im know, and last night 'e was all in the dark."

Donovan helps him tie the handkerchiefs about his eyes. 36 "Thanks, chum," he says. Donovan asks him if there are any messages he would like to send. "Naow, chum," he says, "none for me. If any of you likes to write to 'Awkins's mother you'll find a letter from 'er in 'is pocket. But my missus left me eight years ago. Went away with another fellow and took the kid with her. I likes the feelin' of a 'ome (as you may 'ave noticed) but I couldn't start again after that."

We stand around like fools now that he can no longer see 37 us. Donovan looks at Noble and Noble shakes his head. Then Donovan raises his Webley again and just at that moment Belcher laughs his queer nervous laugh again. He must think we are talking of him; anyway, Donovan lowers his gun. "'Scuse me, chums," says Belcher, "I feel I'm talking the 'ell of a lot . . . and so silly . . . abaout me being so 'andy abaout a 'ouse. But this thing come on me so sudden. You'll forgive me, I'm sure." "You don't want to say a prayer?" asks Jeremiah Donovan. "No, chum," he replies, "I don't think that'd 'elp. I'm ready if you want to get it over." "You understand," says Jeremiah Donovan, "it's not so much our doing. It's our duty, so to speak." Belcher's head is raised like a real blind man's, so that you can only see his nose and chin in the lamplight. "I never could make out what duty was myself," he said, "but I think you're all good lads, if that's what you mean. I'm not complaining." Noble, with a look of desperation, signals to Donovan, and in a flash Donovan raises his gun and fires. The big man goes over like a sack of meal, and this time there is no need of a second shot.

I don't remember much about the burying, but that it was 38 worse than all the rest, because we had to carry the warm corpses a few yards before we sunk them in the windy bog.

It was all mad lonely, with only a bit of lantern between ourselves and the pitch blackness, and birds hooting and screeching all round disturbed by the guns. Noble had to search 'Awkins first to get the letter from his mother. Then having smoothed all signs of the grave away, Noble and I collected our tools, said good-bye to the others, and went back along the desolate edge of the treacherous bog without a word. We put the tools in the houseen and went into the house. The kitchen was pitch black and cold, just as we left it, and the old woman was sitting over the hearth telling her beads. We walked past her into the room, and Noble struck a match to light the lamp. Just then she rose quietly and came to the doorway, being not at all so bold or crabbed as usual.

"What did ye do with them?" she says in a sort of whisper, and Noble took such a mortal start the match quenched in his trembling hand. "What's that?" he asks without turning round. "I heard ye," she said. "What did you hear?" asks Noble, but sure he wouldn't deceive a child the way he said it. "I heard ye. Do you think I wasn't listening to ye putting the things back in the houseen?" Noble struck another match and this time the lamp lit for him. "Was that what ye did with them?" she said, and Noble said nothing—after all what could he say?

So then, by God, she fell on her two knees by the door, and began telling her beads, and after a minute or two Noble went on his knees by the fireplace, so I pushed my way out past her, and stood at the door, watching the stars and listening to the damned shrieking of the birds. It is so strange what you feel at such moments, and not to be written afterwards. Noble says he felt he seen everything ten times as big, perceiving nothing around him but the little patch of black bog with the two Englishmen stiffening into it; but with me it was the other way, as though the patch of bog where the two Englishmen were was a thousand miles away from me, and even Noble mumbling just behind me and the old woman and the birds and the bloody stars were all far away, and I was somehow very small and very lonely. And anything that ever happened to me after I never felt the same about again.

COMMENT ON
"GUESTS OF THE NATION"

The setting for Frank O'Connor's "Guests of the Nation" is the Anglo-Irish war, in which the Irish fought for independence in 1919–1921. Two Englishmen, Belcher and Hawkins, are held hostages by the Irish, but an amiable relationship develops among them suggesting that they are more "chums" than enemies. But one of the Irishmen, Donovan, learns that several Irish hostages have been killed by the English. He therefore insists that the Englishmen be killed in relatiation. As the execution is carried out in a dreary bog, the story raises all sorts of comparisons—i.e., how would you compare a guest and a hostage, a home and a nation, loyalty to friends and duty to a cause?

Comparison and Contrast as a Writing Strategy

1. Select a place in your childhood neighborhood—perhaps a garden, a playground, or a movie theater. Then, in an essay addressed to your writing class, write a short comparison of the way the place used to be and the way it is now. Consider the example of Mark Twain's "Two Views of the River" as you compare your childhood and adult visions. Consider also what you have learned about the place or about yourself by making the comparison. That lesson should help control your decisions about purpose and audience.

2. Select two people who embody odd characteristics—athletes, musicians, movie stars. Then, like Pico Iyer, compare and contrast their strengths and weaknesses. Include information on how they might see each other. Cite biographical information that accounts for their similarities and differences.

3. Conduct some research on the conversational patterns in your home (or dormitory) and in your classroom. Keep track of who talks, what they talk about, and how they use conversation—for example, to make friends, to report information, to win approval. Keep track of who doesn't talk and in what situations they are likely to stay silent. Then write an essay in which you compare the patterns of home and school conversation.

4. In "Nature and Televised Nature" Bill McKibben contrasts what he learned from observing the world firsthand and from watching it on television. Select a subject you know well—your job, your hometown, your favorite sport or hobby—and then compare your firsthand experience with the subject with the way it is represented on television.

5. Write an essay comparing the way two magazines or newspapers cover the same story. You could select magazines that have opposing political philosophies or newspapers that are published in different parts of the country. For

example, compare American and Palestinian statements on terrorism, American and Korean views on economic aid, or American and Mexican policies on immigration.

6. Compare and contrast arguments on both sides of a controversial issue such as welfare reform or gun control. Such issues produce controversy because there are legitimate arguments on each side. They also produce controversy because people can simplify them in slogans (Reading is good; television is bad). Select two slogans that present the opposing sides of the controversy you are writing about. Compare and contrast the assumptions, evidence, and logic of both slogans. Like Deborah Tannen, avoid choosing sides. Maintain a neutral tone as you assess the motives, methods, and reasons for each argument.

DIVISION
AND
CLASSIFICATION

࿏

Division and **classification** are mental processes that often work together. When you *divide,* you separate something (a college, a city) into sections (departments, neighborhoods). When you *classify,* you place examples of something (restaurants, jobs) into categories or classes (restaurants: moderately expensive, very expensive; jobs: unskilled, semiskilled, and skilled).

When you divide, you move downward from a concept to the subunits of that concept. When you classify, you move upward from specific examples to classes or categories that share a common characteristic. For example, you could *divide* a television news program into subunits such as news, features, editorials, sports, and weather. And you could *classify*

some element of that program—such as the editorial commentator on the six o'clock news—according to his or her
style, knowledge, and trustworthiness. You can use either
division or classification singly, depending on your purpose,
but most of the time you will probably use them together
when you are writing a classification essay. First you might
identify the subunits in a college sports program—football,
basketball, hockey, volleyball, tennis; then you could classify
them according to their budgets—most money budgeted for
football, the least budgeted for volleyball.

PURPOSE

When you write a classification essay, your chief purpose is to
explain. You might want to explain an established method for
organizing information, such as the Library of Congress system, or a new plan for arranging data such as the Internal
Revenue Service's latest schedule for itemizing tax deduc-
tions. On one level, your purpose in such an essay is simply
to show how the system works. At a deeper level, your purpose is to define, analyze, and justify the organizing principle
that underlies the system.

You can also write a classification essay to *entertain* or to
persuade. If you classify to entertain, you have an opportunity
to be clever and witty. If you classify to persuade, you have a
chance to be cogent and forceful. If you want to entertain,
you might concoct an elaborate scheme for classifying fools,
pointing out the distinguishing features of each category and
giving particularly striking examples of each type. But if you
want to persuade, you could explain how some new or controversial plan, such as the metric system or congressional
redistricting, is organized, pointing out how the schemes use
new principles to identify and organize information. Again,
although you may give your readers a great deal of information in such an essay, your main purpose is to persuade them
that the new plan is better than the old one.

AUDIENCE

As with any writing assignment, when you write a classification essay, you need to think carefully about what your readers already know and what they need to get from your writing. If you're writing on a new topic (social patterns in a primitive society) or if you're explaining a specialized system of classification (the botanist's procedure for identifying plants), your readers need precise definitions and plenty of illustrations for each subcategory. If your readers already know about your subject and the system it uses for classification (the movies' G, PG, PG–13, R, and NC–17 rating codes), then you don't need to give them an extensive demonstration. In that kind of writing situation, you might want to sketch the system briefly to refresh your readers' memories but then move on, using examples of specific movies to analyze whether the system really works.

You also need to think about how your readers might use the classification system that you explain in your essay. If you're classifying rock musicians, your readers are probably going to regard the system you create as something self-enclosed—interesting and amusing, perhaps something to quibble about, but not something they're likely to use in their everyday lives. On the other hand, if you write an essay classifying stereo equipment, your readers may want to use your system when they shop. For the first audience, you can use an informal approach to classification, dividing your subject into interesting subcategories and illustrating them with vivid examples. For the other audience, you need to be careful and strict in your approach, making sure you divide your topic into all its possible classes and illustrating each class with concrete examples.

STRATEGIES

When you write a classification essay, your basic strategy for organization should be to *divide your subject* into major categories that exhibit a common trait, then subdivide those categories into smaller units. Next, *arrange your categories* into a sequence that shows a logical or a dramatic progression. Finally, *define each of your categories.* First, show how each category is different from the others; then discuss its most vivid examples.

To make this strategy succeed, you must be sure that your classification system is *consistent, complete, emphatic,* and *significant.* Here is a method for achieving this goal. First, when you divide your subject into categories, *apply the same principle of selection to each class.* You may find this hard to do if you're trying to explain a system that someone else has already established but that is actually inconsistent. You have undoubtedly discovered that record stores use overlapping and inconsistent categories. Linda Ronstadt albums, for example, may be found in sections labeled *country, rock, pop, standards,* and *female vocal.* You can avoid such tangles if you create and control your own classification system.

For instance, in "The Extendable Fork" Calvin Trillin classifies eaters by how they eat off other people's plates. James Austin follows a similar strategy when he classifies "four kinds of chance." By contrast, the other three writers in this section explain existing systems of classification. In "Shades of Black" Mary Mebane classifies the arbitrary and unfair assessment of students by color and class. In "The Technology of Medicine," Lewis Thomas classifies medical technologies by their cost effectiveness. And Gail Sheehy classifies human development in terms of "predictable crises of adulthood."

After you have divided your subject into separate and consistent categories, *make sure your division is complete.* The simplest kind of division separates a subject into two categories: A and Not-A (for example, conformists and nonconformists). This kind of division, however, is rarely encouraged. It allows you to tell your readers about category A (conformists), but you won't tell them much about Not-A (nonconformists). For this reason, you should try to "exhaust" your subject by finding at least three separate categories and by acknowledging any examples that don't fit into the system. When an author writes a formal classification essay, like Sheehy's in this section, he or she tries to be definitive—to include everything significant. Even when an author is writing less formal classification essays, such as Trillin's, he or she tries to set up a reasonably complete system.

Once you have completed your process of division, *arrange your categories and examples in an emphatic order.* Thomas arranges his categories of medical technology from least effective to most effective. Sheehy arranges her categories of human development chronologically, from the rebellion of eighteen-year-olds to the mellowing of fifty-year-olds. Austin arranges his classification of chance from blind luck to personal sensibility. Mebane arranges her categories into increasingly subtle codes of class and color. The authors of these essays reveal the principal purpose underlying their classification schemes: to show variety in similarity, to point out how concepts change, and to challenge the arbitrariness of an established system.

Finally, *you need to show the significance of your system of classification.* The strength of the classification process is that you can use it to analyze a subject in any number of ways. Its weakness is that you can use it to subdivide a subject into all kinds of trivial or pointless categories. You can classify people by their educational backgrounds, their work experience, or their significant achievements. You can also classify them by their shoe size, the kind of socks they wear, or their tastes in ice cream. Notice that when Mary Mebane explains her classification system, she questions the social and psychological impact it has on self-esteem. Even a writer who chooses a subject that doesn't seem particularly significant—such as Calvin Trillin's eaters—must convince readers that his or her *system* counts in some way, if only because it lays out and demonstrates, consistently and completely, the significant subdivisions of the subject.

USING DIVISION AND CLASSIFICATION IN PARAGRAPHS

Here are two division-and-classification paragraphs. The first is written by a professional writer and is followed by an analysis. The second is written by a student writer and is followed by questions.

WENDELL BERRY
"Conservation Is Good Work"

Divides conservation into three categories: 1. <u>preservation of wild</u> or"scenic" 2. <u>conservation of natural resources</u> 3. <u>limit, stop,</u> or <u>remedy</u> abuses Concludes that all three are inadequate.	There are, as nearly as I can make out, three kinds of conservation currently operating. The first is the preservation of places that are grandly wild or "scenic" or in some other way spectacular. The second is what is called "conservation of natural resources"—That is, of the things of nature that we intend to use: soil, water, timber, and minerals. The third is what you might call industrial troubleshooting: the attempt to limit or stop or remedy the most flagrant abuses of the industrial system. All three kinds of conservation are inadequate, both separately and together.

Comment In this paragraph, Wendell Berry points out the "three kinds of conservation currently operating" in our culture. As his last sentence suggests, Berry's purpose for establishing these categories is to demonstrate—in subsequent paragraphs—why they are "inadequate, both separately and together."

GARETH TUCKER
"Gentlemen! Start Your Engines"

On a typical weekend, most couch potatoes can channel-surf past about a dozen car races. As they watch brightly colored machines circling the track again and again, like images on some manic video game, they may conclude that a race is a race is a race. Actually automobile racing is divided into many subtle subcategories. For example, the three most popular forms can be identified by the image of the car and driver. Stock cars are perceived as souped-up versions of "stock" cars driven by "good ole boys" who talk as if they have just outrun the local police. Indy cars are perceived as masterpieces of engineering driven by "test pilots" who speak the technobabble of rocket scientists. Formula One cars are almost as technologically advanced as Indy cars, but they still retain the image of the European "Grand Prix" car—the sports car driven by some count who talks as if he's just finished a jolly little tour through the countryside.

1. What principle does Tucker use to establish his three categories?
2. How does his characterization of the race car driver help clarify each category?

DIVISION AND CLASSIFICATION

Points to Remember

1. Determine whether you want to (a) explain an existing system of classification or (b) create your own system.
2. Divide your subject into smaller categories by applying the same principle of selection to each category.
3. Make sure that your division is complete by establishing separate and consistent types of categories.
4. Arrange your categories (and the examples you use to illustrate each category) in a logical and emphatic sequence.
5. Demonstrate the significance of your system by calling your readers' attention to its significance.

Calvin Trillin was born in Kansas City, Missouri, in 1935 and was educated at Yale University. He began his career by working as a reporter for *Time* magazine, then as a columnist for *The New Yorker*. In recent years, he has written a national newspaper column and staged a one-man show off-Broadway. His writing includes two novels, *Runestruck* (1977) and *Floater* (1980); several collections of reporting, *U.S. Journal* (1971), *Killings* (1982), and *American Stories* (1991); a best selling memoir, *Remembering Denny* (1993); and numerous books of humor. In "The Extendable Fork," reprinted from his syndicated column, Trillin classifies eaters by how they eat off other people's plates.

The Extendable Fork

IN OUR HOUSE, news that the extendable fork had been invented was greeted with varying degrees of enthusiasm. I think it's fair to say that I was the most enthusiastic of all. I eat off of other people's plates. My wife was mildly enthusiastic. She figures that if I use an extendable fork I'm less likely to come away from the table with gravy on my cuff. 1

People who eat off of other people's plates can be categorized in four types—The Finisher, The Waif, The Researcher and The Simple Thief. I might as well admit right here at the beginning that I am all four. 2

The Finisher demonstrates concern that food may be left uneaten even though the starving children your mother told you about are still hungry. Once the pace of eating begins to slacken off a bit, he reaches across to spear a roast potato off 3 of someone's plate a nanosecond after saying, "If you're not planning to finish these . . ."

The long-reach eater I think of as The Waif often doesn't 4
order much himself at a restaurant, claiming that he's not terribly hungry or that he's trying to lose weight. Then, he gazes at his dinner companions' plates, like a hungry urchin who has his nose pressed up against the window of a restaurant where enormously fat rich people are slurping oysters and shoveling down mounds of boeuf bourguignon. Occasionally, he murmurs something like, "That looks delicious." Answering "Actually, it's not all that good" does not affect

---

People who eat off other people's plates come in four categories: The Finisher, The Waif, The Researcher, and The Simple Thief.

---

him—although it may slow down the Researcher, who, as he extends his fork usually says something like, "I'm curious how they do these fried onions."

The Simple Thief simply waits for his dining companions 5
to glance away, then confidently grabs what he wants. If he's desperate, he may actually take measures to distract them, saying something like, "Is it my imagination, or could that be Michael Jackson and Lisa Marie Presley at the table over by the door?"

That sort of subterfuge is not necessary, by the way, if the 6
plate I have singled out as a target is my wife's. She does not object to my sampling—a reflection, I've always thought, of her generous heart. In fact, I have said in the past that if a young groom on his honeymoon reaches over for the first time to sample his bride's fettuccine only to be told "Don't you like what you're having?" or "There really isn't that much of this," he knows he's in for a long haul.

Actually, my wife might be called a Finisher herself. If 7

we're having fried chicken, she will stare at what's on my plate after I have indeed finished. "Look at all the chicken you left," she'll say. Or "There's a ton of meat still on that chicken."

Oddly enough, this is precisely the sort of thing that I 8
heard from my mother, who was also fond of saying that I didn't "do a good job" on the chicken. The way my wife eats chicken is to eat every speck of meat off the bones, so that the chicken looks as if it had been staked out on an anthill by a tribe of crazed chicken torturers. She treats a lobster the same way.

I eat more the way a shark eats—tearing off whatever 9
seems exposed and easy to get at. I have suggested, in fact, that in fried-chicken or lobster restaurants we could economize by getting only one order, which I could start and my wife could finish.

My wife's approach to finishing does not, of course, re- 10
quire an extendable fork, but I intend to be an early customer myself. According to an item in the *New York Times,* the fork is nearly two feet long when fully opened. It's being marketed under the name of Alan's X-Tenda Fork.

I might have chosen another name, but this one is, 11
I'll admit, evocative. For me, it conjures up visions of a Limbaugh-sized man named Alan sitting in a restaurant with friends and family. He seems to be engaging in normal conversation, but his tiny eyes dart from plate to plate; occasionally, with a fork as quick as the strike of an adder, he helps with the finishing.

In fact, I can imagine Alan inventing other needed imple- 12
ments—a sort of vacuum tube, for instance, that can suck up french fries from three feet away. I can see him improving on Alan's X-Tenda Fork. He might install a tiny tape recorder in it, so when you pulled it out to its full length and moved it quickly across the table a voice said, "If you're not planning to finish these . . ."

For Study and Discussion

QUESTIONS FOR RESPONSE

1. How do you respond when someone eats off your plate?
2. What explanations do you offer when you want to sample something from someone else's plate?

QUESTIONS ABOUT PURPOSE

1. How does Trillin use the news of the invention of the "extendable fork" to justify his classification of eaters?
2. What purpose does Trillin accomplish by admitting that he fits into all four categories?

QUESTIONS ABOUT AUDIENCE

1. What assumptions does Trillin make about the eating habits of his readers?
2. How do his comments about his wife's and mother's behavior clarify his attitude toward his readers?

QUESTIONS ABOUT STRATEGIES

1. What principle does Trillin use to divide and identify his four types of eaters?
2. How does he use dialogue to illustrate the strategies of each eater?

QUESTIONS FOR DISCUSSION

1. What do books of etiquette say about the practice of eating from another's plate?
2. How does the concept of *finishing* fit into our cultural attitudes toward efficiency and economy?

JAMES H. AUSTIN

James H. Austin was born in 1925 in Cleveland,
Ohio, and educated at Brown University and Harvard University Medical School. After an intern-
ship at Boston City Hospital and a residency at the
Neurological Institute of New York, Austin established a private practice in neurology, first in Port-
land, Oregon, and then in Denver, Colorado. He
currently serves as professor and head of the department of neurology at the University of Colorado Medical School. His major publication,
*Chase, Chance, and Creativity: The Lucky Art of
Novelty* (1978), addresses the issue of how
"chance and creativity interact in biomedical research." In this essay, published originally in *Saturday Review*, Austin distinguishes four kinds of
chance by the way humans react to their environment.

Four Kinds of Chance

W HAT IS CHANCE? Dictionaries define it as something 1
fortuitous that happens unpredictably without discernible human intention. Chance is unintentional and capri-
cious, but we needn't conclude that chance is immune from
human intervention. Indeed, chance plays several distinct
roles when humans react creatively with one another and with
their environment.

We can readily distinguish four varieties of chance if we 2
consider that they each involve a different kind of motor
activity and a special kind of sensory receptivity. The varieties
of chance also involve distinctive personality traits and differ
in the way one particular individual influences them.

Chance I is the pure blind luck that comes with no effort 3

240

on your part. If, for example, you are sitting at a bridge table of four, it's "in the cards" for you to receive a hand of all 13 spades, but it will come up only once in every 6.3 trillion deals. You will ultimately draw this lucky hand—with no intervention on your part—but it does involve a longer wait than most of us have time for.

Chance II evokes the kind of luck Charles Kettering had in mind when he said: "Keep on going and the chances are you will stumble on something, perhaps when you are least expecting it. I have never heard of anyone stumbling on something sitting down."

In the sense referred to here, Chance II is not passive, but springs from an energetic, generalized motor activity. A cer-

> *The term* serendipity *describes the facility for encountering unexpected good luck as the result of accident, general exploratory behavior, or sagacity.*

tain basal level of action "stirs up the pot," brings in random ideas that will collide and stick together in fresh combinations, lets chance operate. When someone, *anyone,* does swing into motion and keeps on going, he will increase the number of collisions between events. When a few events are linked together, they can then be exploited to have a fortuitous outcome, but many others, of course, cannot. Kettering was right. Press on. Something will turn up. We may term this the Kettering Principle.

In the two previous examples, a unique role of the individual person was either lacking or minimal. Accordingly, as we move on to Chance III, we see blind luck, but in camouflage. Chance presents the clue, the opportunity exists, but it would be missed except by that one person uniquely equipped to observe it, visualize it conceptually, and fully grasp its significance. Chance III involves a special receptivity and discernment unique to the recipient. Louis Pasteur characterized it for all time when he said: "Chance favors only the prepared mind."

Pasteur himself had it in full measure. But the classic example of his principle occurred in 1928, when Alexander Fleming's mind instantly fused at least five elements into a conceptually unified nexus. His mental sequences went something like this: (1) I see that a mold has fallen by accident into my culture dish; (2) the staphylococcal colonies residing near it failed to grow; (3) the mold must have secreted something that killed the bacteria; (4) I recall a similar experience once before; (5) if I could separate this new "something" from the mold, it could be used to kill staphylococci that cause human infections.

Actually, Fleming's mind was exceptionally well prepared for the penicillin mold. Six years earlier, while he was suffering from a cold, his own nasal drippings had found their way into a culture dish, for reasons not made entirely clear. He noted that nearby bacteria were killed, and astutely followed up the lead. His observations led him to discover a bactericidal enzyme present in nasal mucus and tears, called lysozyme. Lysozyme proved too weak to be of medical use, but imagine how receptive Fleming's mind was to the penicillin mold when it later happened on the scene!

One word evokes the quality of the operations involved in the first three kinds of chance. It is *serendipity*. The term describes the facility for encountering unexpected good luck, as the result of: accident (Chance I), general exploratory behavior (Chance II), or sagacity (Chance III). The word itself was coined by the Englishman-of-letters Horace Walpole, in 1754. He used it with reference to the legendary tales of the Three Princes of Serendip (Ceylon), who quite unexpectedly encountered many instances of good fortune on their travels. In today's parlance, we have usually watered down *serendipity* to mean the good luck that comes solely by accident. We think of it as a result, not an ability. We have tended to lose sight of the element of sagacity, by which term

Walpole wished to emphasize that some distinctive personal receptivity is involved.

There remains a fourth element in good luck, an unintentional but subtle personal prompting of it. The English Prime Minister Benjamin Disraeli summed up the principle underlying Chance IV when he noted that "we make our fortunes and we call them fate." Disraeli, a politician of considerable practical experience, appreciated that we each shape our own destiny, at least to some degree. One might restate the principle as follows: *Chance favors the individualized action.* 10

In Chance IV the kind of luck is peculiar to one person, and like a personal hobby, it takes on a distinctive individual flavor. This form of chance is one-man-made, and it is as personal as a signature. . . . Chance IV has an elusive, almost miragelike, quality. Like a mirage, it is difficult to get a firm grip on, for it tends to recede as we pursue it and advance as we step back. But we still accept a mirage when we see it, because we vaguely understand the basis for the phenomenon. A strongly heated layer of air, less dense than usual, lies next to the earth, and it bends the light rays as they pass through. The resulting image may be magnified as if by a telescopic lens in the atmosphere, and real objects, ordinarily hidden far out of sight over the horizon, are brought forward and revealed to the eye. What happens in a mirage then, and in this form of chance, not only appears farfetched but indeed is farfetched. 11

About a century ago, a striking example of Chance IV took place in the Spanish cave of Altamira.* There, one day in 1879, Don Marcelino de Sautuola was engaged in his hobby of archaeology, searching Altamira for bones and stones. With him was his daughter, Maria, who had asked him if she could come along to the cave that day. The indulgent father had said she could. Naturally enough, he first looked where he had always found heavy objects before, on the *floor* of the cave. But Maria, unhampered by any such preconceptions, 12

*The cave had first been discovered some years before by an enterprising hunting dog in search of game. Curiously, in 1932 the French cave of Lascaux was discovered by still another dog.

looked not only at the floor but also all around the cave with the open-eyed wonder of a child! She looked up, exclaimed, and then he looked up, to see incredible works of art on the cave ceiling! The magnificent colored bison and other animals they saw at Altamira, painted more than 15,000 years ago, might lead one to call it "the Sistine Chapel of Prehistory." Passionately pursuing his interest in archaeology, de Sautuola, to his surprise, discovered man's first paintings. In quest of science, he happened upon Art.

Yes, a dog did "discover" the cave, and the initial recep- 13 tivity was his daughter's, but the pivotal reason for the cave paintings' discovery hinged on a long sequence of prior events originating in de Sautuola himself. For when we dig into the background of this amateur excavator, we find he was an exceptional person. Few Spaniards were out probing into caves 100 years ago. The fact that he—not someone else—decided to dig that day in the cave of Altamira was the culmination of his passionate interest in his hobby. Here was a rare man whose avocation had been to educate himself from scratch, as it were, in the science of archaeology and cave exploration. This was no simple passive recognizer of blind luck when it came his way, but a man whose unique interests served as an active creative thrust—someone whose own actions and personality would focus the events that led circuitously but inexorably to the discovery of man's first paintings.

Then, too, there is a more subtle matter. How do you give 14 full weight to the personal interests that imbue your child with your own curiosity, that inspire her to ask to join you in your own musty hobby, and that then lead you to agree to her request at the critical moment? For many reasons, at Altamira, more than the special receptivity of Chance III was required—this was a different domain, that of the personality and its actions.

A century ago no one had the remotest idea our caveman 15 ancestors were highly creative artists. Weren't their talents rather minor and limited to crude flint chippings? But the paintings at Altamira, like a mirage, would quickly magnify this diminutive view, bring up into full focus a distant, hidden era of man's prehistory, reveal sentient minds and well-developed aesthetic sensibilities to which men of any age might aspire. And like a mirage, the events at Altamira grew out of de Sautuola's heated personal quest and out of the invisible forces of chance we know exist yet cannot touch. Accordingly, one may introduce the term *altamirage* to identify the quality underlying Chance IV. Let us define it as the facility for encountering unexpected good luck as the result of highly individualized action. *Altamirage* goes well beyond the boundaries of serendipity in its emphasis on the role of personal action in chance.

Chance IV is favored by distinctive, if not eccentric, hobbies, personal life-styles, and modes of behavior peculiar to one individual, usually invested with some passion. The farther apart these personal activities are from the area under investigation, the more novel and unexpected will be the creative product of the encounter.

16

For Study and Discussion

QUESTIONS FOR RESPONSE

1. Would you consider yourself a lucky or an unlucky person? What evidence would you use to support your case?
2. Do you agree with Austin's assessment of the dictionary's definitions of the word *chance*? How would you define the word?

QUESTIONS ABOUT PURPOSE

1. What elements of human behavior and attitude does Austin demonstrate by dividing chance into four varieties?
2. What relationship does Austin discover between the words "luck," "serendipity," "sagacity," and "altamirage"?

QUESTIONS ABOUT AUDIENCE

1. What assumptions does Austin make about his readers when he offers them *the best example* rather than several examples to illustrate each category?
2. How does Austin's attitude toward his audience change during

the essay? For example, why does he speak directly to his readers when he explains Chance I but address them more formally in his discussion of other categories?

QUESTIONS ABOUT STRATEGIES

1. How does Austin arrange his four categories? Why doesn't he give equal treatment to each category?
2. How does Austin use transitions and summaries to clarify the differences between the major categories? In particular, see paragraphs 6 and 9.

QUESTIONS FOR DISCUSSION

1. What incidents in your personal experience would support Austin's classification system? How many examples can you cite in each category?
2. What do you think is the relationship between *ability* and *result*? For example, what is your opinion of Disraeli's assertion that "we make our fortunes and we call them fate"?

LEWIS THOMAS

Lewis Thomas (1913–1993) was born in Flushing, New York, and was educated at Princeton University and Harvard University Medical School. He held appointments at numerous research hospitals and medical schools before assuming his last position as president of the Sloan-Kettering Cancer Center in New York City. Thomas's early writing, on the subject of pathology, appeared in scientific journals. In 1971 he began contributing a popular column, "Notes of a Biology Watcher," to the *New England Journal of Medicine*. In 1974 his collection of these essays, *The Lives of a Cell: Notes of a Biology Watcher*, won the National Book Award for Arts and Letters. His other books include *The Medusa and the Snail: More Notes of a Biology Watcher* (1979), *The Youngest Science* (1983), *Late Night Thoughts on Listening to Mahler's Ninth Symphony* (1983), and *The Fragile Species* (1992). In "The Technology of Medicine," from *The Lives of a Cell*, Thomas classifies "three quite different levels of technology in medicine."

The Technology of Medicine

TECHNOLOGY ASSESSMENT HAS become a routine exercise 1
for the scientific enterprises on which the country is obliged to spend vast sums for its needs. Brainy committees are continually evaluating the effectiveness and cost of doing various things in space, defense, energy, transportation, and the like, to give advice about prudent investments for the future.

Somehow medicine, for all the $80-odd billion that it is   2
said to cost the nation, has not yet come in for much of this
analytical treatment. It seems taken for granted that the technology of medicine simply exists, take it or leave it, and the
only major technologic problem which policy-makers are interested in is how to deliver today's kind of health care, with
equity, to all the people.

When, as is bound to happen sooner or later, the analysts   3
get around to the technology of medicine itself, they will have
to face the problem of measuring the relative cost and effectiveness of all the things that are done in the management of
disease. They make their living at this kind of thing, and I

---

*There are three quite different levels of
technology in medicine, so unlike each other
as to seem altogether different undertakings.*

---

wish them well, but I imagine they will have a bewildering
time. For one thing, our methods of managing disease are
constantly changing—partly under the influence of new bits
of information brought in from all corners of biologic science. At the same time, a great many things are done that are
not so closely related to science, some not related at all.

In fact, there are three quite different levels of technology   4
in medicine, so unlike each other as to seem altogether different undertakings. Practitioners of medicine and the analysts will be in trouble if they are not kept separate.

1. First of all, there is a large body of what might be termed   5
"nontechnology," impossible to measure in terms of its capacity to alter either the natural course of disease or its even-
tual outcome. A great deal of money is spent on this. It is
valued highly by the professionals as well as the patients. It
consists of what is sometimes called "supportive therapy." It
tides patients over through diseases that are not, by and large,

understood. It is what is meant by the phrases "caring for" and "standing by." It is indispensable. It is not, however, a technology in any real sense, since it does not involve measures directed at the underlying mechanism of disease.

It includes the large part of any good doctor's time that is 6 taken up with simply providing reassurance, explaining to patients who fear that they have contracted one or another lethal disease that they are, in fact, quite healthy.

It is what physicians used to be engaged in at the bedside 7 of patients with diphtheria, meningitis, poliomyelitis, lobar pneumonia, and all the rest of the infectious diseases that have since come under control.

It is what physicians must now do for patients with intrac- 8 table cancer, severe rheumatoid arthritis, multiple sclerosis, stroke, and advanced cirrhosis. One can think of at least twenty major diseases that require this kind of supportive medical care because of the absence of an effective technology. I would include a large amount of what is called mental disease, and most varieties of cancer, in this category.

The cost of this nontechnology is very high, and getting 9 higher all the time. It requires not only a great deal of time but also very hard effort and skill on the part of physicians; only the very best of doctors are good at coping with this kind of defeat. It also involves long periods of hospitalization, lots of nursing, lots of involvement of nonmedical professionals in and out of the hospital. It represents, in short, a substantial segment of today's expenditures for health.

2. At the next level up is a kind of technology best termed 10 "halfway technology." This represents the kinds of things that must be done after the fact, in efforts to compensate for the incapacitating effects of certain diseases whose course one is unable to do very much about. It is a technology designed to make up for disease, or to postpone death.

The outstanding examples in recent years are the trans- 11 plantations of hearts, kidneys, livers, and other organs, and the equally spectacular inventions of artificial organs. In the public mind, this kind of technology has come to seem like the equivalent of the high technologies of the physical sciences. The media tend to present each new procedure as though it represented a breakthrough and therapeutic triumph, instead of the makeshift that it really is.

In fact, this level of technology is, by its nature, at the same time highly sophisticated and profoundly primitive. It is the kind of thing that one must continue to do until there is a genuine understanding of the mechanisms involved in disease. In chronic glomerulonephritis, for example, a much clearer insight will be needed into the events leading to the destruction of glomeruli by the immunologic reactants that now appear to govern this disease, before one will know how to intervene intelligently to prevent the process, or turn it around. But when this level of understanding has been reached, the technology of kidney replacement will not be much needed and should no longer pose the huge problem of logistics, cost, and ethics that it poses today.

An extremely complex and costly technology for the management of coronary heart disease has evolved—involving specialized ambulances and hospital units, all kinds of electronic gadgetry, and whole platoons of new professional personnel—to deal with the end results of coronary thrombosis. Almost everything offered today for the treatment of heart disease is at this level of technology, with the transplanted and artificial hearts as ultimate examples. When enough has been learned to know what really goes wrong in heart disease, one ought to be in a position to figure out ways to prevent or reverse the process, and when this happens the current elaborate technology will probably be set to one side.

Much of what is done in the treatment of cancer, by surgery, irradiation, and chemotherapy, represents halfway technology, in the sense that these measures are directed at the existence of already established cancer cells, but not at the mechanisms by which cells become neoplastic.

It is a characteristic of this kind of technology that it costs an enormous amount of money and requires a continuing expansion of hospital facilities. There is no end to the need for new, highly trained people to run the enterprise. And there is really no way out of this, at the present state of knowledge. If the installation of specialized coronary-care units can result in the extension of life for only a few patients with coronary disease (and there is no question that this technology is effective in a few cases), it seems to me an inevitable fact of life that as many of these as can be will be put together, and as much money as can be found will be spent. I do not see that anyone has much choice in this. The only thing that can move medicine away from this level of technology is new information, and the only imaginable source of this information is research.

3. The third type of technology is the kind that is so 16 effective that it seems to attract the least public notice; it has come to be taken for granted. This is the genuinely decisive technology of modern medicine, exemplified best by modern methods for immunization against diphtheria, pertussis, and the childhood virus diseases, and the contemporary use of antibiotics and chemotherapy for bacterial infections. The capacity to deal effectively with syphilis and tuberculosis represents a milestone in human endeavor, even though full use of this potential has not yet been made. And there are, of course, other examples: the treatment of endocrinologic disorders with appropriate hormones, the prevention of hemolytic disease of the newborn, the treatment and prevention of various nutritional disorders, and perhaps just around the corner the management of Parkinsonism and sickle-cell anemia. There are other examples, and everyone will have his favorite candidates for the list, but the truth is that there are nothing like as many as the public has been led to believe.

The point to be made about this kind of technology—the 17 real high technology of medicine—is that it comes as the result of a genuine understanding of disease mechanisms, and when it becomes available, it is relatively inexpensive, and relatively easy to deliver.

Offhand, I cannot think of any important human disease 18 for which medicine possesses the outright capacity to prevent or cure where the cost of the technology is itself a major problem. The price is never as high as the cost of managing the same diseases during the earlier stages of no-technology or halfway technology. If a case of typhoid fever had to be managed today by the best methods of 1935, it would run to a staggering expense. At, say, around fifty days of hospitalization, requiring the most demanding kind of nursing care, with the obsessive concern for details of diet that characterized the therapy of that time, with daily laboratory monitoring, and, on occasion, surgical intervention for abdominal catastrophe, I should think $10,000 would be a conservative estimate for the illness, as contrasted with today's cost of a bottle of chloramphenicol and a day or two of fever. The halfway technology that was evolving for poliomyelitis in the early 1950s, just before the emergence of the basic research that made the vaccine possible, provides another illustration of the point. Do you remember Sister Kenny, and the cost of those institutes for rehabilitation, with all those ceremonially applied hot fomentations, and the debates about whether the affected limbs should be totally immobilized or kept in passive motion as frequently as possible, and the masses of statistically tormented data mobilized to support one view or the other? It is the cost of that kind of technology, and its relative effectiveness, that must be compared with the cost and effectiveness of the vaccine.

Pulmonary tuberculosis had similar episodes in its history. 19 There was a sudden enthusiasm for the surgical removal of infected lung tissue in the early 1950s, and elaborate plans were being made for new and expensive installations for major pulmonary surgery in tuberculosis hospitals, and the INH and streptomycin came along and the hospitals themselves were closed up.

It is when physicians are bogged down by their incomplete 20 technologies, by the innumerable things they are obliged to do in medicine when they lack a clear understanding of disease mechanisms, that the deficiencies of the health-care system are most conspicuous. If I were a policy-maker, interested in saving money for health care over the long haul, I would regard it as an act of high prudence to give high priority to a lot more basic research in biologic science. This is the only way to get the full mileage that biology owes to the science of medicine, even though it seems, as used to be said in the days when the phrase still had some meaning, like asking for the moon.

For Study and Discussion

QUESTIONS FOR RESPONSE

1. What kind of medical tests have you experienced or seen conducted on friends or family? What kind of emotional reaction do you feel toward the imposing machines used for such tests?
2. What does the word *technology* mean? What do you expect when you hear phrases such as "the latest in medical technology"?

QUESTIONS ABOUT PURPOSE

1. Is Thomas's primary purpose to explain the various kinds of medical technology or to argue that certain technologies are more useful than others? Explain your answer.
2. What does Thomas demonstrate about the relationship between cost-effective technology and a genuine understanding of the disease mechanism?

QUESTIONS ABOUT AUDIENCE

1. How does Thomas's assertion that policy makers are interested in "how to deliver today's kind of health care, with equity, to all the people" suggest that he is aware of his readers' interest in the issue he will discuss?
2. To what extent does Thomas assume that his readers are familiar with the diseases he uses to illustrate each category? How does he provide assistance to his readers when the disease may be unfamiliar? See, for example, his discussion of typhoid fever in paragraph 18.

QUESTIONS ABOUT STRATEGIES

1. How does Thomas's definition of his three categories—nontechnology, halfway technology, and effective technology—clarify the single principle he has used to establish his classification system?

2. How does Thomas's discussion of specific diseases demonstrate that his divisions are complete? What aspect of his system enables him to discuss cancer as an illustration in two categories?

QUESTIONS FOR DISCUSSION

1. Why does Thomas believe so strongly in "basic research in biologic science"? Why would an investment in such research save money for "health care over the long haul"?
2. What is Thomas's attitude toward his second category, halfway technology? Why does he call it "at the same time highly sophisticated and profoundly primitive"?

Mary Mebane was born in 1933 in Durham, North Carolina, and educated at North Carolina Central University and the University of North Carolina. She taught in the public schools of North Carolina before moving on to teaching writing at the University of South Carolina and the University of Wisconsin. She has written essays for the *New York Times;* a two-act play, *Take a Sad Song* (1975); and two volumes of her autobiography, *Mary: An Autobiography* (1981) and *Mary, Wayfarer* (1983). In "Shades of Black," excerpted from the first autobiographical volume, Mebane reveals how class and color have been used to classify members of the African-American community.

Shades of Black

D URING MY FIRST week of classes as a freshman, I was stopped one day in the hall by the chairman's wife, who was indistinguishable in color from a white woman. She wanted to see me, she said. 1

This woman had no official position on the faculty, except that she was an instructor in English; nevertheless, her summons had to be obeyed. In the segregated world there were (and remain) gross abuses of authority because those at the pinnacle, and even their spouses, felt that the people "under" them had no recourse except to submit—and they were right except that sometimes a black who got sick and tired of it would go to the whites and complain. This course of action was severely condemned by the blacks, but an interesting thing happened—such action always got positive results. Power was thought of in negative terms: I can deny someone 2 something, I can strike at someone who can't strike back, I can ride someone down; that proves I am powerful. The concept of power as a force for good, for affirmative response to people or situations, was not in evidence.

When I went to her office, she greeted me with a big smile.   3 "You know," she said, "you made the highest mark on the verbal part of the examination." She was referring to the examination that the entire freshman class took upon entering the college. I looked at her but I didn't feel warmth, for in spite of her smile her eyes and tone of voice were saying, "How could this black-skinned girl score higher on the verbal than some of the students who've had more advantages than she? It must be some sort of fluke. Let me talk to her." I felt it, but I managed to smile my thanks and back off. For here at North Carolina College at Durham, as it had been since the beginning, social class and color were the primary criteria used in determining status on the campus.

First came the children of doctors, lawyers, and college   4 teachers. Next came the children of public-school teachers, businessmen, and anybody else who had access to more money than the poor black working class. After that came the

> *At my college, social class and color were the primary criteria in determining status on campus.*

bulk of the student population, the children of the working class, most of whom were the first in their families to go beyond high school. The attitude toward them was: You're here because we need the numbers, but in all other things defer to your betters.

The faculty assumed that light-skinned students were more   5 intelligent, and they were always a bit nonplussed when a dark-skinned student did well, especially if she was a girl. They had reason to be appalled when they discovered that I planned to do not only well but better than my light-skinned peers.

I don't know whether African men recently transported to ⁶ the New World considered themselves handsome or, more important, whether they considered African women beautiful in comparison with Native American Indian women or immigrant European women. It is a question that I have never heard raised or seen research on. If African men considered African women beautiful, just when their shift in interest away from black black women occurred might prove to be an interesting topic for researchers. But one thing I know for sure: by the twentieth century, really black skin on a woman was considered ugly in this country. This was particularly true among those who were exposed to college.

Hazel, who was light brown, used to say to me, "You are ⁷ *dark,* but not *too* dark." The saved commiserating with the damned. I had the feeling that if nature had painted one more brushstroke on me, I'd have had to kill myself.

Black skin was to be disguised at all costs. Since a black ⁸ face is rather hard to disguise, many women took refuge in ludicrous makeup. Mrs. Burry, one of my teachers in elementary school, used white face powder. But she neglected to powder her neck and arms, and even the black on her face gleamed through the white, giving her an eerie appearance. But she did the best she could.

I observed all through elementary and high school that for ⁹ various entertainments the girls were placed on the stage in order of color. And very black ones didn't get into the front row. If they were past caramel-brown, to the back row they would go. And nobody questioned the justice of these decisions—neither the students nor the teachers.

One of the teachers at Wildwood School, who was from ¹⁰ the Deep South and was just as black as she could be, had been a strict enforcer of these standards. That was another irony—that someone who had been judged outside the realm of beauty herself because of her skin tones should have adopted them so wholeheartedly and applied them herself without question.

One girl stymied that teacher, though. Ruby, a black   11
cherry of a girl, not only got off the back row but off the
front row as well, to stand alone at stage center. She could
outsing, outdance, and outdeclaim everyone else, and talent
proved triumphant over pigmentation. But the May Queen
and her Court (and in high school, Miss Wildwood) were
always chosen from among the lighter ones.

When I was a freshman in high school, it became clear that   12
a light-skinned sophomore girl named Rose was going to get
the "best girl scholar" prize for the next three years, and there
was nothing I could do about it, even though I knew I was
the better. Rose was caramel-colored and had shoulder-
length hair. She was highly favored by the science and math
teacher, who figured the averages. I wasn't. There was only
one prize. Therefore, Rose would get it until she graduated.
I was one year behind her, and I would not get it until after
she graduated.

To be held in such low esteem was painful. It was difficult   13
not to feel that I had been cheated out of the medal, which
I felt that, in a fair competition, I perhaps would have won.
Being unable to protest or do anything about it was a traumatic experience for me. From then on I instinctively tended
to avoid the college-exposed, dark-skinned male, knowing
that when he looked at me he saw himself and, most of the
time, his mother and sister as well, and since he had rejected
his blackness, he had rejected theirs and mine.

Oddly enough, the lighter-skinned black male did not   14
seem to feel so much prejudice toward the black black
woman. It was no accident, I felt, that Mr. Harrison, the
eighth-grade teacher, who was reddish-yellow himself, once
protested to the science and math teacher about the fact that
he always assigned sweeping duties to Doris and Ruby Lee,
two black black girls. Mr. Harrison said to them one day,
right in the other teacher's presence, "You must be some bad
girls. Every day I come down here ya'll are sweeping." The
science and math teacher got the point and didn't ask them
to sweep anymore.

Uneducated black males, too, sometimes related very well   15 to the black black woman. They had been less firmly indoctrinated by the white society around them and were more securely rooted in their own culture.

Because of the stigma attached to having dark skin, a black   16
black woman had to do many things to find a place for herself. One possibility was to attach herself to a light-skinned woman, hoping that some of the magic would rub off on her. A second was to make herself sexually available, hoping to attract a mate. Third, she could resign herself to a more chaste life-style—either (for the professional woman) teaching and work in established churches or (for the uneducated woman) domestic work and zealous service in the Holy and Sanctified churches.

<u>Even</u> as a young girl, Lucy had chosen the first route. Lucy   17
was short, skinny, short-haired, and black black, and thus unacceptable. So she made her choice. She selected Patricia, the lightest-skinned girl in the school, as her friend, and followed her around. Patricia and her friends barely tolerated Lucy, but Lucy smiled and doggedly hung on, hoping that some who noticed Patricia might notice her, too. Though I felt shame for her behavior, even then I understood.

As is often the case of the victim agreeing with and adopt-   18
ing the attitudes of oppressor, so I have seen it with black black women. I have seen them adopt the oppressor's attitude that they are nothing but "sex machines," and their supposedly superior sexual performance becomes their sole reason for being and for esteeming themselves. Such women learn early that in order to make themselves attractive to men they have somehow to shift the emphasis from physical beauty to some other area—usually sexual performance. Their constant talk is of their desirability and their ability to gratify a man sexually.

I knew two such women well—both of them black black.   19
To hear their endless talk of sexual conquests was very sad. I have never seen the category that these women fall into described anywhere. It is not that of promiscuity or nymphomania. It is the category of total self-rejection: "Since I am black, I am ugly, I am nobody. I will perform on the level

that they have assigned to me." Such women are the pitiful results of what not only white America but also, and more important, black America has done to them.

Some, not taking the sexuality route but still accepting black society's view of their worthlessness, swing all the way across to intense religiosity. Some are staunch, fervent workers in the more traditional Southern churches—Baptist and Methodist—and others are leaders and ministers in the lower status, more evangelical Holiness sects.   20

Another avenue open to the black black woman is excellence in a career. Since in the South the field most accessible to such women is education, a great many of them prepared to become teachers. But here, too, the black black woman had problems. Grades weren't given to her lightly in school, nor were promotions on the job. Consequently, she had to prepare especially well. She had to pass examinations with flying colors or be left behind; she knew that she would receive no special consideration. She had to be overqualified for a job because otherwise she didn't stand a chance of getting it—and she was competing only with other blacks. She had to have something to back her up: not charm, not personality—but training.   21

The black black woman's training would pay off in the 1970's. With the arrival of integration the black black woman would find, paradoxically enough, that her skin color in an integrated situation was not the handicap it had been in an all-black situation. But it wasn't until the middle and late 1960s, when the post-1945 generation of black males arrived on college campuses, that I noticed any change in the situation at all. *He* wore an afro and *she* wore an afro, and sometimes the only way you could tell them apart was when his afro was taller than hers. Black had become beautiful, and the really black girl was often selected as queen of various campus activities. It was then that the dread I felt at dealing with the college-educated black male began to ease. Even now, though, when I have occasion to engage in any type of transaction with a college-educated black man, I gauge his age. If I guess he was born after 1945, I feel confident that   22 the transaction will turn out all right. If he probably was born before 1945, my stomach tightens, I find myself taking shallow breaths, and I try to state my business and escape as soon as possible.

For Study and Discussion

QUESTIONS FOR RESPONSE

1. How do you respond when you or your friends are judged by some physical feature—weight, height, hair?
2. How do you and your friends identify various social classes? What assumptions do you make about people in each class?

QUESTIONS ABOUT PURPOSE

1. Why does Mebane use the concept of power to introduce her classification?
2. How does Mebane use her essay to explain the impulse of the victim to adopt the attitudes of the oppressor?

QUESTIONS ABOUT AUDIENCE

1. Does Mebane envision her readers as primarily black or primarily white, primarily men or primarily women? Explain your answer.
2. In what way do you think Mebane's system may apply to the attitudes of today's African-American students? Explain your answer.

QUESTIONS ABOUT STRATEGIES

1. How does Mebane classify her college classmates by color and class? What assumptions do her teachers make about black black working-class women?
2. What options does Mebane suggest are available to black black women? How are these options enforced?

QUESTIONS FOR DISCUSSION

1. How did the civil rights movement of the 1950s and black consciousness movement of the 1960s change the African-American community's definition of beauty?
2. Do subtle judgments about class and color still control the power structure of the African-American community? In what way?

GAIL SHEEHY

Gail Sheehy was born in 1937, attended the University of Vermont and Columbia University Journalism School, and worked as contributing editor for *New York* magazine for ten years. Her writing has appeared in *Esquire, McCall's, Ms.,* and *Rolling Stone.* Although Sheehy's first book was a novel, *Lovesounds* (1970), she soon turned to nonfiction, writing *Panthermania: The Clash of Black Against Black in One American City* (1971), *Hustling: Prostitution in Our Wide Open Society* (1973), and her best-selling *Passages: Predictable Crises of Adult Life* (1976). Her more recent books include *The Spirit of Survival* (1986), a history of Cambodia; *The Silent Passage* (1992), a study of the social and psychological effects of menopause; and *New Passages* (1995), an analysis of adult behavior beyond the age of fifty. In "Predictable Crises of Adulthood," excerpted from the second chapter of *Passages,* Sheehy identifies six stages that most adults experience between the ages of eighteen and fifty.

Predictable Crises of Adulthood

W E ARE NOT unlike a particularly hardy crustacean. 1
The lobster grows by developing and shedding a series of hard, protective shells. Each time it expands from within, the confining shell must be sloughed off. It is left exposed and vulnerable until, in time, a new covering grows to replace the old.

With each passage from one stage of human growth to the 2 next we, too, must shed a protective structure. We are left exposed and vulnerable—but also yeasty and embryonic again, capable of stretching in ways we hadn't known before. These sheddings may take several years or more. Coming out of each passage, though, we enter a longer and more stable period in which we can expect relative tranquillity and a sense of equilibrium regained. . . .

As we shall see, each person engages the steps of develop- 3
ment in his or her own characteristic *step-style*. Some people never complete the whole sequence. And none of us "solves" with one step—by jumping out of the parental home into a job or marriage, for example—the problems in separating from the caregivers of childhood. Nor do we "achieve" autonomy once and for all by converting our dreams into concrete goals, even when we attain those goals. The central

---

On the developmental ladder, the mastery of one set of tasks may fortify us for the next period and the next set of challenges.

---

issues or tasks of one period are never fully completed, tied up, and cast aside. But when they lose their primacy and the current life structure has served its purpose, we are ready to move on to the next period.

Can one catch up? What might look to others like listless- 4
ness, contrariness, a maddening refusal to face up to an ob-vious task may be a person's own unique detour that will bring him out later on the other side. Developmental gains won can later be lost—and rewon. It's plausible, though it can't be proven, that the mastery of one set of tasks fortifies us for the next period and the next set of challenges. But it's important not to think too mechanistically. Machines work by units. The bureaucracy (supposedly) works step by step. Human beings, thank God, have an individual inner dynamic that can never be precisely coded.

Although I have indicated the ages when Americans are 5

likely to go through each stage, and the differences between men and women where they are striking, do not take the ages too seriously. The stages are the thing, and most particularly the sequence.

Here is the briefest outline of the developmental ladder.   6

PULLING UP ROOTS

Before 18, the motto is loud and clear: "I have to get away   7
from my parents." But the words are seldom connected to action. Generally still safely part of our families, even if away at school, we feel our autonomy to be subject to erosion from moment to moment.

After 18, we begin Pulling Up Roots in earnest. College,   8
military service, and short-term travels are all customary vehicles our society provides for the first round trips between family and a base of one's own. In the attempt to separate our view of the world from our family's view, despite vigorous protestations to the contrary—"I know exactly what I want!"—we cast about for any beliefs we can call our own. And in the process of testing those beliefs we are often drawn to fads, preferably those most mysterious and inaccessible to our parents.

Whatever tentative memberships we try out in the world,   9
the fear haunts us that we are really kids who cannot take care of ourselves. We cover that fear with acts of defiance and mimicked confidence. For allies to replace our parents, we turn to our contemporaries. They become conspirators. So long as their perspective meshes with our own, they are able to substitute for the sanctuary of the family. But that doesn't last very long. And the instant they diverge from the shaky ideals of "our group," they are seen as betrayers. Rebounds to the family are common between the ages of 18 and 22.

The tasks of this passage are to locate ourselves in a peer   10
group role, a sex role, an anticipated occupation, an ideology or world view. As a result, we gather the impetus to leave home physically and the identity to *begin* leaving home emotionally.

Even as one part of us seeks to be an individual, another   11
part longs to restore the safety and comfort of merging with
another. Thus one of the most popular myths of this passage
is: We can piggyback our development by attaching to a
Stronger One. But people who marry during this time often
prolong financial and emotional ties to the family and relatives that impede them from becoming self-sufficient.

A stormy passage through the Pulling Up Roots years will   12
probably facilitate the normal progression of the adult life
cycle. If one doesn't have an identity crisis at this point, it
will erupt during a later transition, when the penalties may
be harder to bear.

THE TRYING TWENTIES

The Trying Twenties confront us with the question of how   13
to take hold in the adult world. Our focus shifts from the
interior turmoils of late adolescence—"Who am I?" "What is
truth?"—and we become almost totally preoccupied with
working out the externals. "How do I put my aspirations into
effect?" "What is the best way to start?" "Where do I go?"
"Who can help me?" "How did *you* do it?"

In this period, which is longer and more stable compared   14
with the passage that leads to it, the tasks are as enormous as
they are exhilarating: To shape a Dream, that vision of ourselves which will generate energy, aliveness, and hope. To
prepare for a lifework. To find a mentor if possible. And to
form the capacity for intimacy, without losing in the process
whatever consistency of self we have thus far mustered. The
first test structure must be erected around the life we choose
to try.

Doing what we "should" is the most pervasive theme of   15
the twenties. The "shoulds" are largely defined by family
models, the press of the culture, or the prejudices of our
peers. If the prevailing cultural instructions are that one
should get married and settle down behind one's own door,
a nuclear family is born. If instead the peers insist that one
should do one's own thing, the 25-year-old is likely to har-

ness himself onto a Harley-Davidson and burn up Route 66 in the commitment to have no commitments.

One of the terrifying aspects of the twenties is the inner conviction that the choices we make are irrevocable. It is largely a false fear. Change is quite possible, and some alteration of our original choices is probably inevitable.   16

Two impulses, as always, are at work. One is to build a firm, safe structure for the future by making strong commitments, to "be set." Yet people who slip into a ready-made form without much self-examination are likely to find themselves *locked in.*   17

The other urge is to explore and experiment, keeping any structure tentative and therefore easily reversible. Taken to the extreme, these are people who skip from one trial job and one limited personal encounter to another, spending their twenties in the *transient* state.   18

Although the choices of our twenties are not irrevocable, they do set in motion a Life Pattern. Some of us follow the locked-in pattern, others the transient pattern, the wunderkind pattern, the caregiver pattern, and there are a number of others. Such patterns strongly influence the particular questions raised for each person during each passage. . . .   19

Buoyed by powerful illusions and belief in the power of the will, we commonly insist in our twenties that what we have chosen to do is the one true course in life. Our backs go up at the merest hint that we are like our parents, that two decades of parental training might be reflected in our current actions and attitudes.   20

"Not me," is the motto, "I'm different."   21

CATCH-30

Impatient with devoting ourselves to the "shoulds," a new vitality springs from within as we approach 30. Men and women alike speak of feeling too narrow and restricted. They blame all sorts of things, but what the restrictions boil down to are the outgrowth of career and personal choices of the twenties. They may have been choices perfectly suited to that stage. But now the fit feels different. Some inner aspect that   22 was left out is striving to be taken into account. Important new choices must be made, and commitments altered or deepened. The work involves great change, turmoil, and often crisis—a simultaneous feeling of rock bottom and the urge to bust out.

One common response is the tearing up of the life we spent most of our twenties putting together. It may mean striking out on a secondary road toward a new vision or converting a dream of "running for president" into a more realistic goal. The single person feels a push to find a partner. The woman who was previously content at home with children chafes to venture into the world. The childless couple reconsiders children. And almost everyone who is married, especially those married for seven years, feels a discontent.

If the discontent doesn't lead to a divorce, it will, or should, call for a serious review of the marriage and of each partner's aspirations in the Catch-30 condition. The gist of that condition was expressed by a 29-year-old associate with a Wall Street law firm:

"I'm considering leaving the firm. I've been there four years now; I'm getting good feedback, but I have no clients of my own. I feel weak. If I wait much longer, it will be too late, too close to that fateful time of decision on whether or not to become a partner. I'm success-oriented. But the concept of being 55 years old and stuck in a monotonous job drives me wild. It drives me crazy now, just a little bit. I'd say that 85 percent of the time I thoroughly enjoy my work. But when I get a screwball case, I come away from court saying, 'What am I doing here?' It's a *visceral* reaction that I'm wasting my time. I'm trying to find some way to make a social contribution or a slot in city government. I keep saying, 'There's something more.'"

Besides the push to broaden himself professionally, there is a wish to expand his personal life. He wants two or three more children. "The concept of a home has become very meaningful to me, a place to get away from troubles and relax. I love my son in a way I could not have anticipated. I never could live alone."

Consumed with the work of making his own critical life-   27
steering decisions, he demonstrates the essential shift at this
age: an absolute requirement to be more self-concerned. The
self has new value now that his competency has been proved.

His wife is struggling with her own age-30 priorities. She   28
wants to go to law school, but he wants more children. If she
is going to stay home, she wants him to make more time for
the family instead of taking on even wider professional commitments. His view of the bind, of what he would most like
from his wife, is this:

"I'd like not to be bothered. It sounds cruel, but I'd like   29
not to have to worry about what she's going to do next week.
Which is why I've told her several times that I think she
should do something. Go back to school and get a degree in
social work or geography or whatever. Hopefully that would
fulfill her, and then I wouldn't have to worry about her line
of problems. I want her to be decisive about herself."

The trouble with his advice to his wife is that it comes out   30
of concern with *his* convenience, rather than with *her* development. She quickly picks up on this lack of goodwill: He is
trying to dispose of her. At the same time, he refuses her the
same latitude to be "selfish" in making an independent decision to broaden her own horizons. Both perceive a lack of
mutuality. And that is what Catch-30 is all about for the
couple.

ROOTING AND EXTENDING

Life becomes less provisional, more rational and orderly in   31
the early thirties. We begin to settle down in the full sense.
Most of us begin putting down roots and sending out new
shoots. People buy houses and become very earnest about
climbing career ladders. Men in particular concern themselves with "making it." Satisfaction with marriage generally
goes downhill in the thirties (for those who have remained together) compared with the highly valued, vision-supporting
marriage of the twenties. This coincides with the couple's

reduced social life outside the family and the in-turned focus on raising their children.

THE DEADLINE DECADE

In the middle of the thirties we come upon a crossroads. We   32
have reached the halfway mark. Yet even as we are reaching our prime, we begin to see there is a place where it finishes. Time starts to squeeze.

The loss of youth, the faltering of physical powers we have   33
always taken for granted, the fading purpose of stereotyped roles by which we have thus far identified ourselves, the spiritual dilemma of having no absolute answers—any or all of these shocks can give this passage the character of crisis. Such thoughts usher in a decade between 35 and 45 that can be called the Deadline Decade. It is a time of both danger and opportunity. All of us have the chance to rework the narrow identity by which we defined ourselves in the first half of life. And those of us who make the most of the opportunity will have a full-out authenticity crisis.

To come through this authenticity crisis, we must reexam-   34
ine our purposes and reevaluate how to spend our resources from now on. "Why am I doing all this? What do I really believe in?" No matter what we have been doing, there will be parts of ourselves that have been suppressed and now need to find expression. "Bad" feelings will demand acknowledgment along with the good.

It is frightening to step off onto the treacherous footbridge   35
leading to the second half of life. We can't take everything with us on this journey through uncertainty. Along the way, we discover that we are alone. We no longer have to ask permission because we are the providers of our own safety. We must learn to give ourselves permission. We stumble upon feminine or masculine aspects of our natures that up to this time have usually been masked. There is grieving to be done because an old self is dying. By taking in our suppressed and even our unwanted parts, we prepare at the gut level for the reintegration of an identity that is ours and ours alone—not

some artificial form put together to please the culture or our mates. It is a dark passage at the beginning. But by disassembling ourselves, we can glimpse the light and gather our parts into a renewal.

Women sense this inner crossroads earlier than men do. 36 The time pinch often prompts a woman to stop and take an all-points survey at age 35. Whatever options she has already played out, she feels a "my last chance" urgency to review those options she has set aside and those that aging and biology will close off in the *now foreseeable* future. For all her qualms and confusion about where to start looking for a new future, she usually enjoys an exhilaration of release. Assertiveness begins rising. There are so many firsts ahead.

Men, too, feel the time push in the mid-thirties. Most men 37 respond by pressing down harder on the career accelerator. It's "my last chance" to pull away from the pack. It is no longer enough to be the loyal junior executive, the promising young novelist, the lawyer who does a little *pro bono* work on the side. He wants now to become part of top management, to be recognized as an established writer, or an active politician with his own legislative program. With some chagrin, he discovers that he has been too anxious to please and too vulnerable to criticism. He wants to put together his own ship.

During this period of intense concentration on external 38 advancement, it is common for men to be unaware of the more difficult, gut issues that are propelling them forward. The survey that was neglected at 35 becomes a crucible at 40. Whatever rung of achievement he has reached, the man of 40 usually feels stale, restless, burdened, and unappreciated. He worries about his health. He wonders, "Is this all there is?" He may make a series of departures from well-established lifelong base lines, including marriage. More and more men are seeking second careers in midlife. Some become self-destructive. And many men in their forties experience a major shift of emphasis away from pouring all their energies into their own advancement. A more tender, feeling side comes into play. They become interested in developing an ethical self.

RENEWAL OR RESIGNATION

Somewhere in the mid-forties, equilibrium is regained. A new   39
stability is achieved, which may be more or less satisfying.

If one has refused to budge through the midlife transition,   40
the sense of staleness will calcify into resignation. One by one,
the safety and supports will be withdrawn from the person
who is standing still. Parents will become children; children
will become strangers; a mate will grow away or go away; the
career will become just a job—and each of these events will
be felt as an abandonment. The crisis will probably emerge
again around 50. And although its wallop will be greater, the
jolt may be just what is needed to prod the resigned middle-
ager toward seeking revitalization.

On the other hand . . .   41

If we have confronted ourselves in the middle passage and   42
found a renewal of purpose around which we are eager to
build a more authentic life structure, these may well be the
best years. Personal happiness takes a sharp turn upward for
partners who can now accept the fact: "I cannot expect
anyone to fully understand me." Parents can be forgiven for
the burdens of our childhood. Children can be let go without
leaving us in collapsed silence. At 50, there is a new warmth
and mellowing. Friends become more important than ever,
but so does privacy. Since it is so often proclaimed by people
past midlife, the motto of this stage might be "No more
bullshit."

For Study and Discussion

QUESTIONS FOR RESPONSE

1. Does it reassure or infuriate you when what you assume is your
   own idiosyncratic behavior is classified as "normal" for your age?
   Explain your answer.
2. How much confidence do you have in Sheehy's system? What
   kinds of evidence do you think she used to organize it?

QUESTIONS ABOUT PURPOSE

1. What is Sheehy's purpose—to define the various stages of human development or to analyze the process of moving (or the consequences of not moving) from one stage to another?
2. What do the words *predictable* and *crisis* contribute to Sheehy's purpose?

QUESTIONS ABOUT AUDIENCE

1. Who does Sheehy imagine as the readers of her essay: general readers, psychologists, people who are stuck in one stage, or people who have successfully navigated the passage from stage to stage?
2. How does Sheehy use the pronoun *we* to establish a relationship with her readers?

QUESTIONS ABOUT STRATEGIES

1. How does Sheehy use the opening metaphor of the lobster shedding its shell to clarify the system of development she intends to classify?
2. How effective are the headings Sheehy uses to identify the six stages of development?

QUESTIONS FOR DISCUSSION

1. What assumptions about growth does Sheehy make by stopping her system at age fifty? Suggest some crises (and stages) for the years after fifty.
2. What problems do psychologists encounter when they try to make generalizations about human behavior? For example, how does Sheehy's classification system compare with those designed for early childhood and adolescence?

FLANNERY O'CONNOR

Flannery O'Connor (1925–1964) was born in Savannah, Georgia, and was educated at the Women's College of Georgia and the University of Iowa. She returned to her mother's farm near Milledgeville, Georgia, when she discovered that she had contracted lupus erythematosus, the systemic disease that had killed her father and of which she herself was to die. For the last fourteen years of her life, she lived a quiet, productive life on the farm—raising peacocks, painting, and writing the extraordinary stories and novels that won her worldwide acclaim. Her novels, *Wise Blood* (1952), which was adapted for film in 1979, and *The Violent Bear It Away* (1960), deal with fanatical preachers. Her thirty-one carefully crafted stories, combining grotesque comedy and violent tragedy, appear in *A Good Man Is Hard to Find* (1955), *Everything That Rises Must Converge* (1965), and *The Complete Stories* (1971), which won the National Book Award. "Revelation" dramatizes the ironic discoveries a woman makes about how different classes of people fit into the order of things.

Revelation

T HE DOCTOR'S WAITING room, which was very small, was almost full when the Turpins entered and Mrs. Turpin, who was very large, made it look even smaller by her presence. She stood looming at the head of the magazine table set in the center of it, a living demonstration that the room was inadequate and ridiculous. Her little bright black eyes took in all the patients as she sized up the seating situation. There was one vacant chair and a place on the sofa occupied by a blond child in a dirty blue romper who should have been told to move over and make room for the lady. He was five or six, but Mrs. Turpin saw at once that no one was going to tell him to move over. He was slumped down in the seat, his arms idle at his sides and his eyes idle in his head; his nose ran unchecked.

Mrs. Turpin put a firm hand on Claud's shoulder and said   2 in a voice that included anyone who wanted to listen, "Claud, you sit in that chair there," and gave him a push down into the vacant one. Claud was florid and bald and sturdy, somewhat shorter than Mrs. Turpin, but he sat down as if he were accustomed to doing what she told him to.

Mrs. Turpin remained standing. The only man in the room   3 besides Claud was a lean stringy old fellow with a rusty hand spread out on each knee, whose eyes were closed as if he were asleep or dead or pretending to be so as not to get up and offer her his seat. Her gaze settled agreeably on a well-dressed gray-haired lady whose eyes met hers and whose expression said: if that child belonged to me, he would have some manners and move over—there's plenty of room there for you and him too.

Claud looked up with a sigh and made as if to rise.   4

"Sit down," Mrs. Turpin said. "You know you're not   5 supposed to stand on that leg. He has an ulcer on his leg," she explained.

Claud lifted his foot onto the magazine table and rolled   6 his trouser leg up to reveal a purple swelling on a plump marble-white calf.

"My!" the pleasant lady said. "How did you do that?"   7

"A cow kicked him," Mrs. Turpin said.   8

"Goodness!" said the lady.   9

Claud rolled his trouser leg down.   10

"Maybe the little boy would move over," the lady sug-   11 gested, but the child did not stir.

"Somebody will be leaving in a minute," Mrs. Turpin said.   12 She could not understand why a doctor—with as much money as they made charging five dollars a day to just stick

their head in the hospital door and look at you—couldn't
afford a decent-sized waiting room. This one was hardly
bigger than a garage. The table was cluttered with limp-
looking magazines and at one end of it there was a big green
glass ash tray full of cigarette butts and cotton wads with little
blood spots on them. If she had had anything to do with the
running of the place, that would have been emptied every so
often. There were no chairs against the wall at the head of
the room. It had a rectangular-shaped panel in it that permitted a view of the office where the nurse came and went and
the secretary listened to the radio. A plastic fern in a gold pot
sat in the opening and trailed its fronds down almost to the
floor. The radio was softly playing gospel music.

Just then the inner door opened and a nurse with the   13
highest stack of yellow hair Mrs. Turpin had ever seen put
her face in the crack and called for the next patient. The
woman sitting beside Claud grasped the two arms of her chair
and hoisted herself up; she pulled her dress free from her legs
and lumbered through the door where the nurse had disappeared.

Mrs. Turpin eased into the vacant chair, which held her   14
tight as a corset. "I wish I could reduce," she said, and rolled
her eyes and gave a comic sigh.

"Oh, *you* aren't fat," the stylish lady said.   15

"Ooooo I am too," Mrs. Turpin said. "Claud he eats all   16
he wants to and never weighs over one hundred and seventy-
five pounds, but me I just look at something good to eat and
I gain some weight," and her stomach and shoulders shook
with laughter. "You can eat all you want to, can't you,
Claud?" she asked, turning to him.

Claud only grinned.   17

"Well, as long as you have such a good disposition," the   18
stylish lady said, "I don't think it makes a bit of difference
what size you are. You just can't beat a good disposition."

Next to her was a fat girl of eighteen or nineteen, scowling   19
into a thick blue book which Mrs. Turpin saw was entitled
Human Development. The girl raised her head and directed
her scowl at Mrs. Turpin as if she did not like her looks. She

appeared annoyed that anyone should speak while she tried
to read. The poor girl's face was blue with acne and Mrs.
Turpin thought how pitiful it was to have a face like that at
that age. She gave the girl a friendly smile but the girl only
scowled the harder. Mrs. Turpin herself was fat but she had
always had good skin, and, though she was forty-seven years
old, there was not a wrinkle in her face except around her
eyes from laughing too much.

Next to the ugly girl was the child, still in exactly the same 20
position, and next to him was a thin leathery old woman in
a cotton print dress. She and Claud had three sacks of chicken
feed in their pump house that was in the same print. She had
seen from the first that the child belonged with the old
woman. She could tell by the way they sat—kind of vacant
and white-trashy, as if they would sit there until Doomsday
if nobody called and told them to get up. And at right angles
but next to the well-dressed pleasant lady was a lank-faced
woman who was certainly the child's mother. She had on
a yellow sweat shirt and wine-colored slacks, both gritty-
looking, and the rims of her lips were stained with snuff. Her
dirty yellow hair was tied behind with a little piece of red
paper ribbon. Worse than niggers any day, Mrs. Turpin
thought.

The gospel hymn playing was, "When I looked up and He 21
looked down," and Mrs. Turpin, who knew it, supplied the
last line mentally, "And wona these days I know I'll weear a
crown."

Without appearing to, Mrs. Turpin always noticed people's 22
feet. The well-dressed lady had on red and gray suede shoes
to match her dress. Mrs. Turpin had on her good black
patent leather pumps. The ugly girl had on Girl Scout
shoes and heavy socks. The old woman had on tennis shoes
and the white-trashy mother had on what appeared to be
bedroom slippers, black straw with gold braid threaded
through them—exactly what you would have expected her to
have on.

Sometimes at night when she couldn't go to sleep, Mrs. 23
Turpin would occupy herself with the question of who she

would have chosen to be if she couldn't have been herself. If Jesus had said to her before he made her, "There's only two places available for you. You can either be a nigger or white-trash," what would she have said? "Please, Jesus, please," she would have said, "just let me wait until there's another place available," and he would have said, "No, you have to go right now and I have only those two places so make up your mind." She would have wiggled and squirmed and begged and pleaded but it would have been no use and finally she would have said, "All right, make me a nigger then—but that don't mean a trashy one." And he would have made her a neat clean respectable Negro woman, herself but black.

Next to the child's mother was a red-headed youngish woman, reading one of the magazines and working a piece of chewing gum, hell for leather, as Claud would say. Mrs. Turpin could not see the woman's feet. She was not white-trash, just common. Sometimes Mrs. Turpin occupied herself at night naming the classes of people. On the bottom of the heap were most colored people, not the kind she would have been if she had been one, but most of them; then next to them—not above, just away from—were the white-trash; then above them were the home-owners, and above them the home-and-land-owners, to which she and Claud belonged. Above she and Claud were people with a lot of money and much bigger houses and much more land. But here the complexity of it would begin to bear in on her, for some of the people with a lot of money were common and ought to be below she and Claud and some of the people who had good blood had lost their money and had to rent and then there were colored people who owned their homes and land as well. There was a colored dentist in town who had two red Lincolns and a swimming pool and a farm with registered white-face cattle on it. Usually by the time she had fallen asleep all the classes of people were moiling and roiling around in her head, and she would dream they were all crammed in together in a box car, being ridden off to be put in a gas oven.

"That's a beautiful clock," she said and nodded to her   25 right. It was a big wall clock, the face encased in a brass sunburst.

"Yes, it's very pretty," the stylish lady said agreeably. "And right on the dot too," she added, glancing at her watch. 26

The ugly girl beside her cast an eye upward at the clock, smirked, then looked directly at Mrs. Turpin and smirked again. Then she returned her eyes to her book. She was obviously the lady's daughter because, although they didn't look anything alike as to disposition, they both had the same shape of face and the same blue eyes. On the lady they sparkled pleasantly but in the girl's seared face they appeared alternately to smolder and to blaze. 27

What if Jesus had said, "All right, you can be white-trash or a nigger or ugly"! 28

Mrs. Turpin felt an awful pity for the girl, though she thought it was one thing to be ugly and another to act ugly. 29

The woman with the snuff-stained lips turned around in her chair and looked up at the clock. Then she turned back and appeared to look a little to the side of Mrs. Turpin. There was a cast in one of her eyes. "You want to know wher you can get you one of themther clocks?" she asked in a loud voice. 30

"No, I already have a nice clock," Mrs. Turpin said. Once somebody like her got a leg in the conversation, she would be all over it. 31

"You can get you one with green stamps," the woman said. "That's most likely wher he got hisn. Save you up enough, you can get you most anythang. I got me some joo'ry." 32

Ought to have got you a wash rag and some soap, Mrs. Turpin thought. 33

"I get contour sheets with mine," the pleasant lady said. 34

The daughter slammed her book shut. She looked straight in front of her, directly through Mrs. Turpin and on through the yellow curtain and the plate glass window which made the wall behind her. The girl's eyes seemed lit all of a sudden with a peculiar light, an unnatural light like night road signs give. Mrs. Turpin turned her head to see if there was anything going on outside that she should see, but she could not see anything. Figures passing cast only a pale shadow through the curtain. There was no reason the girl should single her out for her ugly looks.

"Miss Finley," the nurse said, cracking the door. The   36
gum-chewing woman got up and passed in front of her and Claud and went into the office. She had on red high-heeled shoes.

Directly across the table, the ugly girl's eyes were fixed on   37
Mrs. Turpin as if she had some very special reason for disliking her.

"This is wonderful weather, isn't it?" the girl's mother said.   38

"It's good weather for cotton if you can get the niggers   39
to pick it," Mrs. Turpin said, "but niggers don't want to pick cotton any more. You can't get the white folks to pick it and now you can't get the niggers—because they got to be right up there with the white folks."

"They gonna *try* anyways," the white-trash woman said,   40
leaning forward.

"Do you have one of the cotton-picking machines?" the   41
pleasant lady asked.

"No," Mrs. Turpin said, "they leave half the cotton in the   42
field. We don't have much cotton anyway. If you want to make it farming now, you have to have a little of everything. We got a couple of acres of cotton and a few hogs and chickens and just enough white-face that Claud can look after them himself."

"One thang I don't want," the white-trash woman said,   43
wiping her mouth with the back of her hand. "Hogs. Nasty stinking things, a-gruntin and a-rootin all over the place."

Mrs. Turpin gave her the merest edge of her attention.   44
"Our hogs are not dirty and they don't stink," she said. "They're cleaner than some children I've seen. Their feet never touch the ground. We have a pig-parlor—that's where you raise them on concrete," she explained to the pleasant lady, "and Claud scoots them down with the hose every afternoon and washes off the floor." Cleaner by far than that child right there, she thought. Poor nasty little thing. He had not moved except to put the thumb of his dirty hand into his mouth.

The woman turned her face away from Mrs. Turpin. "I 45 know I wouldn't scoot down no hog with no hose," she said to the wall.

You wouldn't have no hog to scoot down, Mrs. Turpin 46 said to herself.

"A-gruntin and a-rootin and a-groanin," the woman mut- 47 tered.

"We got a little of everything," Mrs. Turpin said to the 48 pleasant lady. "It's no use in having more than you can handle yourself with help like it is. We found enough niggers to pick our cotton this year but Claud he has to go after them and take them home again in the evening. They can't walk that half a mile. No they can't. I tell you," she said and laughed merrily, "I sure am tired of buttering up niggers, but you got to love em if you want em to work for you. When they come in the morning, I run out and I say, 'Hi yawl this morning?' and when Claud drives them off to the field I just wave to beat the band and they just wave back." And she waved her hand rapidly to illustrate.

"Like you read out of the same book," the lady said, 49 showing she understood perfectly.

"Child, yes," Mrs. Turpin said. "And when they come in 50 from the field, I run out with a bucket of icewater. That's the way it's going to be from now on," she said. "You may as well face it."

"One thang I know," the white-trash woman said. "Two 51 thangs I ain't going to do: love no niggers or scoot down no hog with no hose." And she let out a bark of contempt.

The look that Mrs. Turpin and the pleasant lady exchanged 52 indicated they both understood that you had to *have* certain things before you could *know* certain things. But every time Mrs. Turpin exchanged a look with the lady, she was aware that the ugly girl's peculiar eyes were still on her, and she had trouble bringing her attention back to the conversation.

"When you got something," she said, "you got to look 53 after it." And when you ain't got a thing but breath and britches, she added to herself, you can afford to come to town every morning and just sit on the Court House coping and spit.

A grotesque revolving shadow passed across the curtain   54
behind her and was thrown palely on the opposite wall. Then
a bicycle clattered down against the outside of the building.
The door opened and a colored boy glided in with a tray from
the drugstore. It had two large red and white paper cups on
it with tops on them. He was a tall, very black boy in discolored white pants and a green nylon shirt. He was chewing
gum slowly, as if to music. He set the tray down in the office
opening next to the fern and stuck his head through to look
for the secretary. She was not in there. He rested his arms on
the ledge and waited, his narrow bottom stuck out, swaying
to the left and right. He raised a hand over his head and
scratched the base of his skull.

"You see that button there, boy?" Mrs. Turpin said. "You   55
can punch that and she'll come. She's probably in the back
somewhere."

"Is thas right?" the boy said agreeably, as if he had never   56
seen the button before. He leaned to the right and put his
finger on it. "She sometime out," he said and twisted around
to face his audience, his elbows behind him on the counter.
The nurse appeared and he twisted back again. She handed
him a dollar and he rooted in his pocket and made the change
and counted it out to her. She gave him fifteen cents for a tip
and he went out with the empty tray. The heavy door swung
to slowly and closed at length with the sound of suction. For
a moment no one spoke.

"They ought to send all them niggers back to Africa," the   57
white-trash woman said. "That's wher they come from in the
first place."

"Oh, I couldn't do without my good colored friends," the   58
pleasant lady said.

"There's a heap of things worse than a nigger," Mrs.   59
Turpin agreed. "It's all kinds of them just like it's all kinds of
us."

"Yes, and it takes all kinds to make the world go round,"   60
the lady said in her musical voice.

As she said it, the raw-complexioned girl snapped her teeth   61
together. Her lower lip turned downwards and inside out,

revealing the pale pink inside of her mouth. After a second it rolled back up. It was the ugliest face Mrs. Turpin had ever seen anyone make and for a moment she was certain that the girl had made it at her. She was looking at her as if she had known and disliked her all her life—all of Mrs. Turpin's life, it seemed too, not just all the girl's life. Why, girl, I don't even know you, Mrs. Turpin said silently.

She forced her attention back to the discussion. "It wouldn't be practical to send them back to Africa," she said. "They wouldn't want to go. They got it too good here." 62

"Wouldn't be what they wanted—if I had anythang to do with it," the woman said. 63

"It wouldn't be a way in the world you could get all the niggers back over there," Mrs. Turpin said. "They'd be hiding out and lying down and turning sick on you and wailing and hollering and raring and pitching. It wouldn't be a way in the world to get them over there." 64

"They got over here," the trashy woman said. "Get back like they got over." 65

"It wasn't so many of them then," Mrs. Turpin explained. 66

The woman looked at Mrs. Turpin as if here was an idiot indeed but Mrs. Turpin was not bothered by the look, considering where it came from. 67

"Nooo," she said, "they're going to stay here where they can go to New York and marry white folks and improve their color. That's what they all want to do, every one of them, improve their color." 68

"You know what comes of that, don't you?" Claud asked. 69

"No, Claud, what?" Mrs. Turpin said. 70

Claud's eyes twinkled. "White-faced niggers," he said with never a smile. 71

Everybody in the office laughed except the white-trash and the ugly girl. The girl gripped the book in her lap with white fingers. The trashy woman looked around her from face to face as if she thought they were all idiots. The old woman in the feed sack dress continued to gaze expressionless across the floor at the high-top shoes of the man opposite her, the one who had been pretending to be asleep when the Turpins 72

came in. He was laughing heartily, his hands still spread out
on his knees. The child had fallen to the side and was lying
now almost face down in the old woman's lap.

While they recovered from their laughter, the nasal chorus   73
on the radio kept the room from silence.

> *"You go to blank blank*
> *And I'll go to mine*
> *But we'll all blank along*
> *To-geth-ther,*
> *And all along the blank*
> *We'll hep eachother out*
> *Smile-ling in any kind of*
> *Weath-ther!"*

Mrs. Turpin didn't catch every word but she caught   74
enough to agree with the spirit of the song and it turned her
thoughts sober. To help anybody out that needed it was her
philosophy of life. She never spared herself when she found
somebody in need, whether they were white or black, trash
or decent. And of all she had to be thankful for, she was most
thankful that this was so. If Jesus had said, "You can be high
society and have all the money you want and be thin and
svelte-like, but you can't be a good woman with it," she
would have had to say, "Well don't make me that then. Make
me a good woman and it don't matter what else, how fat or
how ugly or how poor!" Her heart rose. He had not made
her a nigger or white-trash or ugly! He had made her herself
and given her a little of everything. Jesus, thank you! she said.
Thank you thank you thank you! Whenever she counted her
blessings she felt as buoyant as if she weighed one hundred
and twenty-five pounds instead of one hundred and eighty.

"What's wrong with your little boy?" the pleasant lady   75
asked the white-trashy woman.

"He has a ulcer," the woman said proudly. "He ain't give   76
me a minute's peace since he was born. Him and her are just
alike," she said, nodding at the old woman, who was running
her leathery fingers through the child's pale hair. "Look like
I can't get nothing down them two but Co' Cola and candy."

That's all you try to get down em, Mrs. Turpin said to   77
herself. Too lazy to light the fire. There was nothing you
could tell her about people like them that she didn't know
already. And it was not just that they didn't have anything.
Because if you gave them everything, in two weeks it would
all be broken or filthy or they would have chopped it up for
lightwood. She knew all this from her own experience. Help
them you must, but help them you couldn't.

All at once the ugly girl turned her lips inside out again.   78
Her eyes fixed like two drills on Mrs. Turpin. This time there
was no mistaking that there was something urgent behind
them.

Girl, Mrs. Turpin exclaimed silently, I haven't done a thing   79
to you! The girl might be confusing her with somebody else.
There was no need to sit by and let herself be intimidated.
"You must be in college," she said boldly, looking directly at
the girl. "I see you reading a book there."

The girl continued to stare and pointedly did not answer.   80

Her mother blushed at this rudeness. "The lady asked you   81
a question, Mary Grace," she said under her breath.

"I have ears," Mary Grace said.   82

The poor mother blushed again. "Mary Grace goes to   83
Wellesley College," she explained. She twisted one of the
buttons on her dress. "In Massachusetts," she added with a
grimace. "And in the summer she just keeps right on studying. Just reads all the time, a real book worm. She's done real
well at Wellesley; she's taking English and Math and History
and Psychology and Social Studies," she rattled on, "and I
think it's too much. I think she ought to get out and have
fun."

The girl looked as if she would like to hurl them all   84
through the plate glass window.

"Way up north," Mrs. Turpin murmured and thought,   85
well, it hasn't done much for her manners.

"I'd almost rather to have him sick," the white-trash   86
woman said, wrenching the attention back to herself. "He's
so mean when he ain't. Look like some children just take
natural to meanness. It's some gets bad when they get sick
but he was the opposite. Took sick and turned good. He

don't give me no trouble now. It's me waitin to see the doctor," she said.

If I was going to send anybody back to Africa, Mrs. Turpin 87
thought, it would be your kind, woman. "Yes, indeed," she
said aloud, but looking up at the ceiling, "it's a heap of things
worse than a nigger." And dirtier than a hog, she added to
herself.

"I think people with bad dispositions are more to be pitied 88
than anyone on earth," the pleasant lady said in a voice that
was decidedly thin.

"I thank the Lord he has blessed me with a good one," 89
Mrs. Turpin said. "The day has never dawned that I couldn't
find something to laugh at."

"Not since she married me anyways," Claud said with a 90
comical straight face.

Everybody laughed except the girl and the white-trash. 91

Mrs. Turpin's stomach shook. "He's such a caution," she 92
said, "that I can't help but laugh at him."

The girl made a loud ugly noise through her teeth. 93

Her mother's mouth grew thin and tight. "I think the 94
worst thing in the world," she said, "is an ungrateful person.
To have everything and not appreciate it. I know a girl," she
said, "who has parents who would give her anything, a little
brother who loves her dearly, who is getting a good education, who wears the best clothes, but who can never say a
kind word to anyone, who never smiles, who just criticizes
and complains all day long."

"Is she too old to paddle?" Claud asked. 95

The girl's face was almost purple. 96

"Yes," the lady said, "I'm afraid there's nothing to do but 97
leave her to her folly. Some day she'll wake up and it'll be too
late."

"It never hurt anyone to smile," Mrs. Turpin said. "It just 98
makes you feel better all over."

"Of course," the lady said sadly, "but there are just some 99
people you can't tell anything to. They can't take criticism."

"If it's one thing I am," Mrs. Turpin said with feeling, "it's 100
grateful. When I think who all I could have been besides
myself and what all I got, a little of everything, and a good

disposition besides, I just feel like shouting, 'Thank you, Jesus, for making everything the way it is!' It could have been different!" For one thing, somebody else could have got Claud. At the thought of this, she was flooded with gratitude and a terrible pang of joy ran through her. "Oh thank you, Jesus, Jesus, thank you!" she cried aloud.

The book struck her directly over her left eye. It struck almost at the same instant that she realized the girl was about to hurl it. Before she could utter a sound, the raw face came crashing across the table toward her, howling. The girl's fingers sank like clamps into the soft flesh of her neck. She heard the mother cry out and Claud shout, "Whoa!" There was an instant when she was certain that she was about to be in an earthquake.   101

All at once her vision narrowed and she saw everything as if it were happening in a small room far away, or as if she were looking at it through the wrong end of a telescope. Claud's face crumpled and fell out of sight. The nurse ran in, then out, then in again. Then the gangling figure of the doctor rushed out of the inner door. Magazines flew this way and that as the table turned over. The girl fell with a thud and Mrs. Turpin's vision suddenly reversed itself and she saw everything large instead of small. The eyes of the white-trashy woman were staring hugely at the floor. There the girl, held down on one side by the nurse and on the other by her mother, was wrenching and turning in their grasp. The doctor was kneeling astride her, trying to hold her arm down. He managed after a second to sink a long needle into it.   102

Mrs. Turpin felt entirely hollow except for her heart which swung from side to side as if it were agitated in a great empty drum of flesh.   103

"Somebody that's not busy call for the ambulance," the doctor said in the off-hand voice young doctors adopt for terrible occasions.   104

Mrs. Turpin could not have moved a finger. The old man who had been sitting next to her skipped nimbly into the office and made the call, for the secretary still seemed to be gone.   105

"Claud!" Mrs. Turpin called.   106

He was not in his chair. She knew she must jump up and   107
find him but she felt like some one trying to catch a train in
a dream, when everything moves in slow motion and the
faster you try to run the slower you go.

"Here I am," a suffocated voice, very unlike Claud's, said.   108

He was doubled up in the corner on the floor, pale as   109
paper, holding his leg. She wanted to get up and go to him
but she could not move. Instead, her gaze was drawn slowly
downward to the churning face on the floor, which she could
see over the doctor's shoulder.

The girl's eyes stopped rolling and focused on her. They   110
seemed a much lighter blue than before, as if a door that had
been tightly closed behind them was now open to admit light
and air.

Mrs. Turpin's head cleared and her power of motion re-   111
turned. She leaned forward until she was looking directly into
the fierce brilliant eyes. There was no doubt in her mind that
the girl did know her, knew her in some intense and personal
way, beyond time and place and condition. "What you got
to say to me?" she asked hoarsely and held her breath, waiting, as for a revelation.

The girl raised her head. Her gaze locked with Mrs. Tur-   112
pin's. "Go back to hell where you came from, you old wart
hog," she whispered. Her voice was low but clear. Her eyes
burned for a moment as if she saw with pleasure that her
message had struck its target.

Mrs. Turpin sank back in her chair.   113

After a moment the girl's eyes closed and she turned her   114
head wearily to the side.

The doctor rose and handed the nurse the empty syringe.   115
He leaned over and put both hands for a moment on the
mother's shoulders, which were shaking. She was sitting on
the floor, her lips pressed together, holding Mary Grace's
hand in her lap. The girl's fingers were gripped like a baby's
around her thumb. "Go on to the hospital," he said. "I'll call
and make the arrangements."

"Now let's see that neck," he said in a jovial voice to Mrs.   116
Turpin. He began to inspect her neck with his first two
fingers. Two little moon-shaped lines like pink fish bones

were indented over her windpipe. There was the beginning of an angry red swelling above her eye. His fingers passed over this also.

"Lea' me be," she said thickly and shook him off. "See about Claud. She kicked him." 117

"I'll see about him in a minute," he said and felt her pulse. He was a thin gray-haired man, given to pleasantries. "Go home and have yourself a vacation the rest of the day," he said and patted her on the shoulder. 118

Quit your pattin me, Mrs. Turpin growled to herself. 119

"And put an ice pack over that eye," he said. Then he went and squatted down beside Claud and looked at his leg. After a moment he pulled him up and Claud limped after him into the office. 120

Until the ambulance came, the only sounds in the room were the tremulous moans of the girl's mother, who continued to sit on the floor. The white-trash woman did not take her eyes off the girl. Mrs. Turpin looked straight ahead at nothing. Presently the ambulance drew up, a long dark shadow, behind the curtain. The attendants came in and set the stretcher down beside the girl and lifted her expertly onto it and carried her out. The nurse helped the mother gather up her things. The shadow of the ambulance moved silently away and the nurse came back in the office. 121

"That ther girl is going to be a lunatic, ain't she?" the white-trash woman asked the nurse, but the nurse kept on to the back and never answered her. 122

"Yes, she's going to be a lunatic," the white-trash woman said to the rest of them. 123

"Po' critter," the old woman murmured. The child's face was still in her lap. His eyes looked idly out over her knees. He had not moved during the disturbance except to draw one leg up under him. 124

"I thank Gawd," the white-trash woman said fervently, "I ain't a lunatic." 125

Claud came limping out and the Turpins went home. 126

As their pick-up truck turned into their own dirt road and made the crest of the hill, Mrs. Turpin gripped the window ledge and looked out suspiciously. The land sloped gracefully 127 down through a field dotted with lavender weeds and at the start of the rise their small yellow frame house, with its little flower beds spread out around it like a fancy apron, sat primly in its accustomed place between two giant hickory trees. She would not have been startled to see a burnt wound between two blackened chimneys.

Neither of them felt like eating so they put on their house clothes and lowered the shade in the bedroom and lay down, Claud with his leg on a pillow and herself with a damp washcloth over her eye. The instant she was flat on her back, the image of a razor-backed hog with warts on its face and horns coming out behind its ears snorted into her head. She moaned, a low quiet moan. 128

"I am not," she said tearfully, "a wart hog. From hell." But the denial had no force. The girl's eyes and her words, even the tone of her voice, low but clear, directed only to her, brooked no repudiation. She had been singled out for the message, though there was trash in the room to whom it might justly have been applied. The full force of this fact struck her only now. There was a woman there who was neglecting her own child but she had been overlooked. The message had been given to Ruby Turpin, a respectable, hard-working, church-going woman. The tears dried. Her eyes began to burn instead with wrath. 129

She rose on her elbow and the washcloth fell into her hand. Claud was lying on his back, snoring. She wanted to tell him what the girl had said. At the same time, she did not wish to put the image of herself as a wart hog from hell into his mind. 130

"Hey, Claud," she muttered and pushed his shoulder. 131

Claud opened one pale baby blue eye. 132

She looked into it warily. He did not think about any thing. He just went his way. 133

"Wha, whasit?" he said and closed the eye again. 134

"Nothing," she said. "Does your leg pain you?" 135

"Hurts like hell," Claud said. 136

"It'll quit terreckly," she said and lay back down. In a moment Claud was snoring again. For the rest of the afternoon they lay there. Claud slept. She scowled at the ceiling. 137

Occasionally she raised her fist and made a small stabbing motion over her chest as if she was defending her innocence to invisible guests who were like the comforters of Job, reasonable-seeming but wrong.

About five-thirty Claud stirred. "Got to go after those niggers," he sighed, not moving.   138

She was looking straight up as if there were unintelligible handwriting on the ceiling. The protuberance over her eye had turned a greenish-blue. "Listen here," she said.   139

"What?"   140

"Kiss me."   141

Claud leaned over and kissed her loudly on the mouth. He pinched her side and their hands interlocked. Her expression of ferocious concentration did not change. Claud got up, groaning and growling, and limped off. She continued to study the ceiling.   142

She did not get up until she heard the pick-up truck coming back with the Negroes. Then she rose and thrust her feet in her brown oxfords, which she did not bother to lace, and stumped out onto the back porch and got her red plastic bucket. She emptied a tray of ice cubes into it and filled it half full of water and went out into the back yard. Every afternoon after Claud brought the hands in, one of the boys helped him put out hay and the rest waited in the back of the truck until he was ready to take them home. The truck was parked in the shade under one of the hickory trees.   143

"Hi yawl this evening?" Mrs. Turpin asked grimly, appearing with the bucket and the dipper. There were three women and a boy in the truck.   144

"Us doin nicely," the oldest woman said. "Hi you doin?" and her gaze stuck immediately on the dark lump on Mrs. Turpin's forehead. "You done fell down, ain't you?" she asked in a solicitous voice. The old woman was dark and almost toothless. She had on an old felt hat of Claud's set back on her head. The other two women were younger and lighter and they both had new bright green sunhats. One of them had hers on her head; the other had taken hers off and the boy was grinning beneath it.   145

Mrs. Turpin set the bucket down on the floor of the truck.   146
"Yawl hep yourselves," she said. She looked around to make
sure Claud had gone. "No, I didn't fall down," she said,
folding her arms. "It was something worse than that."

"Ain't nothing bad happen to you!" the old woman said.   147
She said it as if they all knew that Mrs. Turpin was protected
in some special way by Divine Providence. "You just had you
a little fall."

"We were in town at the doctor's office for where the cow   148
kicked Mr. Turpin," Mrs. Turpin said in a flat tone that
indicated they could leave off their foolishness. "And there
was this girl there. A big fat girl with her face all broke out.
I could look at that girl and tell she was peculiar but I
couldn't tell how. And me and her mama was just talking and
going along and all of a sudden WHAM! She throws this big
book she was reading at me and . . ."

"Naw!" the old woman cried out.   149

"And then she jumps over the table and commences to   150
choke me."

"Naw!" they all exclaimed, "naw!"   151

"Hi come she do that?" the old woman asked. "What ail   152
her?"

Mrs. Turpin only glared in front of her.   153

"Somethin ail her," the old woman said.   154

"They carried her off in an ambulance," Mrs. Turpin con-   155
tinued, "but before she went she was rolling on the floor and
they were trying to hold her down to give her a shot and she
said something to me." She paused. "You know what she said
to me?"

"What she say?" they asked.   156

"She said," Mrs. Turpin began, and stopped, her face very   157
dark and heavy. The sun was getting whiter and whiter,
blanching the sky overhead so that the leaves of the hickory
tree were black in the face of it. She could not bring forth
the words. "Something real ugly," she muttered.

"She sho shouldn't said nothin ugly to you," the old   158
woman said. "You so sweet. You the sweetest lady I know."

"She pretty too," the one with the hat on said.   159

"And stout," the other one said. "I never knowed no sweeter white lady." 160

"That's the truth befo' Jesus," the old woman said. "Amen! You des as sweet and pretty as you can be." 161

Mrs. Turpin knew exactly how much Negro flattery was worth and it added to her rage. "She said," she began again and finished this time with a fierce rush of breath, "that I was an old wart hog from hell." 162

There was an astounded silence. 163

"Where she at?" the youngest woman cried in a piercing voice. 164

"Lemme see her. I'll kill her!" 165

"I'll kill her with you!" the other one cried. 166

"She b'long in the sylum," the old woman said emphatically. "You the sweetest white lady I know." 167

"She pretty too," the other two said. "Stout as she can be and sweet. Jesus satisfied with her!" 168

"Deed he is," the old woman declared. 169

Idiots! Mrs. Turpin growled to herself. You could never say anything intelligent to a nigger. You could talk at them but not with them. "Yawl ain't drunk your water," she said shortly. "Leave the bucket in the truck when you're finished with it. I got more to do than just stand around and pass the time of day," and she moved off and into the house. 170

She stood for a moment in the middle of the kitchen. The dark protuberance over her eye looked like a miniature tornado cloud which might any moment sweep across the horizon of her brow. Her lower lip protruded dangerously. She squared her massive shoulders. Then she marched into the front of the house and out the side door and started down the road to the pig parlor. She had the look of a woman going single-handed, weaponless, into battle. 171

The sun was a deep yellow now like a harvest moon and was riding westward very fast over the far tree line as if it meant to reach the hogs before she did. The road was rutted and she kicked several good-sized stones out of her path as she strode along. The pig parlor was on a little knoll at the end of a lane that ran off from the side of the barn. It was a 172 square of concrete as large as a small room, with a board fence about four feet high around it. The concrete floor sloped slightly so that the hog wash could drain off into a trench where it was carried to the field for fertilizer. Claud was standing on the outside, on the edge of the concrete, hanging onto the top board, hosing down the floor inside. The hose was connected to the faucet of a water trough nearby.

Mrs. Turpin climbed up beside him and glowered down   173
at the hogs inside. There were seven long-snouted bristly shoats in it—tan with liver-colored spots—and an old sow a few weeks off from farrowing. She was lying on her side grunting. The shoats were running about shaking themselves like idiot children, their little slit pig eyes searching the floor for anything left. She had read that pigs were the most intelligent animal. She doubted it. They were supposed to be smarter than dogs. There had even been a pig astronaut. He had performed his assignment perfectly but died of a heart attack afterwards because they left him in his electric suit, sitting upright throughout his examination when naturally a hog should be on all fours.

A-gruntin and a-rootin and a-groanin.   174

"Gimme that hose," she said, yanking it away from Claud.   175
"Go on and carry them niggers home and then get off that leg."

"You look like you might have swallowed a mad dog,"   176
Claud observed, but he got down and limped off. He paid no attention to her humors.

Until he was out of earshot, Mrs. Turpin stood on the side   177
of the pen, holding the hose and pointing the stream of water at the hind quarters of any shoat that looked as if it might try to lie down. When he had had time to get over the hill, she turned her head slightly and her wrathful eyes scanned the path. He was nowhere in sight. She turned back again and seemed to gather herself up. Her shoulders rose and she drew in her breath.

"What do you send me a message like that for?" she said   178
in a low fierce voice, barely above a whisper but with the force of a shout in its concentrated fury. "How am I a hog and me

both? How am I saved and from hell too?" Her free fist was knotted and with the other she gripped the hose, blindly pointing the stream of water in and out of the eye of the old sow whose outraged squeal she did not hear.

The pig parlor commanded a view of the back pasture where their twenty beef cows were gathered around the hay-bales Claud and the boy had put out. The freshly cut pasture sloped down to the highway. Across it was their cotton field and beyond that a dark green dusty wood which they owned as well. The sun was behind the wood, very red, looking over the paling of trees like a farmer inspecting his own hogs.   179

"Why me?" she rumbled. "It's no trash around here, black or white, that I haven't given to. And break my back to the bone every day working. And do for the church."   180

She appeared to be the right size woman to command the arena before her. "How am I a hog?" she demanded. "Exactly how am I like them?" and she jabbed the stream of water at the shoats. "There was plenty of trash there. It didn't have to be me.   181

"If you like trash better, go get yourself some trash then," she railed. "You could have made me trash. Or a nigger. If trash is what you wanted why didn't you make me trash?" She shook her fist with the hose in it and a watery snake appeared momentarily in the air. "I could quit working and take it easy and be filthy," she growled. "Lounge about the sidewalks all day drinking root beer. Dip snuff and spit in every puddle and have it all over my face. I could be nasty.   182

"Or you could have made me a nigger. It's too late for me to be a nigger," she said with deep sarcasm, "but I could act like one. Lay down in the middle of the road and stop traffic. Roll on the ground."   183

In the deepening light everything was taking on a mysterious hue. The pasture was growing a peculiar glassy green and the streak of highway had turned lavender. She braced herself for a final assault and this time her voice rolled out over the pasture. "Go on," she yelled, "call me a hog! Call me a hog again. From hell. Call me a wart hog from hell. Put that bottom rail on top. There'll still be a top and bottom!"   184

A garbled echo returned to her.   185

A final surge of fury shook her and she roared, "Who do   186
you think you are?"

The color of everything, field and crimson sky, burned for   187
a moment with a transparent intensity. The question carried
over the pasture and across the highway and the cotton field
and returned to her clearly like an answer from beyond the
wood.

She opened her mouth but no sound came out of it.   188

A tiny truck, Claud's, appeared on the highway, heading   189
rapidly out of sight. Its gears scraped thinly. It looked like a
child's toy. At any moment a bigger truck might smash into
it and scatter Claud's and the niggers' brains all over the road.

Mrs. Turpin stood there, her gaze fixed on the highway,   190
all her muscles rigid, until in five or six minutes the truck
reappeared, returning. She waited until it had had time to
turn into their own road. Then like a monumental statue
coming to life, she bent her head slowly and gazed, as if
through the very heart of mystery, down into the pig parlor
at the hogs. They had settled all in one corner around the
old sow who was grunting softly. A red glow suffused them.
They appeared to pant with a secret life.

Until the sun slipped finally behind the tree line, Mrs.   191
Turpin remained there with her gaze bent to them as if she
were absorbing some abysmal life-giving knowledge. At last
she lifted her head. There was only a purple streak in the sky,
cutting through a field of crimson and leading, like an extension of the highway, into the descending dusk. She raised her
hands from the side of the pen in a gesture hieratic and
profound. A visionary light settled in her eyes. She saw the
streak as a vast swinging bridge extending upward from the
earth through a field of living fire. Upon it a vast horde of
souls were rumbling toward heaven. There were whole companies of white-trash, clean for the first time in their lives, and
bands of black niggers in white robes, and battalions of freaks
and lunatics shouting and clapping and leaping like frogs.
And bringing up the end of the procession was a tribe of
people whom she recognized at once as those who, like

herself and Claud, had always had a little of everything and the God-given wit to use it right. She leaned forward to observe them closer. They were marching behind the others with great dignity, accountable as they had always been for good order and common sense and respectable behavior. They alone were on key. Yet she could see by their shocked and altered faces that even their virtues were being burned away. She lowered her hands and gripped the rail of the hog pen, her eyes small but fixed unblinkingly on what lay ahead. In a moment the vision faded but she remained where she was, immobile.

At length she got down and turned off the faucet and   192
made her slow way on the darkening path to the house. In the woods around her the invisible cricket choruses had struck up, but what she heard were the voices of the souls climbing upward into the starry field and shouting hallelujah.

COMMENT ON "REVELATION"

Ruby Turpin, the central character in Flannery O'Connor's "Revelation," is obsessed with the classification process. At night she occupies herself "naming the classes of people": most "colored people" are on the bottom; "next to them— not above, just away from—are the white trash"; and so on. Mrs. Turpin puzzles about the exceptions to her system—the black dentist who owns property and the decent white folks who have lost their money—but for the most part she is certain about her system and her place in it. In the doctor's waiting room, she sizes up the other patients, placing them in their appropriate classes. But her internal and external dialogue reveals the ironies and inconsistencies in her rigid system. Self-satisfied, pleased that Jesus is on her side, she is not prepared for the book on *Human Development* that is thrown at her or the events that follow—the transparent flattery of the black workers, her cleaning of the pig parlor, and finally her vision of the highway to heaven that reveals her real place in God's hierarchy.

Division and Classification as a Writing Strategy

1. Write a column for your local newspaper in which you develop a system for classifying a concept such as trash. You may decide to interpret this word literally, developing a scheme to categorize the type of objects people throw away. Or you may decide to interpret the word figuratively, focusing on things that some people consider worthless— gossip columns, romance magazines, game shows. Here are a few possibilities: although people throw trash away, it won't go away; people's distaste for trash is the cause of its creation; people are so saturated by trash that they accept it as part of their culture with its own subtle sub-categories.

2. In an essay addressed to a psychology class, classify various kinds of eaters. Instead of writing a humorous essay like Calvin Trillin's, you may want to write a serious essay that classifies people by what they eat, how fast they eat, or when they eat.

3. Mary Mebane argues that the system of class and color is used to impose power in a negative way. Consider some other system that uses power in a positive way. For example, you may want to classify people by the various ways they empower others.

4. Write an essay that classifies various kinds of bad luck. You may want to follow Austin's pattern by arranging the types of bad luck in an ascending order of complexity. You may also want to consult some of the essays on gambling in *Resources for Writing*. Or you may simply wish to illustrate your categories by using Murphy's law—"If anything can go wrong, it will."

5. Select *one* of Lewis Thomas's categories in "The Technology of Medicine" and classify it into smaller subcategories. For example, you may wish to draft an editorial in which you argue that the various kinds of "supportive therapy,"

while costly and time consuming, are nevertheless very valuable kinds of medical technology.

6. Using Gail Sheehy's crisis/growth model, write an essay in which you classify the predictable crises of a college education. Although you may divide the period into the traditional four years (ages eighteen to twenty-one), remember that the average student takes six years to complete a college education and that the nontraditional student population is the fastest-growing group within the university. Use this information to expand and enrich your classification system. But use your system, as Sheehy does, to illustrate some theory of intellectual development. What are the factors that permit or prevent students from moving from stage to stage?

DEFINITION

❦

As a writer, both in and out of college, you're likely to spend a good deal of time writing definitions. In an astronomy class, you may be asked to explain what the Doppler effect is or what a white dwarf star is. In a literature class, you may be asked to define a sonnet and identify its different forms. If you become an engineer, you may write to define problems your company proposes to solve or to define a new product your company has developed. If you become a business executive, you may have to write a brochure to describe a new service your company offers or draft a letter that defines the company's policy on credit applications.

Writers use definitions to establish boundaries, to show the essential nature of something, and to explain the special

qualities that identify a purpose, place, object, or concept
and distinguish it from others similar to it. Writers often
write extended definitions—definitions that go beyond the
one-sentence or one-paragraph explanations that you find
in a dictionary or encyclopedia to expand on and examine
the essential qualities of a policy, an event, a group, or a
trend. Sometimes an extended definition becomes an entire book. Some books are written to define the good life;
others are written to define the ideal university or the best
kind of government. In fact, many of the books on any
current nonfiction best-seller list are primarily definitions.
The essays in this section of *The Riverside Reader* are all
extended definitions.

PURPOSE

When you write, you can use definitions in several ways. For
instance, you can define to *point out the special nature* of
something. You may want to show the special flavor of San
Francisco that makes it different from other major cities in
the world, or you may want to describe the unique features
that make the Macintosh computer different from other personal computers.

You can also define to *explain*. In an essay about cross-
country skiing, you might want to show your readers what
the sport is like and point out why it's less hazardous and less
expensive than downhill skiing but better exercise. You might
also define to *entertain*—to describe the essence of what it
means to be a "good old boy," for instance. Often you define
to *inform;* that is what you are doing in college papers when
you write about West Virginia folk art or postmodern archi-
tecture. Often you write to *establish a standard,* perhaps for
a good exercise program, a workable environmental policy,
or even the ideal pair of running shoes. Notice that when you
define to set a standard, you may also be defining to *persuade,*
to convince your reader to accept the ideal you describe.
Many definitions are essentially arguments.

Sometimes you may even write to *define yourself.* That is

what you are doing when you write an autobiographical statement for a college admissions officer or a scholarship committee, or when you write a job application letter. You hope to give your readers the special information that will distinguish you from all other candidates. When that is your task, you'll profit by knowing the common strategies for defining and by recognizing how other writers have used them.

AUDIENCE

When you're going to use definition in your writing, you can benefit by thinking ahead of time about what your readers expect from you. Why are they reading, and what questions will they want you to answer? You can't anticipate all their questions, but you should plan on responding to at least two kinds of queries.

First, your readers are likely to ask, "What distinguishes what you're writing about? What's typical or different about it? How do I know when I see one?" For example, if you were writing about the Olympic games, your readers would perhaps want to know the difference between today's Olympic games and the original games in ancient Greece. With a little research, you could tell them about several major differences.

Second, for more complex topics you should expect that your readers will also ask, "What is the basic character or the essential nature of what you're writing about? What do you mean when you say 'alternative medicine,' 'Marxist theory,' or 'white-collar crime?'" Answering questions such as these is more difficult, but if you're going to use terms like these in an essay, you have an obligation to define them, using as many strategies as you need to clarify your terms. To define white-collar crime, for instance, you could specify that it is nonviolent, likely to happen within businesses, and involves illegal manipulation of funds or privileged information. You should also strengthen your definition by giving examples that your readers might be familiar with.

STRATEGIES

You can choose from a variety of strategies for defining and use them singly or in combination. A favorite strategy for all of us is *giving examples,* a technique as natural as pointing to a certain kind of automobile or to the picture of a horse in a children's book. Writers use the same method when they describe a scene or an event to help readers get a visual image. Every writer in this section defines by giving examples, but in "The Hoax" John Berendt uses the greatest number in the shortest article as he describes impostors, forgeries, frauds, and fake radio broadcasts. Kathleen Norris relies on examples to illustrate what she means by *gossip.*

You can define by *analyzing qualities* to show what features or characteristics distinguish the thing you're defining. When you use this strategy, you pick out particular qualities you want your reader to identify with the person, concept, or object you're defining. Richard Rodriguez uses the strategy to define adolescence in "Growing Up in Los Angeles," pointing out that rebellion has been a traditional part of American adolescence, from the earliest settlers to Tom Sawyer and Huck Finn. John Berendt also analyzes qualities when he says, "To qualify as a hoax, a prank must have some magic in it."

A similar strategy is *attributing characteristics.* This is Harrigan's chief tactic in "The Tiger Is God." He starts by describing tigers' characteristic method of attack, points out that zoo keepers know that tigers are supposed to be dangerous, and then identifies tigers as predators whose mission is to kill. Kathleen Norris uses the same strategy in "The Holy Use of Gossip" when she says that telling stories is characteristic of small towns.

Jon Katz uses the strategy of *defining negatively,* the important method of showing what something is not. In "Interactivity" he gives examples of various media that are not interactive: network television, newspapers, and weekly news magazines. Alice Walker also defines negatively in "Everyday Use," when the character of the mother suggests that honoring one's heritage doesn't mean hanging on to relics from the past.

Another way to define is by *using analogies*. Rodriguez uses this strategy in "Growing Up in Los Angeles" when he says that the grafitti done by street gangs is a kind of advertising comparable to a billboard on Sunset Boulevard. Harrigan uses analogy when he compares the window in the tiger's cage to a portal through which mankind's most primeval terrors flow.

You can also define by *giving functions*. Sometimes the most significant feature about a creature, object, or institution is what it does. Function is a key concpet in "Interactivity." For Katz, the important point about all the media he believes will dominate the future is that they allow users to interact with them. In "The Tiger Is God," Harrigan stresses that the function of a tiger is to kill; it's a predator.

COMBINING STRATEGIES

Even when you're writing an article or essay that is primarily a definition, you're not limited to the strategies we've just mentioned. You may want to combine definition with other patterns, as most professional writers do. For example, in "Rapport-Talk and Report-Talk" (see page 183) Deborah Tannen defines men's and women's different communication styles, then argues that many of the problems between men and woman grow out of these differences. In "A Chinaman's Chance" (page 468) Eric Liu gives his own definition of the American Dream, then argues that young people who feel they have no chance to achieve the dream are mistaken.

Some writers also use narration and description as a way of defining. Maya Angelou defines a certain kind of racist attitude in her narrative "My Name Is Margaret" (see page 31).

As you read essays in this section, and especially as you reread them, keep part of your mind alert to spot the strategies the writer is using. You may want to incorporate some of them into your own writing. You may want to define through anecdotes, as the writers do in "The Hoax" and "The Holy Use of Gossip."

USING DEFINITION IN PARAGRAPHS

Here are two definition paragraphs. The first is written by a professional writer and is followed by an analysis. The second is written by a student writer and is followed by questions.

JEREMY RIFKIN
"The Gospel of Mass Consumption"

Historically, word negative— steeped in violence

Term of destruction and disease

The term "consumption" has both English and French roots. In its original form, to consume meant to destroy, to pillage, to subdue, to exhaust. It is a word steeped in violence and until the present century had only negative connotations. As late as the 1920s, the word was still being used to refer to the most deadly disease of the day—tuberculosis. Today the average American is consuming twice as much as he or she did at the end of World War II. The metamorphosis of consumption from vice to virtue is one of the most important yet least examined phenomena of the twentieth century.

Now we worship consumption—has become a virt

Comment In this paragraph, the social critic Jeremy Rifkin goes back to the original meanings of the term "consumption" to stress how ominous the implications of the word really are. He points out that when we consume something, we destroy it, demolish it, wipe it out. He gives us a telling reminder that the deadly disease of tuberculosis was called "consumption"; it literally destroyed the lungs. Now, however, Americans encourage and laud consumption; we've turned it from a vice into a virtue.

Rifkin's paragraph is succinct and forceful; the contrast he sets up works well. He creates a striking metaphor when he says the term "consumption" is "steeped in violence," and his concrete reminder that consumption was once a disease suggests that we should think about what we've created with our changed attitudes.

JASON UTESCH
Personality

"She has a great personality." Translation: she goes to bed early to watch the shopping channel. "He has a great personality." Translation: he tells dirty jokes at funerals. The "p" word is troublesome not only because all the great personalities we've been told about have proved disappointing, but also because all the great personalities we know don't seem to measure up to other people's expectations. Even the old song suggests that personality is a complicated quality to define because to have it a person has to have a special walk, talk, smile, charm, love, and PLUS she (or he) has to have a great big heart.

1. What do you see as Utesch's purpose in listing so many contradictions in the way people define *personality*?
2. What does the writer imply by using the phrase "The 'p' word"?

DEFINITION

Points to Remember

1. Remember that you are obligated to define key terms that you use in your writing—such as Marxism, alternative medicine, nontraditional student.
2. Understand your purpose in defining: to explain, to entertain, to persuade, to set boundaries, or to establish a standard.
3. Understand how writers construct an argument from a definition. For example, by defining the good life or good government, they argue for that kind of life or government.
4. Know the several ways of defining: giving examples, analyzing qualities, attributing characteristics, defining negatively, using analogies, and showing function.
5. Learn to use definition in combination with other strategies, as a basis on which to build an argument, or as supporting evidence.

John Berendt was born in Syracuse, New York, in 1939 and was educated at Harvard University. He began his writing career as an associate editor at *Esquire,* before editing *Holiday Magazine* and writing and producing television programs such as *The David Frost Show* and *The Dick Cavett Show.* In 1979, he returned to *Esquire* as a columnist and began contributing articles to periodicals such as *New York Magazine.* In 1993, he published his first book, *Midnight in the Garden of Good and Evil,* a "nonfiction novel" about a controversial murder in Savannah, Georgia. In "The Hoax," reprinted from *Esquire,* Berendt defines the magical ingredients of a hoax.

The Hoax

WHEN THE HUMORIST Robert Benchley was an under- 1
graduate at Harvard eighty years ago, he and a couple of friends showed up one morning at the door of an elegant Beacon Hill mansion, dressed as furniture repairmen. They told the housekeeper they had come to pick up the sofa. Five minutes later they carried the sofa out the door, put it on a truck, and drove it three blocks away to another house, where, posing as deliverymen, they plunked it down in the parlor. That evening, as Benchley well knew, the couple living in house A were due to attend a party in house B. Whatever the outcome—and I'll get to that shortly—it was guaranteed to be a defining example of how proper Bostonians handle social crises. The wit inherent in Benchley's practical joke elevated it from the level of prank to the more respectable realm of hoax.

To qualify as a hoax, a prank must have magic in it—the 2

word is derived from *hocus-pocus*, after all. Daring and irony are useful ingredients, too. A good example of a hoax is the ruse perpetrated by David Hampton, the young black man whose pretense of being Sidney Poitier's son inspired John Guare's *Six Degrees of Separation*. Hampton managed to insinuate himself into two of New York's most sophisticated households—one headed by the president of the public-television station WNET, the other by the dean of the Columbia School of Journalism. Hampton's hoax touched a number of sensitive themes: snobbery, class, race, and sex, all of which playwright Guare deftly exploited.

Hampton is a member of an elite band of famous impostors that includes a half-mad woman who for fifty years claimed to be Anastasia, the lost daughter of the assassinated   3

To qualify as a hoax, a prank must have magic in it. . . .

---

czar Nicholas II; and a man named Harry Gerguson, who became a Hollywood restaurateur and darling of society in the 1930s and 1940s as the ersatz Russian prince Mike Romanoff.

Forgeries have been among the better hoaxes. Fake Vermeers painted by an obscure Dutch artist, Hans van Meegeren, were so convincing that they fooled art dealers, collectors, and museums. The hoax came to light when Van Meegeren was arrested as a Nazi collaborator after the war. To prove he was not a Nazi, he admitted he had sold a fake Vermeer to Hermann Göring for $256,000. Then he owned up to having created other "Vermeers," and to prove he could do it, he painted *Jesus in the Temple* in the style of Vermeer while under guard in jail.   4

In a bizarre twist, a story much like Van Meegeren's became the subject of the book *Fake!*, by Clifford Irving, who   5 in 1972 attempted to pull off a spectacular hoax of his own: a wholly fraudulent "authorized" biography of Howard Hughes. Irving claimed to have conducted secret interviews with the reclusive Hughes, and McGraw-Hill gave him a big advance. Shortly before publication, Hughes surfaced by telephone and denied that he had ever spoken with Irving. Irving had already spent $100,000 of the advance; he was convicted of fraud and sent to jail.

As it happens, we are used to hoaxes where I come from.   6
I grew up just a few miles down the road from Cardiff, New York—a town made famous by the Cardiff Giant. As we learned in school, a farmer named Newell complained, back in 1889, that his well was running dry, and while he and his neighbors were digging a new one, they came upon what appeared to be the fossilized remains of a man twelve feet tall. Before the day was out, Newell had erected a tent and posted a sign charging a dollar for a glimpse of the "giant"—three dollars for a longer look. Throngs descended on Cardiff. It wasn't long before scientists determined that the giant had been carved from a block of gypsum. The hoax came undone fairly quickly after that, but even so—as often happens with hoaxes—the giant became an even bigger attraction *because* it was a hoax. P. T. Barnum offered Newell a fortune for the giant, but Newell refused, and it was then that he got his comeuppance. Barnum simply made a replica and put it on display as the genuine Cardiff Giant. Newell's gig was ruined.

The consequences of hoaxes are what give them spice.   7
Orson Welles's lifelike 1938 radio broadcast of H. G. Wells's *War of the Worlds* panicked millions of Americans, who were convinced that martians had landed in New Jersey. The forged diary of Adolf Hitler embarrassed historian Hugh Trevor-Roper, who had vouched for its authenticity, and *Newsweek* and *The Sunday Times* of London, both of which published excerpts in 1983 shortly before forensic tests proved that there were nylon fibers in the paper it was written on, which wouldn't have been possible had it originated before 1950. The five-hundred-thousand-year-old remains of Piltdown man, found in 1912, had anthropologists confused

about human evolution until 1953, when fluoride tests exposed the bones as an elaborate modern hoax. And as for Robert Benchley's game on Beacon Hill, no one said a word about the sofa all evening, although there it sat in plain sight. One week later, however, couple A sent an anonymous package to couple B. It contained the sofa's slipcovers.

For Study and Discussion

QUESTIONS FOR RESPONSE

1. What hoaxes do you know about or have you been involved in? Which of them had elements that might be described as daring or witty?
2. What's your reaction to those incidents in Berendt's account that involve criminal fraud? How do you explain that reaction?

QUESTIONS ABOUT PURPOSE

1. How do you think Berendt wants you to respond to the tricksters he describes in his essay? To what extent did you respond that way?
2. Berendt's examples of people duped by hoaxes include scientists, a historian, a college president, an eminent publisher, and curators of several museums. What does he accomplish by telling stories about such a wide range of dupes?

QUESTIONS ABOUT AUDIENCE

1. This essay originally appeared in *Esquire* magazine. What traits and attitudes do you think a writer for *Esquire* assumes characterize its readers? (If necessary, browse through an issue of *Esquire* in the library to get a feel for its audience.)
2. Berendt seems to assume that everyone enjoys stories about tricksters getting the best of their victims. In your case, is the assumption justified? Why or why not?

QUESTIONS ABOUT STRATEGIES

1. What does the writer achieve by opening and closing the essay with the anecdote about the sofa?
2. How would you characterize the tone of this essay? What attitude of the writer toward his subject do you think the tone reflects? Do you find that attitude engaging or off-putting?

QUESTIONS FOR DISCUSSION

1. Which of Berendt's anecdotes do you find the most entertaining? Why?
2. When would you say a deception ceases to be a hoax and turns into something else? What examples can you think of?

Kathleen Norris was born in 1947 in Washington, D.C., and educated at Bennington College. She worked for a brief period as program secretary for the Academy of American Poets in New York before moving to South Dakota, where she became affiliated with Leaves of Grass, Inc. She has contributed poems and essays to *Dragonfly, Sumac,* and *Tennessee Poetry Journal,* published two collections of poetry, *Falling Off* (1971) and *Middle of the World* (1981), and three works of nonfiction, *Dakota: A Spiritual Geography* (1993), *The Cloister Walk* (1996), and *Amazing Grace* (1998). In "The Holy Use of Gossip," reprinted from *Dakota,* Norris defines the various uses of gossip in a small town.

The Holy Use of Gossip

It is the responsibility of writers to listen to gossip and pass it on.
It is the way all storytellers learn about life.
— GRACE PALEY

If there's anything worth calling theology, it is listening to
people's stories, listening to them and cherishing them.
— MARY PELLAUER

I ONCE SCANDALIZED a group of North Dakota teenagers who had been determined to scandalize me. Working as an artist-in-residence in their school for three weeks, I happened to hit prom weekend. Never much for proms in high school, I helped decorate, cutting swans out of posterboard and sprinkling them with purple glitter as the school gym was festooned with lavender and silver crepe paper streamers. 1

On Monday morning a group of the school outlaws was 2

gossiping in the library, just loud enough for me to hear, about the drunken exploits that had taken place at a prairie party in the wee hours after the dance: kids meeting in some remote spot, drinking beer and listening to car stereos turned up loud, then, near dawn, going to one girl's house for breakfast. I finally spoke up and said, "See, it's like I told you: the party's not over until you've told the stories. That's where all writing starts." They looked up at me, pretending that it bothered them that I'd heard.

"And," I couldn't resist adding, "everyone knows you   3
don't get piss-drunk and then eat scrambled eggs. If you

---

*At its deepest level, small-town gossip is
about how we face matters of life and death.*

---

didn't know it before, you know it now." "You're not going to write about *that,* are you?" one girl said, her eyes wide. "I don't know," I replied, "I might. It's all grist for the mill."

When my husband and I first moved to Dakota, people   4
were quick to tell us about an eccentric young man who came from back East and gradually lost his grip on reality. He shared a house with his sheep until relatives came and took him away. "He was a college graduate," someone would always add, looking warily at us as if to say, we know what can happen to Easterners who are too well educated. This was one of the first tales to go into my West River treasure-house of stories. It was soon joined by the story of the man who shot himself to see what it felt like. He hit his lower leg and later said that while he didn't feel anything for a few seconds, after that it hurt like hell.

There was Rattlesnake Bill, a cowboy who used to carry   5
rattlers in a paper sack in his pickup truck. If you didn't believe him, he'd put his hand in without looking and take one out to show you. One night Bill limped into a downtown

bar on crutches. A horse he was breaking had dragged him for about a mile, and he was probably lucky to be alive. He'd been knocked out, he didn't know for how long, and when he regained consciousness he had crawled to his house and changed clothes to come to town. Now Bill thought he'd drink a little whiskey for the pain. "Have you been to a doctor?" friends asked. "Nah, whiskey'll do."

Later that night at the steak house I managed to get Bill to eat something—most of my steak, as it turned out, but he needed it more than I. The steak was rare, and that didn't sit well with Bill. A real man eats his steak well done. But when I said, "What's the matter, are you too chicken to eat rare meat?" he gobbled it down. He slept in his pickup that night, and someone managed to get him to a doctor the next day. He had a broken pelvis.

There was another cowboy who had been mauled by a bobcat in a remote horse barn by the Grand River. The animal had leapt from a hayloft as he tied up a horse, and he had managed to grab a rifle and shoot her. He felt terrible afterwards, saying, "I should have realized the only reason she'd have attacked like that was because she was protecting young." He found her two young cubs, still blind, in the loft. In a desperate attempt to save them he called several veterinarians in the hope that they might know of a lactating cat who had aborted. Such a cat was found, but the cubs lived just a few more days.

There was the woman who nursed her husband through a long illness. A dutiful farm daughter and ranch wife, she had never experienced life on her own. When she was widowed, all the town spoke softly about "poor Ida." But when "poor Ida" kicked up her heels and, entering a delayed adolescence in her fifties, dyed her hair, dressed provocatively, and went dancing more than once a week at the steak house, the sympathetic cooing of the gossips turned to outrage. The woman at the center of the storm hadn't changed; she was still an innocent, bewildered by the calumny now directed at her. She lived it down and got herself a steady boyfriend, but she still dyes her hair and dresses flashy. I'm grateful for the color she adds to the town.

Sometimes it seems as if the whole world is fueled by gossip. Much of what passes for hard news today is the Hollywood fluff that was relegated to pulp movie magazines when I was a girl. From the Central Intelligence Agency to *Entertainment Tonight*, gossip is big business. But in small towns, gossip is still small-time. And as bad as it can be—venal, petty, mean—in the small town it also stays closer to the roots of the word. If you look up gossip in the *Oxford English Dictionary* you find that it is derived from the words for God and sibling, and originally meant "akin to God." It was used to describe one who has contracted spiritual kinship by acting as a sponsor at baptism; one who helps "give a name to." Eric Partridge's *Origins*, a dictionary of etymology, tells you simply to "see God," and there you find that the word's antecedents include gospel, godspell, *sippe* (or consanguinity) and "*sabha*, a village community—notoriously inter-related."

We are interrelated in a small town, whether or not we're related by blood. We know without thinking about it who owns what car; inhabitants of a town as small as a monastery learn to recognize each other's footsteps in the hall. Story is a safety valve for people who live as intimately as that; and I would argue that gossip done well can be a holy thing. It can strengthen communal bonds.

Gossip provides comic relief for people under tension. Candidates at one monastery are told of a novice in the past who had such a hot temper that the others loved to bait him. Once when they were studying he closed a window and the other monks opened it; once, twice. When he got up to close the window for the third time, he yelled at them, "Why are you making me sin with this window?"

Gossip can help us give a name to ourselves. The most revealing section of the weekly *Lemmon Leader* is the personal column in the classified ads, where people express thanks to those who helped with the bloodmobile, a 4-H booth at the county fair, a Future Homemakers of America fashion show,

9

10

11

12

a benefit for a family beset by huge medical bills. If you've been in the hospital or have suffered a death in the family, you take out an ad thanking the doctor, ambulance crew, and wellwishers who visited, sent cards, offered prayers, or brought gifts of food.

Often these ads are quite moving, written from the heart. 13 The parents of a small boy recently thanked those who had remembered their son with

> *prayers, cards, balloons, and gifts, and gave moral support to the rest of the family when Ty underwent surgery. . . . It's great to be home again in this caring community, and our biggest task now is to get Ty to eat more often and larger amounts. Where else but Lemmon would we find people who would stop by and have a bedtime snack and milk with Ty or provide good snacks just to help increase his caloric intake, or a school system with staff that take the time to make sure he eats his extra snacks. May God Bless all of you for caring about our "special little" boy—who is going to gain weight!*

No doubt it is the vast land surrounding us, brooding on 14 the edge of our consciousness, that makes it necessary for us to call such attention to human activity. Publicly asserting, as do many of these ads, that we live in a caring community helps us keep our hopes up in a hard climate or hard times, and gives us a sense of identity.

Privacy takes on another meaning in such an environment, 15 where you are asked to share your life, humbling yourself before the common wisdom, such as it is. Like everyone else, you become public property and come to accept things that city people would consider rude. A young woman using the pay phone in a West River café is scrutinized by several older women who finally ask her, "Who are you, anyway?" On discovering that she is from a ranch some sixty miles south, they question her until, learning her mother's maiden name, they are satisfied. They know her grandparents by reputation; good ranchers, good people.

The *Leader* has correspondents in rural areas within some 16 fifty miles of Lemmon—Bison, Chance, Duck Creek, Howe, Morristown, Rosebud (on the Grand River), Shadehill, Spring Butte, Thunder Hawk, White Butte—as well as at the local nursing home and in the town of Lemmon itself, who report on "doings." If you volunteer at the nursing home's weekly popcorn party and sing-along, your name appears. If you host a card party at your home, this is printed, along with the names of your guests. If you have guests from out of town, their names appear. Many notices would baffle an outsider, as they require an intimate knowledge of family relationships to decipher. One recent column from White Butte, headed "Neighbors Take Advantage of Mild Winter Weather to Visit Each Other," read in part: "Helen Johanssen spent several afternoons with Gaylene Francke; Mavis Merdahl was a Wednesday overnight guest at the Alvera Ellis home."

Allowing yourself to be a subject of gossip is one of the 17 sacrifices you make, living in a small town. And the pain caused by the loose talk of ignorant people is undeniable. One couple I know, having lost their only child to a virulent pneumonia (a robust thirty-five years old, he was dead in a matter of days) had to endure rumors that he had died of suicide, AIDS, and even anthrax. But it's also true that the gossips don't know all that they think they know, and often misread things in a comical way. My husband was once told that he was having an affair with a woman he hadn't met, and I still treasure the day I was encountered by three people who said, "Have you sold your house yet?" "When's the baby due?" and, "I'm sorry to hear your mother died."

I could trade the sources of the first two rumors: we'd 18 helped a friend move into a rented house, and I'd bought baby clothes downtown when I learned that I would soon become an aunt. The third rumor was easy enough to check; I called my mother on the phone. The flip side, the saving grace, is that despite the most diligent attentions of the diehard gossips, it is possible to have secrets.

Of course the most important things can't be hidden: 19
birth, sickness, death, divorce. But gossip is essentially democratic. It may be the plumber and his wife who had a screaming argument in a bar, or it could be the bank president's
wife who moved out and rented a room in the motel; everyone is fair game. And although there are always those who
take delight in the misfortunes of others, and relish a juicy
story at the expense of truth and others' feelings, this may be
the exception rather than the rule. Surprisingly often, gossip
is the way small-town people express solidarity.

I recall a marriage that was on the rocks. The couple had 20
split up, and gossip ran wild. Much sympathy was expressed
for the children, and one friend of the couple said to me,
"The worst thing she could do is to take him back too soon.
This will take time." Those were healing words, a kind of
prayer. And when the family did reunite, the town breathed
a collective sigh of relief.

My own parents' marriage was of great interest in Lem- 21
mon back in the 1930s. My mother, the town doctor's only
child, eloped with another Northwestern University student;
a musician, of all things. A poor preacher's kid. "This will
bear watching," one matriarch said. My parents fooled her.
As time went on, the watching grew dull. Now going on
fifty-five years, their marriage has outlasted all the gossip.

Like the desert tales that monks have used for centuries as 22
a basis for a theology and way of life, the tales of small-town
gossip are often morally instructive, illustrating the ways ordinary people survive the worst that happens to them; or,
conversely, the ways in which self-pity, anger, and despair can
overwhelm and destroy them. Gossip is theology translated
into experience. In it we hear great stories of conversion, like
the drunk who turns his or her life around, as well as stories
of failure. We can see that pride really does go before a fall,
and that hope is essential. We watch closely those who retire,
or who lose a spouse, lest they lose interest in living. When
we gossip we are also praying, not only for them but for
ourselves.

At its deepest level, small-town gossip is about how we face 23 matters of life and death. We see the gossip of earlier times, the story immortalized in ballads such as "Barbara Allen," lived out before our eyes as a young man obsessively in love with a vain young woman nearly self-destructs. We also see how people heal themselves. One of the bravest people I know is a young mother who sewed and embroidered exquisite baptismal clothes for her church with the memorial money she received when her first baby died. When she gave birth to a healthy girl a few years later, the whole town rejoiced.

My favorite gossip takes note of the worst and the best that is in us. Two women I know were diagnosed with terminal cancer. One said, "If I ever get out of this hospital, I'm going to look out for Number One." And that's exactly what she did. Against overwhelming odds, she survived, and it made her mean. The other woman spoke about the blessings of a life that had taken some hard blows: her mother had killed herself when she was a girl, her husband had died young. I happened to visit her just after she'd been told that she had less than a year to live. She was dry-eyed, and had been reading the Psalms. She was entirely realistic about her illness and said to me, "The one thing that scares me is the pain. I hope I die before I turn into an old bitch." I told her family that story after the funeral, and they loved it; they could hear in it their mother's voice, the way she really was.

24

For Study and Discussion

QUESTIONS FOR RESPONSE

1. What stories similar to those Norris tells can you relate about your own community? That community can be an organization or an extended family as well as a town.
2. Norris stresses the positive effects of gossip. What are some of the negative effects that you have witnessed? Overall, how would you describe the balance between positive and negative gossip in your community?

QUESTIONS ABOUT PURPOSE

1. What common attitude about gossip does Norris hope to counteract?
2. What kind of picture of her small town does Norris seek to create? What common beliefs about small towns does she seek to overcome?

QUESTIONS ABOUT AUDIENCE

1. What assumptions do you think Norris makes about the way most people react to stories? How do you yourself feel about stories?
2. Although today relatively few people live in a small town like the one Norris describes, she suggests that her audience should see that her generalizations apply to larger communities. To what extent do you think she is warranted in that assumption?

QUESTIONS ABOUT STRATEGIES

1. How does Norris expand the definition of gossip into something that goes beyond the ordinary use of the term? Why is it important for her to do this?
2. What common themes in the stories Norris tells support her assertions about gossip as a benevolent force in a community?

QUESTIONS FOR DISCUSSION

1. Many magazines, newspaper columns, and radio and television shows make big profits by reporting or even sometimes creating gossip about celebrities. What do you see as some of the consequences of such activity?
2. What purpose do you feel that gossip, as Norris defines it, fills in your life and your community?

RICHARD RODRIGUEZ

Richard Rodriguez was born in San Francisco in 1944 and was educated at Stanford, Columbia, and the University of California at Berkeley. The son of Mexican immigrants and unable to speak English when he started school, he eventually went on to earn a master's degree and was awarded a Fulbright fellowship to study English Renaissance literature at the Warburg Institute in London. His compelling and controversial auto-biography, *Hunger of Memory: The Education of Richard Rodriguez* (1982), provides details of Rodriguez's experiences in the American educational system and his alienation from his own culture. In "Growing Up in Los Angeles," Rodriguez tries to define the idea of adolescence as it is acted out in southern California.

Growing Up in Los Angeles

AMERICA'S GREATEST CONTRIBUTION to the world of ideas is adolescence. European novels often begin with a first indelible memory—a golden poplar, or Mama standing in the kitchen. American novels begin at the moment of rebellion, the moment of appetite for distance, the moonless night Tom Sawyer pries open the back-bedroom window, shinnies down the drainpipe, drops to the ground, and runs.

America invented a space—a deferment, a patch of asphalt between childhood and adulthood, between the child's ties to family and the adult's re-creation of family. Within this space, within this boredom, American teenagers are supposed to innovate, to improvise, to rebel, to turn around three times before they harden into adults.

If you want to see the broadcasting center, the trademark

1

2

3

323

capital of adolescence, come to Los Angeles. The great post-war, postmodern, suburban city in Dolby sound was built by restless people who intended to give their kids an unending spring.

There are times in Los Angeles—our most American of 4
American cities—when teenagers seem the oldest people around. Many seem barely children at all—they are tough and cynical as ancients, beyond laughter in a city that idolizes them. Their glance, when it meets ours, is unblinking.

At a wedding in Brentwood, I watch the 17-year-old 5
daughter of my thrice-divorced friend give her mother away.

---

*The baby boom generation transformed
youth into a lifestyle, a political manifesto,
an aesthetic, a religion.*

The mother is dewey with liquid blush. The dry-eyed daughter has seen it all before.

I know children in Los Angeles who carry knives and guns 6
because the walk to and from school is more dangerous than their teachers or parents realize. One teenager stays home to watch her younger sister, who is being pursued by a teenage stalker. The girls have not told their parents because they say they do not know how their parents would react.

Have adults become the innocents? 7

Adults live in fear of the young. It's a movie script, a boffo 8
science-fiction thriller that has never been filmed but that might well star Jean-Claude Van Damme or Sylvester Stallone.

A friend of mine, a heavyweight amateur wrestler, wonders 9
if it's safe for us to have dinner at a Venice Beach restaurant. (There are, he says, 12-year-old gangsters who prowl the neighborhood with guns.)

Some of the richest people in town have figured out how 10

to sell the idea of American adolescence to the world. The children with the most interesting dilemma are the children of 90210. What does adolescence mean when your father is a record producer who drives to work in a Jeep to audition rap groups? What do you do when your father—who has a drug habit and is nowhere around in the years when you are growing up—is an internationally recognizable 50-foot face on the movie screen?

On the other hand: What can it feel like to grow up a teenager in South Central when your mama is on crack and you are responsible for her five kids? Teenagers who never had reliable parents or knew intimacy are having babies. There are teenagers in East L.A. who (literally) spend their young lives searching for family—"blood"—in some gang that promises what they never had.

It is every teenager's dream to "get big." In L.A. you can be very big, indeed. Fame is a billboard along Sunset Boulevard. Mexican-American gangstas pass the Southern California night by writing crypto-nonsense on sides of buildings, because the biggest lesson they have taken from the city is that advertisement is existence. Los Angeles is a horizontal city of separate freeway exits, separate malls, suburb fleeing suburb. Parents keep moving their children away from what they suppose is the diseased inner city. But there is no possibility of a healthy suburb radiant from a corrupt center. *No man is an island entire of itself.* Didn't we learn that in high school?

The children of East L.A. live in the same city as Madonna and Harvard-educated screenwriters who use cocaine for inspiration, selling a believably tarnished vision of the world to children of the crack mothers in Compton.

And look: There's always a TV in the houses of Watts. And it is always on. In the suburbs, white kids watch black rappers on MTV. Suburbanites use TV to watch the mayhem of the inner city. But on the TV in the inner city, they watch the rest of us. The bejeweled pimp in his gold BMW parodies the Beverly Hills matron on Rodeo Drive.

Elsewhere in America, we like to tell ourselves that Los

Angeles is the exception. The truth is that, for all its eccentricity, Los Angeles tells us a great deal about adolescence in rural Kansas. And postmodern L.A. is linked to colonial Boston. Today's gangsta with a tattooed tear on his face is kin to young men fighting Old Man Europe's wars in the trenches of 1914 or 1941, to the young rebels who overthrew Old Man Englande rather than submit to another curfew, and to Judy Garland, who will always be a stagestruck teenager.

The earliest Americans imagined that they had fled the past—motherland, fatherland—and had come upon land that was without history or meaning. By implication, the earliest Americans imagined themselves adolescent, orphans. Their task was self-creation, without benefit or burden of family. The myth that we must each create our own meaning has passed down through American generations.   16

Young Meriwether Lewis heads out for the territory. He writes to his widowed mother, "I . . . hope therefore you will not suffer yourself to indulge any anxiety for my safety. . . ." The ellipsis is adolescence: estrangement, embarrassment, self-absorption, determination. The adolescent body plumps and furs, bleeds and craves to be known for itself. In some parts of the world, puberty is a secret, a shameful biological event, proof that you have inevitably joined the community of your gender. In America, puberty is the signal to rebel.   17

American teenagers invent their own tongue, meant to be indecipherable to adult hearing. Every generation of adolescents does it. Adults are left wondering what they mean: *Scrilla. Juking. Woop, woop, woop.*   18

"Children grow up too quickly," American parents sigh. And yet nothing troubles an American parent so much as the teenager who won't leave home.   19

Several times in this century, American teenagers have been obliged to leave home to fight overseas. Nineteen-year-old fathers vowed to their unborn children that never again would the youth of the world be wasted by the Potentates of Winter.   20

My generation, the baby boom generation, was the refoliation of the world. We were the children of mothers who   21 learned how to drive, dyed their hair, used Maybelline, and decorated their houses for Christmas against the knowledge that winter holds sway in the world. Fathers, having returned from blackened theaters of war, used FHA loans to move into tract houses that had no genealogy. In such suburbs, our disillusioned parents intended to ensure their children's optimism.

Prolonged adolescence became the point of us—so much 22 the point of me that I couldn't give it up. One night, in the 1950s, I watched Mary Martin, a middle-aged actress, play an enchanted boy so persuasively that her rendition of "I Won't Grow Up" nurtured my adolescent suspicions of anyone over the age of 30.

My generation became the first in human history (only 23 hyperbole can suggest our prophetic sense of ourselves) that imagined we might never grow old.

Jill, a friend of mine whose fame was an orange bikini, 24 whose face has fallen, whose breasts have fallen, whose hair is gray, is telling me about her son who has just gone to New York and has found there the most wonderful possibilities. My friend's eyes fill with tears. She fumbles in her handbag for the pack of cigarettes she had just sworn off.

What's wrong? 25

"Dammit," she says, "I'm a geezer." 26

From my generation arose a culture for which America has 27 become notorious. We transformed youth into a lifestyle, a political manifesto, an aesthetic, a religion. My generation turned adolescence into a commodity that could be sold worldwide by 45-year-old executives at Nike or Warner Bros. To that extent, we control youth.

But is it unreasonable for a child to expect that Mick Jagger 28 or Michael Jackson will grow up, thicken, settle, and slow— relinquish adolescence to a new generation?

At the Senior Ball, teenagers in the ballroom of the Beverly 29 Hills Hotel, beautiful teenagers in black tie and gowns, try very hard not to look like teenagers. But on the other hand, it is very important not to look like one's parents.

The balancing trick of American adolescence is to stand 30 in-between—neither to be a child nor an adult.

Where are you going to college?   31

The question intrudes on the ball like a gong from some   32
great clock. It is midnight, Cinderella. Adolescence must
come to an end. Life is governed by inevitabilities and consequences—a thought never communicated in America's
rock-and-roll lyrics.

American storytellers do better with the beginning of the   33
story than the conclusion. We do not know how to mark the
end of adolescence. Mark Twain brings Huck Finn back to
Missouri, to Hannibal, and forces his young hero to bend
toward inevitability. But Huck yearns, forever, "to light out
for the territory . . . because Aunt Sally she's going to adopt
me and sivilize me, and I can't stand it."

And then comes the least convincing conclusion ever writ-   34
ten in all of American literature: THE END, YOURS TRULY, HUCK
FINN.

For Study and Discussion

QUESTIONS FOR RESPONSE

1. In what ways do Rodriguez's descriptions of teenagers in Los
   Angeles correspond to the behavior of adolescents that you
   know? How do they differ?
2. How do you respond to the advertising strategies that the media,
   especially television, use to appeal to young people? What, if
   anything, would you like to see changed in those strategies?

QUESTIONS ABOUT PURPOSE

1. Rodriguez projects an angry tone in this article. Toward whom
   do you think the anger is directed and what does he hope to
   accomplish by stirring up anger with his readers?
2. What new information or insights about American adolescents
   did you get from this essay? What do you think Rodriguez wants
   you to do with that information?

QUESTIONS ABOUT AUDIENCE

1. This article was originally published in *U.S. News and World Report,* a magazine whose readers are generally well educated, fairly prosperous, and in their late thirties or forties. How do you think they view most adolescents, and what might they learn from Rodriguez that could help them with their own children?
2. What different experiences and attitudes about adolescents do readers under thirty bring to this essay? How do you think their experiences affect their response to the essay?

QUESTIONS ABOUT STRATEGIES

1. Probably most of Rodriguez's readers haven't been to Los Angeles. What details does he use to convey the flavor of that city to a stranger? How well do they work to help you envision Los Angeles?
2. Rodriguez uses exaggeration as a strategy. For example, he says that Los Angeles is the most American of cities, he compares a pimp in his gold BMW to a Beverly Hills matron, and he mentions Madonna and the mothers of crack babies in the same sentence. What effects does he achieve with this strategy? How effective do you find it?

QUESTIONS FOR DISCUSSION

1. Rodriguez says that his generation (the baby boomers) turned adolescence into a commodity to be sold worldwide by sports manufacturers and movie producers. How true does that statement ring with you? What examples come to mind?
2. How would you characterize the persona or role that Rodriguez adopts for himself in this essay? Moralist, social critic, cynic, reformer, disenchanted observer? Might you adopt such a persona in an essay you might write? Why?

JON KATZ

Jon Katz was born in 1947 in Providence, Rhode Island. He was "thrown out of two colleges" before working as a journalist. Eventually, he became executive producer of the *CBS Morning News* and an editor at *The Boston Globe* and *The Washington Post*. He has written several novels, such as *Sign Off* (1991), and worked as a media critic for the *New York Times, Rolling Stone,* and *New York* magazine. He currently serves as a contributing editor of *Wired*. In "Interactivity," reprinted from *Virtuous Reality: How America Surrendered Discussion of Moral Values to Opportunists, Nitwits and Blockheads like William Bennett,* Katz defines the difficulties with the big idea of "interactivity."

Interactivity

PERHAPS THE SINGLE biggest idea is this notion of "inter- 1 activity," one of the words we hear so frequently that they've become background noise, but that we don't really understand. Interactivity isn't about machinery; it's about our relationship with information.

Interactivity—sometimes called "conviviality" by new me- 2 dia theorists—is the participation of individual users in their media. A revolutionary concept for modern America, interactivity will prove the enduring legacy of new media, the powerful force driving and shaping the cultural conflicts we're engulfed in. Interactivity is already reshaping politics, altering the consciousness of the young, sparking a return to media and politics by millions of people long shut out. Interactivity is the big idea our existing news organizations have been slowest to grasp, the pill so bitter many would rather perish than swallow it.

If you're over thirty-five, you probably grew up with non-interactive, or "passive," media. The daily paper came to your door in the morning (evening papers have been dying off for decades). You read what you wanted and ignored the rest. You had no say in determining the content of the paper, and unless you were intensely political or especially outraged, you probably never thought of trying to communicate with it. Nor did its editors think much about hearing from you. Each party's role was clear: They got to pick the stories. You got to read them.

If you read *Time, Newsweek* or *U.S. News & World Report,* the process was similar, except it happened once a week. The

> *One of the things that makes interactivity so big an idea is that it is critically important to the young, who have little experience with the passive media.*

magazines were put together by nameless editors in Washington and New York, and "interacting" with them was even tougher than with local newspapers. If yours was among the more than 90 percent of American households that once watched an evening newscast (the number has now fallen below 50 percent), you had no chance at all of being heard or listened to. You were offered a choice of three newscasts, all strikingly similar.

The information world of the 1990s bears little relationship to that one, which feels as remote as ancient Babylon. Remember those Nintendos and Segas that attached to TV sets and riveted your kids? They were some of the first interactive (and digital) tools we saw. Although typically denounced as hypnotic, violent and mind-numbing, many of the games were sophisticated and challenging. They required kids to actively participate rather than passively watch. Often played in groups rather than individually, they involved social skills and strategizing. They required hand-eye coordination. They could be intensely stimulating, sometimes even addictive. And kids loved them; they took game playing to new levels of engagement and imagination.

And channel switchers—"zappers"—might be the most 6 subversive political gadgets ever invented. Along with VCRs, they were a network mogul's worst nightmare. For decades, broadcasting was owned and operated by three men— William Paley of CBS, David Sarnoff of NBC, and Leonard Goldenson of ABC. We saw only what they wanted us to see, when they wanted to show it to us. Zappers and VCRs broke their grip, giving far more control of the world's most powerful new medium to the people who use it.

TV viewers didn't have to watch ads anymore if they didn't 7 want to. They didn't have to watch boring programs anymore, either; they could instantly shop around. They could go bowling and watch *Melrose Place* on tape later, fast-forwarding through tiresome commercials and station breaks.

Add the development of satellite technology, which made 8 CNN possible, and the unleashing of many-channel cable, which brought real diversity to programming, and the transformation of television was under way.

TV is our most underappreciated medium, mostly por- 9 trayed in terms of stupefying children and inciting violence, the proverbial vast wasteland.

But it is a phenomenal thing. A TV set is easy to install 10 and lasts for years. It brings the whole world into your house, using little power. Lightning storms and freak accidents aside, it turns on every time you want it to, producing clear color pictures and good-quality sound. It costs a fourth the price of a good computer. It can occupy and amuse kids, show the Oklahoma City federal building minutes after a bomb explodes, and go around the world to wars, cultural events and volcanic eruptions. It shows great old movies, history, drama and—yes—lots of trash, too. Far more popular, enduring and important than most people acknowledge or realize, it is becoming one of our most interactive forms of communication.

As we've watched in wonder, the TV has mutated into a full-blown information, amusement and communications center. The "couch potato" is an outdated myth. TV viewers are now entertainment producers and directors. They have options, controls, choices and machinery to run—even products to buy, surveys to vote in, questions to pose, numbers to call.

Cable news—especially CNN—is a prime example of how interactivity is determined by content as well as machinery. In the 1980s, with most women in the workforce and nobody waiting at home to cook dinner for Dad, fewer and fewer families could plump down in the living room to watch the evening news for half an hour. But CNN was on twenty-four hours a day, offering continuous news, not news when David Brinkley or Dan Rather was available to provide it. CNN met viewers' needs, not the networks'. The fixed-time newscast—a longtime staple of commercial broadcasting—began to decline, in the morning as well as the evening. Since 1980, the evening news programs have lost almost half of their viewers.

Notice, too, how many cable broadcasts have built interactivity into their programs. No network newscast or major newspaper would dream of having a viewer or reader pose a question to a politician. What could an ordinary Joe possibly know, compared with a professional journalist? But from C-Span to MTV News, from E! to *Larry King Live,* interactivity—formats and technology that permits viewers to express themselves and participate—was part of the design. Many of these networks and broadcasts featured call-ins, phone polls, fax numbers and voice-mail lines, as well as special phone lines for additional information.

On cable, traditional boundaries between news and entertainment began to blur. MTV News helped register more than a million young voters in the 1992 presidential campaign with its "Rock the Vote" campaign. Comedy Central offered gavel-to-gavel spoofing of the presidential nominating conventions; its commentators were more blunt than any Big Three correspondent about Pat Buchanan's inflammatory speech and how it would hurt Republicans.

And in digital new media, interactivity isn't an added feature, it is the point. Online users have far more control over what they consume than any newspaper or mainstream magazine reader ever had. Online, people are constantly perusing menus, making selections. They can get news or go to live "chat" rooms, exchange e-mail or meet in groups to hear and question guest speakers. They can create new topics of discussion or respond to others'. They can pray with other members of their faith or—on certain "adult" boards, with the help of a credit card—download pornography.   15

Their loss of control has been jarring to our traditional media and political organizations, who had sat astride a tight monopoly over politics and news. They fought back and have been fighting ever since, complaining that these new, interactive media are dangerous and destructive of public discourse. New media have brought with them enormous cultural displacement—the journalists, producers, publishers, editors and academics who controlled most of our information flow have all been, to varying degrees, pushed aside. They don't like it.   16

Yet if some of the technology promoting interactivity is spanking new, the idea behind it has a long history. Our original press, founded by Tom Paine and his fellow hellraisers, was highly interactive. Citizens ticked off about issues hung their arguments up on the sides of buildings. The press then was filled with individual voices.   17

If the founders would be horrified by Olympian journalists and corporate-owned media conglomerates, however, they'd feel quite comfortable with the raucous new media that permit lots of voices to pipe up, to speak directly to politicians and to one another. Our forebears would find radio talk shows familiar as well. An intensely interactive medium—such shows literally depend for their existence on people who call in—talk radio has grown from a couple of hundred programs in 1980 to nearly a thousand now.   18

The long, sad process of corporatizing the press, making 19
users of communications media passive again, disconnecting
journalists from the rest of us, has been under way since the
eighteenth century. But in modern times, the estrangement
has worsened. Reporters became wealthier and better educated, and reporting much more fashionable. For most of
their history considered far too scruffy to hang out with
"decent" people, journalists suddenly were living in Georgetown and summering in the Hamptons.

Watergate and Vietnam, both high-water marks of modern 20
journalism, had the unfortunate side effect of intensifying the
detachment. Having helped stop a war and bring down a
president, journalists' collective sense of self-righteous purpose ballooned. Now reporters began seeing themselves as
an unofficial FBI/morals squad, combing through the private
financial and personal dealings of everyone in public life. That
no one else in America—politicians, the public, historians—
saw this as a suitable role for journalism didn't seem to slow
anybody down. By the eighties, much of the press saw nothing but virtue in the *Miami Herald* reporters who staked out
Gary Hart's Washington town house.

How could any institution so utterly disconnected from 21
its consumers help but become arrogant and remote? And
vulnerable.

Americans began ranking journalists lower than bankers 22
and lawyers in public-confidence ratings in the late eighties
and early nineties. The press's transparent pretense of objectivity didn't fool anybody, either. Sixty-seven percent of people answering a recent *Los Angeles Times* poll agreed with this
statement: "The news media give more coverage to stories
that support their own point of view than to those that
don't." Polls by news organizations themselves, and by organizations like Harris, Gallup and Yankelovich, all show
declining respect for journalism and rising anger over its
intrusions into government and public life.

No wonder the environment was so receptive to new kinds 23
of media. When America Online's news department asked its
"readers" what, if anything, they would change about its

presentation of daily spot news, readers suggested moving hourly updates to the top of the news menus. It was done instantly. They also complained that they didn't always want the pictures that accompany the text of breaking news stories, since downloading takes much longer when graphics are included. They were—again instantly—given the option to eliminate the pictures and just call up the stories.

Interactive media give their users a voice. Of course, CNN   24
as an organization is still far more powerful than the people watching it. America Online is more powerful than its individual subscribers. Both have their flaws. But individual users have more clout—much more—than they used to.

One of the things that makes interactivity so big an idea is   25
that it is critically important to the young, who have little experience with passive media. From Nintendo to cable channels to zapper-controlled TVs and computers, the young are accustomed to varying degrees of choice in all their media. According to a 1993 survey by Peter Hart Research Associates, three-fifths of people under forty-five, if forced to choose between cable or broadcast TV, would opt for cable, a remarkable statistic, given the limited availability and meager programming of cable just twenty years ago. The Hart survey found that "young people prefer choices. A majority of those under age forty-five believe more channels is a step in the right direction. The majority of those age sixty and older disagree."

The survey highlights one of the great generational divides   26
fueling the wars over culture and media. Middle-aged and older people tend to be more reflexively resistant to change, often finding new choices disorienting, even unhealthy. The young can't get enough. Not surprisingly, the differences in the way these groups acquire information are stark, and widening.

The percentage of people under thirty-five who said they   27
"read a newspaper yesterday" has plunged from 67 percent in 1965 to under 30 percent today, newspaper industry surveys show. The number of adults eighteen to twenty-four

reading *Time, Newsweek* or *U.S. News & World Report* has declined by 55 percent in the past fifteen years, according to media consultant David Lehmkuhl. One confidential survey commissioned by a network news division in 1993 found that the percentage of viewers between eighteen and thirty-four watching commercial network newscasts has dropped nearly 50 percent since 1980.

A Yankelovich study says it all. Only 20 percent of people   28 twenty-one to twenty-four watch ABC's *World News Tonight,* it found, but more than 30 percent watch CNN. And 35 percent sit down to savor *The Simpsons.*

The media business is complex; lots of factors determine   29 whether or not ventures succeed. But one of the emerging realities is this: Interactive media—cable, talk radio, audience-participation TV talk shows, digital communities, Web sites, computer-conferencing systems—are mostly ascending. Traditional, passive media are either stagnant or declining. Americans increasingly are coming to see media participation—the opportunity to express themselves—as a right, not a gift conferred by the editors of letters pages.

At least magazines seem to have noticed this trend and   30 have transformed themselves radically in the past decade, reaching for revolutionary new graphic designs, stronger cultural coverage, better writing with more point of view. *Time* and *Newsweek,* among others, have experimented with new formats and looks and have dramatically improved the range and sophistication of their coverage of interactive culture. *Newsweek* has a weekly cyberpage; *Time* was a major presence on America Online (now it's on CompuServe) and, via Pathfinder, on the Web. Even the venerable *New Yorker* began, rather grudgingly, to print occasional letters from readers.

Newspapers are a sadder story. The structure and presen-   31 tation of daily papers have changed remarkably little. They still present "breaking news" we all saw on television the day before; they war relentlessly against the new culture of the young; they seem graphically impaired. Aside from offering unwieldy and clunky electronic versions online, newspapers remain in the grip of cultural paralysis. Not a single major paper has even put e-mail addresses at the end of stories so that readers can communicate easily with reporters, a simple addition most papers have had the technological capacity to do for years.

The same goes for the networks' evening newscasts, which   32 today, as in the late 1950s, feature middle-aged white men in suits reading introductions to other people's stories for eight or nine minutes each weeknight. With information and newscasts emerging on cable, and hard-pressed Americans working longer and longer hours, fixed-time network news broadcasts have a dismal future, at least in their current forms. To date, none seems anxious to experiment with new ones.

For Study and Discussion

QUESTIONS FOR RESPONSE

1. What do you see as some of the consequences of viewers and listeners being able to interact directly with television and radio programs and give their opinions?
2. In what ways are you interacting with radio or television programs or with sites on the Internet? How important and useful is such interactivity to you?

QUESTIONS ABOUT PURPOSE

1. What does Katz achieve with his history of changes in the media in the past fifteen years?
2. What message does Katz have for people who have been prominent figures in the media for the past decades—people like Dan Rather, Barbara Walters, and Bryan Gumbel?

QUESTIONS ABOUT AUDIENCE

1. To whom do you think Katz is directing this article? For what kind of readers is it likely to have the greatest appeal? Why?
2. What audience of older readers might profit substantially by

reading this article? What attempt, if any, does Katz make to appeal to that audience?

QUESTIONS ABOUT STRATEGIES

1. Katz uses a very positive style and tone and makes rosy predictions about the future. How does that affect the way you respond to his predictions? If he is trying to sell you something, what is it?
2. What evidence does Katz give to support his thesis about the coming dominance of interactive media? How convincing is that evidence?

QUESTIONS FOR DISCUSSION

1. Katz claims that interactive media are going to reshape politics and alter the consciousness of the young. What are some of the ways you can imagine that might happen?
2. Katz claims that today's magazine articles are better written and "have more point of view." What do you think that phrase means? What drawbacks might such a change mean?

Stephen Harrigan was born in Oklahoma City in 1948 and educated at the University of Texas. After working as a journalist, including a term as senior editor at *Texas Monthly,* Harrigan turned his attention to fiction and screenplays. His novels include *Aransas* (1980) and *Jacob's Well* (1984) and his screenplays include *The Last of His Tribe* (1992) and *The O.J. Simpson Story* (1995). Harrigan has also published two collections of essays, *Natural State* (1988) and *Comanche Midnight* (1995). In "The Tiger Is God," reprinted from the latter collection, Harrigan provides dramatic examples that help define a tiger "just being a tiger."

The Tiger Is God

W HEN TIGERS ATTACK men, they do so in a characteristic way. They come from behind, from the right side, and when they lunge it is with the intent of snapping the neck of the prey in their jaws. Most tiger victims die swiftly, their necks broken, their spinal cords compressed or severed high up on the vertebral column.

Ricardo Tovar, a fifty-nine-year-old keeper at the Houston Zoo, was killed by a tiger on May 12, 1988. The primary cause of death was a broken neck, although most of the ribs on the left side of his chest were fractured as well, and there were multiple lacerations on his face and right arm. No one witnessed the attack, and no one would ever know exactly how and why it took place, but the central nightmarish event was clear. Tovar had been standing at a steel door separating the zookeepers' area from the naturalistic tiger display outside. Set into the door was a small viewing window—only slightly larger than an average television screen—made of wire-reinforced glass. Somehow the tiger had broken the glass, grabbed the keeper, and pulled him through the window to his death.

Fatal zoo accidents occur more frequently than most peo-   3 ple realize. The year before Tovar died, a keeper in the Fort Worth Zoo was crushed by an elephant, and in 1985, an employee of the Bronx Zoo was killed by two Siberian tigers—the same subspecies as the one that attacked Tovar— when she mistakenly entered the tiger display while the

---

One point is beyond dispute: A tiger is a predator, its mission on earth is to kill, and in doing so it often displays awesome strength and dexterity.

---

animals were still there. But there was something especially haunting about the Houston incident, something that people could not get out of their minds. It had to do with the realization of a fear built deep into our genetic code: the fear that a beast could appear out of nowhere—through a window!—and snatch us away.

The tiger's name was Miguel. He was eleven years old—   4 middle-aged for a tiger—and had been born at the Houston Zoo to a mother who was a wild-caught Siberian. Siberians are larger in size than any of the other subspecies, and their coats are heavier. Fewer than three hundred of them are now left in the frozen river valleys and hardwood forests of the Soviet Far East, though they were once so plentiful in that region that Cossack troops were sent in during the construction of the Trans-Baikal railway specifically to protect the workers from tiger attacks. Miguel was of mixed blood—his father was a zoo-reared Bengal—but his Siberian lineage was dominant. He was a massive 450-pound creature whose disposition had been snarly ever since he was a cub. Some of the other tigers at the zoo were as placid and affectionate as house cats, but Miguel filled his keepers with caution. Oscar Mendietta, a keeper who retired a few weeks before Tovar's death, remembers the way Miguel would sometimes lunge at zoo personnel as they walked by his holding cage, his claws unsheathed and protruding through the steel mesh. "He had," Mendietta says, "an intent to kill."

Tovar was well aware of Miguel's temperament. He had been working with big cats in the Houston Zoo since 1982, and his fellow keepers regarded him as a cautious and responsible man. Like many old-time zookeepers, he was a civil servant with no formal training in zoology, but he had worked around captive animals most of his life (before coming to Houston, he had been a keeper at the San Antonio Zoo) and had gained a good deal of practical knowledge about their behavior. No one regarded Miguel's aggressiveness as aberrant. Tovar and the other keepers well understood the fact that tigers were supposed to be dangerous.

In 1987 the tigers and other cats had been moved from their outdated display cages to brand-new facilities with outdoor exhibit areas built to mimic the animals' natural environments. The Siberian tiger exhibit—in a structure known as the Phase II building—comprised about a quarter of an acre. It was a wide rectangular space decorated with shrubs and trees, a few fake boulders, and a water-filled moat. The exhibit's backdrop was a depiction, in plaster and cement, of a high rock wall seamed with stress fractures.

Built into the wall, out of public view, was a long corridor lined with the cats' holding cages, where the tigers were fed and confined while the keepers went out into the display to shovel excrement and hose down the area. Miguel and the other male Siberian, Rambo, each had a holding cage, and they alternated in the use of the outdoor habitat, since two male tigers occupying the same space guaranteed monumental discord. Next to Rambo's cage was a narrow alcove through which the keepers went back and forth from the corridor into the display. The alcove was guarded by two doors. The one with the viewing window led outside. Another door, made of steel mesh, closed off the interior corridor.

May 12 was a Thursday. Tovar came to work at about 8 six-thirty in the morning, and at that hour he was alone. Rambo was secure in his holding cage and Miguel was outside—it had been his turn that night to have the run of the display.

Thursdays and Sundays were "fast" days. Normally the 9 tigers were fed a daily ration of ten to fifteen pounds of ground fetal calf, but twice a week their food was withheld in order to keep them from growing obese in confinement. The animals knew which days were fast days, and on those mornings they were sometimes balky about coming inside, since no food was being offered. Nevertheless, the tigers had to be secured in their holding cages while the keepers went outside to clean the display. On this morning, Tovar had apparently gone to the viewing window to check the whereabouts of Miguel when the tiger did not come inside, even though the keepers usually made a point of not entering the alcove until they were certain that both animals were locked up in their holding cages. The viewing window was so small and the habitat itself so panoramic that the chances of spotting the tiger from the window were slim. Several of the keepers had wondered why there was a window there at all, since it was almost useless as an observation post and since one would never go through the door in the first place without being certain that the tigers were in their cages.

But that was where Tovar had been, standing at a steel 10 door with a panel of reinforced glass, when the tiger attacked. John Gilbert, the senior zookeeper who supervised the cat section, stopped in at the Phase II building a little after seven-thirty, planning to discuss with Tovar the scheduled sedation of a lion. He had just entered the corridor when he saw broken glass on the floor outside the steel mesh door that led to the alcove. The door was unlocked—it had been opened by Tovar when he entered the alcove to look out the window. Looking through the mesh, Gilbert saw the shards of glass hanging from the window frame and Tovar's cap, watch, and a single rubber boot lying on the floor. Knowing something dreadful had happened, he called Tovar's name, then pushed on the door and cautiously started to enter the alcove. He was only a few paces away from the broken window when the tiger's head suddenly appeared there, filling its jagged frame. His heart pounding, Gilbert backed off, slammed and locked the mesh door behind him and radioed for help.

Tom Dieckow, a wiry, white-bearded Marine veteran of 11 the Korean War, was the zoo's exhibits curator. He was also in charge of its shooting team, a seldom-convened body whose task was to kill, if necessary, any escaped zoo animal that posed an immediate threat to the public. Dieckow was in his office in the service complex building when he heard Gilbert's emergency call. He grabbed a twelve-gauge shotgun, commandeered an electrician's pickup truck, and arrived at the tiger exhibit two minutes later. He went around to the front of the habitat and saw Miguel standing there, calm and unconcerned, with Tovar's motionless body lying face down fifteen feet away. Dieckow did not shoot. It was his clear impression that the keeper was dead, that the harm was already done. By that time the zoo's response team had gathered outside the exhibit. Miguel stared at the onlookers and then picked up Tovar's head in his jaws and started to drag him off.

"I think probably what crossed that cat's mind at that 12 point," Dieckow speculated later, "is 'look at all those scavengers across there that are after my prey. I'm gonna move it.' He was just being a tiger."

Dieckow raised his shotgun again, this time with the in- 13 tention of shooting Miguel, but because of all the brush and ersatz boulders in the habitat, he could not get a clear shot. He fired into the water instead, causing the startled tiger to drop the keeper, and then fired twice more as another zoo worker discharged a fire extinguisher from the top of the rock wall. The commotion worked, and Miguel retreated into his holding cage.

The Houston Zoo opened a half-hour late that day. 14

Miguel and all the other big cats were kept inside until zoo officials could determine if it was safe—both for the cats and for the public—to exhibit them again. For a few days the zoo switchboard was jammed with calls from people wanting to express their opinion on whether the tiger should live or die. But for the people at the zoo that issue had never been in doubt.

"It's automatic with us," John Werler, the zoo director, 15 told me when I visited his office a week after the incident. "To what end would we destroy the tiger? If we followed this argument to its logical conclusion, we'd have to destroy every dangerous animal in the zoo collection."

Werler was a reflective, kindly looking man who was obvi- 16 ously weighed down by a load of unpleasant concerns. There was the overall question of zoo safety, the specter of lawsuits, and most recently the public anger of a number of zoo staffers who blamed Tovar's death on the budget cuts, staffing short-ages, and bureaucratic indifference that forced keepers to work alone in potentially dangerous environments. But the dominant mood of the zoo, the day I was there, appeared to be one of simple sadness and shock.

"What a terrible loss," read a sympathy card from the staff 17 of the Fort Worth Zoo that was displayed on a coffee table. "May you gain strength and support to get you through this awful time."

The details of the attack were still hazy, and still eerie to 18 think about. Unquestionably, the glass door panel had not been strong enough, but exactly how Miguel had broken it, how he had killed Tovar—and why—remained the subjects of numb speculation. One point was beyond dispute: A tiger is a predator, its mission on the earth is to kill, and in doing so it often displays awesome strength and dexterity.

An Indian researcher, using live deer and buffalo calves as 19 bait, found that the elapsed time between a tiger's secure grip on the animal's neck and the prey's subsequent death was anywhere from thirty-five to ninety seconds. In other circum-stances the cat will not choose to be so swift. Sometimes a tiger will kill an elephant calf by snapping its trunk and waiting for it to bleed to death, and it is capable of dragging the carcass in its jaws for miles. (A full-grown tiger possesses the traction power of thirty men.) When a mother tiger is teaching her cubs to hunt, she might move in on a calf, cripple it with a powerful bite to its rear leg, and stand back and let the cubs practice on the helpless animal.

Tigers have four long canine teeth—fangs. The two in the   20
upper jaw are tapered along the sides to a shearing edge. Fourteen of the teeth are molars, for chewing meat and grinding bone. Like other members of the cat family, tigers have keen, night-seeing eyes, and their hearing is so acute that Indonesian hunters—convinced that a tiger could hear the wind whistling through a man's nose hairs—always kept their nostrils carefully barbered. The pads on the bottom of a tiger's paws are surprisingly sensitive, easily blistered or cut on hot, prickly terrain. But the claws within, five on each front paw and four in the hind paws, are protected like knives in an upholstered box.

They are not idle predators; when they kill, they kill to eat.   21
Even a well-fed tiger in a zoo keeps his vestigial repertoire of hunting behaviors intact. (Captive breeding programs, in fact, make a point of selecting in favor of aggressive predatory behavior, since the ultimate hope of these programs is to bolster the dangerously low stock of free-living tigers.) In the zoo, tigers will stalk birds that land in their habitats, and they grow more alert than most people would care to realize when children pass before their gaze. Though stories of man-eating tigers have been extravagantly embellished over the centuries, the existence of such creatures is not legendary. In the Sunderbans, the vast delta region that spans the border of India and Bangladesh, more than four hundred people have been killed by tigers in the last decade. So many fishermen and honey collectors have been carried off that a few years ago officials at the Sunderbans tiger preserve began stationing electrified dummies around the park to encourage the tigers to seek other prey. One percent of all tigers, according to a German biologist who studied them in the Sunderbans, are "dedicated" man-eaters: when they go out hunting, they're

after people. Up to a third of all tigers will kill and eat a human if they come across one, though they don't make a special effort to do so.

It is not likely that Miguel attacked Ricardo Tovar out of 22 hunger. Except for the killing wounds inflicted by the tiger, the keeper's body was undisturbed. Perhaps something about Tovar's movements on the other side of the window intrigued the cat enough to make him spring, a powerful lunge that sent him crashing through the glass. Most likely the tiger was surprised, and frightened, and reacted instinctively. There is no evidence that he came all the way through the window. Probably he just grabbed Tovar by the chest with one paw, crushed him against the steel door, and with unthinkable strength pulled him through the window and killed him outside.

John Gilbert, the senior keeper who had been the first on 23 the scene that morning, took me inside the Phase II building to show me where the attack had taken place. Gilbert was a sandy-haired man in his thirties, still shaken and subdued by what he had seen. His recitation of the events was as formal and precise as that of a witness at an inquest.

"When I got to this point," Gilbert said as we passed 24 through the security doors that led to the keepers' corridor, "I saw the broken glass on the floor. I immediately yelled Mr. Tovar's name . . ."

The alcove in which Tovar had been standing was much 25 smaller than I had pictured it, and seeing it firsthand made one thing readily apparent: it was a trap. Its yellow cinder-block walls were no more than four feet apart. The ceiling was made of steel mesh and a door of the same material guarded the exit to the corridor. The space was so confined it was not difficult to imagine—it was impossible *not* to imagine—how the tiger had been able to catch Tovar by surprise with a deadly swipe from his paw.

And there was the window. Covered with a steel plate now, 26 its meager dimensions were still visible. The idea of being hauled through that tiny space by a tiger had an almost supernatural resonance—as if the window were a portal through which mankind's most primeval terrors were allowed to pass unobstructed.

Gilbert led me down the corridor. We passed the holding cage of Rambo, who hung his head low and let out a grumbling basso roar so deep it sounded like a tremor in the earth. Then we were standing in front of Miguel.   27

"Here he is," Gilbert said, looking at the animal with an expression on his face that betrayed a sad welter of emotions. "He's quite passive right now."   28

The tiger was reclining on the floor, looking at us without concern. I noticed his head, which seemed to me wider than the window he had broken out. His eyes were yellow, and when the great head pivoted in my direction and Miguel's eyes met mine I looked away reflexively, afraid of their hypnotic gravity. The tiger stood up and began to pace, his gigantic pads treading noiselessly on the concrete. The bramble of black stripes that decorated his head was as neatly symmetrical as a Rorschach inkblot, and his orange fur—conceived by evolution as camouflage—was a florid, provocative presence in the featureless confines of the cage.   29

Miguel idly pawed the steel guillotine door that covered the entrance to his cage, and then all of a sudden he reared on his hind legs. I jumped back a little, startled and dwarfed. The top of Miguel's head nestled against the ceiling mesh of his cage, his paws were spread to either side. In one silent moment, his size and scale seemed to have increased exponentially. He looked down at Gilbert and me. In Miguel's mind, I suspected, his keeper's death was merely a vignette, a mostly forgotten moment of fright and commotion that had intruded one day upon the tiger's torpid existence in the zoo. But it was hard not to look up at that immense animal and read his posture as a deliberate demonstration of the power he possessed.   30

I thought of Tipu Sultan, the eighteenth-century Indian mogul who was obsessed with the tiger and used its likeness as his constant emblem. Tipu Sultan's imperial banner had borne the words "The Tiger Is God." Looking up into Miguel's yellow eyes I felt the strange appropriateness of   31 those words. The tiger was majestic and unknowable, a beast of such seeming invulnerability that it was possible to believe that he alone had called the world into being, and that a given life could end at his whim. The truth, of course, was far more literal. Miguel was a remnant member of a species never far from the brink of extinction, and his motivation for killing Ricardo Tovar probably did not extend beyond a behavioral quirk. He had a predator's indifference to tragedy; he had killed without culpability. It was a gruesome and unhappy incident, but as far as Miguel was concerned most of the people at the zoo had reached the same conclusion: he was just being a tiger.

For Study and Discussion

QUESTIONS FOR RESPONSE

1. In your visits to zoos, how have you responded to tigers you've seen? With admiration? With awe? With fear? How do you think reading Harrigan's essay might affect your feelings on any future visit?
2. How do you respond to the zoo professionals' feeling that Miguel was "just being a tiger?" Does that reflect a callous or careless attitude?

QUESTIONS ABOUT PURPOSE

1. What attitude about the tiger do you think Harrigan wants to bring about in his readers?
2. Why does Harrigan go into minute detail about the physical arrangements of the zoo and about the schedules? Why would readers want to know these details?

QUESTIONS ABOUT AUDIENCE

1. On what basis do you think that Harrigan can assume that a general audience would want to read about tigers and about the fatal incident at the Houston zoo?

2. What questions does Harrigan anticipate that his readers will have? How does he attempt to answer those questions?

QUESTIONS ABOUT STRATEGIES

1. What is the impact on the reader of Harrigan's first paragraph? What tone does it set for the essay?
2. What details does the author give that are most important in defining the nature of the tiger? Pick out three or four specific paragraphs that are most important.

QUESTIONS FOR DISCUSSION

1. In what ways are zoos important institutions in this country? Does their value to the public warrant their cost in money, in risk, and in the treatment of animals?
2. What do you think is the appeal of an article such as this? What special significance does it have that the animal was a tiger rather than other animals that can be just as dangerous, for instance, elephants or rhinoceroses?

ALICE WALKER

Alice Walker was born in 1944 in Eatonton, Georgia, attended Spelman College in Atlanta, and graduated from Sarah Lawrence College. She then became active in the civil rights movement, helping to register voters in Georgia, teaching in the Head Start program in Mississippi, and working on the staff of the New York City welfare department. In subsequent years, she began her own writing career while teaching at Wellesley College, the University of California at Berkeley, and Brandeis University. Her writing reveals her interest in the themes of sexism and racism, themes she embodies in her widely acclaimed novels: *The Third Life of Grange Copeland* (1970), *Meridian* (1976), *The Color Purple* (1982), and *Possessing the Secret of Joy* (1992). Her stories, collected in *In Love and Trouble: Stories of Black Women* (1973) and *You Can't Keep a Good Woman Down* (1981); essays, found in *Living by the Word* (1988), and *The Same River Twice* (1996), examine the complex experiences of black women. "Everyday Use," reprinted from *In Love and Trouble,* focuses on a reunion that reveals two contrasting attitudes toward the meaning of family heritage.

Everyday Use
for your grandmama

I WILL WAIT for her in the yard that Maggie and I made so   1
clean and wavy yesterday afternoon. A yard like this is
more comfortable than most people know. It is not just a
yard. It is like an extended living room. When the hard clay

is swept clean as a floor and the fine sand around the edges lined with tiny, irregular grooves anyone can come and sit and look up into the elm tree and wait for the breezes that never come inside the house.

Maggie will be nervous until after her sister goes: she will 2 stand hopelessly in corners homely and ashamed of the burn scars down her arms and legs, eyeing her sister with a mixture of envy and awe. She thinks her sister has held life always in the palm of one hand, that "no" is a word the world never learned to say to her.

You've no doubt seen those TV shows where the child who 3 has "made it" is confronted, as a surprise, by her own mother and father, tottering in weakly from backstage. (A pleasant surprise, of course: What would they do if parent and child came on the show only to curse out and insult each other?) On TV mother and child embrace and smile into each other's faces. Sometimes the mother and father weep, the child wraps them in her arms and leans across the table to tell how she would not have made it without their help. I have seen these programs.

Sometimes I dream a dream in which Dee and I are sud- 4 denly brought together on a TV program of this sort. Out of a dark and soft-seated limousine I am ushered into a bright room filled with many people. There I meet a smiling, gray, sporty man like Johnny Carson who shakes my hand and tells me what a fine girl I have. Then we are on the stage and Dee is embracing me with tears in her eyes. She pins on my dress a large orchid, even though she has told me once that she thinks orchids are tacky flowers.

In real life I am a large, big-boned woman with rough, 5 man-working hands. In the winter I wear flannel nightgowns to bed and overalls during the day. I can kill and clean a hog as mercilessly as a man. My fat keeps me hot in zero weather. I can work all day, breaking ice to get water for washing. I can eat pork liver cooked over the open fire minutes after it comes steaming from the hog. One winter I knocked a bull calf straight in the brain between the eyes with a sledge hammer and had the meat hung up to chill before nightfall. But of course all this does not show on television. I am the way my daughter would want me to be: a hundred pounds lighter, my skin like an uncooked barley pancake. My hair glistens in the hot bright lights. Johnny Carson has much to do to keep up with my quick and witty tongue.

But that is a mistake. I know even before I wake up. Who ever knew a Johnson with a quick tongue? Who can even imagine me looking a strange white man in the eye? It seems to me I have talked to them always with one foot raised in flight, with my head turned in whichever way is farthest from them. Dee, though. She would always look anyone in the eye. Hesitation was no part of her nature.   6

"How do I look, Mama?" Maggie says, showing just enough of her thin body enveloped in pink skirt and red blouse for me to know she's there, almost hidden by the door.   7

"Come out into the yard," I say.   8

Have you ever seen a lame animal, perhaps a dog run over by some careless person rich enough to own a car, sidle up to someone who is ignorant enough to be kind to him? That is the way my Maggie walks. She has been like this, chin on chest, eyes on ground, feet in shuffle, ever since the fire that burned the other house to the ground.   9

Dee is lighter than Maggie, with nicer hair and a fuller figure. She's a woman now, though sometimes I forget. How long ago was it that the other house burned? Ten, twelve years? Sometimes I can still hear the flames and feel Maggie's arm sticking to me, her hair smoking and her dress falling off her in little black papery flakes. Her eyes seemed stretched open, blazed open by the flames reflected in them. And Dee. I see her standing off under the sweet gum tree she used to dig gum out of; a look of concentration on her face as she watched the last dingy gray board of the house fall in toward the red-hot brick chimney. Why don't you do a dance around   10 the ashes? I'd wanted to ask her. She had hated the house that much.

I used to think she hated Maggie, too. But that was before 11 we raised the money, the church and me, to send her to Augusta to school. She used to read to us without pity; forcing words, lies, other folks' habits, whole lives upon us two, sitting trapped and ignorant underneath her voice. She washed us in a river of make-believe, burned us with a lot of knowledge we didn't necessarily need to know. Pressed us to her with the serious way she read, to shove us away at just the moment, like dimwits, we seemed about to understand.

Dee wanted nice things. A yellow organdy dress to wear 12 to her graduation from high school; black pumps to match a green suit she'd made from an old suit somebody gave me. She was determined to stare down any disaster in her efforts. Her eyelids would not flicker for minutes at a time. Often I fought off the temptation to shake her. At sixteen she had a style of her own: and knew what style was.

I never had an education myself. After second grade the 13 school was closed down. Don't ask me why: in 1927 colored asked fewer questions than they do now. Sometimes Maggie reads to me. She stumbles along good-naturedly but can't see well. She knows she is not bright. Like good looks and money, quickness passed her by. She will marry John Thomas (who has mossy teeth in an earnest face) and then I'll be free to sit here and I guess just sing church songs to myself. Although I never was a good singer. Never could carry a tune. I was always better at a man's job. I used to love to milk till I was hoofed in the side in '49. Cows are soothing and slow and don't bother you, unless you try to milk them the wrong way.

I have deliberately turned my back on the house. It is three 14 rooms, just like the one that burned, except the roof is tin; they don't make shingle roofs any more. There are no real windows, just some holes cut in the sides, like the portholes in a ship, but not round and not square, with rawhide holding the shutters up on the outside. This house is in a pasture,

too, like the other one. No doubt when Dee sees it she will
want to tear it down. She wrote me once that no matter
where we "choose" to live, she will manage to come see us.
But she will never bring her friends. Maggie and I thought
about this and Maggie asked me, "Mama, when did Dee ever
have any friends?"

She had a few. Furtive boys in pink shirts hanging about   15
on washday after school. Nervous girls who never laughed.
Impressed with her they worshiped the well-turned phrase,
the cute shape, the scalding humor that erupted like bubbles
in lye. She read to them.

When she was courting Jimmy T she didn't have much   16
time to pay to us, but turned all her faultfinding power on
him. He *flew* to marry a cheap gal from a family of ignorant
flashy people. She hardly had time to recompose herself.

When she comes I will meet—but there they are!   17

Maggie attempts to make a dash for the house, in her   18
shuffling way, but I stay her with my hand. "Come back
here," I say. And she stops and tries to dig a well in the sand
with her toe.

It is hard to see them clearly through the strong sun. But   19
even the first glimpse of leg out of the car tells me it is Dee.
Her feet were always neat-looking, as if God himself had
shaped them with a certain style. From the other side of the
car comes a short, stocky man. Hair is all over his head a foot
long and hanging from his chin like a kinky mule tail. I hear
Maggie suck in her breath. "Uhnnnh," is what it sounds like.
Like when you see the wriggling end of a snake just in front
of your foot on the road. "Uhnnnh."

Dee next. A dress down to the ground, in this hot weather.   20
A dress so loud it hurts my eyes. There are yellows and
oranges enough to throw back the light of the sun. I feel my
whole face warming from the heat waves it throws out. Earrings, too, gold and hanging down to her shoulders. Bracelets
dangling and making noises when she moves her arm up to
shake the folds of the dress out of her armpits. The dress is
loose and flows, and as she walks closer, I like it. I hear
Maggie go "Uhnnnh" again. It is her sister's hair. It stands

straight up like the wool on a sheep. It is black as night and around the edges are two long pigtails that rope about like small lizards disappearing behind her ears.

"Wa-su-zo-Tean-o!" she says, coming on in that gliding   21
way the dress makes her move. The short stocky fellow with the hair to his navel is all grinning and he follows up with "Asalamalakim, my mother and sister!" He moves to hug Maggie but she falls back, right up against the back of my chair. I feel her trembling there and when I look up I see the perspiration falling off her chin.

"Don't get up," says Dee. Since I am stout it takes some-   22
thing of a push. You can see me trying to move a second or two before I make it. She turns, showing white heels through her sandals, and goes back to the car. Out she peeks next with a Polaroid. She stoops down quickly and lines up picture after picture of me sitting there in front of the house with Maggie cowering behind me. She never takes a shot without making sure the house is included. When a cow comes nibbling around the edge of the yard she snaps it and me and Maggie *and* the house. Then she puts the Polaroid in the back seat of the car, and comes up and kisses me on the forehead.

Meanwhile Asalamalakim is going through the motions   23
with Maggie's hand. Maggie's hand is limp as a fish, and probably as cold, despite the sweat, and she keeps trying to pull it back. It looks like Asalamalakim wants to shake hands but wants to do it fancy. Or maybe he don't know how people shake hands. Anyhow, he soon gives up on Maggie.

"Well," I say. "Dee."   24

"No, Mama," she says. "Not 'Dee,' Wangero Leewanika   25
Kemanjo!"

"What happened to 'Dee'?" I wanted to know.   26

"She's dead," Wangero said. "I couldn't bear it any longer   27
being named after the people who oppress me."

"You know as well as me you was named after your aunt   28
Dicie," I said. Dicie is my sister. She named Dee. We called her "Big Dee" after Dee was born.

"But who was *she* named after?" asked Wangero.   29

"I guess after Grandma Dee," I said.   30

"And who was she named after?" asked Wangero.   31

"Her mother," I said, and saw Wangero getting tired. 32
"That's about as far back as I can trace it," I said. Though,
in fact, I probably could have carried it back beyond the Civil
War through the branches.

"Well," said Asalamalakim, "there you are." 33

"Uhnnnh," I heard Maggie say. 34

"There I was not," I said, "before 'Dicie' cropped up in 35
our family, so why should I try to trace it that far back?"

He just stood there grinning, looking down on me like 36
somebody inspecting a Model A car. Every once in a while
he and Wangero sent eye signals over my head.

"How do you pronounce this name?" I asked. 37

"You don't have to call me by it if you don't want to," 38
said Wangero.

"Why shouldn't I?" I asked. "If that's what you want us 39
to call you, we'll call you."

"I know it might sound awkward at first," said Wangero. 40

"I'll get used to it," I said. "Ream it out again." 41

Well, soon we got the name out of the way. Asalamalakim 42
had a name twice as long and three times as hard. After I
tripped over it two or three times he told me to just call him
Hakim-a-barber. I wanted to ask him was he a barber, but I
didn't really think he was, so I didn't ask.

"You must belong to those beef-cattle peoples down the 43
road," I said. They said "Asalamalakim" when they met you,
too, but they didn't shake hands. Always too busy: feeding
the cattle, fixing the fences, putting up salt-lick shelters,
throwing down hay. When the white folks poisoned some of
the herd the men stayed up all night with rifles in their hands,
I walked a mile and half just to see the sight.

Hakim-a-barber said, "I accept some of their doctrines, 44
but farming and raising cattle is not my style." (They didn't
tell me, and I didn't ask, whether Wangero [Dee] had really
gone and married him.)

We sat down to eat and right away he said he didn't eat 45
collards and pork was unclean. Wangero, though, went on
through the chitlins and corn bread, the greens and everything else. She talked a blue streak over the sweet potatoes.
Everything delighted her. Even the fact that we still used the

benches her daddy made for the table when we couldn't afford to buy chairs.

"Oh, Mama!" she cried. Then turned to Hakim-a-barber. 46 "I never knew how lovely these benches are. You can feel the rump prints," she said, running her hands underneath her and along the bench. Then she gave a sigh and her hand closed over Grandma Dee's butter dish. "That's it!" she said. "I knew there was something I wanted to ask you if I could have." She jumped up from the table and went over in the corner where the churn stood, the milk in its clabber by now. She looked at the churn and looked at it.

"This churn top is what I need," she said. "Didn't Uncle 47 Buddy whittle it out of a tree you all used to have?"

"Yes," I said. 48

"Uh huh," she said happily. "And I want the dasher, too." 49

"Uncle Buddy whittle that, too?" asked the barber. 50

Dee (Wangero) looked up at me. 51

"Aunt Dee's first husband whittled the dash," said Maggie 52 so low you almost couldn't hear her. "His name was Henry, but they called him Stash."

"Maggie's brain is like an elephant's," Wangero said, 53 laughing. "I can use the churn top as a centerpiece for the alcove table," she said, sliding a plate over the churn, "and I'll think of something artistic to do with the dasher."

When she finished wrapping the dasher the handle stuck 54 out. I took it for a moment in my hands. You didn't even have to look close to see where hands pushing the dasher up and down to make butter had left a kind of sink in the wood. In fact, there were a lot of small sinks; you could see where thumbs and fingers had sunk into the wood. It was beautiful light yellow wood, from a tree that grew in the yard where Big Dee and Stash had lived.

After dinner Dee (Wangero) went to the trunk at the foot 55 of my bed and started rifling through it. Maggie hung back in the kitchen over the dishpan. Out came Wangero with two quilts. They had been pieced by Grandma Dee and then Big Dee and me had hung them on the quilt frames on the front porch and quilted them. One was in the Lone Star pattern.

The other was Walk Around the Mountain. In both of them were scraps of dresses Grandma Dee had worn fifty and more years ago. Bits and pieces of Grandpa Jarrell's Paisley shirts. And one teeny faded blue piece, about the size of a penny matchbox, that was from Great Grandpa Ezra's uniform that he wore in the Civil War.

"Mama," Wangero said sweet as a bird. "Can I have these old quilts?" 56

I heard something fall in the kitchen, and a minute later the kitchen door slammed. 57

"Why don't you take one or two of the others?" I asked. "These old things was just done by me and Big Dee from some tops your grandma pieced before she died." 58

"No," said Wangero. "I don't want those. They are stitched around the borders by machine." 59

"That'll make them last better," I said. 60

"That's not the point," said Wangero. "These are all pieces of dresses Grandma used to wear. She did all this stitching by hand. Imagine!" She held the quilts securely in her arms, stroking them. 61

"Some of the pieces, like those lavender ones, come from old clothes her mother handed down to her," I said, moving up to touch the quilts. Dee (Wangero) moved back just enough so that I couldn't reach the quilts. They already belonged to her. 62

"Imagine!" she breathed again, clutching them closely to her bosom. 63

"The truth is," I said, "I promised to give them quilts to Maggie, for when she marries John Thomas." 64

She gasped like a bee had stung her. 65

"Maggie can't appreciate these quilts!" she said. "She'd probably be backward enough to put them to everyday use." 66

"I reckon she would," I said. "God knows I been saving 'em for long enough with nobody using 'em. I hope she will!" I didn't want to bring up how I had offered Dee (Wangero) a quilt when she went away to college. Then she had told me they were old-fashioned, out of style. 67

"But they're *priceless!*" she was saying now, furiously; for 68 she has a temper. "Maggie would put them on the bed and in five years they'd be in rags. Less than that!"

"She can always make some more," I said. "Maggie knows how to quilt." 69

Dee (Wangero) looked at me with hatred. "You just will not understand. The point is these quilts, *these* quilts!" 70

"Well," I said, stumped. "What would *you* do with them?" 71

"Hang them," she said. As if that was the only thing you *could* do with quilts. 72

Maggie by now was standing in the door. I could almost hear the sound her feet made as they scraped over each other. 73

"She can have them, Mama," she said, like somebody used to never winning anything, or having anything reserved for her. "I can 'member Grandma Dee without the quilts." 74

I looked at her hard. She had filled her bottom lip with checkerberry snuff and it gave her face a kind of dopey, hangdog look. It was Grandma Dee and Big Dee who taught her how to quilt herself. She stood there with her scarred hands hidden in the folds of her skirt. She looked at her sister with something like fear but she wasn't mad at her. This was Maggie's portion. This was the way she knew God to work. 75

When I looked at her like that something hit me in the top of my head and ran down to the soles of my feet. Just like when I'm in church and the spirit of God touches me and I get happy and shout. I did something I never had done before: hugged Maggie to me, then dragged her on into the room, snatched the quilts out of Miss Wangero's hands and dumped them into Maggie's lap. Maggie just sat there on my bed with her mouth open. 76

"Take one or two of the others," I said to Dee. 77

But she turned without a word and went out to Hakim-a-barber. 78

"You just don't understand," she said, as Maggie and I came out to the car. 79

"What don't I understand?" I wanted to know. 80

"Your heritage," she said. And then she turned to Maggie, kissed her and said, "You ought to try to make something of yourself, too, Maggie. It's really a new day for us. But from the way you and Mamma still live you'd never know it." 81

She put on some sunglasses that hid everything above the tip of her nose and her chin. 82

Maggie smiled; maybe at the sunglasses. But a real smile, not scared. After we watched the car dust settle I asked Maggie to bring me a dip of snuff. And then the two of us sat there just enjoying, until it was time to go in the house and go to bed. 83

COMMENT ON "EVERYDAY USE"

Alice Walker's "Everyday Use" describes a difference between a mother's and her visiting daughter's understanding of the word "heritage." For Mama and her daughter Maggie, heritage is a matter of everyday living, of "everyday use." For Mama's other daughter, Dee (Wangero), however, heritage is a matter of style, a fashionable obsession with one's roots. These comparisons are revealed first in Walker's description of the physical appearance of the characters. Mama is fat and manly, and Maggie bears the scars from a fire. By contrast, Dee (Wangero) is beautiful and striking in her brightly colored African dress, earrings, sunglasses, and Afro hair style. Next, Walker compares the characters' skills. Mama can butcher a hog or break ice to get water, and Maggie is able to make beautiful quilts. Dee (Wangero), on the other hand, thinks of herself as outside this domestic world, educated by books to understand the cultural significance of her heritage. The problem posed by the debate over family possessions is whether heritage is an object to be preserved, like a priceless painting, or a process, to be learned, like the creation of a quilt.

Definition as a Writing Strategy

1. Reread the strategies section on pages 304–305. Then for your classmates and instructor, write a definition essay about your high school that will give your audience a vivid idea of what that high school was like. What was valued most in the school? Describe some of the admired students. What were the most important activities? Define by giving examples, analyzing qualities, attributing characteristics, drawing analogies when possible, and telling stories about particular individuals that illustrate the flavor and character of the school. This kind of assignment provides a great opportunity to tell stories about people.

2. For a challenging assignment focusing on a person, pick someone you find especially interesting—an athlete such as Michael Jordan, a businessperson such as Bill Gates or Michael Dell, an entertainment personality such as Oprah Winfrey or Barbra Streisand, a public figure such as Al Gore or Hillary Rodham Clinton. Through a computer search, locate several magazine articles on that person, and read them. Be sure to use substantial articles, not just items from gossip columns. Write a definition essay in which you describe the person—his or her professional activities and personal interests—trying to bring out the unique traits that have made the person successful. Remember that anecdotes are useful in this kind of essay. Your hypothetical audience could be readers of a magazine like *Parade* or *Esquire*.

3. If you are a person with special knowledge about a particular kind of animal, reread Harrigan's essay, "The Tiger Is God," paying special attention to his strategies for defining the nature of the tiger. Then write an essay in which you describe and define a breed or type of animal you know well. Some possibilities are the cutting horse, the dressage horse, hunting dogs or sheep dogs, a particular breed of dog such as Golden Retrievers or Weimaraners, or a particular breed of cat such as Burmese or Russian

Blues. Certainly there are many other possibilities. Use concrete details and examples of particular actions that illustrate the animal's distinctive temperament and behavior.

4. Choose a term that interests you—for example, *camaraderie, sportsmanship, sex appeal, gutsiness, good taste*—and for your campus newspaper write a guest column defining that term with examples and anecdotes. What are the necessary characteristics of someone who has the quality? What is the opposite quality? Who epitomizes the term for you?

5. Richard Rodriguez's "Growing Up in Los Angeles" defines one kind of adolescent, a young person who seems to be the product of that city of glitz and excesses. Write a similar essay, though shorter and less complex, that defines one kind of adolescent in the community where you grew up. You could describe what such a person wears, what extracurricular activities he or she excels at, what he or she drives, and so on. Some possibilities are a rodeo cowboy from west Texas, a gymnast, a member of the school band, a debater, a computer genius, or a popular athlete. You could create a character that would be a composite of several young people you knew. Your audience could be your classmates and instructor.

6. Writers and speakers often argue from definition, trying to get their audiences to agree with or approve of something by defining it positively (for example, a good education) or to criticize something by defining it negatively (for example, a bad grading policy). Drawing on material and information you are getting in one of your courses, write a paper suitable for that course defining a concept, policy, theory, or event either negatively or positively. For a course in early childhood development, you could define a good day-care center. For a chemistry course, you could do a process paper on how to set up a good laboratory experiment. For a government course, you could define a well-run local campaign. For a speech course, you could define an effective speaking style.

CAUSE
AND
EFFECT

If you are like most people, you were born curious and will stay that way all your life, always wondering why things happen, wanting to know reasons. You want to know why the wind blows or what makes some young people dye their hair green, but you also want to know how to control your life and your environment. You can't have that control unless you understand **causes.** That is why so much writing is cause-and-effect writing. You need it to help you understand more about your world so you can improve it. Writing about causes plays an important role in almost all the professions, and it certainly figures prominently in writing in college.

You also want to know about **effects.** Will A lead to B? And also to C, D, and E? Such questions also arise partly from pure curiosity—a youngster will pull any string or push any button just to find out what will happen—but they stem too from a need to regulate your life, to understand how your acts affect the lives of others. You want to predict consequences so you can manage your existence in ways that other creatures cannot manage theirs. You see an effect and look for explanations, usually in writing; and when you try to explain an effect to someone else, you often do it in writing.

PURPOSE

When you write cause-and-effect essays, you're likely to have one of three purposes. Frequently, you will write *to explain*. You want your readers to know how and why things happen, to satisfy their curiosity or to educate them on some issue. You could write a paper in science or economics to lay out logical explanations and show connections for your readers. At other times, you might use a cause-and-effect pattern simply *to speculate* about an interesting topic—for example, to theorize about why a new style has become popular or what the effects will be of a new "no pass/no play" law for high school athletes.

You can also use cause-and-effect writing *to argue*. That may be the way you will use it most often, particularly when you are making an argument to pragmatic people who will pay attention to practical, common-sense reasons. When you cannot get someone to listen to arguments that something is right or wrong, you may be able to persuade by arguing not that a policy is wrong but that it is foolish or impractical—that it will have bad effects.

AUDIENCE

You can assume that cause-and-effect arguments appeal to most audiences because the pattern is such a natural one that readers are used to seeing it. Whether they are teachers, lawyers, parents, doctors, or politicians, your readers will expect you to explain and argue from cause and effect.

When you are thinking about your readers for such arguments, you will find that it helps greatly to think about them as jurors for whom you are going to present a case. You can make up a list of questions about your readers just as a lawyer would to help him or her formulate an argument. Here are some suggested questions: How ready are your readers to hear your arguments? Do you need to give them background information to prepare them? How skeptical are they likely to be? How much evidence will they require? What kind of evidence will they require: factual, statistical? Are your readers bright and well informed, likely to see the connections you want them to make, or will you have to spell everything out? Like a lawyer, you're trying to establish *probable* cause-and-effect sequences. You have the best chance of doing that if you think ahead of time about the expectations, questions, and doubts your readers will have.

STRATEGIES

When you make a cause-and-effect argument, you want your readers to accept your analysis—to agree that when A occurs, then B will probably follow. Thus Cathy Young argues in "Keeping Women Weak" that radical feminists weaken rather than empower women when they claim that women need to be protected by special regulations and conduct codes. She develops her essay by drawing an analogy between paranoia and suspicion in the Soviet Union, where she grew up, and the radical feminists' tendency to see sexism and oppression in virtually all male-female relationships. You could use the same kind of argument if you wanted to write a primarily cause-and-effect paper claiming that a culture that glorifies competition, particularly in bruising sports like football and hockey, shouldn't be surprised at gangs and street violence among young males. You could support your claims with articles you find by using the key words *sports, violence,* and *gangs* for a computerized search.

When you are arguing about effects, you want your audience to accept your analysis of a situation and agree that behavior Y is the result of event X. Robert Coles uses this pattern throughout his essay "Uniforms" when he argues that requiring young people to dress in a certain way puts pressure on them to control their behavior and become part of a respected community. Although Coles isn't dogmatic—that's never his style—he firmly asserts that clothes send signals and that uniforms can help young people who are adrift to find a direction.

You could use the same kind of pattern if you wanted to argue, for instance, that physical punishment is almost never a good idea for children or anyone else. To support your claim you would need to research the issue and then cite studies that show the effects of violence on both those who receive it and those who practice it.

Some of the strategies you can use for cause-and-effect papers resemble those used by lawyers in making an argument. For instance, it's a good idea to *state your claim early* and then *show the connection* you're setting up. Then *present supporting evidence*—past experience, research findings, documentation, personal observation, expert testimony, and so on. Pay special attention to establishing links between the claim and the evidence. It's crucial to show that connection.

You don't have to write every cause-and-effect paper to prove something or as if you were conducting a major court case. You can also write interesting speculative papers in which you theorize about certain trends—for instance, wearing baseball caps backward or athletic shoes with the laces untied—and try to find who initiated the trends and why. Or you could write satirically about some of the annoyances in our culture—for instance, the 800 "help" numbers that keep you on hold or phone menus that go on forever.

POTENTIAL PITFALLS IN CAUSE-AND-EFFECT PAPERS

Although cause and effect is a powerful writing strategy, it can also be a hazardous one. When it comes to dealing with the difficult, ongoing problems of people and societies, you can almost never prove simple cause-and-effect relationships. Many serious human problems really have no good, single solutions because our lives and cultures are so complex. Thus, to keep from looking naive or poorly informed, avoid hasty statements such as "I know what causes X, and we can fix it if we just do Y." To avoid such pitfalls, you should observe the following cautions in writing about cause and effect.

First, as in all expository writing, be careful about how much you claim. Instead of insisting that if A happens, B is inevitable, write, "I believe if A occurs, B is very likely to happen" or "B will probably follow if A happens." For instance, you might feel absolutely sure that if the university opened a child-care center for students' children, attendance at classes would be higher, but you can't prove it. You would gain more credibility with university administrators if you were careful not to overstate your case.

Second, be careful not to oversimplify cause-and-effect connections. Experienced writers and observers know that most major problems and important events have not one cause but several. Daniel Goleman makes this clear in "Peak Performance: Why Records Fall" when he points out that many elements have contributed to better performance among athletes—better coaching, improved equipment, and more knowledge about physiology. Nevertheless, he points out, intensive, longer practicing seems to be the major cause of better performance in most activities.

A less complicated, because more easily analyzed, effect that one might explore is the significant decline in deaths from heart disease in the United States in the last thirty years. There are many reasons for this decline, not just one or two. Increasingly, people smoke less, eat healthier foods, exercise more, and try to control their blood pressure. New treatments for heart problems also make a difference. Similarly, when major events occur, such as the disintegration of socialism in eastern Europe or the Los Angeles riots of May, 1992, knowledgeable observers know that they have multiple and complex causes. Thus, prudent writers qualify their claims about causes and effects by using phrases such as "a major cause," "an important result," or "an immediate effect."

You should also take care to distinguish between immediate, obvious causes for something and more remote, less apparent causes. You may feel that the immediate cause of the distressing rise in teenage pregnancies in the United States is movies and television programs that are much more sexually explicit than those of fifteen years ago, but it's important to recognize that there are more far-reaching, long-term reasons, such as poor sex education programs, many taboos on dispensing birth control information, and the increased focus on sexuality in ads.

Third, avoid confusing coincidence or simple sequence for cause and effect. Just because X follows Y doesn't mean Y causes X—that assumption is the basis of superstitions. If an increase in the automobile accident rate follows a drop in gasoline prices, you can't conclude there is a necessary connection between the two events. There might be, but a prudent investigator would want much more data before drawing such a conclusion. If you jump to quick conclusions about causes and effects, you risk falling into the "false cause" or "after this, therefore because of this" fallacy.

So working with cause and effect in a paper can be tricky and complex. That doesn't mean, however, that you should refrain from using cause-and-effect explanations or arguments until you are absolutely sure of your ground. You can't always wait for certainty to make an analysis or a forecast. The best you can do is observe carefully, speculate intelligently, and add qualifications.

USING CAUSE AND EFFECT IN PARAGRAPHS

Here are two cause-and-effect paragraphs. The first is written by a professional writer and is followed by an analysis. The second is written by a student writer and is followed by questions.

WINIFRED GALLAGHER
From "From the Nest to the Global Village"

We also look to our territories to serve the needs of a loftier order. Studies of hunter–gatherer societies show that a person's turf helps provide identity, privacy, intimacy, and protection from stress. One reason our homes are so precious to us—and being homeless is so debilitating—is that every time we cross the threshold, we wrap ourselves in a cozy, protective mantle of memories that help sustain our persona. In the effort to extend the deep psychological meaning and comfort that our special places impart, we even invest particular objects with their values. The most obvious example is the flag, which conjures up the whole heartland in many breasts, just as a family snapshot or portable heirloom can turn a hotel room into a home away from home. Such territorial symbols not only help us unify our past and present, but also help us forge the future. In one study, researchers found the best inidcation of which students were likeliest to drop out of college was the decor of their dorm rooms during freshman year; the kids who embellished them lavishly with local touches, such as university posters, were far more apt to stick it out than those who made little effort or decked their rooms with hometown memorabilia, say, a dried corsage from the high school prom.

Person's turf important to sense of self

Home a protective wrap

We invest objects with home values

Example of stuff in college dorm rooms that makes a nest

Comment Starting with a reference to anthropological research, Gallagher explains how our homes help us forge a sense of self. Every time we come into our homes, we "wrap ourselves in a protective mantle of memories"; we even transfer these associations to objects like a picture or a memento. She reinforces her thesis by citing a piece of research showing that first-year college students who put up university posters and other reminders of their new identity in their dorm rooms were more likely to stay in school than those who made little attempt to create a home environment.

EMILY LINDERMAN
Barrier-Free Design

Many merchants view the Americans with Disabilities Act as expensive social engineering. They have established an attractive and affordable space for their businesses. Their customers seem satisfied. Then the federal government requires them to provide accessible ramps and elevators, wider doorways and halls, larger bathrooms, and lower drinking fountains. Seen from another perspective, however, making these changes may pay off in the long run. How many times have you tried to move furniture into a building or up to the third floor? How many times have you tried to find a place for your packages in a cramped bathroom stall? And how many times have you had to lift your little brother up to the fountain to get a drink? All customers, not simply disabled customers, will benefit from and reward merchants who invest in these barrier-free buildings.

1. Whom do you think Linderman is addressing with her argument for the benefits of barrier-free buildings?
2. How does the significance of the extra benefits that Linderman mentions compare with the significance of the benefits that the Disabilities Act was designed to provide?

CAUSE AND EFFECT

Points to Remember

1. Remember that in human events you can almost never prove direct, simple, cause-and-effect relationships. Qualify your claims.
2. Be careful not to oversimplify your cause-and-effect statements; be cautious about saying that a cause always produces a certain effect or that a remedy never succeeds.
3. Distinguish between the immediate, obvious cause of something and more long-range, less apparent causes for that effect.
4. Avoid confusing coincidence or simple sequence with cause and effect; because B follows A doesn't mean that A caused B.
5. Build your cause-and-effect argument as a trial lawyer would. Present as much evidence as you can and argue for your hypothesis.

Robert Coles was born in Boston, Massachusetts, in 1929 and educated at Harvard University and Columbia Medical School. He worked as a member of the psychiatric staff at several hospitals before assuming the position of professor of psychiatry and medical humanities at the Harvard Medical School. Although he has contributed essays to journals as diverse as *The Atlantic* and the *American Journal of Psychiatry,* he is best known for his multivolume study of children in various stressful situations, *Children of Crisis* (1967–1978). He has also written books such as *Erik H. Erikson: The Growth of His Work* (1970); *Irony in the Mind's Life: Essays on Novels by James Agee, Elizabeth Bowen and George Eliot* (1974); *The Call of Stories* (1989); *The Call of Service* (1993); and, together with his wife, Jane Hallowell Coles, the multivolume *Women of Crisis* (1978–1980). In "Uniforms," reprinted from *Harvard Diary II,* Coles describes the possible effects of wearing a uniform.

Uniforms

WE HAVE BEEN hearing a good deal, of late, about the value of uniforms as a means of encouraging young people to be more disciplined, law-abiding. The rationale goes like this: children and young people need a sense of order; need firm rules with respect to how they ought to look, behave; need to feel themselves very much part of particular institutions whose educational and ethical principles are meant to strengthen our various communities and, by extension, our nation—and uniforms help address that necessary psychological and moral aspect of child-rearing. Not that clothes in and of themselves possess magical transformative powers. A child (or adult) bent on being rowdy, mean, hurtful, criminal can do so wearing a coat and tie, and shoes polished to a sparkle, whereas youngsters who appear to certain fastidious and formal adults as slobs and worse (their pants uncreased and wrinkled, their shirts sloppily worn) can be conscientious, decent, considerate, kindly—respectful of others, if not respectful of the notion some of us have as to

> *In a sense, all clothes are . . . symbolic—*
> *we send signals, thereby, as to who we are,*
> *what we hold dear, with whom we wish to*
> *connect, and affiliate ourselves.*

how they ought to be attired. Moreover, for some young people, such casual, laid-back garb is itself a uniform—to appear relaxed and "cool" is felt to be a mandatory manner of self-presentation.

For years, actually, I have heard the word "uniform" used by certain Harvard college students of mine, who have arrived in Cambridge from small towns in the South or the Midwest, and aren't familiar with a kind of constraint that is imposed by indirection: "I went to a Catholic school in Minnesota, and we were told we didn't all have to wear the same kind of blouse and skirt and socks and shoes, the way it used to be—but, you know, we did have to wear some kind of blouse and skirt: I mean, no jeans and no T-shirts. So, when I came here I wasn't as uptight as some people I met here [during the first days of orientation] who came from schools where there really were uniforms and everyone had to wear them, be dressed the same. But it doesn't take long to discover that there's a 'uniform' here too—and if you

2

don't wear it, you'll pay a price. I mean [I had, obviously, asked] here, if you wear a skirt and blouse to class, you can feel out of it: too formal. Here, the scruffier the better, that's what you learn right off, boy or girl! There's a way to dress when you go to class, just as there was when I was in high school, only the clothes are different—and Lord help you at breakfast if you come into the dining room looking neat and tidy, and your hair is combed and you're wearing a dress (a dress!) and some jewelry, a bracelet or a necklace: people will think you're on your way to a job interview, or something has *happened*—you have to go to a hospital, or a funeral, or church, something unusual! You'll hear, 'Is everything all right?' Now, I hear myself thinking those words—if I get the urge to wear clothes that are just the slightest bit 'formal,' the way I used to all the time! If I told my roommates or others in the [freshman] dorm what I've just said, they'd think I was odd—making a case out of nothing, one guy put it when I got into a discussion with him about all this, and made the mistake of pointing out that all the boys here wear khakis or jeans, and sneakers, the dirtier the better, and open shirts, work shirts, a lot of them, as if we're in a logging camp out West!"

She was exaggerating a little, but her essential point was quite well taken—that in a setting where studied informality rules supreme, and where individualism is highly touted, there are, nevertheless, certain standards with respect to the desirable, the decidedly unattractive, so that a dress code certainly asserts itself, however informally, unofficially: a uniform of sorts, as the young man she mentioned did indeed agree to call it, a range of what is regarded as suitable, and what is unusual, worth observing closely, even paying the notice of a comment, a question. Nor is such a college environment all that unusual, with respect to a relative consistency of attire that is, surely, more apparent to the outsider. We all tend to fall in line, accommodate the world (of work, of study, of travel and relaxation, of prayer) we have chosen, for varying lengths of time, to join. We take notice of others, ascertain a given norm, with respect to what is (and is not) worn, and make the necessary choices for our wardrobe, our use—or we don't do so, thereby, of course, for one reason or another of our own, setting ourselves apart, even as others promptly do the same in the way they regard us.

All of the above is unsurprising: the stuff of our daily   4
unselfconscious living, yet, an aspect of our existence that ought to be remembered when a topic such as "uniforms" is brought up for public consideration—a necessary context. Still, these days, when the subject of "uniforms" comes up, it is meant to help us consider how to work more effectively in our schools with young people who are in trouble, who aren't doing well in school, who may be drop-outs and already up to no good—well on their way to delinquency, criminality. To ask such individuals (to demand of them when they are under the jurisdiction of a court) that they adhere to a certain dress code is to put them on due and proper notice: a certain kind of behavior is expected, and no ifs, ands, buts—the uniform as an exterior instance of what has to take place within: obedience, self-restraint, a loyalty to institutional authority. True, to repeat, clothes don't make us decent, cooperative, respectful human beings, in and of themselves—but they are an aspect of the way we present ourselves to others, and they are also daily reminders to us of the world to which we belong, and by extension, the values and customs and requirements of that world. To tell a child, a young man or woman, that he or she has to "shape up" in a certain way, dress in a certain manner, speak a certain language (and not another kind!) is to indicate a determination that a particular community's jurisdiction, its sovereignty will be asserted, maintained, upheld, from moment to moment.

I hear all the time, of course, that in our fancy private   5
schools and colleges such an institutional insistence with regard to dress has been, by and large, abandoned in the name of a modern individualism, a lack of pretentiousness, a respect for our variousness, a refusal of "authoritarianism," of the "repressiveness" of yore. To be sure, clothes can be a badge, an instrument of fearful, blind submission, of snobbish, cliquish affiliation, of gratuitous and relentless and unthinking indoctrination. On the other hand, as mentioned earlier, even

the most vigorously iconoclastic, even those righteously en-
amored of a social or political or educational privatism that
resists compliance with any number of conventions or habits,
will not easily escape their own, ironic nod (and more) to
social cohesion—one uniform replacing another, ties and
skirts abandoned in a compulsory stampede for jeans or
sweatpants, or for undershirts become all there is above the
waist.

Many of the youngsters I have met, taught in ghetto   6
schools, many of the youngsters I've known who are in
trouble at first-rate suburban or private school, have enormous need for "control": they haven't learned to subordinate
their impulses to the needs of others; they are self-absorbed
to their own detriment, never mind the harm that such a
tenaciously reflexic egoism can cause to others in a classroom,
on a team, a playground, anywhere in a neighborhood. Such
boys and girls, such youths can often be desperately in search
of the very commitment to an (educational, religious, civic)
community they seem flagrantly to refuse, scorn. Indeed,
their only hope may be the moment when a school or judge
acts on behalf of a rehabilitative or corrective program that
draws the line, insists that a uniform be a step (a mere step,
but nonetheless, a significant first move) toward integration
into a world outside any given self, a world in which others
count, are respected, a world of obedience and self-control,
as well as self-regard and self-assertion (the nature of the mix
is all-important).

In a sense then all clothes are, as Freud, not to mention   7
Shakespeare, reminded us, symbolic—we send signals,
thereby, as to who we are, what we hold dear, with whom we
wish to connect, affiliate ourselves. Moreover, it works both
ways: we receive messages with respect to our appearance
from the nation, the culture, the various institutions or communities to which we belong (or which we are *told* we must
join, such as the schools)—as anyone will realize upon visiting
a foreign land, a different continent, but also while here at
home, where what we wear can tell a lot about our hopes,
inclinations, dispositions, aspirations, loyalties, and, too, our

fears and worries, and worse. Small wonder then, that uniforms worn by young people adrift, wayward in various ways, can bring a promise of direction, can offer a community with a shared purpose certain values and ideals, all of which, literally, are worn on the sleeves of its members. Of course, the heart of the matter is a person's interior moral life, but some of us badly need to be reminded, again and again, that there are others out there to whom, so to speak, we belong, and of whom we have to think with consideration and respect. We do, indeed, dress for those others, not only for ourselves—and for all of us that daily gesture has meaning, even as for some of us such a gesture may mark the beginning of a life that itself has, finally, come to possess some meaning.

For Study and Discussion

QUESTIONS FOR RESPONSE

1. If you or someone close to you wore uniforms to school, what effect do you think they had on those who wore them? Give some examples.
2. Would you say there is an unofficial uniform on your campus? If so, what is it and why do you think it has been adopted? How strong do you think the pressure is to conform?

QUESTIONS ABOUT PURPOSE

1. What significant points does Coles make about the role that clothes play in most of our lives? How valid do you find his reasoning?
2. How does Coles suggest that uniforms can play a part in helping young people to establish their place in a community?

QUESTIONS ABOUT AUDIENCE

1. The original audience for this essay probably consisted of Coles's colleagues and other adults who know of and are interested in his work with children. In what ways do you think that the

response of those readers and those of first-year college students are likely to differ?

2. What negative feelings do many people have about uniforms that Coles has to overcome in order to make his argument? What do you think is the source of those feelings?

QUESTIONS ABOUT STRATEGIES

1. In the course of the essay, what details does Coles reveal about his professional dealings with children? What weight do those details give to his argument?
2. What kind of reasoning does Coles use to counteract the reaction against school uniforms that he knows many students are likely to have?

QUESTIONS FOR DISCUSSION

1. What are some of "the constraints imposed by indirection," as Coles puts it (paragraph 2), that you feel in your life? What would the result be if you defied some of those constraints?
2. What are some of the common reasons school administrators and parents give for wanting youngsters to wear school uniforms? What is your response to those reasons?

CATHY YOUNG

Cathy Young was born in 1963 in Moscow, in the former Soviet Union, and was educated at Rutgers University. After writing a weekly column for the college newspaper, she began contributing articles to the *New York Times* and *American Spectator.* One year after graduating from Rutgers, she published *Growing Up in Moscow: Memoirs of a Soviet Girlhood* (1989). She is currently at work on *The Virgin of Terror: A Biography of Charlotte Corday,* a book on the political activism of women in Russia. In "Keeping Women Weak," reprinted from *NEXT: Young American Writers on the New Generation* (1994), Young analyzes the effects of feminism on her generation's attitudes toward women's liberation.

Keeping Women Weak

NOT LONG AGO, I attended a conference on women's research and activism in the nineties, attended by dozens of feminist academics, writers, and public figures. At the wrap-up session, a middle-aged history professor from the Midwest introduced a discordant note into the spirit of celebration. "The fact," she said, "is that young women just aren't interested in feminism or feminist ideas, even though they are leading feminist lives—planning to become lawyers, doctors, professionals. What is it about feminism, and about our approach, that puts young women off?"

In response, some blamed "the backlash," others "homophobia." One woman protested that there *were* young feminists out there, citing sexual harassment lawsuits filed by high-school girls—apparently a greater accomplishment than merely preparing for a career. Another declared that what

1

2

feminist educators needed to give their students was "an understanding of the power dynamic," not "quote-unquote objectivity." (Could it be something about comments like these that turns female students off?) Missing from this picture was any serious discussion of what modern feminism has to offer modern young women.

Feminism meant a great deal to me when I came to the United States thirteen years ago, after a childhood spent in the Soviet Union. Indeed, one of the things that elated me the most about America was women's liberation.   3

The society in which I had grown up was one that officially proclaimed sexual equality and made it a point of great pride   4

The new radical feminism seeks to regulate personal relationships to a degree unprecedented since the Puritans roamed the earth.

---

yet stereotyped men and women in ways reminiscent of the American fifties. At school, we had mandatory home economics for girls and shop for boys, a practice no one thought of challenging. At the music school for the gifted where my mother taught piano, to say that someone played "like a girl"—pleasantly, neatly, and without substance—was a commonly used putdown; in literary reviews, the highest compliment to be paid a woman writer or poet was that she wrote like a man.

As I approached college age, I learned that there was tacit but widely known discrimination against women in the college-entrance exams, on the assumption that a less-capable male would in the end be a more valuable asset than a bright female, who would have boys and makeup and marriage on her mind. And all too many smart, ambitious girls seemed to accept this injustice as inevitable, assuming simply that they had to be twice as good as the boys to prove themselves.   5

It was just as unquestioningly accepted that housework, 6
including the arduous task of Soviet shopping, was women's
work; when the problem of women's excessive double burden at home and on the job was mentioned at all, the proposed solution was always for men to be paid more and for
women to spend more time at home, not for men to pitch
in with domestic chores. And although my parents' relationship was an uncommonly equal one, my father still quoted
to me the dictum (coming from Karl Marx, a thinker he
generally did not regard as much of an authority) that
"woman's greatest strength is her weakness."

My discovery of America was also a discovery of femi- 7
nism—not only *Ms.* magazine and *The Feminine Mystique* but
also the open and straightforward manner of young American
women I met. This was in stark contrast to the style that so
many Russian women reverently equated with "femininity"—
a more-or-less affected air of capriciousness and frailty, a
flirtatious deference to men. I admired the easy camaraderie
between boys and girls on American college campuses, the
independence and self-confidence of young women who invited guys on dates and picked up the tab, drove when they
were out with male companions, and wouldn't let anyone
treat them like frail, helpless little things.

Those early impressions may have been too optimistic, 8
perhaps somewhat superficial, perhaps incomplete. But I
don't think they were wrong.

Becoming an American as a teenager in 1980, I joined the 9
first generation of American women who had grown up assuming not only that they would work most of their lives but
also that they were the equals of men and that they could be
anything they wanted to be (except maybe a full-time home-
maker). This was also the first generation, really, to have
grown up after the sexual revolution—at a time when, at least
among the educated, the nice-girls-don't sexual standard
vanished almost completely. In a somewhat dizzying reversal
of traditional norms, many girls felt embarrassed telling their
first lovers that they were virgins (at least that's how I felt).

Of course new choices meant new pressures. I never 10
thought a world of sexual equality would be a utopia of peace

and harmony. I did believe that our generation of women, and men, was on its way to achieving a world in which people were judged as individuals and not on the basis of their gender; a world in which men and women worked and loved in equal partnership—even if, inevitably, they continued every so often to make each other miserable and furious.

And then something funny happened on the way to that   11
feminist future. We were told that we were victims, with little control over our lives and our choices; we were told that we needed to be protected.

When the right said that women were victimized by career   12
opportunities and sexual freedom, it didn't matter much—at least to the middle-class, college-educated women who were the main beneficiaries of these new opportunities. Who, in those social circles, was going to listen to people who said that wives should obey their husbands and stick to the kitchen and nursery—to Phyllis Schlafly or Jerry Falwell, notorious reactionaries with little impact on mass culture?

But the message of victimhood also came from the feminist   13
left. Everywhere around us, we were told, was a backlash seeking to snatch from us the freedoms we had gained. We were told that we were the targets of a hidden war and had better start acting like one, searching for subtle signs of enemy forays everywhere. If we believed that we had never experienced gender-based injustice and had never felt particularly restricted by our gender, we were not just naive but dangerous: we were turning our backs on feminism and fostering the myth that its major battles had been won.

Whenever a campus study has shown that young people of   14
both sexes increasingly share the same values and aspirations and that most college women are quite confident of their ability to succeed in the workplace and to combine family and career, older feminists seem far from pleased. Their warnings—oh, just wait until these young women get a taste of the real world and find that they still face prejudice and discrimination—can sound almost gleeful.

Older feminists talk a good line about empowering young   15
women and letting them speak in their own voices; but that

goes only as long as these voices say all the approved things. At a university workshop on peer sexual harassment in schools I attended in the spring of 1993, some of the panelists complained that many girls didn't seem to understand what sexual harassment was; when boys made passes or teased them sexually they just shrugged it off, or they thought it was funny and actually liked it. "They need to be educated," one speaker said earnestly, "that the boys aren't just joking around with you, that it's harassment."

Ignored in all this discussion was intriguing evidence of the assertive, even aggressive sexuality of many of today's teenage girls, who apparently do a bit of harassing of their own. If girls seemed to revel in sexual attention, that could only be a sign of "low self-esteem" or inability to say no. 16

Judging by all those complaints about the unraised consciousness of the young, the preoccupation with the sexual and other victimization of high-school and college females is not coming, by and large, from young women themselves. Most of them, I believe, tend to regard all the extreme rhetoric as a sort of background noise; if they think about feminism at all, they often decide that they want no part of it—even if they're all for equal rights. The kind of feminists they usually see in their midst may further contribute to this alienation. 17

When I was still in college, I began to notice, alongside the spirited, independent, ambitious young women I admired, a different product of the feminist age: the ever-vigilant watchdog on the alert for signs of sexism. Occasionally, she made a good point; when our environmental science professor blamed overpopulation in part on Third World women "choosing" to have lots of babies, a student spoke up to note that for most Third World women, childbearing was hardly a matter of choice. 18

More typical, alas, was the young woman in my human sexuality class who was constantly pouncing on the professor for saying something like "People who suffer from premature ejaculation . . ." ("Are you implying that only men are people?"). When he had the audacity to cite data indicating that 19 some rapists were motivated primarily by hatred of women and the desire to dominate them but others were driven primarily by sexual impulses, she went ballistic: "The ONLY thing that causes rape is men wanting to control and terrorize women, and you're trying to make it SEXY!" Later, this person bragged about having caused the poor prof "a lot of trouble" by filing a complaint with the dean.

Paranoid is a red-flag word to many feminists—under- 20
standably so, since it has been used all too often to dismiss women's rightful concerns about sexism. But what other word can come to mind when a woman claims that her writing instructor's selection of a sample of bad writing—a conservative Christian screed linking pornography and communism—was a personal insult directed at her, since she had sometimes worn a Women Against Pornography button in school?

And what can one expect when Naomi Wolf, a writer 21
hailed as a trailblazer of a new "Third Wave" of feminism for the younger generation, urges women to undertake—and men, to gracefully (and gratefully) second—"the arduous, often boring, nonnegotiable *daily chore of calling attention to sexism*" (emphasis mine)? In the essay "Radical Heterosexuality, or, How to Love a Man and Save Your Feminist Soul" (published in the twentieth-anniversary issue of *Ms.*), Wolf describes how even well-intentioned men tend to be blind to the horrific things women have to put up with:

> *Recently, I walked down a New York City avenue with a woman friend, X, and a man friend, Y. I pointed out to Y the leers, hisses, and invitations to sit on faces. Each woman saw clearly what the other woman saw, but Y was baffled. . . . A passerby makes kissy-noises with his tongue while Y is scrutinizing the menu of the nearest bistro. "There, there! Look! Listen!" we cried. "What? Where? Who?" wailed poor Y, valiantly, uselessly spinning.*

Like poor Y, I am baffled. God knows, I've been taking 22
walks in Manhattan at least once or twice a week for nearly

thirteen years now, and not a single invitation to sit on a face, not even a single hiss as far as I recall—nothing more dramatic than the occasional "You look gorgeous today" or "That's a pretty outfit," and certainly nothing like the constant barrage Wolf describes. Even the time I wore a new dress that exposed much more cleavage than I realized, all it cost me was one fairly tame remark (as I was stepping into a subway car, a man who was stepping off stared at my bosom and muttered, "Very nice"). Applied to everyday life and interpersonal relations, "eternal vigilance is the price of liberty" strikes me as a rather disastrous motto to adopt.

Like all would-be revolutionaries, the radical feminists seek   23
to subordinate private life to ideology—an endeavor that I find, quite simply, frightening. You don't have to spend part of your life under a totalitarian system (though maybe it helps) to realize that social and political movements that subordinate life to ideology have a nasty way of turning coercive, whether it's the mass violence of communism or the neo-Puritan controls of "P.C."

This is not to say that there is no room for rethinking   24
traditional attitudes, on things ranging from who picks up the check in the restaurant to who takes care of the baby. Millions of women and men are grappling with these issues at home and in the workplace, some more successfully than others. But that doesn't mean they have to walk around with their eyes glued to a microscope.

Eternal vigilance is a tempting trap for post-baby-boomer   25
feminists. It has been often remarked that women of earlier generations had to struggle against visible and overt barriers, such as being denied admission to law school, or told that only men need apply for certain jobs or that married women shouldn't work. It seemed that once such barriers dropped, equality would come quickly. It didn't quite turn out that way; there were other, more insidious roadblocks, from a working mother's guilt over taking a business trip to a professor's unconscious tendency to call on the boys in the class. The problem, however, is that subtle sexism is an elusive target, with plenty of room for error and misinterpretation. If you complain to your professor that you find the course

work too difficult and he says, "Well, I've always thought girls didn't belong in this class anyway," there's not a shadow of a doubt that he's a sexist pig. But suppose he says, "Hey, start working harder or drop the class, but don't come whining to me." Is he being insensitive to you as a woman? (An incident of this sort figured in a recent sex-discrimination suit at the University of Minnesota.) Or is he simply a blunt fellow who believes people should stand on their own two feet and who would have treated a male student exactly the same? And if he had been tough on a man but sensitive and solicitous toward a woman student, wouldn't that have been exactly the kind of paternalism feminists used to oppose?

But then, certain aspects of cutting-edge feminism do   26
smack of a very old-fashioned paternalism, a sort of chivalry without the charm. At some campus meetings, it is considered P.C. for men who are first in line for the microphone to cede their place to a woman in order to ensure that female speakers—apparently too timid to just get up and get in line—get a proper hearing. Ladies first?

Definitions of "hostile environment" sexual harassment   27
often seem like a throwback to prefeminist, if not positively Victorian, standards of how to treat a lady: no off-color jokes, no sexual remarks, no swearing and, God forbid, no improper advances. Surveys purporting to gauge the prevalence of harassment lump together sexual blackmail—demands for sex as a condition of promotion, good grades, or other rewards—with noncoercive advances from coworkers or fellow students, with sexual jokes or innuendo, "improper staring" or "winking."

Well, guess what: women too make off-color jokes and   28
risqué comments, and even sexual advances. Sure, many women at one time or another also have to deal with obnoxious, lecherous, and/or sexist jerks. But in most cases, especially if the man is not a superior, they're perfectly capable of putting a jerk back in his place. Of course, radical feminists such as Catharine MacKinnon tell us that there is *always* an imbalance of power between a man and a woman: even if you're studying for an MBA and have a prestigious job lined

up, you're still powerless. Now there's a message guaranteed to build up self-confidence and self-esteem.

A video on sexual harassment, broadcast on public television twice in January 1993 and available free through an 800 number, includes a segment on a university experiment in which unwitting male students are assigned to supervise the computer work of an attractive girl. Before leaving them alone, the male research assistant pretends to take small liberties with the young woman (putting a hand on her shoulder, bending closely over her) while explaining the work process, and in most cases the male student proceeds to imitate this behavior or even push it a little further.

Then, the young woman—who, of course, has known what's been going on the whole time—talks on camera about how the experience has helped her understand what it's like to feel powerless. But doesn't this powerlessness have at least something to do with the fact that she was undoubtedly instructed not to show displeasure? Is it such a good idea to teach young women that, short of legal intervention, they have no way of dealing with such annoyances?

I don't believe that our views or our allegiances are determined solely or primarily by age. Still, one might have expected our generation to articulate a feminism rooted in the experience of women who have never felt subordinated to men, have never felt that their options were limited by gender in any significant way or that being treated as sexual beings diminished their personhood. This is not, of course, the experience of all young women; but it is the experience of many, and an experience that should be taken as a model. Perhaps those of us who have this positive view of our lives and our relationships with men have not lived up to our responsibility to translate that view into a new feminist vision.

In an *Esquire* article about sexual politics and romantic love on campus in the nineties, Janet Viggiani, then–assistant dean for coeducation at Harvard, was quoted as saying, "I think young women now are very confused. . . . They don't have many models for how to be strong females and feminine. Many of their models are victim models—passive, weak, endangered." In recent years, feminist activism has focused almost entirely on negatives, from eating disorders to sexual violence and abuse. Sadly, these problems are all too real, and they certainly should be confronted; what they should not be is the central metaphor for the female condition or for relations between women and men, or for feminism. What does it mean when the only time young women and girls think of feminism is not when they think of achievement but when they think of victimization?

The emphasis on victimhood has had an especially dramatic effect on attitudes toward sexuality. We didn't revel in our sexual freedom for too long; as if the shadow of AIDS weren't bad enough, sex was suddenly fraught with danger and violence as much as possibilities of pleasure, or even more so. A cartoon in the *Nation* shows a girl grooming herself before a mirror, with the caption, "Preparing for a date"— and in the next frame, a boy doing the same, with the caption, "Preparing for a date rape." Pamphlets on sexual assault warn that one out of every five dates ends in a rape, and that up to 25 percent of college women become victims: "Since you can't tell who has the potential for rape by simply looking, be on your guard with every man." 33

If these numbers are true, women would be well advised either to forswear dating altogether or to carry a can of Mace on every date. But what about these numbers? When one looks at how they are obtained, and how rape is defined, it becomes clear that the acquaintance-rape hysteria not only gives young women an exaggerated picture of the dangers they face in the company of men but essentially demeans women, absolving or stripping them of all responsibility for their behavior. 34

The question is not whether a woman's provocative dress, flirtatious behavior, or drinking justifies sexual assault; that attitude is now on the wane, for which the women's movement certainly deserves credit. It's not even a question of whether a woman should have to fight back and risk injury to prove that she did not consent to sex. The latest crusade makes a woman a victim of rape if she did not rebuff a man's 35 sexual advances because she was too shy or didn't want to hurt his feelings, or if she had sex while drunk (not passed out, just sufficiently intoxicated so that her inhibitions were loosened) and felt bad about it afterwards. In a typical scenario, a couple is making out and then the woman pulls back and says, "I really think we shouldn't," and the man draws her back toward him, *nonforcibly,* and continues to fondle her, or says, "Oh come on, you know you want it," and eventually they end up having sex. If the woman feels that the intercourse was "unwanted," she can—according to the anti-date-rape activists—claim to be a victim, no different from the woman who's attacked at knifepoint in a dark, empty parking lot.

A few years ago, I was at the apartment of an ex-boyfriend 36 with whom I was still on friendly terms; after a couple of beers, we started kissing. When his hand crept under my skirt, I suddenly sobered up and thought of several good reasons why I should not go to bed with the guy. I wriggled out of his arms, got up, and said, "That's enough." Undaunted, he came up from behind and squeezed my breasts. I rammed my elbow into his chest, forcefully enough to make the point, and snapped, "Didn't you hear me? I said, enough."

Some people might say that I overreacted (my ex- 37 boyfriend felt that way), but the logic of modern-day radical feminists suggests the opposite: that I displayed a heroism that cannot be required of any woman in a situation like that because she could expect the guy to beat her up, to maim her, even if he hadn't made any threats or shown any violent tendencies. A "reasonable" woman would have passively submitted and then cried rape.

Even "no means no" is no longer enough; some activists 38 want to say that yes means no, or at least the absence of an explicit yes means no. Feminist legal theorist MacKinnon suggests that much of what our society regards as consensual sex hardly differs from rape and that, given women's oppression, it is doubtful "whether consent is a meaningful concept" at all. Which is to say that, like underage children and the mentally retarded, women are to be presumed incapable of valid consent. MacKinnon's frequent ally, polemicist Andrea Dworkin, states bluntly that all intercourse is rape.

This reasoning is still very far from mainstream acceptance. 39 Even MacKinnon only expresses such views when addressing fairly narrow and converted audiences, not when she's interviewed on TV. Yet a 1992 report by the Harvard Date Rape Task Force recommended that university guidelines define rape as "any act of sexual intercourse that occurs without the expressed consent of the person." What does this mean—that a consent form must be signed before a date? Or that, as a couple moves toward the bed after passionate and mutual heavy petting, the man should ask the woman if she's quite sure she wants to? (A friend who just graduated from college tells me that some men are actually beginning to act that way.) And perhaps he has to keep asking every time: the couple's prior sexual relationship, the advocates say, makes no difference whatsoever.

Clearly, this vision leaves no room for spontaneity, for 40 ambiguity, for passionate, wordless, animal sex. What's more, it is, in the end, deeply belittling to women, who apparently cannot be expected to convey their wishes clearly or to show a minimum of assertiveness. It also perpetuates a view of woman as the passive and reticent partner who may or may not want sex and man as the pursuer who is naturally presumed to want it: *she* is not required to ask for *his* consent (even though, given some current definitions, plenty of women must have committed rape at least a few times in their lives; I'm sure I have). Sex is something men impose on women. We're back full circle to fragile, chaste, nineteenth-century womanhood.

And some people think that's good. Recently, I got into a 41 discussion with a conservative Catholic male who vehemently argued that the campaign against date rape was nothing more than a distorted expression of women's legitimate rejection of sexual freedom, a thing so contrary to their chaste natures. Casual sex, he said, makes women (but not men) feel cheap and used, and what they're doing now is using the extreme language of rape to describe this exploitation; things were really better under the much-maligned double standard, when women were expected to say no to sex, and thus accorded more protection from male lust. To some conservatives, the outcry about sexual harassment confirms what conservatives have known all along: women want to be put on a pedestal and treated like ladies; they find sexual advances insulting because they are chaster than men.

I don't think that's true. Most young women have no wish   42
to return to the days when they were branded as sluts if they said yes. It may be, however, that this generation's confusion over sexual boundaries has to do with the pains of transition from one set of morals to another, of contradictory cultural messages: the traditional ones of chastity as the basis of female self-respect and reputation and the new ones of sexual liberation and female desire. Sometimes, we may not think we're "cheap" if we go to bed with a man we just met—at least, we're no worse than the guy is for going to bed with a woman he just met—yet when we wake up the next morning we may find that *he* thinks less of us but not of himself. And we may find, to our chagrin, that feminine coyness is not quite as extinct as we might like to think. The other day, a very liberated fortysomething friend of mine breezily said, "Oh, of course no modern woman says no when she means yes." Alas, recent studies (done by feminist researchers) show that *by their own admission,* about half of college women sometimes do.

But there may be another reason, too, for this generation's   43
susceptibility to the victim mentality: overconfidence in the perfectibility of life. The sexual-liberation rhetoric itself overlooked the complexity of human emotions and fostered the belief that sexual relationships could be free of all manipulation or unfair pressure. More generally, there is the idealistic arrogance of middle-class boys and girls who have grown up in a sheltered, affluent environment, accustomed to the notion that getting one's way is a basic right. The old cliché "Life isn't fair" is not only unpopular nowadays but profoundly suspect, seen as a smokescreen designed by the oppressors to keep the oppressed—women and minorities, in

particular—in their place. Yes, it has been used for such purposes often enough. But often it happens to be true, and to disregard that is to invite disastrous consequences—like the belief that anyone, male or female, is entitled to an annoyance-free life.

The danger in the new radical feminism is not only that it   44
legitimizes what is, deep down, an extremely retrograde view of women; it also seeks to regulate personal relationships to a degree unprecedented since the Puritans roamed the earth. If you feel that a man has enticed or pressured you into having unwanted sex, you don't confront him and call him a manipulative creep; you run to a campus grievance committee and demand redress. If you don't like the way a coworker has been putting his hand on your shoulder, you don't have to tell him to stop it—you can go and file a lawsuit instead. Courts and law-enforcement authorities are being asked to step into situations where, short of installing hidden cameras in every bedroom and every office hallway, they have no way of finding out on whose side the truth is. Of course, many millions of women and men remain relatively unaffected by this relentless politicization of the personal. Still, the damage is being done.

Again, it may be my Soviet background that makes me   45
especially sensitive to the perils of this aggressive, paternalistic interventionism. In the Soviet *ancien régime*, it was not uncommon to report one's unfaithful spouse to the Communist party bureau at his (or, less commonly, her) workplace, and conflicts between husband and wife—particularly if both were party members—were often settled at public meetings that satisfied both the voyeuristic and the viciously moralistic impulses of the other comrades.

What are we going to be, then? Assertive, strong women   46
(and sometimes, surely, also needy and vulnerable, because we *are* human), seeing ourselves as no better or worse than men; aware of but not obsessed with sexism; interested in loving and equal relationships but with enough confidence in ourselves, and enough understanding of human foibles, to know better than to scrutinize every move we or our partners

make for political incorrectness? Or full-time agents of the gender-crimes police?

Women's liberation is not yet a completed task. Sexism still 47 lingers and injustice toward women still exists, particularly in the distribution of domestic tasks. We are still working on new standards and values to guide a new, equal relationship between men and women. But "Third Wave" feminism, which tries to fight gender bias by defining people almost entirely in terms of gender, is not the way to go.

We need a "Third Way" feminism that rejects the excesses 48 of the gender fanatics *and* the sentimental traditionalism of the Phyllis Schlaflys; one that does not seek special protections for women and does not view us as too socially disadvantaged to take care of ourselves. Because on the path that feminism has taken in the past few years, we are allowing ourselves to be treated as frail, helpless little things—by our would-be liberators.

For Study and Discussion

QUESTIONS FOR RESPONSE

1. For women: Describe an incident with a man in which someone might have seen you as a victim. What was your own reaction to the incident?
2. For men: How do you distinguish for yourself between behavior you mean to be friendly and attentive and behavior that might be interpreted as sexist or patronizing?

QUESTIONS ABOUT PURPOSE

1. What changes in behavior and attitude among today's college students do you think Young wants to help bring about with this essay? How could those changes come about?
2. What does Young mean by claiming that the new radical feminism legitimizes an extremely retrograde view of women? See paragraph 44.

QUESTIONS ABOUT AUDIENCE

1. Most of us write for readers with whom we believe we share experiences and concerns. To what extent do you feel that you share Young's experiences and concerns, and how does that feeling affect the way you respond to her essay?
2. Assuming that Young realizes she is not likely to persuade the radical feminists she is criticizing, to what other groups do you think she directs her essay? Give some of their characteristics.

QUESTIONS ABOUT STRATEGIES

1. How does Young go about establishing her credentials as a modern young woman who is concerned about women's issues?
2. How does Young use material from her seventeen years in Russia to strengthen her argument? How well does the strategy work?

QUESTIONS FOR DISCUSSION

1. What do you see as the differences between pioneer feminists such as Gloria Steinem and Betty Friedan—often called radicals in their day—and those feminists of today whom Young calls "radical"?
2. What are some of the consequences for members of a group who become persuaded that they are victims?

DANIEL GOLEMAN

Daniel Goleman was born in 1946 in Stockton, California, and was educated at Amherst College and Harvard University. After working for several years as a professor of psychology, he began his career as an editor for *Psychology Today*. He has contributed more than fifty articles to psychology journals and has written a dozen books, including *The Meditative Mind* (1988), *The Creative Spirit* (1992), *Mind, Body Medicine: How to Use Your Mind for Better Health* (1993), and *Emotional Intelligence* (1995). In "Peak Performance: Why Records Fall," reprinted from a 1994 *New York Times* article, Goleman analyzes how dedication to practice contributes to "peak performances."

Peak Performance: Why Records Fall

THE OLD JOKE—How do you get to Carnegie Hall? Practice, practice, practice—is getting a scientific spin. Researchers are finding an unexpected potency from deliberate practice in world-class competitions of all kinds, including chess matches, musical recitals and sporting events.

Studies of chess masters, virtuoso musicians and star athletes show that the relentless training routines of those at the top allows them to break through ordinary limits in memory and physiology, and so perform at levels that had been thought impossible.

World records have been falling inexorably over the last century. For example, the marathon gold medalist's time in the 1896 Olympics Games was, by 1990, only about as good as the qualifying time for the Boston Marathon.

"Over the last century Olympics have become more and 4
more competitive, and so athletes steadily have had to put in
more total lifetime hours of practice," said Dr. Michael Mahoney, a psychologist at the University of North Texas in
Denton, who helps train the United States Olympic weight-
lifting team. "These days you have to live your sport."

That total dedication is in contrast to the relatively leisurely 5
attitude taken at the turn of the century, when even world-
class athletes would train arduously for only a few months
before their competition.

"As competition got greater, training extended to a whole 6
season," said Dr. Anders Ericsson, a psychologist at Florida

---

*Through their hours of practice, elite
performers of all kinds master shortcuts
that give them an edge.*

State University in Tallahassee who wrote an article on the
role of deliberate practice for star performance recently in the
journal *American Psychologist*. "Then it extended through the
year, and then for several years. Now the elite performers start
their training in childhood. There is a historical trend toward
younger starting ages, which makes possible a greater and
greater total number of hours of practice time."

To be sure, there are other factors at work: coaching meth- 7
ods have become more sophisticated, equipment has improved and the pool of people competing has grown. But
new studies are beginning to reveal the sheer power of training itself.

Perhaps the most surprising data show that extensive prac- 8
tice can break through barriers in mental capacities, particularly short-term memory. In short-term memory, information
is stored for the few seconds that it is used and then fades, as
in hearing a phone number which one forgets as soon as it is
dialed.

The standard view, repeated in almost every psychology 9
textbook, is that the ordinary limit on short-term memory is
for seven or so bits of information—the length of a phone
number. More than that typically cannot be retained in short-
term memory with reliability unless the separate units are
"chunked," as when the numbers in a telephone prefix are
remembered as a single unit.

But, in a stunning demonstration of the power of sheer 10
practice to break barriers in the mind's ability to handle
information, Dr. Ericsson and associates at Carnegie-Mellon
University have taught college students to listen to a list of
as many as 102 random digits and then recite it correctly.
After 50 hours of practice with differing sets of random digits,
four students were able to remember up to 20 digits after a
single hearing. One student, a business major not especially
talented in mathematics, was able to remember 102 digits.
The feat took him more than 400 hours of practice.

The ability to increase memory in a particular domain is 11
at the heart of a wide range high-level performance, said Dr.
Herbert Simon, professor of computer science and psychol-
ogy at Carnegie-Mellon University and a Nobel laureate. Dr.
Ericsson was part of a team studying expertise led by Dr.
Simon.

"Every expert has acquired something like this memory 12
ability" in his or her area of expertise, said Dr. Simon. "Memory is like an index; experts have approximately 50,000
chunks of familiar units of information they recognize. For a
physician, many of those chunks are symptoms."

A similar memory training effect, Dr. Simon said, seems 13
to occur with many chess masters. The key skill chess players
rehearse in practicing is, of course, selecting the best move.
They do so by studying games between two chess masters
and guessing the next move from their own study of the
board as the game progresses.

Repeated practice results in a prodigious memory for chess 14
positions. The ability of some chess masters to play blind-
folded, while simply told what moves their opponents make,
has long been known; in the 1940's Adrian DeGroot, himself
a Dutch grandmaster, showed that many chess masters are

able to look at a chess board in midgame for as little as five seconds and then repeat the position of every piece on the board.

Later systematic studies by Dr. Simon's group showed that 15 the chess masters' memory feat was limited to boards used in actual games; they had no such memory for randomly placed pieces. "They would see a board and think, that reminds me of Spassky versus Lasker," said Dr. Simon.

This feat of memory was duplicated by a college student 16 who knew little about chess, but was given 50 hours of training in remembering chess positions by Dr. Ericsson in a 1990 study.

Through their hours of practice, elite performers of all 17 kinds master shortcuts that give them an edge. Dr. Bruce Abernathy, a researcher at the University of Queensland in Australia, has found that the most experienced players in racquet sports like squash and tennis are able to predict where a serve will land by cues in the server's posture before the ball is hit.

A 1992 study of baseball greats like Hank Aaron and Rod 18 Carew by Thomas Hanson, then a graduate student at the University of Virginia in Charlottesville, found that the all-time best hitters typically started preparing for games by studying films of the pitchers they would face, to spot cues that would tip off what pitch was about to be thrown. Using such fleeting cues demands rehearsing so well that the response to them is automatic, cognitive scientists have found.

The maxim that practice makes perfect has been borne out 19 through research on the training of star athletes and artists. Dr. Anthony Kalinowski, a researcher at the University of Chicago, found that swimmers who achieved the level of national champion started their training at an average age of 10, while those who were good enough to make the United States Olympic teams started on average at 7. This is the same age difference found for national and international chess champions in a 1987 study.

Similarly, the best violinists of the 20th century, all with 20 international careers as soloists for more than 30 years, were found to have begun practicing their instrument at an average age of 5, while violinists of only national prominence, those affiliated with the top music academy in Berlin, started at 8, Dr. Ericsson found in research reported last year in *The Psychological Review.*

Because of limits on physical endurance and mental alertness, world-class competitors—whether violinists or weight lifters—typically seem to practice arduously no more than four hours a day, Dr. Ericsson has found from studying a wide variety of training regimens.   21

"When we train Olympic weight lifters, we find we often have to throttle back the total time they work out," said Dr. Mahoney. "Otherwise you find a tremendous drop in mood, and a jump in irritability, fatigue and apathy."   22

Because their intense practice regimen puts them at risk for burnout or strain injuries, most elite competitors also make rest part of their training routine, sleeping a full eight hours and often napping a half-hour a day, Dr. Ericsson found.   23

Effective practice focuses not just on the key skills involved, but also systematically stretches the person's limits. "You have to tweak the system by pushing, allowing for more errors at first as you increase your limits," said Dr. Ericsson. "You don't get benefits from mechanical repetition, but by adjusting your execution over and over to get closer to your goal."   24

Violin virtuosos illustrate the importance of starting early in life. In his 1993 study Dr. Ericsson found that by age 20 top-level violinists in music academies had practiced a lifetime total of about 10,000 hours, while those who were slightly less accomplished had practiced an average of about 7,500 hours.   25

A study of Chinese Olympic divers, done by Dr. John Shea of Florida State University, found that some 11-year-old divers had spent as many hours in training as had 21-year-old American divers. The Chinese divers started training at age 4.   26

"It can take 10 years of extensive practice to excel in   27 anything," said Dr. Simon. "Mozart was 4 when he started composing, but his world-class music started when he was about 17."

Total hours of practice may be more important than time   28
spent in competition, according to findings not yet published by Dr. Neil Charness, a colleague of Dr. Ericsson at Florida State University. Dr. Charness, comparing the rankings of 107 competitors in the 1993 Berlin City Tournament, found that the more time they spent practicing alone, the higher their ranking as chess players. But there was no relationship between the chess players' rankings and the time they spent playing others.

As has long been known, the extensive training of an elite   29
athlete molds the body to fit the demands of a given sport. What has been less obvious is the extent of these changes.

"The sizes of hearts and lungs, joint flexibility and bone   30
strength all increase directly with hours of training," said Dr. Ericsson. "The number of capillaries that supply blood to trained muscles increases."

And the muscles themselves change, Dr. Ericsson said.   31
Until very recently, researchers believed that the percentage of muscle fiber types was more than 90 percent determined by heredity. Fast-twitch muscles, which allow short bursts of intense effort, are crucial in sports like weight lifting and sprinting, while slow-twitch muscles, richer in red blood cells, are essential for endurance sports like marathons. "Muscle fibers in those muscles can change from fast twitch to slow twitch, as the sport demands," said Dr. Ericsson.

Longitudinal studies show that years of endurance training   32
at champion levels leads athletes' hearts to increase in size well beyond the normal range for people their age.

Such physiological changes are magnified when training   33
occurs during childhood, puberty and adolescence. Dr. Ericsson thinks this may be one reason virtually all top athletes today began serious practice as children or young adolescents, though some events, like weight training, may be exceptions because muscles need to fully form before intense lifting begins.

The most contentious claim made by Dr. Ericsson is that   34 practice alone, not natural talent, makes for a record-breaking performance. "Innate capacities have very little to do with becoming a champion," said his colleague, Dr. Charness. "What's key is motivation and temperament, not a skill specific to performance. It's unlikely you can get just any child to apply themselves this rigorously for so long."

But many psychologists argue that the emphasis on practice alone ignores the place of talent in superb performance. "You can't assume that random people who practice a lot will rise to the top," said Dr. Howard Gardner, a psychologist at Harvard University. Dr. Ericsson's theories "leave out the question of who selects themselves—or are selected—for intensive training," adding, "It also leaves out what we most value in star performance, like innovative genius in a chess player or emotional expressiveness in a concert musician." 35

Dr. Gardner said: "I taught piano for many years, and there's an enormous difference between those who practice dutifully and get a little better every week, and those students who break away from the pack. There's plenty of room for innate talent to make a difference over and above practice time. Mozart was not like you and me." 36

For Study and Discussion

QUESTIONS FOR RESPONSE

1. Think of some top performers who started very young—for instance, violinist Midori, chess prodigy Bobby Fisher, or tennis player Jennifer Capriati. What do you know about their subsequent lives? To what extent can you generalize about such individuals?

2. If you hope to be a top performer in your chosen field, does this essay encourage you or discourage you? Explain why.

QUESTIONS ABOUT PURPOSE

1. What message do you think the experts quoted in this essay are giving to young people who want to excel in something? What do you see as the impact of that message?

2. What role do you think science plays in sports these days? What is your feeling about that role?

QUESTIONS ABOUT AUDIENCE

1. What groups of readers do you see as people who would particularly benefit from learning about the research reported here? In what way would they benefit?
2. How would the value system of a reader—that is, the complex of things that the reader thinks is important—affect the way he or she responds to this essay?

QUESTIONS ABOUT STRATEGIES

1. What is the impact of Goleman's pointing out that the marathon runner who won an Olympic gold medal a hundred years ago could barely qualify for the Boston Marathon today?
2. How does Goleman's use of diverse authorities strengthen his essay?

QUESTIONS FOR DISCUSSION

1. What impact do you think the new realities about becoming a winner will have on the families of young artists and athletes? How might it differ among families?
2. What factors in a competitor's performance that are not discussed here might affect his or her achievement? How important are those elements?

BRUCE SHAPIRO

Bruce Shapiro was born in 1959 in Westchester County, New York, and educated at the University of Chicago. In the early 1980s he was a staff writer for the *New Haven Advocate,* and in 1986 he was co-founder and editor of the *New Haven Independent,* a weekly newspaper noted for its innovative, hard-hitting urban muckraking. Shapiro's work has appeared in *Harper's,* the *Village Voice,* and the *Guardian* of London. He currently writes a column, "Law and Order," for *The Nation.* In "One Violent Crime," reprinted from *The Nation,* Shapiro describes how his experience as a victim of crime causes him to rethink our culture's attitude toward the justice system.

One Violent Crime

A LONE IN MY home, I am staring at the television screen and shouting. On the evening local news I have unexpectedly encountered video footage, several months old, of myself writhing on an ambulance gurney, bright green shirt open and drenched with blood, skin pale, knee raised, trying desperately and with utter futility to find relief from pain.

On the evening of August 7, 1994, I was among seven people stabbed and seriously wounded in a coffee bar a few blocks from my house. Any televised recollection of this incident would be upsetting. But the anger that has me shouting tonight is quite specific, and political, in origin: my picture is being shown on the news to illustrate why Connecticut's legislature plans to lock up more criminals for a longer time. A picture of my body, contorted and bleeding, has become a propaganda image in the crime war.

I had not planned to write about this assault. But for

months now the politics of the nation have in large part been the politics of crime, from last year's federal crime bill through the fall elections through the Contract with America proposals awaiting action by the Senate. Among a welter of reactions to the attack, one feeling is clear: I am unwilling to be a silent poster child in this debate.

The physical and political truth about violence and crime   4
lies in their specificity, so here is what happened: I had gone out for after-dinner coffee that evening with two friends and New Haven neighbors, Martin and Anna Broell Bresnick. At 9:45 we arrived at a recently opened coffeehouse on Audubon Street, a block occupied by an arts high school

---

The answer to violent crime will not be found in social Darwinism and individualism, in racism, and in dismantling cities and increasing the destitution of the poor.

---

where Anna teaches, other community arts institutions, a few pleasant shops and upscale condos. Entering, we said hello to another friend, a former student of Anna's named Christina Koning, who the day before had started working behind the counter. We sat at a small table near the front of the café; about fifteen people were scattered around the room. Just before ten o'clock, the owner announced closing time. Martin stood up and walked a few yards to the counter for a final refill.

Suddenly there was chaos—as if a mortar shell had landed.   5
I looked up, heard Martin call Anna's name, saw his arm raised and a flash of metal and people leaping away from a thin bearded man with a ponytail. Tables and chairs toppled. Without thinking I shouted to Anna, "Get down!" and pulled her to the floor, between our table and the café's outer

wall. She clung to my shirt, I to her shoulders, and, crouch-
ing, we pulled each other toward the door.

What actually happened I was only able to tentatively 　6
reconstruct many weeks later. Apparently, as Martin headed
toward the counter the thin bearded man, whose name we
later learned was Daniel Silva, asked the time from a young
man named Richard Colberg, who answered and turned to
leave.

Without any warning, Silva pulled out a hunting knife with 　7
a six-inch blade and stabbed in the lower back a woman
leaving with Colberg, a medical technician named Kerstin
Braig. Then he stabbed Colberg, severing an artery in his
thigh. Silva was a slight man, but he moved with demonic
speed and force around the café's counter. He struck Martin
in the thigh and in the arm he raised to protect his face. Our
friend Chris Koning had in a moment's time pushed out the
screen in a window and helped the wounded Kerstin Braig
through it to safety. Chris was talking on the phone with the
police when Silva lunged over the counter and stabbed her
in the chest and abdomen. He stabbed Anna in the side as
she and I pulled each other along the wall. He stabbed Emily
Bernard, a graduate student who had been sitting quietly
reading a book, in the abdomen as she tried to flee through
the café's back door. All of this happened in about the time
it has taken you to read this paragraph.

Meanwhile, I had made it out the café's front door onto 　8
the brick sidewalk with Anna, neither of us realizing yet that
she was wounded. Seeing Martin through the window, I
returned inside and we came out together. Somehow we
separated, fleeing opposite ways down the street. I had gone
no more than a few steps when I felt a hard punch in my
back, followed instantly by the unforgettable sensation of skin
and muscle tissue parting. Silva had stabbed me about six
inches above my waist, just beneath my rib cage. (That single
deep stroke cut my diaphragm and sliced my spleen in half.)
Without thinking, I clapped my left hand over the wound
even before the knife was out, and its blade caught my hand,
leaving a slice across my palm and two fingers.

"Why are you doing this?" I cried out to Silva in the 　9

moment after feeling his knife punch in and yank out. As I fell to the street he leaned over my face; I vividly remember the knife's immense and glittering blade. He directed the point through my shirt into the flesh of my chest, beneath my left shoulder. I remember his brown beard, his clear blue-gray eyes looking directly into mine, the round globe of a street lamp like a halo above his head. Although I was just a few feet from a café full of people, and although Martin and Anna were only yards away, the street, the city, the world felt utterly empty except for me and this thin bearded stranger with clear eyes and a bowie knife. The space around us—well-lit, familiar Audubon Street, where for six years I had taken a child to music lessons—seemed literally to have expanded into a vast and dark canyon.

"You killed my mother," he answered. My own desperate 10
response: "Please don't." Silva pulled the knifepoint out of my chest and disappeared. A moment later I saw him flying down the street on a battered, ungainly bicycle, back straight, vest flapping and ponytail flying.

After my assailant had gone I lay on the sidewalk, hand 11
still over the wound on my back, screaming. Pain ran over me like an express train; it felt as though every muscle in my back were locked and contorted; breathing was excruciating. A security guard appeared across the street from me. I called out to him but he stood there frozen, or so it seemed. (A few minutes later, he would help police chase Silva down.) I shouted to Anna, who was hiding behind a car down the street. Still in shock and unaware of her own injury, she ran for help, eventually collapsing on the stairs of a nearby brownstone where a prayer group that was meeting upstairs answered her desperate ringing of the doorbell. From where I was lying, I saw a second-floor light in the condo complex across the way. A woman's head appeared in the window. "Please help me," I implored. "He's gone. Please help me." She shouted back that she had called the police, but she did not come to the street. I was suddenly aware of a blond woman—Kerstin Braig, though I did not know her name then—in a white-and-gray-plaid dress, sitting on the curb. I

asked her for help. "I'm sorry, I've done all I can," she muttered. She raised her hand, like a medieval icon; it was covered with blood. So was her dress. She sank into a kind of stupor. Up the street I saw a police car's flashing blue lights, then another's, then I saw an officer with a concerned face and a crackling radio crouched beside me. I stayed conscious as the medics arrived and I was loaded into an ambulance—being filmed for television, as it turned out, though I have no memory of the crew's presence.

Being a victim is hard to accept, even while lying in a 12 hospital bed with tubes in veins, chest, penis, and abdomen. The spirit rebels against the idea of oneself as fundamentally powerless. So I didn't think much for the first few days about the meaning of being a victim; I saw no political dimension to my experience.

As I learned in more detail what had happened, I thought, 13 in my jumbled-up, anesthetized state, about my injured friends—although everyone survived, their wounds ranged from quite serious to critical—and about my wound and surgery. I also thought about my assailant. A few facts about him are worth repeating. Until August 7 Daniel Silva was a self-employed junk dealer and a homeowner. He was white. He lived with his mother and several dogs. He had no arrest record. A New Haven police detective who was hospitalized across the hall from me recalled Silva as a socially marginal neighborhood character. He was not, apparently, a drug user. He had told neighbors about much violence in his family— indeed, not long before August 7 he showed one neighbor a scar on his thigh he said was from a stab wound.

A week earlier, Silva's seventy-nine-year-old mother had 14 been hospitalized for diabetes. After a few days the hospital moved her to a new room; when Silva saw his mother's empty bed he panicked, but nurses swiftly took him to her new location. Still, something seemed to have snapped. Earlier on the day of the stabbings, police say, Silva released his beloved dogs, set fire to his house, and rode away on his bicycle as it burned. He arrived on Audubon Street with a single dog on a leash, evidently convinced his mother was dead. (She actually did die a few weeks after Silva was jailed.)

While I lay in the hospital, the big story on CNN was the   15
Clinton administration's 1994 crime bill, then being debated
in Congress. Even fogged by morphine I was aware of the
irony. I was flat on my back, the result of a particularly violent
assault, while Congress eventually passed the anti-crime package I had editorialized against in *The Nation* just a few weeks
earlier. Night after night in the hospital, unable to sleep, I
watched the crime-bill debate replayed and heard Republicans and Democrats (who had sponsored the bill in the first
place) fall over each other to prove who could be the toughest
on crime.

The bill passed on August 21, a few days after I returned   16
home. In early autumn I read the entire text of the crime
bill—all 412 pages. What I found was perhaps obvious, yet
under the circumstances compelling: not a single one of those
412 pages would have protected me or Anna or Martin or
any of the others from our assailant. Not the enhanced prison
terms, not the forty-four new death-penalty offenses, not the
three-strikes-you're-out requirements, not the summary deportations of criminal aliens. And the new tougher-than-tough anti-crime provisions of the Contract with America,
like the proposed abolition of the Fourth Amendment's
search and seizure protections, offer no more practical protection.

On the other hand, the mental-health and social-welfare   17
safety net shredded by Reagonomics and conservatives of
both parties might have made a difference in the life of
someone like my assailant—and thus in the life of someone
like me. My assailant's growing distress in the days before
August 7 was obvious to his neighbors. He had muttered
darkly about relatives planning to burn down his house. A
better-funded, more comprehensive safety net might just
have saved me and six others from untold pain and trouble.

From my perspective—the perspective of a crime victim—   18
the Contract with America and its conservative Democratic

analogs are really blueprints for making the streets even less safe. Want to take away that socialist income subsidy called welfare? Fine. Connecticut Governor John Rowland proposes cutting off all benefits after eighteen months. So more people in New Haven and other cities will turn to the violence-breeding economy of crack, or emotionally implode from sheer desperation. Cut funding for those soft-headed social workers? Fine; let more children be beaten without the prospect of outside intervention, more Daniel Silvas carrying their own traumatic scars into violent adulthood. Get rid of the few amenities prisoners enjoy, like sports equipment, musical instruments, and the right to get college degrees, as proposed by the congressional right? Fine; we'll make sure that those inmates are released to their own neighborhoods tormented with unchanneled rage.

One thing I could not properly appreciate in the hospital 19 was how deeply many friends, neighbors, and acquaintances were shaken by the coffeehouse stabbings, let alone strangers who took the time to write. The reaction of most was a combination of decent horrified empathy and a clear sense that their own presumption of safety was undermined.

But some people who didn't bother to acquaint themselves 20 with the facts used the stabbings as a sort of Rorschach test on which they projected their own preconceptions about crime, violence, and New Haven. Some present and former Yale students, for instance, were desperate to see in my stabbing evidence of the great dangers of New Haven's inner city. One student newspaper wrote about "New Haven's image as a dangerous town fraught with violence." A student reporter from another Yale paper asked if I didn't think the attack proved New Haven needs better police protection. Given the random nature of this assault—it could as easily have happened in wealthy, suburban Greenwich, where a friend of mine was held up at an ATM at the point of an assault rifle—it's tempting to dismiss such sentiments as typical products of an insular urban campus. But city-hating is central to today's political culture. Newt Gingrich excoriates cities as

hopelessly pestilential, crime-ridden, and corrupt. Fear of
urban crime and of the dark-skinned people who live in cities
is the right's basic text, and defunding cities a central agenda
item for the new congressional majority.

Yet in no small measure it was the institutions of an urban   21
community that saved my life last August 7. That concerned
police officer who found Kerstin Braig and me on the street
was joined in a moment by enough emergency workers to
handle the carnage in and around the coffeehouse, and his
backups arrived quickly enough to chase down my assailant
three blocks away. In minutes I was taken to Yale–New Haven
Hospital, less than a mile away—built in part with the kind
of public funding so hated by the right. As I was wheeled
into the ER, several dozen doctors and nurses descended to
handle all the wounded.

By then my abdomen had swelled from internal bleeding.   22
Dr. Gerard Burns, a trauma surgeon, told me a few weeks
later that I arrived on his operating table white as a ghost;
my prospects, he said, would have been poor had I not been
delivered so quickly, and to an ER with the kind of trauma
team available only at a large metropolitan hospital. In other
words, if my stabbing had taken place in the suburbs, I would
have bled to death.

"Why didn't anyone try to stop him?" That question was   23
even more common than the reflexive city-bashing. I can't
even begin to guess the number of times I had to answer it.
Each time, I repeated that Silva moved too fast, that it was
simply too confusing. And each time, I found the question
not just foolish but offensive.

"Why didn't anyone stop him?" To understand that ques-   24
tion is to understand, in some measure, why crime is such a
potent political issue. To begin with, the question carries not
empathy but an implicit burden of blame; it really asks "Why
didn't *you* stop him?" It is asked because no one likes to
imagine oneself a victim. It's far easier to graft onto oneself
the aggressive power of the attacker, to embrace the delusion
of oneself as Arnold Schwarzenegger defeating a multitude

single-handedly. *If I am tough enough and strong enough, I can take out the bad guys.*

The country is at present suffering from a huge version of this same delusion. This myth is buried deep in the political culture, nurtured in the historical tales of frontier violence and vigilantism and by the action-hero fantasies of film and television. Now, bolstered by the social Darwinists of the right, who see society as an unfettered marketplace in which the strongest individuals flourish, this delusion frames the crime debate. ₂₅

I also felt that the question "Why didn't anybody stop him?" implied only two choices: Rambo-like heroism or abject victimhood. To put it another way, it suggests that the only possible responses to danger are the individual biological imperatives of fight or flight. And people don't want to think of themselves as on the side of flight. This is a notion whose political moment has arrived. In last year's debate over the crime bill, conservatives successfully portrayed themselves as those who would stand and fight; liberals were portrayed as ineffectual cowards. ₂₆

"Why didn't anyone stop him?" That question and its underlying implications see both heroes and victims as lone individuals. But on the receiving end of a violent attack, the fight-or-flight dichotomy didn't apply. Nor did that radically individualized notion of survival. At the coffeehouse that night, at the moments of greatest threat, there were no Schwarzeneggers, no stand-alone heroes. (In fact, I doubt anyone could have "taken out" Silva; as with most crimes, his attack came too suddenly.) But neither were there abject victims. Instead, in the confusion and panic of life-threatening attack, *people reached out to one another.* This sounds simple, yet it suggests there is an instinct for mutual aid that poses a profound challenge to the atomized individualism of the right. Christina Koning helped the wounded Kerstin Braig to escape, and Kerstin in turn tried to bring Christina along. Anna and I, and then Martin and I, clung to each other, pulling one another toward the door. And just as Kerstin found me on the sidewalk rather than wait for help ₂₇

alone, so Richard and Emily, who had never met before, together sought a hiding place around the corner. Three of us even spoke with Silva either the moment before or the instant after being stabbed. My plea to Silva may or may not have been what kept him from pushing his knife all the way through my chest and into my heart; it's impossible to know what was going through his mind. But this impulse to communicate, to establish human contact across a gulf of terror and insanity, is deeper and more subtle than the simple formulation of fight or flight, courage or cowardice, would allow.

I have never been in a war, but I now think I understand   28
a little the intense bond among war veterans who have survived awful carnage. It is not simply the common fact of survival but the way in which the presence of these others seemed to make survival itself possible. There's evidence, too, that those who try to go it alone suffer more. In her insightful study *Trauma and Recovery,* Judith Herman, a psychiatrist, writes about rape victims, Vietnam War veterans, political prisoners, and other survivors of extreme violence. "The capacity to preserve social connection . . . ," she concludes, "even in the face of extremity, seems to protect people to some degree against the later development of post-traumatic syndromes. For example, among survivors of a disaster at sea, the men who had managed to escape by cooperating with others showed relatively little evidence of post-traumatic stress afterward." On the other hand, she reports that the "highly symptomatic" ones among those survivors were 'Rambos,' men who had plunged into impulsive, isolated action and not affiliated with others."

The political point here is that the Rambo justice system   29
proposed by the right is rooted in that dangerous myth of the individual fighting against a hostile world. Recently that myth got another boost from several Republican-controlled state legislatures, which have made it much easier to carry concealed handguns. But the myth has nothing to do with the reality of violent crime, the ways to prevent it, or the needs of survivors. Had Silva been carrying a handgun

instead of a knife on August 7, there would have been a massacre.

I do understand the rage and frustration behind the crime- 30
victim movement, and I can see how the right has harnessed
it. For weeks I thought obsessively and angrily of those minutes on Audubon Street, when first the nameless woman in
the window and then the security guard refused to approach
me—as if I, wounded and helpless, were the dangerous one.
There was also a subtle shift in my consciousness a few days
after the stabbing. Up until that point, the legal process and
press attention seemed clearly centered on my injuries and
experience, and those of my fellow victims. But once Silva
was arraigned and the formal process of prosecution began,
it became *his* case, not mine. I experienced an overnight sense
of marginalization, a feeling of helplessness bordering on
irrelevance.

Sometimes that got channeled into outrage, fear, and 31
panic. After arraignment, Silva's bail was set at $700,000.
That sounds high, but just 10 percent of that amount in cash,
perhaps obtained through some relative with home equity,
would have bought his pretrial release. I was frantic at even
this remote prospect of Silva walking the streets. So were the
six other victims and our families. We called the prosecutor
virtually hourly to request higher bail. It was eventually raised
to $800,000, partly because of our complaints and partly
because an arson charge was added. Silva remains in the
Hartford Community Correctional Center awaiting trial.

Near the six-month anniversary of the stabbings I called 32
the prosecutor and learned that in December Silva's lawyer
filed papers indicating that he intends to claim a "mental
disease or defect" defense. If successful, it would send him to
a maximum-security hospital for the criminally insane for the
equivalent of the maximum criminal penalty. In February the
court was still awaiting a report from Silva's psychiatrist. Then
the prosecution will have him examined by its own psychiatrist. "There's a backlog," I was told; the case is not likely to
come to trial until the end of 1995 at the earliest. Intellectu-

ally, I understand that Silva is securely behind bars, that the court system is overburdened, that the delay makes no difference in the long-term outcome. But emotionally, viscerally, the delay is devastating.

Another of my bursts of victim consciousness involved the press. Objectively, I know that many people who took the trouble to express their sympathy to me found out only through news stories. And sensitive reporting can for the crime victim be a kind of ratification of the seriousness of an assault, a reflection of the community's concern. One reporter for the daily *New Haven Register*, Josh Kovner, did produce level-headed and insightful stories about the Audubon Street attack. But most other reporting was exploitative, intrusive, and inaccurate. I was only a few hours out of surgery, barely able to speak, when the calls from television stations and papers started coming to my hospital room. Anna and Martin, sent home to recover, were ambushed by a Hartford TV crew as they emerged from their physician's office, and later rousted from their beds by reporters from another TV station ringing their doorbell. The *Register*'s editors enraged all seven victims by printing our home addresses (a company policy, for some reason) and running spectacularly distressing full-color photos of the crime scene, complete with the coffee bar's bloody windowsill.   33

Such press coverage inspired in all of us a rage it is impossible to convey. In a study commissioned by the British Broadcasting Standards Council, survivors of violent crimes and disasters "told story after story of the hurt they suffered through the timing of media attention, intrusion into their privacy and harassment, through inaccuracy, distortion and distasteful detail in what was reported." This suffering is not superficial. To the victim of violent crime the press may reinforce the perception that the world is an uncomprehending and dangerous place.   34

The very same flawed judgments about "news value" contribute significantly to a public conception of crime that is as completely divorced from the facts as a Schwarzenegger   35 movie. One study a few years ago found that reports on crime and justice constitute 22 to 28 percent of newspaper stories, "nearly three times as much attention as the presidency or the Congress or the state of the economy." And the most spectacular crimes—the stabbing of seven people in an up-scale New Haven coffee bar, for instance—are likely to be the most "newsworthy" even though they are statistically the least likely. "The image of crime presented in the media is thus a reverse image of reality," writes sociologist Mark Warr in a study commissioned by the National Academy of Sciences.

Media coverage also brings us to another crucial political moral: the "seriousness" of crime is a matter of race and real estate. This has been pointed out before, but it can't be said too often. Seven people stabbed in a relatively affluent, mostly white neighborhood near Yale University—this was big news on a slow news night. It went national over the AP wires and international over CNN's *Headline News.* It was covered by the *New York Times,* and words of sympathy came to New Haven from as far as Prague and Santiago. Because a graduate student and a professor were among those wounded, the university sent representatives to the emergency room. The morning after, New Haven Mayor John DeStafano walked the neighborhood to reassure merchants and office workers. For more than a month the regional press covered every new turn in the case.

Horrendous as it was, though, no one was killed. Four weeks later, a fifteen-year-old girl named Rashawnda Crenshaw was driving with two friends about a mile from Audubon Street. As the car in which she was a passenger turned a corner, she was shot through the window and killed. Apparently her assailants mistook her for someone else. Rashawnda Crenshaw was black, and her shooting took place in the Hill, the New Haven neighborhood with the highest poverty rate. No Yale officials showed up at the hospital to comfort Crenshaw's mother or cut through red tape. The *New York Times* did not come calling; there were certainly no bulletins flashed around the world on CNN. The local news coverage lasted just long enough for Rashawnda Crenshaw to be buried.

Anyone trying to deal with the reality of crime, as opposed to the fantasies peddled to win elections, needs to understand the complex suffering of those who are survivors of traumatic crimes, and the suffering and turmoil of their families. I have impressive physical scars: there is a broad purple line from my breastbone to the top of my pubic bone, an X-shaped cut into my side where the chest tube entered, a thick pink mark on my chest where the point of Silva's knife rested on a rib. On my back is the unevenly curving horizontal scar where Silva thrust the knife in and yanked it out, leaving what looks like a crooked smile. But the disruption of my psyche is, day in and day out, more noticeable. For weeks after leaving the hospital I awoke nightly agitated, drenched with perspiration. For two months I was unable to write; my brain simply refused to concentrate. Into any moment of mental repose would rush images from the night of August 7; or alternatively, my mind would not tune in at all. My reactions are still out of balance and disproportionate. I shut a door on my finger, not too hard, and my body is suddenly flooded with adrenaline and I nearly faint. Walking on the arm of my partner, Margaret, one evening I abruptly shove her to the side of the road; I have seen a tall, lean shadow on the block where we are headed and am alarmed out of all proportion. I get into an argument and find myself quaking with rage for an hour afterward, completely unable to restore calm. Though to all appearances normal, I feel at a long arm's remove from all the familiar sources of pleasure, comfort, and anger that shaped my daily life before August 7.

What psychologists call post-traumatic stress disorder is, among other things, a profoundly political state in which the world has gone wrong, in which you feel isolated from the broader community by the inarticulate extremity of experience. I have spent a lot of time in the past few months thinking about what the world must look like to those who have survived repeated violent attacks, whether children bat-

38

39

tered in their homes or prisoners beaten or tortured behind bars; as well as those, like rape victims, whose assaults are rarely granted public ratification.

The right owes much of its success to the anger of crime victims and the argument that government should do more for us. This appeal is epitomized by the rise of restitution laws—statutes requiring offenders to compensate their targets. On February 7 the House of Representatives passed, by a vote of 431 to 0, the Victim Restitution Act, a plank of the Contract with America that would supposedly send back to jail offenders who don't make good on their debts to their victims. In my own state, Governor Rowland recently proposed a restitution amendment to the state constitution.
₄₀

On the surface it is hard to argue with the principle of reasonable restitution—particularly since it implies community recognition of the victim's suffering. But I wonder if these laws really will end up benefiting someone like me—or if they are just empty, vote-getting devices that exploit victims and could actually hurt our chances of getting speedy, substantive justice. H. Scott Wallace, former counsel to the Senate Judiciary Subcommittee on Juvenile Justice, writes in *Legal Times* that the much-touted Victim Restitution Act is "unlikely to put a single dollar into crime victims' pockets, would tie up the federal courts with waves of new damages actions, and would promote unconstitutional debtors' prisons."
₄₁

I also worry that the rhetoric of restitution confuses—as does so much of the imprisonment-and-execution mania dominating the political landscape—the goals of justice and revenge. Revenge, after all, is just another version of the individualized, take-out-the-bad-guys myth. Judith Herman believes indulging fantasies of revenge worsens the psychic suffering of trauma survivors: "The desire for revenge . . . arises out of the victim's experience of complete helplessness," and forever ties the victim's fate to the perpetrator's. Real recovery from the cataclysmic isolation of trauma comes only when "the survivor comes to understand the issues of principle that transcend her personal grievance against the
₄₂

perpetrator . . . [a] principle of social justice that connects the fate of others to her own." The survivors and victims' families of the Long Island Rail Road massacre have banded together not to urge that Colin Ferguson be executed but to work for gun control.

What it all comes down to is this: What do survivors of violent crime really need? What does it mean to create a safe society? Do we need courts so overburdened by nonviolent drug offenders that Daniel Silvas go untried for eighteen months, delays that leave victims and suspects alike in limbo? Do we need to throw nonviolent drug offenders into mandatory-sentence proximity with violent sociopaths and career criminals? Do we need the illusory bravado of a Schwarzenegger film—or the real political courage of those LIRR survivors? 43

If the use of my picture on television unexpectedly brought me face to face with the memory of August 7, some part of the attack is relived for me daily as I watch the gruesome, voyeuristically reported details of the stabbing deaths of two people in California, Nicole Brown Simpson and Ronald Goldman. It was relived even more vividly by the televised trial of Colin Ferguson. (One night soon after watching Ferguson on the evening news, I dreamed that I was on the witness stand and Silva, like Ferguson, was representing himself and questioning me.) Throughout the trial, as Ferguson spoke of falling asleep and having someone else fire his gun, I heard neither cowardly denial nor what his first lawyer called "black rage"; I heard Daniel Silva's calm, secure voice telling me I killed his mother. And when I hear testimony by the survivors of that massacre—on a train as comfortable and familiar to them as my neighborhood coffee bar—I feel a great and incommunicable fellowship. 44

But the public obsession with these trials, I am convinced, has no more to do with the real experience of crime victims than does the anti-crime posturing of politicians. I do not know what made my assailant act as he did. Nor do I think crime and violence can be reduced to simple political categories. I do know that the answers will not be found in social 45

Darwinism and atomized individualism, in racism, in disman-tling cities and increasing the destitution of the poor. To the contrary: every fragment of my experience suggests that the best protections from crime and the best aid to victims are the very social institutions most derided by the right. As crime victim and citizen, what I want is the reality of a safe community—not a politician's fantasyland of restitution and revenge. That is my testimony.

For Study and Discussion

QUESTIONS FOR RESPONSE

1. If you or some person close to you has been injured through a violent crime, how has that fact affected your attitude about crime legislation? Why?
2. What is your response to Shapiro's suggestion that more spend-ing on social programs could help prevent the kind of violent attack he suffered?

QUESTIONS ABOUT PURPOSE

1. What does Shapiro mean when he says, "I am unwilling to be a silent poster child in this debate." How does the essay follow up on that remark?
2. How does Shapiro try to move his readers beyond their imme-diate reactions to the horrifying details on the attack on him to grasp a broader picture?

QUESTIONS ABOUT AUDIENCE

1. How are today's readers conditioned to be very aware of and fearful about violent urban crime even though the crime rate has declined significantly in most cities in the last five years?
2. This article first appeared in *The Nation* and later, in shorter form, in *Harper's* magazine. What do you know or infer about the readers of both these magazines that makes it likely they would be open to the argument Shapiro is making?

QUESTIONS ABOUT STRATEGIES

1. What does Shapiro accomplish by going into such graphic detail about the attack on him and about his injuries?
2. How does Shapiro use his reaction to the question, "Why didn't anyone try to stop him?" to illustrate one of his important points?

QUESTIONS FOR DISCUSSION

1. How are you affected by television images of the kind that Shapiro describes in his first paragraph? Why do you think such images are played up on television and in political advertising?
2. Do you feel resistant to or sympathetic with Shapiro's argument? What do you think is the basis of your reaction?

Terry McMillan was born in 1951 in Port Huron, Michigan, and educated at the University of California at Berkeley and Columbia University. She taught at the University of Wyoming and the University of Arizona before the critical success of her first novel, *Mama* (1987), and the controversy surrounding her second novel, *Disappearing Acts* (1989), encouraged her to devote her full attention to writing. Her third novel, *Waiting to Exhale* (1992), a story of the romantic complications besetting four contemporary African-American women friends, was adapted into an extremely popular film. Her most recent work is *How Stella Got Her Groove Back* (1996). In "The Movie That Changed My Life," McMillan analyzes her positive and negative reaction to watching *The Wizard of Oz*.

The Movie That Changed My Life

I GREW UP in a small industrial town in the thumb of Michigan: Port Huron. We had barely gotten used to the idea of color TV. I can guess how old I was when I first saw *The Wizard of Oz* on TV because I remember the house we lived in when I was still in elementary school. It was a huge, drafty house that had a fireplace we never once lit. We lived on two acres of land, and at the edge of the back yard was the woods, which I always thought of as a forest. We had weeping willow trees, plum and pear trees, and blackberry bushes. We could not see into our neighbors' homes. Railroad tracks were part of our front yard, and the house shook when a train

passed—twice, sometimes three times a day. You couldn't
hear the TV at all when it zoomed by, and I was often afraid
that if it ever flew off the tracks, it would land on the sun
porch, where we all watched TV. I often left the room during
this time, but my younger sisters and brother thought I was
just scared. I think I was in the third grade around this time.

It was a raggedy house which really should've been con-   2
demned, but we fixed it up and kept it clean. We had our
German shepherd, Prince, who slept under the rickety steps
to the side porch that were on the verge of collapsing but
never did. I remember performing a ritual whenever *Oz* was
coming on. I either baked cookies or cinnamon rolls or

The movie [The Wizard of Oz] *taught me
that it's okay to be an idealist,
that you have to imagine something
better and go for it.*

---

popped popcorn while all five of us waited for Dorothy to
spin from black and white on that dreary farm in Kansas to
the luminous land of color of Oz.

My house was chaotic, especially with four sisters and   3
brothers and a mother who worked at a factory, and if I'm
remembering correctly, my father was there for the first few
years of the *Oz* (until he got tuberculosis and had to live in
a sanitarium for a year). I do recall the noise and the fighting
of my parents (not to mention my other relatives and neighbors). Violence was plentiful, and I wanted to go wherever
Dorothy was going where she would not find trouble. To put
it bluntly, I wanted to escape because I needed an escape.

I didn't know any happy people. Everyone I knew was   4
either angry or not satisfied. The only time they seemed to
laugh was when they were drunk, and even that was short-
lived. Most of the grown-ups I was in contact with lived their

lives as if it had all been a mistake, an accident, and they were paying dearly for it. It seemed as if they were always at someone else's mercy—women at the mercy of men (this prevailed in my hometown) and children at the mercy of frustrated parents. All I knew was that most of the grown-ups felt trapped, as if they were stuck in this town and no road would lead out. So many of them felt a sense of accomplishment just getting up in the morning and making it through another day. I overheard many a grown-up conversation, and they were never life-affirming: "Chile, if the Lord'll just give me the strength to make it through another week . . ."; "I just don't know how I'ma handle this, I can't take no more. . . ." I rarely knew what they were talking about, but even a fool could hear that it was some kind of drudgery. When I was a child, it became apparent to me that these grown-ups had no power over their lives, or, if they did, they were always at a loss as to how to exercise it. I did not want to grow up and have to depend on someone else for my happiness or be miserable or have to settle for whatever I was dished out—if I could help it. That much I knew already.

I remember being confused a lot. I could never understand 5 why no one had any energy to do anything that would make them feel good, besides drinking. Being happy was a transient and very temporary thing which was almost always offset by some kind of bullshit. I would, of course, learn much later in my own adult life that these things are called obstacles, barriers—or again, bullshit. When I started writing, I began referring to them as "knots." But life wasn't one long knot. It seemed to me it just required stamina and common sense and the wherewithal to know when a knot was before you and you had to dig deeper than you had in order to figure out how to untie it. It could be hard, but it was simple.

The initial thing I remember striking me about *Oz* was 6 how nasty Dorothy's Auntie Em talked to her and everybody on the farm. I was used to that authoritative tone of voice because my mother talked to us the same way. She never asked you to do anything; she gave you a command and never said "please," and, once you finished it, rarely said "thank you." The tone of her voice was always hostile, and Auntie Em sounded just like my mother—bossy and domineering. They both ran the show, it seemed, and I think that because my mother was raising five children almost single-handedly, I must have had some inkling that being a woman didn't mean you had to be helpless. Auntie Em's husband was a wimp, and for once the tables were turned: he took orders from her! My mother and Auntie Em were proof to me that if you wanted to get things done you had to delegate authority and keep everyone apprised of the rules of the game as well as the consequences. In my house it was punishment— you were severely grounded. What little freedom we had was snatched away: As a child, I often felt helpless, powerless, because I had no control over my situation and couldn't tell my mother when I thought (or knew) she was wrong or being totally unfair, or when her behavior was inappropriate. I hated this feeling to no end, but what was worse was not being able to do anything about it except keep my mouth shut.

So I completely identified when no one had time to listen   7
to Dorothy. That dog's safety was important to her, but no one seemed to think that what Dorothy was saying could possibly be as urgent as the situation at hand. The bottom line was, it was urgent to her. When I was younger, I rarely had the opportunity to finish a sentence before my mother would cut me off or complete it for me, or, worse, give me something to do. She used to piss me off, and nowadays I catch myself—stop myself—from doing the same thing to my seven-year-old. Back then, it was as if what I had to say wasn't important or didn't warrant her undivided attention. So when Dorothy's Auntie Em dismisses her and tells her to find somewhere where she'll stay out of trouble, and little Dorothy starts thinking about if there in fact is such a place— one that is trouble free—I was right there with her, because I wanted to know, too.

I also didn't know or care that Judy Garland was supposed   8
to have been a child star, but when she sang "Somewhere Over the Rainbow," I *was* impressed. Impressed more by the

song than by who was singing it. I mean, she wasn't exactly Aretha Franklin or the Marvelettes or the Supremes, which was the only vocal music I was used to. As kids, we often laughed at white people singing on TV because their songs were always so corny and they just didn't sound anything like the soulful music we had in our house. Sometimes we would mimic people like Doris Day and Fred Astaire and laugh like crazy because they were always so damn happy while they sang and danced. We would also watch square-dancing when we wanted a real laugh and try to look under the women's dresses. What I hated more than anything was when in the middle of a movie the white people always had to start singing and dancing to get their point across. Later, I would hate it when black people would do the same thing—even though it was obvious to us that at least they had more rhythm and, most of the time, more range vocally.

We did skip through the house singing "We're off to see the Wizard," but other than that, most of the songs in this movie are a blank, probably because I blanked them out. Where I lived, when you had something to say to someone, you didn't sing it, you told them, so the cumulative effect of the songs wore thin.   9

I was afraid for Dorothy when she decided to run away, but at the same time I was glad. I couldn't much blame her—I mean, what kind of life did she have, from what I'd seen so far? She lived on an ugly farm out in the middle of nowhere with all these old people who did nothing but chores, chores, and more chores. Who did she have to play with besides that dog? And even though I lived in a house full of people, I knew how lonely Dorothy felt, or at least how isolated she must have felt. First of all, I was the oldest, and my sisters and brothers were ignorant and silly creatures who often bored me because they couldn't hold a decent conversation. I couldn't ask them questions, like: Why are we living in this dump? When is Mama going to get some more money? Why can't we go on vacations like other people? Like white people? Why does our car always break down? Why are we poor? Why doesn't Mama ever laugh? Why do we have   10

to live in Port Huron? Isn't there someplace better than this
we can go live? I remember thinking this kind of stuff in
kindergarten, to be honest, because times were hard, but I'd
saved twenty-five cents in my piggy bank for hotdog-and-
chocolate-milk day at school, and on the morning I went to
get it, my piggy bank was empty. My mother gave me some
lame excuse as to why she had to spend it, but all I was
thinking was that I would have to sit there (again) and watch
the other children slurp their chocolate milk, and I could see
the ketchup and mustard oozing out of the hot-dog bun that
I wouldn't get to taste. I walked to school, and with the
exception of walking to my father's funeral when I was sixteen, this was the longest walk of my entire life. My plaid
dress was starched and my socks were white, my hair was
braided and not a strand out of place; but I wanted to know
why I had to feel this kind of humiliation when in fact I had
saved the money for this very purpose. Why? By the time I
got to school, I'd wiped my nose and dried my eyes and
vowed not to let anyone know that I was even moved by this.
It was no one's business why I couldn't eat my hot dog and
chocolate milk, but the irony of it was that my teacher, Mrs.
Johnson, must have sensed what had happened, and she
bought my hot dog and chocolate milk for me that day. I can
still remember feeling how unfair things can be, but how they
somehow always turn out good. I guess seeing so much
negativity had already started to turn me into an optimist.

I was a very busy child, because I was the oldest and had   11
to see to it that my sisters and brother had their baths and
did their homework; I combed my sisters' hair, and by fourth
grade I had cooked my first Thanksgiving dinner. It was my
responsibility to keep the house spotless so that when my
mother came home from work it would pass her inspection,
so I spent many an afternoon and Saturday morning mopping
and waxing floors, cleaning ovens and refrigerators, grocery
shopping, and by the time I was thirteen, I was paying bills
for my mother and felt like an adult. I was also tired of it,
sick of all the responsibility. So yes, I rooted for Dorothy
when she and Toto were vamoosing, only I wanted to know:

Where in the hell was she going? Where would I go if I were to run away? I had no idea because there was nowhere to go. What I did know was that one day I would go somewhere— which is why I think I watched so much TV. I was always on the lookout for Paradise, and I think I found it a few years later on "Adventures in Paradise," with Gardner McKay, and on "77 Sunset Strip." Palm trees and blue water and islands made quite an impression on a little girl from a flat, dull little depressing town in Michigan.

Professor Marvel really pissed me off, and I didn't believe for a minute that that crystal ball was real, even before he started asking Dorothy all those questions, but I knew this man was going to be important, and I just couldn't figure out how. Dorothy was so gullible, I thought, and I knew this word because my mother used to always drill it in us that you should "never believe everything somebody tells you." So after Professor Marvel convinced Dorothy that her Auntie Em might be in trouble, and Dorothy scoops up Toto and runs back home, I was totally disappointed, because now I wasn't going to have an adventure. I was thinking I might actually learn how to escape drudgery by watching Dorothy do it successfully, but before she even gave herself the chance to discover for herself that she could make it, she was on her way back home. "Dummy!" we all yelled on the sun porch. "Dodo brain!"

The storm. The tornado. Of course, now the entire set of this film looks so phony it's ridiculous, but back then I knew the wind was a tornado because in Michigan we had the same kind of trapdoor underground shelter that Auntie Em had on the farm. I knew Dorothy was going to be locked out once Auntie Em and the workers locked the door, and I also knew she wasn't going to be heard when she knocked on it. This was drama at its best, even though I didn't know what drama was at the time.

In the house she goes, and I was frightened for her. I knew that house was going to blow away, so when little Dorothy gets banged in the head by a window that flew out of its casement, I remember all of us screaming. We watched everybody fly by the window, including the wicked neighbor who turns out to be the Wicked Witch of the West, and I'm sure I probably substituted my mother for Auntie Em and fantasized that all of my siblings would fly away, too. They all got on my nerves because I could never find a quiet place in my house—no such thing as peace—and I was always being disturbed.

It wasn't so much that I had so much I wanted to do by myself, but I already knew that silence was a rare commodity, and when I managed to snatch a few minutes of it, I could daydream, pretend to be someone else somewhere else—and this was fun. But I couldn't do it if someone was bugging me. On days when my mother was at work, I would often send the kids outside to play and lock them out, just so I could have the house to myself for at least fifteen minutes. I loved pretending that none of them existed for a while, although after I finished with my fantasy world, it was reassuring to see them all there. I think I was grounded.   15

When Dorothy's house began to spin and spin and spin, I was curious as to where it was going to land. And to be honest, I didn't know little Dorothy was actually dreaming until she woke up and opened the door and everything was in color! It looked like Paradise to me. The foliage was almost an iridescent green, the water bluer than I'd ever seen in any of the lakes in Michigan. Of course, once I realized she was in fact dreaming, it occurred to me that this very well might be the only way to escape. To dream up another world. Create your own.   16

I had no clue that Dorothy was going to find trouble, though, even in her dreams. Hell, if I had dreamed up something like another world, it would've been a perfect one. I wouldn't have put myself in such a precarious situation. I'd have been able to go straight to the Wizard, no strings attached. First of all, that she walked was stupid to me; I would've asked one of those Munchkins for a ride. And I never bought into the idea of those slippers, but once I bought the whole idea, I accepted the fact that the girl was definitely lost and just wanted to get home. Personally, all I   17 kept thinking was, if she could get rid of that Wicked Witch of the West, the Land of Oz wasn't such a bad place to be stuck in. It beat the farm in Kansas.

At the time, I truly wished I could spin away from my family and home and land someplace as beautiful and surreal as Oz—if only for a little while. All I wanted was to get a chance to see another side of the world, to be able to make comparisons, and then decide if it was worth coming back home. 18

What was really strange to me, after the Good Witch of the North tells Dorothy to just stay on the Yellow Brick Road to get to the Emerald City and find the Wizard so she can get home, was when Dorothy meets the Scarecrow, the Tin Man, and the Lion—all of whom were missing something I'd never even given any thought to. A brain? What did having one really mean? What would not having one mean? I had one, didn't I, because I did well in school. But because the Scarecrow couldn't make up his mind, thought of himself as a failure, it dawned on me that having a brain meant you had choices, you could make decisions and, as a result, make things happen. Yes, I thought, I had one, and I was going to use it. One day. And the Tin Man, who didn't have a heart. Not having one meant you were literally dead to me, and I never once thought of it as being the house of emotions (didn't know what emotions were), where feelings of jealousy, devotion, and sentiment lived. I'd never thought of what else a heart was good for except keeping you alive. But I did have feelings, because they were often hurt, and I was envious of the white girls at my school who wore mohair sweaters and box-pleat skirts, who went skiing and tobogganing and yachting and spent summers in Quebec. Why didn't white girls have to straighten their hair? Why didn't their parents beat each other up? Why were they always so goddamn happy? 19

And courage. Oh, that was a big one. What did having it and not having it mean? I found out that it meant having guts and being afraid but doing whatever it was you set out to do anyway. Without courage, you couldn't do much of 20 anything. I liked courage and assumed I would acquire it somehow. As a matter of fact, one day my mother *told* me to get her a cup of coffee, and even though my heart was pounding and I was afraid, I said to her pointblank, "Could you please say please?" She looked up at me out of the corner of her eye and said, "What?" So I repeated myself, feeling more powerful because she hadn't slapped me across the room already, and then something came over her and she looked at me and said, "Please." I smiled all the way to the kitchen, and from that point forward, I managed to get away with this kind of behavior until I left home when I was seventeen. My sisters and brother—to this day—don't know how I stand up to my mother, but I know. I decided not to be afraid or intimidated by her, and I wanted her to treat me like a friend, like a human being, instead of her slave.

I do believe that Oz also taught me much about friendship. 21 I mean, the Tin Man, the Lion, and the Scarecrow hung in there for Dorothy, stuck their "necks" out and made sure she was protected, even risked their own "lives" for her. They told each other the truth. They trusted each other. All four of them had each other's best interests in mind. I believe it may have been a while before I actually felt this kind of sincerity in a friend, but really good friends aren't easy to come by, and when you find one, you hold on to them.

Okay. So Dorothy goes through hell before she gets back 22 to Kansas. But the bottom line was, she made it. And what I remember feeling when she clicked those heels was that you have to have faith and be a believer, for real, or nothing will ever materialize. Simple as that. And not only in life but even in your dreams there's always going to be adversity, obstacles, knots, or some kind of bullshit you're going to have to deal with in order to get on with your life. Dorothy had a good heart and it was in the right place, which is why I suppose she won out over the evil witch. I've learned that one, too. That good *always* overcomes evil; maybe not immediately, but in the long run, it does. So I think I vowed when I was little to try to be a good person. An honest person. To care about others and not just myself. Not to be a selfish person, because my heart would be of no service if I used it only for myself. And I had to have the courage to see other people and myself as not being perfect (yes, I had a heart and a brain, but some other things would turn up missing, later), and I would have to learn to untie every knot that I encountered— some self-imposed, some not—in my life, and to believe that if I did the right things, I would never stray too far from my Yellow Brick Road.

I'm almost certain that I saw *Oz* annually for at least five   23 or six years, but I don't remember how old I was when I stopped watching it. I do know that by the time my parents were divorced (I was thirteen), I couldn't sit through it again. I was a mature teen-ager and had finally reached the point where Dorothy got on my nerves. Singing, dancing, and skipping damn near everywhere was so corny and utterly sentimental that even the Yellow Brick Road became sickening. I already knew what she was in for, and sometimes I rewrote the story in my head. I kept asking myself, what if she had just run away and kept going, maybe she would've ended up in Los Angeles with a promising singing career. What if it had turned out that she hadn't been dreaming, and the Wizard had given her an offer she couldn't refuse—say, for instance, he had asked her to stay on in the Emerald City, that she could visit the farm whenever she wanted to, but, get a clue, Dorothy, the Emerald City is what's happening; she could make new city friends and get a hobby and a boyfriend and free rent and never have to do chores . . .

I had to watch *The Wizard of Oz* again in order to write   24 this, and my six-and-a-half-year-old son, Solomon, joined me. At first he kept asking me if something was wrong with the TV because it wasn't in color, but as he watched, he became mesmerized by the story. He usually squirms or slides to the floor and under a table or just leaves the room if something on TV bores him, which it usually does, except if he's watching Nickelodeon, a high-quality cable kiddie channel. His favorite shows, which he watches with real consistency, and, I think, actually goes through withdrawal if he can't get them for whatever reason, are "Inspector Gadget,"

"Looney Tunes," and "Mr. Ed." "Make the Grade," which is sort of a junior-high version of "Jeopardy," gives him some kind of thrill, even though he rarely knows any of the answers. And "Garfield" is a must on Saturday morning. There is hardly anything on TV that he watches that has any real, or at least plausible, drama to it, but you can't miss what you've never had.

The Wicked Witch intimidated the boy no end, and he was afraid of her. The Wizard was also a problem. So I explained—no, I just told him pointblank—"Don't worry, she'll get it in the end, Solomon, because she's bad. And the Wizard's a fake, and he's trying to sound like a tough guy, but he's a wus." That offered him some consolation, and even when the Witch melted he kind of looked at me with those *Home Alone* eyes and asked "But where did she go, Mommy?" "She's history," I said. "Melted. Gone. Into the ground. Remember, this is pretend. It's not real. Real people don't melt. This is only TV," I said. And then he got that look in his eyes as if he'd remembered something.

Of course he had a nightmare that night and of course there was a witch in it, because I had actually left the sofa a few times during this last viewing to smoke a few cigarettes (the memory bank is a powerful place—I still remembered many details), put the dishes in the dishwasher, make a few phone calls, water the plants. Solomon sang "We're off to see the Wizard" for the next few days because he said that was his favorite part, next to the Munchkins (who also showed up in his nightmare).

So, to tell the truth, I really didn't watch the whole movie again. I just couldn't. Probably because about thirty or so years ago little Dorothy had made a lasting impression on me, and this viewing felt like overkill. You only have to tell me, show me, once in order for me to get it. But even still, the movie itself taught me a few things that I still find challenging. That it's okay to be an idealist, that you have to imagine something better and go for it. That you have to believe in *something,* and it's best to start with yourself and take it from there. At least give it a try. As corny as it may sound, sometimes I am afraid of what's around the corner, or what's not around the corner. But I look anyway. I believe that writing is one of my "corners"—an intersection, really; and when I'm confused or reluctant to look back, deeper, or ahead, I create my own Emerald Cities and force myself to take longer looks, because it is one sure way that I'm able to see.

Of course, I've fallen, tumbled, and been thrown over all kinds of bumps on my road, but it still looks yellow, although every once in a while there's still a loose brick. For the most part, though, it seems paved. Perhaps because that's the way I want to see it.

28

For Study and Discussion

QUESTIONS FOR RESPONSE

1. Can you name any movie or book that you remember so vividly that you feel it influenced you strongly? If so, what was the movie or book and what effect do you think it had on you?
2. What was your own response to the movie *The Wizard of Oz?* Would you call it a significant movie for you? Why?

QUESTIONS ABOUT PURPOSE

1. In the process of showing why the movie was significant for her, what does McMillan reveal about herself?
2. What advantages does McMillan suggest that fantasy has for children? What effects might fantasies other than *The Wizard of Oz* have, perhaps books like C.S. Lewis's Narnia Chronicle or a movie like *Star Trek?*

QUESTIONS ABOUT AUDIENCE

1. How justified do you think McMillan is in assuming that her readers are very familiar with the movie *The Wizard of Oz?* What would be the effect if they're not familiar with the movie?
2. What personality traits and outlook on life do you think readers

are likely to have who like this essay and find it persuasive? To what extent do you think you and your friends share those traits?

QUESTIONS ABOUT STRATEGIES

1. How does McMillan tie the attraction that the Oz movie has for her to conditions in her own life? How well does that strategy work?
2. How does McMillan fill in details of the movie for readers who may have forgotten or didn't know the story of *The Wizard of Oz*? How good a job does she do?

QUESTIONS FOR DISCUSSION

1. What place do you think the movie *The Wizard of Oz* has in our contemporary culture? What associations do most people have with it and what phrases from it are commonplace? If some people in your class do not share in that culture, how well does McMillan's essay work with them?
2. What contemporary movies or television shows are so familiar to you and your circle of friends that they serve as common ground that everyone can refer to? How do you use incidents from those shows as points of reference in your conversations?

SANDRA CISNEROS

Sandra Cisneros was born in 1954 in Chicago and spent much of her childhood living in Chicago and Mexico City. A graduate of the University of Iowa Writer's Workshop, she has taught writing at the University of California at Berkeley and the University of Michigan. She has also taught in the San Antonio Public Schools and worked as literary director of the Guadalupe Cultural Arts Center. She has contributed stories and poems to periodicals such as *Imagine, Contact II,* and *Revista Chicano-Riquena.* Her poems appear in *Bad Boys* (1980), *The Rodrigo Poems* (1985), and *My Wicked, Wicked Ways* (1987); her stories are collected in *Woman Hollering Creek* (1991). Cisneros's book for young adults, *The House on Mango Street* (1983), won the American Book Award. In "One Holy Night," reprinted from *Woman Hollering Creek,* Cisneros's narrator analyzes the impact of her "holy night" with a man who claims he is descended from Mayan kings.

One Holy Night

About the truth, if you give it to a person, then he has power over you. And if someone gives it to you, then they have made themselves your slave. It is a strong magic. You can never take it back.

—CHAQ UXMAL PALOQUÍN

HE SAID HIS name was Chaq. Chaq Uxmal Paloquín. That's what he told me. He was of an ancient line of Mayan kings. Here, he said, making a map with the heel of his boot, this is where I come from, the Yucatán, the ancient cities. This is what Boy Baby said.

It's been eighteen weeks since Abuelita chased him away   2
with the broom, and what I'm telling you I never told nobody, except Rachel and Lourdes, who know everything. He
said he would love me like a revolution, like a religion.
Abuelita burned the pushcart and sent me here, miles from
home, in this town of dust, with one wrinkled witch woman
who rubs my belly with jade, and sixteen nosy cousins.

I don't know how many girls have gone bad from selling   3
cucumbers. I know I'm not the first. My mother took the
crooked walk too, I'm told, and I'm sure my Abuelita has
her own story, but it's not my place to ask.

Abuelita says it's Uncle Lalo's fault because he's the man   4
of the family and if he had come home on time like he was
supposed to and worked the pushcart on the days he was
told to and watched over his goddaughter, who is too foolish
to look after herself, nothing would've happened, and I
wouldn't have to be sent to Mexico. But Uncle Lalo says if
they had never left Mexico in the first place, shame enough
would have kept a girl from doing devil things.

I'm not saying I'm not bad. I'm not saying I'm special.   5
But I'm not like the Allport Street girls, who stand in doorways and go with men into alleys.

All I know is I didn't want it like that. Not against the   6
bricks or hunkering in somebody's car. I wanted it to come
undone like gold thread, like a tent full of birds. The way it's
supposed to be, the way I knew it would be when I met Boy
Baby.

But you must know, I was no girl back then. And Boy Baby   7
was no boy. Chaq Uxmal Paloquín. Boy Baby was a man.
When I asked him how old he was he said he didn't know.
The past and the future are the same thing. So he seemed
boy and baby and man all at once, and the way he looked at
me, how do I explain?

I'd park the pushcart in front of the Jewel food store   8
Saturdays. He bought a mango on a stick the first time. Paid
for it with a new twenty. Next Saturday he was back. Two
mangoes, lime juice, and chili powder, keep the change. The
third Saturday he asked for a cucumber spear and ate it slow.

I didn't see him after that till the day he brought me Kool-Aid in a plastic cup. Then I knew what I felt for him.

Maybe you wouldn't like him. To you he might be a bum. Maybe he looked it. Maybe. He had broken thumbs and burnt fingers. He had thick greasy fingernails he never cut and dusty hair. And all his bones were strong ones like a man's. I waited every Saturday in my same blue dress. I sold all the mango and cucumber, and then Boy Baby would come finally. 9

What I knew of Chaq was only what he told me, because nobody seemed to know where he came from. Only that he could speak a strange language that no one could understand, said his name translated into boy, or boy-child, and so it was the street people nicknamed him Boy Baby. 10

I never asked about his past. He said it was all the same and didn't matter, past and the future all the same to his people. But the truth has a strange way of following you, of coming up to you and making you listen to what it has to say. 11

Night time. Boy Baby brushes my hair and talks to me in his strange language because I like to hear it. What I like to hear him tell is how he is Chaq, Chaq of the people of the sun, Chaq of the temples, and what he says sounds sometimes like broken clay, and at other times like hollow sticks, or like the swish of old feathers crumbling into dust. 12

He lived behind Esparza & Sons Auto Repair in a little room that used to be a closet—pink plastic curtains on a narrow window, a dirty cot covered with newspapers, and a cardboard box filled with socks and rusty tools. It was there, under one bald bulb, in the back room of the Esparza garage, in the single room with pink curtains, that he showed me the guns—twenty-four in all. Rifles and pistols, one rusty musket, a machine gun, and several tiny weapons with mother-of-pearl handles that looked like toys. So you'll see who I am, he said, laying them all out on the bed of newspapers. So you'll understand. But I didn't want to know. 13

The stars foretell everything, he said. My birth. My son's. The boy-child who will bring back the grandeur of my people 14 from those who have broken the arrows, from those who have pushed the ancient stones off their pedestals.

Then he told how he had prayed in the Temple of the   15
Magician years ago as a child when his father had made him promise to bring back the ancient ways. Boy Baby had cried in the temple dark that only the bats made holy. Boy Baby who was man and child among the great and dusty guns lay down on the newspaper bed and wept for a thousand years. When I touched him, he looked at me with the sadness of stone.

You must not tell anyone what I am going to do, he said.   16
And what I remember next is how the moon, the pale moon with its one yellow eye, the moon of Tikal, and Tulum, and Chichén, stared through the pink plastic curtains. Then something inside bit me, and I gave out a cry as if the other, the one I wouldn't be anymore, leapt out.

So I was initiated beneath an ancient sky by a great and   17
mighty heir—Chaq Uxmal Paloquín. I, Ixchel, his queen.

The truth is, it wasn't a big deal. It wasn't any deal at all.   18
I put my bloody panties inside my T-shirt and ran home hugging myself. I thought about a lot of things on the way home. I thought about all the world and how suddenly I became a part of history and wondered if everyone on the street, the sewing machine lady and the *panadería* saleswomen and the woman with two kids sitting on the bus bench didn't all know. *Did I look any different? Could they tell?* We were all the same somehow, laughing behind our hands, waiting the way all women wait, and when we find out, we wonder why the world and a million years made such a big deal over nothing.

I know I was supposed to feel ashamed, but I wasn't   19
ashamed. I wanted to stand on top of the highest building, the top-top floor, and yell, *I know.*

Then I understood why Abuelita didn't let me sleep over   20
at Lourdes's house full of too many brothers, and why the Roman girl in the movies always runs away from the soldier, and what happens when the scenes in love stories begin to

fade, and why brides blush, and how it is that sex isn't simply a box you check *M* or *F* on in the test we get at school.

I was wise. The corner girls were still jumping into their stupid little hopscotch squares. I laughed inside and climbed the wooden stairs two by two to the second floor rear where me and Abuelita and Uncle Lalo live. I was still laughing when I opened the door and Abuelita asked, Where's the pushcart? 21

And then I didn't know what to do. 22

It's a good thing we live in a bad neighborhood. There are always plenty of bums to blame for your sins. If it didn't happen the way I told it, it really could've. We looked and looked all over for the kids who stole my pushcart. The story wasn't the best, but since I had to make it up right then and there with Abuelita staring a hole through my heart, it wasn't too bad. 23

For two weeks I had to stay home. Abuelita was afraid the street kids who had stolen the cart would be after me again. Then I thought I might go over to the Esparza garage and take the pushcart out and leave it in some alley for the police to find, but I was never allowed to leave the house alone. Bit by bit the truth started to seep out like a dangerous gasoline. 24

First the nosy woman who lives upstairs from the laundromat told my Abuelita she thought something was fishy, the pushcart wheeled into Esparza & Sons every Saturday after dark, how a man, the same dark Indian one, the one who never talks to anybody, walked with me when the sun went down and pushed the cart into the garage, that one there, and yes we went inside, there where the fat lady named Concha, whose hair is dyed a hard black, pointed a fat finger. 25

I prayed that we would not meet Boy Baby, and since the gods listen and are mostly good, Esparza said yes, a man like that had lived there but was gone, had packed a few things and left the pushcart in a corner to pay for his last week's rent. 26

We had to pay $20 before he would give us our pushcart back. Then Abuelita made me tell the real story of how the 27 cart had disappeared, all of which I told this time, except for that one night, which I would have to tell anyway, weeks later, when I prayed for the moon of my cycle to come back, but it would not.

When Abuelita found out I was going to *dar a luz,* she cried until her eyes were little, and blamed Uncle Lalo, and Uncle Lalo blamed this country, and Abuelita blamed the infamy of men. That is when she burned the cucumber push-cart and called me a *sinvergüenza* because I *am* without shame. 28

Then I cried too—Boy Baby was lost from me—until my head was hot with headaches and I fell asleep. When I woke up, the cucumber pushcart was dust and Abuelita was sprinkling holy water on my head. 29

Abuelita woke up early every day and went to the Esparza garage to see if news about that *demonio* had been found, had Chaq Uxmal Paloquín sent any letters, any, and when the other mechanics heard that name they laughed, and asked if we had made it up, that we could have some letters that had come for Boy Baby, no forwarding address, since he had gone in such a hurry. 30

There were three. The first, addressed "Occupant," de-manded immediate payment for a four-month-old electric bill. The second was one I recognized right away—a brown envelope fat with cake-mix coupons and fabric-softener sam-ples—because we'd gotten one just like it. The third was addressed in a spidery Spanish to a Señor C. Cruz, on paper so thin you could read it unopened by the light of the sky. The return address a convent in Tampico. 31

This was to whom my Abuelita wrote in hopes of finding the man who could correct my ruined life, to ask if the good nuns might know the whereabouts of a certain Boy Baby—and if they were hiding him it would be of no use because God's eyes see through all souls. 32

We heard nothing for a long time. Abuelita took me out of school when my uniform got tight around the belly and said it was a shame I wouldn't be able to graduate with the other eighth graders. 33

Except for Lourdes and Rachel, my grandma and Uncle   34
Lalo, nobody knew about my past. I would sleep in the big
bed I share with Abuelita same as always. I could hear
Abuelita and Uncle Lalo talking in low voices in the kitchen
as if they were praying the rosary, how they were going to
send me to Mexico, to San Dionisio de Tlaltepango, where
I have cousins and where I was conceived and would've been
born had my grandma not thought it wise to send my mother
here to the United States so that neighbors in San Dionisio
de Tlaltepango wouldn't ask why her belly was suddenly big.

I was happy. I liked staying home. Abuelita was teaching   35
me to crochet the way she had learned in Mexico. And just
when I had mastered the tricky rosette stitch, the letter came
from the convent which gave the truth about Boy Baby—
however much we didn't want to hear.

He was born on a street with no name in a town called   36
Miseria. His father, Eusebio, is a knife sharpener. His mother,
Refugia, stacks apricots into pyramids and sells them on a
cloth in the market. There are brothers. Sisters too of which
I know little. The youngest, a Carmelite, writes me all this
and prays for my soul, which is why I know it's all true.

Boy Baby is thirty-seven years old. His name is Chato   37
which means fat-face. There is no Mayan blood.

I don't think they understand how it is to be a girl. I don't   38
think they know how it is to have to wait your whole life. I
count the months for the baby to be born, and it's like a ring
of water inside me reaching out and out until one day it will
tear from me with its own teeth.

Already I can feel the animal inside me stirring in his own   39
uneven sleep. The witch woman says it's the dreams of wea-
sels that make my child sleep the way he sleeps. She makes
me eat white bread blessed by the priest, but I know it's the
ghost of him inside me that circles and circles, and will not
let me rest.

Abuelita said they sent me here just in time, because a little   40
later Boy Baby came back to our house looking for me, and

she had to chase him away with the broom. The next thing we hear, he's in the newspaper clippings his sister sends. A picture of him looking very much like stone, police hooked on either arm . . . *on the road to* Las Grutas de Xtacumbilxuna, *the Caves of the Hidden Girl . . . eleven female bodies . . . the last seven years . . .*

Then I couldn't read but only stare at the little black-and-white dots that make up the face I am in love with. 41

All my girl cousins here either don't talk to me, or those who do, ask questions they're too young to know *not* to ask. What they want to know really is how it is to have a man, because they're too ashamed to ask their married sisters. 42

They don't know what it is to lay so still until his sleep breathing is heavy, for the eyes in the dim dark to look and look without worry at the man-bones and the neck, the man-wrist and man-jaw thick and strong, all the salty dips and hollows, the stiff hair of the brow and sour swirl of sideburns, to lick the fat earlobes that taste of smoke, and stare at how perfect is a man. 43

I tell them, "It's a bad joke. When you find out you'll be sorry." 44

I'm going to have five children. Five. Two girls. Two boys. And one baby. 45

The girls will be called Lisette and Maritza. The boys I'll name Pablo and Sandro. 46

And my baby. My baby will be named Alegre, because life will always be hard. 47

Rachel says that love is like a big black piano being pushed off the top of a three-story building and you're waiting on the bottom to catch it. But Lourdes says it's not that way at all. It's like a top, like all the colors in the world are spinning so fast they're not colors anymore and all that's left is a white hum. 48

There was a man, a crazy who lived upstairs from us when we lived on South Loomis. He couldn't talk, just walked 49 around all day with this harmonica in his mouth. Didn't play it. Just sort of breathed through it, all day long, wheezing, in and out, in and out.

This is how it is with me. Love I mean.   50

COMMENT ON "ONE HOLY NIGHT"

In her story "One Holy Night" Sandra Cisneros uses a first-person narrative to take us into the mind of a fourteen-year-old girl who has romanticized her seduction—really rape—by a stranger into "one holy night," a night that leaves her pregnant. Sure that she is better than the girls who slip into alleys with boys, the girl imagines her first sexual experience will be as if something will "come undone like gold thread, like a tent full of birds." And because her seducer convinces her that he is like a god, the descendant of an ancient line of Mayan kings, and that his son will be the boy-child who will bring back the grandeur of his people, she thinks of losing her virginity as an initiation "beneath an ancient sky" that makes her his queen. Her romanticism and her longing to be someone special betray her into giving herself to a man she really knows nothing about.

Reality takes over when she is sent away to relatives to have her baby, still mooning over the child's father and convinced she's still in love with him. The truth about that father is stark, even dangerous. He was a thirty-seven-year-old man from nowhere with no trace of Mayan blood, much less royal blood. It's also probable that he has killed and hidden the bodies of eleven women. But at the end, we're still not quite sure if the title "One Holy Night" is ironic or if the girl will always look back on her sex with a stranger as "one holy night."

Cause and Effect as a Writing Strategy

1. For a short opinion piece in some magazine you enjoy reading, write an essay in which you describe the fashions adopted by a certain group of people and then theorize about why the fashion is popular and how it affects the behavior of the people who follow it. Give specific examples that illustrate the fashion.

   Some possibilities that you might consider:

   - Where did the fashion of untied shoelaces on athletic shoes come from and why? Of baseball caps turned backward? Of tattered jeans?
   - In an office you know, what does casual attire on Fridays look like and how does it affect the behavior of people who adopt it?
   - How do instructors dress on your campus? What do you see as the message of their attire?
   - What was the approved attire in your high school? How did it influence the behavior of those who observed it most faithfully?
   - What was approved prom attire in your high school? How did those clothes influence the behavior of the people who wore them?
   - What is the accepted clothes style for the place where you work? How do you think the style affects the employees and the people they serve?

2. For an editorial in your campus newspaper, write an essay of between 300 and 500 words about an incident on your campus that involved allegations of racist or sexist behavior. In your editorial, take sides. In your opinion, were the people who claimed they had been discriminated against justified in their accusations? Were they indeed victims, and if so, what should their response have been? If you don't think they were justified in the complaint, explain why. Conclude with a suggestion about how such incidents might be avoided in the future.

3. You may strongly disagree with one of the cause-and-effect essays in this section and want to refute what the author is saying or at least argue against a part of his or her thesis. If so, develop a paper by supposing that the writer has appeared as a speaker in your college's Ideas and Issues lecture series and has given his or her essay as a talk. Write your counterargument as a guest editorial for your campus newspaper, assuming that your readers will be other students and the college faculty.

   Here are some of the strategies you might use for your argument:

   a. Challenge the cause-and-effect relationships that the author claims.

   b. Citing information you have from different sources or from your experience, argue that the writer's conclusions are faulty.

   c. Challenge the accuracy of some of the writer's evidence, or show weak links in his or her reasoning.

   d. Show that the writer has failed to take certain things into account about his or her readers or their situation and has thus weakened the thesis of the essay.

   e. Demonstrate that the writer has let his or her biases distort the argument.

   f. Show that the writer claims too much, more than the evidence warrants.

   Keep in mind how skillfully the writers in this section of the book use facts and examples to support their essays, and be sure you do the same.

4. Write an essay for your classmates telling why you have chosen the profession you currently plan to go into. What are your reasons? Why do you think it will be rewarding? What caused you to choose this profession? Whom do you know in the profession, and how have their experiences affected your choice? What kind of training and education will be necessary, and what sacrifices, both financial and personal, might be involved? What kind of conflicts, if any, do you think you might experience between your personal and professional lives? What effects do you think those conflicts might have on you?

5. Movies, on and off television, play a major role in modern culture, yet no one seems to have a clear idea of how much influence they have on young people. Write a short essay, perhaps for the movie section of your local newspaper, in which you speculate about the influence a very popular movie or kind of movie has on the under twenty-one viewers who are a major market for Hollywood. Mention specific movies and discuss ways in which they could influence young viewers.

    As an alternative topic, consider this. American movies, particularly action movies with stars like Bruce Willis and Tom Cruise, are extremely popular in other countries. What effect do you think such movies—name some you've seen recently—may have on the image of the United States abroad? If you're a student from another country, draw on your own experience in seeing American movies and discuss how they colored your opinions.

6. In his essay "One Violent Crime," Bruce Shapiro claims that politicians in both parties use scare tactics and promote drastic anticrime legislation to garner votes, yet they do little to support measures that might prevent crime. Write a short argument to be shared with others in your class in which you choose one community program you know of that is designed to help an at-risk group develop skills or improve conditions with the goal of reducing crime. Some possibilities are tutoring programs to keep students in school, apprentice programs that help young people to learn marketable skills such as carpentry, programs that help people get their GED certificates, or mentoring programs such as Big Brothers and Big Sisters. Describe the program and its goals and argue for funding for it from the United Way or a municipal grant.

PERSUASION
AND
ARGUMENT

૮౿ౢ

Intuitively, you already know a good deal about **argument.**
For one thing, you use it all the time as you go through the
day talking or writing and making claims and giving reasons.
But you also live surrounded by arguments. They come not
only from people you talk to and deal with in everyday
personal or business situations, but also from television, radio, newspapers, subway posters, billboards, and signs and
brochures of all kinds. Any time someone is trying to persuade you to buy something, contribute money, take action,
make a judgment, or change your mind about anything, that
person is arguing with you.

People write entire books showing how to argue effectively, how to analyze arguments, and how to refute them.

Colleges offer complete courses in the subject. Obviously, then, the subject is too complex and extensive for us to do more than skim the surface in this brief discussion. This introduction offers a quick overview of some important argument theory, tips about the kinds of arguments you can make, some concerns and strategies to keep in mind as you write arguments, and a reminder about pitfalls to avoid. If you want to learn more about making better arguments and criticizing them effectively, you can find useful books in your college bookstore or library or take an argumentation course in your speech department.

In college writing, you're not likely to spend time writing arguments about matters of taste—that is, debates in which you're saying little more than "I like it" or "I don't like it." You may enjoy talking with friends about whether you'd rather watch soccer or rugby, but mere preferences don't make workable topics for writing arguments in college. Nor do matters of fact, such as whether Mount Hood or Mount Whitney is the highest peak in the United States. Such disputes can be quickly settled by research and aren't worth the time it takes to write about them.

But in college you will probably write a wide variety of other kinds of arguments, ranging from strong personal opinion essays to closely reasoned position statements. At one extreme, in the personal opinion essays, you may make emotional claims and support them with moving and colorful language. At the other extreme, in the position statements, you try to make strictly logical claims and support them with factual, research-based data. Traditionally, your emotional argument would be classified as *persuasive,* and your logical argument would be classified as *rational.* In practice, however, most arguments mix emotion and reason in various degrees. In this section, the argumentative essays are arranged along a continuum; the more emotional, opinion-focused essays appear at the beginning, and the more objective, fact-focused essays are at the end of the section.

It's also important to remember that writing that is primarily rational isn't necessarily better than writing that is mainly emotional. Some occasions call for appeals to pride, loyalty, or compassion; for using vivid metaphors that reach the senses; and for strong language that touches the passions. When someone is speaking at a political rally or graduation ceremony or giving a eulogy, the audience wants not statistics and intellectual reasoning but emotional satisfaction and inspiration. The kind of writing done for such occasions is called *ceremonial discourse,* and often it is successful precisely because it is emotional.

When you write arguments for college instructors or your fellow students, however, you should assume that you face a skeptical audience, one that wants explanations and good reasons. Thus you need to write primarily rational arguments built mostly on evidence and logical appeal, although at times you might bring in emotional elements. You can take your cue from lawyers pleading a courtroom case. You should argue as persuasively as you can, but you should also make reasonable claims and support them with strong evidence.

PURPOSE

When you hear the term *argument,* you may automatically connect it with controversy and conflict. That's not necessarily the case, however, particularly in academic writing. There—and at other times too—you may have many purposes other than winning a dispute.

Sometimes you may argue *to support a cause.* For instance, you might write an editorial in favor of subsidized child care on your campus. You may also argue *to urge people to action* or *to promote change*—for instance, when you write a campaign brochure or a petition to reduce student fees. Sometimes you may argue *to refute a theory*—perhaps a history paper claiming that antislavery sentiment was not the chief cause of the Civil War. You can also write arguments *to arouse sympathy*—for better laws against child abuse, for example; *to stimulate interest*—for more participation in student government; *to win agreement*—to get condominium residents to agree to abolish regulations against pets; and *to provoke anger*—to arouse outrage against a proposed tax. And, of course, you might incorporate several of these purposes into one piece of writing.

AUDIENCE

When you write arguments, you must think about your readers. Who are they, what do they know, what do they believe, and what do they expect? Unless you can answer these questions at least partially, you cannot expect to write an effective argument. There simply is no such thing as a good argument in the abstract, separated from its purpose and its audience. Any argument you write is a good one only if it does what you want it to do with the particular readers who are going to read it. So by no later than the second draft of any argument you write, you need to know why you are writing and for whom you are writing.

Often it's not easy to analyze your readers. You have to work partly by instinct. Sometimes you adjust the tone of your writing almost automatically to suit a particular group of readers, and often you know intuitively that certain strategies won't work with certain readers. But you don't have to depend only on hunches. Working through a set of questions as part of your preparation to write will yield important information about your readers and will help you gradually form a sense of audience to guide you as you write and revise.

If you are trying to choose an audience for your paper, ask yourself the following questions:

1. Who is likely to be interested in what I am writing about?
2. What groups could make the changes I'm arguing for?

When you know the answers to these questions, you can direct your writing to readers to whom you have something to say—otherwise, there's little point in writing.

Once you have settled on your audience, ask yourself these questions:

1. What do my readers already know about my topic?
   a. What experience and knowledge do they have that I can use?
   b. Can I use specialized language? Should I?
   c. How can I teach them something they want to know?
2. How do my readers feel about my topic?
   a. What shared values can I appeal to?
   b. What prejudices or preconceptions must I pay attention to?
   c. What kind of approach will work best with them— casual or formal, objective or personal, factual or anecdotal?
3. What questions will my readers want me to answer?

You may find it especially useful to write out the answers to that last question.

When you have worked your way through all of these questions, either as a brainstorming exercise or in a prewriting group discussion, you'll have a stronger sense of who your readers are and how you can appeal to them.

STRATEGIES

When you are writing arguments, you can use a wide range of strategies, but most of them will fall into one of these three categories: *emotional appeal, logical appeal,* or *ethical appeal.*

Emotional Appeal

You argue by emotional or nonlogical appeal when you appeal to the emotions, the senses, and to personal biases or prejudices. You incorporate such appeals into your writing when you use *connotative language* that elicits feelings or reactions—words like *melancholy, crimson, slovenly,* or *villainous.* Usually you're also using nonlogical appeal when you use *figurative language*—metaphors, allusions, or colorful phrases that make the reader draw comparisons or make associations. Phrases like "environmental cancer" or "industrial Goliath" evoke images and comparisons and play on the emotions.

Creating a tone is also a nonlogical strategy and an important one. The tone you choose can exert a powerful force on your readers, catching their attention, ingratiating you into their favor, conveying an air of authority and confidence. You can establish a friendly, close-to-your-reader tone by using contractions and the pronouns *I, we,* and *you.* You can create a relaxed tone by bringing in humor or personal anecdote, or you can give your writing an air of authority and detachment by avoiding personal pronouns and writing as objectively as possible.

All the writers in this section use emotional appeal, but those who rely on it most heavily are Martin Luther King, Jr., and, perhaps surprisingly, Esther Dyson. In "I Have a Dream," King appeals to the feelings of his listeners through the extensive use of metaphor and impassioned language. In "A Design for Living on the Internet," Dyson appeals to her readers' emotions through her consistently upbeat tone, her promises of a rosy future for Internet users, and her continual use of terms with relentlessly positive connotations: *freedom, creativity, choice, opportunity, honesty,* and *participation.* In "A Chinaman's Chance" Eric Liu also makes an emotional appeal through his stories and through phrases like "a nation of second chances" and "freedom and opportunity"; his language is, however, more restrained than King's.

Logical Appeal

You argue with logical or rational strategies when you appeal mainly to your readers' intelligence, reason, and common sense. Here you depend heavily on *making claims* and *using supporting evidence.* Like a lawyer arguing a case, you may *bring in testimony* (including statistics and reports), *cite authorities,* and *argue from precedent.* You *make comparisons* and *use analogies* to strengthen your presentation, and you *theorize about cause and effect.* You also *de-emphasize personal feelings,* although you may not eliminate them completely, and *focus on facts and research.*

David Denby's "What the Great Books Do" and Mike Rose's "The Limits of the Great Books" are complex and closely reasoned arguments. Each author draws heavily on historical examples and on his own experience in the classroom, quotes authorities, and refers to traditions from the past. But each also incorporates considerable emotional appeal. In a powerful closing paragraph, Denby says, "What *can* be achieved through culture is the greatest range of pleasure that any of us is capable of." Rose concludes like this: "We'll need a revised store of images . . . that embody the reward and turmoil of education in democracy, that celebrate the plural, messy human reality of it all."

In "The Coming White Underclass" Charles Murray makes a logical appeal by using statistics to indicate the dimensions of the illegitimacy problem, then suggesting that there is a rational solution: stop subsidizing unwed mothers, and the births will stop. Nevertheless, emotional appeal runs throughout the essay in his phrasing: "wrong-headed social policy," "degraded cultural and social norms," and "Dickensian barracks," for example. Rosemary Bray uses logic and evidence in "So How Did I Get Here?" Arguing forcefully from statistics and history, she demolishes the common misconceptions about welfare. But the factual account of her family's years on welfare has great emotional impact, and the tone of her article is strong and angry when she attacks the patriarchal attitudes that perpetuate stereotypes.

Ethical Appeal

An ethical appeal is the most subtle and often the most powerful because it comes from character and reputation, not words. As a writer your ethical appeal stems from your ability to convince your readers that you are a reliable, intelligent person who knows what you're talking about and cares about the issues. Building this kind of appeal into your argument isn't easy. You have to know your readers and respect them, and you have to show that you've done your homework. For most readers, you also have to be careful not to exaggerate or make excessive claims; otherwise, you'll destroy your credibility.

Most of the writers in this section demonstrate strong ethical appeal, partly because they all have excellent credentials in their fields, but also because they show respect for their readers and have done their homework. Martin Luther King's ethical appeal is the strongest because it rests on his record as a fighter for civil rights and his own history of being willing to sacrifice for his beliefs. In the companion essay, "A Chinaman's Chance," Eric Liu's ethical appeal comes from his family's experience as aliens in the United States and his thoughtful analysis of how the American Dream has affected him. Rosemary Bray's ethical appeal comes from the dramatic story of her family's struggle during their years on welfare. Charles Murray's ethical appeal seems mixed. It may be strong for readers of the *Wall Street Journal,* his original audience, who might feel he's making a sensible argument about a serious problem, but it may lack authenticity for other readers, who feel he shows little empathy for or knowledge of the people he's talking about.

Ultimately, ethical appeal is the strongest of all argument strategies because it comes from the image and presence that the writer projects to her or his audience. If you show your readers that you are honest, knowledgeable, thoughtful, and genuinely committed to your position, your arguments are likely to be well received.

POTENTIAL PITFALLS IN ARGUMENT

This brief introduction to argument cannot point out all the things that can go wrong in arguments—the so-called logical fallacies—but adhering to the following guidelines should keep you from getting into too much trouble.

1. *Don't claim too much.* Avoid suggesting that the proposal you're arguing for will solve all the problems involved— for instance, implying that legalizing drugs would get rid of drug-related crimes or that openly paying college football players would eliminate recruitment scandals. Settle for suggesting that your ideas may be worth considering or that you have thought of a new approach.

2. *Don't oversimplify complex issues.* Usually when an issue is serious enough and interesting enough for you to spend your time writing about it, it's a complicated matter with a tangled history and involves difficult issues. If you try to reduce it to simplistic terms and come up with an easy solution, you'll lose credibility quickly. Instead, acknowledge that the matter defies easy analysis but suggest that some things could be done.

3. *Support your arguments with concrete evidence and specific proposals, not with generalizations and conventional sentiments.* Always assume you are arguing for skeptical readers who expect you to demonstrate your case and won't be impressed by opinion alone. You can hold their interest and gain their respect only if you teach them something as you argue and present an old problem in a new light.

As you read the essays in this section, try to identify how these writers are arguing and what strategies they are using to convince you. As you get in the habit of reading arguments analytically and appreciatively, you will move toward writing arguments more easily and effectively. None of these strategies is new, after all, and seeing what other writers have done can give you an idea of what is possible.

USING PERSUASION AND ARGUMENT IN PARAGRAPHS

Here are two persuasive paragraphs. The first is written by a professional writer and is followed by an analysis. The second is written by a student and is followed by questions.

BARBARA KINGSOLVER
from "Jabberwocky"

This subterfuge use of the word "political," which doesn't show up in my Random House Unabridged, means only that a thing runs counter to prevailing assumptions. **[Critics call art political if it goes against majority opinion]** If 60 percent of us support the war, then the expressions of the other 40 percent are political—and can be disallowed in some contexts for that reason alone. The really bad news is that the charter of the shopping mall seems to be standing in as a national artistic standard. Cultural workers in the U.S. are prone to be bound and gagged by a dread of being called political, for that word implies the art is not quite pure. **[Artists intimidated by implication their art isn't pure]** Real art, the story goes, does not endorse a point of view. This is utter nonsense, of course (try to imagine a story or a painting with no point of view) and also the most thorough and invisible form of censorship **[To say art shouldn't be political is form of censorship]** I've ever encountered. **[She contends that controversial topics are good subjects for literature]** When I'm interviewed about writing, I spend a good deal of time defending the possibility that such things as environmental ruin, child abuse, or the hypocrisy of U.S. immigration policy are appropriate subjects for a novel. I keep waiting for the interviewer to bring up *art* things, like voice and metaphor; usually I'm still waiting for that when the cows come home.

Comment In this paragraph from a collection of her spirited and opinionated essays, Kingsolver ridicules what she sees as a hypocritical attack on literature that expresses strong feelings about social issues. When certain critics try to discredit such art by calling it "political," she feels they are really trying to censor ideas they don't agree with. Still, some artists are intimidated by the label, which suggests that their art isn't pure. She dismisses such concerns as nonsense.

Kingsolver's argument is a protest against what she sees as a slippery use of language to suppress unpopular ideas. She calls such tactics a subterfuge, an attack on ideas that is disguised as high-minded criticism. She points out that such critics are seldom interested in discussing more legitimate issues about art.

JIM F. SALOMAN
Genetic Engineering

We need to regulate experiments in genetic engineering. Scientists can reconfigure the genetic makeup of an organism. They can literally change life. But without appropriate controls, such tampering can lead to unpredictable and violent results. What would happen if scientists were able to resurrect an extinct species that would reverse the order of natural selection? And what would happen if they produced a superior organism that destroyed the balance of our present ecosystem? And what would happen if they started "creating" people for particular tasks? They could design aggressive men to fight wars and passive women to breed children. Whole new social classes could be created, some genetically advanced, some genetically restricted. If we are to protect the rights of individuals and prevent evolutionary chaos, we must create a thoughtful public policy that protects us from our own scientific experiments.

1. How might Saloman go on to develop this paragraph into a full-length persuasive essay?
2. Saloman gives several examples of what he calls "unpredictable and violent results." How would you evaluate the persuasive value of the several generalizations that he gives as examples of such results?

ARGUMENT AND PERSUASION

Points to Remember

1. Remember that in order to argue well, you must understand your audience and know your purpose.
2. Understand the three principal kinds of appeal: emotional appeal, the appeal to feelings and senses; logical appeal, the appeal to intelligence and reason; and ethical appeal, the appeal from the character and competence of the author. The most effective arguments combine all three.
3. Construct an argument as a lawyer would construct a case to present to a jury; state your assertions and back them up with evidence and reason, appealing to your readers' intellect and feelings.
4. Always assume your audience is intelligent, although some members of it may be uninformed on a particular issue.
5. Avoid three common pitfalls: (a) don't overstate your claims; (b) be careful not to oversimplify complex issues; and (c) support your arguments with concrete evidence, not generalizations.

MARTIN LUTHER KING, JR.

Martin Luther King, Jr. (1929–1968) was born in Atlanta, Georgia, and was educated at Morehouse College, Crozer Theological Seminary, and Boston University. Ordained a Baptist minister in his father's church in 1947, King soon became involved in civil rights activities in the South. In 1957 he founded the Southern Christian Leadership Conference and established himself as America's most prominent spokesman for nonviolent racial integration. In 1963 he was named *Time* magazine's Man of the Year; in 1964 he was given the Nobel Peace Prize. In 1968 he was assassinated in Memphis, Tennessee. His writing includes *Letter from Birmingham Jail* (1963), *Why We Can't Wait* (1964), and *Where Do We Go from Here: Chaos or Community?* (1967). "I Have a Dream" is the famous speech King delivered at the Lincoln Memorial at the end of the "March on Washington" in 1963 to commemorate the one hundredth anniversary of the Emancipation Proclamation. King argues that realization of the dream of freedom for all American citizens is long overdue.

I Have a Dream

FIVE SCORE YEARS ago, a great American, in whose symbolic shadow we stand, signed the Emancipation Proclamation. This momentous decree came as a great beacon light of hope to millions of Negro slaves who had been seared in the flames of withering injustice. It came as a joyous daybreak to end the long night of captivity.

But one hundred years later, we must face the tragic fact

that the Negro is still not free. One hundred years later, the life of the Negro is still sadly crippled by the manacles of segregation and the chains of discrimination. One hundred years later, the Negro lives on a lonely island of poverty in the midst of a vast ocean of material prosperity. One hundred years later, the Negro is still languishing in the corners of American society and finds himself an exile in his own land. So we have come here today to dramatize an appalling condition.

In a sense we have come to our nation's Capitol to cash a   3 check. When the architects of our republic wrote the magnificent words of the Constitution and the Declaration of

---

There will be neither rest nor tranquility in America until the Negro is granted his citizenship rights.

Independence, they were signing a promissory note to which every American was to fall heir. This note was a promise that all men would be guaranteed the unalienable rights of life, liberty, and the pursuit of happiness.

It is obvious today that America has defaulted on this   4 promissory note insofar as her citizens of color are concerned. Instead of honoring this sacred obligation, America has given the Negro people a bad check; a check which has come back marked "insufficient funds." But we refuse to believe that the bank of justice is bankrupt. We refuse to believe that there are insufficient funds in the great vaults of opportunity of this nation. So we have come to cash this check—a check that will give us upon demand the riches of freedom and the security of justice. We have also come to this hallowed spot to remind America of the fierce urgency of *now*. This is no time to engage in the luxury of cooling off or to take the tranquilizing drug of gradualism. *Now* is the time to make real the promises of Democracy. *Now* is the time to rise from the dark and desolate valley of segregation to the sunlit path of racial justice. *Now* is the time to open the doors of opportunity to all of God's children. *Now* is the time to lift our nation from the quicksands of racial injustice to the solid rock of brotherhood.

It would be fatal for the nation to overlook the urgency of the moment and to underestimate the determination of the Negro. This sweltering summer of the Negro's legitimate discontent will not pass until there is an invigorating autumn of freedom and equality. 1963 is not an end, but a beginning. Those who hope that the Negro needed to blow off steam and will now be content will have a rude awakening if the nation returns to business as usual. There will be neither rest nor tranquility in America until the Negro is granted his citizenship rights. The whirlwinds of revolt will continue to shake the foundations of our nation until the bright day of justice emerges.

But there is something I must say to my people who stand on the warm threshold which leads into the palace of justice. In the process of gaining our rightful place we must not be guilty of wrongful deeds. Let us not seek to satisfy our thirst for freedom by drinking from the cup of bitterness and hatred. We must forever conduct our struggle on the high plane of dignity and discipline. We must not allow our creative protest to degenerate into physical violence. Again and again we must rise to the majestic heights of meeting physical force with soul force. The marvelous new militancy which has engulfed the Negro community must not lead us to a distrust of all white people, for many of our white brothers, as evidenced by their presence here today, have come to realize that their destiny is tied up with our destiny and their freedom is inextricably bound to our freedom. We cannot walk alone.

And as we walk, we must make the pledge that we shall march ahead. We cannot turn back. There are those who are asking the devotees of civil rights, "When will you be satisfied?" We can never be satisfied as long as the Negro is the victim of the unspeakable horrors of police brutality. We can never be satisfied as long as our bodies, heavy with the fatigue of travel, cannot gain lodging in the motels of the highways and the hotels of the cities. We cannot be satisfied as long as the Negro's basic mobility is from a smaller ghetto to a larger one. We can never be satisfied as long as a Negro in Mississippi cannot vote and a Negro in New York believes he has nothing for which to vote. No, no, we are not satisfied, and we will not be satisfied until justice rolls down like waters and righteousness like a mighty stream.

I am not unmindful that some of you have come here out   8
of great trials and tribulations. Some of you have come fresh from narrow jail cells. Some of you have come from areas where your quest for freedom left you battered by the storms of persecution and staggered by the winds of police brutality. You have been the veterans of creative suffering. Continue to work with the faith that unearned suffering is redemptive.

Go back to Mississippi, go back to Alabama, go back to   9
South Carolina, go back to Georgia, go back to Louisiana, go back to the slums and ghettoes of our northern cities, knowing that somehow this situation can and will be changed. Let us not wallow in the valley of despair.

I say to you today, my friends, that in spite of the difficul-   10
ties and frustrations of the moment I still have a dream. It is a dream deeply rooted in the American dream.

I have a dream that one day this nation will rise up and   11
live out the true meaning of its creed: "We hold these truths to be self-evident; that all men are created equal."

I have a dream that one day on the red hills of Georgia   12
the sons of former slaves and the sons of former slaveowners will be able to sit down together at the table of brotherhood.

I have a dream that the state of Mississippi, a desert state   13
sweltering with the heat of injustice and oppression, will be transformed into an oasis of freedom and justice.

I have a dream that my four little children will one day live   14
in a nation where they will not be judged by the color of their skin but by the content of their character.

I have a dream today.   15

I have a dream that the state of Alabama, whose governor's   16 lips are presently dripping with the words of interposition and nullification, will be transformed into a situation where little black boys and black girls will be able to join hands with little white boys and white girls and walk together as sisters and brothers.

I have a dream today.   17

I have a dream that one day every valley shall be exalted,   18
every hill and mountain shall be made low, the rough places will be made plain, and the crooked places will be made straight, and the glory of the Lord shall be revealed, and all flesh shall see it together.

This is our hope. This is the faith with which I return to   19
the South. With this faith we will be able to hew out of the mountain of despair a stone of hope. With this faith we will be able to transform the jangling discords of our nation into a beautiful symphony of brotherhood. With this faith we will be able to work together, to pray together, to struggle together, to go to jail together, to stand up for freedom together, knowing that we will be free one day.

This will be the day when all of God's children will be able   20
to sing with new meaning.

> *My country, 'tis of thee*
> *Sweet land of liberty,*
>   *Of thee I sing:*
> *Land where my fathers died,*
> *Land of the pilgrims' pride,*
> *From every mountainside*
>   *Let freedom ring.*

And if America is to be a great nation this must become   21
true. So let freedom ring from the prodigious hilltops of New Hampshire. Let freedom ring from the mighty mountains of New York. Let freedom ring from the heightening Alleghenies of Pennsylvania!

Let freedom ring from the snowcapped Rockies of   22
Colorado!

Let freedom ring from the curvaceous peaks of California! 23

But not only that; let freedom ring from Stone Mountain 24
of Georgia!

Let freedom ring from Lookout Mountain of Tennessee! 25

Let freedom ring from every hill and molehill of Missis- 26
sippi. From every mountainside, let freedom ring.

When we let freedom ring, when we let it ring from every 27
village and every hamlet, from every state and every city, we
will be able to speed up that day when all of God's children,
black men and white men, Jews and Gentiles, Protestants and
Catholics, will be able to join hands and sing in the words of
the old Negro spiritual, "Free at last! free at last! thank God
almighty, we are free at last!"

For Study and Discussion

QUESTIONS FOR RESPONSE

1. What experiences of injustice have you had (or perhaps witnessed,
   read about, or seen in a movie) that help you to identify with
   King's dreams and feel the force of his speech?
2. What did you already know about the life of King and of his place
   in modern U.S. history that prepared you for reading "I Have a
   Dream"? How well did the speech live up to what you expected
   of it?

QUESTIONS ABOUT PURPOSE

1. King has at least two strong messages. One message is local and
   immediate; the other one is national and long-range. How would
   you summarize those two messages?
2. How does King use his speech to reinforce his belief in nonvio-
   lence as the appropriate tool in the struggle for civil rights?

QUESTIONS ABOUT AUDIENCE

1. King gave this speech to a huge live audience that had come to
   Washington for a march for freedom and civil rights. How much

larger is the national audience he is addressing, and why is that audience also important?
2. This speech is one of the most widely anthologized of modern speeches. What audiences does it continue to appeal to and why?

QUESTIONS ABOUT STRATEGIES

1. How does King draw on metaphor to engage his listeners' feelings of injustice and give them hope for a new day? What are some of the most powerful metaphors?
2. In what way do King's talents as a minister serve his purposes in the speech? What African-American leader today do you think most resembles King in style and in mission?

QUESTIONS FOR DISCUSSION

1. If King were alive today, more than thirty years after this speech, how much of his dream do you think he would feel has come true? Look particularly at the visions he speaks of in paragraph 7 and paragraphs 11 through 16.
2. What elements in the speech reveal those qualities that contributed to King's power as a major civil rights leader, effective with whites as well as with blacks?

Eric Liu was born in Poughkeepsie, New York, in
1968, and was educated at Yale University. He
worked as a legislative aide for Senator David
Boren of Oklahoma and then as a speechwriter for
Secretary of State Warren Christopher and President Bill Clinton. He is currently the publisher
and editor of *The Next Progressive,* a journal of
opinion, and the editor of *NEXT: Young American Writers on the New Generation* (1994). In "A
Chinaman's Chance: Reflections on the American
Dream," reprinted from *NEXT,* Liu argues that
the American Dream is more about seizing opportunity than about claiming prosperity.

A Chinaman's Chance:
Reflections on the American
Dream

A LOT OF people my age seem to think that the American   1
Dream is dead. I think they're dead wrong.

Or at least only partly right. It is true that for those of us   2
in our twenties and early thirties, job opportunities are scarce.
There looms a real threat that we will be the first American
generation to have a lower standard of living than our parents.

But what is it that we mean when we invoke the American   3
Dream?

In the past, the American Dream was something that held   4
people of all races, religions, and identities together. As James
Comer has written, it represented a shared aspiration among
all Americans—black, white, or any other color—"to provide
well for themselves and their families as valued members of a

democratic society." Now, all too often, it seems the American Dream means merely some guarantee of affluence, a birthright of wealth.

At a basic level, of course, the American Dream is about [5] prosperity and the pursuit of material happiness. But to me, its meaning extends beyond such concerns. To me, the dream is not just about buying a bigger house than the one I grew up in or having shinier stuff now than I had as a kid. It also represents a sense of opportunity that binds generations together in commitment, so that the young inherit not only property but also perseverance, not only money but also a

---

*I want to prove that a Chinaman's chance
is as good as anyone else's.*

---

mission to make good on the strivings of their parents and grandparents.

The poet Robert Browning once wrote that "a man's reach [6] must exceed his grasp—else what's a heaven for?" So it is in America. Every generation will strive, and often fail. Every generation will reach for success, and often miss the mark. But Americans rely as much on the next generation as on the next life to prove that such struggles and frustrations are not in vain. There may be temporary setbacks, cutbacks, recessions, depressions. But this is a nation of second chances. So long as there are young Americans who do not take what they have—or what they can do—for granted, progress is always possible.

My conception of the American Dream does not take [7] progress for granted. But it does demand the *opportunity* to achieve progress—and values the opportunity as much as the achievement. I come at this question as the son of immigrants. I see just as clearly as anyone else the cracks in the idealist vision of fulfillment for all. But because my parents came here with virtually nothing, because they did build something, I see the enormous potential inherent in the ideal.

I happen still to believe in our national creed: freedom and   8
opportunity, and our common responsibility to uphold them.
This creed is what makes America unique. More than any
demographic statistic or economic indicator, it animates the
American Dream. It infuses our mundane struggles—to plan
a career, do good work, get ahead—with purpose and possibility. It makes America the only country that could produce
heroes like Colin Powell—heroes who rise from nothing,
who overcome the odds.

I think of the sacrifices made by my own parents. I appre-   9
ciate the hardship of the long road traveled by my father—
one of whose first jobs in America was painting the yellow
line down a South Dakota interstate—and by my mother—
whose first job here was filing pay stubs for a New York
restaurant. From such beginnings, they were able to build a
comfortable life and provide me with a breadth of resources—through arts, travel, and an Ivy League education.
It was an unspoken obligation for them to do so.

I think of my boss in my first job after college, on Capitol   10
Hill. George is a smart, feisty, cigar-chomping, take-no-shit
Greek-American. He is about fifteen years older than I, has
different interests, a very different personality. But like me,
he is the son of immigrants, and he would joke with me that
the Greek-Chinese mafia was going to take over one day. He
was only half joking. We'd worked harder, our parents doubly
harder, than almost anyone else we knew. To people like
George, talk of the withering of the American Dream seems
foreign.

It's undeniable that principles like freedom and opportu-   11
nity, no matter how dearly held, are not enough. They can
inspire a multiracial March on Washington, but they can not
bring black salaries in alignment with white salaries. They can
draw wave after wave of immigrants here, but they can not
provide them the means to get out of our ghettos and barrios
and Chinatowns. They are not sufficient for fulfillment of the
American Dream.

But they are necessary. They are vital. And not just to the 12
children of immigrants. These ideals form the durable thread
that weaves us all in union. Put another way, they are one of
the few things that keep America from disintegrating into a
loose confederation of zip codes and walled-in communities.

What alarms me is how many people my age look at our 13
nation's ideals with a rising sense of irony. What good is such
a creed if you are working for hourly wages in a dead-end
job? What value do such platitudes have if you live in an urban
war zone? When the only apparent link between homeboys
and housepainters and bike messengers and investment bankers is pop culture—MTV, the NBA, movies, dance music—
then the social fabric is flimsy indeed.

My generation has come of age at a time when the country 14
is fighting off bouts of defeatism and self-doubt, at a time
when racism and social inequities seem not only persistent
but intractable. At a time like this, the retreat to one's own
kind is seen by more and more of my peers as an advance.
And that retreat has given rise again to the notion that there
are essential and irreconcilable differences among the races—
a notion that was supposed to have disappeared from American discourse by the time my peers and I were born in the
sixties.

Not long ago, for instance, my sister called me a "banana." 15

I was needling her about her passion for rap and hip-hop 16
music. Every time I saw her, it seemed, she was jumping and
twisting to Arrested Development or Chubb Rock or some
other funky group. She joked that despite being the daughter
of Chinese immigrants, she was indeed "black at heart." And
then she added, lightheartedly, "You, on the other hand—
well, you're basically a banana." Yellow on the outside, but
white inside.

I protested, denied her charge vehemently. But it was too 17
late. She was back to dancing. And I stood accused.

Ever since then, I have wondered what it means to be 18
black, or white, or Asian "at heart"—particularly for my
generation. Growing up, when other kids would ask whether
I was Chinese or Korean or Japanese, I would reply, a little

petulantly, "American." Assimilation can still be a sensitive subject. I recall reading about a Korean-born Congressman who had gone out of his way to say that Asian-Americans should expect nothing special from him. He added that he was taking speech lessons "to get rid of this accent." I winced at his palpable self-hate. But then it hit me: Is this how my sister sees me?

There is no doubt that minorities like me can draw strength from our communities. But in today's environment, anything other than ostentatious tribal fealty is taken in some communities as a sign of moral weakness, a disappointing dilution of character. In times that demand ever-clearer thinking, it has become too easy for people to shut off their brains: "It's a black/Asian/Latino/white thing," says the variable T-shirt. "You wouldn't understand." Increasingly, we don't.   19

The civil-rights triumphs of the sixties and the cultural revolutions that followed made it possible for minorities to celebrate our diverse heritages. I can appreciate that. But I know, too, that the sixties—or at least, my generation's grainy, hazy vision of the decade—also bequeathed to young Americans a legacy of near-pathological race consciousness.   20

Today's culture of entitlement—and of race entitlement in particular—tells us plenty about what we get if we are black or white or female or male or old or young.   21

It is silent, though, on some other important issues. For instance: What do we "get" for being American? And just as importantly, What do we owe? These are questions around which young people like myself must tread carefully, since talk of common interests, civic culture, responsibility, and integration sounds a little too "white" for some people. To the new segregationists, the "American Dream" is like the old myth of the "Melting Pot": an oppressive fiction, an opiate for the unhappy colored masses.   22

How have we allowed our thinking about race to become so twisted? The formal obstacles and the hateful opposition to civil rights have long faded into memory. By most external measures, life for minorities is better than it was a quarter century ago. It would seem that the opportunities for toler-   23

ance and cooperation are commonplace. Why, then, are so
many of my peers so cynical about our ability to get along
with one another?

The reasons are frustratingly ambiguous. I got a glimpse   24
of this when I was in college. It was late in my junior year,
and as the editor of a campus magazine, I was sitting on a
panel to discuss "The White Press at Yale: What Is to Be
Done?" The assembly hall was packed, a diverse and noisy
crowd. The air was heavy, nervously electric.

Why weren't there more stories about "minority issues" in   25
the Yale *Daily News*? Why weren't there more stories on
Africa in my magazine, the foreign affairs journal? How many
"editors of color" served on the boards of each of the major
publications? The questions were volleyed like artillery, one
round after another, punctuated only by the applause of an
audience spoiling for a fight. The questions were not at all
unfair. But it seemed that no one—not even those of us on
the panel who *were* people of color—could provide, in this
context, satisfactory answers.

Toward the end of the discussion, I made a brief appeal   26
for reason and moderation. And afterward, as students milled
around restlessly, I was attacked: for my narrowmindedness—
How dare you suggest that Yale is not a fundamentally preju-
diced place!—for my simplemindedness—Have you, too,
been co-opted?

And for my betrayal—Are you just white inside?   27

My eyes were opened that uncomfortably warm early sum-   28
mer evening. Not only to the cynical posturing and the com-
bustible opportunism of campus racial politics. But more
importantly, to the larger question of identity—my identity—
in America. Never mind that the aim of many of the loudest
critics was to generate headlines in the very publications they
denounced. In spite of themselves—against, it would seem,
their true intentions—they got me to think about who I am.

In our society today, and especially among people of my   29
generation, we are congealing into clots of narrow common-
ality. We stick with racial and religious comrades. This tribal
consciousness-raising can be empowering for some. But while

America was conceived in liberty—the liberty, for instance, to associate with whomever we like—it was never designed to be a mere collection of subcultures. We forget that there is in fact such a thing as a unique American identity that transcends our sundry tribes, sets, gangs, and cliques.

I have grappled, wittingly or not, with these questions of identity and allegiance all my life. When I was in my early teens, I would invite my buddies overnight to watch movies, play video games, and beat one another up. Before too long, my dad would come downstairs and start hamming it up—telling stories, asking gently nosy questions, making corny jokes, all with his distinct Chinese accent. I would stand back, quietly gauging everyone's reaction. Of course, the guys loved it. But I would feel uneasy.   30

What was then cause for discomfort is now a source of strength. Looking back on such episodes, I take pride in my father's accented English; I feel awe at his courage to laugh loudly in a language not really his own.   31

It was around the same time that I decided that continued attendance at the community Chinese school on Sundays was uncool. There was no fanfare; I simply stopped going. As a child, I'd been too blissfully unaware to think of Chinese school as anything more than a weekly chore, with an annual festival (dumplings and spring rolls, games and prizes). But by the time I was a peer-pressured adolescent, Chinese school seemed like a badge of the woefully unassimilated. I turned my back on it.   32

Even as I write these words now, it feels as though I am revealing a long-held secret. I am proud that my ancestors—scholars, soldiers, farmers—came from one of the world's great civilizations. I am proud that my grandfather served in the Chinese Air Force. I am proud to speak even my clumsy brand of Mandarin, and I feel blessed to be able to think idiomatically in Chinese, a language so much richer in nuance and subtle poetry than English.   33

Belatedly, I appreciate the good fortune I've had to be the son of immigrants. As a kid, I could play Thomas Jefferson in the bicentennial school play one week and the next week   34 play the poet Li Bai at the Chinese school festival. I could come home from an afternoon of teen slang at the mall and sit down to dinner for a rollicking conversation in our family's hybrid of Chinese and English. I understood, when I went over to visit friends, that my life was different. At the time, I just never fully appreciated how rich it was.

Yet I know that this pride in my heritage does not cross 35 into prejudice against others. What it reflects is pride in what my country represents. That became clear to me when I went through Marine Corps Officer Candidates' School. During the summers after my sophomore and junior years of college, I volunteered for OCS, a grueling boot camp for potential officers in the swamps and foothills of Quantico, Virginia.

And once I arrived—standing 5'4", 135 pounds, bespec- 36 tacled, a Chinese Ivy League Democrat—I was a target straight out of central casting. The wiry, raspy-voiced drill sergeant, though he was perhaps only an inch or two taller than I, called me "Little One" with as much venom as can be squeezed into such a moniker. He heaped verbal abuse on me, he laughed when I stumbled, he screamed when I hesitated. But he also never failed to remind me that just because I was a little shit didn't mean I shouldn't run farther, climb higher, think faster, hit harder than anyone else.

That was the funny thing about the Marine Corps. It is, 37 ostensibly, one of the most conservative institutions in the United States. And yet, for those twelve weeks, it represented the kind of color-blind equality of opportunity that the rest of society struggles to match. I did not feel uncomfortable at OCS to be of Chinese descent. Indeed, I drew strength from it. My platoon was a veritable cross section of America: forty young men of all backgrounds, all regions, all races, all levels of intelligence and ability, displaced from our lives (if only for a few weeks) with nowhere else to go.

Going down the list of names—Courtemanche, Dough- 38 erty, Grella, Hunt, Liu, Reeves, Schwarzman, and so on— brought to mind a line from a World War II documentary I once saw, which went something like this: The reason why it seemed during the war that America was as good as the rest of the world put together was that America *was* the rest of the world put together.

Ultimately, I decided that the Marines was not what I [39] wanted to do for four years and I did not accept the second lieutenant's commission. But I will never forget the day of the graduation parade: bright sunshine, brisk winds, the band playing Sousa as my company passed in review. As my mom and dad watched and photographed the parade from the rafters, I thought to myself: this is the American Dream in all its cheesy earnestness. I felt the thrill of truly being part of something larger and greater than myself.

I do know that American life is not all Sousa marches and [40] flag-waving. I know that those with reactionary agendas often find it convenient to cloak their motives in the language of Americanism. The "American Party" was the name of a major nativist organization in the nineteenth century. "America First" is the siren song of the isolationists who would with-draw this country from the world and expel the world from this country. I know that our national immigration laws were once designed explicitly to cut off the influx from Asia.

I also know that discrimination is real. I am reminded of [41] a gentle old man who, after Pearl Harbor, was stripped of his possessions without warning, taken from his home, and thrown into a Japanese internment camp. He survived, and by many measures has thrived, serving as a community leader and political activist. But I am reluctant to share with him my wide-eyed patriotism.

I know the bittersweet irony that my own father—a strong [42] and optimistic man—would sometimes feel when he was alive. When he came across a comically lost cause—if the Yankees were behind 14–0 in the ninth, or if Dukakis was down ten points in the polls with a week left—he would often joke that the doomed party had "a Chinaman's chance" of success. It was one of those insensitive idioms of a generation ago, and it must have lodged in his impressionable young mind when he first came to America. It spoke of a perceived stacked deck.

I know, too, that for many other immigrants, the dream [43] simply does not work out. Fae Myenne Ng, the author of

Bone, writes about how her father ventured here from China under a false identity and arrived at Angel Island, the detention center outside the "Gold Mountain" of San Francisco. He got out, he labored, he struggled, and he suffered "a bitter no-luck life" in America. There was no glory. For him, Ng suggests, the journey was not worth it.

But it is precisely because I know these things that I want   44 to prove that in the long run, over generations and across ethnicities, it *is* worth it. For the second-generation American, opportunity is obligation. I have seen and faced racism. I understand the dull pain of dreams deferred or unmet. But I believe still that there is so little stopping me from building the life that I want. I was given, through my parents' labors, the chance to bridge that gap between ideals and reality. Who am I to throw away that chance?

Plainly, I am subject to the criticism that I speak too much   45 from my own experience. Not everyone can relate to the second-generation American story. When I have spoken like this with some friends, the issue has been my perspective. *What you say is fine for you. But unless you grew up where I did, unless you've had people avoid you because of the color of your skin, don't talk to me about common dreams.*

But are we then to be paralyzed? Is respect for different   46 experiences supposed to obviate the possibility of shared aspirations? Does the diversity of life in America doom us to a fractured understanding of one another? The question is basic: Should the failure of this nation thus far to fulfill its stated ideals incapacitate its young people, or motivate us?

Our country was built on, and remains glued by, the idea   47 that everybody deserves a fair shot and that we must work together to guarantee that opportunity—the original American Dream. It was this idea, in some inchoate form, that drew every immigrant here. It was this idea, however sullied by slavery and racism, that motivated the civil-rights movement. To write this idea off—even when its execution is spotty—to let American life descend into squabbles among separatist tribes would not just be sad. It would be a total mishandling of a legacy, the squandering of a great historical inheritance.

Mine must not be the first generation of Americans to lose   48

America. Just as so many of our parents journeyed here to find their version of the American Dream, so must young Americans today journey across boundaries of race and class to rediscover one another. We are the first American generation to be born into an integrated society, and we are accustomed to more race mixing than any generation before us. We started open-minded, and it's not too late for us to stay that way.

Time is of the essence. For in our national political culture today, the watchwords seem to be *decline* and *end*. Apocalyptic visions and dark millennial predictions abound. The end of history. The end of progress. The end of equality. Even something as ostensibly positive as the end of the Cold War has a bittersweet tinge, because for the life of us, no one in America can get a handle on the big question, "What Next?" 49

For my generation, this fixation on endings is particularly enervating. One's twenties are supposed to be a time of widening horizons, of bright possibilities. Instead, America seems to have entered an era of limits. Whether it is the difficulty of finding jobs from some place other than a temp agency, or the mountains of debt that darken our future, the message to my peers is often that this nation's time has come and gone; let's bow out with grace and dignity. 50

A friend once observed that while the Chinese seek to adapt to nature and yield to circumstance, Americans seek to conquer both. She meant that as a criticism of America. But I interpreted her remark differently. I *do* believe that America is exceptional. And I believe it is up to my generation to revive that spirit, that sense that we do in fact have control over our own destiny—as individuals and as a nation. 51

If we are to reclaim a common destiny, we must also reach out to other generations for help. It was Franklin Roosevelt who said that while America can't always build the future for its youth, it can—and must—build its youth for the future. That commitment across generations is as central to the American Dream as any I have enunciated. We are linked, black and white, old and young, one and inseparable. 52

I know how my words sound. I am old enough to perceive 53

my own naïveté but young enough still to cherish it. I realize that I am coming of age just as the American Dream is showing its age. Yet I still have faith in this country's unique destiny—to create generation after generation of hyphenates like me, to channel this new blood, this resilience and energy into an ever more vibrant future for *all* Americans.

And I want to prove—for my sake, for my father's sake, and for my country's sake—that a Chinaman's chance is as good as anyone else's.   54

For Study and Discussion

QUESTIONS FOR RESPONSE

1. Do you endorse or discount Liu's argument? How do you think your family background and history affect your response?
2. How would you define the American Dream? To what extent do you think it has been or will be fulfilled for you?

QUESTIONS ABOUT PURPOSE

1. To what criticisms *about* his generation is Liu responding? To what criticisms *from* his generation is he responding?
2. What specific attitudes among young people does Liu challenge?

QUESTIONS ABOUT AUDIENCE

1. Liu wrote this essay for a 1994 book titled *NEXT: Young American Writers on the New Generation,* a book he conceived of and also edited. What kind of readers do you think he envisioned for the book? How do you think you fit into that group?
2. What do you think Liu's appeal might be to generations older than his? Why?

QUESTIONS ABOUT STRATEGIES

1. What is the impact of Liu's writing about his parents' experience?
2. Liu was once one of President Clinton's speechwriters. What

strategies does he use that he might have learned through that experience?

QUESTIONS FOR DISCUSSION

1. What evidence, if any, do you see that students are splitting into separate groups on your campus? What is your view of such splits? Why?
2. What factors in Liu's life and experiences do you think played a significant part in his success in college and beyond? How would those factors affect his outlook on life?

Judith Levine was born in Queens, New York, in 1952, and educated at the City College of the City University of New York and Columbia School of Journalism. An activist in the National Writers Union, she has published articles on sex and politics in magazines such as *Mother Jones* and *Village Voice.* Her books include *My Enemy, My Love: Man Hating and Ambivalence in Women's Lives* (1992) and *Harmful to Minors: How We Are Hurting Children by Protecting Them from Sex* (1999). In "I Surf, Therefore I Am," reprinted from the Internet magazine *Salon,* Levine argues that there are significant limits to the power of the Internet.

I Surf, Therefore I Am

O BVIOUSLY, I'M SOMEBODY who believes that personal computers are empowering tools," Bill Gates said after he bestowed a $200 million gift to America's public libraries so they could hook up to the Internet.

"People are entitled to disagree," Gates said. "But I would invite them to visit some of these libraries and see the impact on kids using this technology."

Well, I have seen the impact, and I disagree. Many of my students—undergraduate media and communications majors at a New York university—have access to the endless information bubbling through cyberspace, and *it is not* empowering.

Most of the data my students Net is like trash fish—and it is hard for them to tell a dead one-legged crab from a healthy sea bass. Scant on world knowledge and critical thinking skills, they are ill-equipped to interpret or judge the so-called facts, which they insert into their papers confidently but in no discernible order.

Their writing often "clicks" from info-bit to info-bit, their arguments free of that gluey, old-fashioned encumbrance—the transitional sentence. When I try to help them corral their impressions into coherent stories, I keep hearing the same complaint: "I can't concentrate." I've diagnosed this phenomenon as epidemic attention deficit disorder. And I can't help but trace its etiology, at least in part, to the promiscuous pointing and clicking that has come to stand in for intellectual inquiry.

These students surf; therefore, they do not read. They do not read scholarly articles—which can be trusted because they

---

On the Internet, nobody knows if any particular "fact" is a dog.

---

are juried or challenged because they are footnoted. They do not read books—which tell stories and sustain arguments by placing idea and metaphor one on top of the other, so as to hold weight, like a stone wall. Even the journalism students read few magazines and even fewer newspapers, which are edited by people with recognizable and sometimes even admitted cultural and political biases and checked by fact-checkers using other edited sources.

On the Net, nobody knows if any particular "fact" is a dog. One student handed in a paper about tobacco companies' liability for smokers' health, which she had gleaned almost entirely from the Web pages of the Tobacco Institute. Did she know what the Tobacco Institute is? Apparently not, because she had done her research on the Net, and was deprived of the modifying clause, "a research organization supported by the tobacco industry," obligatory in any edited news article.

Another young woman, writing about teen pregnancy, 8
used data generated by the Family Research Council, which,
along with other right-wing Christian think tanks, dominates
the links on many subjects related to family and sexuality and
offers a decidedly one-sided view.

A teacher at another school told me one of her students 9
had written a paper quoting a person who had a name but
no identifying characteristics. "Who's this?" the professor
asked. "Someone with a Web page," the young man said.

If there is no context on the Net, neither is there history. 10
My friend who teaches biology told me her students propose
research that was completed, and often discredited, 50 years
ago. "They go online," she said, "where nothing has been
indexed before 1980."

A San Francisco librarian interviewed on National Public 11
Radio worried that, space and resources strained as they are,
more computers will inevitably mean fewer books. Another
commentator on the Gates gift suggested that the computers
would not be very valuable without commensurate human
resources—that is, trained workers to help people use them.

At New York's gleaming new Science, Industry, & Busi- 12
ness Library (SIBL), you can sit in an ergonomically correct
chair at one of several hundred lovely color computer terminals and call up, among hundreds of other databases, the
powerful journalistic and legal service Nexis/Lexis. But since
Nexis/Lexis is in great demand, you have about 45 minutes
at the screen, half of which the inexperienced user will blow
figuring out the system, because there is only one harassed
staff person to assist all the computer-users. Then you'll learn
that the library cannot afford the stratospheric fees for downloading the articles. So most users, I imagine, will manage to
copy out quotes from a couple of articles before relinquishing
the seat to the next person waiting for the cyber-kiosk.

Unlike a paper or microfilm version of the same pieces, 13
which could be photocopied or copied at leisure onto a pad
or laptop, the zillion articles available on the library's
Nexis/Lexis are more or less unavailable—that is, to no avail.
Useless.

Technology may empower, but how and to what end will   14
that power be used? What else is necessary to use it well and
wisely? I'd suggest, for a start, reading books—literature and
history, poetry and politics—and listening to people who
know what they're talking about. Otherwise, the brains of
those kids in Gates' libraries will be glutted with "information" but bereft of ideas, rich in tools but clueless about what
to build or how to build it. Like the search engines that
retrieve more than 100,000 links or none at all, they will be
awkward at discerning meaning, or discerning at all.

For Study and Discussion

QUESTIONS FOR RESPONSE

1. If you use the Internet frequently, how do your experiences with
   its resources compare with Levine's evaluation? What specific
   successes or problems have you had?
2. In what ways is the Internet important in your life? In what ways
   do you expect to make use of it in the future?

QUESTIONS ABOUT PURPOSE

1. In what ways does Levine think the Internet must be supplemented if it is to become reliable and valuable to students?
2. What attitudes and publicity about the Internet and its potential
   is Levine trying to counteract in her article?

QUESTIONS ABOUT AUDIENCE

1. Levine's article was published on line through an Internet magazine called *Salon*. What experiences with such on-line journals
   do you think those reading her article on the Net might have
   had that would affect their reaction to the article?
2. Teachers form an important part of the audience Levine wants
   to reach with this essay. What experiences are they likely to have
   had with students using the Internet that would make them a
   good audience for this piece?

QUESTIONS ABOUT STRATEGIES

1. What specific examples does Levine bring in to support her claims? In your experience, how widespread are the problems these examples illustrate? What similar problems have you had?
2. What advantage does Levine gain by publishing the article on the Internet?

QUESTIONS FOR DISCUSSION

1. What groups do you think are getting the most benefits from the Internet? In what ways?
2. What issues about access to the Internet are you aware of right now? What problems about access may arise in the future? What are the implications of access to the Net being difficult for certain groups?

ESTHER DYSON

Esther Dyson was born in 1951 in Zurich, Switzerland, and educated at Harvard University. She has worked as a reporter and columnist for *Forbes* magazine, vice president of New Court Securities, and president of EDventure Holdings. She also is the publisher and editor of *Computer Industry Daily* and *Release 1.0,* and the moderator of an annual Personal Computer Forum. Her recent book, *Release 2.0: A Design for Living in the Digital Age,* outlines the profound changes that "the Net will bring to human *institutions.*" In "A Design for Living on the Internet," reprinted from *Release 2.0,* Dyson argues that people will have more opportunities for choice and creative action on the Internet.

A Design for Living on the Internet

MANY THINGS ARE familiar on the Net: the same people   1
with the same emotions and motivations, the same frailties. But the Net puts the same people in a new situation. In doing so, it makes everything different: power shifting away from the center toward individuals and small organizations, more fluidity and continuous change, increasingly irrelevant national boundaries. The markets for attention and information are almost as friction-free as those for money.

In each sphere of life on the Net, the opportunities for   2
individuals (and the potential for conflicts between individuals exercising their rights) are enhanced. In work and education and your personal life, you have greater choice—and a greater role not just in choosing but in shaping the organi-

zations and people with whom you deal. You can set your own rules of engagement. In the sphere of intellectual property, you can be not just a consumer but also a creator: an ongoing participant in commercial and noncommercial intellectual processes. You can set your own standards for content, for privacy, for anonymity, for security.

On the Net politics and the general welfare is a part of life. ₃ The choices you make affect others, because this new world depends on its citizens rather than its history. On the Net, your choices and actions in living will have an impact on the texture of life for the people around you on the Net, an impact potentially far broader than in the terrestrial world. In

---

The Internet provides an exceptional opportunity for you to find what you want—whether it's a product, a group of friends, or a merchant who respects your privacy.

---

the terrestrial world, the choices you make in voting or buying products are mostly limited to options offered by established institutions, and the results are summed up centrally. On the Net, you can range more broadly, and your behavior will help create the tone of the communities you live in. Your choices for disclosure and security can foster an atmosphere of trust and openness, as will your demands for the same from others.

Even in the terrestrial world, "government" means more ₄ than legislation and funding and administration of programs. Governments can also set a moral tone and influence what we consider proper behavior. Unfortunately, they don't always do it right. But the kind of governance I'm talking about on the Net (through agencies that are truly chosen and managed by citizens) does have a chance of getting it right, if *we* get it right. We have to do it for ourselves. Like businesses of the future, the governing bodies of the Net will focus more on design of rules and their enforcement, and less on administration, regulation, and routine processes.

You could read all this and say, "All this idealistic stuff will never happen. People are passive. Lots of them can't even read. Every time I open a newspaper I read about another vicious crime, venal politician, or unscrupulous businessman. The rich are greedy and the poor are lazy."   5

It's true that every time I read a newspaper, I wonder about my hopes for the new good life on the Net. But in the end, this is not a book of description; it's prescription. It's what you *can* do . . . That's why I'm addressing this book to individuals, not to governments or businesses (although it *is* also addressed to individuals in government and business). Whatever sphere you operate in, you have a broader capability than ever before to change it for the good.   6

As you go out and explore the Net, you have to trust yourself and your own common sense. In a decentralized world, you no longer can or should leave all the decisions up to someone else. Precisely because the Net has and needs fewer broad rules than most environments, it depends more on the good sense and participation of each of its citizens. Broadly speaking, the real world gets its flavor from institutions; the Net gets its flavor from its citizens.   7

The one thing required of you is to make use of the Net's powers. They are like a Bible on a shelf or an exercise machine in a den—not worth much unless you do something with them. The Net is a tool *for* some purpose, whether that's getting ahead at work or avoiding work to do something more amusing or fulfilling. You now have more freedom and more responsibilities in everything from how you handle (or change) your job, to how you interact with the government, to how you establish a new friendship.   8

On the Net, there's a profusion of choices—content, places, shopping environments, discussion groups. Most things are free. Even—especially—the pleasures. You may   9 complain that you're overwhelmed with choices. In the old days, life was simple. Not too many choices, and a structure you could easily complain about because you could never hope to win.

Now you've won, and the world is asking you to make some proposals. You could just leave all this opportunity alone and probably carve out a fairly pleasant life for yourself anyway. The Net will offer you wonderful opportunities as a consumer, and it will make your daily life easier.

But when you have choices, making no choices is itself a choice.

Indeed, the biggest opportunity of the Net is that it allows you to go beyond choosing and start creating. The Net is uniquely malleable: It lets you build communities, find ideas, share information, connect with other people.

Exactly what you do with all this is up to you. You have your own interests and capabilities. My hope is that what you do on the Net will change your offline life, too, by making you less willing to accept things the way they are and more sure of your ability to build a life to suit yourself and your family. The trick is to set your own priorities.

The point is not that everyone should do the same thing, but that everyone should contribute in his own way, for his own online communities. It's the very diversity of approaches that makes the Net, and life, so exciting and so rich. I would hate for us all to do good the same way.

Nonetheless, there are some underlying principles—design rules, if you will—that do hold true across a broad range of situations. Most of them have very little to do with the Net per se, although they have their own character on the Net. Basically, they foster involvement, disclosure, clarity, honesty, respect for yourself and others.

Like most design rules, they're general. The magic is in how you actually apply them. And like most rules, they can and should be broken on certain occasions. In fact, that's the first rule:

USE YOUR OWN
JUDGMENT

This rule applies off the Net, too, of course, but many new-   17
comers are tempted to defer to other people in a new environment. You should defer to their knowledge, yes, but you
can still make up your mind for yourself. As I've tried to show
in many ways, the technology really doesn't change most
relations between human beings or what's right and wrong.
The Net simply gives you greater ability to find a situation
you like or abandon one you don't.

The Net provides an exceptional opportunity for you to   18
find what you want—whether it's a product, a group of
friends, or a merchant who respects your privacy. If you're a
parent, you can control what your child sees or where she
goes to school. If you're looking for work, you can find an
employer you like and work you respect. Does your business
respect its customers? If not, move on. Remember that the
market doesn't run on money alone. It means you have
choice.

DISCLOSE YOURSELF

Let people know who you are and what you stand for. Explain   19
your biases and vested interests. Ask the same of the people
and organizations you deal with. Especially on the Net, clarity
is helpful. Remember how confusing things can be to someone without context. For example, don't assume that the
person you're dealing with knows who you are or what your
motivations are. Explain whether you're looking to do business or just trying to be helpful when you answer someone's
question. Let people know (politely) if you disagree with
them; they may have a good answer to your arguments.

And don't regard secret information as power. Hoarding   20
information and secrets doesn't really make you powerful; it
just leaves you vulnerable to exposure.

And, of course, don't let other people (even me) tell you   21
what to do.

DON'T GET INTO SILLY FIGHTS

If you forget this rule, the visibility you will have on the Net [22] is likely to remind you. (Too often, people get into ridiculous flame wars that are embarrassing to all who watch.) In general, it is easier to walk away from conflicts on the Net than it may be in real life. You can refuse to read someone's mail and refuse to let him provoke you once you've left an argument. Just don't let public postings lure you back in.

If something or someone is holding you back or annoying [23] you, you don't need to take on the system as a whole. In many cases, you can bypass the offending person or entity. You don't need to overcome it; maybe, you can compete with it.

ASK QUESTIONS

There's no other good way to learn. Being a reporter taught [24] me how much you can find out by asking questions and listening to the answers, even if you thought you already knew the subject. You have to be humble and willing to appear stupid. It's amazing how willing people are to tell you things if you're only ready to listen. I built my career on it. (Just don't ask the same question twice!) The Net is a great place to ask questions, because you are more likely to be able to find someone who knows the answer.

BE A PRODUCER

Being a consumer is fine; it helps the economy, and it lets [25] you get the products you want. But don't let the real promise of the Net pass you by: to be a producer without all the overhead that used to accompany producing—factories, printing presses, broadcast stations, government infrastructure. On the Net, you have the choice of all the things that are offered—and the choice to make and offer your own.

For example, you can design your own Web page. For a [26]

bigger challenge, you can design a whole community. Look at any of the 79,000 (at last count) online discussion forums. Most of them were designed by individuals with something on their minds.

BE GENEROUS

My aunt Alice (really!) has been important in my life, offering   27
support and counsel and unconditional love. I have never really paid her back; there's no way to. But whenever some young woman asks me for a favor, I think of the real Alice, who lives in Winchester, England. So when someone does you a truly generous favor, don't worry about paying them back (if they want to be paid back, they weren't being generous). Do a favor to someone else. When I help people, it's often in honor of my aunt.

This rule, too, is not Net-specific. But the Net often makes   28
it easier to be generous and do small but important favors— anything from forwarding a résumé from one friend to another, to sending an e-mail of congratulations to a friend, to posting a message asking if anyone could use the old sofa you no longer need.

Of course, true generosity is when it *does* cost you some-   29
thing. Give your time. Give your attention. It's the only thing you have to give that's uniquely yours.

HAVE A SENSE OF HUMOR

Enough of "In cyberspace no one knows you're a dog"   30
already! The Net is the all-time best medium for the dissemination of jokes, and I find new ones every day. The Net will be a dull and sterile place if we can't also have a little fun. But a sense of humor is more than just laughing at jokes. It means not taking life too seriously. Laugh at problems even as you try to fix them. A perfect world would be boring; an imperfect world offers opportunities for humor.

ALWAYS MAKE NEW MISTAKES!

This is my all-time favorite rule for living. I like it so much 31
that I use it as my sig file—the little quote that gets inserted
along with my address and other coordinates at the end of
each of my e-mails. I still have new mistakes to make. The
challenge is not to avoid mistakes, but to learn from them.
And then to go forward and make new ones and learn again.
There's no shame in making new mistakes if you acknowledge
them and benefit from them.

NOW DESIGN YOUR OWN

Please feel free to borrow these rules. Or improve on them 32
for yourself. Good luck!

For Study and Discussion

QUESTIONS FOR RESPONSE

1. In what ways does Dyson's expansive and optimistic visions of
   "life on the Net" appeal to you? What, if anything, do you find
   unappealing about the vision?
2. What kind of persona or image of herself does Dyson project in
   this selection? How do you think you would respond to her if
   you were to meet her or hear her speak?

QUESTIONS ABOUT PURPOSE

1. Dyson is in the computer business and the publisher of a magazine for the computer industry. What does she have to gain by
   persuading people to become active participants in the Internet
   culture?
2. What perceptions and reservations about the Internet and people
   who are heavily involved in it do you think Dyson is trying to
   overcome in this essay?

QUESTIONS ABOUT AUDIENCE

1. Reread the headnote that gives you information about Dyson, then reflect that this selection is the final chapter from her book, *Release 2.0: A Design for Living in the Digital Age.* Who do you envision as the audience for such a book? What feelings are such readers likely to have toward computer users and the information age?

2. What do you think readers who have begun to use the Internet only recently would want to learn from someone like Dyson? How helpful would they find this article?

QUESTIONS ABOUT STRATEGIES

1. What is the effect of Dyson's addressing her reader as "you?" Why do you think she chooses this direct and personal pronoun?

2. How would you describe the emotional tone of Dyson's selection? What effect does that tone have on you as a reader?

QUESTIONS FOR DISCUSSION

1. How useful do you find Dyson's eight rules for living on the Net? In what ways might you put some of them into effect?

2. What proportion of your close community of friends and/or workers use the Internet extensively? In what ways do you think the Net affects your life or their lives? How would you feel about losing access to the Internet?

Rosemary L. Bray was born in Chicago in 1955 and was educated at Yale University. She has worked as an editor for the *Wall Street Journal, Essence, Ms.,* and the *New York Times Book Review.* She has contributed articles to magazines such as *Redbook, Savvy,* and *Glamour* and has written a children's biography, *Martin Luther King* (1995), and a memoir, *Unafraid of the Dark* (1998). In "So How Did I Get Here?," first printed in the *New York Times Magazine* in 1993, Bray uses her own experiences to show how the "welfare question" has become "the race question and the woman question in disguise."

So How Did I Get Here?

Growing up on welfare was a story I had planned to tell a long time from now, when I had children of my own. My childhood on Aid to Families with Dependent Children (A.F.D.C.) was going to be one of those stories I would tell my kids about the bad old days, an urban legend equivalent to Abe Lincoln studying by firelight. But I know now I cannot wait, because in spite of a wealth of evidence about the true nature of welfare and poverty in America, the debate has turned ugly, vicious and racist. The "welfare question" has become the race question and the woman question in disguise, and so far the answers bode well for no one.

In both blunt and coded terms, comfortable Americans more and more often bemoan the waste of their tax money on lazy black women with a love of copulation, a horror of birth control and a lack of interest in marriage. Were it not for the experiences of half my life, were I not black and female and of a certain age, perhaps I would be like so many people who blindly accept the lies and distortions, half-truths and wrongheaded notions about welfare. But for better or worse, I do know better. I know more than I want to know about being poor. I know that the welfare system is designed to be inadequate, to leave its constituents on the edge of survival. I know because I've been there.

And finally, I know that perhaps even more dependent on   3 welfare than its recipients are the large number of Americans who would rather accept this patchwork of economic horrors than fully address the real needs of real people.

My mother came to Chicago in 1947 with a fourth-grade   4

The rage I feel about the welfare debate comes from listening to a host of lies, distortions, and exaggerations.

---

education, cut short by working in the Mississippi fields. She pressed shirts in a laundry for a while and later waited tables in a restaurant, where she met my father. Mercurial and independent, with a sixth-grade education, my Arkansas-born father worked at whatever came to hand. He owned a lunch wagon for a time and prepared food for hours in our kitchen on the nights before he took the wagon out. Sometimes he hauled junk and sold it in the open-air markets of Maxwell Street on Sunday mornings. Eight years after they met—seven years after they married—I was born. My father made her quit her job; her work, he told her, was taking care of me. By the time I was 4, I had a sister, a brother and another brother on the way. My parents, like most other American couples of the 1950's, had their own American dream—a husband who worked, a wife who stayed home, a family of smiling children. But as was true for so many African-American couples, their American dream was an illusion.

The house on the corner of Berkeley Avenue and 45th   5

Street is long gone. The other houses still stand, but today
the neighborhood is an emptier, bleaker place. When we
moved there, it was a street of old limestones with beveled
glass windows, all falling into vague disrepair. Home was a
four-room apartment on the first floor, in what must have
been the public rooms of a formerly grand house. The rent
was $110 a month. All of us kids slept in the big front room.
Because I was the oldest, I had a bed of my own, near a big
plate-glass window.

My mother and father had been married for several years   6
before she realized he was a gambler who would never stay
away from the track. By the time we moved to Berkeley
Avenue, Daddy was spending more time gambling, and
bringing home less and less money and more and more anger.
Mama's simplest requests were met with rage. They fought
once for hours when she asked for money to buy a tube of
lipstick. It didn't help that I always seemed to need a doctor.
I had allergies and bronchitis so severe that I nearly died one
Sunday after church when I was about 3.

It was around this time that my mother decided to sign   7
up for A.F.D.C. She explained to the caseworker that Daddy
wasn't home much, and when he was he didn't have any
money. Daddy was furious; Mama was adamant. "There were
times when we hardly had a loaf of bread in here," she told
me years later. "It was close. I wasn't going to let you all go
hungry."

Going on welfare closed a door between my parents that   8
never reopened. She joined the ranks of unskilled women
who were forced to turn to the state for the security their
men could not provide. In the sterile relationship between
herself and the State of Illinois, Mama found an autonomy
denied her by my father. It was she who could decide, at last,
some part of her own fate and ours. A.F.D.C. relegated
marginally productive men like my father to the ranks of
failed patriarchs who no longer controlled the destiny of their
families. Like so many of his peers, he could no longer afford
the luxury of a woman who did as she was told because her
economic life depended on it. Daddy became one of the

shadow men who walked out back doors as caseworkers came in through the front. Why did he acquiesce? For all his anger, for all his frightening brutality, he loved us, so much that he swallowed his pride and periodically ceased to exist so that we might survive.

In 1960, the year my mother went on public aid, the poverty threshold for a family of five in the United States was $3,560 and the monthly payment to a family of five from the State of Illinois was $182.56, a total of $2,190.72 a year. Once the $110 rent was paid, Mama was left with $72.56 a month to take care of all the other expenses. By any standard, we were poor. All our lives were proscribed by the narrow line between not quite and just enough.

What did it take to live?

It took the kindness of friends as well as strangers, the charity of churches, low expectations, deprivation and patience. I can't begin to count the hours spent in long lines, long waits, long walks in pursuit of basic things. A visit to a local clinic (one housing doctors, a dentist and pharmacy in an incredibly crowded series of rooms) invariably took the better part of a day; I never saw the same doctor twice.

It took, as well, a turning of our collective backs on the letter of a law that required reporting even a small and important miracle like a present of $5. All families have their secrets, but I remember the weight of an extra burden. In a world where caseworkers were empowered to probe into every nook and cranny of our lives, silence became defense. Even now, there are things I will not publicly discuss because I cannot shake the fear that we might be hounded by the state, eager to prosecute us for the crime of survival.

All my memories of our years on A.F.D.C. are seasoned with unease. It's painful to remember how much every penny counted, how even a gap of 25 cents could make a difference in any given week. Few people understand how precarious life is from welfare check to welfare check, how the word "extra" has no meaning. Late mail, a bureaucratic mix-up . . . and a carefully planned method of survival lies in tatters.

What made our lives work as well as they did was my

mother's genius at making do—worn into her by a childhood of rural poverty—along with her vivid imagination. She worked at home endlessly, shopped ruthlessly, bargained, cajoled, charmed. Her food store of choice was the one that stocked pork and beans, creamed corn, sardines, Vienna sausages and potted meat all at 10 cents a can. Clothing was the stuff of rummage sales, trips to Goodwill and bargain basements, where thin cotton and polyester reigned supreme. Our shoes came from a discount store that sold two pairs for $5.

It was an uphill climb, but there was no time for reflection; 15 we were too busy with our everyday lives. Yet I remember how much it pained me to know that Mama, who recruited a neighbor to help her teach me how to read when I was 3, found herself left behind by her eldest daughter, then by each of us in turn. Her biggest worry was that we would grow up uneducated, so Mama enrolled us in parochial school.

When one caseworker angrily questioned how she could 16 afford to send four children to St. Ambrose School, my mother, who emphatically declared "My kids need an education," told her it was none of her business. (In fact, the school had a volume discount of sorts; the price of tuition dropped with each child you sent. I still don't know quite how she managed it.) She organized our lives around church and school, including Mass every morning at 7:45. My brother was an altar boy; I laid out the vestments each afternoon for the next day's Mass. She volunteered as a chaperone for every class trip, sat with us as we did homework she did not understand herself. She and my father reminded us again and again and again that every book, every test, every page of homework was in fact a ticket out and away from the life we lived.

My life on welfare ended on June 4, 1976—a month after 17 my 21st birthday, two weeks after I graduated from Yale. My father, eaten up with cancer and rage, lived just long enough to know the oldest two of us had graduated from college and were on our own. Before the decade ended, all of us had left the welfare rolls. The eldest of my brothers worked at the post office, assumed support of my mother (who also went to work, as a companion to an elderly woman) and earned his master's degree at night. My sister married and got a job at a bank. My baby brother parked cars and found a wife. Mama's biggest job was done at last; the investment made in our lives by the State of Illinois had come to fruition. Five people on welfare for 18 years had become five working, taxpaying adults. Three of us went to college, two of us finished; one of us has an advanced degree; all of us can take care of ourselves.

Ours was a best-case phenomenon, based on the synergy of church and state, the government and the private sector and the thousand points of light that we called friends and neighbors. But there was something more: What fueled our dreams and fired our belief that our lives could change for the better was the promise of the civil rights movement and the war on poverty—for millions of African-Americans the defining events of the 1960's. Caught up in the heady atmosphere of imminent change, our world was filled not only with issues and ideas but with amazing images of black people engaged in the struggle for long-denied rights and freedoms. We knew other people lived differently than we did, we knew we didn't have much, but we didn't mind, because we knew it wouldn't be long. My mother borrowed a phrase I had read to her once from Dick Gregory's autobiography: Not poor, just broke. She would repeat it often, as often as she sang hymns in the kitchen. She loved to sing a spiritual Mahalia Jackson had made famous: "Move On Up a Little Higher." Like so many others, Mama was singing about earth as well as heaven. 18

These are the things I remember every time I read another article outlining America's welfare crisis. The rage I feel about the welfare debate comes from listening to a host of lies, distortions and exaggerations—and taking them personally. 19

I am no fool. I know of few women—on welfare or off— with my mother's grace and courage and stamina. I know not all women on welfare are cut from the same cloth. Some are lazy; some are ground down. Some are too young; many are without husbands. A few have made welfare fraud a lucrative 20 career; a great many more have pushed the rules on outside income to their very limits.

I also know that none of these things justify our making welfare a test of character and worthiness, rather than an acknowledgment of need. Near-sainthood should not be a requirement for financial and medical assistance.

But all manner of sociologists and policy gurus continue to equate issues that simply aren't equivalent—welfare, race, rates of poverty, crime, marriage and childbirth—and to reach conclusions that serve to demonize the poor. More than one social arbiter would have us believe that we have all been mistaken for the last 30 years—that the efforts to relieve the most severe effects of poverty have not only failed but have served instead to increase and expand the ranks of the poor. In keeping women, children and men from starvation, we are told, we have also kept them from self-sufficiency. In our zeal to do good, we have undermined the work ethic, the family and thus, by association, the country itself.

So how did I get here?

Despite attempts to misconstrue and discredit the social programs and policies that changed—even saved—my life, certain facts remain. Poverty was reduced by 39 percent between 1960 and 1990, according to the Census Bureau, from 22.2 percent to 13.5 percent of the nation's population. That is far too many poor people, but the rate is considerably lower than it might have been if we had thrown up our hands and reminded ourselves that the poor will always be with us. Of black women considered "highly dependent," that is, on welfare for more than seven years, 81 percent of their daughters grow up to live productive lives off the welfare rolls, a 1992 Congressional report stated; the 19 percent who become second-generation welfare recipients can hardly be said to constitute an epidemic of welfare dependency. The vast majority of African-Americans are now working or middle class, an achievement that occurred in the past 30 years, most specifically between 1960 and 1973, the years of expansion in the very same social programs that it is so popular now to savage. Those were the same years in which I changed from girl to woman, learned to read and think, graduated from high school and college, came to be a working woman, a taxpayer, a citizen.

In spite of all the successes we know of, in spite of the reality that the typical welfare recipient is a white woman with young children, ideologues have continued to fashion from whole cloth the specter of the mythical black welfare mother, complete with a prodigious reproductive capacity and a galling laziness, accompanied by the uncaring and equally lazy black man in her life who will not work, will not marry her and will not support his family. 25

Why has this myth been promoted by some of the best (and the worst) people in government, academia, journalism and industry? One explanation may be that the constant presence of poverty frustrates even the best-intentioned among us. It may also be because the myth allows for denial about who the poor in America really are and for denial about the depth and intransigence of racism regardless of economic status. And because getting tough on welfare is for some a first-class career move; what better way to win a position in the next administration than to trash those people least able to respond? And, finally, because it serves to assure white Americans that lazy black people aren't getting away with anything. 26

Many of these prescriptions for saving America from the welfare plague not only reflect an insistent, if sometimes unconscious, racism but rest on the bedrock of patriarchy. They are rooted in the fantasy of a male presence as a path to social and economic salvation and in its corollary—the image of woman as passive chattel, constitutionally so afflicted by her condition that the only recourse is to transfer her care from the hands of the state to the hands of a man with a job. The largely ineffectual plans to create jobs for men in communities ravaged by disinvestment, the state-sponsored dragnets for men who cannot or will not support their children, the exhortations for women on welfare to find themselves a man and get married, all are the institutional expressions of the same worn cultural illusion—that women 27 and children without a man are fundamentally damaged goods. Men are such a boon, the reasoning goes, because they make more money than women do.

Were we truly serious about an end to poverty among women and children, we would take the logical next step. We would figure out how to make sure women who did a dollar's worth of work got a dollar's worth of pay. We would make sure that women could go to work with their minds at ease, knowing their children were well cared for. What women on welfare need, in large measure, are the things key to the life of every adult woman: economic security and autonomy. Women need the skills and the legitimate opportunity to earn a living for ourselves as well as for people who may rely on us; we need the freedom to make choices to improve our own lives and the lives of those dear to us.

"The real problem is not welfare," says Kathryn Edin, a professor of sociology at Rutgers University and a scholar in residence at the Russell Sage Foundation. "The real problem is the nature of low-wage work and lack of support for these workers—most of whom happen to be women raising their children alone."

Completing a five-year study of single mothers—some low-wage workers, some welfare recipients—Edin is quantifying what common sense and bitter experience have told millions of women who rotate off and on the welfare rolls: Women, particularly unskilled women with children, get the worst jobs available, with the least amount of health care, and are the most frequently laid off. "The workplace is not oriented toward people who have family responsibilities," she says. "Most jobs are set up assuming that someone else is minding the kids and doesn't need assistance."

But the writers and scholars and politicians who wax most rhapsodic about the need to replace welfare with work make their harsh judgments from the comfortable and supportive environs of offices and libraries and think tanks. If they need to go to the bathroom midsentence, there is no one timing their absence. If they take longer than a half-hour for lunch, there is no one waiting to dock their pay. If their baby sitter gets sick, there is no risk of someone having taken their place at work by the next morning. Yet these are conditions that low-wage women routinely face, which inevitably lead to the cyclical nature of their welfare histories. These are the realities that many of the most vocal and widely quoted critics of welfare routinely ignore. In his book *The End of Equality*, for example, Mickey Kaus discusses social and economic inequity, referring to David Ellwood's study on long-term welfare dependency without ever mentioning that it counts anyone who uses the services for at least one month as having been on welfare for the entire year.

In the heated atmosphere of the welfare debate, the larger 32 society is encouraged to believe that women on welfare have so violated the social contract that they have forfeited all rights common to those of us lucky enough not to be poor. In no area is this attitude more clearly demonstrated than in issues of sexuality and childbearing. Consider the following: A *Philadelphia Inquirer* editorial of Dec. 12, 1990, urges the use of Norplant contraceptive inserts for welfare recipients— in spite of repeated warnings from women's health groups of its dangerous side effects—in the belief that the drug "could be invaluable in breaking the cycle of inner-city poverty." (The newspaper apologized for the editorial after it met widespread criticism, both within and outside the paper.) A California judge orders a woman on welfare, convicted of abusing two of her four children, to use Norplant; the judge's decision was appealed. The Washington state legislature considers approving cash payments of up to $10,000 for women on welfare who agree to be sterilized. These and other proposals, all centering on women's reproductive capacities, were advanced in spite of evidence that welfare recipients have fewer children than those not on welfare.

The punitive energy behind these and so many other Dra- 33 conian actions and proposals goes beyond the desire to decrease welfare costs; it cuts to the heart of the nation's racial and sexual hysteria. Generated neither by law nor by fully informed public debate, these actions amount to social control over "those people on welfare"—a control many Americans feel they have bought and paid for every April 15. The question is obvious: If citizens were really aware of who receives welfare in America, however inadequate it is, if they acknowledged that white women and children were welfare's primary beneficiaries, would most of these things be happening?

Welfare has become a code word now. One that enables white Americans to mask their sometimes malignant, sometimes benign racism behind false concerns about the suffering ghetto poor and their negative impact on the rest of us. It has become the vehicle many so-called tough thinkers use to undermine compassionate policy and engineer the reduction of social programs. 34

So how *did* I get here? 35

I kept my drawers up and my dress down, to quote my mother. I didn't end up pregnant because I had better things to do. I knew I did because my uneducated, Southern-born parents told me so. Their faith, their focus on our futures are a far cry from the thesis of Nicholas Lemann, whose widely acclaimed book *The Promised Land* perpetuates the myth of black Southern sharecropping society as a primary source of black urban malaise. Most important, my family and I had every reason to believe that I had better things to do and that when I got older I would be able to do them. I had a mission, a calling, work to do that only I could do. And that is knowledge transmitted not just by parents, or school, or churches. It is a palpable thing, available by osmosis from the culture of the neighborhood and the world at large. 36

Add to this formula a whopping dose of dumb luck. It was my sixth-grade teacher, Sister Maria Sarto, who identified in me the first signs of a stifling boredom and told my mother that I needed a tougher, more challenging curriculum than her school could provide. It was she who then tracked down the private Francis W. Parker School, which agreed to give me a scholarship if I passed the admissions test. 37

Had I been born a few years earlier, or a decade later, I might now be living on welfare in the Robert Taylor Homes 38 or working as a hospital nurse's aide for $6.67 an hour. People who think such things could never have happened to me haven't met enough poor people to know better. The avenue of escape can be very narrow indeed. The hope and energy of the 1960's—fueled not only by a growing economy but by all the passions of a great national quest—is long gone. The sense of possibility I knew has been replaced with the popular cultural currency that money and those who have it are everything and those without are nothing.

Much has been made of the culture of the underclass, the 39 culture of poverty, as though they were the free-floating illnesses of the African-American poor, rendering them immune to other influences: the widespread American culture of greed, for example, or of cynicism. It is a thinly veiled continuation of the endless projection of "dis-ease" onto black life, a convenient way to sidestep a more painful debate about the loss of meaning in American life that has made our entire nation depressed and dispirited. The malaise that has overtaken our country is hardly confined to African-Americans or the poor, and if both groups should disappear tomorrow, our nation would still find itself in crisis. To talk of the black "underclass threat" to the public sphere, as Mickey Kaus does, to demonize the poor among us and thus by association all of us—ultimately this does more damage to the body politic than a dozen welfare queens.

When I walk down the streets of my Harlem neighbor- 40 hood, I see women like my mother, hustling, struggling, walking their children to school and walking them back home. And I also see women who have lost both energy and faith, talking loud, hanging out. I see the shadow men of a new generation, floating by with a few dollars and a toy, then drifting away to the shelters they call home. And I see, a dozen times a day, the little girls my sister and I used to be, the little boys my brothers once were.

Even the grudging, inadequate public help I once had is 41 fading fast for them. The time and patience they will need to re-create themselves is vanishing under pressure for the big, quick fix and the crushing load of blame being heaped upon them. In the big cities and the small towns of America, we have let theory, ideology and mythology about welfare and poverty overtake these children and their parents.

For Study and Discussion

QUESTIONS FOR RESPONSE

1. What beliefs about families on welfare did you bring to this essay? What effect do you think reading the essay has had on those beliefs?
2. How does talk about welfare reform focus on women? What is your response to that focus?

QUESTIONS ABOUT PURPOSE

1. What stereotypes about welfare recipients does Bray seek to break? What is the origin of those stereotypes?
2. What do you think Bray wants her readers to learn from her account of her family's struggle to achieve independence? What action would she like for them to take?

QUESTIONS ABOUT AUDIENCE

1. This article was first published in the *New York Times Magazine*. Why is the *New York Times* audience an important one for Bray to reach?
2. How do you think college readers differ from readers of the *New York Times*? How do you think college readers' responses might differ from those of *Times* readers?

QUESTIONS ABOUT STRATEGIES

1. Bray spends almost half the essay giving an account of her family's experiences on welfare. How does this strategy help her advance her argument?
2. How does Bray go about counteracting the myth she describes in paragraph 25?

QUESTIONS FOR DISCUSSION

1. Welfare is only one of many entitlement programs administered by the federal government. Some of the others are Social Security, farm subsidies, Medicare, and military and veterans' benefits. How do most of the public's feelings about these entitlement programs compare to their feelings about welfare? Why?
2. How is the welfare question "the race question and the woman question in disguise," as Bray asserts in the first paragraph of her essay?

CHARLES MURRAY

Charles Murray was born in Newton, Iowa, in 1943 and was educated at Harvard University. Upon graduation, he worked in the Peace Corps in Thailand and as a research assistant for the American Institute for Research before attending Massachusetts Institute of Technology to complete his graduate studies. He returned to the American Institute for Research to supervise and evaluate federal welfare, urban education, and criminal justice programs. His assessment of this experience appears in books such as *Beyond Probation: Juvenile Corrections and the Chronic Delinquent* (1979) and *Safety Nets and the Truly Needy* (1982). The impact of these books encouraged Murray to conduct the research that produced two extremely controversial books, *Losing Ground: American Social Policy, 1950–1980* (1984) and *The Bell Curve: Intelligence and Class Structure in American Life* (1994). Murray currently works for the American Enterprise Institute. In "The Coming White Underclass," printed in the *Wall Street Journal* in 1993, he argues that the increasing number of white illegitimate children will have a severe social and economic impact on American culture.

The Coming White Underclass

EVERY ONCE IN a while the sky really is falling, and this 1
seems to be the case with the latest national figures on illegitimacy. The unadorned statistic is that, in 1991, 1.2 million children were born to unmarried mothers, within a hair of 30% of all live births. How high is 30%? About four

percentage points higher than the black illegitimacy rate in
the early 1960s that motivated Daniel Patrick Moynihan to
write his famous memorandum on the breakdown of the
black family.

The 1991 story for blacks is that illegitimacy has now   2
reached 68% of births to black women. In inner cities, the
figure is typically in excess of 80%. Many of us have heard
these numbers so often that we are inured. It is time to think
about them as if we were back in the mid-1960s with the
young Moynihan and asked to predict what would happen if
the black illegitimacy rate were 68%.

Impossible, we would have said. But if the proportion of   3

---

*Illegitimacy is the single most important
social problem of our time because it drives
everything else.*

---

fatherless boys in a given community were to reach such
levels, surely the culture must be *Lord of the Flies* writ large,
the values of unsocialized male adolescents made norms—
physical violence, immediate gratification and predatory sex.
That is the culture now taking over the black inner city.

But the black story, however dismaying, is old news. The   4
new trend that threatens the U.S. is white illegitimacy. Matters have not yet quite gotten out of hand, but they are on
the brink. If we want to act, now is the time.

In 1991, 707,502 babies were born to single white   5
women, representing 22% of white births. The elite wisdom
holds that this phenomenon cuts across social classes, as if the
increase in Murphy Browns were pushing the trendline.
Thus, a few months ago, a Census Bureau study of fertility
among all American women got headlines for a few days
because it showed that births to single women with college

degrees doubled in the last decade to 6% from 3%. This is an interesting trend, but of minor social importance. The real news of that study is that the proportion of single mothers with less than a high school education jumped to 48% from 35% in a single decade.

These numbers are dominated by whites. Breaking down   6 the numbers by race (using data not available in the published version), women with college degrees contribute only 4% of white illegitimate babies, while women with a high school education or less contribute 82%. Women with family incomes of $75,000 or more contribute 1% of white illegitimate babies, while women with family incomes under $20,000 contribute 69%.

The National Longitudinal Study of Youth, a Labor De-   7 partment study that has tracked more than 10,000 youths since 1979, shows an even more dramatic picture. For white women below the poverty line in the year prior to giving birth, 44% of births have been illegitimate, compared with only 6% for women above the poverty line. White illegitimacy is overwhelmingly a lower-class phenomenon.

This brings us to the emergence of a white underclass. In   8 raw numbers, European-American whites are the ethnic group with the most people in poverty, most illegitimate children, most women on welfare, most unemployed men, and most arrests for serious crimes. And yet whites have not had an "underclass" as such, because the whites who might qualify have been scattered among the working class. Instead, whites have had "white trash" concentrated in a few streets on the outskirts of town, sometimes a Skid Row of unattached white men in the large cities. But these scatterings have seldom been large enough to make up a neighborhood. An underclass needs a critical mass, and white America has not had one.

But now the overall white illegitimacy rate is 22%. The   9 figure in low-income, working-class communities may be twice that. How much illegitimacy can a community tolerate? Nobody knows, but the historical fact is that the trendlines on black crime, dropout from the labor force, and illegitimacy all shifted sharply upward as the overall black illegitimacy rate passed 25%.

The causal connection is murky—I blame the revolution   10
in social policy during that period, while others blame the sexual revolution, broad shifts in cultural norms, or structural changes in the economy. But the white illegitimacy rate is approaching that same problematic 25% region at a time when social policy is more comprehensively wrongheaded than it was in the mid-1960s, and the cultural and sexual norms are still more degraded.

The white underclass will begin to show its face in isolated   11
ways. Look for certain schools in white neighborhoods to get a reputation as being unteachable, with large numbers of disruptive students and indifferent parents. Talk to the police; listen for stories about white neighborhoods where the incidence of domestic disputes and casual violence has been shooting up. Look for white neighborhoods with high concentrations of drug activity and large numbers of men who have dropped out of the labor force. Some readers will recall reading the occasional news story about such places already.

As the spatial concentration of illegitimacy reaches critical   12
mass, we should expect the deterioration to be as fast among low-income whites in the 1990s as it was among low-income blacks in the 1960s. My proposition is that illegitimacy is the single most important social problem of our time—more important than crime, drugs, poverty, illiteracy, welfare or homelessness because it drives everything else. Doing something about it is not just one more item on the American policy agenda, but should be at the top. Here is what to do:

In the calculus of illegitimacy, the constants are that boys   13
like to sleep with girls and that girls think babies are endearing. Human societies have historically channeled these elemental forces of human behavior via thick walls of rewards and penalties that constrained the overwhelming majority of births to take place within marriage. The past 30 years have seen those walls cave in. It is time to rebuild them.

The ethical underpinning for the policies I am about to   14 describe is this: Bringing a child into the world is the most important thing that most human beings ever do. Bringing a child into the world when one is not emotionally or financially prepared to be a parent is wrong. The child deserves society's support. The parent does not.

The social justification is this: A society with broad legal 15 freedoms depends crucially on strong nongovernmental institutions to temper and restrain behavior. Of these, marriage is paramount. Either we reverse the current trends in illegitimacy—especially white illegitimacy—or America must, willy-nilly, become an unrecognizably authoritarian, socially segregated, centralized state.

To restore the rewards and penalties of marriage does not 16 require social engineering. Rather, it requires that the state stop interfering with the natural forces that have done the job quite effectively for millennia. Some of the changes I will describe can occur at the federal level; others would involve state laws. For now, the important thing is to agree on what should be done.

I begin with the penalties, of which the most obvious are 17 economic. Throughout human history, a single woman with a small child has not been a viable economic unit. Not being a viable economic unit, neither have the single woman and child been a legitimate social unit. In small numbers, they must be a net drain on the community's resources. In large numbers, they must destroy the community's capacity to sustain itself. *Mirabile dictu,* communities everywhere have augmented the economic penalties of single parenthood with severe social stigma.

Restoring economic penalties translates into the first and 18 central policy prescription: to end all economic support for single mothers. The AFDC (Aid to Families with Dependent Children) payment goes to zero. Single mothers are not eligible for subsidized housing or for food stamps. An assortment of other subsidies and in-kind benefits disappear. Since universal medical coverage appears to be an idea whose time has come, I will stipulate that all children have medical coverage. But with that exception, the signal is loud and unmistakable: From society's perspective, to have a baby that you cannot care for yourself is profoundly irresponsible, and the government will no longer subsidize it.

How does a poor young mother survive without government support? The same way she has since time immemorial. If she wants to keep a child, she must enlist support from her parents, boyfriend, siblings, neighbors, church or philanthropies. She must get support from somewhere, anywhere, other than the government. The objectives are threefold. 19

First, enlisting the support of others raises the probability that other mature adults are going to be involved with the upbringing of the child, and this is a great good in itself. 20

Second, the need to find support forces a self-selection process. One of the most short-sighted excuses made for current behavior is that an adolescent who is utterly unprepared to be a mother "needs someone to love." Childish yearning isn't a good enough selection device. We need to raise the probability that a young single woman who keeps her child is doing so volitionally and thoughtfully. Forcing her to find a way of supporting the child does this. It will lead many young women who shouldn't be mothers to place their babies for adoption. This is good. It will lead others, watching what happens to their sisters, to take steps not to get pregnant. This is also good. Many others will get abortions. Whether this is good depends on what one thinks of abortion. 21

Third, stigma will regenerate. The pressure on relatives and communities to pay for the folly of their children will make an illegitimate birth the socially horrific act it used to be, and getting a girl pregnant something boys do at the risk of facing a shotgun. Stigma and shotgun marriages may or may not be good for those on the receiving end, but their deterrent effect on others is wonderful—and indispensable. 22

What about women who can find no support but keep the baby anyway? There are laws already on the books about the right of the state to take a child from a neglectful parent. We have some 360,000 children in foster care because of them. Those laws would still apply. Society's main response, how- 23 ever, should be to make it as easy as possible for those mothers to place their children for adoption at infancy. To that end, state governments must strip adoption of the nonsense that has encumbered it in recent decades.

The first step is to make adoption easy for any married 24
couple who can show reasonable evidence of having the resources and stability to raise a child. Lift all restrictions on interracial adoption. Ease age limitations for adoptive parents.

The second step is to restore the traditional legal principle 25
that placing a child for adoption means irrevocably relinquishing all legal rights to the child. The adoptive parents are parents without qualification. Records are sealed until the child reaches adulthood, at which time they may be unsealed only with the consent of biological child and parent.

Given these straightforward changes—going back to the 26
old way, which worked—there is reason to believe that some extremely large proportion of infants given up by their mothers will be adopted into good homes. This is true not just for flawless blue-eyed blond infants but for babies of all colors and conditions. The demand for infants to adopt is huge.

Some small proportion of infants and larger proportion of 27
older children will not be adopted. For them, the government should spend lavishly on orphanages. I am not recommending Dickensian barracks. In 1993, we know a lot about how to provide a warm, nurturing environment for children, and getting rid of the welfare system frees up lots of money to do it. Those who find the word "orphanages" objectionable may think of them as 24-hour-a-day preschools. Those who prattle about the importance of keeping children with their biological mothers may wish to spend some time in a patrol car or with a social worker seeing what the reality of life with welfare-dependent biological mothers can be like.

Finally, there is the matter of restoring the rewards of 28
marriage. Here, I am pessimistic about how much government can do and optimistic about how little it needs to do. The rewards of raising children within marriage are real and deep. The main task is to shepherd children through adoles-

cence so that they can reach adulthood—when they are likely
to recognize the value of those rewards—free to take on
marriage and family. The main purpose of the penalties for
single parenthood is to make that task easier.

One of the few concrete things that the government can   29
do to increase the rewards of marriage is make the tax code
favor marriage and children: Those of us who are nervous
about using the tax code for social purposes can advocate
making the tax code at least neutral.

A more abstract but ultimately crucial step in raising the   30
rewards of marriage is to make marriage once again the sole
legal institution through which parental rights and responsibilities are defined and exercised.

Little boys should grow up knowing from their earliest   31
memories that if they want to have any rights whatsoever
regarding a child that they sire—more vividly, if they want to
grow up to be a daddy—they must marry. Little girls should
grow up knowing from their earliest memories that if they
want to have any legal claims whatsoever on the father of their
children, they must marry. A marriage certificate should establish that a man and a woman have entered into a unique
legal relationship. The changes in recent years that have
blurred the distinctiveness of marriage are subtly but importantly destructive.

Together, these measures add up to a set of signals, some   32
with immediate and tangible consequences, others with long-
term consequences, still others symbolic. They should be
supplemented by others based on a re-examination of divorce
law and its consequences.

That these policy changes seem drastic and unrealistic is a   33
peculiarity of our age, not of the policies themselves. With
embellishments, I have endorsed the policies that were the
uncontroversial law of the land as recently as John Kennedy's
presidency. Then, America's elites accepted as a matter of
course that a free society such as America's can sustain itself
only through virtue and temperance in the people, that virtue
and temperance depend centrally on the socialization of each
new generation, and that the socialization of each generation

depends on the matrix of care and resources fostered by marriage.

Three decades after that consensus disappeared, we face an emerging crisis. The long, steep climb in black illegitimacy has been calamitous for black communities and painful for the nation. The reforms I have described will work for blacks as for whites, and have been needed for years. But the brutal truth is that American society as a whole could survive when illegitimacy became epidemic within a comparatively small ethnic minority. It cannot survive the same epidemic among whites. 34

For Study and Discussion

QUESTIONS FOR RESPONSE

1. What do you know firsthand of single white mothers like those Murray talks about or about divorced single mothers who are raising their children alone? What is your impression of how they manage their lives? To what extent does it correspond to Murray's impression?
2. Murray says in paragraph 4, "the black story, however dismaying, is old news." What is your response to that statement?

QUESTIONS ABOUT PURPOSE

1. What immediate actions does Murray hope to initiate among his readers? What long-range actions?
2. Why does Murray focus on white illegitimacy? How would his recommendations about single mothers affect all ethnic groups?

QUESTIONS ABOUT AUDIENCE

1. This article was first published in the *Wall Street Journal*. What do you know about its readers? What attitudes and concerns can Murray assume are likely to exist among these readers?
2. How do you think the experiences and attitudes of college readers at your institution compare with those of readers of the *Wall*

Street Journal? What differences would those experiences make in their response?

QUESTIONS ABOUT STRATEGIES

1. What effect does Murray hope to achieve with the statistics he quotes in the first seven paragraphs?
2. Murray lays out a specific plan for reducing illegitimacy, saying decisively, "Here is what to do." How do you think *Wall Street Journal* readers would react to this strategy and the remedies he proposes? How do you react to them? Why?

QUESTIONS FOR DISCUSSION

1. What issues do Murray's statements about adoption and orphanages (paragraphs 23 through 27) raise? How do you respond to the claims he makes in those paragraphs? Discuss his recommendations.
2. Read what Rosemary Bray says in paragraph 28 of "So How Did I Get Here?" To what extent do Murray's proposed solutions to illegitimacy problems resemble what she regards as a patriarchal fantasy? Explain.

DAVID DENBY

David Denby was born in 1943 in New York City and educated at Columbia University. He has contributed articles to magazines such as the *New Republic* and *The New Yorker,* and has served as movie reviewer for *New York* magazine. He is the editor of *Awake in the Dark: An Anthology of American Film Criticism, 1915 to the Present* (1977). In 1991, Denby decided to return to Columbia College to retake the two core Great Books courses. His description of that experience appears in his intellectual memoir, *Great Books: My Adventures with Homer, Rousseau, Woolf, and Other Indestructible Writers of the Western World* (1996). In "What the Great Books Do," reprinted from the "Epilogue" of *Great Books,* Denby argues that great books "force us to ask all those questions about self and society we no longer address without embarrassment."

What the Great Books Do

B Y THE END of my year in school, I knew that the culture-   1
ideologues, both left and right, are largely talking nonsense. Both groups simplify and caricature the Western tradition. They ignore its ornery and difficult books; they ignore its actual students, most of whom have been dispossessed. Whether white, black, Asian, or Latino, American students rarely arrive at college as habitual readers, which means that few of them have more than a nominal connection to the past. It is absurd to speak, as does the academic left, of classic Western texts dominating and silencing everyone but a ruling elite of white males. The vast majority of white

students do not know the intellectual tradition that is allegedly theirs any better than black or brown ones do. They have
not read its books, and when they do read them, they may
respond well, but they will not respond in the way that the
academic left supposes. For there is only one "hegemonic
discourse" in the lives of American undergraduates, and that
is the mass media. Most high schools can't begin to compete
against a torrent of imagery and sound that makes every
moment but the present seem quaint, bloodless, or dead.

When I began writing movie criticism in 1969, I could   2
assume in my readers a stable background of respect (unex-
amined respect, perhaps) for traditional high culture against

---

*The [Great Books] core curriculum courses
jar so many student habits, violate so many
contemporary pieties, and challenge so
many forms of laziness that . . . they are
the most radical courses in the
undergraduate curriculum.*

---

which the immediacy of pop was startling and liberating—a
blow against timidity, schoolroom piety, and complacence. I
was drawn to movie reviewing myself by the daring of the
best movies of the late sixties and early seventies, and by the
absence of a strong academic tradition in writing about them.
But the only thing I can assume now is that there isn't much
traditional culture left to explode. The situation has gone into
reverse: The movies have declined; *pop* has become a field of
conformity and complacency, while the traditional high culture, by means of its very strangeness and difficulty, strikes
students as odd. They may even be shocked by it.

So the left-academic critics of the canon and of core-cur-   3
riculum courses have got things comically wrong. They are

eager to empower minority students and women; they want to make white male students recognize "the other"—the voices allegedly silenced by the traditional canon. But it is just such an experience as reading the canon which now forces students to confront the other. All students, not just white students, confront it when they read of Homer's pitiless warriors and of such women as Antigone or Dido who choose death as a matter of honor. They confront it in Plato's insistence on an education sanitized of representations of evil or weakness, in Aristotle's ideal of participation in government as a duty of citizenship. The students may be alarmed by the physicality of Dante's torments and, in a different way, by the sexual eagerness of women in Boccaccio. Rousseau's loathing of society and Marx's insistence that alienated labor is an unnatural state of being are both startling rebukes to our present arrangements. The style, manner, and thought of these books are all a long way from us. Yet they are part of us, too, fixed in our language and institutions, in our ideals and habits.

At Columbia, the Literature Humanities course was set up in the late 1930s by humanists eager to preserve the culture of white male Christian Europe in a country increasingly populated with immigrants. These men, I suppose, may be described as hegemonists in the sense that the academic left means. But history has transformed Lit Hum (and also C.C.). After World War II, the courses were taught by intellectuals absorbed in the classics of modernism (Conrad, Yeats, Eliot, Joyce, Woolf, Kafka) and schooled by the disasters of totalitarianism and war. The teachers brought a special consciousness to their work: They taught the premodernist classics in a modernist way, emphasizing the elements of internal dissonance and conflict, the darker ironies, and the arguments between books. They saw the threats to community, the centrifugal forces that destroy human society. The way the books are taught now—and this should be true at most colleges—guarantees that no single or unitary meaning can

be found in them. Reading again, I was not surprised that I
loved the Western classics, but I was surprised by what they
are. The books are less a conquering army than a kingdom
of untamable beasts, at war with one another and with readers. Reading the books, the students receive an ethically
strenuous education, a set of bracing intellectual habits,
among them skepticism and self-criticism. They may be impelled to advocacy and belief as well, but they will not be
impelled to any doctrine in particular—except perhaps the
notion that a Western education, opening many doors at
once, is an extraordinarily useful experience. In brief, the
intended "hegemonic" celebration of the West became a
continuing interrogation (as well as celebration) of the West.

Think double! as Professor Tayler says. To the left, I would   5
say that reading the canon in the 1990s is unlikely to turn
anyone into a chauvinist or an imperialist. The left should
stop misstating the issue of elitism; it should stop confusing
the literary hierarchy and the social hierarchy. The two must
be disentangled. As the late Irving Howe liked to say: To
believe that some books and traditions are more worthy than
others is not to endorse the inequality of American society.
A literary judgment may represent class prejudice, but it is
naïve or dishonest to assume that it represents nothing more
than class prejudice. People who deny the power of aesthetic
experience or the possibility of disinterested judgment may
well have cynical and careerist reasons for doing so.

And to the right, I would say that however instructive the   6
great works might be in building the moral character of the
nation's citizens, the books were more likely, in the initial
brush, to mean something idiosyncratic and personal. First
comes the personal reckoning, the summoning into existence
of the self. A good teacher sets in motion a lifelong process
of students' knowing themselves through their most complex
pleasures and knowing their societies through a fundamental
analysis of the principles on which they are based. I agree with
William Bennett and other traditionalists to this extent: Men
and women educated in the Western tradition will have the
best possible shot at the daunting task of reinventing morality

and community in a republic now badly tattered by fear and mistrust. These books—or any such representative selection—speak most powerfully of what a human being can be. They dramatize the utmost any of us is capable of in love, suffering, and knowledge. They offer the most direct representation of the possibilities of civil existence and the disaster of its dissolution. Reading and discussing the books, the students begin the act of repossession. They scrape away the media haze of secondhandedness.

By definition, that is an arduous and painful experience.   7 Taking my own pulse, and watching the students struggle, fail, and succeed, I came to a conclusion that surprised me: The core-curriculum courses jar so many student habits, violate so many contemporary pieties, and challenge so many forms of laziness that so far from serving a reactionary function, they are actually the most radical courses in the undergraduate curriculum.

The question of exclusion remains. Many African-Ameri-   8 can students enjoy the core-curriculum courses or at least give them grudging assent. I interviewed many students, and attended meetings on the core curriculum in which complaints were aired, and though many African-Americans wanted a more historicized consciousness around the books (what, for instance, was the role of Egypt in forming Greek culture?), few wanted a different set of texts. Yet I was haunted all year by the black student who was furious that she had been made to listen to Mozart and by other minority students I heard who insisted the courses were racist and blind and made them feel inferior.

As I listened to their complaints, I couldn't help noticing   9 the words the students used: The West, they said, had failed in justice and equality. They employed the vocabulary and values of the West to attack the West for not living up to its own highest standards. They spoke against the courses in terms they may well have gleaned from the books. And I couldn't help noticing something else: They knew that a great culture had flourished in Europe, that the United States has inherited some of it and has been partly shaped by it. They might consider that culture their enemy, but they were not indifferent to it. They had taken its measure and they knew its power. That knowledge alone put them in a small minority of Americans.

At the risk of contradicting them, I would say that I came   10 away with the impression that their identity as African-Americans had not been hurt or shriveled at all. People who feel inferior are not likely to stand up in public meetings and question institutional policy. (The beaten stay quiet.) Leaving college, such students would combine what they knew and what they had fought against; they would use both knowledge and resistance for their own purpose. Not the white man's purpose: their own purpose. Their identity as African-Americans would likely be strengthened by the experience.

If they refuse to consider the classics of Western culture as   11 a "common" heritage, but use the books instead as a resource and a tool, that seems to me allegiance enough to "the West." The great thing about Western culture is that any American can stand on it, or on some small part of it. In this country, we take what we want and mix it with our own composition. No one here but the paranoid or simpleminded demands purity; no one plausibly accuses anyone else of cultural bastardy when all are truly bastards. But at the end of education, something both flexible and strong emerges from the meeting of influence and identity and takes its place in the world with a defiant freedom that no other modern culture can match.

For surely the game has changed. In the past, in the United   12 States, we had a grave problem of access: Who writes, who reads, who composes, who publishes? Minority groups and women had no more than severely limited hold on what Marxists call "the means of cultural production." But no one can now say that women have been shut out of education, and when blacks are shut out, the reason is that they are poor and therefore suffer the dilemmas and demoralization of poverty. Inequality—power and powerlessness, the rich and the poor—remains the problem for African-Americans, not the cultural domination of white people. African-Americans now have an abundant access to the presses, the media, the museums, the art galleries, the recording studios. What they absorb of the older "white" culture they will remake as their own; it cannot hurt them. Demagogues and ambitious academics who turn the culture of the past into a turf war are playing a diversionary game, drawing attention away from political and economic problems that can be solved only by studying, earning, voting, organizing, and taking power. None of these activities but the first can be accomplished in the English or Black Studies departments. The curriculum debate is not a tempest in a teapot but a teapot in a tempest. The storm rages outside the university.

What *can* be achieved through culture is the greatest range 13 of pleasure and soulfulness and reasoning power that any of us is capable of. The courses in the Western classics force us to ask all those questions about self and society we no longer address without embarrassment—the questions our media-trained habits of irony have tricked us out of asking. In order to ask those questions, students need to be enchanted before they are disenchanted. They need to love the text before they attack the subtext. They need to read before they disappear into the aridities of electronic "information." They need a chance at making a self before they are told that it doesn't exist. They need a strong taste of Europe so they can become better Americans. Walt Whitman said it this way in *Leaves of Grass:*

> Dead poets, philosophs, priests,
> Martyrs, artists, inventors, governments long since,
> Language-shapers on other shores,
> Nations once powerful, now reduced, withdrawn, or desolate,
> I dare not proceed till I respectfully credit what you have left
>   wafted hither,
> I have perused it, own it is admirable, (moving awhile among it,)
> Think nothing can ever be greater, nothing can ever deserve more
>   than it deserves,
> Regarding it all intently a long while, then dismissing it,
> I stand in my place with my own day here.

Here lands female and male,
Here the heir-ship and heiress-ship of the world, here the flame
  of materials,
Here spirituality the translatress, the openly-avow'd,
The ever-tending, the finalè of visible forms,
The satisfier, after due long-waiting now advancing,
Yes here comes my mistress the soul.

For Study and Discussion

QUESTIONS FOR RESPONSE

1. Denby argues that the dominant source of information ("hege-monic discourse" is the academic term) for young people today is not the books of white male authors that some faculty dislike and distrust, but the mass media of movies and television. Judg-ing by your own experience and perceptions of our culture, how do you respond to his claim?
2. Among the great books you may have read in high school, on your own, or in your first years of college are some of Shake-speare's plays, the Gettysburg Address, portions of the Bible, and perhaps some Greek plays or portions of the Odyssey and the Iliad. How did you respond to the ones you've read? In what ways do they seem important to you?

QUESTIONS ABOUT PURPOSE

1. Denby's essay raises recurring questions about what the required reading should be in college courses. What reasons does he give for thinking that today's students should read some of the tradi-tional classics of Western literature?
2. What is the issue of exclusion that he raises in paragraph 8? How does he deal with that issue?

QUESTIONS ABOUT AUDIENCE

1. What questions do you think Denby's audience might have for him about his experience of going to Columbia University to reread the classics of Western literature and philosophy that he first read there as an eighteen-year-old? What are some of his answers?

2. What preconceptions and assumptions about the classic books of Western literature is an audience of first-year college readers likely to have? How does Denby address those assumptions?

QUESTIONS ABOUT STRATEGIES

1. How do Denby's references to his own experiences in rereading the classics affect the strength of his argument?
2. What does Denby achieve by calling the great books "the most radical texts in the undergraduate curriculum"?

QUESTIONS FOR DISCUSSION

1. At forty-eight, while still holding down his day jobs as movie critic and magazine writer, Denby went back to Columbia University and took the two Western civilization courses he had first taken thirty years before; in doing so he reread many of the classic books of Western literature and philosophy. Imagine yourself taking such a step; what do you think the experience might be like?
2. The average age of college students is now twenty-six, which means that many students are reentering college after an interruption of several years. If you are such a student, how does being older and more experienced affect your attitude toward your courses? What do you think are the advantages and disadvantages of being a student past the traditional college age? Do you think being older makes you more or less interested in reading some of the classics of Western literature?

Mike Rose was born in 1944 in Altoona, Pennsylvania, and was educated at Loyola College at Los Angeles, the University of Southern California, and the University of California, Los Angeles. He has taught elementary students in the Teacher's Corps, adult writers in UCLA's extension program for Vietnam veterans, and basic writers in UCLA's writing program. He has published articles on writer's anxiety, theories of cognition, and assessment in academic journals such as *College English, College Composition and Communication,* and *Written Communication.* In 1989, Rose published *Lives on the Boundary: The Struggles and Achievements of America's Underprepared,* an extraordinary fusion of autobiography, case study, and cultural criticism. His most recent book is a study of "the promise of public education in America," *Possible Lives* (1995). In "The Limits of the Great Books," excerpted from *Lives on the Boundary,* Rose argues that the canon of great books pushes much of our culture to the margins.

The Limits of the Great Books

T HERE IS A strong impulse in American education—curious in a country with such an ornery streak of antitraditionalism—to define achievement and excellence in terms of the acquisition of a historically validated body of knowledge, an authoritative list of books and allusions, a canon. We seek a certification of our national intelligence, indeed, our national virtue, in how diligently our children can display this central corpus of information. This need for certification tends to emerge most dramatically in our educational policy debates during times of real or imagined threat: economic hard times, political crises, sudden increases in immigration. Now is such a time, and it is reflected in a number of influential books and commission reports. E. D. Hirsch argues that a core national vocabulary, one oriented toward the English literature tradition—Alice in Wonderland to zeitgeist—will build a knowledge base that will foster the literacy of all Americans. Diane Ravitch and Chester Finn call for a return to a traditional historical and literary curriculum: the valorous historical figures and the classical literature of the once-elite course of study. Allan Bloom, Secretary of Education William

> *We need a revised store of images of educational excellence, ones that embody the reward and turmoil of education in a democracy, that celebrate the plural, messy human reality of it all.*

Bennett, Mortimer Adler and the Paideia Group, and a number of others have affirmed, each in their very different ways, the necessity of the Great Books: Plato and Aristotle and Sophocles, Dante and Shakespeare and Locke, Dickens and Mann and Faulkner. We can call this orientation to educational achievement the canonical orientation.

At times in our past, the call for a shoring up of or return to a canonical curriculum was explicitly elitist, was driven by a fear that the education of the select was being compromised. Today, though, the majority of the calls are provocatively framed in the language of democracy. They assail the mediocre and grinding curriculum frequently found in remedial and vocational education. They are disdainful of the patronizing perceptions of student ability that further restrict the already restricted academic life of disadvantaged youngsters.

2

They point out that the canon—its language, conventions, and allusions—is central to the discourse of power, and to keep it from poor kids is to assure their disenfranchisement all the more. The books of the canon, claim the proposals, the Great Books, are a window onto a common core of experience and civic ideals. There is, then, a spiritual, civic, and cognitive heritage here, and *all* our children should receive it. If we are sincere in our desire to bring Mario, Chin, the younger versions of Caroline, current incarnations of Frank Marrell, and so many others who populate this book—if we truly want to bring them into our society—then we should provide them with this stable and common core. This is a forceful call. It promises a still center in a turning world.

I see great value in being challenged to think of the curriculum of the many in the terms we have traditionally reserved for the few; it is refreshing to have common assumptions about the capacities of underprepared students so boldly challenged. . . . Too many people are kept from the books of the canon, the Great Books, because of misjudgments about their potential. Those books eventually proved important to me, and, as best I know how, I invite my students to engage them. But once we grant the desirability of equal curricular treatment and begin to consider what this equally distributed curriculum would contain, problems arise: If the canon itself is the answer to our educational inequities, why has it historically invited few and denied many? Would the canonical orientation provide adequate guidance as to how a democratic curriculum should be constructed and how it should be taught? Would it guide us in opening up to Olga that "fancy talk" that so alienated her?

Those who study the way literature becomes canonized, how linguistic creations are included or excluded from a tradition, claim that the canonical curriculum students would most likely receive would not, as is claimed, offer a common core of American experience. Caroline would not find her life represented in it, nor would Mario. The canon has tended to push to the margin much of the literature of our nation: from American Indian songs and chants to immigrant fiction to working-class narratives. The institutional messages that students receive in the books they're issued and the classes they take are powerful and, as I've witnessed since my Voc. Ed. days, quickly internalized. And to revise these messages and redress past wrongs would involve more than adding some new books to the existing canon—the very reasons for linguistic and cultural exclusion would have to become a focus of study in order to make the canon act as a democratizing force. Unless this happens, the democratic intent of the reformers will be undercut by the content of the curriculum they propose.

And if we move beyond content to consider basic assumptions about teaching and learning, a further problem arises, one that involves the very nature of the canonical orientation itself. The canonical orientation encourages a narrowing of focus from learning to that which must be learned: It simplifies the dynamic tension between student and text and reduces the psychological and social dimensions of instruction. The student's personal history recedes as the what of the classroom is valorized over the how. Thus it is that the encounter of student and text is often portrayed by canonists as a transmission. Information, wisdom, virtue will pass from the book to the student if the student gives the book the time it merits, carefully traces its argument or narrative or lyrical progression. Intellectual, even spiritual, growth will *necessarily* result from an encounter with Roman mythology, *Othello,* and "I heard a Fly buzz—when I died—," with biographies and historical sagas and patriotic lore. Learning is stripped of confusion and discord. It is stripped, as well, of strong human connection. My own initiators to the canon—Jack MacFarland, Dr. Carothers, and the rest—knew there was more to their work than their mastery of a tradition. What mattered most, I see now, were the relationships they established with me, the guidance they provided when I felt inadequate or threatened. This mentoring was part of my entry into that solemn library of Western thought—and even with such support, there were still times of confusion, anger, and fear. It is telling, I think, that once that rich social network

5

slid away, once I was in graduate school in intense, solitary encounter with that tradition, I abandoned it for other sources of nurturance and knowledge.

The model of learning implicit in the canonical orientation   6
seems, at times, more religious than cognitive or social: Truth resides in the printed texts, and if they are presented by someone who knows them well and respects them, that truth will be revealed. Of all the advocates of the canon, Mortimer Adler has given most attention to pedagogy—and his Paideia books contain valuable discussions of instruction, coaching, and questioning. But even here, and this is doubly true in the other manifestos, there is little acknowledgment that the material in the canon can be not only difficult but foreign, alienating, overwhelming.

We need an orientation to instruction that provides gui-   7
dance on how to determine and honor the beliefs and stories, enthusiasms, and apprehensions that students reveal. How to build on them, and when they clash with our curriculum—as I saw so often in the Tutorial Center at UCLA—when they clash, how to encourage a discussion that will lead to reflection on what students bring and what they're currently confronting. Canonical lists imply canonical answers, but the manifestos offer little discussion of what to do when students fail. If students have been exposed to at least some elements of the canon before—as many have—why didn't it take? If they're encountering it for the first time and they're lost, how can we determine where they're located—and what do we do then?

Each member of a teacher's class, poor *or* advantaged,   8
gives rise to endless decisions, day-to-day determinations about a child's reading and writing: decisions on how to tap strength, plumb confusion, foster growth. The richer your conception of learning and your understanding of its social and psychological dimensions, the more insightful and effective your judgments will be. Consider the sources of literacy we saw among the children in El Monte: shopkeepers' signs, song lyrics, auto manuals, and conventions of the Western, family stories and tales, and more. Consider Chin's sources—

television and *People* magazine—and Caroline's oddly generative mix of the Bible and an American media illusion. Then there's the jarring confluence of personal horror and pop cultural flotsam that surfaces in Mario's drawings, drawings that would be a rich, if volatile, point of departure for language instruction. How would these myriad sources and manifestations be perceived and evaluated if viewed within the framework of a canonical tradition, and what guidance would the tradition provide on how to understand and develop them? The great books and central texts of the canon could quickly become a benchmark against which the expressions of student literacy would be negatively measured, a limiting band of excellence that, ironically, could have a dispiriting effect on the very thing the current proposals intend: the fostering of mass literacy.

To understand the nature and development of literacy we   9
need to consider the social context in which it occurs—the political, economic, and cultural forces that encourage or inhibit it. The canonical orientation discourages deep analysis of the way these forces may be affecting performance. The canonists ask that schools transmit a coherent traditional knowledge to an ever-changing, frequently uprooted community. This discordance between message and audience is seldom examined. Although a ghetto child can rise on the lilt of a Homeric line—books *can* spark dreams—appeals to elevated texts can also divert attention from the conditions that keep a population from realizing its dreams. The literacy curriculum is being asked to do what our politics and our economics have failed to do: diminish differences in achievement, narrow our gaps, bring us together. Instead of analysis of the complex web of causes of poor performance, we are offered a faith in the unifying power of a body of knowledge, whose infusion will bring the rich and the poor, the longtime disaffected and the uprooted newcomers into cultural unanimity. If this vision is democratic, it is simplistically so, reductive, not an invitation for people truly to engage each other at the point where cultures and classes intersect.

I worry about the effects a canonical approach to educa-   10 tion could have on cultural dialogue and transaction—on the involvement of an abandoned underclass and on the movement of immigrants like Mario and Chin into our nation. A canonical uniformity promotes rigor and quality control; it can also squelch new thinking, diffuse the generative tension between the old and the new. It is significant that the canonical orientation is voiced with most force during times of challenge and uncertainty, for it promises the authority of tradition, the seeming stability of the past. But the authority is fictive, gained from a misreading of American cultural history. No period of that history was harmoniously stable; the invocation of a golden age is a mythologizing act. Democratic culture is, by definition, vibrant and dynamic, discomforting and unpredictable. It gives rise to apprehension; freedom is not always calming. And, yes, it can yield fragmentation, though often as not the source of fragmentation is intolerant misunderstanding of diverse traditions rather than the desire of members of those traditions to remain hermetically separate. A truly democratic vision of knowledge and social structure would honor this complexity. The vision might not be soothing, but it would provide guidance as to how to live and teach in a country made up of many cultural traditions.

We are in the middle of an extraordinary social experiment: 11
the attempt to provide education for all members of a vast pluralistic democracy. To have any prayer of success, we'll need many conceptual blessings: A philosophy of language and literacy that affirms the diverse sources of linguistic competence and deepens our understanding of the ways class and culture blind us to the richness of those sources. A perspective on failure that lays open the logic of error. An orientation toward the interaction of poverty and ability that undercuts simple polarities, that enables us to see simultaneously the constraints poverty places on the play of mind and the actual mind at play within those constraints. We'll need a pedagogy that encourages us to step back and consider the threat of the standard classroom and that shows us, having stepped back, how to step forward to invite a student across the boundaries of that powerful room. Finally, we'll need a revised store of

images of educational excellence, ones closer to egalitarian ideals—ones that embody the reward and turmoil of education in a democracy, that celebrate the plural, messy human reality of it. At heart, we'll need a guiding set of principles that do not encourage us to retreat from, but move us closer to, an understanding of the rich mix of speech and ritual and story that is America.

For Study and Discussion

QUESTIONS FOR RESPONSE

1. In paragraph 2, Rose says that many people believe that knowing the traditional works of Western literature is central to "the discourse of power"; that is, they think a person has to have some knowledge of those traditional works to function effectively in the power circles of business and government. How do you respond to such a claim? On what experiences, impressions, or knowledge do you base your response?
2. To what extent do you see the argument between Denby ("What the Great Books Do") and Rose as a serious issue affecting your own education? What is your reasoning?

QUESTIONS ABOUT PURPOSE

1. Rose has taught students from many different ethnic and economic backgrounds and written two books about teaching marginal and disadvantaged students. What is his position on making the classic works of Western literature an essential part of the education of such students?
2. What books and literature would Rose introduce into the curriculum as a result of his experience with students of different ethnic and economic backgrounds?

QUESTIONS ABOUT AUDIENCE

1. Educated people usually believe that their children should get the same kind of education that they received. What challenge does that pose for the author of this selection if he wants to reach the general public?
2. As a college student reading this essay, what do you believe you

want to get from the literature you will read in college? What are your reasons?

QUESTIONS ABOUT STRATEGIES

1. How does Rose use his own experience as an educator to support his argument against making certain classics of Western literature an important part of the college curriculum?
2. What appeals to diversity and fairness does Rose make in the last three paragraphs of his essay?

QUESTIONS FOR DISCUSSION

1. Name some specific works of literature that you think a person should be familiar with if he or she wants to be considered educated. Why are such works important? If you don't think knowledge of any particular literature is important, give your reasons.
2. What experience have you had with studying literary classics; for example, such Shakespeare plays as *Hamlet* or *Othello,* a book like Dostoyevsky's *Crime and Punishment* or Joyce's *The Dubliners,* or the poetry of Emily Dickinson or Walt Whitman? What pleasure or benefit do you think you derived from such study? What works do you know of that you might have preferred to study?

KURT VONNEGUT, JR.

Kurt Vonnegut, Jr., was born in 1922 in Indianapolis, Indiana, and attended Cornell University, where he studied biochemistry before being drafted into the infantry in World War II. Vonnegut was captured by the Germans at the Battle of the Bulge and sent to Dresden, where he worked in the underground meat locker of a slaughterhouse. He miraculously survived the Allied firebombing of Dresden and, following the war, returned to the United States to study anthropology at the University of Chicago and to work for a local news bureau. In 1947 Vonnegut accepted a position writing publicity for the General Electric Research Laboratory in Schenectady, New York, but left the company in 1950 to work on his own writing. His first three novels, *Player Piano* (1952), a satire on the tyrannies of corporate automation, *The Sirens of Titan* (1959), a science-fiction comedy on the themes of free will and determination, and *Cat's Cradle* (1963), a science fantasy on the amorality of atomic scientists, established Vonnegut's reputation as a writer who could blend humor with serious insights into the human experience. His most successful novel, *Slaughterhouse-Five, or the Children's Crusade* (1969), is based on his wartime experiences in Dresden. His other works include *God Bless You, Mr. Rosewater* (1966), *Breakfast of Champions* (1973), *Jailbird* (1979), *Palm Sunday* (1981), *Galapagos* (1985), *Hocus Pocus* (1990), and *Timequake* (1997). His best-known short stories are collected in *Canary in the Cat House* (1961) and *Welcome to the Monkey House* (1968). "Harrison Bergeron," reprinted from the latter collection, is the story of the apparatus that a future society must create to make everyone equal.

Harrison Bergeron

T HE YEAR WAS 2081, and everybody was finally equal. 1
They weren't only equal before God and the law. They
were equal every which way. Nobody was smarter than anybody else. Nobody was better looking than anybody else.
Nobody was stronger or quicker than anybody else. All this
equality was due to the 211th, 212th, and 213th Amend-
ments to the Constitution, and to the unceasing vigilance of
agents of the United States Handicapper General.

Some things about living still weren't quite right, though. 2
April, for instance, still drove people crazy by not being
springtime. And it was in that clammy month that the H-G
men took George and Hazel Bergeron's fourteen-year-old
son, Harrison, away.

It was tragic, all right, but George and Hazel couldn't 3
think about it very hard. Hazel had a perfectly average intelligence, which meant she couldn't think about anything except in short bursts. And George, while his intelligence was
way above normal, had a little mental handicap radio in his
ear. He was required by law to wear it at all times. It was
tuned to a government transmitter. Every twenty seconds or
so, the transmitter would send out some sharp noise to keep
people like George from taking unfair advantage of their
brains.

George and Hazel were watching television. There were 4
tears on Hazel's cheeks, but she'd forgotten for the moment
what they were about.

On the television screen were ballerinas. 5

A buzzer sounded in George's head. His thoughts fled in 6
panic, like bandits from a burglar alarm.

"That was a real pretty dance, that dance they just did," 7
said Hazel.

"Huh?" said George. 8

"That dance—it was nice," said Hazel. 9

"Yup," said George. He tried to think a little about the 10
ballerinas. They weren't really very good—no better than
anybody else would have been, anyway. They were burdened

with sashweights and bags of birdshot, and their faces were masked, so that no one, seeing a free and graceful gesture or a pretty face, would feel like something the cat drug in. George was toying with the vague notion that maybe dancers shouldn't be handicapped. But he didn't get very far with it before another noise in his ear radio scattered his thoughts.

George winced. So did two of the eight ballerinas. 11

Hazel saw him wince. Having no mental handicap herself, she had to ask George what the latest sound had been. 12

"Sounded like somebody hitting a milk bottle with a ball peen hammer," said George. 13

"I'd think it would be real interesting, hearing all the different sounds," said Hazel, a little envious. "All the things they think up." 14

"Um," said George. 15

"Only, if I was Handicapper General, you know what I would do?" said Hazel. Hazel, as a matter of fact, bore a strong resemblance to the Handicapper General, a woman named Diana Moon Glampers. "If I was Diana Moon Glampers," said Hazel, "I'd have chimes on Sunday—just chimes. Kind of in honor of religion." 16

"I could think, if it was just chimes," said George. 17

"Well—maybe make 'em real loud," said Hazel. "I think I'd make a good Handicapper General." 18

"Good as anybody else," said George. 19

"Who knows better'n I do what normal is?" said Hazel. 20

"Right," said George. He began to think glimmeringly about his abnormal son who was now in jail, about Harrison, but a twenty-one-gun salute in his head stopped that. 21

"Boy!" said Hazel, "that was a doozy, wasn't it?" 22

It was such a doozy that George was white and trembling, and tears stood on the rims of his red eyes. Two of the eight ballerinas had collapsed on the studio floor, were holding their temples. 23

"All of a sudden you look so tired," said Hazel. "Why don't you stretch out on the sofa, so's you can rest your handicap bag on the pillows, honeybunch." She was referring to the forty-seven pounds of birdshot in a canvas bag, which was padlocked around George's neck. "Go on and rest the 24 bag for a little while," she said. "I don't care if you're not equal to me for a while."

George weighed the bag with his hands. "I don't mind   25
it," he said. "I don't notice it any more. It's just a part of me."

"You been so tired lately—kind of wore out," said Hazel.   26
"If there was just some way we could make a little hole in the bottom of the bag, and just take out a few of them lead balls. Just a few."

"Two years in prison and two thousand dollars fine for   27
every ball I took out," said George. "I don't call that a bargain."

"If you could just take a few out when you came home   28
from work," said Hazel. "I mean—you don't compete with anybody around here. You just set around."

"If I tried to get away with it," said George, "then other   29
people'd get away with it—and pretty soon we'd be right back to the dark ages again, with everybody competing against everybody else. You wouldn't like that, would you?"

"I'd hate it," said Hazel.   30

"There you are," said George. "The minute people start   31
cheating on laws, what do you think happens to society?"

If Hazel hadn't been able to come up with an answer to   32
this question, George couldn't have supplied one. A siren was going off in his head.

"Reckon it'd fall all apart," said Hazel.   33

"What would?" said George blankly.   34

"Society," said Hazel uncertainly. "Wasn't that what you   35
just said?"

"Who knows?" said George.   36

The television program was suddenly interrupted for a   37
news bulletin. It wasn't clear at first as to what the bulletin was about, since the announcer, like all announcers, had a serious speech impediment. For about half a minute, and in a state of high excitement, the announcer tried to say, "Ladies and gentlemen—"

He finally gave up, handed the bulletin to a ballerina to   38
read.

"That's all right—" Hazel said to the announcer, "he tried. 39
That's the big thing. He tried to do the best he could with
what God gave him. He should get a nice raise for trying so
hard."

"Ladies and gentlemen—" said the ballerina, reading the 40
bulletin. She must have been extraordinarily beautiful, because the mask she wore was hideous. And it was easy to see
that she was the strongest and most graceful of all the dancers, for her handicap bags were as big as those worn by
two-hundred-pound men.

And she had to apologize at once for her voice, which was 41
a very unfair voice for a woman to use. Her voice was a warm,
luminous, timeless melody. "Excuse me—" she said, and she
began again, making her voice absolutely uncompetitive.

"Harrison Bergeron, age fourteen," she said in a grackle 42
squawk, "has just escaped from jail, where he was held on
suspicion of plotting to overthrow the government. He is a
genius and an athlete, is under-handicapped, and should be
regarded as extremely dangerous."

A police photograph of Harrison Bergeron was flashed on 43
the screen upside down, then sideways, upside down again,
then right side up. The picture showed the full length of
Harrison against a background calibrated in feet and inches.
He was exactly seven feet tall.

The rest of Harrison's appearance was Halloween and 44
hardware. Nobody had ever borne heavier handicaps. He had
outgrown hindrances faster than the H-G men could think
them up. Instead of a little ear radio for a mental handicap,
he wore a tremendous pair of earphones, and spectacles with
thick wavy lenses. The spectacles were intended to make him
not only half blind, but to give him whanging headaches
besides.

Scrap metal was hung all over him. Ordinarily, there was 45
a certain symmetry, a military neatness to the handicaps issued to strong people, but Harrison looked like a walking
junkyard. In the race of life, Harrison carried three hundred
pounds.

And to offset his good looks, the H-G men required that 46

he wear at all times a red rubber ball for a nose, keep his eyebrows shaved off, and cover his even white teeth with black caps at snaggle-tooth random.

"If you see this boy," said the ballerina, "do not—I repeat, do not—try to reason with him." 47

There was the shriek of a door being torn from its hinges. 48

Screams and barking cries of consternation came from the television set. The photograph of Harrison Bergeron on the screen jumped again and again, as though dancing to the tune of an earthquake. 49

George Bergeron correctly identified the earthquake, and well he might have—for many was the time his own home had danced to the same crashing tune. "My God—" said George, "that must be Harrison!" 50

The realization was blasted from his mind instantly by the sound of an automobile collision in his head. 51

When George could open his eyes again, the photograph of Harrison was gone. A living, breathing Harrison filled the screen. 52

Clanking, clownish, and huge, Harrison stood in the center of the studio. The knob of the uprooted studio door was still in his hand. Ballerinas, technicians, musicians, and announcers cowered on their knees before him, expecting to die. 53

"I am the Emperor!" cried Harrison. "Do you hear? I am the Emperor! Everybody must do what I say at once!" He stamped his foot and the studio shook. 54

"Even as I stand here—" he bellowed, "crippled, hobbled, sickened—I am a greater ruler than any man who ever lived! Now watch me become what I *can* become!" 55

Harrison tore the straps of his handicap harness like wet tissue paper, tore straps guaranteed to support five thousand pounds. 56

Harrison's scrap-iron handicaps crashed to the floor. 57

Harrison thrust his thumbs under the bars of the padlock that secured his head harness. The bar snapped like celery. Harrison smashed his headphones and spectacles against the wall. 58

He flung away his rubber-ball nose, revealed a man that   59
would have awed Thor, the god of thunder.

"I shall now select my Empress!" he said, looking down   60
on the cowering people. "Let the first woman who dares rise
to her feet claim her mate and her throne!"

A moment passed, and then a ballerina arose, swaying like   61
a willow.

Harrison plucked the mental handicap from her ear,   62
snapped off her physical handicaps with marvelous delicacy.
Last of all, he removed her mask.

She was blindingly beautiful.   63

"Now—" said Harrison, taking her hand, "shall we show   64
the people the meaning of the word dance? Music!" he commanded.

The musicians scrambled back into their chairs, and Har-   65
rison stripped them of their handicaps, too. "Play your best,"
he told them, "and I'll make you barons and dukes and earls."

The music began. It was normal at first—cheap, silly, false.   66
But Harrison snatched two musicians from their chairs,
waved them like batons as he sang the music as he wanted it
played. He slammed them back into their chairs.

The music began again and was much improved.   67

Harrison and his Empress merely listened to the music for   68
a while—listened gravely, as though synchronizing their
heartbeats with it.

They shifted their weights to their toes.   69

Harrison placed his big hands on the girl's tiny waist,   70
letting her sense the weightlessness that would soon be hers.

And then, in an explosion of joy and grace, into the air   71
they sprang!

Not only were the laws of the land abandoned, but the law   72
of gravity and the laws of motion as well.

They reeled, whirled, swiveled, flounced, capered, gam-   73
boled, and spun.

They leaped like deer on the moon.   74

The studio ceiling was thirty feet high, but each leap   75
brought the dancers nearer to it.

It became their obvious intention to kiss the ceiling.   76

They kissed it.   77

And then, neutralizing gravity with love and pure will, they   78
remained suspended in air inches below the ceiling, and they
kissed each other for a long, long time.

It was then that Diana Moon Glampers, the Handicapper   79
General, came into the studio with a double-barreled ten-
gauge shotgun. She fired twice, and the Emperor and the
Empress were dead before they hit the floor.

Diana Moon Glampers loaded the gun again. She aimed   80
it at the musicians and told them they had ten seconds to get
their handicaps back on.

It was then that the Bergerons' television tube burned out.   81

Hazel turned to comment about the blackout to George.   82
But George had gone out into the kitchen for a can of beer.

George came back in with the beer, paused while a handi-   83
cap signal shook him up. And then he sat down again. "You
been crying?" he said to Hazel.

"Yup," she said.   84

"What about?" he said.   85

"I forgot," she said. "Something real sad on television."   86

"What was it?" he said.   87

"It's all kind of mixed up in my mind," said Hazel.   88

"Forget sad things," said George.   89

"I always do," said Hazel.   90

"That's my girl," said George. He winced. There was the   91
sound of a rivetting gun in his head.

"Gee—I could tell that one was a doozy," said Hazel.   92

"You can say that again," said George.   93

"Gee—" said Hazel, "I could tell that one was a doozy."   94

COMMENT ON "HARRISON BERGERON"

Known for his offbeat and sometimes bizarre vision of reality,
Kurt Vonnegut, Jr., has created in "Harrison Bergeron" a
science fiction story full of black humor and grotesque details.
The society he creates in the story is reminiscent of the society
pictured in Orwell's *1984*, totally controlled by a government

that invades and interferes in every facet of its citizens' lives. In a travesty of the famous declaration that "All men are created equal," the government has set out to legislate equality. Vonnegut portrays the results of such legislation in macabre images of people forced to carry weighted bags to reduce their strength, wear grotesque masks to conceal their beauty, and suffer implants in their brain to disrupt their thinking. When a fourteen-year-old boy, Harrison Bergeron, shows signs of excellence, he is first arrested, then ruthlessly destroyed when he throws off his restraints and literally rises to the top.

Underneath the farce, Vonnegut has created a tragic picture of a culture so obsessed with equality that people must be leveled by decree. Mediocrity reigns; any sign of excellence or superiority threatens law and order and must be suppressed immediately. Ultimately, of course, such a society will perish because it will kill its talent and stagnate.

Vonnegut wrote this story in 1961, after the repressive Stalinist regime that wiped out thousands of leaders and intellectuals in Russia; it precedes by a few years the disastrous era of Mao's Red Guards in China, when hundreds of thousands of intellectuals and artists were killed or imprisoned in the name of equality. Is Vonnegut commenting on the leveling tendencies of these totalitarian societies? Or does he see such excesses reflected in our own society? No one knows, but it's the genius of artists to prod us to think about such concerns.

Persuasion and Argument as a Writing Strategy

1. Reread several of the essays in this section, and decide which one or two appeal to you most. Then analyze your response to those essays—to their topic, their tone, their vocabulary, their use of personal anecdotes or narratives, and to the kind of arguments the author presented. Why do you think you liked your one or two choices better than the rest or found them more convincing? What was it about them that appealed to you, a college student, even though you were not the intended reader for that essay? Finally, draw a general conclusion about what you think the author or authors have done that made their work effective for you and what lesson you could take for your own writing.

2. Reread "I Have a Dream" by Martin Luther King, Jr., and "A Chinaman's Chance" by Eric Liu. Write an essay comparing King's dreams and hopes for African Americans with the American Dream that Liu wants to hang on to for his generation. What components of the two dreams are similar? To what extent do you think King and Liu would agree with each other? Conclude on a personal note by sketching out your own version of the American Dream and indicating how you hope to achieve it.

3. For an opinion column for your campus newspaper or perhaps for an on-line magazine like *Salon*, write a persuasive essay pointing out the advantages and rewards of investing substantial chunks of time in learning to navigate the Internet. Such advantages could be financial, recreational, academic, or intellectual—or you might argue that the Internet is just a lot of fun. On the other hand, you could write a comparable essay for the same audience pointing out the disadvantages and frustrations of investing your time on the Internet. For either essay, use specific examples of items you've encountered on the Net and

describe personal experiences to illustrate your claims and enliven your writing.

4. Write a persuasive article for either your hometown newspaper or your campus newspaper in which you try to get a local company or industry to contribute its support to a civic project, either one that exists or one that you design. Such a project might be restoring dilapidated homes for people who need housing, sponsoring a literacy project, or sponsoring a remodeling project for a public playground. Be specific about how the company could help and how it would benefit. You might reread the introduction to this section to help you frame your argument and establish your tone.

5. For an audience of your classmates and instructor, write an essay in which you analyze how Rosemary Bray uses narration and personal examples in "So How Did I Get Here?" Citing several examples, show how this strategy affects the appeal of her essay. Compare her primarily emotional and ethical appeal with Charles Murray's primarily logical appeal in "The Coming White Underclass." Which appeal do you find more effective and why?

6. By having a core of basic requirements that everyone must meet in order to get a degree, most colleges and universities affirm that to be considered educated, a person needs to have mastered a certain body of knowledge. Usually the requirements include history, literature, and science courses, and often some courses in philosophy and fine arts. Check out the requirements for a liberal arts degree at your institution. Then, for an audience of your classmates and instructor, discuss what the required courses should cover. For instance, should everyone have to take American history and literature, should everyone have to pass a proficiency test in writing and mathematics, should everyone have to take at least two science courses? Or are requirements superfluous and stifling? Support your argument with reasons and evidence.

RESOURCES
FOR
WRITING

ↂ

As you worked your way through this book, you discovered that you already possess many resources for reading and writing. You read essays on a wide variety of subjects. You encountered new and complicated information shaped by unusual and unsettling assertions. But you discovered experiences and feelings that you recognize—the challenge of learning, the ordeal of disappointment, the cost of achievement. As you examined these essays, you realized that you had something to say about your reading, something to contribute to the writers' interpretation of some complex subjects. Your reading revealed your resources for writing.

Your work with this book has also enabled you to identify and practice using patterns that at each stage of the writing process will help you transform your resources into writing. In the beginning, these patterns give rise to questions that you might ask about any body of information.

Suppose you want to write an essay on women's contributions to science. You might begin by asking why so few women are ranked among the world's great scientists. You might continue asking questions: What historical forces have discouraged women from becoming scientists (cause and effect)? How do women scientists define problems, analyze evidence, formulate conclusions (process analysis), and do they go about these processes in ways different from the ways used by men scientists (comparison and contrast)? If women scientists look at the world differently from the way men do, does this difference have an effect on the established notions of inquiry (argument)? Such questions work like the different lenses you attach to a camera: each lens gives you a slightly different perspective on your subject.

Your initial questions enable you to envision your subject from different perspectives. Answering one question encourages you to develop your subject according to a purpose associated with one of the common patterns of organization. For instance, if you decide to write about your first scuba dive, your choice of purpose seems obvious: to answer the question, What happened? You would then proceed to write a narrative essay. In drafting this essay, however, you may discover questions you had not anticipated, such as: What factors led to the development of scuba diving? How do you use scuba equipment? How is scuba diving similar to or different from swimming?

Responding to these new questions forces you to decide whether your new information develops or distorts your draft. The history of underwater diving—from diving bells to diving suits to self-contained equipment—may help your readers see a context for your narrative. On the other hand, such information may confuse them, distracting them from your original purpose: to tell what happened.

As you struggle with your new resources, you may decide that your original purpose no longer drives your writing. You may decide to change your purpose and write a cause-and-effect essay. Instead of telling what happened on your first scuba dive, you might decide to use your personal experience, together with some reading, to write a more scientific essay analyzing the effects of underwater swimming on your senses of sight and hearing.

This book has helped you make such decisions by showing you how the common patterns of organization evoke different purposes, audiences, and strategies. In this final section, you will have the opportunity to make such decisions about a new collection of resources—an anthology of writing on the subject of gambling.

Before you begin reading these selections, take an initial inventory.

> What kind of direct experience have you had with gambling?
>> What kind of games have you played?
>> How much money have you won or lost?
> What kind of indirect experience have you had with gambling?
>> What has happened to the gamblers among your relatives or family?
>> How has gambling been portrayed in the novels you have read or the television programs and movies you have watched?
> What do you know about the place of gambling in American culture?
>> What games of chance have Americans played throughout their history?
>> Why has gambling been illegal for most of our history?
>> Why has gambling recently become acceptable in our culture?
> What do you believe about the role of luck in life?
>> Who taught you to believe or distrust luck?
>> What people do you know who are lucky?

Why do you think they are lucky?
If you had to choose, would you rather be talented
or lucky?

Thinking about such questions will remind you of the
extensive resources you bring to the subject of gambling. It
is a subject that touches all of our lives in some way. And it
affects our behavior in countless other ways—what we do
with our spare time, with whom we associate, how we spend
our money, and how we think about ourselves (i.e., winners
or losers).

After you have made a preliminary inventory of your
knowledge and attitudes toward gambling, read the writings
in this section. You will notice that each selection asks you to
look at gambling from a different perspective:

1. *What happened? (narration and description).* Joseph Epstein recounts his adolescent admiration for those who live
   the gambler's life.
2. *How do you do it? (process analysis).* Bill Barich analyzes the
   procedures for handicapping horses and the consequences
   of impulsive gambling.
3. *How is it similar to or different from something else? (comparison and contrast).* Clyde Brion Davis compares the
   risks of growing wheat and throwing craps. He also suggests other comparisons between those who invest and
   those who bet.
4. *What kind of subdivision does it contain? (division and
   classification).* Charlotte Olmsted explains the historical
   symbolism in the most prominent divisions in a pack of
   cards.
5. *How would you characterize it? (definition).* Margaret O.
   Hyde points out the distinguishing characteristics of a
   compulsvie gambler.
6. *How did it happen? (cause and effect).* James Popkin analyzes the techniques casinos use to encourage gamblers to
   stay longer and lose more.

7. *How can you prove it? (persuasion and argument)*. Robert Goodman, director of the United States Gambling Research Institute, provides ample evidence to demonstrate that, as a public policy, gambling has been a bad investment.

The collection ends with Louise Erdrich's story, "Lyman's Luck" and student Jason Rex's essay, "Not a Bad Night." The story focuses on a man's attempt to acquire a symbol of his heritage—a pipe—and his reaction to losing it in a spree of compulsive gambling. The student essay provides a look at the types of students who entertain themselves at a weekly poker game.

Both selections raise questions that weave their way throughout the other writing in the section: Is gambling a serious, corrupting force in American culture? Is gambling a harmless form of entertainment?

As you examine these selections, keep track of how your reading expands your resources—provoking memories, adding information, and suggesting questions you had not considered when you made your initial inventory about gambling. Because this information will give you new ways to think about your original questions, you will want to explore your thinking in writing.

The assignments that follow each selection suggest several ways that you can use these resources for writing:

1. You can *respond* to the essay by shaping a similar experience according to its method of organization.
2. You can *analyze* the essay to discover how the writer uses specific strategies to communicate a purpose to an audience.
3. You can use the essay as a springboard for an essay that *argues* a similar thesis in a different context.
4. You can *compare* the essay to other selections in the anthology that raise similar questions about gambling. At the

end of each writing assignment, one or two selections are suggested as Resources for Comparison.

5. You can follow Jason Rex's example and explore some aspect of gambling by using a specific writing strategy.

Drawing on your experience, reading, and familiarity with writing strategies, you are ready to work up a writing assignment on any subject.

Joseph Epstein was born in 1937 in Chicago and was educated at the University of Chicago. For many years he edited *American Scholar,* the quarterly journal of the national honor society Phi Beta Kappa, and is currently a visiting lecturer in English at Northwestern University. His learned essays on American life and letters, sometimes written under the pseudonym Aristides, have appeared in magazines such as *American Scholar, Harper's, The New Yorker,* and the *New York Times Magazine.* His books include *Divorced in America: Marriage in an Age of Possibility* (1974), *Ambition: The Secret Passion* (1981), *The Middle of My Tether: Familiar Essays* (1983), *Plausible Prejudices: Essays on American Writing* (1985), and *Partial Payments* (1989). In "Confessions of a Low Roller," Epstein describes the glamorous appeal of the gambling life.

Confessions of a Low Roller

M Y OWN INTEREST in gambling . . . initially derived 1 from the social atmosphere in which I came of age. By this I certainly don't mean my home. My father had not the least interest in cards, sports, or gambling generally, preferring situations, such as the one he had inserted himself into as the owner of a small business, in which as far as possible he could control his own destiny. Most of the men in the rising middle-class Jewish milieu that I grew up in felt much the same. They were physicians and lawyers and businessmen, and worked hard so that their children could have an easier life than they, as the sons of immigrants, had had. Some among them gambled—played a little gin rummy or in a small-stakes poker game, bet $50 on a prizefight—but clearly work was at the center of their lives. They believed in personal industry, in thrift, in saving for the future. Entrepreneurial in spirit, they also believed that only a fool works for someone else.

On the periphery, though, were a small number of men who lived and believed otherwise. Two boys among my school friends and acquaintances had fathers who were bookies, and rather big-time ones, judging by the scale on which they lived. Nothing back of the candy store or Broadway cigar stand about them; they were rather like the rest of our fathers, but home more often and with better tans and more telephones in the house. They lived on the edge of the criminal

2

I learned that in gambling, as in life, you could figure the odds, the probabilities, the little and the large likelihoods, and still, when lightning struck in the form of ill luck, logic was no help.

---

world. So, too, I gather did the father of a girl I knew in high school; he played golf from April until October and from October until April played high-stakes gin rummy at a place atop the Sheraton Hotel called The Town Club; the younger brother of a Capone lieutenant, he was rumored to collect a dollar a month on every jukebox installed in Chicago. The brother of a man I once worked for when I was in high school was said to be a full-time gambler, making his living (he was a bachelor) betting on sports events. In his forties then, he carried the nickname "Acey"; if he is still alive, he would now be in his seventies, which is a bit old to carry around such a nickname. I would often see him at baseball games on weekday afternoons, where, well groomed and well rested, he looked as if his personal motto, an edited version of my father's and my friends' fathers', might read: "Only a fool works."

When young, I felt a strong attraction to such men. The attraction was to their seemingly effortless access to what I then took to be the higher and finer things of life. Their connection to corruption also excited me. Corruption was endemic to Chicago, a city that prided itself on its gangsters the way that other cities were proud of their artists, and one had to be brought up in a glass bubble—make that an isinglass bubble—not to come in contact with it. Dickens, Dostoyevsky, Dreiser, and many a novelist since knew that corruption is more alluring, and more convincingly described, than goodness. Goodness, on first acquaintance, is a bit boring—and, when young, the only thing duller than goodness is common sense.

I had an acquaintance whose father became a very rich man in a very brief time through selling very ugly aluminum awnings. One Saturday afternoon I went with him to his father's small factory, where, among his father and his father's salesmen, each with a high stack of bills in front of him, a serious poker game was in progress. My own father often used the phrase "place of business" with something of the same reverence that some reserve for the phrase "place of worship," and the idea of a poker game on the site of his business would have appalled him. At the time, it rather thrilled me. But then it would be many years until I came round to my father's view, which was essentially the view set out by Henry James in a youthful letter to his friend Charles Eliot Norton: "I have in my own fashion learned the lesson that life is effort, unremittingly repeated. . . . I feel somehow as if the real pity was for those who had been beguiled into the perilous delusion that it isn't."

So beguiled, I spent much of my adolescence in imitation of what I took to be the model of the gambler. During our last year of grammar school, my friends and I met for penny poker games on Saturday afternoons before ballroom dancing lessons. There we sat, at thirteen years old, neckties loosened, jackets draped over the backs of chairs, cigarettes depending unsteadily from the sides of our mouths, smoke causing our eyes to water and squint, playing seven-card stud, deuces usually wild. Quite a scene. Each of us must have thought himself some variant of George Raft, James Cagney, Humphrey Bogart, or John Garfield, when Leo Gorcey and the Dead End Kids gone middle class was much more like it. "My pair of jacks sees your three cents, Ronald, and I bump you a nickel."

A misspent youth? I suppose it was, though I never 6 thought of it as such. Perhaps this was owing to its being so immensely enjoyable. In high school, gambling went from an occasional to an almost incessant activity. Although we never shot dice, my friends and I played every variation of poker, blackjack, and gin rummy. From city newsstand vendors we acquired and bet football parlay cards. Every so often, on weekend nights, we would travel out of the city to the sulky races, or "the trotters" as we called them, at Maywood Park. Some unrecognized genius invented a game called "potluck," a combination of blackjack and in-between, which guaranteed that, no matter how minimal the stakes to begin with, one would soon be playing for more than one could afford. With its built-in escalation element, potluck was a game that produced high excitement, for it was not unusual for someone to walk away from these games a $200 winner. I won my share, but more vividly than any win do I remember one gray wintry afternoon when, between four and six o'clock, I lost $125—this at a time when that figure might pay a month's rent on a two-bedroom apartment in a respectable middle-class neighborhood. If the end of the world had been announced on that evening's news, I, at seventeen, shouldn't in the least have minded. In fact, as I recall, I felt it already had.

Gambling, though scarcely a valuable education in itself, 7 did teach a thing or two about one's own nature. I learned about the limits of my courage with money, for one thing; for another, I learned that, in gambling, as in life, you could figure the odds, the probabilities, the little and large likelihoods, and still, when lightning struck in the form of ill luck, logic was no help. I learned I had to put a good, and insofar as possible stylish, face on defeat, even though losing was very far from my idea of a nice time. If you were even mildly attentive, gambling revealed your character to you, showed it in operation under pressure, often taught you the worst about yourself. Some people wanted to win too sorely; they whined and moaned, banged the table and cursed the gods when they lost and seemed smug and self-justified in victory. Others sat grim and humorless over their cards, gloomy in defeat and always ready to settle for a small win. Still others exhibited, even at sixteen or seventeen, a certain largeness of spirit; they were ready to trust their luck; they had a feeling for the game, which I took to be a feeling for life itself, and were delighted to be in action.

"In action" is an old gambler's phrase; and "the action" 8 used to refer to gambling generally. Yet, for all its insistence on action, gambling can be excruciatingly boring. During one stretch in the army, I played poker at Fort Chaffee, in Arkansas, almost nightly for roughly six weeks; I played less for the excitement of gambling than to combat the boredom of army life when one is confined to a post. It turned out to be boredom pitted against boredom. In a rather low-stakes game over this period I emerged roughly a $400 winner. Some of this money I sent to a friend to buy me books in Chicago. The rest I spent on a steak and champagne dinner in the town of Fort Smith, Arkansas, for eight or nine barracks mates. Doing this seemed to me at the time a gesture of magnificence befitting a gambling man.

Topics for Writing
Narration and Description

1. *Respond.* In an essay for the Guest Opinion column of your state's educational journal (e.g., *The Indiana School Journal*), recount your experiences as a young gambler. Describe why you were attracted to gambling and what you learned about your "nature" when you won and lost. (*Resources for Comparison:* Judith Ortiz Cofer, "Silent Dancing," page 56; Richard Rodriguez, "Growing Up in Los Angeles," page 323).

2. *Analyze.* For many years, Joseph Epstein edited *The American Scholar* (the official magazine of the Phi Beta Kappa society). Write an essay for the chapter of the Phi Beta Kappa society on your campus in which you analyze how Epstein illustrates the following mottos: (1) only a fool works for someone else and (2) only a fool works. You might also speculate on what caused Epstein to finally agree with Henry James that "life is effort." (*Resources for Comparison:* Lars Eighner, "My Daily Dives in the Dumpster," page 111; Eric Liu, "A Chinaman's Chance: Reflections on the American Dream," page 468).

3. *Argue.* In a column for the newsletter of your church, argue the merits of Epstein's contention that *corruption* is more alluring than *goodness.* Or that the only thing more boring (and duller) than *goodness* is *common sense.* You may want to interview your minister or several youth counselors to see how they would challenge Epstein's assertions. (*Resources for Comparison:* Terry Tempest Williams, "The Village Watchman," page 46; Flannery O'Connor, "Revelation," page 274).

BILL BARICH

Bill Barich was born in 1943 in Winona, Minnesota, and educated at Colgate University. After serving in the Peace Corps in Nigeria and Biafra, Barich returned to the United States to work in publishing. He began as editorial assistant at the *New Yorker* and then began contributing essays on sports and travel. His semi-autobiographical research on horse racing appears in *Laughing in the Hills* (1980). His more recent publications include a collection of essays, *Traveling Light* (1984), a collection of short stories, *Hard to Be Good* (1987), a travel narrative, *Big Drama: Into the Heart of California* (1994), and a novel, *Carson Valley* (1996). In "Handicapping," reprinted from *Laughing in the Hills,* Barich analyzes the complicated process of handicapping race horses.

Handicapping

T HE NIGHT BEFORE the meet began, I sat at my unconventionally four-legged Terrace desk and prepared to handicap the following day's races. I had no system or standard approach, but there were a few things I always took into account before making a tentative selection: *speed,* which could be gauged in general fashion from a horse's recent running times; *class,* which was a function both of breeding and the level (races were ranked by the size of the purse offered, handicap first, then stakes, allowance, and claiming) at which a horse had been competing; and *condition,* which meant fitness and was expressed by a horse's recent finishes (if they were good or improving, the horse was said to be "on form") and its showing during the daily exercise period, morning workouts (recent workout times were given at the

1

bottom of each horse's chart). The trainer and jockey associated with a horse also affected my decision. Certain trainers
were downright inept and never won a race regardless of their
stock, and not a few riders at Golden Gate were incapable of
handling their mounts.

I also considered post position as a potential factor in the   2
outcome of a race. Before leaving home I'd compiled a post-
position survey of races run during the Pacific meeting that
was just ending. I'd done this to see if there was an advantage
to be gained by breaking from a particular post (the slot a
horse is assigned in the starting gate; there are rarely more
than twelve horses entered in a race), and to determine

---

*My five hundred dollars in twenty dollar
bills looked pitiful stacked on the desk,
the smallest stake any would-be gambler
ever started with.*

---

whether front-runners, horses who broke quickly, took the
lead, and tried to hold it throughout (going *wire-to-wire*)
fared better at Golden Gate than one would expect. The
survey proved instructive. In races over a mile, called *routes*,
the outside posts, seven through twelve, were as disadvanta-
geous as usual; horses stuck out there had more ground to
cover. In races under a mile, called *sprints*, the survey turned
up a surprise. Ordinarily, the best posts in a short race are
those closest to the rail, but during the Pacific meet horses
starting near the middle of the track, posts four and five, had
won more often than horses inside them. Furthermore,
horses breaking from the seven slot had won almost as often
as those breaking from the one slot. The survey indicated as
well that front-runners won over thirty percent of all sprints
at Golden Gate. Facts like these were invaluable when trying

to choose between two otherwise closely matched thorough-breds.

As an additional edge I'd brought along three books on handicapping technique: Tom Ainslie's *Complete Guide to Thoroughbred Racing*, Andy Beyer's *Picking Winners*, and Steve Davidowitz's *Betting Thoroughbreds*. These books were not typical of the genre; most handicapping tracts are lurid affairs that sucker readers into parting with a few dollars in exchange for an easy-to-follow system guaranteed to produce eight million dollars in just three short weeks. Ainslie, Beyer, and Davidowitz were serious, intelligent men who never underestimated the complexity of the sport. Ainslie was the dean of the company. His book was the most informative about all aspects of racing and is still the best primer around. He favored a balanced approach to making a selection, weighing all the factors much as I had been doing. ⒊

Beyer was more dogmatic. As an undergraduate at Harvard he'd gotten hooked on racing and had since "perfected" a system based on the digital-computer research of Sheldon Kovitz, a fellow student and doctoral candidate in mathematics. Apparently, Kovitz was too busy feeding numbers into his IBM 360 Model 40 to succeed himself, but Beyer saw in his calculations the seed of Something Big, a way to incorporate relativity into speed ratings. Most ratings, like those given in the *Form*, were suspect because they were derived from non-existent absolutes. A horse who'd earned an 80 on Tuesday was not *exactly* as fast as a horse who'd earned an 80 on Wednesday because the track surface changed every day (or even from moment to moment), and Tuesday's conditions were always different from Wednesday's—faster or slower by critical fractions. Beyer adopted Kovitz's method, improved it, and parlayed the results into a complicated mathematical system. It was the best in the world, he claimed. ⒋

"Speed figures are the way, the truth and the light," wrote Beyer. "And my method of speed handicapping is, I believe, without equal." ⒌

I found Davidowitz's book the most pithy and available. He seemed a little tougher than the other men, more hard- ⒍ nosed, and it showed in his jacket photo. While Ainslie looked like a businessman and Beyer like a computer programmer with a side interest in recreational drugs, Davidowitz looked mean. His face had a demonic cast; an eyebrow was arched in perpetual scrutiny. I liked the knack he had for making direct, incontrovertible statements: *When a three-year-old is assigned actual top weight in a race for horses three years and up, the three-year-old has little or no chance of winning.* Such gems were inlaid throughout the text, always supported by statistics. Davidowitz further endeared himself by being quick to point a finger at the criminal element in racing whenever he encountered it. Most turf writers were unwilling to print anything but bland idealizations of the sport.

After skimming through the books, I put all the materials   7
aside and reached into my pocket, as I'd been doing every hour or so since leaving home. Again I counted my money— five hundred dollars in twenty-dollar bills. It looked pitiful stacked on the desk, the smallest stake any would-be gambler ever started with. I felt embarrassed. I thought the stake was correlated directly with my life: impoverished spirit, empty wallet. Such stupid flashes of guilt often overtook me after midnight. I tried to ignore this one, though, and took a shower and went to bed.

Early the next morning, April 19, the first morning of   8
Tanforan, I went to Golden Gate Fields ready to win. The grandstand was empty and quiet, with the cool feel of an aluminum mixing bowl waiting for ingredients. The sun climbed slowly over the eucalyptus trees on Albany Hill, huge blue gums planted there a century ago to shield the town from the reports of Industry on the Point. From the club-house rail I could see the backstretch and the neat rows of wooden barns and the soiled straw piled high at the corners of the rows. The hotwalking machines were turning. They were a recent addition to the track and had made obsolete a job grooms used to do, walking horses until they'd cooled down after exercising. There was a power pack at the base of each machine, and from it rose a thin shaft with four metal arms arranged in the shape of a cross. The arms were about

six feet long and resembled in their positioning the blades of a propeller. When the power was on, the shaft revolved slowly and the horses, hitched by their halters to insulated cords dangling from the arms, were forced to circle until their pulse rates dropped and their breathing was not so labored. As they circled they looked like flywheels turning within the greater geometry of the backstretch, suggesting an intricate time-piece thrown open to bits of biology.

I took the escalator to the ground floor and walked through the paddock area. The green wear-forever carpet was worn thin, the railings were chipped and needed paint, and the saddling stalls, green and white, were scarred with half-moons incised by hoofs. The Par Three course laid out on the infield grass was soon to be closed for lack of patronage, but an OPEN sign hung in the pro shop window. I saw my face reflected among irons sticking out of a plaid bag. House sparrows pecked at seeds the harrow had uncovered, hopping around among the horse apples. The turf course surprised me. It was rough and stubby, spiked with crabgrass and not nearly as smooth as it looked from above. Two redwing blackbirds were mating in the caked mud of a drainage ditch. The male's epaulets were scarlet, brilliantly exposed as he drew his lover into a caped embrace.

Near the winner's circle I found a monument to Silky Sullivan. It was built of bricks and mortar and looked like the chimney of a backyard barbecue pit. A bronze plaque was set into the center of the chimney, and on it was inscribed a celebratory poem written by Elaine Marfoglia of Pasadena.

Out of the gate like a bullet of red,
Dropping behind as the rest speed ahead,
Loping along as the clubhouse fans cheer,
Leisurely stalking the field in first gear.

Down the backstretch forty lengths far behind,
Unconcerned—strictly the following kind;
Muscles in motion, nostrils aflare,
Holding the pace with a casual air.

The poem continued for a few more stanzas, then galloped   11
toward a finish as heart-tugging as any of Silky's.

> *And now he's at rest, where all champions go;*
> *We'll miss the parade of his "Derby Day" show.*
> *As he pranced and kicked up his heels for the crowd,*
> *He was loved—he was big, he was gentle and proud.*

About eleven-thirty fans began arriving in steady streams,   12
and as I watched them come in I had the sense of a jointly
imagined form evolving, something entirely apart from
horses and jockeys. Each person seemed to carry a narrative
element in his head, and these elements were being woven
gradually into the prevailing fiction. It was modeled on notions of symmetry and coherence. The electronic devices
around the track reinforced the fiction in the warm-up patterns they flashed: the infield toteboard showed four rows of
zeros balanced one on top of another, the smaller totes inside
offered odds of five to five at every slot, and the closed-circuit
TVs featured tiny dots boxed at perfect intervals within a
neatly squared grid. The gift shop lady displayed her horse-
head bookends in a horseshoe-shaped arc, and the popcorn
lady, her striped smock in harmony with the trim of her
booth, checked to see that the empty cardboard boxes she
would later fill were distributed in evenly matched stacks. The
fiction was carefully, if unconsciously, projected and didn't
begin to dissipate until the National Anthem had been played
and the horses came sauntering up from the barns in single
file. Then order gave way to chaos.

The moment when horses enter the paddock before a race   13
can be a bad one. Statistics that had earlier seemed so definitive are translated peremptorily into flesh, and flesh is heir to
miseries, bandaged legs, a limp, a nervous froth bubbling on
a filly's inner thighs. Many times I've heard people groan
when they saw what their figures had led them to, some
scarred creature with downcast eyes. I was fortunate on the
opening day of Tanforan. The horse I'd chosen at the Ter-

race, Southern Gospel, looked good. He was a rangy chestnut
gelding with a polish to his coat. He was breaking from the
preferential four hole, too, which should have set my mind
at ease, but I was feeling anxious. I'd been away from the
track for some time and my responses to its stimuli were
heightened, exaggerated. Every flickering movement made
an impression on me, and I tried to take them all into account. Suddenly other horses began looking good. Folklore's
Lite, who'd earned a high Beyer speed rating, was up on his
toes. When I opened the *Form* to compare him with Southern Gospel, I saw instead something I'd missed before, excellent workouts for Top Pass. Was Top Pass ready to make
his bid? Davidowitz might think so. The more I read, the
more confused I became. The *Form* kept bursting open,
punctured by discoveries, ruining my cartographic efforts.

Next I felt the concentrative energy of the bettors around
me. They were staring at the paddock just as piercingly as I
was, working hard to affect the outcome of the race. It was
as though many versions of reality were competing for a
chance to obtain. The man next to me was steaming. He wore
the blissful expression of a monk in his tenth hour of *zazen;*
smoke was about to issue from his ears. I stood there paralyzed, unable to make a choice. I was afraid that if I lost my
first bet, a downward trend would be irreversibly established.
With three minutes to go I ran to the windows and bet a
horse I hadn't even considered before, Spicy Gift, because
I'd noticed that he'd had some bad luck last time out, which
indicated, absolutely, that he was bound, perhaps even *compelled*, to win. When I walked away I realized I'd just put ten
bucks on a twenty-to-one shot. Handicapping overkill, the
brain weaving useless webs. Spicy Gift finished somewhere in
the middle of the field, beaten by Bargain Hostess, a filly and
first-time starter who broke from the outermost post. These
factors had eliminated her from contention in my mind; now
I saw them for what they were, markers of talent.

But it was too late, I was locked into a loser's mind-set
and couldn't shake free of it. All day long I compounded my
mistakes, playing the most improbable nags on the card,

hoping to get even, to start over, the slate wiped clean. Hong Kong Flew, Skinny Dink, throwing what little expertise I had out the window, Hey Mister M.A., a toad at fifty-seven to one, *giving* it away, then Queequeg in the eighth race because of Melville and what they'd found taped under his desk after he'd died, a scrap of paper on which he'd written, *Be true to the dreams of your youth;* but Queequeg drowned too, leaving me adrift, not even a coffin for support, and in the ninth, a broken man, I latched on to the favorite, Crazy Wallet, and watched in disgust as he hobbled home fifth. Down I went, spiraling, down and down, done in but good, sixty dollars fed irretrievably into the belly of the beast and still the breeze did blow.

Topics for Writing
Process Analysis

1. *Respond.* Barich says that he was a victim of "handicapping overkill." Write an essay for your student newspaper illustrating how too much "studying" confuses learning. For example, demonstrate how knowing too much can make you overanalyze (and misread) simple and obvious questions. (*Resources for Comparison:* Nikki Giovanni, "Campus Racism 101," page 119; Mike Rose, "The Limits of the Great Books," page 528).

2. *Analyze.* Barich is convinced that applying his criteria, studying his survey, and consulting his experts will make him ready to win. For a class in research design or statistics, analyze the effectiveness of Barich's preparation. You may want to "recrunch" the numbers in his survey given the "facts" in Beyer's comments on relativity. (*Resources for Comparison:* James H. Austin, "Four Kinds of Chance," page 240; Daniel Goleman, "Peak Performance: Why Records Fall," page 397).

3. *Argue.* Despite Barich's lengthy preparation, he quickly develops a "loser's mind-set" and starts "giving it away." For a psychology class, describe those factors that enable the mind to affect the outcome of events. What factors create a "winner's mind-set"? (*Resources for Comparison:* Alice Adams, "Truth or Consequences," page 78; Stephen Harrigan, "The Tiger Is God," page 340).

Clyde Brion Davis (1894–1962) was born in Unadilla, Nebraska, and educated in the public schools of Chillicothe and Kansas City, Missouri. He worked as a reporter for the *Denver Post* and the *San Francisco Examiner* before assuming positions with Knight Newspapers and the Rinehart Publishing Company. His books include *Nebraska Coast* (1939), *The Stars Incline* (1946), *The Age of Indiscretion* (1950), and *Something for Nothing* (1956). In "The Wheat Farmer and the Crap Shooter," excerpted from *Something for Nothing,* Davis compares the risks of farming and gambling.

The Wheat Farmer and the Crap Shooter

S PEAKING OF GAMBLING in a pessimistic sort of way, you may say that life itself is a one-armed bandit slot machine which, in the end, takes all your nickels. Once in a while you get two cherries and a bar or three oranges or even three plums and the light clatter of coins down the pipe is very pleasant and encouraging, although you really should know you're bound to drop those winnings back into the machine before you stop playing. 1

But hope in man is eternal. 2

Speaking of the gamble of life in a more optimistic way, you'll have faith that eventually you'll hit the jackpot and be transported to everlasting bliss. 3

If you're a hedonist or an esthete, you'll gain a quiet pleasure merely from watching those spinning bands of fluctuating color, which represent the communion of human with human, and human with nature. 4

But if you are a matter-of-fact realist, you may sit back 5 grumpily refusing to play at all. Then you'll have no fun and your nickels will mold in your pocket.

Well, not *everyone* is a gambler. 6

There is, however, the wheat farmer. And in a less general 7 vein you might observe that the soil of the western plains is an extraordinarily liberal one-armed bandit slot machine into which the owner or lessee drops his money and then anxiously watches the spinning cycles of hot, dry days and rainy days and line squalls and hail, hoping against hope that they finally will resolve themselves into a happy pattern which will

---

Psychologically and philosophically, there is little difference between a wheat farmer and the fellow who takes a flier at roulette—except the farmer's under nervous tension for a long time and his chances of winning are materially better.

---

produce a shiny new Cadillac, but quite aware that early drought or late hail may well send him to the banker petitioning for a loan.

Once the soil is prepared and the wheat sowed, there is 8 literally nothing he can do except hope and pray until—luck being with him—the harvesting combines move into the field of ripened grain.

Objections can be raised that the wheatgrower is not a 9 gambler because he is producing wealth, adding to the world's tangible assets, providing the material for bread. A potent and legal argument can be made that in a true gambling transaction nothing of value is produced or transported or jobbed or wholesaled or distributed, that on a basis of sheer chance one individual seeking to gain something for nothing ventures some legal tender and loses while another individual also seeking something for nothing wins. Under the law, of course, that will hold up—and so will speculating on the stock market and in grain futures.

From a philosophical or a psychological point of view, however, I think one might take into account the emotional reaction of the wheatgrower at sight of his expanse of waving grain. In the unlikely event that his predominant reaction is a warm satisfaction at the thought of his capital and his direction producing bread for thousands of fellow humans, then it must be granted that he is not essentially a gambler.

Yet I think a more typical case would be a South Dakotan who is a wheat farmer because his background has given him a knowledge of that sort of enterprise and he either owns the land or has the capital or bank credit to lease land, acquire seeds and prepare the soil, and I think also that his probable reaction as he surveys the ripening wheat would be voiced to himself in somewhat this fashion: "Man, oh, man, it looks like we got it this year. And it's going to be a good market on account the radio said Kansas and Oklahoma is burned out. Oh, God, give us just a week more good weather and we got it in the bag. Sweet Jesus, just a week more and Mamie's got a new fur coat. Not a cloud in the sky and the barometer's riding high. Hold it off, God, and I'll surprise you what I give to the church, and I wonder if the new Chryslers will outperform the big Buicks? Well, brother, I'll try 'em both. I'll try 'em both."

Is it a coincidence that this quasi-prayer closely resembles in essence the fervent appeal of a crap shooter to the rattling dice?

There are, of course, certain differences between the wheatgrower and the crap shooter. For instance, the wheat-grower usually is playing for much bigger stakes and he is allowed but one cast a year. Then, while the dice-thrower is seeking to propitiate his particular gods or saints or strange forces which control or influence his fortunes, those other players who have him "faded" are appealing to other mystic agencies to thwart and circumvent him, and not only the

wheatgrower's wheat-growing neighbors are praying and offering promises and sacrifices with him but the ministers of
the Gospel in the region are employing their talents and
eloquence over heaven's own wave-length in the interest of
a fine crop and good market and, concomitant, a probable
new Sunday School room and a possible increase in salary
which, considering the cost of living these days, goodness
knows, the ministers could use.

Legally, of course, the wheat farmer is not a gambler any   14
way you look at it. And perhaps he is not morally. But psychologically and philosophically, I should say there is little
difference between him an the fellow who takes a flier at
roulette—except that he is under a nervous tension for a
longer time and his chances of winning are materially better.

Topics for Writing
Comparison and Contrast

1. *Respond.* Consider the various "quasi-prayers" you have chanted in your life as you have waited for grades, watched a game, or listened to the weather report. Then write a humorous column for your local newspaper describing the language you have used to bring about good results. (*Resources for Comparison:* Maya Angelou, "My Name Is Margaret," page 31; Deborah Tannen, "Rapport-talk and Report-talk," page 183).

2. *Analyze.* Davis suggests that the wheat farmer and the stock investor are gamblers. Make a list of people in other professions—teachers, doctors, politicians—who might be considered gamblers. Show how one profession requires investment, involves risk, and may result in failure. Consider your audience as students who are about to begin a job search. (*Resources for Comparison:* George Orwell, "Shooting an Elephant," page 68; Lewis Thomas, "The Technology of Medicine," page 247).

3. *Argue.* Davis contends that gambling produces nothing of value and, on the basis of sheer chance, rewards an individual rather than the community. Conduct some research on the gambling industry in your state. Then argue that the industry does produce something of value—jobs, related industries, and money for community projects. Your argument might be directed at those people who object to your state lottery. (*Resources for Comparison:* Edward Hoagland, "In the Toils of the Law," page 132; Charles Murray, "The Coming White Underclass," page 509).

CHARLOTTE OLMSTED

Charlotte Olmsted was born in 1912 in Brookline, Massachusetts (a descendant of the famous city planner, Frederick Law Olmsted), and educated at Sweet Briar College and Stanford University. She worked as a research associate at the Mental Research Institute in Palo Alto, California, where she served as an editorial assistant on *Etiology of Schizophrenia*. Her own books include *Heads I Win Tails You Lose* (1962). In "Analyzing a Pack of Cards," reprinted from *Heads I Win Tails You Lose,* Olmsted explains the symbolism of the most prominent divisions in a pack of cards.

Analyzing a Pack of Cards

A s GOOD A place as any to start our analysis is with a very familiar but somewhat complex game tool—the pack of cards. Looked at as a symbolic system, the card pack is compact and ingenious, with a maximum number of variables handled in a neat and economical way. It lends itself extremely well to expressing a wide variety of human conflicts and problems, and to all sorts of interactions between the variables that can symbolize many different styles of human interaction. This is, of course, why it has retained its popularity so long. You are not confined to one sort of game or one style of play, but can vary both to suit your individual needs.

The most prominent divisions in the card pack are the four suits, the two colors, and the face-card, numbered-card divisions. Two other features are the movable ace (which can be either top or bottom and can be used to make the suits circular at will), plus the highly variable joker. Several packs can be used in any individual games, or part of the pack can be dropped out for particular purposes. All of these various divisions are interrelated in a way that is both complex and flexible, but which is clear, unambiguous, and easily learned—all highly desirable characteristics in a symbolic system.

Historically the English pack, which is the one with which we are most familiar, arose out of an earlier French pack. Modern French packs use different figures for the court cards, but otherwise the two packs are interchangeable. The Spanish pack and some local German and Italian packs differ in the suit symbols, don't have distinctive suit colors, and don't employ a queen, but are otherwise similarly organized. 3

The suits [in a deck of cards] have picked up emotional connotations with the years: spades—aggression, hostility; hearts—courage, love; diamonds—ambition, greed; clubs—fear.

Linguistic clues point to a probable Persian source for our European pack (as in the case of chess), but forerunners can be traced back to China, where many similar devices are used. The most familiar Chinese example to the Western world is probably mahjong. The mahjong tiles are organized in a very similar way to the card pack, although they differ widely in detail.

Among the ancestors of the card pack is the sun-game series. The clockwise, circular direction of play is retained, and a number of calendrical features—the four-part division into suits, and the fifty-two card series (with a sort of fractional extra card in the form of the joker), which can stand for the weeks in a year. But these very slight traces, while they may help to form a framework for the world of the card pack, have been subordinated to other features. 4

The four-part division is so fundamental in early thought 5 (and even in modern thought, because of the conservative tendency of linguistic habits) that it can stand for many things, and the most important immediate point of reference in the card pack is social. The four suits historically represent the four estates of medieval social theory, identical in composition to the four castes of intellectual Indian theory. Spades, whose name is taken from the old southern pack, still retained in Spain, come from "spada," "swords," although the symbol used is borrowed from the old German pack and represents a leaf. They represent the fighting man, the nobility. Hearts, whose name and form both come from the German pack and which correspond to cups in the southern pack, stand for the church, religion (Brahmins in Indian theory). In early games from the Renaissance period they ranked above spades but have since been downgraded. Diamonds stand for merchants, and clubs for the peasantry. The name of clubs, like that of spades, was borrowed from the southern pack, while the symbol is a copyist's version of the old German acorn. Acorns were very important in old German peasant economy, as providing food for pigs. Diamonds are interesting; in France they are called "carreaux," from the shape, a word also used to mean paving tile. The same suit is coins in the southern pack, while the old German pack used hawkbells, an extremely old medium of exchange and trade article. The English pack retained the idea of article-of-concentrated-value in the name "diamonds," but the shape is probably ultimately derived from a hasty copying of the bell symbol. When we refer to "diamond-shaped" we are borrowing from the card pack itself, as real diamonds are not customarily of this shape; the older English word for the shape was "lozenge."

These suits have also picked up emotional connotations 6 with the years. Spades—aggression, hostility; hearts—courage, love (both in the churchly meaning of altruism, good will, and in the sense of sexual love); diamonds—ambition, greed; clubs—fear, the state of being exploited. The association of courage and love in the hearts does not quite fit modern notions and may need a little explanation. The basic idea seems to be that these people have the supreme courage to drop their weapons, their defenses, and are thus able to love. It at least avoids the confusion of courage with overt aggression and (by implication) hostility which our age seems particularly prone to make.

The face cards represent the old European family system 7 of father, mother, and eldest son or heir; our pack is very good at playing out family role conflicts and is often so used. It does reflect a particular type of family structure—one where father-son conflicts are seen as more important than mother-daughter conflicts, since there is only one female in the pack, wife to one and mother to the other. The unattached female is not seen as important enough to have a card to herself, although the mother-wife is central to the family structure. You would expect such a society to have a great many Oedipus conflicts—they would probably be based so solidly on family structure as to be all but universal. There would also probably be a strong drive on the part of unmarried females to secure a husband and thus a place in the family structure for themselves, probably not matched by a like desire on the part of the male, who could continue to use his mother for emotional support if he chose. These are, of course, all features that are very prominent in the European area where this pack arose. The Spanish and German packs do not employ a queen, but have king, knight, foot soldiers, or servant instead—they are more useful for playing out social role conflicts than intrafamily conflicts.

The face-card, numbered-card division is often used to 8 symbolize people versus things, or significant people in one's life versus strangers, people in the mass. Ace represents ego, and can be either top or bottom of the pack at will, depending on a variety of factors and corresponding to one's own self-image. Ace of spades (aggression-ego), possibly one's own death, has a very special marking in the English pack. This originated in the custom of printing this one card separately in the government printing office to facilitate collecting taxes, but the particular card chosen may have a certain symbolic significance as representing the ultimate sanction of government.

The joker is the last lingering remnant of the tarot pack. 9
This tarot pack is sometimes considered the oldest form of
cards in Europe—there has been some controversy on this,
but it is certainly very old. There are the usual four suits,
usually employing the symbols of the southern pack, and with
four face cards (king, queen, knight, jack), plus a special series
of twenty-one cards that are symbolically very interesting,
representing as they do late medieval ideas. The number one
of this suit is the bateleur or juggler, and he is sometimes
duplicated by an extra card. The earliest mention of cards in
Europe is from Italy in 1379, and it may have been this tarot
deck. It is occasionally still used for fortune telling purposes.
The juggler or jester is the only tarot card that retains a
somewhat precarious toe hold in the modern deck. His wandering presence lends a certain flexibility and picturesque
disorder to the rather rigid pack, and he still finds employment in certain modern games. Since he was originally number one, or ace, in the tarot suit, he usually also represents
ego, and a particularly free and independent ego at that, not
attached to the social order at all.

The English and French packs employ color in addition to 10
symbolism. Red and black are used in many games, especially
in the European area. In Europe in general, especially western
Europe, they both carry slightly hostile and derogatory connotations—devils come in both colors. White is too good a
color—the color of angels—to be much used in games, since
if the two colors were black and white, few people would
voluntarily choose black. The one exception is chess, and in
chess white does have the advantage—it always plays first.
This white and black (or occasionally white and red) colora-
tion of the chessmen is found both in Europe and in India—
both areas where there tend to be rather elaborate social
distinctions based on skin color. Chess sets from the farther
Orient seldom use these distinctions—either they use red and
green with the Asian connotation of red-good, green-evil, or
they employ distinctions of shape and direction-in-which-

pointed, like "shogi," the Japanese form of chess, and not color distinctions at all.

Red and black as used in Europe usually represent revolu- 11 tion, change versus conservatism, *status quo*. It is probably significant of the Renaissance origin of our modern pack that the nobility and the peasantry are seen as conservative, while the church and the merchants are seen as the party of change. This reflects the Reformation and the Counterreformation. It is appropriate in emotional terms, also, with altruism, courage, and ambition seen as forces working toward change, while aggression, greed, and fear try to maintain the *status quo*.

Incidentally, since Russia overlaps both the European and 12 the Asian area, it can be seen why she uses red so extensively as a symbol—it can stand for revolution and change, and also carry overtones of the Asian good versus evil.

There are three one-eyed face cards, probably representing 13 the most single-minded of the people; these are the jack of spades (the young aggressive or hostile male) and the jack of hearts (the young, either altruistic or amorous male)—both representing different aspects of the conventional mythic hero of the West. The other single-minded character is the king of diamonds—the mature businessman. All the queens hold flowers—old symbols of female sexuality—and the queen of spades (the aggressive or hostile female) has a scepter of rule as well. The jack of spades holds a rather twiddly object in his hand that has completely lost its meaning—it looks more like a mathematical symbol of infinity than anything else—but it was originally a sword hilt.

The jack of hearts has suffered a sad fate. Originally he 14 held a splendid torch as tall as himself, the torch of Hymen, a phallic symbol, neatly symbolizing the source of his drive— either directly for an amorous male or sublimated for an idealistic one. Generations of copyists have reduced this once proud symbol to the wilted leaf he now holds—no wonder he looks depressed! Three of the kings carry swords; spades and clubs directly, ready to be used as weapons. Both nobles and peasants may use these, and in emotional terms both aggression and fear may use weapons. Or if one prefers to take the sword as a phallic symbol (remember that games are overdetermined), the nobility and the peasantry, both country dwellers, are apt to have larger families than either church or merchant, seen as town dwellers. The king of hearts has a sword, but he has buried it in his own head. He has suppressed his aggression, or if you prefer to see it as a phallic symbol, he has suppressed his own sexuality, either by becoming a celibate priest, or as the kindly, benevolent head of a family who must use his libidinous impulses to be especially nice to the daughters in the family while holding tight to his incest taboos.

The ambitious and single-minded king of diamonds and the jack of hearts not only do not carry weapons, they are driven by a weapon back of them. Apparently the love that drives the young, amorous male and the ambition that drives the mature businessman may not be wholly his own, but forced on him from outside; these are seen as in some sense the most driven members of the society. The battle-axes back of them may be among the forces that have helped to castrate them—I wonder if the queen of spades and her scepter had a hand in this? It may not have been conscious, but it makes a fairly sharp social commentary all the same. 15

Although very few people are consciously aware of the meanings of the card pack, it has retained sufficient unconscious force so that practically all games use the pack in very similar ways to play out various interaction patterns. It does this so efficiently that I think we might well begin to make use of this tool consciously for working out the implications and probable results of a variety of human systems of organizing relationships. 16

Topics for Writing
Division and Classification

1. *Respond.* Classify a symbolic system you encounter every day. You may want to focus on a physical system (signs, letters, and pictures) or a social system (dress, behavior, credentials). Then describe how your knowledge of the system enables you to make choices in crucial situations. (*Resources for Comparison:* Doris Kearns Goodwin, "Keeping the Scorebook," page 39; Mary Melane, "Shades of Black," page 255).

2. *Analyze.* Olmsted points out that there is only one female face card in a deck. How does she interpret this face in social (family) and psychological (Oedipal) terms? Write an essay for your history class in which you analyze certain events from the queen's perspective. (*Resources for Comparison:* Natalie Angier, "Dolphin Courtship: Brutal, Cunning and Complex," page 125; Cathy Young, "Keeping Women Weak," page 381).

3. *Argue.* Consider the dominant race or social class of the players of a game—basketball, golf, ice hockey. Then argue that in playing one of these games the players enact some larger social drama. Identify your audience as people who are familiar with the history of the game you choose to interpret. (*Resources for Comparison:* Terry McMillan, "The Movie That Changed My Life," page 423; Kurt Vonnegut, Jr., "Harrison Bergeron," page 537).

MARGARET O. HYDE

Margaret O. Hyde was born in 1917 in Philadelphia, Pennsylvania, and educated at Beaver College, Columbia University, and Temple University. When Hyde was a young girl, her ambition was to become a doctor. Instead, she became one of the most prolific and respected writers on science for young readers. She has written about "new ideas in science" on subjects as diverse as *Molecules Today and Tomorrow* (1963), *The New Genetics: Promises and Perils* (1974), and *Artificial Intelligence* (1986). In "Compulsive Gambling," reprinted from *Addictions: Smoking, Gambling, Cocaine Use and Others* (1978), Hyde defines the distinguishing characteristics of a compulsive gambler.

Compulsive Gambling

C AN GAMBLING BE an addiction? Experts believe that there are between 4 and 10 million people in the United States whose lives are dominated by gambling. Although not everyone agrees, many experts feel that most of these people have a problem of addiction. Certainly, these individuals proceed from occasional to habitual gambling, risking higher and higher stakes. They develop a craving for the pleasurable yet painful tension that accompanies the uncertainty of winning or losing. As compulsive gamblers, they continue their risky activities no matter how self-destructive, compelled by forces over which they have no control. Gambling is irresistible to them, even though material gain is far from certain. Unlike casual gamblers who usually go to the track or casino with friends, compulsive gamblers usually go alone.

Age, social background, education, and other factors vary   2 widely. Dr. Robert L. Custer, a psychiatrist with the Veterans Administration, is an expert on alcohol, drug abuse, and gambling. He suggests the following composite picture of a compulsive gambler in an advanced stage: male, age thirty to forty, drinks heavily, sleeps poorly, no financial resources, tense, irritable, has considered suicide, and gambles constantly. The larger percentage of males than females is often considered due to the environment. Then, too, males have greater opportunity to gamble. Dr. Custer suggests that the availability of easy money through a bookie is a factor in the

---

The act of gambling becomes an outlet for stress, and the enjoyment of betting, the sense of being important in the action, are more important than winning or losing money.

---

addiction process. He also observes that almost all the gamblers he has treated began gambling when they were adolescents. Opportunity to gamble is only one of the factors involved. Most compulsive gamblers share certain personality characteristics.

Consider the case of Mary. Except for her sex, she has 3 many typical characteristics of problem gamblers. She lives for gambling while neglecting her husband, children, and home. Every cent that she can get goes to the casino with her. She even steals money from her children's piggy banks to gamble, hoping to "make it big." Mary, like other compulsive gamblers, feels important when she is betting. While holding the dice, she feels in control of her world. Through the rituals of gambling, she enjoys an altered state of consciousness, a kind of high that some people obtain from climbing a mountain, walking alone by the ocean's edge, winning a tennis game, or through drug or alcohol use. Mary is not usually a happy person. Her behavior at home is immature and demanding. She is irritable, suffers feelings of unworthiness, helplessness, and inadequacy.

Mary, as most compulsive gamblers, sees herself as a winner. She lives in a dream world in which she is a charming philanthropist. She plans to do wonderful things for her family and friends "when she wins big." Then she hopes to make up for all the problems she has caused by her gambling. Gambling addicts share a desire to have tremendous amounts of material things without making a great effort to obtain them. They maintain a self-image of being all-powerful when gambling, and many say they feel secure only when they are participating in risking their money for big winnings or dreaming about making their betting systems work to bring great luxuries. When they are losing, they continue to gamble, for they feel that they will win everything they have lost if they bet just one more time. 4

Compulsive gamblers rarely stop betting until they have lost all available money. Then they promise themselves that they will give up their habit. Many individuals go to work, earn enough money to keep themselves and to save thousands of dollars. But then they are tempted to bet some or all of their savings, with the hope that they will win a huge amount. Even though they know that the odds are against them, such gamblers believe they can beat the system and win. 5

Many people gamble within the limits they set for themselves, and most agree that risk taking is part of everyday living. There is risk involved when one plants seeds in a garden, rides in an automobile, or participates in an almost endless number of activities. But some individuals carry their risk taking to extremes, and will continue to gamble until they have lost all their material possessions. 6

Gambling is usually defined as betting or wagering, whether or not money is involved. A compulsive gambler bets on all kinds of things, including those in which money is involved. He or she is dominated by the irresistible urge to bet and by an obsessive idea that he or she can win. 7

Some gamblers realize that their behavior is destructive. 8
They see marriages deteriorating, friends suffering, careers
lost, and in many cases they become involved with the law.
They rationalize that passing bad checks for cash needed to
gamble is just a sort of borrowing since they plan to pay back
the money with interest when they make a financial coup. But
money that is won usually finds its way back to the gambling
scene with the hope that it will bring even more money.

Since money appears to be a major incentive for compul- 9
sive gambling, and gamblers cannot manage their finances for
everyday living, people ask if the need for money is at the
root of the problem. Experts think not. Emotional problems
play a much more important part than financial need in this
type of addiction.

One man who was imprisoned for gambling read the 10
sports column of a newspaper each morning in jail and picked
the likely winners, even though he could not bet on them.
Although no money was involved, he waited anxiously each
day for the sports results.

The causes of compulsive gambling are not completely 11
understood, though many theories have been offered. Some
are extremely complicated and beyond the scope of this book,
but there are ideas that may help lay people in the understanding of the problem. Compulsive gambling has been
described as a ritualistic response to anxiety. The compulsive
gambler continues to ask, "Is Lady Luck with me?" somewhat the way a child asks a parent, "Do you love me? Do you
approve of me?" Since this question can never be satisfactorily
answered through gambling, the gambler continues to pose
the question and continues to lose until all funds are de-
pleted. Experts say release can be found only by losing.

There is a theory in which compulsive gambling is de- 12
scribed as a phase of a high, or manic, reaction; the stage at
which all money has been lost is the painful low, or depression, afterward.

According to another theory, the compulsive gambler 13
wants to lose in order to be punished for subconscious
thoughts about sex and parents. The wish to lose, of course,

is also subconscious. Few dispute the fact that most compulsive gamblers are losers, since even after winning (which is considered to strengthen unconscious guilt feelings), the winnings are used up in an effort to make even larger amounts of money.

Even gamblers who know they cannot win act as if they 14 might. The act of gambling becomes an outlet for stress, and the enjoyment of betting or risk taking, the sense of being important in the action, are more important than the winning or losing of money.

Just as a first drink can lead an alcoholic back to a drunken 15 spree, a first bet can lead a compulsive gambler back to uncontrollable risk taking. In spite of the fact that there may be as many as 10 million compulsive gamblers in the United States, comparatively little research has been done on the subject.

Not only is permanent cure questionable, but many problem gamblers who claim they want to stop would not accept 16 therapy even if it were available. Perhaps one of the reasons that problem gamblers resist treatment is that their symptoms are enjoyable. People who suffer from phobias are more apt to want to relieve their symptoms because their excessive fears are unpleasant. Gambling involves enjoyable feelings, such as the love of conflict, the satisfaction of being an object of jealousy when they are winning, and the pleasure that gamblers derive from using their cunning, concealment, and deceit. The courting of fear adds spice and color to the quality of some gamblers' lives. There is a theory that gambling satisfies certain qualities, such as the need for stimulation and change, that are present in human beings. The fluctuation between self-faith and fear provides a kind of tension that is necessary to life.

The first in-patient program in which professional thera- 17 pists work with gamblers reports only limited success. Since there appears to be a similarity in the way addictive behavior serves to help both alcoholics and gamblers avoid psychological pain and prevent psychological growth, a treatment program for both kinds of addicts was combined at the Veterans

Administration Hospital in Cleveland, Ohio. Dr. Alida Glen, psychologist and program coordinator, believes that both illnesses begin in adolescence, although they have roots in childhood when, in most cases, there appears to have been considerable psychological deprivation. She describes the typical compulsive gambler as appearing to have a personality disorder when first interviewed. The patient shows little remorse for antisocial behavior, offers many rationalizations for it, and is ready to blame others for his/her problems. Other symptoms include being out of touch with one's own feelings, lacking insight, not expecting to be understood, and doubting that she can be helped. Dr. Glen says that if one doubts that gambling can be addictive, interviews with compulsive gamblers can be very revealing.

Many patients who have been treated in the program at 18 Cleveland Veterans Administration Hospital were already members of Gamblers Anonymous. G.A., as it is commonly called, is similar in many ways to Alcoholics Anonymous, or A.A. Today, G.A. has about 450 chapters throughout the United States as well as some in other countries, and it has fostered two offshoots for families of addicts. Gam-Anon is the organization for spouses of compulsive gamblers. Gam-A-Teen sponsors weekly meetings for children of hard-core gamblers, where they help one another to understand their parents' problems.

Gamblers Anonymous began in Los Angeles, California, 19 in 1957 after two compulsive gamblers began leaning on each other for support in controlling their habits. One man, Jim W., had been trying for several years to establish a group of individuals who wanted to overcome gambling problems. After some unsuccessful attempts with others who claimed they wanted to stop, he was discouraged. Then he met Sam, who identified himself as having a problem with gambling. These two men tried with little success to get others to join them, until they were given publicity by Paul Coates. He wrote about them in his newspaper column in the *Los Angeles Mirror* and gave them radio and television time. This column and the TV programs opened the door to those who wanted to share experiences and help each other through such an organization. Today, Gamblers Anonymous has about five-thousand members in the United States alone. Therapeutic talk sessions help some of the members to control their gambling, but many drop out when they relapse into old habits. The cure rate is about 10 percent and the cure is not necessarily permanent.

A combination of Gamblers Anonymous and therapy such as that offered in the program at Cleveland Veterans Administration Hospital may be more successful in arresting the problem than one alone, but even this is not considered a cure. The therapy program helps patients to think more realistically and to accept support from people who have a different value system. Changing a life-style from one in which gambling is completely dominant is far from easy. [20]

A second in-patient program for compulsive gamblers evolved at the Veterans Administration Hospital in Brooklyn, New York. Under the direction of Dr. Abe S. Kramer, this program involves the same kind of intensive therapy used by Dr. Glen. Patients spend two or three weeks in the hospital, where they are not only isolated from gambling but are helped to cope with the more profound emotional problems that trouble them and which are masked by the gambling addiction. Dr. Kramer, who has treated many compulsive gamblers in private therapy, notes that it is difficult for people to admit that they have a gambling problem. They come to him explaining that they have other problems; the gambling habit is revealed at later sessions. [21]

A new, nonprofit organization, the National Council for Compulsive Gambling, is working toward more funds for research and education. Its founders believe that states that collect revenues from legalized gambling should reserve some of the revenue to publicize the dangers of gambling and pay for research and treatment for the victims. [22]

Efforts are underway to provide treatment at a third hospital, the Veterans Administration Hospital in Palo Alto, California, but treatment facilities are minimal. [23]

While there is no physical withdrawal in overcoming the [24] excessive urge to gamble, some experts believe there may be psychological withdrawal. At this stage, patients suffer from depression and feel guilt-ridden. Support from peers as well as staff members is extremely important at all times. Those in therapy receive support from friends they have made in the program, as well as from successful members of Gamblers Anonymous.

Only a very, very small percentage of people who want help 25 with gambling addictions can take part in hospital therapy programs, even though this approach seems far more helpful than prison. Consider the gambler who went to prison for swindling banks so that he could support his habit. When he was released, he visited seven racetracks in one weekend. Experts agree that prison is no more of a cure for gambling than it is for other addictions.

A person may become a compulsive gambler in as little as 26 six months, although it takes a much longer time for many gamblers to become addicted. How does one know if s/he has a problem? Gamblers who visit offtrack betting parlors in New York City may see a sign that reads, "IS GAMBLING MAKING YOUR LIFE UNHAPPY?" Those who answer this question in the affirmative are directed to dial the number of the National Council on Compulsive Gambling. There they will be invited to attend meetings of Gamblers Anonymous.

According to Gamblers Anonymous, most compulsive 27 gamblers will answer yes to at least seven of the following questions:*

1. Do you lose time from work due to gambling? 28
2. Is gambling making your home life unhappy? 29
3. Is gambling affecting your reputation? 30
4. Have you ever felt remorse after gambling? 31
5. Do you ever gamble to get money with which to pay debts or 32 to otherwise solve financial difficulties?
6. Does gambling cause a decrease in your ambition or efficiency? 33

*Reprinted through the courtesy of Gamblers Anonymous, National Service Office, P.O. Box 17173, Los Angeles, CA 90017.

7. After losing do you feel you must return as soon as possible and win back your losses?   34

8. After a win do you have a strong urge to return and win more?   35

9. Do you often gamble until your last dollar is gone?   36

10. Do you ever borrow to finance your gambling?   37

11. Have you ever sold any real or personal property to finance gambling?   38

12. Are you reluctant to use "gambling money" for normal expenditures?   39

13. Does gambling make you careless of the welfare of your family?   40

14. Do you ever gamble longer than you planned?   41

15. Do you ever gamble to escape worry or trouble?   42

16. Have you ever committed, or considered committing, an illegal act to finance gambling?   43

17. Does gambling cause you to have difficulty sleeping?   44

18. Do arguments, disappointments, or frustrations create within you an urge to gamble?   45

19. Do you have an urge to celebrate any good fortune by a few hours of gambling?   46

20. Have you ever considered self-destruction as a result of your gambling?   47

Topics for Writing
Definition

1. *Respond.* Consider the list of questions from Gamblers Anonymous. Select one that might apply to you or your friends. Then write a narrative illustrating your personal experiences with the situation—e.g., have you felt remorse after gambling, have you gambled longer than you planned, have you celebrated by gambling? (*Resources for Comparison:* Calvin Trillin, "The Extendable Fork," page 236; Sandra Cisneros, "One Holy Night" page 437).

2. *Analyze.* Compare and contrast the various theories Hyde presents to explain compulsive gambling. Think of your audience as students who are training to be legal and/or medical professionals. Use the theories to demonstrate that compulsive gamblers require special legal considerations and/or medical treatment. (*Resources of Comparison:* Gail Sheehy, "Predictable Crises of Adulthood" page 263; Rosemary L. Bray, "So How Did I Get Here?" page 495).

3. *Argue.* Hyde asserts that the need for money is not what causes compulsive gambling. Interview the people who buy lottery tickets at the convenience stores in your area. How often do they buy tickets? How often have they won? What have they done with the money? How would they respond to Hyde's assertion? Present their argument that the need for money *is* the reason they gamble. (*Resources for Comparison:* Pico Iyer, "Of Weirdos and Eccentrics," page 165; Bruce Shapiro, "One Violent Crime," page 405).

JAMES POPKIN

James Popkin was born in 1961 in Trenton, New Jersey, and educated at Northwestern University and Yale Law School. After working as a reporter for the Trenton *Times*, Popkin became a writer and senior editor for *U.S. News and World Report*. He currently works as a television reporter for NBC news in Washington, D.C. In "Tricks of the Trade," reprinted from *U.S. News and World Report*, Popkin analyzes the various "tricks" that casinos use to encourage heavy gambling.

Tricks of the Trade

A T PRECISELY MIDNIGHT on October 11, 1991, an obscure Chicago neurologist slipped behind a row of quarter slot machines at the Las Vegas Hilton and switched on a homemade contraption of cardboard, black metal and old fan parts. For the next forty-eight hours, the hidden device pumped a pleasant-smelling vapor into the stale casino air.

GETTING GAMBLERS TO GAMBLE LONGER

The neurologist was not an intruder but a scent expert invited to the Hilton by casino manager Lee Skelley to test whether certain smells can subtly influence slot machine players to wager more. Over the next two days, Hilton gamblers poured thousands of quarters into the eighteen nearby slot machines—45 percent more than usual for an October weekend.

> *Our goal is not to get more out of a customer in three*   3
> *hours but to get him to stay for four hours.*

—Bob Renneisen, President and CEO
Claridge's Casino, Atlantic City

The days of shaved dice, missing face cards and rigged   4
roulette wheels are long gone. But the pursuit of profitability
in the corporate era of gambling has turned the average
casino into a financially hazardous place for bettors. In Nevada and Atlantic City, for example, confidential documents
reveal that five casinos now pump Chicago neurologist Alan

Modern slot machines reward players with
small, frequent payoffs that entice gamblers
to keep chasing their dreams.

Hirsch's secret scent—Odorant 1—into the slot machine pits
twenty-four hours a day. (The Las Vegas Hilton never took
the idea beyond the testing stage.) Some casinos have even
studied how the controversial psychologist B. F. Skinner altered the behavior of rats and pigeons. But of all the tricks in
the casino manager's Psych 101 Handbook, the subtle manipulation of time is by far the most common.

In 1980, a math whiz named Jess Marcum spelled out   5
exactly how time affects a gambler's odds. Marcum, who
helped to develop radar and the neutron bomb before becoming a casino consultant, figured that a craps player who
wagered just $1 every bet for two months straight would have
only one chance in 2 trillion to win $1,000 before he lost
$1,000. On the other hand, by decreasing his exposure at the
craps table to just 25 minutes and wagering $200 every bet,
that same gambler would increase his odds to 1.15 to 1. Even
the lowest-ranking casino official knows the concept: Since
all casino games give the house a mathematical edge, the

longer a player gambles, the greater the house's chance of winning.

That helps explain why gamblers frequently get lost in a maze of slot machines and why down-home gambling halls offer free "Ladies Breakfasts" at 6 a.m., a slow point in the casino day. Over a year, a special promotion or interior-design element that somehow keeps gamblers at play for just five more minutes a night can add millions to a casino's gross, or "hold." The Harrah's Casino spends tens of thousands of dollars a year studying whether fresher air, wider aisles and even back supports on slot-pit stools will make customers comfortable. And slog it out longer, too. "We're now developing technology that's just lighting the felt" on blackjack tables, says Harrah's president, Phil Satre. "We're trying to keep [light] off the forehead of the customers, which is draining on them from an energy standpoint."

Such sensitivity to customer comfort abounds. For example, nearly all new slot machines sold in the United States have built-in bill acceptors. Gamblers like the devices because they no longer have to wait in line for change, and casino managers love them because they keep slot hounds glued to their stools.

CASINOS STRESS "PRODUCTIVITY"

Like car plants, casinos also stress productivity. The hidden cameras above the casino floor scan for fast-fingered dealers and card cheats. But the ubiquitous "eye in the sky" also enables casino officials to conduct regular "game-pace audits." At the Aladdin Casino in Las Vegas, blackjack dealers are instructed to deal at least 75 to 80 hands per hour. They are also supposed to shuffle six decks of cards in less than 80 seconds. The reason: Shuffles can eat up eight rounds of playing time an hour. In a year, the Aladdin could earn an extra $1.2 million if its blackjack dealers never had to shuffle.

Penny-pinching casinos set faster production schedules, especially when the nightly cash hold tumbles. "We don't instruct people to deal faster," says Bob Stupak, owner of the

Vegas World Casino in Las Vegas. "They better deal as fast as they [expletive] can or they're gonna work someplace else."

> *If you give a guy a $100 bill he looks at it like a*   10
> *round of golf, a golf cart, two beers and a hot dog.*
> *But if you give him chips, it's just betting units and*
> *it loses its value.*

—Bill Zender, Operations Chief
Aladdin Casino, Las Vegas

Casinos have become pop-psych laboratories. When a   11 player at a low-limit blackjack table flashes a $100 bill and asks for chips, for example, dealers at many casinos are under orders to dole out chips of the lowest-possible denomination. Partly a convenience for gamblers, the practice also is meant to discourage low bettors from pocketing higher value chips when they leave the table. Such players are likely to blow all twenty of their $5 chips one at a time, the thinking goes, but might hold onto a $25 chip and never gamble it away. "Psychologically, casinos don't want gamblers to realize how much they're losing," explains one Atlantic City dealer.

But slot pits are the true training grounds for casino mind   12 games. Deep, dark colors like black, red, purple and blue trigger a strong response in slot players, research shows. So, slot machine manufacturers like International Game Technology (IGT), based in Reno, Nevada, prominently feature those hues. IGT North American President Bob Bittman says research also shows that gamblers no longer associate winning with the cherry and plum symbols on many slot machine reels. Poof, they're gone. "Fruit is a dinosaur. Ninety-nine percent of the machines we sell now will not have fruit." Bittman says.

Some casinos go to even greater lengths to exploit gam-   13 blers' subconscious preferences. Casino consultant David Britton says that after surveying dozens of Nevada-based slot players he confirmed a hunch that they are drawn to bright-red machines. But after several minutes, the players subconsciously tire of red and seek softer hues. Since casinos want to avoid "transitional periods," when players leave one machine in search of another, Britton devised a new system where players are now lured to the brightly colored machines at the end of a long row of slots. But the machines closer to the middle of the row feature softer colors, like blues and greens.

> *What is gambling? It's really just a hype on emotion.*   14
>
> —Jack Binion, owner
> Horeshoe Casino, Las Vegas

Sometimes casino operators look to actual psychology for   15
inspiration. In 1966, University of Nevada undergrad Larry Andreotti was studying Skinner, one of the first scientists to demonstrate how positive reinforcement can influence animal behavior. Andreotti told his father, the late Rome Andreotti, who at the time was one of the rising stars on the operations side of the growing Harrah's chain. "A lot of the behavior I saw in the lab seemed comparable to the control one has over behavior in casinos," explains Larry Andreotti, who today is a college psychology professor and Skinner specialist in Canada.

In 1937, Skinner taught a white lab rat named Pliny to   16
operate a rudimentary slot machine. After Pliny pulled a chain with its teeth, a marble would fall. The rat would then drop the marble in a slot and receive its reward, 1/20 of a gram of a dog biscuit. By tracking Pliny's reactions over time, Skinner learned that the rat became more motivated when he got a biscuit only occasionally, and randomly. Pliny would drop even more marbles into the slot, in other words, when he was not sure when the biscuit would fall next.

Rome Andreotti applied Skinner's findings to the casino.   17
If most slots were set at about the same payout rate, recalls a former Harrah's president, Richard Goeglein, Andreotti would slip in a few machines with a much more generous jackpot percentage. The casino wouldn't indicate which machines offered better odds, but gamblers soon learned that there were a few ringers in the crowd. And the search for

those machines sent gamblers into a Pliny-like, quarter-dropping frenzy. "Rome knew how to reward people for continual, consistent play," says Goeglein.

Coincidentally, slot machine makers have also put Skinner's theories into practice. Modern slots reward players with frequent, small payoffs—often as inconsequential as one quarter—that entice gamblers to keep chasing their dream. Thirty years ago, by contrast, small, frequent payoffs were unheard of, says slot machine historian Marshall Fey. The new payout system works. "It's like eating popcorn. It's very hard to stop playing," says Jeffrey Lowenhar, senior management consultant with the Resorts casino in Atlantic City.   18

One firm took gambler manipulation too far. In 1986, Universal Distributing began selling slots that produced "near miss" combinations. Instead of running randomly, the slot reels often stopped so that players could see the symbols of a payout just above or below the pay line, giving the false impression that gamblers had missed a massive jackpot. Although the machines quickly became a hit with customers and slot managers, Nevada gaming authorities outlawed the near-miss illusion in 1989.   19

PROFILING GAMBLERS

Push a button and they can find out everything about you. Sometimes it's scary.   20

—Gambler Sam Roberts

It was a Sunday afternoon, and Pennsylvania jewelry salesman Sam Roberts was bellied up to a roulette table at his favorite Las Vegas casino. Dressed in what he described as his "Mr. T starter set"—three gold necklaces, four gold bracelets, a gold watch and four gold rings—Roberts seemed to epitomize the successful Vegas man about town. When asked whether he was ahead after three days of roulette, Roberts said he wasn't "paying any attention."   21

But the casino certainly was. On a computer screen just   22 off the casino floor, the file on Sam Roberts (not his real name) was extensive. Not only did it reveal his exact losses on his current trip ($2,092) but it had already figured his average bet ($20.88), time spent gambling (11 hours and 39 minutes) and "average worth," or how much Roberts should lose ($528) based on time and the house's 5.26 percent edge at roulette. It also contained personal data like Sam's height (5'10"), weight (300), hair color (brown)—even whether he needed corrective eyewear (yes).

Casinos amass personal information to enhance customer service and reward steady players with "comps"—complimentary meals, show tickets and hotel stays. (They never reveal internal data, although Roberts agreed to for this article.) But there's a hidden agenda. Casino marketers need detailed histories to keep old customers loyal and, more important, to "capture" new ones. 23

If marketers learn, for instance, that divorced slot players from Cleveland who love boxing lose big and often, the casino will buy mailing lists and try to find sucker clones. Gamblers who can be lured to the hotel are especially prized. "If we can get you to stay in our hotel, we can bump up your average trip worth," one marketer says. Everyone gets in on the hustle. When a casino hotel is nearly full, reservationists will scan the computer and open remaining rooms only to known gamblers with a high trip worth. 24

TARGETING THE MEAT-AND-POTATOES GAMBLER

A decade ago, most casinos bothered to gather data only on high rollers. Now they use slot-club cards to snare the meat-and-potatoes guy, too. After filling out a survey and receiving an ATM-like card, slot junkies insert them into a "reader" built into almost all slot machines. In a distant computer room, casinos track the action twenty-four hours a day down to the last quarter. 25

Players who use the cards the longest get the most comps, somewhat like a frequent-flier giveback. At the Trump Castle in Atlantic City, an internal document shows that 64 percent 26 of all slot players now use the Castle slot card. The cardholders lost $109 million to the slots last fiscal year, or about $101 per player per trip. Slot players who never bothered with the card, by contrast, lost $31 per trip on average.

> *The stickman controls the pace of the crap game like* 27
> *a barker at a carnival. He pushes the "proposition"*
> *bets, which have a much greater house advantage.*

—Al Glasgow, consultant and editor
Atlantic City Action newsletter

For an industry governed by odds, casinos leave little to 28 chance. To line their pockets just a wee bit more, they've added games with stunning house odds. Many casinos now offer "double-exposure blackjack," for example, in which the dealers reveal all their cards; players keep trying to top the dealer's hand without going over 21. Novices fall for the ruse, overlooking the rule allowing the house to win all ties. "That one rule change is worth about 8 or 9 percent in favor of the house," explains Arnold Snyder, editor of the *Blackjack Forum* newsletter.

Many riverboat casinos also offer "multiple-action black- 29 jack," with complex rules that encourage gamblers to place three bets on every hand. "It causes players to play dumb and put more money on the table," Snyder says. If gambling critics can be believed, that neatly sums up the danger of America's latest entertainment craze. As any old Vegas hand will tell you, "If you wanna make money in a casino, own one."

Topics for Writing
Cause and Effect

1. *Respond.* Write a personal experience essay in which you describe how a "near miss" experience compelled you to try again at some enterprise. Or you may want to reflect on how this "near miss" experience convinced you that you had had enough. (*Resources for Comparison:* Elizabeth Winthrop, "The Golden Darters," page 142; Mark Twain, "Two Views of the River," page 161).

2. *Analyze.* Instead of a casino, select another site that works like a psychology laboratory. For example, analyze the way supermarket displays or web page designs can keep people shopping or surfing the Internet longer than they planned. (*Resources for Comparison:* Naomi Shihab Nye, "My Brother's House," page 171; Judith Levine, "I Surf, Therefore I Am," page 481).

3. *Argue.* In an essay written for your marketing class, argue the case for or against profiling customers: *pro*—if customers are studied, their needs can be satisfied, *con*—if customers are studied, their privacy is invaded. You may want to focus your argument on one type of profiling—e.g., the selling of specific mailing lists. (*Resources for Comparison:* Robert Coles, "Uniforms," page 374; Esther Dyson, "A Design for Living on the Internet," page 486).

Robert Goodman was born in 1936 in Brooklyn, New York, and educated at the Massachusetts Institute of Technology. He has worked as an urban planner, economic development consultant, and architect. He currently teaches at Hampshire College and serves as the executive director of the United States Gambling Research Institute. His books include *After the Planners* (1978): *The Last Entrepreneurs: America's Regional Wars for Jobs and Dollars* (1979); and *The Luck Business: The Devastating Consequences and Broken Promises of America's Gambling Explosion* (1995). In "Grand Illusions," adapted from *The Luck Business,* Goodman argues that as a public policy gambling creates more problems than it solves.

Grand Illusions

T HE UNITED STATES has embarked on an unprecedented   1
experiment with legalized gambling. At times in the past, everything from lotteries to roulette was tolerated and even exploited for public revenues. But recognizing the moral and material hazards involved, public authorities generally acted cautiously, subjecting such ventures to tight controls. Today, gambling enterprises of various kinds, including casinos and riverboats, are not only permitted but actively promoted by many state and city political leaders as a magic bullet for ailing local economies. Indeed, only a belief in magic can explain the willingness of so many people to accept the proposition that legalized gambling can provide jobs and tax revenues at virtually no cost to society. We are only beginning to recognize the real costs.

The rapid spread of legalized gambling has been hard to   2 miss in recent years, insistently announcing itself through clamorous advertisements for lotteries and casino outings. Yet the numbers are still startling. As recently as 1988, casino gambling was legal in only two states: Nevada and New Jersey. By 1994, casinos were either authorized or operating in 23 states, and legalization was being proposed in many others. Casinos sprang up on more than 70 Indian reservations, thanks in large part to powers granted the tribes under the federal Indian Gaming Regulatory Act of 1988. The state of Mississippi alone was home by last year to one million square feet of riverboat casinos—in the four years since legalization Mississippi acquired more gambling space than Atlan-

---

The sad lesson of gambling as an economic development strategy is that it creates far more problems than it solves.

---

tic City, New Jersey, did in 16 years. Within three years after the introduction of casino riverboats in Illinois, per capita spending on gambling in that state doubled.

Between 1988 and 1994, casino revenues in the United States nearly doubled—from $8 billion to about $15 billion annually. Overall, Americans wagered $482 billion in casinos and other legal betting venues in 1994, a jump of 22 percent over the previous year. Gambling has expanded at all levels— and has even brought a rise in attendance at church bingo games. The new gambling outlets were impressive for their variety: electronic slot machines in rural South Dakota bars; imitation Wild West casinos in old Colorado mining towns; riverboats along the Mississippi River, from the distressed industrial cities of Iowa to the Gulf of Mexico; and gambling establishments on Indian reservations from coast to coast. New Orleans is now building what promoters tout as the world's largest casino, while the mayors of Chicago, Philadelphia, and other big cities enthusiastically embrace gambling proposals.

Casino companies often enjoy economic advantages that are available to few other businesses. Since they are usually granted exclusive government franchises, they are able to generate short-term profits on a scale that proprietors of other businesses can only dream about. Earnings of five to eight percent of revenues are the norm for most American businesses. In the gambling industry, however, yearly profits between 30 and 50 percent are not unusual. It is not extraordinary for companies to be able to pay off their total investments in one or two years. One Illinois riverboat company reportedly tripled the return on its investment in just six months.

More and more Americans are being persuaded to try their luck. According to casino industry sources, the number of American households in which at least one member visited a casino doubled between 1990 and '93—from 46 million to 92 million. More than three-quarters of this upsurge was the result of people visiting casinos outside Nevada and Atlantic City. In 1994, gambling industry leaders and other business observers were predicting even more spectacular growth. "By the year 2000," said Phil Satre, president of Harrah's Casinos, one of the world's largest casino companies, "95 percent of all Americans will most likely live in a state with legal casino entertainment." By then, according to Mark Manson, a vice president of Donaldson, Lufkin & Jenrette, a stock brokerage firm, lotteries, casinos, and other kinds of legal gambling "could surpass all other forms of entertainment in terms of total revenue." Manson concluded that "the movement towards gaming appears unstoppable for the foreseeable future."

The amount of money in play is huge. Between the early 1980s and the early '90s, betting on legal games, including the lotteries that were conducted by 37 states and the District of Columbia, grew at almost twice the rate of personal incomes. Last year, legal gambling in the United States generated nearly $40 billion in revenues for its public- and private-sector proprietors.

What has made gambling attractive to politicians and local business leaders is the prospect of new jobs for workers and easy money to fill the coffers of local government and business. An activity that was once feared for its ability to sow moral corruption, its corrosive impact on the work ethic, and its potential to devastate family savings has suddenly been transformed into a leading candidate to revive the fortunes of towns and cities across America. In Chicago, casinos were proposed to bail out the city's overbuilt hotel sector. In Gary, Indiana, they were supposed to offset declines in a once-booming steel industry. In Detroit, they were touted as a way to replace lost jobs in automobile manufacturing. In New Bedford, Massachusetts, gambling was going to provide jobs for fishing industry workers thrown out of work by the exhaustion of Atlantic fisheries. 7

Advocates eagerly seek to cleanse gambling of its traditional connotations. It certainly looks on the surface more reputable than it once did. An industry created by the likes of "Bugsy" Siegel and Meyer Lansky and financed with laundered drug money and other ill-gotten gains is now operated by business school graduates, financed by conglomerates, and listed on the New York Stock Exchange. "Much of the moral argument against legalization is based upon the belief that gaming is mainly about money or greed," Harrah's president Satre told the National Press Club in 1993. "It is not. It is about entertainment. . . . It is a true social experience. And there are no gender-based, race-based, or physical barriers to access." Politicians and others have joined in the effort to de-moralize the debate over gambling. No longer do they speak of "gambling," with all its unsavory overtones, but in euphemisms such as "gaming" and "casino entertainment." 8

Legalization tends to have a snowball effect. When one state allows games of chance, other states have a greater incentive to do so as well. If your citizens are going to gamble anyway, why not at least reap some of the benefits by letting them do so at home? In 1985, Montana became the first state 9 to allow slot machines in bars, effectively creating minicasinos throughout the state. Four years later, South Dakota's legislature gave its state lottery agency authority to install "video lottery terminals"—which in reality are little more than slot machines—in bars and convenience stores. Soon afterward, Oregon, Rhode Island, West Virginia, and Louisiana legalized similar machines. By 1991, Oregon had also legalized betting on sports teams and electronic keno machines through its state lottery.

Iowa took a much bigger leap into gambling in 1991 when   10
it became the first state to legalize casino gambling on riverboats. To ensure that the floating casinos would remain low-key tourist operations, the state government limited stakes to $5 per bet and total losses of any player to $200 per cruise. But these restrictions were soon dropped, after politicians in Illinois, Mississippi, and Louisiana authorized riverboat gambling with unrestricted betting. Iowa had to keep up with the competition.

By late 1994, however, there were signs that the days of   11
expansion without end were over. The casino boom of the early 1990s was not built on a broad base of popular support for legalization. The laws were changed in response to unprecedented, well-financed campaigns by the gambling industry, countered only by the underfunded, ad hoc efforts of opposition groups. But as casinos proliferated and their social and economic costs became more widely recognized, more and more communities rallied to defeat them.

Where statewide referendums have been held on casino   12
gambling, voters have mostly voted no. In 1994, despite the gambling industry's promises of riches to come, not a single one of the four state casino referendums passed. (In seven other states where gambling was already legal, measures to expand it got mixed results.) In Florida, casino companies mounted their costliest promotional campaign ever, yet the voters rendered a decisive no. Where casino gambling has been legalized, it usually has been by direct action of state legislators or by legislature-approved referendums on the town, city, or country level. When the target is a single

community starved for jobs and tax revenues, the industry
has regularly been able to gain approval.

Yet Americans appear to be recognizing that the promises   13
made by gambling proponents are rarely if ever realized by
cash-strapped cities and towns. The municipalities' hopes are
based largely on what happened in Las Vegas—a remote
desert city that for decades held a virtual monopoly on gambling. The city was able to draw huge numbers of tourists
who spent freely, not only at the tables and slots but in local
hotels, restaurants, and stores. Something at least remotely
similar has been achieved at the reservation-based casinos.
The Indian reservations have several things in common with
early Las Vegas, notably, remote locations and no existing
economic bases to speak of. They have, in short, nothing to
lose.

But there aren't likely to be any more Las Vegas-style   14
success stories. With the proliferation of casinos around the
country, the nature of the game has changed. Cities and
towns entering the gambling market now face fierce competition, and they will be hard-pressed to draw patrons from
outside their regions. Most of the people pumping money
into their slot machines will be local residents. Instead of
bringing in new dollars from outside the local economy,
gambling will siphon away consumer dollars from other local
businesses. At the same time, these communities will be sad-
dled with enormous new costs as they deal with the economic
and social consequences of open gambling. Not the least of
these costs is an increase in the local population of chronic
gamblers, who bring with them not only their personal trage-
dies but a host of related problems, from bad debts and family
breakups to crime, often of the white-collar variety. Estimates
of the annual private and public costs imposed by each problem gambler range from my own $13,200 (in 1993 dollars)
up to $52,000. A mere 100 additional problem gamblers, in
other words, exact a monetary toll of more than $1 million.

The sad lesson of gambling as an economic-development   15
strategy is that it creates far more problems than it solves. It
doesn't even deliver the goods it promises. In Atlantic City,

for example, about one-third of the city's retail establishments shut their doors during the first four years after the casinos' arrival. Many could not compete with the low-price restaurants and services offered by the casinos to lure customers. In 1993, unemployment at Atlantic City was double the state average.

One of the worst long-term consequences of legalizing 16
gambling is the difficulty, if not impossibility, of undoing the decision. New gambling ventures create powerful new political constituencies that fight to keep gambling legal and expanding. These operations can radically alter the balance of power in state and local politics.

"Casino gambling is not a 'try it and see' experiment," 17
observes Stephen P. Perskie, the politician who led the battle to legalize gambling in Atlantic City, and a former chair of New Jersey's Casino Control Commission. "Once the casino opens and the dice begin to roll, gambling creates an instant constituency. People depend on it for jobs. Governments depend on it for revenues." Perskie, who went on to become vice president of Players International, a casino development company, elaborates: "You've got economic realities created. You've got infrastructure investments, you've got public policy commitments. . . . The public official who will stand up and say close that casino and put those 4,000 people out of work is somebody I haven't met yet."

Once the novelty of a new casino or a new game wears off, 18
as it inevitably does, revenues tend to fall or flatten, forcing legislators to look for new gambling ventures and gimmicks to keep the money coming in. And as enterprises suffer lower revenues from increased competition or fading consumer interest, they turn to government for regulatory relief and sometimes direct subsidies.

Even in New Jersey, where the casino industry is prohib- 19
ited by law from lobbying, casino operators wield enormous political power. The state's experience offers an instructive example of the ways in which gambling regulations weaken over time. In Atlantic City, the original rules governing casinos included regulations that sought to reduce problem gam-

bling. They prohibited 24-hour gambling, restricted the amount of floor space that could be dedicated to slot machines (considered by many experts one of the most addictive forms of gambling), outlawed games such as electronic keno, poker, and sports betting, and created rules for jackpots and prizes designed to ensure that players wouldn't be taken advantage of too outrageously. But over time, especially as competition from casinos in other states increased during the early 1990s, casino companies pressed for relief from these restrictions. Gambling got its way. By 1994, all these rules had been dropped, with the single exception of limits on sports betting. (New Jersey's Casino Control Commission ruled that it simply had no legal power to change these rules because federal law restricts sports betting.)

New Jersey's powerful casino constituency was the force 20 behind a number of public projects that were designed to restore Atlantic City's luster as a tourist destination—and thereby bolster the gambling business. In 1993, the state announced plans to spend about $100 million to expand Atlantic City's airport, rebuild the city's convention center, and beautify the approach roads to the casinos and their surrounding boardwalk areas. The plans had little to do with reversing the massive deterioration of the other Atlantic City beyond the boardwalk. In fact, they were aimed at concealing the city's mean streets from casino visitors. As an article in the *New Jersey Casino Journal,* a voice for local casino owners, explained, "The need to negotiate passage through a depressed and deteriorated urban war zone is not especially conducive to a memorable entertainment experience."

The public debt that many cash-poor communities must 21 assume to build or improve boat docks, parking facilities, highways, water and sewer systems, and other infrastructure creates problems of its own. The hope is that a continuous stream of revenue from taxes on casino income will help pay off this debt. But the community is also in a trap. To close down or curtail these operations if they falter or prove disruptive would be almost impossible—indeed, the community has every incentive to promote even more gambling.

Some of the biggest costs of gambling expansion are the   22
hardest to quantify. They are what economists refer to as
"opportunity costs." The more energy government officials
and business leaders expend on gambling as an economic
development strategy, the less they can devote to the cultiva-
tion of other kinds of business enterprises that may be less
flashy and more difficult to establish. Over the long term,
such businesses would almost certainly be more beneficial to
towns and cities than those built on the exploitation of the
gambling itch.

If gambling ventures continue to proliferate and expand,   23
the political power of the gambling industry will grow as well,
making it increasingly difficult to control gambling. A taste
of what may come was provided in the spring of 1994, when
the Clinton administration proposed a four percent federal
tax on gross gambling revenues to fund its new welfare reform programs. The industry's response was swift and forceful. Thirty-one governors promptly wrote to the president
complaining of the potential damage to their gambling-de-
pendent state budgets. Governor Bob Miller of Nevada flew
to Washington and presented President Clinton with a scenario of silent casinos and layoffs by the thousands in the
gambling industry. Owners of horse and dog racetracks lob-
bied Congress with similar visions of economic devastation.
The administration quickly withdrew its tax proposal.

The seed planted in the Nevada desert some 50 years ago   24
is now bearing very dangerous fruit indeed. America's unprecedented gambling boom has created grand illusions worthy of the gaudiest and most grandiose Las Vegas casino.
Only in one place could the notion flourish that a magical
way could be found to create new jobs, generate fresh revenues for public coffers, and revive cities at virtually no cost:
a fantasy land.

Topics for Writing
Persuasion and Argument

1. *Respond.* Consider all the ways gambling might be considered entertainment. Then using as your title "Time Well Spent," write an essay addressed to the students at your school explaining more "profitable" forms of entertainment—e.g., participation in sports, tutoring programs, or computer workshops. (*Resources for Comparison:* Ann Zwinger, "Drawing on Experience," page 103; Bill McKibben, "Nature and Televised Nature," page 198).

2. *Analyze.* Read through your local newspaper—sports, entertainment, religion, and business sections—for evidence to support Goodman's assertion that gambling has been made more attractive to politicians and local business leaders. In the past, why did these people object to gambling? What evidence in your paper suggests that they now embrace it? (*Resources for Comparison:* Frank O'Connor, "Guests of the Nation," page 213; Kathleen Norris, "The Holy Use of Gossip," page 314).

3. *Argue.* Look for evidence in your community to support Goodman's argument that gambling rarely delivers on its promise to improve infrastructure, social programs, education, and employment. Then write an essay to convince your state legislator that gambling is a bad public policy. (*Resources for Comparison:* John Berendt, "The Hoax," page 309; Martin Luther King, Jr., "I Have A Dream," page 461).

LOUISE ERDRICH

Louise Erdrich was born in 1954 in Little Falls, Minnesota, and grew up in Wahpeton, North Dakota, as a member of the Turtle Mountain Band of Chippewa. She was educated at Dartmouth College and Johns Hopkins University, taught poetry in both schools and prisons, and edited the Boston *Indian Council* newspaper before accepting a position as writer-in-residence at Dartmouth College. Her first work of fiction, *Love Medicine* (1984), won the National Book Critics Circle Award. Her recent novels, continuing the saga she began in *Love Medicine,* include *The Beet Queen* (1986), *Tracks* (1988), *The Bingo Palace* (1994) and *The Antelope Wife* (1998). She has also published several collections of poetry, including *Jacklight* (1984) and *Baptism of Desire* (1989), and a personal narrative, *The Blue Jay's Dance: A Birth Year* (1995). In "Lyman's Luck," reprinted from *The Bingo Palace,* Erdrich creates the psychological appeal of winning and the cultural consequences of losing.

Lyman's Luck

THE TWO MEN sat across from one another at a scratched plastic table in the palace bar. Lipsha Morrissey hunched over his arms, cradled his hand, rocked forward in his chair. Lyman leaned back slightly, palms placed neatly on the tabletop. Ever since he'd seen the pipe returned from the authorities and put back into the boy's possession, Lyman hadn't been able to get the thought of it from his head. He wanted that pipe with a simple finality that had nothing to do with its worth as a historical artifact. Although he didn't examine all of his motivations, he knew that the desire had something to do with his natural father, for when he imagined himself smoking the pipe that had once belonged to Nector Kashpaw, he saw himself drawing the sacred object solemnly from its bag and also presenting it to friends, to officials, always with the implication that it had, somehow, been passed down to him by right.

The prestige of owning that pipe had dogged Lyman's   2
thoughts so consistently that he had tried several times to actually buy it from Lipsha. Always, he'd been shyly refused, but now he thought he might reason a little more aggressively. Lyman knotted his square, heavy hands, looked down at his blue class ring. The stone drank deep light. He cocked his head to one side and his wide-spaced eyes figured.

"I'm not trying to persuade you for myself," he said to   3
Lipsha. "Consider it this way—you would be donating the pipe back to your people."

Lipsha licked the end of a straw and shook his head with   4
a distracted smile.

"I'd keep it on permanent display," Lyman continued.   5
"Put it out where the public could look at it, in a glass case maybe, right at the casino entrance. Keep it yourself and you're liable to lose it. Something might happen, just like at the border crossing."

"We got it returned though," Lipsha reminded Lyman.   6
"They took it illegal, they admitted that."

"I'm not saying the loss was your fault," Lyman shook his   7
head, frowning into the steeple of his fingers. "I'm just saying *things happen.*"

"Things do happen," Lipsha agreed.   8

"To you, they happen all the time."   9

"I guess." Lipsha crumpled his fingers together in a tight   10
package, and looked down at the little star that shot across the back of his hand. Titus, the bartender, placed a hamburger before him. Titus was dressed in black—black jeans, biker's boots, T-shirt, black plastic diver's watch. His long curls, dry and electric, hung about his shoulders. He gazed at Lyman, then back at Lipsha.

"You ain't got a hangover, do you?" Titus asked Lipsha.   11
"Never deal with Lyman when you're not a hundred percent.
He's after that pipe."

"Tell me about it." Lipsha kept on eating. His jaws slowed   12
until he was merely pretending to chew, once, twice. His hair
fell out of its band and he suddenly stuffed the rest of the
burger into his mouth. He swallowed, staring down at the
table, hair flopped across his face, then tossed his head back,
hooked the loose strands behind his ears.

"I don't think I better sell."   13

"Why not?" Lyman's face clouded over as he attempted   14
to control his irritation.

"You ever heard the story about the mess of porridge?"   15
"What?"   16

"One brother gives his birthright to the other for some   17
breakfast. It's in the Bible."

Lyman's look eased slightly and he almost started to laugh.   18

"That hamburger's on the house." He then frowned in   19
deepening suspicion. He began to smooth one hand over the
other, back and forth, like he was petting a dog. He worked
his hands together faster, faster, and then finally spoke in a
quick, dry tone.

"Nector Kashpaw was *my* real father."   20
"What does that have to do with it?"   21

"Goddamn it, Lipsha! Think about it once. Everybody   22
could be getting inspiration from this pipe, it's a work of
genuine art, it's spiritual. Only you'd rather keep it in your
leaky trunk, or stuffed in your footlocker. Somewhere like
that. You don't deserve it!"

Lipsha stared at his uncle's face, his mouth slightly open,   23
dazed, strangely serene in his contemplation.

Lyman's voice lowered to its most persuasive register. "It   24
belongs to all of us, Lipsha. It especially belongs to me."

"Like Shawnee Ray?"   25

Lyman tucked his mouth in at the corners, reeled back a   26
little as if at the surprising unfairness of the question. He
clenched his jaw, spoke sternly, adopting a minister's logical,
reasoning tones.

"Shawnee Ray doesn't 'belong' to me, Lipsha. She goes   27

out with me because she chooses to, because she sees something in me she admires, because she has, I like to think, good taste—she values hard work, intelligence. She goes out with me because of *her*, Lipsha, not because I make her do it."

As Lipsha listened, his stare became wide-eyed, almost frantic, piercing. 28

"I'll trade you the pipe!" he suddenly cried out. 29

"For what?" 30

"Shawnee Ray. Here's the deal: I give you the pipe, and you lay low, step aside." 31

"You sonofabitch!" 32

Lipsha raised his hands, palms out, grinning crazily as Lyman jumped up, unable to contain his agitation. He went about the bar, straightening stools, dusting off tables, lifting the chairs and setting them down. He took a grape soda from the glass-door cooler, sat down again with a bowl of popcorn. 33

"You want me to go get the pipe now?" Lipsha asked, his grin stretching huger. 34

Lyman halted with a handful of popcorn halfway to his mouth, one eye glinting past his fist. 35

"I'll write the check," he said. 36

"It's not for *sale*." Lipsha was composed and patient now. "Trade only. You get the pipe, I get to let Shawnee make her own decision." 37

Lyman drew his head back, sank his chin to his chest in thought. He stared at the counter, his eyes staring blank, then shrewd. 38

"She's going to love hearing that you tried to do this," he said. 39

Lipsha turned away, at a loss. For moment after long moment neither man said anything. The only sounds in the bar were a low cloud of conversation around the pool table, the intermittent clicking of balls, Titus in the back room on the phone. The popcorn machine popped over, spilled, and a last kernel exploded, weakly, in the yellow air. 40

Packing his suitcase for the Indian Gaming Conference, Lyman weighed the pipe for a moment in his hands. Quickly, carefully, he set the pipe, in its pouch, within the inside pocket 41

of his carry-on case and pulled all of the zippers shut. He
shuffled through his tickets: Bismarck to Denver, Denver to
Reno. His reservations: Sands Regency. The confirmation
card was inked in purple with tiny stars flying off the letters
of the hotel. He went through everything twice, picked up
his bag, and carried it to the spare living room of his government house. He shrugged his arms into his leather suit jacket,
brown and supple, made sure all his windows were shut, then
locked and triple-locked his front door.

Lyman hadn't been to desert country before. He followed   42
the signs to Ground Transportation, and stood alongside the
service way, waiting for the hotel shuttle. The air passing in
and out of his lungs tasted of the color of dust, faintly tinged,
a dry and melancholy tone. All the buildings he could see
were a washed-out yellow margarine color. He strolled to
stretch his legs. The buckets of palms, set here and there,
smelled of cat piss. He was already sweating in his leather
jacket, boiling. His hair fell in limp, damp clumps. Although
he had helped to organize the conference, he felt anxious and
uncertain, ready to turn around and fly back home. Then the
shuttle pulled to the curb and he put his bag inside and tipped
his head back and was convinced, suddenly, that something
was going to happen to him. His mouth watered, tears
formed at the corners of his eyes, his thoughts were eager,
and his heart pumped, hot and alert. He tried to contain it
but a kick of adrenaline surged up when he walked into the
lobby of the Sands and heard the high, manic warble of the
slot machines, the controlled shouts of pit bosses, the whine
and crash of someone's bad hand sinking, dark, out of view.
    He forced himself to get his key at the front desk, and then   43
he made himself go to his room. The decor was jungle
bronze, the bed vast and tigerish. Foil and black leopard spots
surrounded the mirror and trimmed the desk, table, the
chairs of molded plastic. Green shag carpeted the floor, long
flows of greasy yarn. He took his wallet out of his pocket, put
it in his bag, set the bag down inside his room, backed out,
and shut the door.

Crossing the grand floor of the casino, the biggest he'd   44
ever been in, Lyman passed through windows—areas of noise
and intensity blocked off from other shapes of smoke and
voice. The ceiling was low and mirrored, the cushioned floor
spread, the rug endless, the color of good barbecue. The
place was dizzyingly lighted, divided by pathways and velvet-
roped rotundas into dreamlike parkways. Pleasure soaked
into him like resin. He entered caves of darkness where ice
cream, chilled in blue polar cases, was sold in a thousand
flavors. A doorway crusted in rhinestones. A great orange
containing Orange Julius. An elevator dispensing trim host-
esses smelling of chlorine from the upstairs swimming pool
and offering to spray you with Obsession. Fascinated, awed,
he watched a couple of elderly women in identical lime green
pantsuits play the quarter slots. He waited, like them, for the
glad sound of the payout. He navigated the banks of video
poker machines and came out the other side with his hands
still clenched in his pockets. A red Camaro. Vintage baby blue
Mustang. Lyman ran his fingers over the hoods of the cars
that people were playing for in the rear bank of the casino.
He passed the five-dollar blackjack tables, passed the ten. He
doubled back to show that he could do it. He passed the
hundred and then the five-hundred tables. He ambled the
entire circle again and as he stood, not watching, looking
sideways, breathing carefully, his hands lifted from his pockets
in a magical arc.

That was when he whirled, almost ran to the elevators, got   45
on, and rode up to his floor. The attraction and detail of it
all was too much, overwhelming, and his eyes fairly ached
from straining to see it all. Once inside his room, he reached
immediately for the phone, dialed room service, ordered a
large fruit salad with cottage cheese. He called back, added
a diet soda, called back again, ordered a plate of Super Grande
Nachos, then sat in front of the window and willed himself
to wait. There was a long blank, a space of time which he
knew that he should fill in by focusing on the presentation
that he had to deliver the next day. Or he could make a
telephone call—surely someone he knew from other, more

local tribal gaming conferences had arrived. Surely he was not the only one to book his flight so early, to arrive so soon. He looked at his watch. So slow! He would have done better going out onto the streets, getting directions to a real restaurant, or just walking around to burn away his appetite.

And why not? So what?   46

He jumped to his feet and searched out his wallet, patted   47
his pockets. Outside the door, he passed the waiter with the cart, making for his room with bored determination, and nearly stopped. But then he saw the salad—large quarter of a pineapple, spiky top still attached, and watermelon, slices of honeydew, red grapes. It looked as though the plastic wrap was molded to the fruit. He kept walking, took the elevator down to the lobby. Just before he went out into the street, he veered around the shining columns, past the churning machines, to the tables where the same people were still tapping and releasing their cards.

People drifted away, the air dimmed and brightened under   48
sizzling marquees. Five hours later, Lyman got up from the blackjack table. He stretched his arms and tipped the dealer. He was seven hundred dollars happier than he was when he sat down. "Now," he said to himself, "*now*." He was advising himself to go, to leave, to find the Italian restaurant recommended to him by the dealer, who clearly wanted to get rid of him. "La Florentine," he said definitively, and stood up. He nodded at the other players, still absorbed in the next hand, counting chips and cards in their heads. Lyman's winnings made a cool package in his hands and he walked to the cashier, but then, as there was a short line, he decided not to wait. He would walk around the slot machines again, uncramp his legs. He passed the ice cream stand and ordered a peanut butter parfait, then put the package under his arms and ate the sundae, standing there, watching people move and shuffle about, jingling their white plastic buckets of quarters.

His features were a mask. His outside expression was fixed,   49
serene, but beneath that, on the real face that was hidden, he could feel his look of bewildered dread. A sudden jittery

anxiety coursed through him along with the cold ice cream.
His senses dulled. His mouth went numb, he could not taste,
couldn't hear above casino clatter, couldn't feel his own
hands spooning the peanut sauce between his lips. A certainty
clapped down like a wet hand and his brain let go. Fixed hard
on the dim comfort of his own surrender he relaxed into it,
threw away the rest of his ice cream, and carried the seven
hundred dollars in chips back to the high stakes table.

He would have played it, too, but for the accident. An   50
elderly man in a neat white shirt and plaid pants bumped into
him halfway across the room, and the jolt sent the chips to
the ground. Lyman, ashamed after they were picked up,
mumbled that he had been on his way to the cashier. Then,
as if a different program had taken over in his brain, he
actually did go there, cashed the chips, walked back through
the crowd. It was as though he was now surrounded by a
force field. He was immune. He got into the elevator and let
himself back into his room. Sitting by the window, watching
other windows and lights, he peeled off layers of plastic wrap
from the tray of food, ate the warm fruit, the corn-chip
wedges disintegrating into salsa and sour cream. He ate
everything and drank the watery soda. Then he slept, dream-
less, the seven hundred curled in an ashtray beside his head.

It was two A.M. when he woke, starting into clarity, his brain   51
on and humming like a machine connected to that money.
He dressed quickly and combed his hands through his hair,
went downstairs knowing that he couldn't miss. And he
couldn't. For the next hour he played perfect games, steadily
and easily accumulating chips until he was far ahead. The wins
came slower for a while, but the chips kept accumulating. A
thousand, then two, then more. Right about there, when he
perched just under three thousand, he felt a low wave, a green
slide of nausea, and told himself to leave. But he was two
people then, split, and could not unstick himself. He started
losing his way in a muddy sluice of sloppy plays, and he got
desperate. His luck turned unpredictable and he played on,
but the momentum had died. The spell was slack. Slowly and
unremittingly, things soured. It was for the nostalgia of feel-

ing the luck, wanting it to return, as much as for the money, that he kept playing after he had nothing left.

At four A.M. he stood before the cash machine and punched   52
in his PIN number again and again, unbelieving, but he'd gone beyond his limit.

At four fifteen he cashed the loan from the Bureau of   53
Indian Affairs that had just come in to finance the tribal gaming project. He put half in chips and half in another cashier's check. He started hitting, then the losses dragged him down again and he went bust.

At five he cashed the other check.   54

At six he brought Nector's pipe to the all-night pawnshop   55
and got a hundred dollars for it.

"I'll be back by noon," he promised the clerk.   56

At seven in the morning he had nothing left that he could   57
turn to collateral, but he still felt good, drained but on top of things, alert and clean. He walked straight out the double glass doors and stood quietly, hands hanging at his sides, in the cool, dry Nevada dawn. In the Sands parking lot, he watched the sky go from silver to blue and felt the sun's light strengthen. Beyond the railroad tracks, he remembered a bridge, and as though he could smell the water, taste it now, he walked toward it. The trees, the grassy park at its edge, lay only two blocks off and he soon entered the sounds of morning, the click of aspen, a lower murmur. Mild breezes swelled against him, and he smelled the sage in dry flower and the oils of broken cedar twigs. He walked over to the rail beside the river's bank, thought hopefully of jumping in, but the Truckee River was only a foot or so in depth, wandering among gray rocks, too weak to flow, too shallow to run.

Topics for Writing
Story

1. *Respond.* For a psychology class, describe the ways in which Lyman's behavior matches the definition of a "compulsive gambler" provided by Margaret O. Hyde. In particular, note Lyman's emotional reactions once he arrives at the casino and when he loses everything at the end of the story. (*Resources for Comparison:* Margaret O. Hyde, "Compulsive Gambling," page 583; Brent Staples, "The Chain Gang Show," page 12).

2. *Analyze.* Write an essay for your literature class in which you analyze Lyman's "pipe." Why did he want it? What did it represent? How did he get it? How did he lose it? Consider as a possible title "Lyman's Heritage." (*Resources for Comparison:* Alice Walker, "Everyday Use," page 351, David Denby, "What the Great Books Do," page 519).

3. *Argue.* Conduct some research on the controversy about gambling on Indian reservations. Look at the controversy from several perspectives: Why are Indian tribes given special privileges to operate casinos? Do the Indian tribes get what they want by operating casinos? Why do gamblers go to the reservations rather than Las Vegas, Reno, or Atlantic City? Using your research, argue that Indians should or should not have special casino privileges. (*Resources for Comparison:* Jon Katz, "Interactivity," page 330; Rosemary L. Bray "So How Did I Get Here?" page 495).

Jason Rex was born in 1976 in Joliet, Illinois, and is currently enrolled at Ball State University where he is majoring in elementary education. He works as a resident assistant (RA) in one of the dormitories where he hosts a weekly poker game. In "Not a Bad Night," he classifies the types of players at his game.

Not a Bad Night

I T'S FRIDAY NIGHT. The dead spot on the college weekend. Saturdays are for home games and special parties. Sundays are for sleeping in and catching up. But Fridays. Ah, Fridays. What to do? My solution was to organize a poker game. But the project was more complicated than finding a deck of cards and a couple of guys. I had to host several experimental games before I found the right mix of personalities to create an entertaining evening. The five "studs" that sit around the table at what has become our weekly game seem to possess the right characteristics for a lively Friday. They can be classified according to their preference for food, reason for gambling, strategy in betting, and attitude toward winning and losing.

The key to the weekly ritual is—of course—the Host. He organizes the game because he has the biggest room and the strongest urge to make everyone happy. Like Martha Stewart, he anticipates the needs of his guests by providing a variety of drinks (soda, club soda, beer) and chips (Bar-BQ, Sour Cream, and Ruffles). He is not particularly interested in gambling. In fact he rarely plays every hand and has trouble remembering the betting sequence. Instead, he seems to be in constant motion, picking up empty cans, filling up the chip bowl, and trying to collect each guest's promised contribu-

1

2

tion to the food bill. Because he does not play every hand, the Host loses less than the other players. But because he rarely collects enough money for the food bill, he feels like he has lost. He takes solace in the social success of the evening.

The first player to arrive every Friday is the Happy Loser. 3 He has probably skipped dinner at the cafeteria so that he can chow down on some real "guy" food, but he is not very discriminating about what he eats. He is simply happy to be anywhere. He tends to have a hard time finding dates on the

---

The five "studs" that sit around the table at what has become our weekly game seem to possess the right characteristics for a lively Friday.

---

weekend, so when he has an opportunity to play cards and bond with the guys, he's in heaven. Anything is better than watching the tube or playing one player Nintendo in your room alone. The Happy Loser knows very little about the rules of poker, so he bets foolishly and loses on a grand scale. But he doesn't seem to care. His game strategy is to talk about how great it is to be with everyone, talking "guy" talk and eating "guy" food. He is the favorite among the players because he keeps their spirits up, and he always loses.

Next to arrive is the Serious Player. He has been thinking 4 about the game all week, plotting how he is going to correct last week's mistakes and play this week's hands. He is very particular about food—drinking only club soda so that he has a clear head and avoiding the chips so he won't mark the cards with grease. He usually brings his own cards because any other deck might have been tampered with. His years of study have taught him the odds of getting dealt a Queen of

Spades with 16 already played, and he shuffles and reshuffles his hand as if his life depended on arranging them in the right order. Although he rarely talks during play, except to "raise," "call," or "fold," he is important to the game because he always knows the betting sequence. The only thing that prevents him from moving to Las Vegas is that he isn't very good. Despite his intricate knowledge of the game, he always manages to lose more than he wins. But he does have an explanation: "You guys talk too much. I can't concentrate when you are babbling."

The main object of his scorn is the Talker. Like the Happy   5
Loser, the Talker shows up as much for the fellowship as for the game. He has a story for everything and he loves a captive audience. Even the food provides an opportunity for a long rambling tale about the last time he and his best buddy ate Sour Cream Chips. Whatever the topic the talker has a story—usually about some "incredible" escapade with people none of the players knows. The Talker can be very tiring—he is especially irritating to the Serious Player—but he is important to the game because as long as he is at the table there will never be a lull in the conversation. And amazingly enough, even though the Talker appears more interested in his stories than the game, he usually wins. But as he pulls in the pot, he's off on another story, seemingly unaware of his victory.

The fifth player at the table is the Bluffer. He doesn't eat   6
or drink anything because he is convinced that every move signals something about his intentions. In some ways, he is like the Serious Player. The game is important because he might win and therefore be able to pay off his many debts. But like the Happy Loser, the Bluffer doesn't know that much about poker. His characteristic betting strategy is to bet big—thinking he can bluff his way to a win. Occasionally, he does win. But unlike the Talker, he feels compelled to rub everyone's nose in his victory: "I don't even need a job." The players put up with these taunts because they know the Bluffer is a bluffer. He is important to the game because despite his grandstand moves he usually loses and loses big.

On a given night, all the players at the table could probably 7
change chairs (and personalities)—the Happy Loser outtalk-
ing the Talker; the Serious Player outbluffing the Bluffer; and
the Host getting more serious than the Serious Player to win
enough to pay the food bill plus a little profit. But for the
most part, the players stay in character, acting out their assigned roles as they eat, drink, and deal their way through
another Friday evening.

In one sense, everybody wins. They pay about five dollars 8
for food and could lose about ten dollars at cards. If, instead,
they took a date to dinner and the movies (plus drinks and
popcorn), their evening could cost about forty dollars. Given
those odds, the five players, despite their differences, conclude that the Friday game is entertaining enough. As they
depart, they agree: "Not a bad night! Same time next week!"

For Study and Discussion

QUESTIONS ABOUT RESOURCES AND STRATEGY

1. What assumption does Rex make about the purpose of gambling?
2. What major strategy does he use to illustrate this purpose?
3. How would the writers in this section (e.g., Joseph Epstein,
   Margaret O. Hyde, Robert Goodman) respond to Rex's presentation of the various characters at his Friday night game?

ACKNOWLEDGMENTS

ALICE ADAMS "Truth or Consequences," from *To See You Again* by Alice Adams. Copyright © 1982 by Alice Adams. Reprinted by permission of Alfred A. Knopf, Inc.

MAYA ANGELOU "My Name Is Margaret," from *I Know Why the Caged Bird Sings* by Maya Angelou. Copyright © 1969 by Maya Angelou. Reprinted by permission of Random House, Inc.

NATALIE ANGIER "Dolphin Courtship: Brutal, Cunning, and Complex," from *The Beauty of the Beastly*. Copyright © 1995 by Natalie Angier. Reprinted by permission of Houghton Mifflin Co. All rights reserved.

JAMES AUSTIN "Four Kinds of Chance," reprinted from *Saturday Review/ World,* November 2, 1974.

BILL BARICH "Handicapping," from *Laughing in the Hills* by Bill Barich. Copyright © 1980 by Bill Barich. Used by permission of Viking Penguin, a division of Penguin Putnam, Inc.

JOHN BERENDT "The Hoax." Copyright © 1994 by John Berendt. Reprinted by permission of the author.

WENDELL BERRY From "Conservation Is Good Work," *Sex, Economy, Freedom & Community*. New York: Pantheon, 1993:27.

ROSEMARY BRAY Reprinted by permission of Rosemary Bray. "So How Did I Get Here?" *New York Times Magazine,* 1993. Copyright © 1993. All rights reserved.

LAUREN BRINER "Deloris," by Lauren Briner is reprinted by permission of the author.

SANDRA CISNEROS "One Holy Night," from *Woman Hollering Creek*. Copyright © 1991 by Sandra Cisneros. Published by Vintage, a division of Random House, Inc. and in hardcover by Random House. Reprinted by permission of Susan Bergholtz Literary Services, New York. All rights reserved.

JUDITH ORTIZ COFER "Silent Dancing" by Judith Ortiz Cofer is reprinted with permission from the publisher of *Silent Dancing: A Partial Remembrance of a Puerto Rican Childhood* (Houston: Arte Publico Press—University of Houston, 1990).

ROBERT COLES "Uniforms," from *Harvard Diary II*. Copyright 1997. Reprinted by permission of The Crossroad Publishing Company.

CLYDE BRION DAVIS "The Wheat Farmer and the Crap Shooter," from *Something for Nothing: The Lore and Lure of Gambling* by Clyde Brion Davis. Copyright © 1955 by Clyde Brion Davis. Reprinted by permission of HarperCollins Publishers, Inc.

DAVID DENBY "What the Great Books Do," reprinted with the permission of Simon & Schuster from *Great Books: My Adventure with Homer, Rousseau, Woolf, and Other Indestructible Writers of the Western World* by David Denby. Copyright © 1996 by David Denby.

ESTHER DYSON "A Design for Living on the Internet," from *Release 2.0* by Esther Dyson. Copyright © 1997 by Esther Dyson. Reprinted by permission of Doubleday Dell Publishing Group.

LARS EIGHNER "My Daily Dives in the Dumpster." *The Threepenny Review*. (Fall 1988): 19–22. Reprinted by permission of the author.

JOSEPH EPSTEIN Excerpts from "Confession of a Low Roller" by Joseph Epstein is reprinted from *The American Scholar*, Volume 57, Number 2, Spring 1988. Copyright © 1988 by the author. Reprinted with permission.

LOUISE ERDRICH "Lyman's Luck," from *The Bingo Palace* by Louise Erdrich. Copyright © 1994 by Louise Erdrich. Reprinted by permission of HarperCollins Publishers, Inc.

WINIFRED GALLAGHER From "From the Nest to the Global Village," *The Power of Place: How Our Surroundings Shape Our Thoughts, Emotions, and Actions*. New York: HarperCollins Publishers, Inc., 1993: 187–88.

NIKKI GIOVANNI "Campus Racism 101," from *Racism 101* by Nikki Giovanni. Copyright © 1994 by Nikki Giovanni. By permission of William Morrow & Company, Inc.

ROBERT GOODMAN "Grand Illusions," reprinted by permission of Robert Goodman from *The Wilson Quarterly* (Autumn 1995). Copyright 1995 by Robert Goodman. All rights reserved.

DANIEL GOLEMAN "Peak Performances: Why Records Fall," *New York Times*. Copyright © 1994 by The New York Times Company. Reprinted by permission.

DORIS KEARNS GOODWIN Reprinted with permission of Simon & Schuster, "Keeping the Scorebook," from *Wait till Next Year* by Doris Kearns Goodwin. Copyright © 1997 by Blithdale Productions.

NATHAN M. HARMS "Howard and Rush" by Nathan M. Harms is reprinted by permission of the author.

STEPHEN HARRIGAN "The Tiger Is God," from *The Natural State* by Stephen Harrigan. Copyright © 1988 by Gulf Publishing Company. Used with permission. All rights reserved.

EDWARD HOAGLAND "In the Toils of the Law," from *Walking the Dead Diamond River,* published by Lyons & Burford. Copyright © 1972, 1973, 1993 by Edward Hoagland. Reprinted by permission of Lescher & Lescher, Ltd.

MARGARET HYDE "Compulsive Gambling," from *Addictions: Gambling, Smoking, Cocaine Use, and Others* by Margaret Hyde. Copyright 1978. Reprinted by permission of The McGraw-Hill Companies.

PICO IYER "Of Weirdos and Eccentrics," excerpt from *Tropical Classical: Essays from Several Directions* by Pico Iyer. Copyright © 1997 by Pico Iyer. Reprinted by permission of Alfred A. Knopf, Inc.

JON KATZ "Interactivity," from *Virtuous Reality* by Jon Katz. Copyright © 1997 by Jon Katz. Reprinted by permission of Random House, Inc.

MARTIN LUTHER KING, JR. "I Have a Dream" by Martin Luther King, Jr., is reprinted by arrangement with The Heirs to the Estate of Martin Luther King, Jr., c/o Writer's House, Inc. as agent for the proprietor. Copyright © 1963 by Martin Luther King, Jr., copyright renewed 1991 by Coretta Scott King.

BARBARA KINGSOLVER "Jabberwocky," from *High Time in Tucson: Essays from Now or Never.* New York: HarperCollins Publishers, Inc., 1996: 228–229.

MAXINE HONG KINGSTON Excerpts from "A Song for a Barbarian Reed Pipe," from *The Woman Warrior* by Maxine Hong Kingston. Copyright © 1975, 1976 by Maxine Hong Kingston. Reprinted by permission of Alfred A. Knopf, Inc.

JUDITH LEVINE "I Surf, Therefore I Am," *Salon Magazine,* July 1997. http://www.salonmagazine.com/july97/mothers/surfing.970729.html. Reprinted by permission of Judith Levine.

EMILY LINDERMAN "Barrier-Free Design" by Emily Linderman is reprinted by permission of the author.

ERIC LIU "A Chinaman's Chance: Reflections on the American Dream," from *Next: Young American Writers on the New Generation.* Copyright © 1994. Reprinted by permission of the author and W. W. Norton & Company, Inc.

DAVID McCULLOUGH Reprinted with the permission of Simon & Schuster. "FDR and Truman," from *Truman* by David McCullough. Copyright © 1992 by David McCullough.

BILL McKIBBEN "Nature and Televised Nature," from *The Age of Missing Information* by Bill McKibben. Copyright © 1992 by Bill McKibben. Reprinted by permission of Random House, Inc.

TERRY McMILLAN "The Movie That Changed My Life," by Terry McMillan, copyright © 1991 by Terry McMillan, from *The Movie That Changed My Life* by David Rosenberg. Used by permission of Viking Penguin, a division of Penguin Putnam, Inc.

MARY MEBANE "Shades of Black," from *Mary* by Mary Mebane. Copyright © 1981 by Mary Elizabeth Mebane. Used by permission of Viking Penguin, a division of Penguin Putnam, Inc.

CHARLES MURRAY "The Coming White Underclass." Reprinted with permission of *The Wall Street Journal,* © 1993 Dow Jones & Company, Inc. All rights reserved.

KATHLEEN NORRIS "The Holy Use of Gossip," from *Dakota.* Copyright © 1993 by Kathleen Norris. Reprinted by permission of Ticknor & Fields/Houghton Mifflin Company. All rights reserved.

NAOMI SHIHAB NYE "My Brother's House," from *Homeground* by Naomi Shihab Nye. Copyright © 1996. Reprinted by permission of the author.

FLANNERY O'CONNOR "Revelation," from *Everything That Rises Must Converge* by Flannery O'Connor. Copyright © 1962, 1965 by the Estate of Mary Flannery O'Connor and copyright renewed © 1993 by Regina O'Connor. Reprinted by permission of Farrar, Straus & Giroux, Inc.

FRANK O'CONNOR "Guests of the Nation," from *Collected Stories* by Frank O'Connor. Copyright © 1981 by Harriet O'Donovan Sheehy, Executrix of the Estate of Frank O'Connor. Reprinted by permission of Alfred A. Knopf, Inc., and by arrangement with Harriet O'Donovan Sheehy, c/o Joan Daves Agency as agent for the proprietor.

CHARLOTTE OLMSTED "Analyzing a Pack of Cards," reprinted with the permission of Simon & Schuster from *Heads I Win, Tails You Lose* by Charlotte Olmsted. Copyright © 1962 by Charlotte Olmsted, renewed 1990 by Charlotte Kursch.

GEORGE ORWELL "Shooting an Elephant," from *Shooting an Elephant and Other Essays* by George Orwell. Copyright © 1950 by Sonia Brownell Orwell and renewed 1978 by Sonia Pitt-Rivers, reprinted by permission of Harcourt Brace & Company.

JAMES POPKIN "Tricks of the Trade" by James Popkin from *US News & World Report,* March 14, 1994. Copyright © March 14, 1994, *US News & World Report.* Reprinted by permission.

JASON REX "Not a Bad Night" by Jason Rex is reprinted by permission of the author.

JEREMY RIFKIN "The Gospel of Mass Consumption," from *The End of Work: The Decline of the Global Labor Force and the Dawn of the Post-Market Era.* New York: Putnam, 1995: 19.

RICHARD RODRIGUEZ "Growing Up in Los Angeles." Copyright, April 7, 1997, *US News & World Report.* Reprinted by permission.

MIKE ROSE Reprinted with the permission of the Free Press, a Division of Simon & Schuster. "The Limits of the Great Books," from *Lives on the Boundary: The Struggles and Achievements of America's Underprepared* by Mike Rose. Copyright © 1989 by Mike Rose.

JIM F. SALOMAN "Genetic Engineering" by Jim F. Saloman is reprinted by permission of the author.

SCOTT RUSSELL SANDERS "Digging Limestone," from *Paradise of Bombs* by Scott Russell Sanders. Copyright © 1982 by Scott Russell Sanders; first appeared in *The North American Review.* Reprinted by permission of the author and Virginia Kidd Agency, Inc.

BRUCE SHAPIRO "One Violent Crime" by Bruce Shapiro reprinted with permission from the April 3, 1995 issue of *The Nation*. Copyright © 1995.

GAIL SHEEHY "Predictable Crises of Adulthood," from *Passages* by Gail Sheehy. Copyright © 1974, 1976 by Gail Sheehy. Used by permission of Dutton, a division of Penguin Putnam, Inc.

BRENT STAPLES "The Chain Gang Show," *New York Times Magazine*, September 17, 1995. Copyright © 1995 by The New York Times Company. Reprinted by permission.

DEBORAH TANNEN "Rapport-Talk and Report-Talk," from *You Just Don't Understand* by Deborah Tannen, Ph.D. Copyright © 1990 by Deborah Tannen, Ph.D. By permission of William Morrow & Company, Inc.

SARA TEMPLE "Making Stained Glass," by Sara Temple is reprinted by permission of the author.

LEWIS THOMAS "The Technology of Medicine," copyright © 1971 by The Massachusetts Medical Society, from *The Lives of a Cell* by Lewis Thomas. Used by permission of Viking Penguin, a division of Penguin Putnam, Inc.

CALVIN TRILLIN "The Extendable Fork." Copyright © 1995 by Calvin Trillin. Reprinted by permission of Lescher & Lescher, Ltd.

GARETH TUCKER "Gentlemen! Start Your Engines" by Gareth Tucker is reprinted by permission of the author.

JASON UTESCH "Personality" by Jason Utesch is reprinted by permission of the author.

KURT VONNEGUT, JR. "Harrison Bergeron" by Kurt Vonnegut, Jr., from *Welcome to the Monkey House* by Kurt Vonnegut, Jr. Copyright © 1961 by Kurt Vonnegut, Jr. Used by permission of Delacorte Press/Seymour Lawrence, a division of Bantam Doubleday Dell Publishing Group, Inc.

ALICE WALKER "Everyday Use," from *In Love and Trouble: Stories of Black Women*, copyright © 1973 by Alice Walker. Reprinted by permission of Harcourt Brace & Company.

TERRY TEMPEST WILLIAMS "The Village Watchman," from *An Unspoken Hunger* by Terry Tempest Williams. Copyright © 1994 by Terry Tempest Williams. Reprinted by permission of Pantheon Books, a division of Random House, Inc.

ELIZABETH WINTHROP "The Golden Darters," by Elizabeth Winthrop. First published in *American Short Fiction*. Copyright © 1991 by Elizabeth Winthrop. Reprinted by permission of the author.

CATHY YOUNG "Keeping Women Weak," from *Next: Young American Writers on the New Generation*, edited by Eric Liu. Copyright © 1994 by Cathy Young. Reprinted by permission of the author and W. W. Norton & Company, Inc.

ANN ZWINGER "Drawing on Experience," from *Finding Home* by *Orion* Magazine. Copyright © 1992 by the Myrin Institute. Reprinted by permission of Beacon Press, Boston.

INDEX